"Children's Voices"

Learn, Earn

& Become Famous!

Eleanor J. Marks

2016 Holocaust Essay Contest

Sponsored by Bernard Marks

Sacramento, California

Printed in the United States of America
I Street Press
Sacramento Public Library Authority
828 I Street
Sacramento, CA 95814

Marks, Bernard, Editor
    "Children's Voices" Learn, earn & become famous! / Eleanor J. Marks Holocaust Essay Contest

Book One ISBN: 978-1-941125-96-0
Book Two ISBN: 978-1-941125-97-7

1. Holocaust, Jewish (1939-1945). 2. Jews – Persecution – Germany. 3. Jews – Persecution – Poland. I. "Children's Voices". II. Eleanor J. Marks Holocaust Essay Contest, 2016. III. Bernard Marks.

ISSN: 2377-2565

Cover design by: Bernard Marks and Gerald F. Ward
Text interior design by: Gerald F. Ward

Cover Pictures on Book One: Gabriella Gutierrez, Allison Metter, Maximillian Schweizer, Libby Slater, Anusha Srinivasan, Jonah Stafford, C.K. McClatchy German Class

Cover Pictures on Book Two: Zlata Arestove, Marion Conus (from 2015), Jacob Dean, Anthony Isca, YounFen Lei (Sally), Livia Antonella Parisella

www.ejmholocaustproject.com

2 3 4 5 6 7 8 9 10

2016 Eleanor J. Marks Holocaust Writing Project

History:

The essay-writing project began in 2008 at Congregation B'nai Israel, Sacramento, California with only four entries. In 2012 the project was opened to 6th-12th grade for public, religious and private schools in California as well as European schools. In 2014 undergraduate students from colleges and universities all over the world were eligible to participate. Over the past seven years the writing project grew to over 500 entries in 2016 alone.

Purpose:

The Eleanor J. Marks Worldwide Holocaust Essay Writing Project honors her memory by promoting remembrance and study of the Holocaust. It is also intended to enhance education in the schools through the annual essay-writing project.

The annual scholarship awards are given to winning students in each participating school:

One award of $150.00 to a student 6th –12th grades in each school

One award of $75.00 for runner-up in each school,

One award $150.00 for undergraduate college/university student.

Special awards of $50.00 selected by the Founder, Bernard Marks

Over fifty (50) judges evaluated the essays and determined the award recipients in each school.

Eleanor J. Marks Holocaust Essay Writing Project
Established 2008

Eleanor (Ellie) Marks (1931-2008) was the wife of Bernard (Bernie) Marks. These essays are dedicated to her memory.

Goals & Rules:

The goal of this annual writing project is for students to understand what the Holocaust means and why we say "Never Again."

The annual project commences no later than November 1 of each year. Essays are due no later than February 28 of the following year and must be submitted electronically as a Microsoft Word® document to **< hagibor52@gmail.com >**

To accomplish this task in a timely manner, the Judging Committee for 2016 consisted 50 plus community members. (See Judges names starting on page _____.)

Presentation of awards will be made during the Yom HaShoah (Day of Remembrance) Community event on April 23, 2017.

Awards:

1) $150.00 to one student from each school from grade 6 –12th, grade

2) $75.00 to one the runner up in each school grades 6 – 12ᵗʰ grade

3) $150 to the selected undergraduate essayist from a College/University

4) Special awards of $50.00 are selected by the Founder of the Eleanor J. Marks Holocaust Project.

PREFACE

How do you honor the victims of the Holocaust? The answer for Bernie Marks is to not let their spirit or memory fade. He does this by sharing their courageous stories with each new generation. His amazing personal story of survival, orchestrated by his father, illustrates how Bernie was able to endure the horrific death camps of the Nazi regime. This treasure of a man now gives first-hand accounts of the shocking truth behind genocide in an effort to ensure that these atrocities never happen again.

Obviously, as time goes on, the remaining survivors of the Holocaust become more rare. The value of Bernie's personal stories is irreplaceable and the youth understand this truth. When a slight man in his 80's can single-handedly engage 450 eighth graders, you know his message is riveting and very well received. After an assembly with Bernie, you will find a multitude of students lining up to simply shake his hand, ask additional questions, and/or take a picture. The students' "rock-star" treatment of Bernie validates the impact his message has on all in attendance.

Bernie Marks also continues to spread the truth of the Holocaust through an essay writing project that honors the memory of his late wife Eleanor J. Marks. This project allows students an opportunity to write an essay about Holocaust victims and the story behind their bravery and struggle to survive. As students research and compose their tributes to these everyday heroes, their awareness grows. At the same time, those who read their essays will understand that it takes purposeful action to prevent similar events. Bernie's message is clear that we must do all that we can to prevent the Holocaust and other events of genocide around the globe from happening again or continuing to take place.

Ron Rammer
Principal
Robert L. McCaffrey Middle School
Galt, California

INTRODUCTION

Near the end of my three-year-long graduate school experience, I was required to take a comprehensive examination on everything I had learned about German history. I recall stepping into the testing room with so little clue as to what would be asked of me. When I opened my blue book, the question that I saw was shorter than I expected: "Germany was the birthplace to the science, literature, and music that would help define culture and progress in the modern era. If this is so, how did Germany also become the birthplace of the Holocaust, an event that came to define so many of the horrors of the modern era?"

The answer was, and is, not an easy one. Simply put, while we think we know what we stand for as a society, humanity can be a fleeting thing. As a culture that prided itself on a nationalized pension plan, the speed of its automobiles, and the splendor of its medieval architecture, so much of Germany's sense of right and wrong faded overnight. Far from placing the west and its traditional bloc of democracies into the shoes of Interwar Germany, the simple take away should be that, as Americans, our own humanity and sensibilities for decency are just as susceptible to the wicked caprices of extremism and racial arrogance that affected Germany in 1933.

It is for this reason that cultivating a strong sense of humanity at the earliest of ages is imperative for a healthy democracy. And while learning from the past is engaging the past, this robust collection of essays provides a window into the bravery and sacrifice of those who stood willing to resist. To resist an ailing moral paradigm takes the strength of holding fast to one's own convictions, while thousands of voices are attempting to convince you otherwise.

What's more, with 70 years having passed between the Holocaust and today, the very act of writing enables tomorrow's leaders to explore the horrors of a broken society, giving them both a context for vigilance and a primer for understanding the earliest of warning signs.

Finally, this compilation showcases the talents and insights of some of today's finest young writers. The essays are written with a passion and dedication that should make the reader feel as if the future is in the hands of those who are willing to learn from the past and guard the sanctity of our collective future.

James C. Scott MA, MLS
Information Services Librarian

8th ANNUAL
Eleanor J. Marks
HOLOCAUST
ESSAY CONTEST

honoring the memory of Eleanor J. Marks; promoting remembrance, awareness, and study of the Holocaust; and enhancing educational experiences.

2016 THEME:

German or Ukrainian Heroes of the Holocaust
1939 -1945

Source: yadvashem.org

Research the theme, write a meaningful essay, and reap the rewards.

Open to students grades 6 –12 in religious, public, and private schools, colleges, and universities.

DEADLINE:

February 28, 2016

QUESTIONS:
Email questions to dov52@rcip.com or contact your teacher.

CASH PRIZES!

Prizes awarded in the following categories, for each school:

- One student winner from grades 6 - 8: $150
- One student runner-up from grades 6 - 8: $75
- One student winner from grades 9 - 12: $150
- One student runner-up from grades 9 - 12: $75
- One college/university student winner: $150

Names of prize winners will be published in *the Voice* (of Sacramento, California), and the Sacramento Community Yom HaShoah Memorial Program, where the awards will be presented at the ceremony. All entries will be published in a special book, *2016 Children's Voices: Volume IV.*

RULES:

- Grades 6 - 8: essays must be 850-1500 words.
- Grades 9 - 12: essays must be 2000-3000 words.
- College/university level: essays must be 3000-5000 words.
- *Submissions must include the following information on page 1, top right hand corner:* entrant's name, address, phone number, email address, and the name of your school.
  Page 1, top left hand corner, please include your personal 2" x 2" photo.

- **Essays must be electronically submitted *as an attachment* in Microsoft Word only**, double-spaced, 12-point font. (Any other format such as Google Docs, cloud or password protected, will not be accepted.)
- **Email essays to:** dov52@rcip.com by the submission deadline of February 28. (Email only, no hard copies.)

Awards will be presented during the Sacramento Community Yom HaShoah commemoration.

„8. jährlich stattfindender Eleanor J. Marks Holocaust Aufsatz Wettbewerb"

„Ehrt und erinnert an Eleanor J. Marks, fördert das Gedenken, die Sensibilisierung sowie die Auseinandersetzung mit dem Holocaust und unterstützt das Lernen aus der Geschichte des Zweiten Weltkriegs."

Thema 2016:
„Deutsche oder ukrainische Helden des Holocaust"
1939 – 1945
Informationen unter: yadvashem.org

| **Learn, Earn and Become Famous**

Offen für Schülerinnen und Schüler der Klassen 6 – 12 des Privatgymnasiums Dr. Richter

Einsende-schluss:
28. Februar 2016

Fragen können elektronisch an:
dov52@rcip.com
gerichtet werden oder persönlich bei der zuständigen Lehrperson gemacht werden | **PREISGELD!**
Preisgeld in jeder Kategorie und für jede Schule:

• 1. Preis: 150$ - ein Schüler der 6. – 8. Klassen
• 1. Preis: 150$ - ein Schüler der 9. – 12. Klassen

• 2. Preis: 75$ - ein Schüler der 6. – 8. Klassen
• 2. Preis: 75$ - ein Schüler der 9.– 12. Klassen

Gewinner werden in Voice of Sacramento, California" und dem "Yom HaShoah Memorial" Programm veröffentlicht. Alle Einträge werden in einem speziellen Buch, "Children´s Voices: Volume IV" publiziert.

REGELN:
• Klasse 6 – 8:   850 – 1500 Wörter pro Essay
• Klasse 9 – 12: 2000 – 3000 Wörter pro Essay

• Einsendungen müssen in der oberen, rechten Ecke den Namen, Adresse, Telefonnummer, Email, Name der Erziehungsberechtigten und Name der Schule beinhalten

• Essays müssen in Schriftgröße12 in Microsoft Word getippt werden. Einsendungen per Email bis zum Einsendeschluss an: dov52@rcip.com schicken |

8ème concours
annuel de rédaction
SUR LE THÈME
DE L'HOLOCAUSTE
à la mémoire de
ELEANOR J. MARKS

Pour encourager la commémoration, sensibiliser les étudiants à l'Holocauste et approfondir ce sujet.

THÈME 2016:
Héros allemands et ukrainiens de l'Holocauste
1939 – 1945
Visitez le site: yadvashem.org

Faites des recherches sur le thème proposé, rédigez une rédaction et gagnez un prix.

Ce concours est ouvert aux étudiants de tous les établissements scolaires privés, publics, religieux et universitaires.

La rédaction doit être envoyée jusqu'au 28 février 2016.

N'hésitez pas à nous contacter par e-mail si vous avez des questions: dov52@rcip.com.

PRIX
Les prix suivants sont attribués à chaque établissement scolaire ayant participé:

- Premier prix pour les classes de niveau secondaire: 150$
- Deuxième prix pour les classes de niveau secondaire: 75$
- Prix pour les étudiants universitaires: 150$

Les gagnants seront publiés dans le journal mensuel "The Voice of Sacramento" et seront également annoncés lors de la cérémonie commémorative du Yom HaShoah, dédiée à la communauté de Sacramento. De plus, toutes les rédactions seront publiées dans un livre intitulé: *Les Voix des Enfants: Volume V.*

REGLEMENTS:
- Niveau secondaire- rédaction de 2000 à 3000 mots.
- Niveau universitaire: rédaction de 3000 à 5000 mots.
- Les rédactions doivent avoir une page titre contenant les informations suivantes: *En haut à droite:* nom, adresse, numéro de téléphone, adresse e-mail et le nom de l'établissement scolaire.
  En haut à gauche: une photo de l'élève qui a rédigé la rédaction.
- Les rédactions doivant êtres rédigées avec un double interlignage en caractère 12.
- Les rédactions doivant êtres transmises au format Microsoft Word jusqu'au 28 février 2016 à l'adresse suivante: dov52@rcip.com (version électronique uniquement).

Les récompenses seront remises le dimanche 1 Mai 2016 durant la cérémonie commémorative du Yom HaShoah, dédiée à la communauté de Sacramento.

Contents

2016 Eleanor J. Marks Holocaust Writing Project
Eleanor J. Marks Holocaust Essay Writing Project
Preface
Introduction

Katherine L. Albiani Middle School. Elk Grove, CA

Brookfield School, Sacramento, CA

Camerado Springs Middle School, Cameron Park, CA

Congregation B'nai Israel, Sacramento, CA

Dallas Ranch Middle School, Antioch, CA

Holmes Jr. High School, Davis, CA

C. K. McClatchy High School, Sacramento, CA

San Juan High School, Citrus Heights, CA

T. R. Smedberg Middle School, Elk Grove, CA

Overseas Schools
Private Gymnasium Dr. Richter, kelkheim, Germany

Technical University431

Katherine L. Albiani Middle School. Elk Grove, CA

Harpreet Sidhu has been teaching for 20 years. She currently teaches middle school at Katherine L. Albiani Middle School in the Elk Grove Unified School District. Mrs. Sidhu is honored to serve as an advisor to the students at her school to participate in this powerfully engaging educational opportunity.

Megan Wojan, a 7th grade middle school teacher in the Elk Grove Unified School District, finds it deeply rewarding to educate her students on the historical truths of the Holocaust. Through participation in the Eleanor J Marks essay contest, her students have developed a deeper understanding of the importance of social equality, dignity, and respect. She hopes that her students will continue to educate future generations allowing us to 'never forget' the victims, survivors, and heroes of the Holocaust.

Dr. Mohamed Helmy- The Man of Moral Righteousness

Noura Mahmoud (Co-Winner)

 "...Dr. Helmy did everything for me out of the generosity of his heart and I will be grateful to him for eternity," Anna Gutman. Anna Gutman was a German of Jewish descent who was saved by Dr. Helmy during the Holocaust. Dr. Mohamed Helmy was a courageous hero who stood in the face of persecution and death to do the most honorable action, defending Jews during the Nazi occupation of Germany. Dr. Helmy dedicated himself to protect the lives of a Jewish family, against all consequences, ensuring their safety and well being.

Born in Egypt, Dr. Helmy grew up in a culture where predominant Islamic belief was the societal norm and where casting aside Judaism and its practices was expected. Seeking higher education, Dr. Helmy went to Berlin, Germany to study medicine. After receiving his medical degree, his dedication and tireless effort was rewarded through a promotion to Chief of Staff of the Urology Department at the Robert Koch Hospital in Berlin. The hospital's policies were dictated by Nazi discrimination against the Jews, which troubled Dr. Helmy. Jewish co-workers, as well as highly skilled Jewish doctors, were dismissed from the hospital. Even Dr. Helmy was soon terminated because of his non-Aryan heritage. Also, German laws invaded his private life when Dr. Helmy was prohibited to wed his German fiancé. These circumstances marked the beginning of Dr. Helmy's dilemmas. Consequently, Dr. Helmy and other Egyptian nationalists were arrested and detained because of birth status. Luckily, he was released a year later based on significant health issues he was experiencing.

Despite fear of being targeted by the Nazi Party, Dr. Helmy spoke out against their anti-Semitic beliefs. Dr. Helmy disagreed with the principle of a superior race and believed extermination of Jews was not needed in order to make Germany great.

In Germany, ghettos were being established, forcing Jews to live in squalor conditions. The deportations of the Jewish people to concentration camps soon began and millions were in danger. One of these endangered individuals was Anna Gutman, a close family friend and former patient of Dr. Helmy. When Anna sought Dr. Helmy's assistance to hide from the Nazis, he took no time in finding a sanctuary for her, and later her family. Dr. Helmy immediately arranged for Anna to relocate to his Berlin cabin, which throughout the war became her safe haven.

Keeping the secret of a hidden Jewish family came at a price. Dr. Helmy was constantly under investigation. If he were to be discovered harboring Jews, jail or death were among the consequences. Dr. Helmy managed to dodge the investigations by moving Anna from his cabin to alternate locations until she was out of danger. "... The Gestapo knew that Dr. Helmy was our family physician, and they knew that he owned a cabin in Berlin-Buch," Anna Gutman wrote after the war. "He managed to evade all their interrogations. In such cases he would bring me to friends where I would stay for several days, introducing me as his cousin from Dresden. When the danger would pass, I would return to his cabin." Dr. Helmy also provided shelter for Anna Gutman's mother, Julie, stepfather, Gerog Wehr, and her grandmother, Cecilie Rudnik. He arranged for Cecilie to be hidden in the house of his close friend, Frieda Szturmann. Frieda did much for the elderly Cecilie; she tended to her needs as if Cecilie was Frieda's own mother.

With investigations dodged and Anna and her family in secured locations, everything seemed to be on a good track for all involved. Suddenly, a great danger arose. Julie and Gerog Wehr were discovered. During the interrogation, the hiding place of Anna Gutman was revealed. With quick thinking, Dr. Helmy moved Anna to Frieda's home and created a bogus letter, allegedly from Anna, stating that she had left the city to go to her aunt's residence in Dessau, Germany. Dr. Helmy used his resourcefulness to cleverly deceive the authorities and evaded all consequences while keeping Anna safe.

Due to Dr. Helmy's heroic actions and compelling generosity, Anna and her three other family members survived the fatal Holocaust during the Nazi reign. After the war, they left the country and immigrated to the United States. Though they were far from the place that had been their worst nightmare, but also safe haven, they never forgot their rescuer. To show their gratitude, during the 1950s and 60s they wrote letters to the Berlin Senate so that Dr. Helmy would be recognized and honored as a Jewish Rescuer.

With the war over, and the Nazi regime toppled, Dr. Helmy was now able to marry his German fiancé. He remained in Berlin, until his death in 1982.

During the process of gathering all possible information to honor Dr. Helmy, The Righteous Among Nations spoke with Anna Gutman's daughter, Clara. Clara provided proof that is astounding in many ways. The evidence reveals that Dr. Helmy did everything possible to protect Anna if she was ever to be discovered. On one occasion, Dr. Helmy gained a falsified certificate from the Central Islamic Institute in Berlin, stating that Anna had been converted to Islam. This protected her from her Jewish identity. Dr. Helmy also cleverly contrived a certificate providing evidence Anna had wed an Egyptian. Dr. Helmy risked his life to protect Anna Gutman and her family, continually performing true acts of heroism during those years.

In March of 2013, Dr. Helmy was honored as a Righteous Among Nations by the organization Yad Vashem. Righteous Among Nations proclaims Dr. Helmy as rescuer of Jews on the basis of uninfluenced generosity, without the impression of receiving a reward or to influence the religious conversion of the Jewish people.

Dr. Mohamed Helmy is a true hero, an inspiring person, and most of all a man who saved a family from being torn apart and forever destroyed. Dr. Helmy did what he believed was right in his heart. He is truly an example of the many who fought so hard and risked their lives to do what was morally right for the Jewish people during their darkest hours.

Works Cited

"Rescued by an Egyptian in Berlin." The Righteous Among Nations. Yad Vashem The Holocaust Martyrs' and Heroes' Remembrance Authority, 2016. Web. 24 Feb. 2016.

Borschel-Dan, Amanda. "First Egyptian Righteous Among the Nations Honored." The Times of Israel. N.p., n.d. Web. 24 Feb. 2016. < http://www.timesofisrael.com/first-egyptian-righteous-among-the-nations-honored/ >.

"Egyptian Doctor Recognized as Righteous Among the Nations by Yad Vashem." Yad Vashem. Yad Vashem The Holocaust Martyrs' and Heroes' Remembrance Authority, 30 Sept. 2013. Web. 24 Feb. 2016.
< http://www.yadvashem.org/yv/en/pressroom/pressreleases/pr_details.asp?cid=812 >.

"Mohamed Helmy." Jewish Virtual Library. N.p., n.d. Web. 24 Feb. 2016.
< https://www.jewishvirtuallibrary.org/jsource/biography/mohamed_helmy.html >.

Charles Joseph Coward

Rohan Menon (Co-Winner)

Four hundred people. That is how many lives that Charles Joseph Coward was rumored to have saved. How many lives he touched, and families he affected. There were many heroes helping the Jewish people during the Holocaust, and Charles Joseph Coward was one such man. Also known as the Count of Auschwitz, he was involved in many resistance efforts in the infamous camps of Auschwitz. He was born in 1905, in England. Coward joined the army in 1937, at the age of 32. Three years later, Coward was captured by the Germans. Coward was moved around to different prisoner-of-war camps, all the while trying to escape. In some camps, Coward saw first-hand the brutal treatment that Jews went through in concentration camps, which strengthened his resolve to help the Jews.He used his position to carry out many of his plans, such as helping Jews escape the gas chamber and saved many lives. Coward died in 1976. Half of this great man's life was dedicated to helping Jewish people escape Nazi persecution.

Charles Coward helped the Jews in many ways. One way that he helped was by purchasing the bodies of dead Jews with Red Cross supplies, like chocolates and such goods. He would then tell fit, able Jews to join the Jews journeying to the gas chamber at night. On the way, these Jews would hide off the path and Coward would lay the bodies that he purchased across the trail, claiming that the escaped Jews had died on the way. He also smuggled weapons to a camp in Birkenau to use in their rebellion efforts. These actions show Coward to be a very courageous man. Contrary to his name, Coward devoted himself to helping others during dark times, and clearly succeeded in saving many. He saw hate and fear in the world and decided to act, something that not many people do. With his courage and willingness to save others, Charles Coward made a difference in the lives of many.

Coward also used his resources to smuggle food to the Jews in need in the concentration camps. Once, this brave man learned of a British doctor, Karel Sperber, a prisoner-of-war, whom the Germans had deported to a concentration camp. He swapped clothes with a Jew in the camp to sneak in, and then looked everywhere he could for the doctor. Although this attempt failed, it showed what lengths Coward was willing to go to save others. He was always risking his life for others, and laid his life on the line on many occasions. He was also involved in the dangerous practice of smuggling bombs to resistance forces against the Nazi regime. He risked everything to help hundreds of people he did not know.

One great example of Coward's kind heart and bravery is his time with the father of the president of Israel Shimmon Peres. Peres's father, Yitzchak Persky, was with Coward on a voyage to Turkey. Coward was always concerned about the welfare of his fellow passengers. He was always thinking ahead. For example, a soldier from New Zealand died on the journey. Although sad, Coward was also practical. He had Persky assume the identity of that soldier for his safety. When they were captured by the Germans, Coward made sure that no one spoke of Persky being Jewish. He valued all lives, and made sure to include Persky in the group who managed to escape and was recaptured. But Coward always had a plan. Yet again they escaped! However, there were still troubles within their groups. A Scottish prisoner became angry with Persky and openly called him a Jew. Persky confided in Coward, who was outraged. He called a meeting of the group and demanded that the Scot leave. However, when the Scot apologized profusely, Coward allowed him to stay. Clearly, Coward was a very virtuous man, who greatly cared for others.

Charles Coward also aided in making the world aware of the plight of the Jews in the concentration camps of the Nazis. He sent back hundreds of coded messages to Great Britain to ensure that the desperation of the situation was widely known. To accomplish this, Coward addressed the messages to his deceased father, through a Mr. William Orange. William Orange was actually the War Office of England, and Coward's wife took some time to figure out that she had to send the letters to the War Office. Coward sent a message almost every day just to keep the British updated. This whole process shows just how devoted Coward was to helping the Jewish people.

In addition to this, Coward testified at the Nuremberg War Trials. He wrote, "I made it a point to get one of the guards to take me to town under the pretense of buying new razor blades and stuff for our boys. For a few cigarettes he pointed out to me the various places where they had the gas chambers and the places where they took them down to be cremated. Everyone to whom I spoke gave the same story – the people in the city of Auschwitz, the SS men, concentration camp inmates, foreign workers – everyone said that thousands of people were being gassed and cremated at Auschwitz, and that the inmates who worked with us and who were unable to continue working because of their physical condition and were suddenly missing, had been sent to the gas chambers. The inmates who were selected to be gassed went through the procedure of preparing for a bath, they stripped their clothes off, and walked into the bathing room. Instead of showers, there was gas. All the camp knew it. All the civilian population knew it. I mixed with the civilian population at Auschwitz. I was at Auschwitz nearly every day...Nobody could live in Auschwitz and work in the plant, or even come down to the plant without knowing what was common knowledge to everybody..." (Affidavit Copy of Document NI-11696, Prosecution Exhibit 1462). Here it is shown that Coward clearly feels disgusted by the practices in the Nazi camps and felt deeply for the Jewish people who were being persecuted.

In 1965, Charles Joseph Coward was recognized as Righteous Among Nations by Yad Vashem, the World Center for Holocaust Research, Documentation, Education and Commemoration. He was the first British citizen to be thus recognized.

When I began this essay, I knew nothing about Charles Joseph Coward. I picked him because his name intrigued me. As I researched him, his story captivated me. His name is a complete antithesis of his character. I came across some reports which mentioned that not all the escapades of Coward could be corroborated and it is unclear how many prisoners were ultimately liberated due to his actions, but I choose to believe that he did all of these things and he did them with audacity, courage, and resourcefulness. Coward's life inspires me. If I had lived around the same time as the Count of Auschwitz, I would like to think that I would have been as brave as he was. His story motivates me to be the best person I can be.

Works Cited

"Charles Joseph Coward." Wollheim Memorial. Rudolf Steiner, n.d. Web. 8 Feb. 2016.

Connifey, Kasey. "Sgt. Major Charles Coward." Prezi.com. Kasey Connifey, 8 Apr. 2014. Web. 08 Feb. 2016.

Crown, Hannah. "Edmonton Soldier Charles Coward May Finally Be Recognised by British Government." Enfield Independent. Independent Press Standards Organization, 21 July 2009. Web. 10 Feb. 2016.

"Issue 17 - Holocaust: The Count of Auschwitz." MQ Magazine. Mark Griffin, Apr. 2006. Web. 27 Feb. 2016.

A Protagonist for Life

Lana Wong

She was courageous with a generous spirit.

She felt that all lives had worth and devoted her life to bringing peace and joy during an appalling time.

She touched the desperate children who were severed from their kin and hidden from dread, concealed at the foot of Mont Blanc. Tears must have rolled down their pink cheeks, and their eyes wet with sadness as they parted from their parents.

She spoke for joy, happiness, and walked the righteous path. Following that path meant protecting the innocent who were the targets of a sharp, murderous arrow even at the cost of her own life.

She didn't believe in the state sponsored persecution and murder of Jews by the Nazi in Germany and in all the lands that they occupied.

She was courageous with a generous spirit.

She was born German to Catholic parents in the town of Nysa.

She dreamed of becoming a teacher.

She abandoned her dream because her father was an unskilled railroad worker, and her family was barely scraping by. This dream withered into sand that fell between her fingers onto the ground to be forgotten. However, forgotten dreams find their way back in other forms.

She knew, not at the time, that abandoning her dream would lead her life into one of great worth.

She etched another path and started working for Father Remillieux, the spiritual leader of the Franco-German religious peace movement, Compagnons de Saint-Francois.

She became a member of Compagnons de Saint-Francois.

She returned to her homeland of Germany and learned how to become a spiritual aid in Freiburg.

She worked for the congregation of Vaujany in the French Alps when she returned to France.

She hid her true identity when the war began as fear surged inside her that she would be caught by the Resistance, a cluster of resistance movements that fought against the Nazi occupation of France, for she was...German. She prayed hoping not to be discovered.

She was courageous with a generous spirit.

She held the words peace and joy, which modeled her whole life.

She saw hatred rise toward the Jews like water bubbling in a kettle ready to burst into burning steam.

She stepped into the shadows of fear when she joined a Catholic family-care clinic in St. Etienne, for the institution she joined helped persecuted Jews.

She helped hide Jewish children who lacked French citizenship from being deported by planting them in non-Jewish families among the rural French population.

She worried that the Jewish children would be discovered, and so she decided on a safer plan.

She volunteered to care for 30 Jewish children who were housed in a summer camp at the foot of Mont Blanc, a place near Chamonix.

She carried the burden of the children's true identity, and she herself didn't even have papers to keep herself safe, but she stayed devoted to the helpless. Every bone in her body must have trembled. The cold had nothing to do with it.

She fought the panic that swelled inside her, dreading the day will come when Nazi soldiers would knock on the door with forceful shouts to open up. Being discovered would destine the children to deportation and possibly death at a Nazi concentration camp.

She must have looked into the eyes of the Jewish children that gave her the power of hope. Their eyes shined with awe and fear. The light in their eyes stood out from the darkness of their pupils, like something good buried under a whole sea of darkness and misery. Maybe it was hope. She smiled, the children shyly smiled back. Warmth and connection bonded in the air. Later, the air was filled with it.

She made the year of 1943 to 1944 a year of peace, joy, trust, and cooperation for her and the children.

She could not remember another time in her life filled with such momentous happiness and worth.

She taught the children how to harness the beautiful art of music through music lessons.

She placed all the children's needs before her own.

She was courageous with a generous spirit.

She saved two orphan infant girls from a bombardment when she was sent on a rescue mission to Lyons. Explosives lit the sky as smoke collected. The infants were crying loudly, but that was nothing compared to the thundering sound of the sky. Finally, everything was alright.

She sighed as relief washed over her when word came that the occupation by the Nazi was over in the summer of 1944. How could it be that they survived the darkness? She prayed thanks to God.

She wrote a final letter to the children. She told them to "Oppose injustice wherever you come across it. Be a protagonist for life, whenever it is in danger. Consider your life as a mission for peace and happiness. Your life would then not be a waste."

She said to always try to promote peace. This means to be a good person no matter what. Serve good even if it puts your life on the line of danger, it is worth it.

She believed that the peace and joy you grant others would make its way back to you.

She said that God had shown her the way of peace and forgiveness.

She was one of many who helped the Jews during this travesty in history and to make the moral choice to prevent the innocent from getting murdered instead of the choice to look the other way or be complicit in the genocide.

She was courageous with a generous spirit.

She was Sister Claire Barwitzky.

Works Cited

"The Righteous Among The Nations Barwitzky FAMILY." Righteous Among The Nations. Yad   Vashem The Holocaust Martyrs' and Heroes' Remembrance Authority, 20 Mar. 1991.   Web. 19 Feb. 2016.

Paldiel, Mordecai. Churches and the Holocaust Unholy Teachings Good Samaritans and

Reconciliation. Jersey City: Ktav House, 2006. Churches and the Holocaust Unholy Teachings Good Samaritans and Reconciliation. Ktav Publishing House, Inc., 2006. Web.   20 Feb. 2016.

Brookfield School, Sacramento, CA

Dr. Jo Gonsalves became Brookfield's instructional leader in 2007. Prior to joining the Brookfield Faculty, she taught middle school and high school English and Science in Sacramento area private and parochial schools for 11 years. She also served as Assistant Principal of Academics at St. Francis High School in Sacramento for 4 years before accepting her current position to lead Brookfield School. Dr. Jo was drawn to Brookfield School because of its reputation for excellence and its commitment to serving the area's brightest and most motivated students, a population that is grossly underserved in most schools today, but is so important to the betterment of our society's future. If you ask Dr. Jo what she sees as her personal mission as Brookfield's principal, she would tell you, "My purpose is to provide a safe and happy environment, combined with a rigorous and creative academic program, and emotional and social support so my bright students have the best opportunity to reach their potential. I see each of my students as a future leader."

Dr. Tracy is the middle school English teacher at Brookfield School in Sacramento, California. As a grades six through eight teacher, she focuses on making her students excellent readers, writers, and world citizens. Students write essays as part of a curriculum involving historical fiction and nonfiction about the Holocaust. It is very important that each new generation learns what happened in the Holocaust, so that we can never forget.

Darth Clurman

Darth Clurman taught Literature and Cultural Studies to College students for 13 years before transitioning to middle school Literature and English Language arts at Brookfield School. Her specialty is the Literature of political resistance and social justice movements.

The Enduring Legacy of a Selfless Act

Olivia M. Ang-Olson

A hero is one who performs affirmative acts of selflessness, bravery, and courage that cannot be fulfilled by positions of neutrality. One is either a hero or not a hero. There is no "in between." Even those who are well-intentioned bystanders still do not qualify as heroes. People become heroes when they put their lives in jeopardy to save that of someone else. Heroes live in our midst, often unrecognized. A true hero doesn't perform their courageous acts for publicity, attention, or fame. They are powered by an inner, moral motivation; something that cannot be touched, but felt. In an event like the Holocaust, people's true colors shone brightly. Some people's colors were of the Nazi flag, as they supported the killers of over 6 million Jews. Others' colors were of neutrality; they refused to save any victims or stop any killers, for the fear of losing their own lives. And lastly, there were those who wore the colors of heroics; they demonstrated acts of selflessness, putting their lives on the line to save those of innocent Jews. "Hero" is the perfect word to describe Gitta Bauer.

Gitta was born into a liberal, Catholic family in Berlin, Germany in 1919. She was one of three girls in the family. She was a member of the Catholic Movement, which was banned in 1935. In 1942, she was mistaken as a Communist and arrested. During the Holocaust, Gitta formed a newspaper that advocated peace. She wasn't afraid of being rebellious, as long as she was fighting for a worthy cause.

Gitta had a good friend named Ilse Baumgart. Ilse was half Jewish and lived in Berlin under an assumed identity, where she worked as a secretary. She heard about an anti-Hitler plot and asked, "Is the swine (Hilter) dead? Then the war is over." Her comment was reported. The officer who came to arrest her gave her 15 minutes to escape. He, himself, was opposed to the Nazis.

It was then, in 1943, at the young age of 24, that Gitta was faced with the life-changing decision; should she or should she not hide a Jew from the Germans during this time?

Haven't we all experienced close bonds of friendship filled with shared struggles, hopes, and dreams? But most of us have not been faced with the morally gripping dilemma of choosing one of two things: to help someone in need or to preserve one's self. Even when in the midst of a "seemingly close" friendship, many of us would hesitate before putting our lives in danger to save the well-being of a friend. Choosing to not take in a friend may not necessarily mean one is a "bad" friend. People have their reasons. After all, hesitation is not always negative. It may be a wise choice. In Gitta's case, time was of the essence, meaning the Nazis were approaching. She did not have the luxury of hesitation, and she was forced into the life-changing decision of taking in or pushing away a good friend.

"This was no big moral or religious decision. She was a friend and she needed help. We knew it was dangerous, and we were careful, but we didn't consider not taking her," she said at a later date. Gitta's quick, reflex-like decision was brave and courageous. She knew, as a friend, it was the right choice to make, and by making this choice, she put her life at risk. This decision may seem rather simple and wise, but in reality, harboring a Jew during World War II was one of the most dangerous acts a person could do. There were severe consequences for those who were caught hiding Jews from the Gestapo. The punishments included death for everyone involved or a one-way ticket to a concentration camp as well as the home and belongings burned. On top of that, hiding someone from the Nazis put a strain on food supplies and other necessities. It was also imperative to take every precaution to keep out of sight of Nazis or any civilians who may give their secrecy away. Gitta was fully aware of this when choosing to put her own life in jeopardy to brighten the chances of her friend's survival.

Many people sided with the Gestapo and Nazis for the fear of being killed by them. Gitta's brave choice proved that her true colors were of heroics as she demonstrated a clear act of selflessness. She put her life on the line to save that of an innocent Jew.

Fifty years later, in a different continent, Gitta Bauer is still talked about. She may not be the most famous hero of the Holocaust, but to me, she is. Gitta may have thought her act during World War II would just affect her friend, Ilse Baumgart, but in reality, it has affected so many more people. Even after receiving the Yad Vashem medal in 1984, Gitta still has not received the recognition I believe a true hero deserves. Regardless, she has touched my life as well as the many others that have learned about her story. Thank you, Gitta Bauer.

Luise W. Elisabeth Abegg: The Guardian Angel

Ayushi Bansal

 Luise Wilhelmine Elisabeth Abegg was a female, German Holocaust hero during the mid-1900s. Luise W. Elisabeth Abegg put her own life on the line to free others from Nazi persecution. Luise W. Elisabeth Abegg was a German teacher and resistance fighter against Nazism. Luise W. Elisabeth Abegg provided shelter for about 80 Jews during the Holocaust and as a result was recognized with the honor of Righteous Among the Nations. Luise Elisabeth Abegg was born on March 3, 1882 in Strasbourg, Alsace, which is now located in France and is the capital of Alsace. Abegg was a social studies teacher at Luisen Mädchenschule, a Fashionable Berlin girls' school, but was forced to retire in 1940, when she was only 52 years old because she refused to teach the children about the Nazis, and also because of her anti-Nazi views. The majority of Abegg's students were Jewish and she wanted to teach them humanistic beliefs that could help them survive during the Holocaust. Elisabeth Abegg was a woman of compassion,

dauntlessness, and bravery, who risked her own life to save others, even though she had no benefits.

The German authorities viewed Elisabeth Abegg as politically undependable and she was once invited by the Gestapo, the German Secret State Police of Nazi Germany, for interrogation. She could not be discouraged from remaining in close contact with many of her Jewish students and friends. With the deportation of her close friend, Anna Hirschberg, to the East, she understood the importance of the Nazi execution of the Jews. Even though it was too late to save her friend, Luise Wilhelmine Elisabeth Abegg devoted the rest of her life in saving other Jews from the Gestapo and removing extermination. In one case, Luise Elisabeth W. Abegg offered some of her own jewelry to finance her operation to bring a handful of Jews to safety. Luise Elisabeth knew what the consequences would be if she got caught. She had seen her friends get taken away and was aware of the horrors of this war. Elisabeth put her own life on the line to help others and to make sure that they were safe and wouldn't be exterminated. She made sure that they didn't get caught. She was conscious of the danger that awaited her. Although she knew she could be sent to work at a concentration camp or to her death, she didn't give up. Luise Elisabeth Abegg continued to fight for justice and succeeded in saving countless Jewish men, women, and children. In 1957, a group of survivors who remained in contact with Abegg after the war dedicated a collection of memoirs to her on her 75th birthday. In 1967, Abegg was recognized as the Righteous Among the Nations by the State of Israel. This honor is given to non-Jews who risked their own lives during the Holocaust to help save Jews from extermination from the Nazis. She risked her life for other people and took the risk of dying to save numerous people. Her actions prove her to be a true hero. Elisabeth Abegg once said "Their fate will be my fate too." Her only goal for her life during this time was to rescue others no matter the consequences. In 1942, at age 60, Abegg turned the four-room apartment that she lived in with her 86 year old mother and disabled sister, Julie, into a shelter and assembly point for Jews who were going underground for safety. Abegg helped several Jews by offering them temporary housing in her own home or directing them to hiding places somewhere else. Abegg also forged papers for them to travel outside the country to safety or to live by a fake identity, so the Gestapo wouldn't exterminate them. She cut corners with her and her sister's food to feed the Jews with food-ration cards. Abegg also invited them each Friday, into her home to special meals. All this activity took place in her apartment which housed some tenants who were active Nazis. Luise Elisabeth Abegg died on August 8th, 1974, in Berlin Germany, as a hero to many families and friends.

Luise Wilhelmine Elisabeth Abegg, a German Holocaust hero during the mid-1900s risked her life to provide food, shelter, and companionship for the Jews. Elisabeth Abegg was an educator and resistance fighter against Nazism. Elisabeth Abegg provided shelter for numerous Jews during the Holocaust and although she didn't receive any money, awards, or certificates for her outstanding commitment and hard work, she received the recognition and honor of being Righteous Among the Nations. Elisabeth Abegg was the guardian angel of countless Jews during a horrific time in history: the Holocaust. It is a relief to know that there were people like Elisabeth Abegg that gave people hope and saved their lives, when no one else stood up to do the deed. This was the story of Luise Wilhelmine Elisabeth Abegg, and the heroism she showed toward the Holocaust victims. Luise Wilhelmine Elisabeth Abegg was, is, and will always be admired for her courage, outstanding achievements, noble qualities, and most of all the bravery she showed toward people she barely knew.

Works Cited

"Elisabeth Abegg - The Righteous Among The Nations - Yad Vashem." Elisabeth Abegg - The Righteous Among the Nations - Yad Vashem. N.P., n.d. Web.

"Elisabeth Abegg - The Righteous Among The Nations." Yad Vashem. N.P., n.d. Web.

"The Righteous During the Holocaust." Holocaust Memorial Center. N.P., n.d. Web.

The Althoff Circus

Adelina Hernandez

 The story of the Althoff family is not one of true adventure or action, but rather a story of compassion, humanity, and tolerance of races, traits that were not that common during Nazi Germany. The Althoff family, specifically Adolf and Maria, ran the well-liked Adolf Althoff Circus in Germany during World War II. Belonging to a circus family, they accepted everyone Adolf lead him to open his arms and his circus to a half Jewish girl, on whom everyone turned their backs. This proves that heroes do not necessarily have to always fly in capes, but rather, saviors are the ones who care for you when everyone else ignores your existence.

Adolf Althoff was born into a circus family in 1913. In 1936, Adolf and his sister, Helene, formed the tenting circus named Circus Geschwister Althoff (Geschwister means siblings). Their father gave them the needed supplies to create a successful circus, including some horses, ponies, and an elephant. In 1939, Helene separated into her own circus company, so Adolf decided to create his own circus: the Adolf Althoff Circus. He found his sweetheart, Maria, who also came from a circus family, and together they toured Europe even throughout the Second World War. During this time, Adolf refused to join the Nazi Party.

During the fateful summer of 1941, the circus was in Germany visiting the city Darmstadt for a prolonged series of shows. One of their visitors happened to be Irene Danner. Born in Belgium, her father Hans Danner was a German artist and her mother, Alice Lorch, belonged to the Jewish circus family Lorch, or rather the German-Jewish dynasty that came to Eschollbruecken near Darmstadt in the 1800s. Unfortunately, the circus went bankrupt in 1930 when workers left and German boycotts against Jews began, driving away business. Irene lived together with her younger sister, Gerda, with her grandmother, Sessy, in Eschollbruecken. Despite the fact that the other side of her family was Christian, she was still a Jew in the eyes of everyone who discriminated against them. At the age of 13, she was denied an education and was prohibited from working as an artist three years later. Around 1938, her grandmother paid for the release of her son, Egon Lorch, from the Dachau concentration camp while it was still possible. Unfortunately he died later on in Italy at the age of 54. Irene's grandfather's business kept him in Belgium and he was not allowed to return to see his family, leaving him to die in exile in great poverty in 1942. In March 1943, Sessy was taken to Auschwitz with her brother-in-law, Eugen Lorch. Neither of them survived.

When Irene visited Adolf, he took her in knowing the consequences of his actions. He was even quoted saying "We circus people see no difference between races or religions." Irene became a bareback rider and soon fell in love with a Belgian circus clown named Peter Storm-Bento and had her first two children with him during hiding. After the war was over, they had three more children. From 1942-1943, there were three deportations of Jews in Darmstadt, including Irene's grandmother. Her mother and sister, Alice and Gerda, were luckily able to join Irene in the circus. Later, her father, Hans Danner, came home from war under the orders to divorce his Jewish wife. He disobeyed orders and instead stayed in the circus. The fear of the Gestapo inspections was always present, but luckily Adolf's connections gave him knowledge of inspections beforehand. This allowed them time to either hide in one of the wagons while Adolf distracted the officers, or Irene and Peter went to the forest on a picnic, acting like a normal family that wasn't being searched for. Adolf even fired another artist for denouncing the family. His wife, Maria, helped Irene and cared for her, especially throughout her pregnancies. Together the couple and the circus ensured the family's survival throughout the war.

In conclusion, the actions of a man and his family lead to the survival and renewal of hope for an unfortunately mistreated family. This man and his wife were heroes not only to the family, but he simultaneously brought joy to others through his own circus throughout the war. With a girl who lost people in her family to the rest of Germany, Irene was eventually saved by the Althoff Circus. In a world that is so large, we need people with hearts large enough to hold people who need to be protected from the villains of the world. If war were to spread across the entire globe again in the future, it would only be a matter of time before new victims would be made, and heroes would be needed again.

Works Cited

"From the Testimony of Irene Danner-Storm, October 1994 - The Righteous Among The Nations - Yad Vashem." From the Testimony of Irene Danner-Storm, October 1994 - The Righteous Among The Nations - Yad Vashem. N.p., n.d. Web. 25 Feb. 2016.

"Adolf and Maria Althoff - The Righteous Among The Nations - Yad Vashem." Adolf and Maria Althoff - The Righteous Among The Nations - Yad Vashem. N.p., n.d. Web. 25 Feb. 2016.

"Althoff, Adolf and Maria - The Jewish Foundation for the Righteous." The Jewish Foundation for the Righteous. N.p., n.d. Web. 25 Feb. 2016.

The Independent. Independent Digital News and Media, n.d. Web. 25 Feb. 2016.

The Story of Marie Burde

Afdithi Benush

Marie Burde was born in 1892. She lived in a small and dark cellar in the Wedding neighborhood of Berlin. She was not well off, and made her living by selling old newspaper, empty bottles and rags. Even though she was not in a good financial position, she went out of her way to help protect three Jewish men, saving their lives. She lived with the danger of being found by the police, and devoted herself to helping these men in any way she could. This bravery and devotion is what made Marie Burde a hero.

Most people in Berlin and throughout Germany were too worried about their own safety to try to protect others, or they just joined the Nazi forces in persecuting and turning in Jews. This was what brothers Alfred and Rolf Joseph found after having escaped the officers who killed their parents and went out into the streets. They asked a former neighbor who had promised to help them when they were in need to take care of them, but he turned them down, saying that his neighbors were now Gestapo agents. The boys went on living in railway stations, public gardens, or woody areas to keep themselves hidden from their persecutors. They used the small amount of money that their parents had left for them with friends to purchase food for themselves on the black market. Soon, Arthur Fondanski, a friend of Alfred, came and joined them. There then came a point where they could no longer stay out on the streets of Berlin. They needed to be hidden and sheltered. They met an acquaintance of Rolf and Alfred's parents who said that though she could not help them herself, they could ask Marie Burde who was known to be against the persecution of Jews, and would be willing to help them out. It was known in Berlin at the time that Burde had been helping Jews escape from the officers.

When Burde received the three men at her home, she immediately agreed to take them into her protection. Because Burde was not in a good living situation, the men slept on piles of newspaper that she had collected to make her living. During the day, Burde had asked the men to leave the apartment. The purpose of the men doing this was to avoid being asked questions by skeptical neighbors. Living in hiding was hard, for both Burde and the men. About a year after Burde took the three men into her shelter, the building was destroyed in an air raid. Following the bombing, Burde set out for a lot she owned in Schoenow, to the north of Berlin, with the three men. Even though Burde had just had her home and lots of her property bombed, she stayed loyal to what she believed was the right thing to do, and continued to help the three men she had agreed to shelter. They used a handcart to transport any remaining property to Schoenow with them, while avoiding authorities by saying that their papers were destroyed in air raid.

Burde and the three men arrived in Schoenow without money to buy a proper house for themselves. They were able to build a small shack out of wood for them to stay in. Burde endured the difficult life in the hut while providing for the men until winter came. It then became impossible for the four to continue living in the small shack. They were forced to return back to Berlin, where they had come from. In Berlin, Burde was able to get a house from the authorities. She told them that her house had been bombed in an air raid and was able to get housing for herself and the men. She continued to shelter and help them, even after all the difficulties that had presented themselves before her. She protected the men through the year of 1943, and most of 1944, until Alfred Joseph was caught and arrested on the streets of Berlin. He was transported to Sachsenhausen, a concentration camp located in Germany. After Sachsenhausen, he was moved to Bergen-Belsen, a concentration camp in Germany with extremely high casualty rates. The two remaining men remained safe under the protection of Burde until liberation.

Miraculously, Alfred was able to survive through both of the concentration camps. Thanks to the tireless efforts of Marie Burde, the other two men were able to come out of the war unscathed. Alfred was reunited with his brother, Rolf, and the two brothers supported Burde, as she did them during the war. Marie Burde passed away in the 1950s, after leading a generous and righteous life.

Marie Burde was a hero of the Holocaust, a righteous gentile. Even though she was not Jewish, she put everything she could into helping and sheltering the persecuted Jewish people who came to her seeking refuge. She was barely able to support herself, yet she was able to put others before her and make sure that they were safe. Burde endured many challenges. She risked her life to protect the three men, and thanks to her efforts, they were able to come out of the Holocaust alive. One of them was caught, but because they were careful, he managed to avoid capture until the closing point of the war, which led to his survival and his reunification with his brother and Burde. Even though the most notable journey of Burde's life was the period of years in the war in which she protected Rolf and Alfred Joseph, as well as their friend Arthur Fondanski, Burde was able to help many more Jewish people through the difficult warring and violent era. Because of her valor and generosity, Marie Burde is a hero. She was recognized as Righteous Among the Nations on February 14, 2012.

Citations:

"Rescue Story Marie Burde." The Righteous Among the Nations. N.p., n.d. Web. 22 Feb. 2016.

"Burde Marie." The Righteous Among the Nations. N.p., n.d. Web. 22 Feb. 2016.

Courage
Charlotte Stiplosek (Co-Winner)

Sometimes the greatest heroes emerge from the most unlikely places. A young boy was born on April 28, 1908 completely unaware of the amazing deeds he would accomplish. Oskar Schindler, a spy, industrialist, and member of the Nazi Party, rescued over 1,200 Jews, by employing them in his factories. Oskar Schindler risked his life to salvage those lives that had not yet been lost. His generosity and courage saved the lives of thousands of people who would otherwise been killed.

A great man was born on April 28, 1908 in Svitavy, Germany. Early on, Schindler learned many trades, including being a farmer, owner of a driving school, and selling government property. He also served in the Czechoslovak army and in 1938 earned the rank of lance corporal in the reserves. Schindler soon began working for the Amt Auslands/Abwehr (Office of the Military Foreign Intelligence) of the German Armed Forces in 1936. Three years later, in February 1939, he joined the Nazi Party. Shortly after, Schindler moved from Svitavy to Krakow where he purchased Rekord Ltd, a Jewish-owned manufacturing plant, renaming this factory Emalia. Though he opened two other factories, Schindler only employed Jewish workers at Emailia.

As Emalia grew, Schindler became richer and more influential in the Nazi Party. At Emalia's peak in 1944, there were more than 1,700 workers; 1,000 were Jewish forced laborers the Germans had relocated from the Krakow ghetto after its dispersion in March 1943, to the concentration camp Krakau-Plaszow. Though these prisoners were still vulnerable to the terrible conditions of the Plasvow Concentration Camp, Schindler often intervened, offering bribes and personal diplomacy in order to stall the deportation of his workers to a more brutal camp. During and after the liquidation of the Krakow ghetto in March 1943, Schindler allowed the Jews to sleep in the factory. However, in 1944 the SS officers forced relocation of the Emalia Jews to Auschwitz, Nazi Germany's largest killing center. Immediately after, Schindler relocated his plant to Brünnlitz, where it reopened solely as a weapons' factory. An assistant then created a list of 1,200 Jews 'needed' to work in this factory. This list later became well known as "Schindler's List." He then made sure this factory met the specifications required for it to be classified as a sub-camp of the Gross-Rosen concentration camp. Though only one wagon-load of live ammunition was produced in eight months, Schindler was able to trick the SS officers, through his bogus statistics that weapons were being produced at a steady rate. Schindler departed Brünnlitz only on May 9, 1945, the day that Soviet troops liberated the camp.

Schindler and his wife Emilie then moved to Regensburg, Germany, until 1949, when they immigrated to Argentina. In 1957, Schindler returned to Germany after permanently separating from his wife. In 1962, Yad Vashem Schindler was awarded the title of "Righteous Among the Nations" in recognition of risking his life to save so many others. Emilie was similarly honored in 1993. Unfortunately, Schindler died in Germany, poor and unknown, in October 1974. However, many of the Jews and the descendants of those he saved paid for his body to be moved and buried in Israel. In 1993, the United States Holocaust Memorial Council awarded the museum's Medal of Remembrance to Schindler. This medal honors those who accomplished extraordinary deeds during the Holocaust. Emilie Schindler accepted the medal on behalf of her ex-husband at a ceremony.

Oskar Schindler was a sentimentalist who loved the simplicity of doing good. He was still full of flaws, but his sheer humanity saved thousands of Jews. Regardless of their difference, even his ex-wife, Emilie Schindler, recalls Schindler this way: "In spite of his flaws, Oscar had a big heart and was always ready to help whoever was in need. He was affable, kind, extremely generous and charitable, but at the same time, not mature at all ..." Schindler was willing to sacrifice his own money, time, and put his life at risk in order to help the greater good. Only once, in a 1964 interview, did Schindler comment on what he did. "The persecution of Jews in occupied Poland meant that we could see horror emerging gradually in many ways. In 1939, they were forced to wear Jewish stars, and people were herded and shut up into ghettos. Then, in the years '41 and '42 there was plenty of public evidence of pure sadism. With people behaving like pigs, I felt the Jews were being destroyed. I had to help them. There was no choice." Schindler's compassion and hope saved thousands of lives, offering justice to those that had been persecuted.

Often, many of our greatest heroes emerge from the most unlikely places. Oskar Schindler was spy, industrialist, and member of the Nazi Party. Regardless, during World War II, Schindler was able to rescue more than 1,000 Jews from deportation by employing them in his ammunitions factories until their liberation. He fell into the background, almost unknown until 1962, when he received his first award for his bravery and willingness to speak against the persecution of Jews and aid towards the betterment of humanity. Oskar Schindler's hope for a better world turned him from an obedient Nazi to a Holocaust hero.

Works Cited:

"Donate Now." Yad Vashem. N.p., n.d. Web. 15 Feb. 2016.

"The Oscar Schindler Story." The Oscar Schindler Story. N.p., n.d. Web. 15 Feb. 2016.

"Oskar Schindler - Why Did He Do It." Oskar Schindler - Why Did He Do It. N.p., n.d. Web. 15 Feb. 2016.

"Oskar Schindler." United States Holocaust Memorial Museum. United States Holocaust Memorial Council, 29 Jan. 2016. Web. 15 Feb. 2016.

http://www.ushmm.org/wlc/en/article.php?ModuleId=10005787

http://www.oskarschindler.com

http://www.oskarschindler.dk/schindler9.htm

Blessed Bernard Lichtenberg

Elliott Lundholm (Co-Winner)

 Because I am going to attend Christian Brothers High School next year, I was hoping that my research would lead me to a Catholic hero of the Holocaust from Germany. I was very pleased to learn that there were several Catholic heroes of from Germany. Among them were truly inspirational men such as Karl Leisner, Rupert Mayer and Joseph Cebula. All showed great compassion and bravery and all would have been great to write about. I chose Bernard Lichtenberg because I discovered that he loved Erich Maria Remaerque's anti-war novel, "All Quiet on the Western Front," one of my favorites. In 1931, he actually called on all Catholics to view a film version of the novel. Also, he was born on December 3, the same day as two of my brothers.

Bernard Lichtenberg, the second oldest of five siblings, was born in Ohlua, a predominantly Protestant city of what was then the Prussian province of Lower Silesia in 1875. In 1886, Catholics made up just under a third of the population of Ohlua, while the Jewish population was less than 1 percent. At an early age, Lichtenberg decided he wanted to become a priest. He studied theology in Innsbruck and in 1899, he was ordained a priest. His career in the Catholic Church took him to Berlin in 1913, where he established a reputation for working with the poor. During World War I, he served as a military chaplain.

Lichtenberg was also known for his politics within the Catholic Church. From 1913 to 1920 he served as a representative in the District Assembly in Charlottenburg and from 1920 to 1930 as a member of the regional parliament of Wedding. He was also a member of the Peace Association of German Catholics and was elected to the board of the Inter-Denominational Working Group for peace in 1929. After the Nazis took over in 1933, he began to express his opinion that as a Catholic priest, he was bound to help the Jewish people or any other group that was being denied civil and human rights. This bought him into some conflict with the majority of the Catholic establishment during the Holocaust. He tried to convince Cardinal Bertram, the Archbishop of Breslau and the president of the German Episcopal Conference, to prevent the anti-Semitic boycott of Jewish businesses planned for April 1, 1933. He even arranged for an influential Jewish banker, Oskar Wassermann to meet with Bertram. Bertram sided with the majority of the Catholic Church establishment and made it clear that the boycott was not something the Catholic Church would do anything about.

Lichtenberg, however, continued to protest the persecution of the Jews as well as the arrest and killing of the mentally ill. In 1935, he actually went to Hermann Goring to personally protest the cruelties of the concentration camps. Although Goring dismissed him as a nuisance, the Nazis soon came to regard Lichtenberg as real menace. He continued to put his life in danger by organizing demonstrations against camps like Dachau and raising his voice publically against Nazi brutality. In 1936, he met with rabbis, Protestant ministers, and "non-Aryan" laymen, all of whom concluded that "the German people have much to atone for with regard to the Jews". Many people tried to warn Lichtenberg that the Nazis would take some sort of action against him, especially after the SS second in command, Reinhard Heydrich, referred to him as "that gutter priest from Berlin". Yet, Lichtenberg was undeterred and enlarged the scope of his protest. In 1937 he was elected Cathedral Provost and in 1938 placed in charge of the Relief Office of the Berlin episcopate. In this capacity, he assisted many Catholics of Jewish descent to emigrate from Germany.

From his pulpit in the St. Hedwig Cathedral in Berlin, he began daily prayers for Jews, Jewish Christians and other victims of the Nazi regime As the German churches continued to keep their silence in the face Nazi brutality during Kristallnacht (9/10 November, 1938), he famously warned a Catholic bishop in the St. Hedwig Cathedral that the burning of a synagogue outside is also a house of God. His exact words were: "We know what happened yesterday. We do not know what lies in store for us tomorrow. But we have experienced what has happened today. Outside burns the temple. This is also a place of worship."

After the outbreak of World War II in 1939, Lichtenberg anti-Nazi statements and protests against the persecution of the Jews and intensified again. He railed against racial segregation in air raid shelters. He protested against the use of euthanasia in the concentration camps. He wrote the Chief Physician of the Third Reich: "I, as a human being, a Christian, a priest and a German, demand of you Chief Physician of the Reich, that you answer for the crimes that have been perpetrated at your bidding, and with your consent, and which will call forth the vengeance of the Lord on the heads of the German people."

By 1941, it became obvious that the Nazis would no longer tolerate Lichtenberg's protest against the persecution of the Jews. Two women who heard him pray publicly for the Jews and concentration camp inmates reported him to the police. The Gestapo searched his home and found a declaration he intended to read following Sunday in Church. The declaration addressed a leaflet circulated by Goebbels' Propaganda Ministry, in which Germans were warned not to offer help to the Jews, not even a friendly greeting. Lichtenberg wrote: "An anonymous slanderous sheet against the Jews is being distributed to Berlin houses. This leaflet states that every German who supports Jews with an ostensibly false sense of sentimentality, be it only friendly kindness, commits treason against his people. Let us not be misled by this un-Christian way of thinking but follow the strict command of Jesus Christ. `You shall love your neighbor as you love yourself."

The Gestapo arrested Lichtenberg on October 23, 1941. He was interrogated and asked to retract his previous statements against the Nazi regime. Not only did he refuse but he also added: "I have made up my mind to accompany the deported Jews and Christian Jews into exile, in order to give them spiritual aid." He was found guilty of abuse of the pulpit and insidious activity and sent to Tegel prison for two years. Toward the end of his sentence after suffering from abuse in prison he became physically frail.

He was visited by Bishop Prysing of Berlin who advised him that the Gestapo would allow him to go free if he refrained from preaching for the duration of the war. Lichtenberg asked instead to accompany deported Jews and Jewish Christians to the Jewish ghetto at Lodz, Poland in order to serve as their pastoral minister. The Gestapo refused and sent him to Dachau. Father Bernard Lichtenberg died in a cattle car on the way to Dachau on November 5, 1943. He was 68 years old.

Lichtenberg's body was returned to Berlin where over more than 4,000 attended his funeral. Many Catholic clergy paid their respects to this great man and acknowledged that he "spoke and acted independently and fearlessly". On June 23, 1996, Pope John Paul II declared Lichtenberg a blessed martyr during a Mass in the Olympic stadium in Berlin.

Father Lichtenberg lived an exceptional life. From the beginning he was an unflinching humanitarian. He first spoke out for the poor then protested against the immoral persecution of innocent people. I am always impressed by people who demonstrate courage whether it be physical courage or moral courage. I believe that Father Lichtenberg exhibited both. He risked his standing in the Catholic Church when repeatedly warned Church officials that their silence in the face of Nazi atrocity was contrary to their Christian principles. When he knew his actions would bring him into direct conflict Nazi leadership and expose him to being jailed or worse, he never backed off. He was an inspiration for us all and a true hero of the Holocaust.

Works Cited

facinghistory.org/Weimar-republic-fragility/personalities/bernard-litchtenberg Feb/23/2016.

catholic.org/saints/saint.php?saint_id=7100 Feb/23/2016

yadvashem.org/yv/righteous/stories/Lichtenberg.asp Feb/23/2016

Johanna Eck: A German Hero of the Holocaust

Emily Sperring (Special Award)

When people think of heroes, many think of brave strong warriors valiantly defeating the villains. However, people who help in more subtle ways are heroes too. A hero is someone who is courageous, has achieved great things, has noble qualities, and is generally admired. Johanna Eck was a brave German hero guided by her strong sense of morality. She sacrificed her own safety and luxuries to save four victims of Nazi persecution, two who were Jews. Eck believed it was her responsibility to help those who were in need. She offered them sanctuary in her own home and provided food, shelter, and false evidence to save them. Eck stepped up when others would not and her resourcefulness and generosity made her a true hero.

Many people are brave, smart, and strong, but they lack important moral values to always assist others. However, that was not the case with Johanna Eck. Johanna Eck was born January 4th 1888 in Berlin, Germany. Not much is known about her childhood. She was a trained nurse and was always very kind. She believed it was the job of the people to help everyone in need, however they could. She once said, "If a fellow human being is in distress and I can help him, then it becomes my duty and responsibility. Were I to refrain from doing so, then I would betray the task that life – or perhaps God? – demands from me." This represents the unique ideology that led her to risk her life repeatedly to help the victims, regardless of who they were or where they were from, unlike most of the people during the war. Her willingness and dedication to serving everyone in any way she could makes her a true hero.

In addition to having strong moral values, to be a hero one needs to be courageous and determined. In Berlin Germany, the Jews were being deported rapidly. When a Jewish family was deported in 1942, one member was left behind: a young man named Heinz Guttmann. Heinz was trying to evade arrest and searching desperately for food and shelter. Everyone refused to help him and turned him away because he was Jewish and they were afraid of getting caught. However, Eck, who had known his family before they got deported, stepped up to aide him. Eck knew it would be very dangerous and that she would be breaking the law but she was determined to help him. She offered him shelter in her own house and shared her rationed portion of food with him. She went around trying to get more food for him from her friends. When her house was destroyed, Eck found a new hiding place for Heinz and continued to provide food for him whenever possible. Although Eck had barely enough food for herself, her determination to assist Heinz led her to successfully scrounge up enough for both him and herself.

Although Eck had already done enough to be considered a hero, she was not finished yet - there were still people suffering and in danger who needed help. Along with her belief in always helping others, her determination, and her bravery; her cleverness and resourcefulness would lead her to another successful rescue. Eck's next act of heroism was when she took in a young Jewish girl named Elfriede Guttmann (not related Heinz Guttmann). Elfriede had been hiding and barely escaped during a raid by the Gestapo. She met Eck, who sheltered her in her own home. One day, Erika Hartmann, a friend of Elfriede, met Elfriede and was concerned about her. Wanting to help her, Hartmann gave Elfriede some of her personal Aryan papers. Eck's most brilliant move was when she used those papers to ensure Elfriede's safety. When Hartmann perished in an air raid, Eck took advantage of the chaos and registered Elfriede as Hartmann, making her a legal citizen and hiding her Jewish heritage from the Nazis. Elfriede survived the rest of the war, thanks to Eck's help. Unfortunately, Elfriede perished due to stomach problems after the war. Eck stayed with her to the end and had her buried in a cemetery. Eck risked her own life to save people in need right under the Germans' noses. Her resourcefulness and determination allowed her to successfully shelter and provide for them all.

Heroes do not have to be brave famous warriors standing in the front. Even if you can't save millions of people, it is important to do whatever possible to help. Johanna Eck was a hero who sacrificed her own safety and luxuries to help the victims of Nazi persecution the best she could, regardless of their background, because she believed it was the right thing to do. She has proven that heroes can help in more subtle ways to change the lives of the victims. We can learn from her example that is important to help everyone in need, in whatever way we can, to stay true to our consciousness, and to always be courageous and clever.

Works Cited

""Women of Valor"" <i>Johanna Eck</i>. N.p., n.d. Web. 09 Feb. 2016.

A Man Who Changed History

Jonathan R. Fong

Oskar Schindler was born in the Czech Republic April 28, 1908, in to a middle class Roman Catholic family. Although he was born in what is today the Czech Republic his family lived in German speaking town of Moravia, and was heavily influenced by German culture. He studied architecture and was expected to follow in the footsteps of his father. Oskar however would do anything except what was expected. He joined the Nazi Party in 1938 and created many friends as being a supplier for the Nazi army.

Oskar started out not as you might expect for being a righteous gentile. He was at first not against the idea that the Jews should be working for them, and he didn't like the Jews. He was a profiteer from the war, as he was a factory owner, and he had many S.S. officers as friends. Later, this would help in in his rescue of the Jews. What really changed Oskar Schindler's perspective was when he saw the treatment of the Jews in the ghetto. Oskar was trying to create livable conditions for the Jews. He would later save more Jews than any other person from the gas chambers.

Oskar would then go to Krakow in 1939 and would take over the formerly Jewish-run factory. He starts producing small cooking wear for the Nazi army, which later would turn into creating ammunition for Oskar's enemy. Instead of fighting, Oskar took an approach for humanitarian issues. Oskar used his old friendships to get Jews out of the gas chambers. He said that he was using them for labor, but he was actually nourishing these Jews back to health. When thousands of Jews were sent to the death camp of Auschwitz, he ran to Auschwitz and convinced the S.S. officer, who was an old drinking buddy, that he needed the men for labor, and later got all the women out of Auschwitz as well.

Nearing the end of the war, in the dead of winter, 120 men were sent to an extermination camp. Oskar Schindler managed to get the head S.S. officer to open the sealed cattle car and hand over the 107 remaining men, saved from frostbite and the bitter cold of winter. He also made sure that those who had died in the car were given a proper Jewish burial. He bought all the burial plots with his own money.

Oskar Schindler tried and was very successful through his humanitarian issues, and saved more Jews than any other individual person. He constantly was doing all he could, spending his own money, and at times risking his own life, like when he would be arrested, just to save the lives of the Jews. Oskar Schindler was repeatedly warned by the Nazi army for helping Jews, by being arrested and put in jail. The lives of people that at first he was against, now turning into the focal point, or what really defined him as a person.

Heroes of the Holocaust: Ludwig Wörl

Lauren Kim

 Ludwig Wörl knew that his life was on the line, yet he continued to assist his fellow prisoners and helped them endure the hardships of the concentration camps. Wörl knew that he could be killed, as assisting the other prisoners was against the laws of the camp, but he was undeterred. Ludwig Wörl spent 11 years as a political prisoner in the Nazi concentration camps. As he rose up in the ranks in the camps, he did his best to try and protect as many of his fellow inmates as he could. Wörl showed true bravery and heroism by putting his life on the line and putting others before himself.

Ludwig Wörl was born in 1906. He was first arrested by the Gestapo in 1934 at the age of 28 for being a (suspected) Communist and for handing out pamphlets informing the public about the horrors of the concentration camp Dachau. At the time, freedom of speech was very limited in Germany, so he was detained. He spend 9 months in a detention cell, and was then sent to work as a medical orderly in Dachau's sick bay. In 1942 he was sent to Monowitz, a sub-camp of Auschwitz, where he worked as a nurse in the infirmary. He had not yet achieved a high status, but had some influence over the medical personnel who were of lower status than him. Wörl was then transferred over to the main camp of Auschwitz to deal with a typhus outbreak, which threatened both the prisoners and the camp personnel. In the concentration camps, Wörl had a hard time until he was finally promoted to a rank of importance. Once he reached the top levels of the concentration camp hierarchy, he had a wide influence over the actions of the camp. The SS tempted Wörl to join them, but he refused to become just a tool used and exploited by the SS. Therefore, he was not able to gain the favor of the authorities consistently for long periods of time. After refusing to work with the SS, Wörl started to assist fellow prisoners, especially Jews who comprised the majority of the imprisoned.

Wörl was eventually appointed to become the Lagerälteste, or camp elder, of the hospital barracks. The Lagerälteste was also in charge of all the inmates in the entire camp. He employed many Jewish doctors, against the explicit orders of the SS. Because of this, many of the Jewish doctors were saved from certain death. Wörl also obtained some of the required medicines and medical instruments needed to treat his patients, and thus put himself at risk. He also forged selection lists to protect his Jewish patients from death by gassing. However, the SS and other top authorities were not very pleased once they found out Wörl had deliberately disobeyed orders. Wörl was dismissed again after not following SS orders to decimate the number of the sick, and was send back to an isolated detention cell.

After being released from the detention cells, Wörl was put in Güntergrube, a forced-labor camp near Auschwitz. In Güntergrube, Wörl protected the Jewish prisoners from maltreatment by the other German Kapos. A Kapo was a prisoner in charge of a group of inmates in Nazi concentration camps. Wörl made sure that each prisoner got their due share of food and clothing. Those with severe illnesses such as tuberculosis were also able to survive because Wörl exempted them from hard work and protected them from "the selection," in which the weak prisoners were gassed and killed. When the prisoners of Auschwitz were evacuated to escape the nearing front and the Allied soldiers, Wörl helped many prisoners escape from the death marches that killed so many others. In the death marches, prisoners were forced to march or run many miles, often in brutal winter conditions, to relocate to a different camp. The SS authorities did not want the prisoners to fall into the hands of Allied soldiers alive to tell their stories to the liberators. They also believed that they could use the prisoners to negotiate a peace that would ensure the survival of the Nazi regime. All in all, an estimated 200,000-250,000 concentration camp prisoners were murdered or died on the forced death marches.

After the war, Wörl became the chairman of the Organization of Former Auschwitz Prisoners in Germany and dedicated his life to preserving the memory of Nazi crimes. He also brought many of the Nazi perpetrators to justice. In 1963, he took the stand as one of the key witnesses in the Auschwitz trial in Frankfurt am Main. On March 19th 1963, Yad Vashem recognized Ludwig Wörl as "Righteous Among the Nations."

Ludwig Wörl risked his life to assist the other prisoners in the concentration camps he worked in. Wörl knew that he could be killed, as what he was doing was against the laws of the camp, yet he continued try to help. Wörl showed true bravery and heroism by putting others before himself and putting his life on the line. He rightfully deserved to be among the Righteous gentiles recognized and commemorated by Yad Vashem. Wörl's life work continues to show today's generation an example on doing one's best to help others, even if peer pressure (and the odds) says one should not. After all, one person can change the world—whether it is for better or for worse.

Works Cited

"The Stories of Six Righteous Among the Nations in Auschwitz." Ludwig Wörl. Yad Vashem, Web. 14 Feb. 2016.

"Death Marches." United States Holocaust Memorial Museum. United States Holocaust Memorial Council, 29 Jan. 2016. Web. 14 Feb. 2016.

Buser, Verena. "Jewish Lagerälteste in the Concentration Camp System: The Yad Vashem Biennial International Conference (15-18 December 2014)." "All People of Israel Are Responsible for Each Other"? Ideals and Reality during the Shoah. Academia.edu, Web. 14 Feb. 2016.

"Death Marches." Yad Vashem. Yad Vashem, Web. 14 Feb. 2016. <http://www.yadvashem.org/odot_pdf/Microsoft%20Word%20-%206260.pdf>.

Camerado Springs Middle School, Cameron Park, CA

Levi Cambridge
Assistant Principal

Levi Cambridge a graduate of California State University Sacramento where he received a Master's degree in Educational Leadership. He taught in the classroom for 13 years at both elementary and secondary levels. He is currently an assistant principal at Camerado Springs Middle School.

Susanna Fong

I have been teaching 8th grade for over twelve years. The past eight have been at Camerado Springs Middle School where we have the absolute best kids around! Being able to teach about the Holocaust is one of the most important units I teach each year.

Heinrich Aschoff: A Holocaust Hero

Aidan Snyder

The Holocaust was a horrible period in time where Adolf Hitler and the Nazi Party took control of Germany's government and started spreading their horrid ideals to people. The Holocaust time period started in 1933 when Adolf Hitler became chancellor of Germany. The Nazi party did not officially start killing Jews until about 1941. It ended in 1945 after many execrating years of pain and suffering when the Allies won World War II. During those years there were many Jews taken away to be killed or put in concentration camps to labor. Many Jews did not know what was happening until it was too late and they were taken. Some were wise or just plain lucky and heard what was happening. They went into hiding and many needed someone to keep watch over them and bring them food and basic necessities. There was a certain man who I thought went above and beyond and his name is Heinrich Aschoff.

Heinrich Aschoff lived in a place called Munsterland that is in lower Saxony, Germany. This is a rural area and was in the countryside. He was called a Munsterland farmer because most people in that area were all farmers and the land in that area has rich soil for farming. Aschoff lived from 1893 to 1958 with had a wife and seven kids. His eighth son was away at the war. Eventually he found out that a Jewish family, Marga and Sigmund Spiegel, who was a local horse handler, with their daughter Karin, need a place of refuge from the Nazis. (Later after the Holocaust, Marga would become famous for writing about her experience surviving the Holocaust). Marga and Sigmund were to report to the Nazis soon and they were desperate to find somebody who would hide them when they found Aschoff. A friend of theirs found Aschoff and the two were very happy that they found somebody to hide them, fearing that they would be shipped off to be killed. Marga was sad when she found out that Aschoff could only house two, and that Sigmund had to hide with Aschoff's brother, Silkenbomer. Marga and Sigmund traveled roughly across the country from Hesse, Germany, which is also in the north, but still quite a way away from Saxony. They hitched rides on trains, carts and camped a lot. Eventually, they met their goal and arrived in Munsterland, Saxony. Aschoff welcomed Marga and her daughter into his house with kindness and hospitality, despite the fact that he had never met either of them before. Even his wife welcomed Marga and Karin with kindness and warmth. As the two settled in, the Aschoff and his wife spread the cover story to their kids and their neighbors that explained that Marga was Mrs. Krone just the wife of a soldier at the front. Out of the seven children in the house, the two eldest were told the truth and Aschoff knew that even that was taking a risk. Aschoff did everything he could to help Marga and keep her hidden. She helped out on the farm, and Aschoff was very thankful for her help and was glad he could help. Marga soon got sad being separated from her husband for so long, so soon after, Aschoff started arranging meeting between Marga and Sigmund since he was staying with his brother,

Silkenbomer. Soon Marga was visiting her husband every few weeks in secret. Aschoff was scared that his and Marga's secret would soon be discovered, but he was relieved to find no one looking for Marga or himself. Soon, Sigmund found problems at Silkenbomer's house, and had to move from hiding place to hiding place. He never stayed in one place and basically lived homeless. Aschoff heard of this from Slikenbomer and miraculously contacted Sigmund telling him he could stay at his farm and hope he wouldn't be noticed or questioned. When he told Marga this she was happy to have her husband safe and on his way to the farm. It was rough for Sigmund, but he made it to Aschoff and lived with him and the rest of his family. Aschoff again had someone to take care of and feed in his house, but he still treated them kindly, and insisted that they needn't help with anything.

Aschoff hid Marga and her family until the end of the Holocaust in 1945 when the Allies officially won the war and the Nazi Party was eradicated. The family stayed with Aschoff for a week more to make sure that they could come out of hiding safely. All of the residents of Aschoff's Munsterland farm in Saxony, Marga, Sigmund, Karin, Aschoff, his wife and kids, all survived the Holocaust. I think that Aschoff is an important Holocaust hero, just like everybody who hid Jews from the Nazis. He was extremely brave hiding Jews voluntarily, and especially since he hid Jews he didn't even know. Heinrich Aschoff was a true German Holocaust hero who will always be remembered.

Sources

The Path of The Righteous N.p., n.d. Web.
< https://books.google.com/books?id=YCz0J-8HIIMC&pg=PA158&lpg=PA158&dq=Heinrich+Aschoff&source=bl&ots=KQI7_4zWPy&sig=Ca1lP64XwTb8GnIwqUOqWEm54io&hl=en&sa=X&ved=0ahUKEwj53rnqwqrKAhUO8WMKHeLkCwEQ6AEIQTAJ#v=onepage&q=Heinrich%20Aschoff&f=false >.

The Righteous Among The Nations N.p., n.d. Web.
< http://db.yadvashem.org/righteous/righteousName.html?language=en&itemId=4013737 >.

The Path Of The Righteous 1. N.p., n.d. Web.
< https://books.google.com/books?id=YCz0J-8HIIMC&pg=PA158&dq=heinrich+aschoff+of+germany&hl=en&sa=X&ved=0ahUKEwi3l-T8t8vKAhVI1GMKHWt4D7MQ6AEIHTAA#v=onepage&q=heinrich%20aschoff%20of%20germany&f=false >.

T8t8vKAhVI1GMKHWt4D7MQ6AEIHTAA#v=onepage&q=heinrich%20aschoff%20of%20germany&f=false >.

A True Hero of the Holocaust

Bella Milliman

I have chosen a female German hero of the Holocaust. Her name is Elisabeth Abegg. Elisabeth Abegg was born in Strasbourg, the capital of Alsace. She was born on March 3, 1882. ("Teachers Who Rescued Jews During the Holocaust." Yad Vashem. N.p., n.d. Web. 20 Jan. 2016.) She was a history teacher. She was majorly influenced by the teachings of Albert Schweitzer, a Christian-universalist. Elisabeth moved to Berlin, where she taught at Luisen Madchenschule, which was a fashionable Berlin girls' school. She taught her students about humanistic beliefs. Humanistic beliefs is basically centering on the sanctity of human life. Many of her students came from Jewish homes. Shortly after the Nazis rose into power, Abegg had a conflict with the new Nazi-appointed director of the school. For that reason, she decided she had to change schools. ("The Righteous Among the Nations." Yad Vashem. N.p., n.d. Web. 21 Jan. 2016.) In 1940, she had to forcibly retire early, and denunciation followed. Despite the authorities marking her as politically unreliable, she refused to be deterred from losing contact with her Jewish friends and students. One of Elisabeth Abegg's dearest friends of 40 years, Anna Hirschberg, was sadly deported because she was a Jew and that really opened up Elisabeth's eyes because now she would really understand the true import of the Nazis persecution of Jews. And she would use every last shred of her power to help the Jews. Just because she was unable to help her friend even though she wanted to and would've. Abegg had lived with her 86 year old mother and invalid sister that goes by the name of Julie. She had made this three and a half room apartment into a temporary assembly and shelter point for Jews that had decided to hide underground. Since Elizabeth worked with her friends in the Quaker movement, she skimped on her and her sisters own food in order to supply her protégés with ration cards. (Steed, Sarah A. "Elisabeth Abegg."Hero Miss. Elisabeth Abegg. N.p., n.d. Web. 21 Jan. 2016.) So she sacrificed herself for the strangers. Elisabeth Abegg would go through anything just to keep these Jews alive and well while they were under her watch. She even went as far as offering to sell her own jewelry for sale. This was all in order to organize the smuggling of Jizchak Schwersenz. Which was occurring in Switzerland. This made sure to procure forged paper for other people. She has also went to Lisolotte Pereles. Lisolette was the director of the day-care center in Berlin. In which she tried to persuade her to go into temporary hiding with her nine year old that went by the name of Susi. Most of the time, the people that would knock on Elisabeth's were completely and utterly strangers. But since Abegg was so compelled to help, she never hesitated to. Which means that there would be a higher and higher risk factor every time she would help someone. She is so brave and courageous which really stands out to me. Not many people have the guts to do that and risk their own lives. Which is why she is a hero in my eyes. ("The Righteous During the Holocaust." Holocaust Memorial Center

Zekelman Family Campus. N.p., n.d. Web. 21 Jan. 2016.) Even though some of Elisabeth's neighbors were active Nazis. There have been many tales in which it states that she helped families go into hiding the night before the very final search. Abegg told them that this would be the right thing to do and she would have to trust her that she knew what she was doing, and making the right decision. Shortly after, the Jews were free. A family of five had survived the Holocaust with her help. She had saved up her money and got the surviving family onto a train afterwards. She did so much for the Jews and is completely respected. In 1957, which was Elisabeth Abegg's 75th birthday, some of the Holocaust survivors that she had saved, dedicated a mimeographed collection of memoirs to her. This was known as "When One Light Pierced the Darkness". ("When One Light Pierced the Darkness." Welcome to the Berlin Quakers. Berlin Quakers, 27 July 2013. Web. 22 Jan. 2016.) Sadly, she later died in 1974. She has no tie to any children or spouse. But that does not matter. She is such a legend in my eyes and I hope her story goes on to teach future generations to stand up for others and not be afraid. She has inspired me in so many ways because of her braveness and her courage to sacrifice her own life for strangers. I really hope that the others that read her story will be inspired too, as much as I was. Her story will live on forever in my heart. Hopefully, it will live on forever in yours as well. "I believe in the sun even when it's not shining. I believe in love even when I cannot feel it. I believe in God even when he is silent." ("Inspiration." Pinterest. N.p., n.d. Web. 22 Jan. 2016.) -Unknown. This quote is for people to not lose hope. Even though there are some rough patches, you will make it tough because it is possible. If people can survive the Holocaust then you can survive what you are going through. Be brave and courageous just like Elisabeth Abegg was. She leaves a legend and hope for others. Her kindness and courage should inspire you to keep moving on, because she never stopped once, and that is what made it possible. Anything is possible.

Works Cited

("Teachers Who Rescued Jews During the Holocaust." Yad Vashem. N.p., n.d. Web. 20 Jan. 2016.)

("The Righteous Among the Nations." Yad Vashem. N.p., n.d. Web. 21 Jan. 2016.)

(Steed, Sarah A. "Elisabeth Abegg."Hero Miss. Elisabeth Abegg. N.p., n.d. Web. 21 Jan. 2016.)

("The Righteous During the Holocaust." Holocaust Memorial Center Zekelman Family Campus. N.p., n.d. Web. 21 Jan. 2016.)

("When One Light Pierced the Darkness." Welcome to the Berlin Quakers. Berlin Quakers, 27 July 2013. Web. 22 Jan. 2016.)

("Inspiration." Pinterest. N.p., n.d. Web. 22 Jan. 2016.)

The Schindler Story

Ethan Layfield

Oskar Schindler is known for one of the most powerful stories of the Holocaust. His story was so powerful Steven Spielberg even made his story into a major motion picture, which one seven Academy Awards. He only joined the Nazi Party to help his business. Schindler ended up saving Jews by making them work for him in his factory. He got away with this by telling Amon Goeth that his factory should be moved to Czechoslovakia so it could be used as a labor camp. In the end Schindler ended up saving thousands of lives by saying that his factory was a labor camp.

Oskar Schindler was born in 1908 in the city of Zwittau Moravia. The area that Schindler grew up in was known as Sudetenland. In his family there was his father Hans Schindler, his mother Louisa Schindler, and his younger sister Elfriede. His father was a factory owner, and his mother was a homemaker. When Schindler was a little boy he was very popular in school but he was not a good student. In the 1920's Oskar worked for his father by selling farm equipment. In 1928 Schindler married a woman named Emilie, which caused tension between him and his father. Oskar left his father's factory to be a sales manager for an electric company in Moravia. As that was happening Adolf Hitler and his Nazi Party was rising to power in Germany. Schindler joined the Nazi Party but only to promote his business not because he believed the same things as the Nazis.

In 1942 the Nazis started to relocate Jews to labor camps. At that time a good number of workers were called to the train station. Schindler rushed to the train station to argue with the SS officer on how vital his workers were to his factory and the war effort. He eventually was able to stop them from getting on the train and safely returned them to his factory. In 1943 the Krakow Ghetto was ordered to have a final liquidation. Amon Goeth, an SS officer, was in charge of the operation. The healthy Jews who would be able to work were sent to the labor camp in Plaszow, and the ones who couldn't were sent to death camps. Schindler bribed Goeth so that his factory could be used as a labor camp. Goeth excepted. From that point on Oskar Schindler's factory was used to secretly rescue Jews.

Schindler ended up moving his factory from Moravia to Czechoslovakia so they could supply Hitler's army, the Third Reich, with vital supplies. Schindler then had to bribe an SS officer to support his plan and he told Schindler to make a list of who would come with him. This meant that Schindler had to make list of whom he would save. Schindler came up with a list of 1,100 names including his employees who were Jews.

In 1944 in the middle of the move to Czechoslovakia 300 women and children were moved to Auschwitz by mistake. Schindler quickly rescued them and sent them on their way to his factory in the town of Brunnlitz. The next several months the factory never produced any supplies. Schindler called it "start-up difficulties," but really Schindler was weakening the manufacturing process on purpose so the bullet shells he was producing failed the quality control tests.

On May 8, 1945 Germany surrendered and the war ended. Schindler told all of his workers that the war was over. He then told them not to seek revenge on the people who did them harm, and called for a moment of silence for the people who were killed. He also thanked the present SS members and told them to go home without bloodshed. Schindler feared being captured so he and his wife fled to the west to avoid Russian troops who were moving from the east. He took his chances with the U.S. forces instead. Days later 1,200 Schindlerjuden or "Schindler's Jews" were freed by a Russian officer.

At the end of the war Oskar Schindler returned to his regular daily life as it was before the war started. His postwar life included more failed business ventures, drinking, overspending, and love affairs. Schindler ended up buying a farm in Argentina in 1949. In 1957 Schindler went bankrupt and relied on B'nai B'rith, which was a Jewish organization. Schindler eventually moved back to West Germany and abandoned his wife. Several grateful people and the Jewish Distribution Committee gave him money. He then started another business in Frankfurt Germany, which failed. Schindler then lived off of funds from the Schindlerjuden and also his retirement money.

After Schindler's 54th Birthday in 1962 he was declared a "Righteous Gentile" and was invited to plant a tree on the Avenue of the Righteous, which led up to a museum in Jerusalem. Schindler ended up dying from liver and heart problems in the year of 1974. He was buried in Israel. Five hundred Scindlerjuden people were at his funeral. His body was laid to rest on Mount Zion in Jerusalem. Six thousand Holocaust survivors as well as their children were alive in the 1990's to tell the wonderful story of Oskar Schindler's List.

Works Cited
"Oskar Schindler Biography." - Life, Family, Childhood, Children, Name, Story, Death, Wife, School. N.p., n.d. Web. 27 Jan. 2016.

Maria von Maltzan: A Hero of the Holocaust

Garrett Hubbard

Maria von Maltzan had an amazing life, which spanned 6 decades. Her life was full of many good as well as bad times, which she experienced during childhood as well as adulthood. As Maria entered adulthood she became very aware of the politics of Hitler and of Germany. During World War II Maria found herself in direct opposition with Hitler and became an unspoken advocate for the Jews. After the war Maria settled into normal life, and she had many different jobs and had a long and frugal life with her husband.

Maria von Maltzan was born March 25th, 1909 and was raised as a countess in a very wealthy German family. She grew up with about 7 or 8 siblings on 18,000 acres in Silesia, Germany. From a very young age it was noticeable that she enjoyed all of the animals in the forest on her estate. When she was 12 years old her father died and she suffered miserably. After Maria's father died her mother wanted her to become an obedient daughter, but that led to many conflicts, which resulted in Maria being moved to a school in Militsch and then to a boarding school in the city of Warmbrunn. Without her mother's knowledge she switched schools because her greatest dream was to become a veterinarian. She wanted to become a veterinarian because she had a love for animals and she thought it fit her just right, therefore that is why she switched from the boarding school in Warmbrunn to high school of Natural Sciences in Berlin. Then in college she continued studying the subjects Zoology, Botany and Anthropology. After her studies she moved to a veterinary clinic in Berlin where she finally got her degree to become a doctor in Natural Science.

Before things got crazy and the war really started, Maria Maltzan was very politically aware with what Adolf Hitler was saying. She had read Adolf Hitler's Mein Kampf where it had clearly stated his hatred of Jews. Shortly later she got in touch with a Catholic resistance group that was making many efforts to help bring the Jews to safety. She took part in an activity that had Jews swim across Lake Constance to Switzerland where they were safe from Adolf Hitler's grip so they were not persecuted. There were also many other organizations that Maria helped in such as a campaign called "Schwedenmobel," which means "furniture for Sweden" in which furniture would be shipped to Sweden, but with Jews inside of the containers with it. She risked it all to help those in need and in this case it was the Jews, she joined another resistance group called "Solf Circle" where unfortunately almost all of the members were arrested and sentenced to death.

Taking in Communist and Jewish refugees always put her life at risk, yet she provided a safe place for these refugees more than 60 times in her life span. The most dangerous time started for her in 1942 when her future husband. Hans Hirchel, a Jewish author, lived with her. When Hans Hirchel moved in he brought with him a large, heavy mahogany sofa bed that had a hollow base. Whenever the Gestapo came (German police) Hans would get under the sofa bed, which had been slightly modified by Maria with breathing holes. Hans had a troublesome chronic cough and to make sure Hans's chronic cough did not happen Maria made sure to give him a bottle of liquid codeine just before the Gestapo came. One time the Gestapo got suspicious of the sofa bed and commanded Maria to open it, (previously Maria had fixed the sofa bed perfectly so it would be nearly impossible to open) instead of opening it Maria said to them," If you're sure someone is in there, shoot. But before you do that, I want a written signed paper from you that you will pay for new material to fix it." Thankfully for Hans and Maria the Gestapo left shortly after not having a reason to stay. Maria became pregnant with Hans's baby, unfortunately the baby did not live long because while in the incubator there was a severe air strike that turned off all the power from what Maria recalled from the time.

  Shortly after the war Maria and Hans got married, but they separated quickly after two years of being married. Many years later they got back together and remarried in 1972. In post-years of the war Maria became a drug addict, she suffered from poor health, gallbladder attacks, and her dependencies on drugs and chemicals. After quite a few attempts she overcame her addictions through rehabilitation. After Hans's death in 1975 she decided to keep following her beloved career of being a veterinarian, and she did many different jobs revolving around that such as being a circus veterinarian, a relief veterinarian in clinics all over Switzerland and Germany and she opened up her own clinic in Berlin-Kruezberg. She became very popular with the punks and alternative young people because she treated their pets for free.

  Maria's life was better than a lot of other peoples' because she died an absolute hero in the fact that she stood up in the darkness of these times to shine an unseen light to help those in need. Over her 60 years, she lived two different lives, one was an unseen hero who did many great things, second she lived a regular life following her dream of being a veterinarian. She may have been born right before a nightmare, but it didn't stop her from doing what was right. She was not scared about what would happen to her for she knew that keeping 60 people alive was more important that just her, one of her quotes that very well describes her life is 'I wasn't bored for a moment.' She is the type of person who inspires others to strive for more in their life.

Works Cited

http://www.auschwitz.dk/maltzan.htm "Maria Countess Von Maltzan." Maria Countess Von Maltzan. N.p., n.d. Web. 28 Jan. 2016.

http://www.imdb.com/name/nm0902658/bio?ref_=nm_ov_bio_sm "Biography." IMDb. IMDb.com, n.d. Web. 28 Jan. 2016.

http://www.fembio.org/english/biography.php/woman/biography/maria-graefin-von-maltzan/ "Maria Gräfin Von Maltzan." Maria Gräfin Von Maltzan. N.p., n.d. Web. 28 Jan. 2016.

http://the-history-girls.blogspot.com/2012/07/maria-von-maltzan-german-resistance.html "The History Girls: Maria Von Maltzan - a German Resistance Heroine, by Leslie Wilson." The History Girls: Maria Von Maltzan - a German Resistance Heroine, by Leslie Wilson. N.p., n.d. Web. 28 Jan. 2016.

Sofka Skipwith: The German War Hero

Hailey Price

During the Holocaust, many people secretly helped the Jewish community in their hiding and surviving the terrible Nazi organization. These people are known, and considered war heroes. The "War Heroes" did things such as hide Jewish people, make fake passports, fake ration books, and risk their lives just to save the people of the Jewish community. A famous war hero was a Russian princess by the name of Sofka Skipwith, who saved numerous Jewish people and risked her life for what was right many times. Sofka Skipwith played an interesting part in helping of the Jewish people, and made this world just a bit better in such a terrible and horrific time.

Sofka Skipwith started in a pampered life in St. Petersburg, with an English governess, nannies, and just about every toy she could dream up. She grew up to marry Leo Zinovieff and live in England and France as n Russian refugee and so was her husband. The two had two sons, Peter and Ian, but eventually she divorced her husband. She proceeded to marry Grey Skipwith, with whome she had a son named Patrick. Unfortunately, her husband died serving in the Royal Air Force. She lived alone with her son Patrick for many years, but when the French Army failed in 1940, she was caught in a situation. She was in Paris, and then arrested by the German Army in November 1940. Along with other British citizens, Sofka was imprisoned in barracks in Besancon, a civilian internee camp. In May 1941, she was sent to Vittel detention camp. Finally, she was released in July 1944.

Sofka then heard of the Jewish prisoners in the beginning of 1943, she was deeply changed. "The thing that struck us about these newcomers was their air of sleep-walkers. They appeared dazed. They spoke little, never seemed to smile, walked slowly in the park, as though nervous of doing wrong," Skipwith said. She worked together with Madeline Steinberg to help the poor Jewish people. The two contacted with the French Resistance, who gave them fake documents, which Sofka gave to young Jewish people in Vittel. Sofka inserted a list of the Jewish people who were holders of the South American passports in a toothpaste tube, which was then delivered to the French partisans. Theses partisans would deliver it then to Lisbon and other western diplomats. The goal was that the Jewish would be protected from deportation.

Things soon took a turn for a worse with Sofka's plan. Unfortunately, the Germans began checking if the Latin American passports owned by the Jewish prisoners at Vittel were indeed valid. The final decision was that these passports were invalid, and the Latin American government admitted they did not recognize any of the fake passports. This put the owners of these passports in grave danger: deportation to the death camps. She attempted to give the poor people valid papers, but when these documents arrived, it way far too late. In April and August of 1944, all for the exception of 60 Jewish people were deported in two different groups to Auschwitz- Birkenau. Sofka could do nothing, and she said, "The Poles knew only too well what that train indicated. To us 'deportation' was just a word... we were incapable of imaging the tortured skeletons later to be associated with the camos. But they had seen." By "Women of Valor"

After her reparation in August 1944, Sofka got back on her feet. She then joined the British Communist Committee, and was the branch secretary for the Chelsea Branch. Then, in 1944, she became an interpreter at the World Peace Congress. She was also an important part in the Party's front tourism agency, Progressive Tours, in which was set up travel from Eastern Europe and the Soviet Union. In this position, she took many tourists to her Grandpa's mansion and the forbidden part of Leningrad. She was arrested and then feted by the security guards. Then, she even let tours in Albania. Proceeding shortly after these events, she was followed, her letters were opened and her phone was tampered with. By her MI5 files, she was "A flamboyant creature who wears rather outre clothes and looks like a typical Chelsea bohemian type" but also as "a brilliant linguist with vast contacts in all spheres.... this woman is an outstanding intelligent courageous and active ." by "Woman Of Valor" It would be said that she had more than hundred lovers in her life\, but then she finally found life with her final love of her life, who she met on a Progressive Tour to the USSR in 1957, Jack King. In 1968, she wrote her own autobiography, a Russian cookbook, a grammar for beginners, and a selection of translations.

In 1970, Sofka was 78 years old, and had a brass and grass-green diary, which she gave to her once 16 year old granddaughter. Later Sofka died at Blisland, Cornwall on 26th February 1944, where she lived for the last 30 years. Sofka did amazing things in her life, helping the Jewish people, writing her stories, and many other accomplishments in her life. Though Sofka was born Russian, she saved numerous Jews as a German war hero during her time in Germany. In conclusion, Sofka Skipwith made a large impact in the Jewish life in Vittel and should be remembered as a great German war hero.

Works Cited
""Women of Valor"" Sofka Skipwith. N.p., n.d. Web. 04 Feb. 2016. < http://www.yadvashem.org/yv/en/exhibitions/righteous-women/skipwith.asp >.

The Kindest Man in Germany

Jacob Patterson (Co-Winner)

Oskar Schindler was a man who, with the help of his wife Emilie Schindler, saved 1,200 Jews during the Holocaust. He was a very great and brave man whose model of citizenship and humanitarianism saved lives. It is because of his greatness that he earned recognition in his life. I believe it is important know about his life and about what made him willing to give up all he held dear to him in an effort to save others. He was one of the few men that started out as a soldier in the Nazi Party who had a change of heart. The majority of the Nazi soldiers fell prey to the persuasive words of Adolf Hitler, but Schindler saw through him and was able to see what was right, even though he could have been put to death and tortured if he were caught. Because of his actions he is known as righteous among the nations. Oskar Schindler was a brave and valiant hero who we should model our lives after and who offered random acts of kindness. So, what made this once Nazi soldier make that leap? In order to evaluate this question we must look into his past. Let's explore his childhood, how he got involved in the Nazi Party, and what made him have a change of heart.

Studying Schindler's childhood is an important step in figuring out why he made the choice to turn on the Nazis and help save so many Jews. He was born April 28, 1914 in a middle class Catholic family. As a child he attended grammar school and studied engineering. After school he was expected to follow in the footsteps of his father and take charge of his family's farm-machinery plant. As a kid some of his classmates and neighbors were Jews but he never appeared to form intimate relationships with any of them. Therefore, a connection could not have been made in terms of how any childhood relationships with Jews may have impacted him to support them over the Nazi party.

So what lead to his involvement in the Nazi party? Originally, he got involved with Konrad Henlein's Sudeten German Party, which was a political party that strongly supported the Nazi Party. This political party was eventually incorporated into the Nazi party in 1938. That was when Schindler officially became a Nazi. He then went to a city called Krakow in order to make a lot of money as an entrepreneur. Overall, Schindler never developed a resistance against the Nazis. What he did do was treat his workers humanely, even Jews. Then, to his horror, he found out how the Jews were being treated. The brutality that was being brought upon them by the Nazis infuriated him as a human being. After that, making money was not nearly as important to him as helping the Jews. He was not only prepared to spend all of his money to help the Jews, but he was also willing to put his own life on the line for them and it paid off.

Now that we know why he saved the Jews it is time to figure out how he did it. As an entrepreneur, he developed a plant and named it "Business Essential to the War Effort." The Nazis did not know that his business was created in an effort to help the Jews. The title of the business alone was in defiance to the Nazis not to mention he was saving Jews right under their noses. This business allowed him to offer refuge to the Jews, for instance when Jews were threatened by the Nazis to be sent to Auschwitz, the death camp, he would pardon them in a way by claiming his plant's production would suffer from the loss of workers and that his plant was essential to the efforts of the war. All the while he was really only saving the Jews from their fate.

When word got out that he may actually be working against the Nazis, he was arrested and interrogated by the Gestapo multiple times. He was charged for things like irregularities and favoring Jews but that never stopped helping them. One of the greatest acts by Schindler was when he saved 107 Jews from dying. They were being transported in sealed cattle wagons when the wagons were opened and a horrific sight of dead bodies and abused Jews was revealed. He used his authority as a Nazi soldier to stop the transport and instead took the surviving Jews to safety. He and his wife then nourished them back to health. But he did not stop there, he even stood up to the Nazi commandant to ensure they were given a proper burial. It was by the grace of God that he himself did not fall victim to the same mistreatment that the Jews endured.

It should come as no surprise that after the war was over he was treated like royalty by all the Jewish survivors. Schindler visited Israel multiple times after that and each time he was treated overwhelmingly well due to his continued support and efforts to save them. He lived out the rest of his life between Germany and Israel. Oskar Schindler died in October of 1974 of liver failure but he will never be forgotten. People will always remember the kindness he stood for in his life and the legacy he left behind. We should all stand in awe of his efforts and take a step forward to stand up for those who cannot.

Works Cited

"Oskar and Emilie Schindler - The Righteous Among The Nations - Yad Vashem." Oskar and Emilie Schindler - The Righteous Among The Nations - Yad Vashem. N.p., n.d. Web. 29 Jan. 2016.

GERMAN HOLOCAUST HERO ESSAY

Kevin Yurgelevic

 After Mr. Marks, the Holocaust survivor, came to our Camerado eighth grade class; he spoke to us about his experience during World War II, the Holocaust, and vividly explained to us more than just what we know. The stories he told of courage and perseverance inspired me to dig deeper into the history of the Jewish people. He has inspired me to learn more about these Holocaust survivors who became heroes from their courageous actions, determination, and survival methods. I was intrigued by the Jewish peoples' strengths and unique survivability under the torture of the harsh Nazi boot.

There are very many heroes of the Holocaust. The one I choose to learn more about is Oskar Schindler. I thought his story was very interesting because Oskar Schindler was the only person whose group mostly survived in one of the harshest camps ever, Plazow, under his leadership. In his group, there were approximately 2.000 Jews who survived. Oskar Schindler spent millions of dollars trying to save as many Jews as he could.

Oskar Schindler was born on the 18th of April in the year of 1908 in Zwitlau, a town in the Czech Republic. (Oskar Schindler The Man and Hero story) He lived and grew up in a highly Christian religious household and family. His family was one of the most prominent and wealthiest families in Zwitlau as also in other places. This was the result of their successful family-owned machinery business.

Oskar was very "tall and handsome'" as April N. Aberly says in her essay on remember.org. All the young women loved and cherished him. He fell for a very attractive girl whose name was Emily. And after just six weeks of dating they decided to get married, but then it took a sad turn after a few months because Oskar began to heavily consume alcohol. From his bad choices, he had multiple affairs resulting in two children out of wedlock. Also, his family business during the Great Depression went bankrupt, and Oskar's father abandoned his mother, who shortly after passed away. With him being without a job he sought out a job in Poland as machinery salesmen. (Oskar Schindler The Man and the Hero story)

Schindler wasn't the brightest of the highest class as you can see. He was a "womanizer" and he was addicted to alcohol. This might make you wonder why is he a hero? Or what made him want to save the lives of so many people and risk his?

He first started to save lives of the innocent Jewish people when he went to Krakow in the beginning of the German invasion, in 1939. There he seized two companies that were previously owned by Jews. The companies dealt with the "manufacture and sales of enamel kitchenware products". He opened a small shop in the Jewish ghetto, where he sold and manufactured enamel. He employed mostly Jewish workers, which then made them unable to be abducted to labor camps. But then in 1942 he found out that most of his workers were being sent to a harsh camp named Plazow. But then his connections came in handy when he convinced the S.S. and the armaments administration who set up the camp to make part of the camp his factory. This one action spared 900 lives.

The next time he saved lives was in October 1944 when the Russian army was approaching. He again used his connections to convince the S.S. again to allow him to restart his factory as a part of camps to work the Jews. He had 700 Jews from the Grossrosen camp, and 300 women from Auschwitz. (Oskar Schindler The Man and the Hero Story) Once they were imported to his factory they were given the best treatment that Oskar could afford. This brought his total up to 1,900 lives. Concluding his previous project he caught word of a group of 100 Jews from the camp of Golezow who were stranded in the city of Svitavy. This group of about 100 Jews was half frozen to death. He pulled his strings once again and was allowed permission to rescue them, and his wife Emile did her best to nurse them back to health.

The ones who perished were given a proper burial paid for by Schindler. Schindler spent unlimited amounts of money, not just paying for the upkeep of workers, but also paying the government. Oskar was arrested two times during his miraculous efforts to save the Jews, but both times he just found a way out, or just pay a little bit more money. By saving these some odd 1,900 Jews he risked not just his life, but also his family's lives, just for a bunch of strangers he hadn't seen in his life. (Oskar Schindler The Man and the Hero story)

Does this answer your question about "why is he a hero?" I'm sure it does, and Oskar Schindler made me ask myself the question of would I be able to risk my life like that or even have to courage to spend millions of dollars saving random people? It was an extremely difficult task and Oskar completed it, not with ease, but somehow he did it. Oskar Schindler's life concluded on October 9th, 1974.

Works cited

Website Title: Oskar Schindler: The Man and the Hero (Holocaust Essays) | Article Title: Oskar Schindler: The Man and the Hero (Holocaust Essays) | Date Accessed: January 28, 2016

Website Title: The Oscar Schindler Story   Article Title: The Oscar Schindler StoryDate Accessed: January 28, 2016

LUDWIG WOERL – A RIGHTEOUS GENTILE

Lauren Kott

"He who saves one life, it is as if he has saved the entire world," is what is written on the medals awarded by Yad Vashem for being a Righteous Gentile.i These were men and women who risked their lives to save Jews in World War II during the Holocaust. Ludwig Woerl was one of these people.

Ludwig Woerl was born in the year 1906 in Germany. He pursued training in the medical field while growing up, and he has always wanted to save people's lives. Ludwig's journey started as a political prisoner in 1934. He was sent to a Nazi concentration camp called Auschwitz after a couple of years. Ludwig switched on and off of being in different camps or in a dark cell for the next eleven years. He was arrested for distributing information to the public to warn them about what the concentration camps really were. Since he had medical training, in 1942 with 17 other male nurses he was sent to Auschwitz to work at the camp's sick-bay. There was an outbreak of typhus at Auschwitz. This disease did not only have to the prisoners at the camp but also affected the Nazi soldiers as well. Ludwig was a person who put himself in danger to protect others from death. He did all he could to help save and protect the people at the concentration camps. Woerl had to decide who got the rations of food and medicine. He also went against many direct orders of the SS by employing Jewish doctors and forging selection lists to save Jewish patients from death by gassing.ii

Ludwig had an inmate, Heinrich Schuster, who worked with Ludwig and his patients. Ludwig and Heinrich were described by fellow inmates "lack of qualifications" and "negative effects on the care of the patients."iii In Ludwig's first year at Auschwitz concentration camp 580 of his patients died of starvation or disease. This shows that even though he might have saved a ton of people, there were people that were in his hands who died.

Ludwig continued these lifesaving actions of saving Jews and doing these good deeds, but these actions also led him back in an isolation cell. He was later released because of his rank and nationality and sent to Guntergrube, a labor camp near Auschwitz. At the labor camp, Ludwig helped 600 prisoners by making sure they had food and clothing. Many prisoners who suffered from tuberculosis were also aided and protected by Ludwig. He would make sure they didn't have to do hard labor and protected them from the Nazi doctors who would have sent them to their deaths.

When War World ll was over, Ludwig spent most of the remainder of his life trying to bring justice and peace to those lives who suffered such tragedy by the Nazis' actions. He was one of many of the key witnesses in trials, recounting one incident where 12 young girls, ages 3-11, came to him begging for their lives to be saved. They claimed they were strong and could work hard for him. They begged for him to please help save their souls before they were forced into the gas chambers. He was unable to help them and helplessly watched SS Kaduk drive them straight into the gas chamber to be killed.iv He also told his memory of a young girl who was shot inside a room where only one other Nazi soldier was in the room with a gun. He remembered this scared girl who was murdered alone in a room and more to redeem and bring justice to himself, the families of the people who had died and the Jewish people, and so we will never forget what the Nazis had done to thousands of human beings including children, parents, and elderly citizens. He has done a favor to the world by helping put many evil men who killed women and children in jail.

It is so hard to understand why people treat others in these ways. As I think about the world we live in today, I wonder if we can learn from our past. Did we already forget our mistakes of the past? Why are we still segregating and spreading hatred toward one another? I would like to see in my lifetime where we can all just be human and truly not care about beliefs or creed or the color of our skin. My hope is that we all can be righteous gentiles in time of need and have the courage to stand up for what is right, rather than follow those who are after power and greed. Ludwig Woerl and many more righteous people should be noticed more often because maybe we as a nation, as people can actually learn from great whole-hearted people who tried to change our world by helping others. Even though there has been thousands of righteous gentiles in this world there have also been thousands of cold-hearted people in this world that might have not wanted peace. More people should try to be the good person to overpower the bad. To do this human beings have to work together and stand out, not fit in.

A HERO OF THE HOLOCAUST, HER STORY

Madison Washburn

I have chosen a female German heroine. She goes by the name of Elisabeth Abegg. As a child Elisabeth Abegg grew up in Strasbourg. Strasbourg is also the capital of Alsace. She was born on May 3, 1882. Her profession in life was a history teacher at a Berlin girls' school known as Luisen Madchenschule. She taught her students about humanistic beliefs. (YadVashem) Humanism is a progressive philosophy of life that, without theism and other supernatural beliefs, affirms our ability and responsibility to lead ethical lives of personal fulfillment that aspire to the greater good of humanity. (Dictionary.com)

This was very impressive to many of her Jewish students. Many students also connected with this lifestyle and philosophy. In Miss Abegg's class she had many students who came from Jewish heritage. She was very familiar with the religion. Her lifelong friend of 40 years was Jewish. After Hitler was anointed as the German dictator; Miss Abegg moved schools because her current school (at the time) retired her for her Quaker and pro-equality beliefs. This belief and religion contradicts Hitler's beliefs in so many ways. Quakers believed that God had come to teach his followers directly and to enjoy life to the fullest. Some early Quaker ministers were women. They based their message on the religious belief that "Christ has come to teach his people himself," stressing the importance of a direct relationship with God through Jesus Christ, and a direct religious belief in the eyes of all believers. Many Christian followers believed in the ideas of Quakers. Quakers also believed in equality for ALL people. As it says in the Christian holy book known as the Bible. Quaker is a form of Christianity. She was therefore anti-Nazi. Quakers also were the ones who believed in women's rights because their holy book they believed everyone was equal under God's law. (Holocaust Center)

The school she moved to many would say was definitely a step down from her original school. After teaching and being around many Jewish students, she was eventually called to the Gestapo for an interrogation. She knew how serious the Nazi deportations were. Her friend of over 40 years, Anne Hirschberg, was sadly deported. Her friend Anna was a Jew. She was devastated by her inability to help her friend so she decided to help other Jews. She was caring for her mother in a three-and-a-half room apartment. Her mother at the time was 86. At that time she was 60 years old. She decided to help Jews. Her apartment was reformed into a shelter and assembly point for Jews underground. She offered shelter to Jews, or redirected them to their next location of shelter. Food was hard to come by. She and her sister ate rarely in order to get ration cards and feed the Jews. Her sister helped get the amount of ration cards needed. She knew almost none of the Jews she was supporting and sheltering. Since she lived in an apartment, all of her anti-Nazi activities had to go unnoticed otherwise the Gestapo would be alerted immediately. Many of her Neighbors were supposed active Nazis. (Brennan Stephens)

Elisabeth Abegg took every opportunity to save lives and contribute, I believe we need more people like this on Earth. Religious or not. Black or white. Female or male. Gay and straight. Transgender or Asexual. American or German. Along with everyone in between...we are all people. People don't hurt people. When Elisabeth had knowledge of Nazi' she did what she could to protect people. As any RIGHTEOUS person would do. Thank you to Elisabeth Abegg. She saved an estimated 80 people. In many circumstances she would go the extra mile. There are stories of her persuading families to go into hiding the night before the Nazis would do their FINAL search of that area. The family had met her through a chain of Jewish shelter owners. Elisabeth told them that it was time and that it was the safe thing to do. She comforted the family by saying that it would be over soon. She was indeed right and she saved this family's life. Shortly after they took shelter at her home the Jews were finally free. The night Elisabeth had persuaded them, the Nazis did their FINAL search. The family of five made it safely. There are stories of her selling her personal items in order to smuggle people into a safe spot. One account says that she sold her jewelry in order to receive a ticket for a smuggled family of three. She had saved the money and got this family onto the train safely. (YadVashem) She did so much. She died in 1974. (FindAGrave) She was cousin to a fairly well known man. William Abegg was a Social Democratic statesman. (YadVashem) She has no known spouse ties as well as ties to children. All I hope is that her story and legend goes on forever. I know it has with me. She inspires me. As she will to whomever her story is told.

Works Cited

"Elisabeth Abegg (1882 - 1974) - Find A Grave Memorial." Elisabeth Abegg (1882 - 1974) - Find A Grave Memorial. N.p., n.d. Web. 28 Jan. 2016. < http://www.findagrave.com/cgi-bin/fg.cgi?page=gr&GRid=32646571 >.

N.p., n.d. Web. 28 Jan. 2016. < http://www.yadvashem.org/ >.

"The Righteous During the Holocaust." Holocaust Memorial Center. N.p., n.d. Web. 28 Jan. 2016. < http://www.holocaustcenter.org/page.aspx?pid=514 >.

"Tribute to Elisabeth Abegg." Brennanstephens. N.p., 23 Oct. 2011. Web. 28 Jan. 2016. < https://brennanstephens.wordpress.com/2011/10/23/tribute-to-elisabeth-abegg/ >.

"Humanism" < http://dictionary.reference.com/ > March. 2009. Web. 29 Jan 2016

True Heroes

Maggie Spring (Special Award)

The Holocaust is a time in history that most people know about, or have learned about in school. However, most people do not know about the countless Ukrainian and German heroes who saved thousands of lives, or more. This time period is undoubtedly known for violence, human suffering, inhumane treatment, and most of all, hatred. Yet, there was much kindness, love, tolerance and sympathy taking place as well. These kind acts, of course were over shadowed by the actions of the Nazis and of the hatred that Hitler spread. During this period, many people sympathized with the Jews and others that were mistreated. These heroes changed the course of history. Although most are not commonly known, these are the true heroes and should be honored and remembered for their brave acts.

One amazing German hero is Johanna Eck. Born in 1888. Johanna, a war widow and nurse, sheltered four innocent people, two of whom were Jewish. (McGreal) She became friends with the refugees and helped them survive. In 1942, she took in a young man named Heinz Guttman. He was a Jew who had no food and no home. Johanna shared her home and rationed food, although she barely had enough for herself. When her home was raided in November 1943, she bravely sought out a new hiding place for Heinz. Even though he moved to another location, Johanna always stayed in contact with him and gave him ration cards for food. Johanna also helped another young Jewish girl named, Elfriede Guttmann. Later, Johanna ended up helping Elfriede change identities so she could remain living in her apartment legally and avoid the Gestapo. Johanna Eck was a true hero that showed devotion and sympathy to those that were shunned by society.

Another heroine of the Holocaust was Ludviga Pukas. She was a Ukrainian citizen who saved two lives, and attempted saving two more. She befriended Frima Sternik, another young lady with two children. Ludviga falsified information so that Frima's two children became her children according to Ukrainian records. This way the two children were not known as Jews, but simply Ukrainian. Although Frima ended up being killed during the "liquidation of the Jews of Proskurov," her two children remained living with Ludviga. After the war, the children changed their name back to "Sternik," but stayed with Ludviga and ultimately considered her their mother. Ludviga also sheltered another young Jewish woman around this same time. When Ludviga's home was raided, the young girl was found, but denied that Ludviga was responsible. The authorities never knew that the children were Jewish, and left them alone. Ludviga most certainly was a savior to this family and to these two children. (Scofield)

Hans Fittko was a German journalist that truly was a hero. He was born in Finsterwalde, Germany in 1903. He wrote about political issues opposing Hitler. Hans and his wife, Lisa were part of the Emergency Rescue Committee. This committee helped political refuges travel from France to Spain in 1941. (Scofield) This organization helped people who were persecuted find safety. Not all of the refugees were Jewish, but all were targeted because they had opposing views of Hitler. Hans and Lisa Fittko helped over 100 people cross into Spain safely. Without a doubt, Hans and Lisa Fittko are protectors of those targeted by Hitler.

Werner Klemke was a German soldier and artist. He is probably the most well-known hero of the Holocaust. He helped a businessman, Sam van Perlstein create a new identity. The new documents that Klemke helped make allowed van Perlstein to fund a network that hid illegal refugees and also supported those who opposed the Nazis. Werner Klemke forged documents like birth certificates, food ration coupons, identification cards, and baptism records, even though he knew he was risking his life. Ultimately, the group that Klemke worked with saved over 500 Jews. Although he was a soldier during World War II and stationed in the Netherlands, he was anti-Nazi. He never shared his story with anyone, and as he was dying, he told his children where to find the documents that told the story of his life and bravery. (Yad Vashem) His amazing courage and bravery will never be forgotten.

One unlikely hero was Major Karl Plagge. He was an engineer that joined the Nazi Party in 1931. Although he was a Wehrmacht staff officer, he felt it was his duty to try and help Jews. Major Plagge began a motor repair station for army vehicles. This is where he sheltered about 1,000 Jewish people. Although some of the men who worked for him were actually mechanics, many people were elderly, hairdressers, teachers, and kitchen staff. He hid them all by telling the forces they were mechanics. (Yad Vashem) He also insisted that the men were allowed to bring their wives and children, saying it was good for production. He ultimately saved over 250 people from their deaths.

Johanna Eck, Ludviga Pukas, Hans and Lisa Fittko, Werner Klemke, and Major Karl Plagge are true heroes of the Holocaust. They showed bravery, empathy, courage and strength during this devastating time period in world history. Their actions saved thousands of lives and should always be remembered as true acts of bravery. These heroes are only a small number of those that helped rewrite history. As we study the Holocaust, these heroes should be celebrated for their strength and courage.

WORKS CITED

McGreal, Chris. "Honour for German Major Who Saved 250 Jews." Theguardian.11 April 2005.theguardian.com. 23 January, 2016.

"The Righteous Among the Nations." Yad Vashem Publications. Yadvashem.org. 1990. 23 January, 2016.

Scofield, Mathew. "How a German Soldier-Artist Saved Dutch Jews From the Nazis."McClathcyDC. 5 September, 2014.mcclatcheydc.com 23 January, 2016.

Ordinary Heroes

Maia Salter (Co-Winner)

What is a hero?

The generic Google definition states that a hero is "a person, typically a man, who is admired or idealized for courage, outstanding achievements, or noble qualities." This definition brings to mind the multitude of dashing male characters ever-present in our culture and literature, including but not limited to: Sir Lancelot, Perseus, Han Solo, and any superhero who has his own movie.

But I am not writing about a hero in that context. I am not writing about a well-known man, nor am I writing about anyone traditionally thought of as extraordinary.

I am writing about a woman. And I am writing about an ordinary woman, a woman who, in dangerous circumstances, chose to do the right thing.

Isn't that what this project is about? Bringing light to those many ordinary people during the Holocaust who selflessly put their lives on the line for others? Everyone knows about Anne Frank, and Miep Gies, and Oskar Schindler. But what about the normal citizens who hid Jews in their hiding places, provided illegal ration cards to those who needed it, and generally did what any decent human being would do? Their stories are every bit as important as the well-known ones, but the difference between them is that one is known, and one is not.

This is the story of Elisabeth Abegg, one of the unknown heroes of the Holocaust.

Elisabeth Abegg's Early Life

Elisabeth Abegg was born in 1882, a time when electricity was still brand new. She grew up in the sprawling city of Strasbourg, surrounded by timber-framed houses and twisting lanes. Strasbourg was also the home of theologian Albert Schweitzer, whose humanist beliefs greatly influenced Elisabeth.

After moving to Berlin, Elisabeth became a teacher at the esteemed Luisen Madchenschule, a school exclusively for girls. Many of her students were Jewish, a fact that would affect her later in life. Elisabeth taught her students the humanist beliefs she valued such as the sanctity of human life.

War Years

Elisabeth's democratic and pacifist principles, and her dedication to them, got her into a conflict with the Nazi director of her school. Labelled as "politically unreliable," she was moved to a teaching position at another, less prestigious school and later faced an early retirement after an accusation.

Even after her premature retirement and a Gestapo interrogation, Elisabeth never lost her devotion to her Jewish students. Her longtime friend Anna Hirschberg's deportation aided Elisabeth in realizing what was actually happening to the Jews, and only strengthened and drove her resolve. Elisabeth knew that Anna couldn't be saved, but other Jewish people could.

Turning her small apartment into a temporary shelter for Jews fleeing the Gestapo, Elisabeth had a new job that was substantially more dangerous than her teaching job. The three-room apartment, which formerly housed just Elisabeth, her elderly mother, and her ill sister, became a brief home for many. The Jews who had gone underground would stay in Elisabeth's residence until Elisabeth found a more permanent hiding place for them.

Many of Elisabeth's neighbors were active Nazis, so she, her family, and the Jews staying at the apartment lived under constant danger of being caught. If they were, they would all be sent to a concentration camp. This didn't stop Elisabeth from helping the Jews and being hospitable to them. She forged papers, gave them some of her own ration cards, and always invited them to have Friday dinner with her. Elisabeth even sold her own jewelry to help smuggle a Jew into Switzerland.

You would think, with the whole operation already very risky and the likelihood of discovery, Elisabeth wouldn't put herself in any more danger. However, that is exactly what she did. The director of the day-care in Berlin, Liselotte Perles, and her niece Susie were living in a "Jew house." Already three of the apartments there were sealed off and the Jews living there deported, but Liselotte still couldn't decide if she wanted to go into hiding. There was the chance that she and her niece could be caught if she fled, but she could be deported and separated from Susie anyway if she stayed in the home.

It was Elisabeth who finally convinced Liselotte and Susie to leave and go into hiding. In doing so, she saved Liselotte and her niece—the day after they went into hiding the Gestapo did their last large scale round up and deportation of Jews.

Elisabeth, by the end of the war, had saved 80 Jews.

Hero, Redefined

Elisabeth has demonstrated that heroism doesn't have to be prodigious—it can be performed in small acts by the ordinary, without fanfare. And Elisabeth was ordinary; she was just a teacher who cared for her students. But she was also a hero, because you can be ordinary and a hero at the same time.

As such, I would like to revise the Google definition of a hero.

Hero, noun: A person, man or woman, who chooses the right thing even in the face of seemingly unsurmountable obstacles.

Elisabeth fits the definition perfectly because she chose to put her life on the line for a good and just cause. She didn't have to help Jewish people, but she did. That sets her out from the many people of her time who chose not to do anything, or who looked the other way.

So, next time you come across the question "What is a hero?" keep in mind the brave individuals who willingly risked their lives for the sake of others at a time of danger. Individuals like Elisabeth Abegg.

Works Cited

"Abegg, Elisabeth." Berliner Themenjahr 2013. N.p., n.d. Web. 28 Jan. 2016.

"Elisabeth Abegg - The Righteous Among The Nations - Yad Vashem." Elisabeth Abegg - The Righteous Among The Nations - Yad Vashem. N.p., n.d. Web. 28 Jan. 2016.

A Hero in the Making

Makenna Swars

Heroes aren't just people you read about in comic books who have superpowers. There are real life heroes who save lives each and every day. Heroes are normal everyday  people who risk their lives so they can help someone they might have never even met before. During the Holocaust there were many heroes in Germany and Ukraine who helped the Jews.

The Holocaust was a time when Jews were persecuted for their beliefs. This happened just after World War I and Germany blamed the Jews for their problems. A man by the name of Adolf Hitler targeted the weak minded so that they felt they would fit in. The Nazi Party patrolled and found Jews. People were turning on their friends and neighbors just because someone told them that is what you have to do. Jews were sent to concentration camps where they were forced to do manual labor and were fed very little. Most contracted typhoid fever or died from poor conditions. The ones who were lucky enough to survive were still in terrible conditions. This reign of terror lasted from 1939-1945, killing over 6 million people.

Some Jews were able to escape before they were sent to camps, but most weren't that lucky. Without the heroes of the Holocaust even more Jews would have died. Can you imagine? These German citizens realized what Hitler and the Nazi Party were doing was wrong and wanted to help. They hid Jews and put their lives in danger to help save another person, most living in fear that they would be discovered. Agnes and Ruth Wendland were two of the heroes during the Holocaust who risked their lives to save others.

Agnes Crawlow was born in the year 1891 and was later married to Walter Wendland. She then was known as Agnes Wendland. She and her husband, Walter, had three children including Ruth (Wendland, Agnes-The Righteous among the Nations). Agnes was a hero who helped Jews who were scapegoats for all of Germany's problems. When she passed away she had a tree planted in her honor after she was recognized as one of the Righteous among the Nations.

Ruth was born on October 9, 1913 in Altfriesland, Kr. Oberbarnim to Walter and Agnes Wendland. She was the eldest of three children in her family. When she was just three years old her father became a minister at Getshemane community in Berlin. In 1934 she joined the Confessing Church that opposed collaboration of German Protestant Church all together. In the years 1936 to 1938 she continued her studies in Basel where she met Karl Barth. When she met him she learned that he had been expelled from Germany (Wendland, Ruth- Righteous among the Nations).

After finding this out she returned to Nazi Germany and joined a small group of Christians ready to assist and help persecuted Jews. The month of August rolled around and she and her mother Agnes offered to house a man named Ralph Newmann and his sister, Rita. They were living underground in Berlin and Ruth and Agnes gave them shelter and food. Ralph slept in a small room in the house and went out during the day to make people assume that he was going to work (Wendland Family-Righteous among the Nations). Only Ruth and her mother knew their identity and for that Ruth's father treated him like a son.

Sadly, in the year 1945 Ralph's real identity was found out and he was arrested by the military patrol that was patrolling the area. When he was arrested they made him tell them who was helping him hide. That's when Ruth and her mother were found out and Ruth's mother Agnes was arrested. In jail, Agnes became ill and would not have made it in jail any longer. Ruth knew her mother would not last and told the authorities to let her take her mother's place (Wendland Family-Righteous among the Nations). Fortunately, the war was near an end and Ruth was able to make it out with little harm.

Her mother ended up getting typhoid fever and died at 55 in the year 1946. Ruth continued her career after getting out of jail. In August 1964 she became the first women pastor of Altstadt community in Mulheim on the Ruhr. Ruth Wendland died in Berlin in 1977. She was recognized August 12, 1975 by Yad Vashem.

There are many other people like Agnes and Ruth who helped the Jews during the Holocaust. I hope that one day I can help someone the way Agnes and Ruth did. They are truly an inspiration the way they helped out of the kindness of their hearts without expecting anything in return. We could use more people like them in the world today. I can only hope that one day I can inspire someone the way they inspired me. We should keep the heroes of the Holocaust in our minds as the real heroes instead of made-up fictional characters who we read about in comic books. Next time you get the chance thank a local hero like military, doctors, police officers, and firefighters. A thank you will make their day and know they are appreciated.

Works Cited

"Wendland Agnes." The Righteous Among The Nation. N.p., n.d. Web. 22 Jan. 2016. http://db.yadvashem.org/righteous/righteousName.html?language=en&itemId=4060110 .

"Wendland Family." The Righteous Among The Nations. N.p., n.d. Web. 22 Jan. 2016. http://db.yadvashem.org/righteous/righteousName.html?language=en&itemId=4044512 .

"Wendland Ruth." The Righteous Among The Nations. N.p., n.d. Web. 22 Jan. 2016. http://db.yadvashem.org/righteous/righteousName.html?language=en&itemId=4044512 .

A Righteous Among Nations

Michaela Stacy

When you imagine a hero you think of a muscular man with superpowers. The traits for this hero would be courageous, selfless, and reliable. More than just superman has these traits, and these heroes have defeated more obstacles than any superhero out there. In a time of great need many brave individuals risked their lives to save many innocent people. One of these heroes went by the name of Hermann Maas. He found himself in a violent period of time called the Holocaust. Every story needs a villain and in this tale his name is Adolf Hitler and his army of Nazis. In this story characters are revealed and risks are taken, but overall true heroes step forward.

Once upon a time on August 5, 1877 in Gernsbach, Hermann Maas was born. In his childhood he played and hung out with some Jewish kids during school and occasionally went to a synagogue, a Jewish church. He grew up in a Christian protestant family and was expected to become a pastor. He studied theology at the universities of Halle, Strasbourg, and Heidelberg. He then moved to Heidelberg in 1915. Maas became a pastor at Holy Spirit Church and ministered there for the next 28 years. Even in Heidelberg he had a close relationship with those in a nearby synagogue and supported the Jewish community and their religion.

50

Over the next few years Maas became close to the Jewish people and supported them. He then got the opportunity to travel to the Holy Lands for three months. The same day the Nazis launched a general economic boycott on the Jews in Germany. In the Holy Lands, Maas had an excellent and educational time. He listened to Hebrew scholars and visited some immigrants from Germany. He had such a wonderful experience and would love to do it again, but he had no idea of what would happen during the time that he left Israel and the next time he would come back.

Change was all he came to when he came back to Heidelberg. He was threatened by a local Nazi group. The Nazi party considered him "Pastor of the Jews" and wanted him out of a Christian church. He was such a looked upon and religious figure in Christianity that the Nazi Party ignored the issue. Maas was furious about the way this group was treating the Jews. During this time of casting out Jews Hermann Maas's relationship with the Jews became even stronger than before. He would invite Jewish religious leaders to his house for a Christmas Eve party and he would go over to their houses for the Jewish celebration of Passover. He attended synagogue services. Maas tried his best to stand up to the Jewish people and their religion and he decided that his best wasn't good enough. Maas offered all his services to the Jews making it his priority to stop this nonsense of inequality and discrimination. He would be so supported to the Jews that Rabbi Dr. Fritz Pinkus would strongly suggest that he should not attend the public prayers because he didn't want to put Maas in danger. Maas became a member of Pfarrernotbund, the emergency association for protestant pastors. He also joined the Confessing Church, the opposition of the pro-Nazi group called German Christians. Hermaan Maas joined many different groups and offered up his help many different times. He would do anything if it meant saving the Jews.

"In October 1940, while the Jews of Baden, the Palatinate and several places in Baden-Württemberg, were being deported to a concentration camp in southern France, Maas succeeded in protecting some of the older and the frail from being included in the deportation. He kept in contact with those who were deported, using his connections to help them obtain exit visas abroad," wrote Yadvashem.org. Maas took on a real responsibility and risked everything hiding Jews, but he did it out of love and compassion.

In March 1942, the Reich Ministry of Education and Cultural Affairs started a campaign against Hermaan Maas, which forced him into retirement. After investigating him more they were not satisfied with his consequence and sent him to a forced labor camp in France. After his entry the Americans released the camp and saved the retired pastor from misery.

Maas then became the first German to be welcomed back to Israel, in 1950. He wrote a few books about Israel and his experience throughout the past years. Hermaan Maas died in 1970 in Heidelberg, but his story still goes on.

Hermaan Maas and his experience was not a tale or a made up story, and it also isn't something that was in the past and doesn't need to be remembered. This story and many others show us an example of bravery and loyalty. These people are an example of what we should do. These people stood up for something and never backed down even in the face of danger. I believe that these people should never be forgotten and should be celebrated for their determination and courage. Hermaan Maas and all of the other Holocaust saviors are the real heroes.

Hans Eiden

Oliver Eagleton

 From 1939-1945, over 2 million people were massacred in Germany in what is now known as the Holocaust. They were killed because of their racial heritage, physical characteristics, and their political beliefs by Nazi fascist forces commanded by Adolf Hitler, who was trying to build a pure (Aryan) race. There were many acts of heroism and self-sacrifice as these innocent victims endeavored to survive and to protect those closest to them. One such hero was Hans Eiden.

Hans Eiden had already come to the attention of the German authorities when they found out that he was part of the German Communist Group (KPD). In 1933, Hans Eiden had already been put into "protective custody," which he had spent in the Gestapo prison in Trier-West. In December 1936 he was sentenced together with Willi and Aurelia Torgau and another 34 mostly communist members of a resistance group in Trier because of "conspiracy to commit high treason". In 1939 his prison time actually ended, but like many others, Hans was immediately arrested again and deported without trial to a concentration camp. In Buchenwald camp, the prisoners were given numbers that took the place of their names. Eiden's number was 6222.

In the concentration camp he learned that there was an illegal camp organization that was driven primarily by communists. He did what he could to assist them and this secret organization succeeded, despite the spy apparatus of the SS, to save fellow prisoners before their assassinations, and to smuggle weapons from the armaments in the camp. He took over the dangerous and important function of a "camp elder." The SS saw how influential he was to everyone so they took advantage of that. He was used by the SS to enforce their orders. He agreed to take this position, but only because he saw the opportunity to protect his fellow inmates. Hans Eiden, being the camp elder, stood between the detainees and the Nazi camp guards. Hans saw his main task in the improvement of their living conditions.

In April 1945, as the Americans were coming closer the SS camp, authorities ordered all Jews to march to the gate. The illegal organizations were to follow the slogan which stated that nobody should leave the camp. Most of the Jews were hidden by comrades in the block for non-Jews. Three-thousand inmates could be saved. On April 11th the first American tanks emerged. The Americans eventually liberated Eiden and his fellow inmates, and ordered the storming of the remaining SS men, but Hans Eiden prevented the captured SS thugs lynched. Deeply moved, he announced on the loud speakers, "The fascist comrades fled an international camp and the American committee has taken power." They were finally liberated and 21,000 inmates in concentration camps were saved and free.

Hans Eiden returned to Trier. He became the First Secretary of Communist Party executive board and worked until September 1946 in the municipal council for the KPD. As deputy, he entered in the Rhineland-Palatinate state parliament, where he entered primarily for social problems and the Committee on Petitions. A year later, he was expelled from the party by the French secret service for alleged contacts with his partner, Margareta Straubing. Hans Eiden died at the age of 49 on December 6, 1950, by the after-effects of incarceration. In the obituary in "Trierischer Volksfreund" it states, "He was the one whose prudent courage owes its unyielding determination to many tens of thousands of Buchenwald prisoners." On 6 December 1995, the city of Trier appreciated this brave man with a memorial stone in front of his birthplace in the Angel Street.

From recognition of these accomplishments, a street and a school in Weimar were named after him. Hans Eiden devoted himself to the mayor at that time, Felix Zimmermann, at the ceremony for the signing of the twinning in the city of Trier Theatre in September 1987. The City Council Group of the Greens-a Hans Eiden Prize in 1988, which should strengthen those who cross campaigning for democratic development to prevailing opinion. A year later, several letter writers sat in Trierischer Volksfreund for a public ceremony in Eidens hometown. Among them the current OB Klaus Jensen, on behalf of the Working Group on Peace (AGF). It took another six years until the city of Trier honored Hans Eiden with a memorial service, and finally installed a memorial plaque at the site of his birthplace in the Angel Street. In 2001, AGF adopted a "walk in the footsteps of Hans Eiden" in the program of its visits. A request in Weimar now brought the message that the country's Hans-Eiden school no longer exists. The school moved in 1990 to a new domicile. The school administration wanted to take the name, but wasn't granted by the School Administration Office in Weimar. The name was linked to the old school building in the Belvedere Alee. This building has since been used by a special school for the mentally handicapped, but no longer under the name of Hans Eiden. They call it the John Landsberger School. Since 1996 there is no longer even the Hans Eiden Prize of Trier countryside. The tour of AGF took place only once and has not been re-booked. Only the memorial plaque in the Engelstrabe left the reminiscence of a man's moral integrity and great courage, has been shown in a time when there are others preferred to look the other way and to duck. Hans Eiden will always be known as a great man and an influential leader.

Bibliography

Beschreibung. "11 April 1945." - Buchenwald Memorial. N.p., n.d. Web. 28 Jan. 2016. < http://www.buchenwald.de/en/473/ >.

"Datenbank Der Kulturgüterin Der Region Trier." Gedenktafel Für Hans Eiden, Trier, Nord. N.p., n.d. Web. 29 Jan. 2016. < http://www.roscheiderhof.de/kulturdb/client/einObjekt.php?id=23110 >.

HANS EIDEN

Spencer Oswald

 Hans Eiden was a soldier who became a Holocaust hero who helped Jews and all others in the concentration camp known as Buchenwald. He was born in 1901 and died in 1950. Hans Eiden lived to the age of forty-nine. He secretly was a communist Nazi resistance fighter and in 1936 he was sentenced to three-year imprisonment because of "high treason." After this, the Nazis sent him to serve as a guard at Buchenwald, a concentration camp near Weimar. He was an officer in the concentration camp who secretly helped the Jewish prisoners. He returned to his home city of Trier in 1937 and was elected into the State Parliament.

While he was in Buchenwald he secretly helped Jewish resistance in that camp. Buchenwald was not a death camp instead it was actually a work camp. There were families and children in the camp, though life was still rough. Just like all concentration camps there was little food and especially bad living conditions. They had to sleep in bunkers and lice was completely rampant.

The resistance Hans aided was constantly being hunted and despised by the Nazi guards running the camp. Joining this group was dangerous. The resistance had been beaten before but they managed to keep fighting. It was hard to fight because the Nazis were always trying to find members. Not only were the guards watching out but their other inmates would turn them in, so they had to be careful who they spoke to about their resisting. These inmates were common criminals to whom the Nazis would show special favor and would reward them with extra food, clothing, and other items of value in the camp for turning in the resistance group. Defeating these common criminal spies was hard since they had had access to more food and resources than the other prisoners.

There was a constant battle going on between the resistance and the common criminals. If the resistance gained the upper hand, because they wanted to help their own people, the Jewish prisoners would be treated as well as possible without the Nazis getting angry. However, if the common criminals won the Jewish prisoners would endure hard times. Hans, being an undercover resistance fighter, was part of this constant battle. He acted as a messenger and gift giver for the resistance. He would deliver whatever the spoils were to the Jewish prisoners.

However, the Nazis' war was not going as planned in the background. The Nazis had suffered defeat after defeat at the hand of the Red Army. The Nazis were eventually forced to retreat from the USSR. They ultimately were pushed back so far that some of the concentrations camps in Poland were liberated.

Because of this, the Nazis ordered the last few concentration camps to be cleared out and the prisoners moved back into Germany. Any Jewish prisoner found in the camp after this was ordered to be shot. This was a problem for the Jewish prisoners because most of them were not in the condition to survive another death march into Germany. Most prisoners hid in order to not have to march to Germany.

Of these people who hid were most of the resistance leaders, including Hans Eiden. They believed the Americans were not for away from their camp. They believed it was just a matter of roughing it for a little bit until the Americans got there. By the resistance's orders no one in the two bunkers, which held mostly Jewish children, reported to the gate to march to Germany. About 2,000 Jewish adults stayed as well. Some prisoners disguised themselves as non-Jewish prisoners of war in hopes of being taken some place safer.

The Jewish children who stayed in the camp were instructed to remove their Stars of David. By taking off the Stars of David, which the Nazis used to identify the Jews, the children became a major morale boost to the other prisoners.

Of the remaining resistance members who stayed was Hans Eiden, Hans falsified identification helping Jewish prisoners escape. Another person of note during this time was Wilhelm Hamman. When the Nazis entered a bunker and asked who of the children there were Jewish he responded that none of the children in the bunker were Jewish. Hamman later survived and died in the 1950s.

Eventually the Nazis decided to flee the camp because of advancing Allied forces and left some lower ranking soldiers to defend the camp. Noticing what had happened the resistance pulled out concealed weapons and took over the concentration camp. The almost ten-day cold war between the camp's officers and the resistance was over. That same afternoon the Allies tank drove into the camp and it was liberated.

As for Hans Eiden, he went on to live until 1950. He went on to become a state parliament member. In Weimar he has a school and street named after him, and he has a plaque in his honor. Most of the Jewish prisoners and the other prisoners as well were freed and sent to Displaced Persons centers.

Zuche, Thomas. http://www.roscheiderhof.de/kulturdb/client/ einObjekt.php?id=23110. Database of Cultural Goods in the Region of Trier. 05/14/2011. Web. 01/27/2016.

n.p. http://jewishcurrents.org/tag/hans-eiden. Jewish Currents. n.d. Magazine. 01/27/2016.

German Hero: Margarete Sommer

Tayla Smith

Margarete Sommer was a Catholic social worker and a woman of her faith, born July 21, 1893 in Berlin, Germany. She lived to be 72 years old. This wonderful woman seemed to be a generous and caring sort of person! During the Holocaust, she helped tormented Jewish people, saving numerous citizens from being deported to concentration camps, otherwise known as death camps because of the way people were treated there and what happened to them. She was quite smart. She became a well-educated teacher at the age of 19, and she studied economics and went to University of Berlin.

Right from the start you could tell that Margarete had a good personality as well as many quality character traits. The year 1924 was a good year for her, as she was honored and awarded her doctoral degree. She was one of the only women of that generation to be awarded this doctoral degree. For almost a decade she gave speeches to people at the School for Social Welfare, full time. Then later on unfortunately she was told to retire because of the fact the she simply refused to teach about the Nazis' racist ideology. She then went to help out at multiple Catholic agencies. Not long after she started participating in Hilfwerk (a relief agency) from 1939 on. She gave food, money, clothes, comfort, and support to the victims that had to deal with the frustration and danger of being racially ridiculed or persecuted. When people talked about Margarete Sommer they used words such as wise and kind.

Okay, that is enough about this magnificent woman's background and childhood. Let's get to the real reason many people view her as a Holocaust hero or an angel, or even a savior! Margarete was the saving grace to a numerous amount of people. A majority of the people who she helped out or saved were "non-Aryan" Christians, but a good amount of them were Jews. Two men named Minister Alfred Brinkmann and his friend who worked at the church and churchyard, Robert Kaminski, were companions with Sommer. She offered and provided a book printer and businessman named Erich Wolff a hiding spot in a specific heating place in a Church named the Herz-Jesu-Church.

Another case that she saved someone in was with a young little Jewish girl named Sonja Goldwerth and her brother named Mojsche Goldwerth. Their parents were quite irresponsible in the fact that they left their little, and very young children home while they went to France and had all this fun while their kids were left alone clueless on what to do. Young Sonja and little Mojsche were then forced to go to an orphanage by their step mother at 17 Ackerstrasse. The two siblings had to fly to go to England, just the two of them, with no adult assisting or watching them. Then the emigration of the children came to a halt and was a huge problem, because there was a war going on at this time and these two kids were roaming around and not being taking care of. So, as you could probably already guess, Margarete jumped in and took the two children and treated them like her own children. She then had to make sure that they had a reliable hiding place to stay, so that they wouldn't be taken away and then get killed and only the ages of 11 and 12 years old. With so much of a life still to live and look forward to! Mojsche, being the little rascal he was, left the hiding place to just go wander around the Berlin Zoo, and he didn't think that this was a problem. At only 11 years old he didn't know what was right from wrong! This was a big mistake, but he didn't realize that until he got taken away and deported to a concentration camp in Buchenwald, yet somehow he managed to stay alive and not killed. As for Sonja, she did what she was supposed to do and stayed in the hiding place where the two siblings were staying, in the small village. Sadly and unfortunately

56

even that that small village in East Prussia she still got her identity discovered. Sonja was too smart though to not try to get back to Sonja! There was a very chaotic and stressful system going on in Kaliningrad, Russia, the main city in the place where the hiding was. She thankfully got out of that terror place and she fled to Berlin and there is where she was able to meet up with Margarete and she could keep Sonja and save and take care of her. Both then went to Sonja's home in Kleinmachow. Margarete was a natural born caregiver and total sweetheart. Once the two of them got all settled in Margarete Sommer gave Sonja some food and made sure she knew not to get anywhere near the authorities or else she would have to go back to the dreadful camp. Many days later Margarete took Sonja to a church that could definitely take care of her, and she even used her connections with the government to monitor her and make sure that nothing bad would happen to her. On May 5, 2003 Margarete was awarded with the fact that she was recognized by Yad Vashem as Righteous Among the Nations! Shout out to Margarete Sommer for her miracle working!

Works Cited

Steinbach, Peter, Johannes Tuchel, and Ute Stiepani. Gedenkstätte Deutscher Widerstand. Gedenkstätte Deutscher Widerstand, n.d. Web. 20 Jan. 2016.

"Righteous Among The Nations." Yad Vashem. N.p., n.d. Web. 20 Jan. 2016. <http://db.yadvashem.org/righteous/family.html?language=en&itemId=4404750>.

"Margarete Sommer." Margarete Sommer. N.p., n.d. Web. 23 Jan. 2016. <http://memim.com/margarete-sommer.html>.

It's a Man! It's a Savior! It's Oskar Schindler!

Yush Raj Kapoor

 Though there were many German Holocaust heroes who were beneficial to the Jews, Oskar Schindler was someone who really caught my attention. He was very important in the freeing of the Jews during the Holocaust era. Schindler was born on April 28, 1908, in Svitavy Moravia, which is in present-day Czech Republic (Holocaust Encyclopedia; Oskar Schindler). He started off like any other citizen of Germany and later on, grew up to become a businessman. He had many jobs before that such as an electric company's representative, a driving teacher, selling poultry, and was even a part of the German Military Intelligence team (Survivor Stories: Oskar Schindler). However, in 1939, he joined the Nazi Party. It seems counterintuitive that a member of the Nazi Party could help Jews during the Holocaust, doesn't it? A few months after he joined, something in his core values drew him to change the way he viewed the Nazi Party. He said, "If you saw a dog going to be crushed under a car, wouldn't you help him?" (Oskar Schindler).

Oskar Schindler was a businessman, and he wanted Jews to be helped and liberated. A brilliant idea then dawned upon him to employ the Jews for his business. In November of 1939, Schindler bought Rekord Ltd. and renamed it, 'German Enamelware Factory Oskar Schindler' (Holocaust Encyclopedia; Oskar Schindler). He employed over 1,500 Jews to work and provided them with food, shelter, and an assurance that they would not be deported to any type of Nazi camp (Holocaust Encyclopedia; Oskar Schindler). He freed the Jews from various concentration camps and ghettos, such as the Krakow ghetto, and the Plaszow camp. The Krakow Ghetto was located in present-day Poland and contained 15,000 to 20,000 Jewish prisoners. Almost half were killed when they were sent to killing camps (Krakow). The Krakow Ghetto sprouted from the Plaszow camp in 1942. In the peak of its power, it held more than 20,000 Jews (Plaszow). Oskar Schindler was arrested multiple times for aiding Jews, but luckily he was never formally charged. In 1943, Oskar Schindler struck a deal with the Nazis to make his factory a sub-camp of the Plaszow concentration camps. This allowed an additional 500 Jews to live at his factory and escape from the death and torture (Holocaust Encyclopedia; Oskar Schindler).

However, in late 1944, tragedy struck. The Nazis forced the Jews who were working at the Enamelware Factory to the Plaszow concentration camp. Schindler then moved the enamelware plant to Brunnlitz, in Moravia, and opened it as an armaments factory (Oskar Schindler). Schindler's Jewish assistant created a list of over 1,000 Jewish prisoners who were in need of work. He employed and freed those 1,000 Jewish men and women who were moving from one concentration camp to another by employing them for the new company. He then signed contracts with the Schutzstaffel (also known as the SS or Protection Squadrons), to produce munitions for the Nazis in World War II. This allowed Schindler to acquire Jewish manpower. Production was fairly slow because it took some time to make and sabotage the ammunitions. It was an ingenious idea to put defects in the ammunitions so that the Nazis were left at a disadvantage. The production was further delayed due to illegally producing counterfeit military travel passes and ration cards along with the defective ammunitions (Survivor Stories: Oskar Schindler).

Though the number of Jews killed in the Holocaust is not certain, many sources estimate around 5 million to 6 million Jews were killed (Basic Questions about the Holocaust). Due to economic advantages, Oskar Schindler managed to free over 1,000 Jews. That is more than 0.0166 percent of the Jewish population that was killed. It may seem insignificant in the large scale of events, but if there were 3,000 Oskar Schindlers who'd have helped the Jews, the death count could have been cut in half. Schindler spent all his money and time into release Jewish prisoners until World War II ended.

When the war ended in 1945, Schindler and his wife Emilie Schindler moved to Argentina to start afresh. Soon he realized that Germany was where his life was and so he left Argentina and moved back to Germany once again. There the Jews he had saved treated him with care. He was given money and shelter but unfortunately, he misused it all. He became an alcoholic and spent all money on alcohol (Biography). He was still respected by his friends whom he saved. In my opinion, we should always respect the part of him that saved many hundreds of Jews.

When he died, he was extremely poor and very few people knew about his contribution to saving the Jews. In the late 1900s, he was honored as a martyr and a man to be respected. He may have died penniless, but his "children," the Jews he saved, took care of his body and sent it to Israel to be properly buried and honored. He was 66 when he died due to heart disease. Unfortunately, he could not witness the impact that he left on the lives of so many. Oskar Schindler may have only helped 1,000 out of the millions of Jews that could be saved then, but now those 1,000 have grown exponentially and will still keep growing as generations pass by. Don't you think Oskar Schindler deserves the title of a God? Personally, I look up to people like Schindler and want to be like him: selfless, honorable, a savior, and maybe a little rich too. "He who saves a single soul, saves the world entire." -Oskar Schindler

Works Cited

"Basic Questions about the Holocaust." Basic Questions about the Holocaust. N.p., n.d. Web. 02 Feb. 2016. <http://www.projetaladin.org/holocaust/en/40-questions-40-answers/basic-questions-about-the-holocaust.html>.

"Biography." Muzeum Svitavy. N.p., n.d. Web. 29 Jan.
2016. <http://www.muzeum.svitavy.cz/stale-exp/oskar-schindler/biography/148-2/>.

"Holocaust Encyclopedia; Oskar Schindler." United States Holocaust Memorial Museum. United States Holocaust Memorial Council, n.d. Web.
<http://www.ushmm.org/wlc/en/article.php?ModuleId=10005787>.

"Krakow." United States Holocaust Memorial Museum. United States Holocaust Memorial Council, 29 Jan. 2016. Web. 02 Feb. 2016.
<http://www.ushmm.org/wlc/en/article.php?ModuleId=10005169>.

"Oskar Schindler." Jewish Virtual Library. N.p., n.d.
Web. <https://www.jewishvirtuallibrary.org/jsource/biography/schindler.html>.

"Plaszow." United States Holocaust Memorial Museum. United States Holocaust Memorial Council, 29 Jan. 2016. Web. 02 Feb. 2016.
<http://www.ushmm.org/wlc/en/article.php?ModuleId=10005301>.

"Survivor Stories: Oskar Schindler." Holocaust Education & Archive Research Team. N.p., n.d.Web. 29 Jan. 2016.
<http://www.holocaustresearchproject.org/survivor/schindler.html>.

Sofka Skipwith, a Holocaust Hero

Sofka Skipwith

Zachary Conwell

The 1940's was a dark time in the world in which a horrible event occurred, the Holocaust. This was a time when people were being beaten and killed in masses by the thousands, simply for being Jewish. These Jews were then thrown into concentration camps, where they would work from dusk to dawn every day, and given 50 calorie meals, often consisting of bread or hot water. Many of these people, oddly enough, weren't Jewish at all. Most were German citizens, or were a part of the Nazis. Most were thrown into these camps simply because they posed threats to the third Reich, or simply said something they didn't like. Luckily for these imprisoned people, they had some hope. Those who were not imprisoned heard about these tragic and inhumane happenings, and they decided to take action. People such as Sofka Skipwith worked tirelessly to rescue and smuggle Jews and others out of concentration camps.

Sofka Skipwith was born in 1907, in St. Petersburg, Russia, and was the daughter to Prince Peter Alexandrovitch Dolgorouky of St. Petersburg, Russia. Her grandfather was Prince Dolgorouky, who was Grand Marshal of the Imperial Court as well as a direct descendant of the founders of Moscow (Women of Valor).She lived in England and France with her husband, because they were both exiled from Russia. They had two children, named Peter and Ian. In 1937 she divorced her husband and married Grey Skipwith, who was from England (Women of Valor). Two years later, their son, Patrick, was born. On June, 1940, the British lost to the Germans. Because of this, Sofka was arrested in Paris by Germany. At first, they were all taken to barracks in Besançon and housed there (Women of Valor). Then, in May 1941, all 400 British citizens who were housed there were sent to a camp known as Vittel detention camp (Women of Valor). While she was there, she became a leading figure among her fellow prisoners. She set up a library and many other benefic activities, along with help from the Red Cross (Skipwith Sofka). She also took part in "la petite famille" where she discussed forbidden subjects that related to Marxism. Four years after Patrick was born, Sofka's husband died while on a mission for the Royal Air Force (Women of Valor). Sofka was so depressed that she refused food in an attempt to starve herself to death. She was then put in a hospital and nursed to health. Sofka was released three years later, on July 1944, in a prisoner exchange between Britain and Germany (Women of Valor).

In 1943, 280 Jews from Poland walked into Vittel holding Latin American passports or visas, in an attempt to avoid being deported to a concentration camp (Women of Valor). Some of these passports were invalid, and were given to Jews without consent of the country in which they came from. Sofka was inspired by what had happened to them, and decided she needed to help these people get the freedom that they deserved.

She and a fellow British prisoner known as Madeline White made attempts to try and help these people. With help of the French Resistance, they were then provided fake documents, which Sofka then gave to the Jewish youth of Vittel (Women of Valor). On April 3, 1943, Sofka put a list of names of the Jews who had legitimate passports in a toothpaste tube (Women of Valor). It was then given to a group known as the French Partisans, who would then distribute the passports to Jews wanting to escape the grasp of Hitler. On the list were not just names, but a note. This note called for diplomats to take action as well as telling them of the horrors that Jews endured while in the camps. In January, 1944 the Germans started checking how up to date the Latin American passports that were owned by those that were in the Vittel camp (Women of Valor). When they realized that the passports were invalid, Sofka knew that the Jews to whome she gave the passports were in grave danger of being taken to a concentration camp. In a desperate attempt to retrieve papers to secure the Jews' safety, she found the papers and shipped them to Vittel, but at that point, it was too late. By the time August was over, only 60 of the 280 of the original Jews remained. The Jews who were taken were split up into groups; one went to Drancy and another to Auschwitz, where their death was probable. Sofka was devastated and felt powerless in trying to save the lives of those taken away. After the Polish Jews were taken away, Sofka and Madeleine took advantage of their contacts to arrange getting children out of the concentration camp, with help of the resistance movement (Skipwith Sofka). Because of their efforts, they managed to save the life of a Jewish baby.

These people, who sacrificed their time, freedom, and even lives to rescue people out of these death camps, are true heroes. If it hadn't been for them, thousands of Jews, old and young, would have their lives cut short, and for no reason. People like Sofka deserve to be recognized, and noticed, for all of their valiant efforts. Sofka Shipwith died on February 26, 1994, (Skipwith Sofka) but in our hearts, she lives on and continues to inspire people with her story from all around the world.

Works Cited

""Women of Valor"" Sofka Skipwith. N.p., n.d. Web. 27 Jan. 2016.

"Skipwith Sofka." Skipwith Sofka. N.p., n.d. Web. 27 Jan. 2016
http://www.southerninstitute.info/holocaust_education/slgide.html
http://www.yadvashhem.org//yv/en/exhibitions/righteous-auschwitz/woerl.asp
http://www.wollheim-memorial.de/en/krankenbau_personal_und_struktur_en
http://www.jta.org/1964/04/07/archive/auschwitz-trial-hears-of-ss-man-who-sent-12-little-jewish-girls-to-death

Congregation B'nai Israel, Sacramento, CA

Denise Crevin is currently the Education Administrator, Congregation B'nai Israel. After graduating from UCLA with a degree in Communication Studies, Denise received a Masters degree in Broadcast and Electronic Communication Arts from San Francisco State University. She worked as a writer for CNN Headline News in Atlanta, did PR for Marriott Hotels during the 1996 Olympics in Atlanta and then returned to the Bay Area to run a business - Service Impressions - with her husband, Dan. She is the proud mom to Ava (age 8) and Max (age 6), and enjoys volunteering for a variety of organizations including the PTO at their school, Hadassah, Girl Scouts and her college sorority, Alpha Epsilon Phi. As the daughter of a Holocaust survivor, she is glad to help review essays for the Eleanor J Marks Holocaust Essay Contest and ensure that future generations never forget.

Joe Gruen works and lives in Sacramento, CA. He is a a full-time accounting student at American River College and works part time teaching Hebrew and Judaica at B'nai Israel Congregation.

Erica Cassman is a California State credentialed teacher. She taught at the elementary school level for ten years in Los Angeles before starting her family and moving to Sacramento. She is currently staying at home with her 3 year old daughter Lilah and 1 year old son Gavin. Since moving to Northern California Erica has become an active member in the Jewish community. Erica's educational background includes a Bachelor of Arts in Liberal Studies with a Concentration in Art and a Master's degree in Educational Administration, both from California State University, Northridge.

A Hero of the Holocaust, Suzanna Braun

Olivia Halseth

Courage is going out of your comfort zone to help someone. People show courage in something as little as when the raise their hand in class or something as important as making a speech to stop segregation as Martin Luther King, Jr. did. There are two types of courage; physical courage and mental courage. Physical courage is going out of your comfort zone to, for example, fight a disease that is hard to fight. Mental courage is going out of your comfort zone to, for example, battle against society's rules. Having courage isn't always easy, though. It can be very hard to gather up enough to even raise your hand in class or to stand up to a school bully. Courage takes guts, and your gut usually tells you what is right.

The Holocaust was a horrifying event. Over 6 million Jewish people, 200,000 Gypsies, 200,000 mentally disabled, 2-3 million prisoners of war, and many other groups were murdered. The man who caused this to happen was Adolf Hitler. He had an idea of a "perfect world," but certain cultures were not in it. These cultures were sent to concentration camps, or death camps, and were separated by their age, gender, and fitness. Certain people were killed, while others were overworked. People were experimented on and tortured. Nazis patrolled through neighborhoods and guarded the camps. How could such a horrifying event happen? Did anyone try to stop it? Actually, some people did.

Suzanna Braun is a hero of the Holocaust. She was a 16-year-old girl in the Holocaust. She was in the concentration camps as well as all the other people, yet she saved many people's lives with her knowledge and skills. She was separated from her dad, and never got a chance to say goodbye. He left telling Suzanna to make sure that she took care of her sister, no matter what obstacles she faced. Her sister was very ill and Suzanna had the responsibility of not only keeping herself alive, but her sister as well. Together, they encountered many near death experiences, yet lived long lives.

Her first near death experience was in the concentration camp, Auschwitz-Birkenau. Suzanna was forced to go into the gas chamber with about 30 other people, including her mom, Elizabeth, and sick sister, Agi. When Suzanna got older and retold this story, she recalled the faint smell of gas, which never got much stronger. The next thing she experienced was that everyone was taken out of the room. She said the group knew something went wrong in the gas chamber. Something malfunctioned and by sheer luck, her life, along with her mom's and her sister's and all the others in the gas chamber were spared.

Suzanna's second experience was probably the most traumatic. She, her sister, and her mother were tossed onto a truck along with many other women. They were driven from Auschwitz-Birkenau to Estonia which was more than one-thousand kilometers away. This is where they were ordered to begin marching south on a death march.

Suzanna's mother was shot dead on the way, and Suzanna was so devastated she was not able to speak for a month. Alongside her sister, Suzanna somehow managed to escape what seemed like a most certain death.

Her third experience was when the Nazis were injecting lethal amounts of strychnine into the arms of the inmates in a line. Suzanna shared that she saw her inmates die instantly once getting the injection in the vein of their wrists. She knew that if the strychnine was not injected directly into her vein, it would not be as lethal and her chance of survival would rise. So, once she was getting her injection of strychnine, she turned her wrist so the needle missed the vein and only pricked her skin. She then used the baling wire from a hay bale to pierce her wrist, getting the poison out. She saved many people who were in line near her, including her own sister by explaining to them to turn their wrists while they were being injected and using this baling wire technique on them.

Suzanna and her sister, Agi, eventually escaped a concentration camp near Danzig. Her sister's illness was getting progressively worse, so Suzanna was dragging her around on a sled in the bitter cold, desperate for shelter. Agi had developed gangrene in her legs, and Suzanna got her to a hospital. Agi's feet were amputated to save her life. Suzanna and Agi eventually immigrated to Israel, and lived next to each other for many years until Agi's death.

Suzanna showed great courage in the situations above, even through pain and loss. She exemplified leadership in saving herself, her sister and others throughout her experience. She is a great example of a hero in the Holocaust. She even fulfilled her father's wish of taking care of her sister. Like all who survived the concentration camps, Suzanna showed great courage in her daily life.

Elisabeth Abegg

Catherine Mastronarde

The Holocaust did not actually start in World War II. It started when Hitler became Chancellor of Germany in 1933. World War II actually started in 1939, and ended in 1945.

We are all really lucky that a lot of people had a lot of courage to help the Jewish refugees during the Holocaust and World War II. If nobody, or only a few people, would have had the courage to help the Jewish people we might not be here today.

Courage is not just about being brave; it is about being brave enough to do the right thing, and the right thing is to follow your heart. People saw what was going on and decided that they wanted to help the Jewish people who were being persecuted in the Holocaust because that was what their hearts were telling them. None of them did it because their friends or parents or the government made them. They did it because they wanted to help. They also knew that they would be punished by the government if they were caught helping the Jewish families and individuals being persecuted, but they did it anyway. They did it because they cared.

It took a lot of courage during World War II for both the Jewish people being hunted down and the people who were helping the Jewish people. They helped the Jewish people in many ways. They gave them food, shelter, money, and even helped smuggle them in to a different country where they would be safe, such as the U.S. One of the people who helped a lot of Jewish people was Elisabeth Abegg.

Elisabeth Abegg was born on May 3,1882 in Strassbourg, Alsace. Before Hitler came to power in 1933 (the same year the Holocaust started), Elisabeth Abegg was a history teacher at the Luisen Mädchenschule, a girls' school in Berlin. It was a fancy private school. A lot of the students there that she taught were Jewish, or had Jewish family members.

When the Nazis hired a new director for the Luisen Mädchenschule, Elisabeth Abegg was forced to teach at a different school that wasn't as fancy. She had to teach at a different school because she had some friends who were Jewish. She got denounced in 1940 and had to retire early.

Elisabeth Abegg kept in touch with a lot of her Jewish friends and students, even after the Holocaust started. Elisabeth Abegg was a part of a peace movement that helped the Jewish individuals and families who were being persecuted by Hitler and the Nazis by giving them clothing, food, a place to stay temporarily, or helping them get tickets and papers to get on a ship to go to a different country.

She was once interrogated by the Gestapo because of her Jewish contacts and their suspicion that she was helping them. She knew where a lot of her friends were hiding, but she did not give them away and tell the Gestapo where they were hiding. (The Gestapo were like the Nazis and they were still working for Hitler, but instead of soldiers they were police.)

When Elisabeth Abegg's friend, Anna Hirschberg, got arrested and killed by the Gestapo because she was Jewish, Elisabeth Abegg realized that even if she could not do anything to help her friend, she could still help other Jews. Even though her apartment was only four rooms, and she was living with her mother and her sister, Julie, she turned it into a meeting place for Jewish families and individuals in hiding.

She had some Jewish families stay in her apartment for a few days until they could find another place to stay, and when there were people who she could not fit in her apartment she showed or told them about places where they could stay. She made sure all of her guests had enough food to eat before she and her sister ate their food. She would sometimes give the Jewish people and families forged papers that would help them get on a ship to go to a different country where they would be safe. Each Friday she would have special meals for the Jewish families or individuals that had gone into hiding.

It was risky for Elisabeth Abegg to be helping the Jewish people, especially because some of her neighbors were Nazis, or they were against Jewish people. Some of the former Jewish refugees still kept in touch with Elisabeth Abegg. One of the things

Elisabeth Abegg did for a Jewish refugee was selling her own jewelry to raise money to send them to Switzerland to be with his family. Elisabeth Abegg had a lot of courage to help the Jewish refugees. Not all superheroes have to have superpowers. Elisabeth Abegg was a superhero because she saved the lives of people who were being persecuted. She followed her heart, even when it was risky at times. What she did made her a better person and made the world a better place. You don't have to do a lot to make the world a better place. You just have to follow your heart.

Citations
http://www.yadvashem.org/
http://www.yadvashem.org/yv/en/righteous/stories/abegg.asp

Who is Elisabeth Abegg?

Maya Moseley

You might ask who is Elisabeth Abegg? Elisabeth Abegg is a woman who went above and beyond to help others during the Holocaust. Other than being a German teacher she also provided shelter to about 80 Jews during the Holocaust. When I was learning about her, it really made me think of what people do to help others. She had risked her own life to save people she didn't even know without any hesitance whatsoever. Elisabeth really was a hero of the Holocaust. That is why I chose to tell you her amazing story.

Abegg was born in Strasbourg in 1882, and was raised in Alsace. She went to college at Leipzig University; where she took history, classical philology, and romance studies. She graduated there with a doctorate in 1916. She moved to Berlin, Germany in 1918 after the region of Alsace was claimed by France. In Berlin she helped a lot with post world war one relief work. After she finished her relief work, she enrolled, and became a teacher in 1924. She was a history teacher at a fashionable girl's school in Berlin. When Abegg openly criticized the Nazis in World War II, she had to be transferred to a different, less good and fashionable school in Berlin. Her ways were not liked there either, and because of it she was forced to retire. But Elisabeth did not stop thinking badly of the Nazis, and she was determined to do what was right.

She began to help Jews find safe shelter in 1942, after the murderous group Gestapo summoned her for interrogation. The interrogation didn't really change a thing, as Gestapo had lost the trial. She then established a large group of rescuers, including former students and Quaker friends of hers to rescue Jews during the holocaust. In one case in January of 1943, she came to a "Jew house" full of many Jews to persuade them to hide underground; the day they finally went underground was the day of the last large sweep of Berlin for Jews by Gestapo. Abegg knew what the consequences would be if she were caught, but she still risked her life to save many others. Abegg wanted to help more so she converted her small, three and a half room apartment that she shared with her mother and sister into a temporary Jewish shelter. She invited people for special meals on Fridays and procured forged papers for them. She did this for over three years but not once was she reported. Abegg housed dozens of people over the three years before the war was over, one time selling her jewelry to pay for their escape. This just shows what she did to give people the freedom they deserved. Abegg still loved teaching though, so she tutored hiding Jewish children in her apartment during their stays at her home. She taught them well enough that they would have more knowledge in the future, to read, to write, and to do math problems. When there were too many people at her home she skimped on food so they could eat. Other than offering people to stay at her house, she also directed them to other houses so they could have the best accommodations possible. She successfully sheltered about 80 Jews herself, even when her neighbors were active Nazis. Abegg continued to help Jews until the war was over in 1945.

After the war was over, Abegg continued her dream of teaching and lived a pretty happy, regular life. The Jews she had rescued deeply appreciated what she had done for them. They appreciated what she did for them so much they even published a book in 1957 called And a Light Shined into the Darkness, which they had dedicated all to her. Many of the authors had probably learned to write because of her tutoring them. In 1967 she was finally recognized as Righteous among the Nations, by Yad Vashem. She then passed away about seven years later to natural causes. In 1991, almost 20 years after her death, her memorial plaque was mounted in her neighborhood where she had rescued Jews. A Street called Elisabeth-Abegg Street was named after her in 2006 in Berlin.

Abegg is a real hero of the Holocaust. She dedicated her time and money to save people she didn't know. She was never hesitant to sell her jewelry to buy their escape. She was never hesitant to give a free, good education to children at her home. She was never hesitant to do what she did knowing the risks that would follow her. She never bragged about what she did, or did it for a prize. She did it because it was the right thing to do. Even though many heroes are not recognized, at least future generations can spread stories, her story. My definition of a hero is someone who helps others knowing the risks that are there, to make things better. That is the exact definition of Elisabeth Abegg.

The Gerasimchik Family

Aubrey Brosnan

In World War II, the Holocaust was a great mass killing of the Jewish people. About 6 million Jews were murdered in World War II by the Nazis. In 1942, the ghettos were first used to cage Jews so that the Nazis could decide what to do with them. The ghettos were also used to keep the Jews together in a small, easily controlled, space and so that they would be easily found and identified. The Nazis killed the Jews because they blamed them for all of the bad things that happened in Germany after the loss of the first World War.

After the ghettos came the death camps. Three million of the Jews died from being gassed to death. All of the dead bodies would have been piled up in an oven and turned to ashes that were then scattered and thrown in the wind. In Nazi death camps there was no way to escape. Guards would shoot anyone who ever tried. Almost everyone who went to the death camps died very painful and gruesome deaths.

The reason Jews are still around today in Europe is that some German and Ukrainian people knew that the killings were not right and risked their lives to help save as many Jews as they could. Those who were caught helping Jews were shot where they were standing. Saving Jews was very dangerous.

This is the story of a poor Ukrainian family who risked everything that they had to help their Jewish friends. Their names were Pavel and Lyubov Gerasimchik and their children Klaudiya, Galina, and Nicolay. They all lived in a small shack in Ukraine. They lived peacefully in the village of Szubkow. Before the war, Pavel Gerasimchik became good friends with a Jew from Tuczyn who was married and had two daughters. The Jewish family's name was Khomut. Unlike most of the locals, the Gerasimchik family did not despise the Jewish family, and they were very good to them. In July 1941, the Germans occupied the area. Unlike most, the Gerasimchik family did not turn their friends in to the Nazis. Instead, Pavel Gerasimchik offered shelter to the Khomut family if they ever needed it.

In September 1942, preparations were made to liquidate the Tuczyn ghetto. That means that everyone living in the Tuczyn ghetto would have been murdered or sent to a concentration camp. The Khomut family tried to flee to Szubkow. They were caught in the act and sent back to their home in the ghetto. The next day, Paul Gerasimchik was at their door, offering once more to hide them. They took him up on his offer and were ready to escape. Pavel drove his cart to his town with the Khomut parents and younger daughter hidden in the cart under some straw. A few days later, the ghetto was liquidated. It turned out that the Khomut's eldest daughter was with another family that was entrusted to save her. Instead, that family broke their promise and handed her over to the Germans. Tragically, she was murdered.

It was very dangerous to hide Jews. Even people who were not Jewish were murdered if it was discovered that they had helped Jews to hide or escape. So, deciding whether or not to save the Jewish family was very hard for the Gerasimchiks. Remembering that their stay would only be for a short while related to their deal, Pavel Gerasimchik asked the Khomut family to leave. But, seeing them packing their few belongings and thinking of the dangers of the public, he changed his mind and instead built a hideout for the three of them under their threshing floor.

For 18 months, the Gerasimchik family hid the Jewish family of three. The Khomuts secretly stayed in the hideout that Pavel Gerasimchik had made for them. Lyubov Gerasimchik and her children cared for and nurtured the Khomuts. They fed, hydrated and sheltered them. They even cleaned the chamber pots. Feeding more people proved to be a difficult task during the war as each person was only allowed a couple of pieces of bread as their ration for the day. All the rest went to soldiers working for the Germans. Money to buy the bread was scarce and buying more bread than you should need was a warning sign that you might be hiding Jews. So, the Gerasimchik family had to be very careful and try to secretly find or grow some extra food to feed three additional people. Towards the end of the occupation, 15 Nazi soldiers suddenly moved onto the Gerasimchik's property. For two weeks, they could not bring food to the hidden Jews because the Germans were staying right over the Jews hideout. The Red Army liberated the area on February 15, 1944.

Afterward, Pavel Gerasimchik returned the gold watch that the Khomuts had given them when they first moved in. Later, the Khomut family immigrated to the United States.

On March 15, 1990, Yad Vashem recognized Pavel and Lyubov Gerasimchik as two of the Righteous Gentiles among the Nations. On December 6, 1999, their children, Klaudia Kucheruk, Galina Gavrishchuk and Nicolay Gerasimchik were also awarded the title.

The Gerasimchik family saved three lives and risked their own in doing so. Even though they didn't have much, they did what they could to save the lives of the Khomut family. They fed them, hydrated them and helped them to survive the dangerous world that was Ukraine under the German occupation during World War II. Pavel Gerasimchik was the most courageous and helpful. He hid the Khomut family in his cart to transport them to his house unseen. He dug them a hideout, which saved the family from the group of German soldiers. He even returned the gold watch to the family even though his own family was very poor. In helping the Jews, he did nothing wrong or unforgivable. By doing this, Pavel and Lyubov Gerasimchik and their children made the world a better place. They displayed t'kun olam, even though they were not Jewish.

I really liked learning about the Gerasimchik family because they helped three people to survive the Holocaust. They helped them in any way that they could and the Khomut family ended up surviving. Their story shows that even the smallest of things help and that it always helps to be kind.

Wilhelm "Wilm" Hosenfeld: A Quiet Voice of Resistance

Ezra William Hammel (Co-Runners up)

The Holocaust is filled with stories of both courage and cowardice. Stories of people who just went along with the evil around them, or made things even worse. But there are other stories as well; stories of people who had the courage to do some good, to speak up publicly or privately, or who tried to save the lives of others. Wilhelm "Wilm" Hosenfeld was one of the people who had the courage to do some good, and the private journals that he kept while he was a soldier helps us understand why he chose to defy the Nazis and save the lives of two Jewish Poles.

Born in Hessen, Germany in 1895, Wilm was raised a religious Catholic. And I believe that it was his faith that helped him do something good and risk his own life when he saw the evil that was going on around him. During World War II, Wilm was a German soldier in the Nazi Army. At first, he did as he was told. But when he saw what the Nazis were doing, he became disillusioned with the fact that they were killing Poles and Jews. We know what Wilm thought about these murders because during the war he kept private journals. The journals survived the war because after completing a journal he would send it home. While this is good for history, it was dangerous for him, because if someone had found his journals, he and his family could have been murdered. In the journals he stressed his growing disgust with the Nazi army oppressing Poles and Jews. In 1943 after witnessing the Warsaw Ghetto Revolt, Wilm's next entry read "With horrible mass murder of the Jews we have lost this war. We have brought an eternal curse on ourselves that will be forever covered with shame. We have no right for compassion or mercy; we all have a share in the guilt. I am ashamed to walk in the city...." These journals are important because it shows us that he was not a regular Nazi, but that he had a conscious, and that there were still people who knew the difference between right and wrong.

The journals also help us understand why he did the most the important thing in his life, the thing we remember him for. The action that made him worth remembering all these after his death is what he did to rescue two Polish Jews. One of those Jews was Waldislaw Szilman a famous composer and pianist. Szilman's story was made into the 2002 film called "The Pianist." Saving Szilman meant Wilm was not only trying to save Szilman's life, but he was also risking his own life. As a Nazi officer, he knew better than anyone the cost of helping a Jewish person. True courage is when you risk everything for the well-being of somebody else, even at great risk to yourself. This ideal is something that Wilm's life is an example of.

After the war, Wilm was captured by the Soviet Army. He died seven years after his capture by the Soviet Army, which is not surprising because the Soviets were known for their harsh and cruel treatment of their prisoners, particularly the Germans.

But, to make things worse, the trial that sentenced him to the Soviet prison was held in his absence. So he did not even get to speak up for his own defense at the trial, he had no real justice, and the trial was just a sham. This is not that different than what happened under the Nazis. Both the Nazis and the Soviets were not interested in truth, justice, or the rule of law. The real goal of the Soviets was to put Wilm in prison, and punish him, as quickly as possible. His real guilt was being a German soldier. The Soviets treated him, similar to the way the Nazis treated the Poles, they were guilty simply for being who they were, not for any specific crime. It is always dangerous when systems of justice are just for appearances and not really for finding out the truth. However, one decent thing the Soviets did after Wilm was captured, was that he was allowed to send letters back to his family.

The story of Wilm Hosenfeld is a of non-Jew who even in the worst of times had the courage to save two Jewish lives. Wilm did something though that bothers me. He saved two Jews, but he might have been able to save more if he spoke up before the war. This made me think about what is going on in society today because the Holocaust started with crazy, irrational, verbal discrimination and blind hatred against "the Jews." This is the same type of crazy, irrational, verbal discrimination that can be heard today by some presidential hopefuls in our country when they talk about "the Muslims" and "the Mexicans." If we forget about Wilm's story we might repeat that same horrible mistakes made by the Nazis and the many ordinary citizens who said nothing to stop them, not so long ago.

At Yad Vashem in Jerusalem, we of course tell the story of our own people and the horrible things that happened to us because of the Nazis. But, we also know that it is important to have hope, so we also tell the story of the Righteous Gentiles who helped us. Stories like this are important for us to remember because it inspires people even in the darkest of times that a single act of goodness can shine brightly through the darkness. Now more than ever, we have to be the light. Stories like Wilm's reminds us that even one person can make a difference.

Works Cited:

Yad Vashem: The Righteous Amongst the Nations: Wilhelm Hosenfeld
{http://www.yadvashem.org/yv/en/righteous/stories/hosenfeld.asp}
Jewish Virtual Library: Wilhelm Hosenfeld
{http://www.jewishvirtuallibrary.org/jsource/biography/Wilhelm_Hosenfeld.html}
'The Good Nazi': Courageous Story of guilt wracked German officer who saved 'The Pianist' and inspired Hollywood blockbuster, by Allan Hall, November 27, 2015, DailyMail.com
{http://www.dailymail.co.uk/news/article-3334954/The-good-Nazi-Courageous-story-guilt-wracked-German-officer-saved-Pianist-inspired-Hollywood-blockbuster.html}

Konyukhs to the Rescue

Harris Prunier

In August 1942 a 20 year old young Jewish woman was wandering through the forest. Her whole family had been killed and she was trying to survive by escaping into the Ukrainian woods. She was walking and trying to find safe shelter. The Germans had announced in all the villages that anyone hiding a Jew would be killed together with his family and their house would be burnt down. Finally, she found a village. A husband and wife who were farmers who took her in for the night. Her rescuers were members of a Baptist community. Through their courage and kindness she survived and even assisted other Jews in escaping. After the war she was able to live in the safety of the newly formed country of Israel. This is the story of Fanya Rozenfeld and her Ukrainian rescuers named Filip and Teklya Konyukh.

In early September 1942, Fanya Rozenfeld from Rafałówka arrived at the home of Filip and Teklya Konyukh, farmers living in the village of Mulczyce in the county of Sarny. Fanya was the only survivor of her family. Everyone else had been killed when the ghetto in Rafałówka was destroyed on August 29, 1942. Fanya was only 20 years old then. At that time she was able to escape.

The Rafalowka ghetto was made in May 1, 1942. Jewish people from Olizarka, Zoludzk, and other villages in the area were brought into this ghetto. At that time its population was around 2,500 people. Then, in July 1942, sixty Jewish forced laborers were murdered outside of this town. On August 29, 1942, the Rafalowka ghetto was destroyed, and 2,250 Jews were taken to pits on the road to Suchowola, where they were murdered. Dozens of others escaped to the forests and other villages.

Even though there was great danger, there were people who were willing to helped the Jews and give them refuges.

Filip and Teklya Konyukhs were Baptists. At first they allowed Fanya to spend the night at their home. The next morning, Fanya told her hosts that she had dreamt at night that she had been reading out words from the Book of Isaiah in front of other Jews. When Filip heard this, he took Fanya to the Batpists' weekly gathering in the home of the preacher, in the village of Młynek. That priest was one of the regional Baptist leaders. Fanya's knowledge of the Bible impressed that congregation deeply, and motivated them to help save her. After the meeting, Fanya returned to the Konyukhs' home, where she was treated as a family member. She helped out with the housework and also offered her own comments on verses from the Old Testament. Consequently, the Baptists named her "Saint Feodosiya."

The Konyukhs also gave shelter to two other Jews, Sender Appelboim and his father Shlomo, who had escaped from the ghetto in Wlodzimierzec. After a few months, in late 1942, the search for more Jews increased and these three Jews were had to leave the

Konyukhs' home. Appelboim and his father turned to someone whom they knew before the war. Fanya Rozenfeld moved to the preacher's home in the village of Młynek.

The preacher, Kaluta, lived with his second wife, Anna, their four children and two daughters from Kaluta's previous marriage. Fanya Rozenfeld stayed with the Kalutas for about a year. Here their Baptist faith played an important role in the life of a Jewish person, and Kaluta would preach in his sermons about the duty to help save Jewish lives.

However Fanya's existence with the Kalutas was threatened toward the end of 1943, when armed Ukrainian fighters arrived in the area. They were deeply anti-Semitic and hated the Jews. Rozenfeld decided to move to the home of Andrey Kuyava, his wife Yarina and their son Nikolay because she thought she would be safe. Kuyava was also a Baptist leader. At the beginning of her stay with this family, Rozenfeld hid in their barn until the fighters left the area. Then it became less dangerous so she left her hiding place and lived free. The area became fully free in 1944.

Fanya's faith probably really helped her to survive. When she told the family her dream about the bible, the farmers knew that she was a religious person. They were too. Maybe they helped her just because of this. Only thirty of Rafalowka's Jews survived, including Fanya. In addition to having been rescued, Fanya also helped other Jews who had escaped. One person described Fanya's help:

"She often received clothes and food from the farmers; dressed as a farmer woman she carried the package on her back and brought it to the Jews in the forest, who didn't have home to live in". She helped many children while in the forest. All of them lived on to have great lives and freedom.

Shortly after the war Fanya Rozenfeld married Yakov Bass, whose daughter had been in hiding with her at the Kaluta family. Together with Yakov's children the couple immigrated to Israel. The Kaluta family never lost touch with Fanya and other wartime rescuers.

1. Memorial book for the towns of Old Rafalowka, New Rafalowka, Olizarka, Zoludzk and vicinity. (Rafalovka, Ukraine) Edited by: Pinhas and Malkah Hagin, Tel Aviv 1996.

Julian Bilecki – Tree to Tree Hero

Henry Goldberg (Co-Runners Up)

 What would you do if 23 helpless people showed up at your doorstep begging to be hidden? The thought of what would happen if the Nazis found them made one teenager take action. Julian Bilecki (bil-LET-ski) and his family took the Jews into hiding, and helped every single one of them.

Julian Bilecki, listed as a Ukrainian hero in Yad Vashem, was born in Zawalow, Poland (now the Ukraine) in 1928. In June 1943, nearly all the families in Jewish communities in nearby Podhajce were being slaughtered by the Nazis. About 3,000 Jews were killed, but once in a while a small group would escape. One of the small groups made it to Bilecki's farm. Julian was a teenager at the time when the Jews came. They asked for help, and Julian helped them hide. The first bunker they built was in a cave. On two occasions, though, neighbors found the bunker, and they had to move hiding spots, so the Nazis wouldn't suspect them. The bunkers were made by digging a hole in the ground and then covering the top with dirt and sticks - hoping the small bunker wouldn't be found. Building the bunker was the first step, but living in it was the next.

One of the reasons why Julian and his family helped them was probably because he was so religious. They were devout Evangelical Christians. Every week he sang hymns, gave clothing, and told news to the Jews during his visits. Julian, with his cousin Roman, also brought food. It was only potatoes, beans, and cornmeal, but it kept the Jews alive and was food for the soul. Since it was a heavy winter, walking would make footprints-which would lead the Nazis to the hiding place. Because of this, Julian and Roman brought food by jumping from tree to tree. Another amazing thing was that the Bileckis were poor farmers, yet still provided food for 23 other people during wartime! The Bileckis had to have rationed food for themselves too, right?

Some of the people who Julian helped already had been in terrible conditions. One was burying a wagon of dead bodies from a ghetto that had just been liquidated, and then ran into the woods to escape. Another survivor, Genia Melzer, was 17 when the Nazis left her for dead in a pile of corpses. She recounts in her gruesome story:

"I lay down on the floor with my head down, and my little cousin, 9 years old, lay down on my right side. They started shooting, but I wasn't shot. They thought I was dead but when the little girl coughed, they came with an ax and started chopping. They took us to this mass grave and they threw all the people into it and I was on top."

She crawled out from the dead bodies and ran into the woods where Julian found her covered with blood. Everyone from her brother, aunts, uncles, cousins, and all her friends were killed. But today she is a great-grandmother, all because of Julian Bilecki

After almost a year of living underground, the Jews heard shots, and knew that at long last they had finally been liberated. On March 27, 1944, the Russians had finally released them from the Nazis' grasp. The Bilecki family had put their own lives in danger to save others. They had saved all 23 Jews just because they thought it was the right thing to do. As the years went on, the remaining survivors sent food and clothing to the Bileckis because they still remained poor. They also kept in touch by mail and became even better friends.

About a half-century later, a gray-haired and 70 year-old Julian Bilecki and five survivors were brought together by the Jewish Foundation of the Righteous. A retired bus driver, Bilecki was flown in from the Ukraine, his first time out of his country. As he walked into a reception room at Kennedy Airport, the five survivors, now with gray hair, too, and some walking with canes, clapped and cheered with joy for the man who, as a teenager, put his life in danger to help them escape the Nazis and survive the Holocaust. Tears welled up in his eyes as he said:

"I see you all have gray hair. I too have gray hair. I thought I would never see you again. I feel lost. I thought this would never happen. All I did was help. It is very pleasant that people remember. Now I am getting paid back by God."

It may seem easy to say, "Yeah, of course I would help people in need," but in wartime it's not that simple. Julian Bilecki endangered his life because he saw the value of Jewish lives as being no less than his own. It is rare to find a person willing to risk his life and the lives of his family to save other people. That is one of the reasons why Julian Bilecki is a holocaust hero not a survivor. He successfully saved 23 people. All out of the kindness in his heart! All in all, Julian Bilecki was an outstanding person because in the words of the Talmud,

"To save one life is as if you have saved the world."

Bibliography
https://jfr.org
http://Auschwitz.dk
Yadvashem.org
Isurvived.org-Bileckihtml

Hermann Graebe – Holocaust Hero

Hudson L Prunier

 Herman Friedrich Graebe is my Hero of the Holocaust because he was an important person who helped the Jews get freed during the Holocaust. He was a German non-Jew and Nazi Party member who stood up for the Jewish people.

Herman was born in 1900 in a small town in Germany. His family was very poor and they were Protestant. When Hermann was twenty four he married and also completed his education to become engineer. A few years later, when he was thirty one, he joined the Nazi Party. However, he soon became unhappy with the movement and actually criticized plans at an open Nazi meeting. He was caught speaking out against the party and was sent to prison for several months.

As an engineer he worked for a construction company on different projects around Germany. When he worked on building a railroad in the Ukraine, he hired teams of people, including thousands of Jewish men and women. In the Ukraine he became aware of horrible crimes committed by the Germans against Jewish people. While doing this work, Graebe became a witness to mass killings of Jewish people in Dubno.

Graebe wrote about what he saw and testified at the war crimes trial at Nurenberg. On a particular day, he was trying to save some Jewish people from being deported and went to their houses to prevent them from being taken. While he was at a certain Jewish area, the German guards came and broke windows and doors to get all the Jewish families to leave. He witnessed them being whipped until they left their homes. He also witnessed the German guards throwing hand grenades at the doors and windows to get inside when people were resisting. He heard parents and children screaming for their lives. Many people tried to get across railroad tracks and across the river in order to be free. However many could not survive capture when they had the German forces running after them. Sometimes he saw parents carrying dead children and children dragging their dead parent. All night he kept hearing the German officers making everyone open their doors.

Then, on October 5, 1942, his foreman told him that many Jewish people from Dubno had been shot and killed in three large holes in the ground. The foreman said that about 1500 people were being killed every day. The foreman said they would all be destroyed. He was very upset because he had witnessed some of these killings. So then, the foreman and Hermann Graebe went to these pits themselves. Mr. Graebe said he saw over 800 pairs of shoes and piles of all sorts of clothes. People were undressing but not complaining. People were standing with their families and kissing and hugging and saying goodbye. The German SS men would give a sign and would start shooting. Mr. Graebe stayed there for about 15 minutes and made some awful observations. He saw young and old people trying to take care of each other in this awful situation. After a while the officers would tell certain groups of people to go behind some mounds and then they were shot and killed.

Mr. Graebe saw dead people, half dead people, and soon to be dead people, laying in the pits. People were laying on top of people who were laying on other people. It must have been awful. Then, he and his foreman went back to Dubno. For all of this that he witnessed, he testified at Nurenburg in front of people who were also horrified.

After these killing he wanted to help save Jewish people. He tried to save as many Jewish people as he could. First in 1942, he obtained protection for 150 Jewish people who were working for him by going to the district commissioner and securing their release in Rovno. Graebe helped these people escape on foot with Ukrainian officers not far behind. Then, a little later, he helped more Jews by providing false Aryan identification papers. He personally took them in his car to a safer place. This safe place, Poltava, was supposed to be his work but it was really just a place that he set up for Jewish people to be safe. When the Red Army advanced to Germany, they escaped to freedom in Russia. If Graebe had been stopped by German officers it would have been dangerous for both him and the Jews.

People were suspicious of his actions but Graebe was able to get to Rhineland and then to the American side where he was still able to be helpful. He worked for the War Crimes branch of the U.S. army and eventually came to America to live. He was the only German to testify at the Nuremberg trials. He settled in San Francisco and continued to bring justice against the German war criminals. For this he was not liked in Germany.

Hermann Graebe was recognized by Yad Vashem for saving Jewish people during the Holocaust. That was on March 23, 1965. He died in 1986 in San Francisco

1. www.holocaustresearchroect.org/einsatz/graebetest.html (Hermann Graebe Evidence testimony at Nuremberg War Crimes trial)

2. www.nytimes.com/108/04/19/obituaries/herman-graebe-85-german-who-saved-jews=from –nazis.html

3. www.yadvashem.org/yv/en/righteous/stories/graebe.asp

Hans Georg Calmeyer

Jacob D. Dean (Winner)

During the Holocaust, Nazi occupation governments were typically tools for the identification and deportation of Jews to concentration and death camps. However, from March 3, 1941, to the end of World War II, a German occupation official and Luftwaffe officer, Hans Georg Calmeyer, courageously used his position and influence in the occupation administration of the Netherlands to save the lives of almost 3,000 Jews. He accomplished this by accepting thousands of petitions from Jews to have their racial status changed to Mischling (half or quarter Jewish) or even Aryan, despite his knowledge that they were forging evidence to escape the Nazis. In this way, Calmeyer managed to delay their deportation until the liberation of the Netherlands. Through cunning and determination, this German lawyer managed to create an efficient system for saving thousands of Jews.

Hans Calmeyer was born on June 23, 1903 in Osnabruck, Germany. His father was a judge, and, as a child, he lost two brothers in the First World War. Calmeyer became an eminent lawyer, but began to have troubles after the rise of the National Socialist party in January of 1933. Due to Calmeyer's defense of several communist clients, he was suspected of disloyal sentiments, and was disbarred after refusing to fire a Jewish employee. However, Calmeyer was conscripted and entered the Netherlands with the invading Nazi army in May of 1940. Some time afterwards, a hometown acquaintance of Calmeyer's in the occupation government, in a remarkable misjudgement, from the Nazi perspective, offered him a job as head of a department of the General Commissariat for Administration and Justice, which dealt with Jews wishing to change their racial status. Upon accepting the position, Calmeyer soon realized that he could use his authority to subvert the Third Reich's racial policies.

In the Nazi racial classification system, there were four categories of person: full Jews, with three or more Jewish grandparents; Mischling A, with two Jewish grandparents; Mischling B, with one Jewish grandparent; and finally, Aryan. A full Jew would be deported quickly, but, if they could prove that they were only Mischling, would be allowed to stay, at least temporarily. Those classified as Mischling still had to contend with severely limited rights, but this was infinitely preferable to being deported to a camp. Calmeyer's job was to assess requests from Jews to have their status changed on the basis of some "new" evidence. Calmeyer thus had significant power to protect Dutch Jews.

The Nazis considered the Dutch to be a "lost tribe" of the Aryan people, and thus expended considerable effort to "purify" the Netherlands of all Jews, so that it could be incorporated into the Reich. Because of this policy, Calmeyer's work was considered very important. When Calmeyer decided to use his influence to aid the Jews, his first task was to secure his department against SS interference. To this end, he began to create a team of people with equally anti-Nazi convictions. These included Gerhard Wander, an influential attorney and Wermacht officer who was of irreplaceable assistance, Heinrich Miessen, a genealogist who added authenticity to the team, and a young Dutch lawyer named J. van Proosdij. With a team of unquestioned loyalty and determination, Calmeyer could begin his work.

In order to change the racial status of an applicant, Calmeyer's office did need some kind of justification to avoid scrutiny. Luckily, Calmeyer and his assistants were extremely creative in this field. One popular deception was for a Jewish mother to claim that her offspring were the result of an illicit relationship with an Aryan, thus making them Mischling. At one point, this strategy became so popular that Calmeyer had to advise petitioners to think of a different explanation, to avoid suspicion. Calmeyer's department also forged baptismal certificates to prove that the grandparents of applicants were not, in fact, Jewish. In addition, Calmeyer allowed Jews to claim that they were Mischling based on supposed evidence in archives in Indonesia, a Dutch colony inaccessible due to the war in the Pacific. Finally, Calmeyer argued to his Nazi superiors that membership in a Jewish community should not necessarily be proof that someone was racially Jewish, and that certain Jews, such as those who were members of the Dutch Nazi Party or had children serving in the Wermacht, should be exempt from deportation. In this way, Calmeyer managed to change official German policy in several instances, in addition to his direct work. However, Calmeyer's team eventually began to encounter problems.

As Calmeyer continued his lenience, he began to come under scrutiny. Worried that an SS investigation could lead to the revoking of decisions that he had made earlier, Calmeyer was forced to begin rejecting some cases. He once even described his position as that of a doctor at an isolated outpost, cut off from help, with only 50 vials of medicine to treat 5,000 critical cases. However, he attempted to turn down only those applicants whose evidence could easily be proven false, and warned those that he could not accept to flee before they were deported. Thus, he managed to ensure the safety of his operation, but still save the lives of many. Some of the cases that Calmeyer approved also began to be rejected by higher authority. For example, in early 1944 Calmeyer argued that the Portuguese Jewish community in the Netherlands, consisting of no less than 4,304 people, should be exempted, as they were of Iberian descent. However, Nazi officials questioned his decision, and, upon further examination, decided that the

Portuguese Jews possessed clearly Jewish racial traits and thus should be deported to Auschwitz, which they promptly were.

As suspicion of Calmeyer's decisions grew, higher authority began to take action. In December 1942 the occupation governor of the Netherlands, Arthur Seyss-Inquart, ordered Calmeyer to cease accepting new applications. However, Calmeyer persisted and so, in 1943, a Dutch Nazi genealogist named Ludo ten Cate was appointed by the head of the SS in the Netherlands, Hanns Rauter, to investigate Calmeyer's department. Ten Cate began to uncover the operation but, luckily for Calmeyer and the Jews he was attempting to save, was recalled in August 1944 due to power struggles between the SS and the Nazi Party establishment. Further investigation was called for by higher officials, but was never carried out due to continuing political backstabbing in Germany. Gerhard Wander, on the other hand, was not so lucky. Because of his perceived leniency to the Jews, he was sent to the Eastern Front in 1944, but managed to desert and sneak back to the Netherlands. He then joined the Dutch underground, but was killed in a shootout with the Gestapo in January 1945, less than two months before the liberation.

The heroic actions of Hans Georg Calmeyer are an excellent example of the extent to which a well-placed official in the Nazi occupation could do enormous good by following his conscience, rather than his orders. I believe Calmeyer's actions are particularly notable first, because he was an official in the Nazi occupation government and former Wermacht officer, but also because he did not just save an individual or family from the Holocaust, but created what was essentially a covert resistance cell within the Nazi administration that was able to save almost 3,000 lives. While he may not have hid Jews in his home or personally smuggled them to safety, Calmeyer managed to use his position to oppose the Final Solution with impressive effectiveness. Hans Calmeyer's rescue of thousands of Jews shows how a courageous, moral individual, working within a tyrannical regime, can thwart its horrific goals.

Works Cited
"Dr. Hans Georg Calmeyer." Dr. Yad Vashem. Web. 21 Feb. 2016.
Gilbert, Martin. The Righteous: The Unsung Heroes of the Holocaust. New York: Henry Holt, 2003. Print.
"Hans-Georg Calmeyer." Jewish Virtual Library. Web. 21 Feb. 2016.
Paldiel, Mordecai. Saving the Jews: Amazing Stories of Men and Women Who Defied the "Final Solution" Rockville, MD: Schreiber, 2000. Print.

The Legacy of Jeanne Daman

Natalie Michaels

We've all heard about the stories of heroes of the Holocaust like Oskar Schindler and the famous stories of those who hid the innocent during World War II like that of Anne Frank, but what about the less known stories, those of the people who risked their lives to stand up and go against what they believed was wrong and aren't remembered like the others today? In the following, you will hear the story of Jeanne Daman, a Catholic woman who decided that no matter who you were, and no matter what others said, everybody deserved an education. Jeanne was a woman of valor, who taught those not given the privilege to learn, who smuggled Jews to safety, and had an impact on the war.

Daman's birth date is unknown, but there are traces that she grew up in Brussels, Belgium. Her parents are unknown. She grew up Catholic, and did not know many Jews growing up, but by the time she became an adult, she had a strong sense of right and wrong, and knew that what was happening to non-gentiles was wrong. In 1942, she took a stand.

She was a young schoolteacher in Brussels when the war was going on, and the perfect person for Fela Perelman. Mrs. Perelman was an active member of many organizations that were trying to set up kindergartens for young Jewish children because of the increasingly pressurized discrimination against the Jewish community that made it nearly impossible for Jewish pupils to attend school. She had began setting up these schools when she realized that she needed a trained person who was qualified enough to teach. Upon receiving the recommendations of the director of educational services in Brussels, Mr. Tits, she asked Jeanne to join her. Jeanne agreed eagerly upon deciding that what was going on was not right, and she wanted to change it. After a little while, she became the head mistres of "Nos Petits.", the school Mrs. Perelman had asked her to join the staff of. Once she claimed this position, she began to truly realize and experience first hand the brutality shown towards the Jews and their families. She then witnessed a mass arrest of Jewish children, and as stated by www.yadvashem.org , "this experience was to change her life." .

After the experience of the mass arrest, it became painful to her every time a child was absent at school, knowing that they and their families had been whisked away by Nazi officers. She also knew that some of them were instantly becoming orphans, as their parents were being rounded up and sent to concentration camps, or instantly sentenced to death because of who and what they believed in and looked like. She and her organization decided that the school was to be closed in order to save the children and conceal them and their identities for as long as possible. They began moving the children into the homes of private Belgian families. Ms. Daman and Mrs. Perelman made contact with ONE (l'Oeuvre Nationale de l'Enfance), and with their cooperation, Daman was able to bring most of the children to safety, although a minor amount were safe, and the increasing number of instant orphans was traumatizing. Once the school was closed officially by the authorities, Mrs. Perelman asked Jeanne to continue working towards the safety of the children. Mrs. Daman then began to escort the children to safety while traveling all over Europe (especially Germany) to drop off and check on the Jewish children and the brave souls who took them in. She often visited Father Rausch, who lived on the French border who took in over 50 of the kids. After a little while, the work became more and more dangerous and was steadily becoming more secretive, to the extent where she was collecting children at different tram-stops.

Once the round ups of Jews became more frequent, Mrs. Perelman and Ms. Daman even had to begin helping adults. The dynamic duo began to develop a chain of Jewish women who were implanted as maids and as working-class people in Belgian homes. Daman gave them fake identity papers and ration cards, which Mrs. Perelman's husband, Chaim, was able to provide for them. Jeanne also tried to inform the mothers and their children who were separated from each other about how they were doing.

Daman was also requested by Albert Domb to coordinate the liquidation of the collaborators as a part of the Jewish underground. She began working at Secours d'Hiver and assumed a new identity as a social worker. Once she did this, she began to find the whereabouts of "the collaborators", and timed the destruction of them. She also collaborated with MRB, an organization that did illegal work connected to the liberation. She transported arms on her bike, and became a spy for the Belgian Partisans Army. Once the war was over, she reunited the families that she had helped escape, and helped those who returned alive from the camps.

In 1946, after her work was done, she moved to the U.S. There, she began fundraising for UJA, an organization that was funding Israel. She received a medal for her hard work and determination, the 'Entr'aide' a medal she received on October 12, 1980 on account of the BJC (the Belgian Jewish Committee), and was recognized on February 2, 1979, by Yad Vashem as "Righteous Among the Nations."

Even though she won only a couple awards, and there is very little information about what she did, she was an extremely important part of the partisan activity and rebellion that went against the cruel war that whisked away and swallowed so many of our people. What she did was a true act of bravery, and it will forever hold a special place in our hearts.

Works Cited

"Women of Valor: Jeanne Daman-Scaglione." www.yadvashem.org. Copyright 2016. Yad Vashem The Holocaust Martyrs' and Heroes' Remembrance Authority. Web. February 22, 2016.

"Cloth Sheet with Three Unused Star of David Badges Owned by a Catholic Rescuer."
http://collections.ushmm.org/search/catalog/irn37011. United State Holocaust Memorial Museum. July 4, 2015. Web. February 22, 2016.

Gertrud Kochanowski

Nate Tochterman

Today I want to tell you about this incredible woman from Germany named Gertrud Kochanowski. She was and is considered a savior of the Jewish people. In the fall of 1942, Gertrud and her father saved a woman named Margot Bloch. Although Gertrud was not the only person to help Margot Bloch through her travels, she helped Margot out most of the way and helped her for a long time. Margot's survival would not be possible without the help of multiple German men and women. Each of them risked their lives and loved ones for this one woman to escape from the Nazis' hatred. This is considered a big achievement by many.

In November 1942, 19-year-old Margot and her father returned home from their forced-labor shift at the electrical engineering firm in Berlin-Tegel. When they arrived home, they found that their flat had been sealed and that Margot's mother had been arrested by the Gestapo pending deportation. The foreman of the Flohr factory, Herbert Patzschke, had told them earlier if any trouble was happening, they should call upon him. The Blochs took advantage of the offer and stayed at his house in Berlin-Tegel, hiding from the authorities. A few days later, the father decided to report to the Gestapo in hope of freeing his wife from custody. As a result, both of her parents got sent to Auschwitz, never to be seen again. After Margot's father was arrested, Patzschke offered to accommodate the young Jewish girl in his house for a few more nights until she could arrange her affairs and escape from Berlin. Margot then called upon Lina Cremer, a Jewish woman who was married to an Aryan; she was invited to Hannover where the Cremers lived. Through Cremer's husband, Margot got in touch with non-Jewish German families with whom she lived with during the last two and a half years of the war.

During that time in Hannover, Margot met Gertrud Kochanowski. Gertrud was a mother of two children ages three to six. Before 1933, Gertrud was a part of the German Social Democratic Party, and retained her political convictions after Hitler's accession to power. During May through June 1943, she was approached by one of her acquaintances if she would be able to accommodate a Jewish girl on the run, and accepted immediately. Her father, a postmaster, arranged for Bloch to obtain a forged postal-identification pass. They also agreed on a foolproof cover–up story where Margot was to pretend and become "Mrs. Fischer from Hilddesheim, the young wife of a solider." All went well until Kochanowski's home in Hannover was destroyed by an air raid on the night of October 8-9, 1943. Because her home was obliterated by the bombs, she received alternative accommodations at Freiheit-Osterode am Harz and invited Bloch to join her. Osterode was a small and intimate area, and seeing a young unemployed woman became too unusual and conspicuous.

Because it was probably not wise to stay in Osterode for too long, Kochanowski turned to her good friend Albert Heuer in Hannover. Mr. Heuer was an old opponent of the National-Socialist regime, and became a target of the regime. He also was previously incarcerated in a concentration camp during 1933 due to his connection with the banned Social Democratic party. After some hesitation, he and his wife Dorle took Bloch into their home, and treated her like family.Only the eldest daughter of the four children was aware of Margot being Jewish. Now in this new home, she could alternate between the Heuer house in Hannover and Kochanowski's house in Osterode Bloch was able to survive for the rest of the war undetected by the Gestapo. After the war, Margot immigrated to England and then to Australia.

This is why Gertrud Kochanowski played a huge role of the survival of Margot Bloch. Gertrud helped her with shelter, food, a forged postal-identification pass, along with many other necessities. But she wasn't the only one to help out Margot; those who also helped were people like Gertrud's father, Lina Cremer and her husband, Dorie and Albert Heuer, and Herbert and Erika Patzschke. Margot started in Berlin-Tegel, then Hanover, Freiheit-Osterode am Harz, then finally went to Britain after the war. While Margot suffered a great tragedy having both of her parents being transported to Auschwitz concentration camp, and having to move to different areas to hide from the Nazis; and there were many other horrible conditions from living during the Holocaust.

Reading about Gertud and Margot makes me appreciate the life that I have as a Jew in a time of peace and calm. I am very grateful to have security and the comforts of home and family. These lessons are certainly a reminder of how things could turn out differently – and it is why I am following the presidential elections closely; I worry that the political system is becoming so problematic and candidates are distorting the truth just as they probably did when Hitler first came into power. It is my hope that we never ever forget – and that we remember that we as humans will always depend on the kindness of other people that we have never met before.

Hermann Maas

Noah Zerbo

Hermann Ludwig Maas was truly an ever so incredible man. Most people see him as a man who was friends with Jews and people from other cultures, and was open to different religions and cultures, but I see him as a man who saved over ten thousand lives of Jewish children at risk of being swallowed up by the monster we now call the Holocaust. Born on August 5, 1877 in Gegenbach/Schwarzwald, Germany, to a family of protestant pastors from both his mother's side, and from his father's side, I don't think he could have pictured attending a Seder in a Jewish home, inviting Jews over for Christmas eve or stopping the deportation of Jewish people to the harsh forced labor camps in France. On top of that, becoming a great friend of the Jewish people after, out of pure curiosity, attended a meeting of the Sixth Zionist Congress.

Hermann Maas spent his childhood growing up in a small forest city called Gernsbach. For the most part, Hermann was a pretty normal kid, playing, and going to school, but now and then, he would go and attend services at the local synagogue. In college, he would major in the study of theology, at the universities of Halle, Heidelberg, and Strafsburg, and later get a doctorate, also in the study of theology.

After college, Maas moved to Heidelberg and assumed the position of pastor at the Holy Spirit Church and take the pulpit, where he would minister for the next 28 years. For a period of four years, Hermann held a political office representing the liberal Deutsch Demokratische Partie. When the Nazis launched the boycott of the Jews in Germany, he set off for the State of Israel. In August, 1933, he financed his daughter in founding a weaving school in Jerusalem. There, she taught Jewish refugees to weave. There, he left a great impression on the people there for his being able to speak Hebrew very fluently – he had been able understand and speak Hebrew fluently ever since he was a young man. When he was a youngster in Gernsbach, he would attend Protestant church regularly. Yet, he would also go to the synagogue with his Jewish friends. This is where he became fluent with Hebrew. In Heidelberg, he had numerous threats from the feared local Nazi propaganda leaders. They demanded that the "pastor of Jews" to be excluded from the pulpit. But, he was too highly honored in the Christian world. He didn't want to risk starting an international scandal.

His fights with the new rulers of Germany only seemed to grow and intensify Hermann's defiance and hatred of what the Nazis were doing. He prevented the old and frail from being shipped off to a forced labor camp in France. During the holiday season, Maas would invite over Jewish friends of his to celebrate Christmas Eve with him. In return, he would attend their Passover Seders.

In 1850, he became the first non-Jewish German to be officially invited into the State of Israel. He had an unusually friendly relationship with the synagogue lead by Rabbi Fritz Pinkuss. Especially for a Christian pastor at the time of the Holocaust. He even joined in establishing the World Alliance for Promoting Friendship through the Churches. This organization communicated with other religious places in Europe to propose disarmament, international cooperation, and also world peace.

Helping Jews was a crime, and he worked with his Berlin colleague and the Kindertransporte, helping children escape the Third Reich, so he was always under the watchful supervision of the Gestapo. The whole time, his church members stood behind him and supported him. Even the ones who worked for or with the Gestapo or had some sort of relation with them had his back. This allowed him to continue his work for another ten years and save a total of 10,000 children. Sadly, in 1944, at 67 years old; Hermann Maas was deported to a forced labor camp in France.

After the war, Hermann worked as a reconciler. In April of 1946, he wrote a religious confession of guilt, which was published in the first post war edition of "Judische Rundschau" in the spring of 1946. In 1967, he was given the honor by Yad Vashem, to be recognized as a Righteous Gentile. He was also the unofficial ambassador between the State of Israel and Germany, to help get their relationship back on their feet. Being a self-acclaimed liberal with pacifist views, he started a scandal in 1925, when he attended the memorial service of a social democratic named Reichsprasident Friedrich Ebert.

In 1977, Hermann Ludwig Maas passed away in his sleep. He was visiting relatives in Mainz. His body still lies at the Handschuhsheim Cemetery in Heidelberg.

Bibliography:
Websites:
United States Holocaust Memorial Museum, Hermann Maas; Maas Foundation.com; Wikipedia the Free Encyclopedia, Hermann Maas; Historic Sullivan, Archives and Tourism Holocaust Heroes, Hermann Maas; Yad Vashem Holocaust Memorial, righteous stories, Hermann Maas; Sensagent.com, Hermann Maas; Hermann Maas and Justice After the Shoah;

Elisabeth Abegg: A German Hero of the Holocaust

Sasha Steinberg

The Holocaust was a very, very horrible and tragic time and was arguably one of the worst things to ever happen in the 20th century, along with World Wars I and II. Over about 6 million Jews were tortured and killed between January of 1933 and May of 1945 in one of the deadliest genocides in history so far. Families were torn apart with some never even reunited, because they were sent to different camps or killed without being able to say goodbye. Although it may have been a devastating event, there can be and are some ways to shine light on the situation. One of these many ways is to honor the people who have saved Jews' lives, may it have been one life or one thousand. These people are the heroes of the Holocaust.

One of these great heroes was Luise Wilhelmine Elisabeth Abegg. She was born on the Third of March, in 1882 to her loving parents, Johann Friedrich Abegg, a jurist, and Marie Caroline Elisabeth (Rähm) Abegg in a city called Strasbourg, the capital of Alsace (today Strasbourg is in the country of France, but at the time, it was in Germany). She was enrolled at Leipzig University in the year of 1912 where she took classes in the subjects of history, classical philology, and Romance studies, and ultimately graduated with a doctorate in 1916. Elisabeth was deeply influenced by the Christian-Universalist teachings and learnings of Albert Schweitzer, a theologian, humanist, and doctor. She moved in to Berlin, Germany after the French reclaimed the Alsace region as their own. In Berlin, she became a history teacher at a girls' school called Luisen Mädchenschule, where she passed on her humanistic beliefs to her students, many of whom were Jewish.

Elisabeth Abegg openly criticized the Nazis after Adolf Hitler assumed power in 1933. She was punished by the Nazis for her criticism and forced to give up teaching entirely and retire. She was even interrogated by the Gestapo (abbreviation for Geheime staatspolize), the official Secret State Police of Nazi Germany and German-occupied Europe. She was marked as "politically unreliable" by the authorities. But Elisabeth could not be deterred and still stayed in contact with her Jewish friends and former students.

When Elisabeth's good friend of 40 years, Anna Hirschberg, was deported to the East, Elisabeth really felt the impact of the Nazi persecution of the Jewish people. She knew too well that it was too late to save her friend, but was deeply determined to help the Jews in need during this hard time. For that very reason, she turned her three-and-a-half room apartment that she shared with her 86 year old mother and her disabled sister, Julie, into a temporary shelter for Jews who needed a place to stay in and an assembly point for Jews who had gone underground.

Working with her friends in the Quaker movement, Elisabeth Abegg helped her many Jewish students by offering to them temporary accommodation in her house or direction to them to other places that could help them, and skimped on her own food and that of her sister's in order to have enough food and other important materials to supply to her students. She also invited them each and every Friday to special meals at her house and got forged papers for them. She sold her precious and valuable jewelry in order organize the smuggling of Jizchak Schwersenz into the country of Switzerland, and even went to Liselotte Pereles, the director of the day-care center in the city of Berlin, to try to convince her to go into hiding with her nine year old niece, Susie, when Liselotte wasn't sure of what to do. Abegg took the time to visit them in the "Jew's House" to which they were moved to. Three of the apartments had already been sealed off after the residents had just been deported from their homes to the East.

Elisabeth succeeded in persuading them into going underground and it was the last possible moment they could, as this was the last unsuspected large Gestapo round-up of all the known Jews in Berlin, Germany. Most people who asked for help from her were complete strangers, yet Elisabeth did not ever hesitate before always lending a hand. She just kept on taking more and more risks, even with some of her close neighbors being active Nazis. She did a wonderful job keeping it a secret from anyone who could hurt them or tell Nazis of it, hiding the obvious right under their little noses.

She resumed teaching in Berlin after the war and some of the students that survived thanks to Elisabeth Abegg's help remained in contact with her even after the war was over. In 1957 for her 75th birthday, they dedicated a book to her, filled with a collection of memoirs. The book is called "When One Light Pierced the Darkness." Elisabeth died on August 8th, 1974 at the age of 92 due to natural causes.

In 1967, Elisabeth was officially recognized as Righteous Among the Nations by Yad Vashem and a memorial plaque was put up in her Tempelhof neighborhood in 1991 and a street in Berlin's Mitte, Elisabeth-Abegg-Straße, was named after her in the year 2006. In total, she sheltered around 80 Jews and maybe even more between 1942 and 1945. It truly takes all the courage a woman could have to do what Elisabeth did for the Jewish people in need. To live out a life like hers must have been such a scary and stressful experience, one that not many people can say they have had. I am glad to share her empowering story of bravery, and to remember her. Heroes like her need to be acknowledged. On this note, I conclude my essay on Elisabeth Abegg: a German hero of the Holocaust.

Fritz and Rosa Hohmann

Sophia Oberst

What is a Righteous Gentile? A Righteous Gentile is someone who is not Jewish who risked their life to save Jews. Righteous Gentiles are recognized by Yad Vashem. It is a tradition to plant a tree in their honor. My Righteous Gentile that I chose has been recognized by Yad Vashem along with many others.

It is important to study Righteous Gentiles. One of the things that makes it important is that you learn so much about our history by just researching on just one couple. Another thing that shows why it is important is the fact that you need to realize that there are good and bad people in every culture/religion. There are so many Germans who did good things when there were so many terrible things happening among them. It's important to not believe that ALL Germans participated or believed in Hitler's plan. Ultimately, it is important to know it does not matter where you live it matters where your heart is and the choices that you make.

I picked Fritz and Rosa Hohmann for my report this year. They have a very interesting and intriguing story. I learned their story from the website yadvashem.org. It starts in 1943 when Fritz was sent by his company to work as a building site manager. He got a labor force allocated to him that had all Jewish women who had been deported in September of the year 1942. Then the big event started. When Hohmann first met the women one of the women said that she missed the sounds of home. The forced laborers lived in an old prison and every day they came and worked for the Hohmanns. Well, it appeared that way. When he got a chance he and his wife would sneak food to them. They did this using a rope and pulley system that went through the prison window. Not only did he and his wife give them food, they also helped the women laborers contact their relatives and close friends. The Hohmanns' children helped pass messages along too. The laborers' friends sent packages and letters to the Hohmanns for them to pass to the laborers. To do all of these great feats it could have cost them their lives. To give more evidence of how dedicated they were, one day Fritz Hohmann was taken to questioning by the Gestapo and that did not even change his mind about what he was doing to help the laborers. When the work assignment ended he was transferred back to Germany. In the summer of 1944 the women were deported to Stuttof Concentration Camp. Those who survived contacted Fritz and his wife to invite them to their homes in New York and Paris. As you can see, the amazing Hohmann couple saved a whole generation of human beings because they saved women. On March 27, 2000, Yad Vashem recognized Fritz and Rosa Hohmann as Righteous Among the Nations.

Works Cited – Yadvashem.org

Johanna Eck, Righteous Woman Among The Nations

Weslie Kliman

 In a time when the Germans were killing and destroying the European Jewish communities, a small quantity of German citizens chose to defend the victims. The world witnessed the Holocaust, a terrible event with so much carnage and so much of the world closed their eyes. On a cellar wall in Cologne, Germany this handwritten quote was found,

"I believe in the sun even when it is not shining. I believe in love even when I cannot feel it. I believe in God even when He is silent."

Some of prayers of the victims were answered, not by the wealthy countries that watched and waited from afar; but rather by a few people who chose not to join the Nazis. In their own back yard German citizens witnessed the violence all around them. Most of them had no choice but to either join the Nazis or at least support them. A few German citizens decided to risk their own lives and help. Johanna Eck, a World War I widow, working as a nurse in Berlin was one such hero. She made a difference for those people that might have been sent to concentration camps, destined to die. The prisoners were forced to work all day and barely got one piece of bread, if they were lucky. Over 6 million Jewish lives were taken during this tragedy. Unfortunately, only a small minority of people were lucky enough to survive this horrible ordeal. It was rare to be saved and in a few situations people were rescued by the very neighbors that could have been their enemies.

The Guttmanns were a Jewish family that had fought beside Johanna Eck's husband during World War I. They were now considered an enemy of Germany and they were under attack. 1942, the Guttmann family was rounded up, forced from their home and deported to the East to a concentration camp. They were never heard from again. Somehow their son, Heinz, escaped the Nazis and found himself left behind without his family, wandering the streets. Heinz asked many of his German family friends and acquaintances to help him. All of them refused to help him because they were afraid of getting in trouble by the Nazis for helping and hiding a Jew. Heinz had no money, no family, no food, no shelter and no food ration cards. He was in a desperate situation. Johanna found the boy. Even though Johanna Eck faced possible death for taking him in, she protected the Jewish boy. She hid and nurtured him back to health. She even found him a new safe hideout after her own house was blown up in November

1943, during an air raid. Beyond this, she monitored his health and used her own personal food rations to feed him until the after the war when Jewish community was finally free.

Johanna Eck said, "The motive for my help? Nothing special in a particular case. In principle what I think is this: If a fellow human being is in distress and I can help him, then it becomes my duty and responsibility. Were I to refrain from doing so, then I would betray the task that life – or perhaps God? – demands from me. Human beings – so it seems to me – make up a big unity; they strike themselves and all in the face when they do injustice to each other. These are my motives." This reflects Johanna Eck's deep caring for all humankind. She proved this courage again when she saved another Jewish woman's life.

In December 1943, Elfreide Guttmann (unrelated to Heinz Guttmann) escaped from her original hiding place under her bed when the German Gestapo raided her home. Johanna Eck welcomed her into her one-room apartment, after she heard Guttmann's very sad story. Since there was so much confusion with all of the air raids, it was very common that people had their identity papers destroyed. Eck was able to use the confusion to register Guttmann with a new identity and make her a legal citizen. She arranged for Elfreide to migrate to the United States. Unfortunately, Elfreide had a problem with her intestines and couldn't travel. When it was obvious that Elfreide was going to die, Eck stayed by her deathbed and comforted her until she passed away in June of 1946 at only 23 years old. She was survived by her parents Markus and Sarah Gutmann.

I believe Johanna Eck was important because she would not stop trying to help out in an impossible situation. Even though Nazi soldiers were against her, the Jewish community appreciated her. Many years later on November 12, 1973 she was commemorated with a tree and a plaque on the Wall of Honor. Johanna Eck rescuing four people made a difference in those lives. Today writing about this German / Ukrainian woman who rescued Holocaust victims helps us to remember this horrible event from so many years ago and recognize their contributions.

Hugo Armann

Will Brosnan

My name is Will Brosnan. I wrote my Holocaust essay about Hugo Armann. It was important for me to write the Holocaust essay for three reasons. My first reason is that I felt bad for the people who got little recognition for the amount of bravery that they showed. This was the main reason that I chose Hugo Armann, because he is one of many who is not widely known for saving Jews during the Holocaust in Germany. The second reason was that I did not know much about the Ukrainian or the German people who helped to save Jews. My third reason is because his last name is the same as the first name of one of my best friends. Another very important reason why I decided to write the Holocaust essay came from my grandmother when she told me about how she knew little about our own family because her parents did not want to talk about the Holocaust because they were traumatized by their own family losses. So, she said that it is important to remember the Holocaust and who died during it, but also those who made it possible for some Jews to survive and escape. Now without further ado, I present to you my Holocaust essay on Hugo Armann.

Hugo Armann was born in Germany on November 8, 1917. He was raised in a Protestant home. While growing up he had Jewish friends and, unlike others, he continued to be friends with them when he could during the war. Hugo Armann was training to become a teacher, but before he could graduate, Hitler rose to power and put him in the army.

Hugo Armann was stationed in Poland on the Baranowicze railway station. He was in charge of the unit that sent soldiers on home leave from the eastern front of the war back to Germany. He was also the only person at the Baranowicze railway station who had access to seat stamps. Seat stamps were like tickets. Passengers had to have a seat stamp in order to ride on the German railway. Because he was the only one with access to the seat stamps and was in charge of coordinating the soldiers' movements from place to place, he had access to practically all military and police instillations in the vicinity. He also had access to the Jewish workshop that was watched by the SD. In English, SD means the Security Service of the Führer. The SD was the intelligence service for the Nazi Party and the SD found most of the top secret information that Hitler needed. Hugo Armann decided to use his power to requisition Jewish workers and, by giving them jobs under his control, he helped to minimize persecution towards them.

One of the many people who Hugo Armann saved was Sarah Czazkes-Manishevitz. At the time, she was 19 and she was one of the people who worked in his house. When Hugo Armann found out that there was going to be a second Aktion, where the Nazis would round up the Jews in the ghetto and kill or deport them, he kept Sarah Czazkes-Manishevitz from returning to the ghetto. He was able to keep her safe in his home for the next seven days. He continued to do what he could for the Jewish workers until the final liquidation of the ghetto on December 17, 1942. Liquidation means that all the people who were in the ghetto would be either gassed, killed or sent to concentration camps. With the imminent liquidation of the ghetto, he would no longer be able to protect the Jewish workers. So, he supplied the workers with food, ammunition and weapons and arranged for them to leave and escape to the partisans. The partisans were the people who hid Jews in their homes. Partisans in general saved many Jewish lives and some were able to help them to further escape from the Nazis.

After the war ended, Hugo Armann finished his schooling and became a headmaster for a primary school. Also, he was able to reconnect and remained in contact with Sarah Czakes-Manishevitz after the war.

On September 5, 1985, Yad Vashem recognized Hugo Armann as one of the Righteous Gentiles Among the Nation and a tree was planted in his honor. Yad Vashem keeps the memories and facts of the Holocaust alive and lists people who lived, died and helped others to survive during the Holocaust. It keeps their stories for future generations so that all can learn and know of what a tragedy the Holocaust was. I used the Yad Vashem website for my main research on Hugo Armann. I am glad that I learned about him. He showed me that even a German army official could and did save Jews.

Hugo Armann is an important Righteous Gentile. In my opinion, Hugo Armann committed Tikun Olam, which means helping the world. He helped the world by sparing Jewish lives and preventing innocent people from getting murdered. Also, by saving Sarah Czazkes-Manishevitz, he saved a Jewish life that, without him, would have probably died. She and all her future family exist because of what he did for her. Hugo Armann risked his own life by hiding her in his house and by supplying the Jews with food, ammunition and weapons. If he had been caught, he would have been killed along with all of the Jews that he had been helping. But this did not stop Hugo Armann. He was one of many who did not agree with Adolf Hitler, but he was one of the few who did anything about it. Hugo Armann knew that massacring Jews because Hitler blamed them and said that they were the reason that Germany lost World War I was both unfair and untrue. So, Hugo Armann helped to make the Jews lives a little easier until he could do so no longer and then he helped them to escape the Nazi concentration camps. Hugo Armann is a true Righteous Gentile and I am glad to have learned his story.

Otto Busse - The Story of a Hero

Steinberg, Zev

The Holocaust: an event that many think of tragically. But amongst all of the tragedies, murders, terror, and violence, there were many heroes during this bereaved time. Otto Busse is one of the thousands of heroes of the Holocaust.

Otto Busse was the seventh son of a farming and agricultural family. Instead of following his family's footsteps, he chose to become a master painter.

Busse founded his first painting business and joined the Nazi Party, as nearly every specialist did in the 30's. After the newly entrenched anti-Jewish policy, Busse left out of disgust and disliking of the new policy. Five years later, in 1939, Busse rejoined the party due to constant pressuring by the officials in his area. During the eruption of the Holocaust, Busse wasn't assigned a spot in the army. Instead, he was appointed to a police reserve unit on the German-Polish border. His commander, Dr. Brix, later went on to become chief of civil defense in Bialystok. After being discharged in March of 1943, he went along with his former reserve commander. They ended up settling down in Bialystok in Eastern Poland. Busse took the opportunity and set up a painting workshop. In Poland, Busse was also able to savor his own special protection because he was a member of the Nazi Party. As a painter, his main goal was to renovate hospitals and apartments in which Jews lived.

Searching for suitable rooms for his labor force, he inspected an apartment in which two girls were staying. A conversation started up, and soon the two German girls were offered jobs as secretaries in Busse's business. Not yet known to Busse, these two girls—Chasia Bilitzka and Chaika Grossman—were leaders of a Jewish Underground Organization going on during all of this. This organization helped save more than hundreds of Jews from the camps, assisting them with escaping.

One of these two girls, Chaika Grossman, organized the Bialystok Ghetto revolt during World War II. She hid her Jewish identity to stay safe when she traveled back and forth between the city and the ghetto. In the ghetto, she met with other underground leaders and was entitled leader of the effort to organize the Bialystok ghetto. She also organized communication between other ghettos. Over time, traveling between these ghettos got more and more difficult. As a result, she mainly focused on the local Bialystok movement where she was more important to the defense strategy there. One of her more well-known activities was when she rescued an explosives expert from a concentration camp. She imported guns and explosives into the ghetto which were vital for the revolt that was up ahead. During the revolt, Grossman fought along with her comrades. Her main objective was to create an opening for the inhabitants of the ghetto to escape. However, their procedure failed and she was one of a couple who were able to survive the ghetto revolt.

After talking for a while and sharing many stories back and forth, Busse quickly began to learn about the horrors of the Holocaust that they had experienced and been exposed to in the extermination campaign that the Nazis were executing against the Jewish people. Otto Busse, being a German employer, was able to stop Jews from being taken to extermination camps by giving them jobs in his workforce. Over time, Busse got more and more involved with the full bounds of Jewish resistance activity. All at his own risk, he got pistols for the fighters and supplied them with warm clothes and medicines. Once, he even participated in a meeting of partisans in the woods. He gave away his office and his typewriter to those who printed anti-fascist leaflets. He also let the Jewish Underground Organization use his apartment as a hiding place for weapons waiting to be delivered to partisans in the woods. However, in 1944, Busse had to leave and go back to Germany.

This time, Busse was drafted into the military. He was captured by the Russians and held for around five years after the war in a Prisoner Of War camp in Kiev. After being released from the camp, Busse couldn't stop thinking about his two Jewish friends that he had left in Bialystok. Otto Busse had to try and find them. In 1958, the Jewish Agency was able to find and locate Chasia Bilitzka and Chaika Grossman. They were located in Isreal, now in contact with the two friends of his, Busse decided to settle down in Nes Ammim. Nes Ammim is a settlement in Western Galilee. Busse kept returning to Germany for visits. Otto Busse eventually died in Germany in 1980 at the age of 78. Amidst all of the horrors and tragedies, Otto Busse was righteous.

To be righteous means to be brave and morally right. In my, and Yad Vashem's, opinion: Otto Busse Definitely qualifies as righteous! On June 25, 1968, Yad Vashem recognized Otto Busse as a Righteous Among the Nations. A memorial plaque on his house in Nes Ammim still stands today to recognize the bravery and heroism of Otto Busse.

Dallas Ranch Middle School, Antioch, CA

Kevin Landski is a 6th grade English and History teacher at Dallas Ranch Middle School in Antioch. He has enjoyed taking courses during the summer to increase the interest and engagement of his students. He recently took a course on the Holocaust from an organization called Facing History, and has enjoyed using that material with his classes beginning in 2015. This is his sixth year teaching 6th grade.

Liselotte Hassenstein – Holocaust Upstander

Ajani Roberts

"The murderers were not content with destroying the communities; they also traced each hidden Jew and hunted down each fugitive. The crime of being a Jew was so great that every single one had to be put to death – the men, the women, the children; the committed, the disinterested, the apostates; the healthy and creative, the sickly and the lazy – all were meant to suffer and die, with no reprieve, no hope, no possible amnesty, nor chance for alleviation (The Holocaust Overview, page 1)" Millions were killed for no good reason. This sad and horrific event that filled many with depression and scarred anyone who survived was known as the Holocaust. The Holocaust was the murder by Nazi Germany of over 6 million Jews. The persecution of the Jews started in 1933. The mass murder was done while World War II was in progress. It took the Germans and their accomplices four and a half years to brutally murder 6 million Jews. They were most brutal from April to November 1942-250 days in which 2.5 million of the Jews were killed. They were relentless and showed no mercy whatsoever. They only slowed down when they ran out of Jews to kill, and only stopped when the Allies beat them in battle. Most of the Jews of Europe were dead by 1945. A civilization that had flourished for over 2,000 years was reduced to nothing by the Nazis. The Jews who survived all the madness didn't swear vengeance on the Germans. They gathered up the rest of their humanity and vitality and rebuilt. No justice could ever be achieved for a crime such as the Holocaust. Liselotte Hassenstein was an upstander during the Holocaust.

Liselotte Hassenstein was an upstander in the Holocaust because she hid Jews away in her own home. Liselotte and Otto arrived in Brody in 1941. Liselotte Hassenstein was the wife of Otto Hassenstein, a German citizen from Lüneburg his career in Forest Administration. Although not a member of the Nazi Party, Otto who had made was sent by the German government to work in Brody during World War II. There he tried to save many Jews by assigning them to forest work, posting special signs on their doors to prevent Nazi officials from apprehending them. It was a ploy that worked only temporarily, as most of these Jews were eventually deported. One day, while Otto was away on a business trip, Liselotte hid in her attic a Jewish woman, Lisa Hecht, who was a seamstress of her acquaintance, together with Lisa Hecht's small son. (I could not Send Them Away- By Liselotte Hassenstein, page1). Eventually, she hid other Jews as well, keeping this secret from her husband and children--a fact that saved the rest of her family from punishment after Liselotte's role in Jewish rescues was revealed to Gestapo officials. Otto had no knowledge of what she was doing. When she was denounced, Otto unknowingly led security police to his home, where the woman and child were found hiding in the attic. They were then sent to Belzec, and were sadly murdered. Liselotte was then arrested and brought before a Sondergericht, a special court for Germans who committed crimes against the state. She was convicted and sentenced to death on the charge Judenbeguenstigung. Judenbeguenstigung was the crime of aiding or abetting a Jew. Considering the fact that Jews were despised by many, this was not just a small crime. Because of bad health, her sentence was later changed to prison and hard labor. When her health deteriorated even further, she was sent to a hospital in Germany. After the war, the German head of the prison and some former prisoners testified to Liselotte's trial and arrest. Otto died trying to save his son from drowning. Liselotte died in May, 2004, at age 99.

Liselotte Hassenstein was an upstander in the Holocaust because she hid Jews in her house so they wouldn't be killed. The fact that she put their lives before her own was astonishing. She paid no attention to the laws and helped them, even though she was going to be killed for helping Jews before her sentence was reduced due to sickness. What I learned from reading about the Holocaust was that we should always help those in need and try to make peace with those against us. Racial and religious rights are yet to be fully achieved across the world. A mass murdering of over 6 million Jews all because they were Jewish. Just because a group of people have a different belief than you doesn't mean they need to be cast out. The Holocaust was just like bullying. Millions of Jews were singled out and murdered. There needed to be more upstanders during that time, people like Liselotte Hassenstein, people who are selfless, not just people who wanted to do something, but just sat there and watched the chaos. For years now, the Holocaust has been something of the past, but we don't know if something similar to it will happen. All we need are more people who care about the world, rather than themselves.

Works Cited

"I Could Not Send Them Away- By Liselotte Hassenstein" Kehilalinks.Jewishgen.org site. 2016   Web 12 Feb. 2016

"The Holocaust Overview." Yad Vashem site. 2016. Web. 12 Feb. 2016

"The Righteous Among The Nations, Liselotte Hassenstein." Yad Vashem site. 2016. Web. 12   Feb. 2016

Otto Busse-Upstanders and the Holocaust

Alex Garcia

 Holocaust is a word of Greek origin meaning "sacrifice by fire (Introduction to the Holocaust, page 1)." The Nazis had a cruel soul and heart to think it was right to do what they did to the Jews; it wasn't right. The Holocaust was the state-sponsored persecution and murder of 6 million Jews by the Nazi regime and its collaborators. The Holocaust was one of the worst times in history. Germany invaded Poland in September 1939, starting World War II. With this said, opponents of the Nazis

were killed, beaten or sent to one of the concentration camps. The Holocaust is a really big issue. It cannot, and should not, be an event by history. Many people do not know of the Holocaust, but if they did, people would learn from it and know not to make the same mistake again. Education is a key that knowing the Holocaust is not forgotten. The Holocaust was a tragic event. So many Jews died because of their religion. They obviously did not deserve the harsh treatment. Today we look back and reflect on the Holocaust. What people learn from this is that no on should be killed because of a certain religion. You shouldn't judge people by their religion, and the Jews did not deserve to die. Violence is never the answer. We should treat people nicely, like them or not. It was not only adults that died in the Holocaust, if a child was too young, they would be sent to concentration camps or shot. A concentration camp is a place where people are detained or confined without trial. Prisoners were kept in extremely harsh conditions and without any rights. It was so horrifying that so many people died in the Holocaust. There were some bright spots during the Holocaust because there were upstanders. Upstanders are able to see the pain the victim experiences and take action. Otto Busse was a German upstander during the Holocaust.

My upstander, Otto Busse, was born in Gillandwirszen in East Prussia. He was German and the youngest of his seven brothers. His main task consisted of renovating hospitals and apartments vacated by the Jewish Residents. As a German employer, he could save the lives of some of the doomed by claiming them as his workers. He obtained pistols for the resistance fighters, and he supplied them with warm clothing and medicine. He let the Jewish underground organization use his apartment as a hiding place for weapons to be delivered to partisans in the woods. One day he went to inspect an apartment where two girls were staying to hide. In the friendly conversation that they had, Busse offered the German-speaking girls work in his business (Yad Vashem, page 1). He died in Germany in 1980. On June 25, 1968, Yad Vashem recognized Otto Busse as Righteous among the Nations. So I think I would call him an Upstander, because he helped those two girls in the apartment hiding. And I learned that the Holocaust can teach us to be kind to others. People would sometimes risk their own lives to save their children, friends, or someone they didn't even know, even if they tried to save someone that still shows that they have a kind heart that you should be nice to others no matter what they truly are inside, and not judge someone because they are different. One day Otto Busse went to inspect an apartment where two girls were staying to hide. In the friendly conversation that they had, Busse offered the German-speaking girls work in his business. He was really kind to help them and supply them with warm clothing. The Holocaust shows that bystanders share an equal level of guilt. Violence is never the answer. You can't judge someone, even if they are red, blue, green, white, or black. Hitler was wrong because of all the stuff that he did. He had kids seeing their teachers hanging right in front of their faces. I learned that you shouldn't judge a book by its cover. Jewish is a religion, not a race.

Work Cited

"The Holocaust Overview". Yad Vashem Site, 2016 Web. 12 Feb 2016

"The Righteous Among the Nations, Otto Busse." Yad Vashem site. 2016 Web. 12   Feb 2016

"Introduction to the Holocaust." Introduction to the Holocaust site, 2016 Web. 12 Feb 2016

Sacrifice by Fire-Willi Garbrecht

Alondra Bruno-Castrejon

"The Holocaust was a murder by the Nazi Germany of 6 million Jews. While the Nazi persecution of the Jews began in 1933, the mass murder was committed during World War II. It took the Germans and their accomplices four and a half years to murder six million Jews. They were at most efficient from April to November 1942-250 days in which they murdered about 2.5 million Jews. They never showed any restraint, they slowed down only when they began to run out of Jews to kill, and they only stopped when the Allies defeated them.   (Holocaust history Yad Vashem)" The Holocaust was a ruthless act that commenced in January 1933 when Adolf Hitler came to power and became chancellor of Germany and technically ended on May 8, 1945. The Holocaust was a murder of over 6 million Jewish men, women, and children. 1.1 million of those were children, since young children were particularly targeted by the Nazis to be executed during the Holocaust. The word Holocaust means "Sacrifice by Fire," but it's also a biblical word meaning "Burnt Offerings". Brutal ways were used to kill these Jews, such as gas chambers, mass shootings, the Nazis would force them to dig there own grave and they were to be shot there, and concentration camps were frequently used during the Holocaust. The most intensive Holocaust killing took place in September 1941 at the Babi Yar Ravine just outside of Kiev, Ukraine, where more than 33,000 Jews were killed in just two days. Jews were forced to undress and walk to the ravine's edge. When German troops shot them, they fell into the abyss. The Nazis then pushed the wall of the ravine over, burying the dead and the living. Police grabbed children and threw them into the ravine as well. Seeing many young people being killed is what caused Willi Garbrecht to do the courageous thing he did in 1941. Willi Garbrecht, a German air force lieutenant, saved about 20-30 Jews during the Holocaust. He saw so many young people and decided to rescue as many as possible. The Jews were assembled in a market place in Auschwitz, about 2,000 of them. When Willi arrived with Antoni Jastrzab, they collected about 20-30 Jews. Regardless of whether or not they were permitted to do so, they began to take people out of the lines, under the pretext that they needed 'professional workers.' They did not meet with any resistance. This caused great panic, because so many people wanted to be saved. They took as many as they could, place them to one side and led them first to the factory and from there to the ghetto. They saved some 20-30 Jews, and the Gestapo did not interfere.

When something disturbed the Gestapo, the two officers took out their guns and shot in the air, insinuating that they would deal with the Jews themselves, but they only did it to camouflage their rescue activity."(Inka Weissbrot. Yad Vashem.) They escaped with the Jews and by then, every child saved knew the name "Garbrecht." He was considered an angel to the Jews.

At the end of May 1942, the first Aktion took place and approximately 2,000 Jews were sent to Auschwitz. They were assembled in the market place, and the selektion began. During the Aktion, Willi Garbrecht [an air force lieutenant who worked in the factor] and Teichert arrived. When they saw so many young people, they decided to save as great a number of them as possible."(Yad Vashem.) Yoel Grinkraut was employed as a tailor in the factory run by the Germans to produce uniforms, where Garbrecht worked at that time. Yoel was in the rescue Garbrecht was committing. He and six other Jews were taken to a basement to be concealed. The reason Yoel and the other Jews in the ghetto weren't killed by the Germans was because the ones who survived the first few waves of assassinations were employed in the air force factory. The only Jewish descendants spared by the Nazis where those with grandparents who converted to Christianity before the founding of the German Empire. Other brutal ways were used for slaughtering these Jews as well. Approximately 100,000 Jews died during "death marches," the forced marches of prisoners over long distances and under intolerable conditions. The prisoners, guarded heavily, were treated brutally and many died from mistreatment or were shot. Carbon monoxide was originally used in gas chambers. Later, the insecticide Zyklon B was developed to kill inmates. Once the inmates were in the chamber, the doors were screwed shut and pellets of Zyklon B were dropped into vents in the side of the walls, releasing toxic gas. SS doctor Joann Kremmler reported that victims would scream and fight for their lives. Victims were found half-squatting in the standing room only chambers, with blood coming out their ears and foam out of their mouths.

We shouldn't be afraid of the Holocaust, but we should learn from what can happen for just a little hatred or beliefs, for who they are. One must think of what can be torn apart for hatred. It has taught us to be better and stop hating, for in fear of a future Holocaust doesn't happen. We learned from it, it was something that could have been handled, we as a people should learn that we should never ever discriminate against any person because of their race, religion or believes. Never should we discriminate against handicapped or gays and lesbians. That we should respect them, not harm them physically or mentally. And above all human life should be respected. We as people should recognize that no leader should ever want death to so many people for any reason. We should never that many in the world would be against and there will be people who will fight so this does not happen again. We should also learn that it could happen to any of us because we are all different. Even a Caucasian could be discriminated against if someone doesn't like your background, your heritage. So respect life and help preserve it. That any nation or group of people, no matter how civilized that they appear to be, is capable of the most terrible evil.

Works Cited

"The Holocaust Overview." Yad Vashem site. 2016. Web. 12 Feb. 2016

"Righteous Among the Nations, Willi Garbrecht." Yad Vashem site. 2016. Web. 12 Feb. 2016

"Fact Slides- 30 facts about the Holocaust" Web. 2016

"90 facts about the Holocaust" Web. 2016

Dr. Fritz Fiedler – Holocaust Upstander

Angel Guerrero

"The Holocaust was the murder by Nazi Germany of six million Jews (The Holocaust Overview How Vast Was the Crime 2016. Web. 19 Feb 2016)." The Holocaust began in 1933, and the mass murder was committed during World War II. It took the Nazis four and a half years to murder 6 million Jews and they were at their most efficient in November 192, when they murdered two in a half million Jews, so when that happened it was harder for the Nazis to find the Jews. There was no escaping the Nazis. They traced every single Jew, because being a Jew was such a crime, you had to be dead. The Nazis didn't care what you were--child, baby, adult, and more. You were meant to suffer and die. Most of the Jews of Europe were gone, dead by 1945. A civilization that lived for over 2,000 years was gone. The survivors gathered the stuff that was left, and the remaining sparks of their humanity, and then the Jews they rebuilt it. They said, "For what justice could ever be achieved after such a crime? (The Holocaust Over, How Vast Was the Crime Yad Vashem site 2016. Web. 19 Feb 2016)." New families forever under those absent, of new life and stories.

"And so, within seven months, I lost my father, my brother, and my mother. I am the only one who survived. This is what the Germans did to us, and these are things that should never be forgotten. On the other hand, we had our revenge; the survivors were able to raise magnificent families – among them myself. This is the revenge and the consolation (Yadvashem.org The Holocaust Overview by author Zui Kopolovich. 2016. Web. 19 Feb 2016.)." The Holocaust ended because of the help of these upstanders. Dr. Fritz Fiedler was a German upstander who saved his Jewish dentist, and more.

Dr. Fritz Fiedler was a German 45-year-old military commander at Horodenka; a town bordering on Soviet Ukraine. Dr. Fritz Fielder was transferred in May 1942; and he didn't like what the SS/Nazis did to the Jewish people. He would never like the cruel SS. In December 1941, the SS were about to kill the first scale Aktion, when that was happening, 2,500 Horodenka Jews were killed. Dr. Fiedler warned his Jewish dentist about the attack, he told his Jewish dentist that they were about to declare the "vaccination action" but really, it was just to lure the Jews to their death. The Jews were ordered to appear at a certain place, but they didn't know they were going to be inside a truck where they were shot. But, Dr. Fritz Fielder swooped in and saved his Jewish dentist, the dentist's Jewish family, and 50 other Jews. He kept them to ask them questions, he detained the Jews so he could gather information. After that, he made his men to fight the SS by force if necessary. Three days later, the SS left, and in May 1942 the Jews were released. In May 1942, Dr. Fiedler moved away from Horodenka. He went to Krasne first and from there, to Russia. Dr. Kaufmann, who managed to survive the Holocaust with his family, got in contact with his German rescuer, Dr. Fritz Fiedler. "On July 26, 1966, Yad Vashem recognized Dr. Fritz Fiedler as Righteous among the Nations. (Righteous Among the Nations, Fiedler Family. Yad Vashem Site 2016. Web. 19 Feb 2016)."

Dr. Fritz Fiedler thought what the Germans/SS did was wrong. The vaccination-action was just to lure the Jews to their deaths, he told his Jewish doctor. Dr. Fritz. Fiedler saved his Jewish doctor, and his Jewish family, and even 50 other Jews. I see why I want to become an upstander, because what if another Holocaust happens? That would be bad. I learned that I must help the people who are having a bad day; I must help anyone getting harassed. I wouldn't want that to happen, people getting harassed, but sometimes people actually ban them if they are different! It is messed up. Killing people if they are not the same like them. They are human beings too, it is messed up that people are actually doing that. That means that they want to start another Holocaust. I don't want that to happen. I wish to be like Dr. Fritz Fiedler, I want to defend the people who are getting harassed. And plus, the scary thing that the Holocaust might have started by harassing people. So let's not start another Holocaust.

Works Cited

"The Holocaust Overview, How Vast Was the Crime." Yad Vashem site. 2016. Web. 10 Feb   2016

"The Righteous Among the Nations, Fiedler Family." Yad Vashem site 2016. Web. 10 Feb   2016.

The Ambruzhuk Family - Holocaust Upstander

Anna Rodriguez

"The crime of being a Jew was so great, that every single one had to be put to death – the men, the women, the children; the committed, the disinterested, the apostates; the healthy and creative, the sickly and the lazy – all were meant to suffer and die, with no reprieve, no hope, no possible amnesty, nor chance for alleviation (The Holocaust Overview, page 1)."
The mass murder of the Jews was during World War II. It took four-and-a-half years for the Germans and their accomplices to murder 6 million Jews. The Germans were most efficient from April to November 1942 - 250 days. They murdered about 2.5 million Jews during that time. The Germans never showed any restraint. They slowed down

only when they started running out of Jews to kill and they stopped only when their Allies defeated them. The murderers were not satisfied with destroying the communities. They also hunted down each fugitive and traced each hidden Jew. Most Jews from Europe were dead by 1945. The civilization that thrived for 2,000 years was gone. The survivors gathered the remnants of their vitality and the remaining sparks of their humanity, and rebuilt. The Holocaust lasted from about 1934 to 1945. Millions of Jews were murdered during that time, but there were some upstanders who saved some Jews lives. Anna and Feodor Ambruzhuk were upstanders during the Holocaust.

Anna and Feodor Ambruzhuk were upstanders by secretly letting their neighbor Leontiy stay at their house for one day. After Leontiy left, he asked Anna to go to Murovanyye Kurilovtsy to give a note to Leontiy's son, Boris, wrapped in a bunch of Ukrainian clothes. They also let Boris stay at their house for a week. Anna and Feodor, a middle-aged, childless Ukrainian couple, worked as farmers in the village of Morozovka with Anna's mother, Yevdokiya. Their friends and neighbors were Dobra and Leontiy Gelin and their four teen-aged children. After occupation of the area, first by Hungarian and then by the German troops in July 1941, the Gelins and the other Jews of the area were expelled from their home and forced to the ghetto in Murovanyye Kurilovtsy, which was established in the worst part of town. Living in harsh conditions and suffering from work and daily humiliations, the people survived one year. Early in the morning on August 21, 1942, the residents of the ghetto were rounded up. About 2,300 women, children, and elderly were murdered. Only 120 young and able-bodied Jews were left for road construction crews. Less than a month later, Leontiy headed back to Morozovka. He believed that somebody there could help him. He stayed one night with Anna and Feodor and then moved to the home of Frosina Chemeriskaya, a religious, elderly farmer that was living with her four-year-old granddaughter, Galya, and her daughter, Nina. He stayed with them for several days and then headed east with Nina to the village of Luchinets, which was controlled by the Romanians. In the meantime, at Leontiy's request, Anna headed to Murovanyye Kurilovtsy and gave Boris, Leontiy's 15-year-old-son, a note wrapped in a bunch of Ukrainian clothes. That night, Boris left the ghetto and went to the Ambruzhuks' house and stayed there for one week and then, like his father, he went to the Chemeriskayas. A week later, he received another note from his father saying it was safe in Luchinets. Two days later they were reunited and moved to the ghetto of Kopaygorod. At the end of 1942, the Chemeriskayas let Benzion Gelin, Boris's cousin, stay with them for a while before he moved to Kopaygorod. Nina visited them until the liberation in March 1944, bringing them food and other supplies. The surviving members of the Gelin family settled in Vinnitsa after the war and kept in touch with their rescuers. Anna and Feodor Ambruzhuk were upstanders because it says, "Leontiy ran away and headed to Morozovka, where, he believed, formed neighbors would help him. He stayed for one night with the Ambruzhuks, and then moved to the home of Frosina Chemeriskaya, an elderly, religious farmer that was living with her daughter, Nina, and her four-year-old granddaughter, Galya (Righteous Among The Nations, page 1)." I think that Anna and Feodor Ambruzhuk really made a difference.

Everybody should be an upstander so that there won't be another Holocaust killing millions of innocent people. Anna and Feodor Ambruzhuk were upstanders by secretly letting their neighbor Leontiy stay at their house for one day. After Leontiy left, he request Anna to go to Murovanyye Kurilovtsy to give a note to Leontiy's son, Boris, wrapped in a bunch of Ukrainian clothes. They also let Boris stay at their house for a week. Anna and Feodor made saved their neighbors Leontiy and Boris lives and that is an example of an upstander. The reason I am learning about the Holocaust is to be an upstander so that they're won't be another Holocaust killing millions of lives, and hopefully there won't be another.

Works Cited

"The Holocaust Overview." Yad Vashem site. 2016. Web. 12 Feb. 2016

"The Righteous Among The Nations, Feodor and Anna Ambruzhuk." Yad Vashem site. 2016.   Web. 12 Feb. 2016

Ruth Andreas-Friedrich – Holocaust Upstander

Anthony Trucks

"It took the Germans and their accomplices four-and-a-half years to murder 6 million Jews (The Holocaust Overview, page 1)." This is terrible because it shows that the Germans were content in destroying the Jewish society. The Holocaust was when 6 million Jews were murdered by Nazi Germany. The mass murder happened in World War II, but the Jews' persecution by the Nazis started in 1933. The Nazis were at their best from April to November 1942 – 250 days when some 2.5 million Jews were murdered. The Nazis never restrained, only slowed down when the number of Jews to kill was going down, and when the Allies defeated them, they stopped. The Holocaust was a horrible thing, but there were some people who stood against it. Ruth Andreas-Friedrich was an upstander.

Ruth, a German upstander, became one by helping Jews hide from the Nazis so they wouldn't get caught and be killed. Not very many people did these kinds of things, but Ruth was one of those people. Following her divorce, Ruth was a freelance journalist who lived with Karin Friedrich, her daughter, and Leo Borchard, her long-time companion and Moscow – born conductor, at no. 6 Hünensteig Street in Berlin Steglitz neighborhood. When the Nazis rose to power, a group of opponents to the regime who initially engaged in a form of resistance that was fairly mild – like passing information that was political to people abroad, and tearing down Nazi posters – was what Ruth became active in. After 1938, the regime upped its anti-Semitic measures, and then the group started helping Jews who were threatened with deportation. In time, the small resistance group – later called "Uncle Emil" – helped "illegals" with accommodations, food ration stamps and papers that weren't right. Karin also became actively involved from 1940 and onward. The most suitable person for carrying out dangerous errands was probably the blond "Aryan" looking girl. In autumn 1943 and onward, someone named Konrad Latte, a Jewish underground musician, frequently visited the Hünensteig address. Leo gave conducting lessons to Konrad, and Konrad could get a meal or food stamps all the time from Ruth and Karin. Karin and Ruth made the acquaintance of Harald Poelchau, the prison chaplain of Berlin – Tegel, through Latte. Poelchau sent persecuted individuals, the regime's opponents and Jews alike, who needed help, to Karin and Ruth. With support from the group, Ruth found Dutch passports and food ration cards that were forged. Konrad, Rita, and Ralph survived. Ruth published her diary entries for 1938-1945 after the war. Ruth was recognized as the Righteous Among the Nations on August 12, 2002 and Karin was recognized as the Righteous Among the Nations on May 30, 2004. Ruth had to spend her time and money to help the Jews who she was going to let stay at her house. For example, "In the spring of 1945, Ralph and Rita Neumann, a Jewish sister and brother who had just escaped from detention, spent the night in Ruth's home (The Righteous Among The Nations, Andreas FAMILY, page 1)."

    Ruth Andreas – Friedrich was an upstander. She became an upstander by helping Jews hide from the Nazis so they wouldn't get caught and be killed. A lot of things happened in the Holocaust, so there are a lot of things that you can learn from it.

Works Cited

"The Holocaust Overview." Yad Vashem site. 2016. Web. 12 Feb. 2016

"The Righteous Among The Nations, Andreas FAMILY." Yad Vashem site. 2016. Web. 12   Feb. 2016

What is Left Unsaid

Aysiana Clark (Winner)

    The imagery of a hero is often an unfailing, flawless person. People picture an honest being, without any mistakes. In other words, they imagine a perfect person. Unfortunately, that kind of person does not exist, as we are all with flaws. The reassuring part, though, is that people can strive to be a better person than they were yesterday, and make better choices. Oskar Schindler was a hero, but he was far from perfect. He was a member of the Nazi Party, a group recognized by the killing of around 14 million people, including 6 million Jews, under Adolf Hitler. Schindler had never had a resistance to the Nazis. His hunger for money only fueled saving Jews, and would let nothing stand in his way. In Oskar and Emilie Schindler, it states that, "Gradually, the egoistic goal of lining his pockets with money took second place to the all-consuming desire of rescuing as many Jews as he could." For some, it is hard to believe that a man with these kinds of values was able to save 1,200 people of different religion without even knowing them personally. Numerous amounts of times, Schindler interfered to save them from concentrations camps. "Today his name is known to the millions as a household word for courage in a world of brutality-the flawed hero who saved Jews from Hitler's gas chambers. A saint walking through hell" (Bülow). He tried his best to provide them the best he could afford, and asking for nothing in return. Against all odds, Schindler was able to outwit the SS, the paramilitary under Hitler, and save Jews from the grasp of cruel fates.

Oskar Schindler was born on April 28th, 1908, in Svitavy (Zwittau), Moravia. Schindler was born into an ethnic German and Catholic family. The Schindlers were a prominent family due to their wealth. It is noted the Schindler was a handsome man, adored by many women. After boarding school, in 1928, he married Emilie Pelzl. Schindler had a handful of odd jobs, such as opening a driving school, serving in the army, and selling government property, yet none of these jobs would be as unique as the one he was about to undertake. He craved a high quality lifestyle, but also became an alcoholic and had multiple intimate relationships with women. "A hedonist and gambler by nature, Schindler soon adopted a profligate lifestyle, coursing into the small hours of the night, hobnobbing with high ranking SS-officers, and philandering with beautiful Polish women," it says in Oskar and Emilie Schindler. It is astounding that a man with these kinds of priorities and questionable morals was able to save the lives of many.

Schindler became a part of the Nazi Party in February 1939. He and his wife moved from Svitavy to Krokow (or Crakow) in October 1939 to exploit a new business. In November of 1939, Oskar Schindler established Deutsche Emalwarenfabrik Oskar Schindler (German Enamelware Factory Oskar Schindler) or "Emalia" to employ Jewish workers in the nearby ghetto and saved them from being deported to nearby labor camps. Furthermore, only at Emilia did he employ Jewish workers, although owning two other factories. In October 1944, he relocated to Brnenec and was reopened exclusively as an armaments factory. Brnenec was then included as a sub-camp of Gross-Rosen, a concentration camp. At the peak of its success, his factory employed 1,700 Jews.

Schindler was arrested several times by the Gestapo, the secret police of the Nazis. He was interrogated and charged of favoring Jews and having an underhanded business. In spite of this, Schindler never detested. Once, he kissed a Jewish girl on the cheek, a forbidden act, and was arrested. His next arrest, in April 1942, he was thought to be bribing people to improve Jewish working conditions. Nevertheless, Schindler stayed less than a week in jail for each of his accusations and got back to managing his factory that protected Jews.

This unlikely hero had no limits when it came to the protection of his Jewish employees. Schindler held a privileged status, as he was thought to be contributing to the war as an owner to an armaments factory. He claimed multiple times that employing more Jews at his factory would keep production up. In 1942, he persuaded the SS into letting him set up a portion of the Plazow labor camp in his factory. "In turn, he spared 900 Jewish lives from this one action" (Paldiel, 1982). Then, in 1944, he transferred 700 Jews from the Gross-Rosen camp, and 300 women from Auschwitz. To fake the legitimacy of his Brnenec factory, they produced one wagonload of ammunition and fake production figures. According to Oskar Schindler, "In addition to the approximately 1,000 Jewish force laborers registered as factory workers, Schindler permitted 450 Jews working in nearby factories to live at Emilia as well, saving them the systematic brutality and arbitrary murder that was part of daily life in Plazow." Emilie Schindler was not useless in his operations, as she helped nurse 100 frozen Jews back to health. Even Jews who passed were given a proper Jewish burial ceremony. His workers were given the best food, clothing, shelter, and medical care that he could afford.

On May 9th, 1945, Schindler left when Soviet troops liberated Brnenec. Oskar and Emilie Schindler stayed in Regensburg, Germany after the war until 1949, when they immigrated to Argentina. In 1957, Oskar Schindler returned to Germany after being separated with Emilie. Yad Vashem, in 1962, rewarded Schindler "Righteous Among the Nations" after saving some 1,200 Jews. He died not a celebrity, but a penniless and unknown man in Germany. If only people understood what this silent man had done.

Schindler was kind to a race that was not even his own, risking his life and asking nothing in return. When asked about his actions, he wouldn't comment. Even the ones closest to him couldn't figure out his motives. Schindler didn't seem to have a resistance against the Nazis, or any motives in general. Besides money, Schindler put everything he had on the line for Jews for no apparent reason. In Oskar and Emilie Schindler it states, "Schindler never developed any ideologically motivated resistance against the Nazi regime."

urvivors have produced what is their hypothesis and wonder with us: What was Oskar Schindler's rationale to want to save so many people? Jonathan Dresner, a survivor, says, "He was an adventurer. He was like an actor who always wanted to be center stage. He got into a play and never could get out of it." On the other hand, Ludwik Feignbaum, another survivor states his opinions. "I don't know what his motives were, even though I knew him very well. I asked him and I never got a clear answer. But I don't give a d---m. What is important is that he saved our lives." "He gave an unselfish kind of love, of sorts, to the Jews" (Aberly). Some might agree, or try to explain why Schindler did it, but we will never truly know. Like the old saying goes, "Some things are better left unsaid."

Works Cited

Aberly, April N. "Oskar Schindler: The Man and the Hero (Holocaust Essays) |. "Oskar Schindler: The Man and the Hero (Holocaust Essays) |. N.p. n.d . Wb. 26 Feb. 2016.

Bülow, Louis. "The Oscar Schindler Story." The Oscar Schindler Story. N.p., n.d. Web. 25 Feb. 2016.

"Oskar and Emilie Schindler - The Righteous Among The Nations - Yad Vashem." Oskar   and Emilie Schindler - The Righteous Among The Nations - Yad Vashem. N.p., n.d. Web. 26 Feb. 2016.

"Oskar Schindler." United States Holocaust Memorial Museum. United States Holocaust   Memorial Council, 29 Jan. 2016. Web. 24 Feb. 2016.

Paldiel, Moredcai. Encyclopedia of the Holocaust. Oskar Schindler. 1982. "Schindler's List." 1995. (8 February 1997). 26 Feb. 2016

Guenther Brandt – Holocaust Upstander

Cayden Depew

"The crime of being a Jew was so great, that every single one had to be put to death – the men, the women, the children; the committed, the disinterested, the apostates; the healthy and creative, the sickly and the lazy – all were meant to suffer and die, with no reprieve, no hope, no possible amnesty, nor chance for alleviation, (Holocaust Overview, page 1)." The Holocaust was the undeniably horifiying mass murder of Jews, starting from 1933, and ending in 1945. The murder was caused by Nazi Germany, and was lead by Adolf Hitler during World War II. The Nazis had killed 6 million Jews, and plenty of other people within four-and-a-half years. These people included homosexuals, gypsies, Polish people, disabled people, and more. The most murders happened between April and November, 1942 in which they had killed 2.5 million Jews. By 1945, most Jews were already dead in Europe. The Nazis would hunt and trace each hidden Jew. They never showed any restraint, and they would not slow down unless they ran out of Jews to kill. They'd also kill anyone who wasn't able to work, which included kids, the disabled, and others. It is absolutely awful that something like this would happen, but with the help of certain upstanders, some Jews were able to survive. Guenther Brandt was an upstander of the Holocaust.

Guenther Brandt was a German upstander, and he helped Jews in many diferent ways during the Holocaust, for instance, Dr. Hans Gumpel. When Gumpel and his wife were living incognito in Potsdam, in 1944, Brandt issued them a stamped comfirmation that they were refugees from Stettin. This helped them pass through various offical controls. The Brandts also cared for and accomodated a Jewish widow by the name of Gertrud Leopold in their house for a few weeks in 1944. They also helped Susanne Vogel, of Jewish descent, by coming to her family one night to tell them of an impending police raid. They then invited the Vogels to shelter at their home, and took in their half-Jewish daughter as their housemaid, saving her from racial persecution. Guenther Brandt was a very brave and kind person, and it was a great thing that he was there to help those people. Guenther Brandt was born March 24, 1912. He died January 1, 1987. He began his job as a pastor at the Confessing Church in Leipzig in 1933. A little more information about Guenther Brandt is: "He was drafted into the army and, in 1941, was severely wounded in action on the eastern front. After a three-year hospital convalescence, he received an assignment as a graves-officer, which meant that he had to keep a register of the graves of fallen war-enemies; for instance, pilots who had been shot down. In addition, he was authorized to help provide bombed-out (German) refugees with new identification papers, food-ration cards, and accommodations, (The Righteous Among The Nations, Brandt Family, page 1)."Guenther Brandt was very heroic, and if it weren't for him, many wouldn't have survied.

Guenther Brandt was an upstander who had helped many Jews in different ways during the Holocaust. These ways include, hiding, taking care of, and disguising Jews to look like the Nazis. Guenther Brandt was very meorable, and was a great and courageous man. I have learned many different things while studying the Holocaust. For instance I am learning how to be an upstander, and how, and when to act in certain situations. I am learning not to tease or hurt people who are victims. I have also learned a lot of information about the Holocaust, like how it was a bad thing and how we should be upstanders so another one won't happen. It would be scary if another Holocaust were to happen, but if more people learn to be an upstander, the less likely it is to occur again. If something like the Holocaust were to take place again, it could happen to women, African-Americans, Mexicans, homosexuals, or other inocent people and races. After all, the main reason that the Holocaust was so scary was because the Nazis were killing off millions of innocent Jews. Learning about the Holocaust has encouraged me to become an upstander, and do what is right whenever I can. But, it has also taught me when, and when not to interfere with a situation. Learning about the Holocaust was a great experience, and I will always remember what I have learned.

Work Cited

"The Holocaust Overview." Yad Vashem site. 2016. Web. 12 Feb. 2016

"The Righteous Among The Nations, Brandt Family." Yad Vashem site. 2016. Web. 12 Feb.   2016

Anna Aksenchuk -- Holocaust Upstander

Chinomso Acholonu

"Anna chose to rescue Kaliszer by herself, she went to the ghetto, rescued Kaliszer and fled with Kaliszer, her daughter Batya and her brother Abraham Wartenfeld" (Holocaust overview page 1). In the Holocaust the Nazi Germans killed 6 million Jews. The destruction of the Jews began in 1933; the mass destruction started in World War II, and it took the Germans four-and-a-half years to murder 6 million Jews. They never slowed down or hesitated when they started running low on Jews to kill. They only stopped when the allies defeated them. Being a Jew was difficult because all men women and children etc. were meant to die, with no hope or possibility of living. Most of the Jews died by 1945. A community that went on for 2,000 years was no more. The murderers were not content with destroying the communities; they also traced each hidden Jew and hunted down each fugitive. The Holocaust was a scary and frightening thing that we should never have again, many people died, but luckily with the help of some upstanders some people were able to survive.

Anna Aksenchuk lived in Czortkow, which is located in the Ukraine. Germans conquered town on July 6, 1941, and in April 1942, established a ghetto there. Anna would've entered the ghetto to exchange food for various other items and then she met Rosa Kaliszer. They together made a friendly relationship, beyond just trading, developed between the two women. Anna soon told Kaliszer that when she was in trouble, she was allowed to come to her home. In June 1943, rumors began to go around Czortkow that the ghetto was going to be liquidated. Anna chose to rescue Kaliszer and, by herself, she went to the ghetto and fled the ghetto with Kaliszer, her daughter Batya and her brother Abraham Wartenfeld. The three Jews were then hidden away in the root cellar, where another Jewish child, Lola Rein joined them two months later. These four Jews remained hidden on the Asenchuks' property until the arrival of the Red Army in late March 1944. Anna's husband, Evstakhiy, played an important role in hiding the Jews, as did their son Bohdan, who was responsible for taking food and water to the hidden wards and concerned himself with regularly emptying the bucket they used as a toilet in the hideout. After the war, Kaliszer, her daughter and brother immigrated to Israel. Lola Rein, who had lost both parents in the ghetto, found her uncle and they left together to the USA.

Anna Asenchuk was an upstander in the Holocaust because she went to the ghetto and helped her friend Rosa Kaliszer and three other Jews flee from the ghetto. They had to hide in the root cellar of the Asenchuk's property, while they were there they discovered another Jewish child named Lola Rein. These four Jews remained hidden on the Asenchuk's property until the arrival of the Red Army, in late March 1944, and that's one reason she's an upstander. What I learned about the Holocaust is that sometimes what other people think is right might not always be right, and I also learned that the Holocaust is something we should never have again. If there is anything I learned about Anna Asenchuk is that she was very brave to go to the ghetto and rescue her friend, Rosa Kaliszer. I also learned that Anna kept her word when she told Rosa that in times of trouble she could come to her home. I think Anna Asenchuk was very caring and loving of others, because she helped Lola Rein reunite with her uncle and leave to the USA, and she is also very brave because no matter what the problem was she would always want to help other.

Work Cited

"The Holocaust Overview." Yad Veshem site. 2016. Web. 12 Feb.2016

"The Righteous Among The Nations, Asenchuk Anna." Yad Vadshem site, 2016. Web. 12   Feb.2016

The Gehre Family- Upstander

Dwayne Eason

"And so, within seven months, I lost my father, my brother, and my mother. I am the only one who survived. This is what Germans did to us, and these are things that should never be forgotten. On the other hand, we had our revenge: the survivors were able to raise magnificent families- among them myself. This is the revenge and the consolation (The Holocaust Overview, page 1)."

This quote represents the revenge of the Jews. It explains that the surviving Jews are going to multiply and increase their numbers as revenge. Adolf Hitler, the leader of the Nazis, was mad at the Jews because he claimed that the Jews stole victory from his country, Germany, in World War I. Adolf Hitler convinced all the Germans that Jews were their enemies. The Nazis forced every Jew out of their home, and told them to pack their bags in 5 minutes and leave. The Nazis started taking Jews on a train to concentration camps. When they arrived they smelled horrible and some of them on the train died. The Nazis lied to them and told them they would be given a shower before they got checked into the camp. The Nazis made them take their clothes off, shave their heads, and put them in a gas chamber and killed them. This terrible crime continued throughout World War II against the Jews. The Germans killed people who couldn't work, like the elderly, babies, and young children. Adolf Hitler killed 6 million Jews. During the time of one of the most hateful acts anybody has ever experienced, there were some Germans who did not agree with Aldolf Hitler's killing of innocent people. The members of the Gehre family were upstanders during the Holocaust.

The Gehres were a German family who were upstanders during the Holocaust because they hid Jews in their small apartment from the German officials and the Nazis. "They were a working class family, in Kottbusser Ufer in Berlin, Germany. Karl Max Otto Gehre was born in 1897 in Berlin, Germany. His wife Aguste was born in 1898 in Altwerp, Northeast Germany. The Gehre family had been patients to a Jewish physician Dr.Arthur Amdt for many years. They were very grateful to him for his treatment to their daughter who was sick at the time with diphtheria. In January 1943, at the peak of deportation of Berlin's Jews, the Gehres had offered their small apartment for Dr. Amdt to hide. Mrs. Gehre was instrumental at finding hiding spots for other members of the Jewish doctor's family and shared what little food they had with them. After the war, the Gehre family moved to Glenn Falls, New York in the United States. They were recognized as righteous among the nations for standing up for Jews (The Righteous Among The Nations, Koehler Family, page 1)."

The members of the Gehre family were upstanders because they hid Jews in their small apartment to keep them safe from the Nazis. What I learned from my upstander during the Holocaust is to stand up to someone who is mistreating others. People should not stand by and do nothing while others are being hurt. Everybody should respect all races and religions. My upstander took a chance and hid people who were innocent, that the Germans wanted dead. My upstanders made a decision that saved their own doctor and his family's life. I'm sorry all the Jews had to suffer all those years in pain. I hope I have the courage to stand up for others like the Gehre family had done.

Work Cited

"The Holocaust Overview." Yad Vashem site. 2016. Web. 12 Feb. 2016
"The Righteous Among The Nations, Koehler Family." 2016. Web. 12 Feb. 2016

Holocaust Hero-Aurelius Arkenau

Edmond Agopian

Have you ever been bullied? Well, Hitler and his Nazi regime killed more than 6 million Jews. Aurelius Arkenau was a Holocaust hero. He worked with other anti-Nazis to rescue dozens of Jews, Communists, and deserters. Aurelius was born in 1900 into a family of farmers in Essen Oldenburg. Sadly, Josef died on October 19, 1991. Aurelius's parents were strict Catholics.

Aurelius's original name was Josef and he received the name Aurelius from a priest. Josef passed his final examinations in 1921. After that Josef followed the example of his older brother and joined the Dominican Order as a novice. In 1940, Aurelius was transferred from Berlin to the Dominican chapel in the working-class district of Leipzig-Wahren. Aurelius found accommodations with Christian families for both mother and child. Aurelius continued to support them with money and food-ration cards throughout their stay. Kathe Sackamdt was a Jew and was saved by Aurelius. Kathe confined in Joshanna Landgraf, who sent her to Father Aurelius. Aurelius said "Unless you want to kill your child, you absolutely must go hiding." (Righteous Among the Nations paragraph one). In one tragic case, a Jewish woman doctor swallowed poison while in the house where she had been hiding for a couple of months. In order to dispose of the body without arousing the Gestapo's suspicion, Father Aurelius arranged a ceremonial Christian burial under an assumed name. On October 27,1998, Yad Vashem recognized Father Aurelius Arkenau as Righteous Among the Nations.

Aurelius was an upstander. He saved many people from the Nazis and helped them hide. Aurelius gave people who were hiding money and food rations. Aurelius inspired me to be an upstander. Whenever I see someone being bullied I will help them and when someone is on the ground I will help them get back up. I will help people who are in need and make a better community. For people who can't always get food, I will help them get all the food and money the people need.

Aurelius Arkenau was one of the most determined Holocaust Heroes. Aurelius helped save many Jews from the Nazi regime. Aurelius was an upstander to Hitler. Hitler was the bully because he killed 6 million Jews. Aurelius died on October 19, 1991.

Elizabeth Abegg

Elizabelle Elevazo Clavido

Did you know there were upstanders in the Holocaust? One known upstander was Elisabeth Abegg. Elisabeth helped many Jews by hiding them. Elisabeth was inspired to help Jews after her friend was taken away. An upstander is someone who stands up for someone who is being bullied. The Holocaust was a horrible event that happened between January 30, 1933 and May 8, 1945. A horrible dictator name Adolf Hitler had his Nazis kill 11 million people. Six million of those people were Polish citizens. Three million of those people were Polish Jews and the other 3 million were Polish Christians. Hitler disposed of disabled humans, children, Roma Gypsies, resistors, and priests. The International Holocaust Day of Remembrance falls on January 27. Adolf Hitler wanted people who had blue eyes, blonde hair, and were tall. Many people thought Hitler was insane not just because he had a lot of people dead but because he didn't have blonde hair and blue eyes either. After the Holocaust, Hitler killed himself with a gunshot. His wife, Eva Braun, killed herself with him using cyanide. In this situation, Adolf Hitler is the bully and the Jews are the victims. Upstanders help because they know what is right and what is wrong. In this essay, you will learn about Elisabeth's personal life, how and why she helped Jews and how Elisabeth Abegg inspired me to help. If you want to learn more, continue reading.

In this paragraph, you will learn about Elisabeth Abegg's personal life. She was born on May 3, 1882 in Strasbourg, the capital of Alsace, which is now part of France. She was a history teacher at the fashionable school, Luisen Madchenschule. When the Holocaust started, she was forced to retire for having anti-Nazi views. She lived in an apartment with her sister and mother. She was a Christian and never married. After the Holocaust, she was recognized as Righteous Among the Nations. She kept in touch with some of the survivors after the Holocaust. On her 75th birthday, some of the people she saved dedicated a mimeographed collection of memoirs entitled, "When One Light Pierced the Darkness." She died at age 92 on August 8, 1974 in Berlin, Germany. Now that you know more about her, you'll be learning how and why she saved Jews.

In this paragraph, you will learn about how and why Elisabeth helped Jews. Before she was forced to retire, most of her students were Jews. After Nazis came in and took the Jewish student, Elisabeth knew it was wrong. Her close friend for 40 years was caught by the Gestapo and sent to Auschwitz. Elisabeth didn't want people to end up like her friend so she helped them. She hid them in her apartment, where her mother and sister lived, from then Nazis. She fed the Jews with her own food and even sold her own jewelry to smuggle Jews underground to Switzerland. Since it was too dangerous for Jewish children to go outside, Elisabeth tutored them during her free time. Although she knew the risks, she also knew that what she was doing was right. Now that we know that she was a hero of many lives, you'll be learning about what I learned had an impact on me.

Elisabeth Abegg was a hero so she inspired me to do the right things as well. Like Elisabeth Abegg, I will stand up for people who are being bullied. I will do that by pulling them out of the situation or telling the bullies to stop. I will also try to be equal to everyone so there is no one special. I will do that by treating everyone the same and be nice to everyone. I will also try to stop people from being racist and discriminant. I will do that by telling them that we are all equal and our looks do not matter. I will also tell them that we are all the same but we have different looks. If the bullies don't stop, I will ask for help from adults. I will tell them that there is someone being bullied. If that adult doesn't help the situation, I won't stop looking for someone who will help. I will try not to be scared when being an upstander and I will try not to hesitate to help someone. When the victim is not being bullied, I will try to be their friend. I will talk to them, do homework with them and try to cheer them up. I will try to have the victim ignore the bullies if they are being bullied verbally. If they are being bullied physically, I will tell the bully to stop.

Now that you know more about Elisabeth Abegg, I hope it helped you realize not to bully. I also hope that you will help people that are being bullied. Don't be scared to stand up for people because you know it's right. Many people want to help someone who is being bullied but are too scared to. That is understandable but if you stand up to a bully, the bully will then know that you are not scared of them. I hope this essay taught you to be an upstander.

Gerhard and Wally Hagemann -- Holocaust Upstanders

Emani Araya

 The history of the Holocaust reflects the reality that Adolph Hitler and the Nazi movement did not invent anti-Semitic hatred against the Jews. What was unique in the Nazi experience was that the Third Reich was the first and only regime in modern history to define anti-Semitism in racial terms and, upon this basis, to use the full weight of the state to legitimize the Ausrottung, or eradication of the Jews. Racial bloodlines defined the essential difference between Aryan Germans and Jews. This distinction, in the words of Victor Klemperer, a philologist and shrewd observer of Nazi language, was everything. What set National Socialism apart from other forms of fascism "is a concept of race reduced solely to anti-Semitism and fired exclusively by it" (Klemperer 2000, p. 135). The racial state conceived by the Nazis as a foundation stone for the Holocaust defined citizenship in biological terms. As one prominent Nazi race eugenicist argued, "National Socialism is nothing but applied

biology" (Baur, Fischer, and Lenz 1931, p. 417) (Macmillan Encyclopedia of Death and Dying | 2003 | WEGNER, GREGORY PAUL)". The Holocaust began in January 1933 when Hitler came to power and technically ended on May 8, 1945. In October 1941, more than 50,000 Jews were killed by Romanian troops in what is now known as the "Odessa Massacre." Between 1933 and 1945 more than 11 million men, women, and children were murdered in the Holocaust. Approximately 6 million were Jews. Over 1.1 million children died during the Holocaust. Young children were particularly targeted by the Nazis to be murdered during the Holocaust. They posed a unique threat because if they lived, they would grow up to parent a new generation of Jews. Many children suffocated in the crowded cattle cars on the way to the camps. Those who survived were immediately taken to the gas chambers. The Nazi were vicious people they murdered 1.1 million children because they thought that they'll start a new generation Jews. Eleven million men, women, and children were murdered, except for two children, a man, and a woman because of Gerhard and Wally Hagemann, who were upstanders during the Holocaust.

Jacob Kahane and his family survived the Holocaust because of Gerhard and Wally Hagemann. Jacob Kahane, his wife, and his 2 children went into hiding. They spent the night in a small room at the Wilhelmshavener Strasse, which they had to vacate before sunrise. Shortly after, the Wilhelmshavener Strasse was burned down in an air raid, Kahane then to his friend Hagemann seeking help. In the end, Hagemann made a desperate decision -- he took his Jewish friend to the mayor's office. Where he declared that his friend, who is now known as alias Hahne – was a refugee from Berlin, and that his family had just barely escaped an air raid in which all their belongings had been destroyed. Thanks to the Hagemanns being upstanders, and vouching for the Kahane family, where able to obtained official Aryan papers. The Hagemann family saved the Kahane family from being murdered. Their two children escaped from being suffocated in the cattle car. The Hagemann family's decision saved lives of four people during the Holocaust. They had a choice to take them to Hitler, but instead they decided to save the life of a friend and be upstanders. "We cannot pretend we do not see, we do not hear, we do not know. We need to take a stand, because history can repeat itself. It can happen to any group of people." – Barbara Turkeltaub

Gerhard and Wally Hagemann were upstanders during the Holocaust, because they saved the life of a Jewish friend of theirs. Jacob Kahane and his family were safe from danger during the Holocaust in the concentration camp. Writing this paper taught me that the Holocaust was a terrible event that occurred in the past and that what you do to help someone can affect their future. The Holocaust was a bad thing, I also learned a lot of information about the holocaust, and I learned that we should do something to help someone. The Holocaust was scary because the Nazis were killing the Jews; the Nazis were led by Adolf Hitler who believed that Jews were a disgrace. The Jews were innocent people they wanted to live in peace with their family, instead their life got interrupted by the Nazis they got sent to gas chambers, they had to dig their own ditches and then get shot, they cremated them, the Nazis took their cloths and let them only

114

take thing that are able to hold in two hands. What I also learned is that you don't have to have a good heart to do something good to help someone, and we can change the world and make sure that there is not another event in time like the Holocaust. Whenever I think about the Holocaust I do so with a certain deep sense of pain. We as a people should learn that we should never discriminate against any person because of their race, religion or believes. Never should we discriminate against handicapped or homosexuals, and that we should respect them and not harm them physically and mentally. And above all human life should be respected. We as people should recognize that no leader should ever want death to so many people for any reason. The Holocaust will become more firmly etched into our mins and hearts. I will always be thinking of the Holocaust and a way to keep it from happening.

Elisabeth Abegg -- Holocaust Upstander

Haley Dunham

"The Holocaust was the murder by the Nazi Germany of 6 million Jews (Holocaust Overview, page 1)". The Nazi persecution of the Jews began in 1933 and took place during World War II. This time period was known for the mass murder of over 6 million Jews. It is estimated that it took the Germans and their accomplices four-and-a-half years to murder this many Jews. The Germans would hunt each Jew down, which would include, all men, women and children as well as the sick and elderly. The Germans wanted the Jews to suffer a slow death. By 1945 most European Jews were dead. Some survivors which were from a small town, or who were able to escape from being found underground were emaciated and dazed beyond recognition. These survivors gathered the remains of their vitality and sparks of their humanity in order to rebuild.

Elisabeth Abegg was born on May 3, 1882 in Strassbourg, Germany. She was the first cousin of William Abegg, a Social Democratic statesmen. Elisabeth was a history teacher at a prestigious Berlin all girls school called Luisen Madchenschule. Almost all of her students came from Jewish homes. Elisabeth Abegg assisted in trying to rebuild the Jewish community by working with her friends in the Quaker movement. She began to help many of her Jewish protégés by offering them to stay at her house or directed them to hiding places elsewhere. Once Hitler's presence in-power she came into conflict with the newly Nazi-appointed director Luisen Madchenschule. Because of the conflict, Elisabeth had to move to another less prestigious school. In 1940, Elisabeth was forced to retire early after someone said she committed a crime. She was then labeled by authorities as politically unreliable. She received this label after a close friend of almost four years was deported to the East. Elisabeth finally understood the true meaning of what the import of Nazi persecution of the Jews was. When it was to late to save her friend, Elisabeth felt her purpose was to save other Jews from the slaying clutches of the

Gestapo. This is when Elisabeth started to house Jews in her three-and-a-half room apartment with her 86-year-old mother and her invalid sister, Julie. Elisabeth's mother and sister were put into a temporary shelter and assembly point for Jews and for people who went underground. While working with her friends in the Quaker movement, she began to help many Jews by offering them to stay in her house or to direct them to hiding places elsewhere. In order to provide food she rationed her meals in order to supply food ration cards to others. She invited other Jews each Friday to her home for special meals and provided forged papers for them. Complete strangers were knocking on her door asking for her help. All the activity took place right under her neighbors' noses even though some of the people who lived in the apartments were active Nazis. Elisabeth did not delay any time trying to help others. With that said, she met Liselotte Perles, the day care director in Berlin, who could not decide whether or not to go into hiding with her nine year old niece, Susie. In late January 1943, Elisabeth decided to go visit the Jews "House" which they were moved to. Three apartments already been sealed after the residents been deported to the east. Elisabeth succeeded on persuading her to go underground and it was the last possible moment as it was the night before of the last and large Gestapo round up of the Jews in Berlin. In order to organize the smuggling of Jizchak Schwerzenz into Switzerland Elisabeth offered her own jewelry for sale. Survivors who remained still kept in touch with Elisabeth after the war, and dedicated a mimeographed collection of memoirs called, "When One Light Pierced the Darkness" for her 75th birthday in 1957.

In conclusion, the Holocaust was a very tragic time in history, and a time that most will never forget. Many movies have been made to retell the individual stories of some of the survivors during this tragic time period. The life or death decisions that were made by Elisabeth show what it means to be an upstander. She sacrificed her safety and the safety of her family in order to save hundreds of lives. She even offered her own jewelry in order to help smuggle another into Switzerland. I have learned what it truly means to give unconditional help. To think of others who are less fortunate and what we can do to help without expecting anything in return. I will try to be more helpful when I see someone who needs help even if it's just saying "Hi" to someone new at school. Sometimes it's the small gestures can make a big impact in someone's life.

Works Cited
"The Holocaust Overview." Yad Vashem site. 2016. Web. 12 Feb. 2016
"The Righteous Among The Nations, Elisabeth Abegg." Yad Vashem site 2016. Web. 12 Feb. 2016

Aurelius Arkenau - Upstander in the Holocaust

Hunter Thomas

"And so, within seven months, I lost my father, my brother, and my mother. I am the only one who survived (Holocaust Overview, page 1)." Being a Jew in the Holocaust was like being in years of nightmares. But this was real. The Holocaust was the murder of 6 million Jews by the Nazis, which took four-and-a-half years. They killed the largest group from April to November in 1942. They only stopped when the Nazis were defeated by the Allies. The crime of being a Jew was so bad that you would be killed no matter what. The persecution began in 1933 but most of the deaths happened during World War II. The survivors were one from town and two from a host. The host would give them shelter, food, or water. There was no escape. Most of the Jews in Europe were killed by 1945. They just rebuilt new families. They were always scared it would happen again. Jews were very afraid and they were very careful. The Jews had it so bad and most people didn't even really care. Aurelius Arkenau was one of the few people who helped out the Jews. Not a lot of people helped, but Aurelius did. Aurelius Arkenau was an upstander in the Holocaust.

Josef Arkenau was an upstander from Germany because he gave Jews water, food, shelter, and money. He was born in 1900 and his parents were strict Catholics. In 1929 he became a priest and his new name was Aurelius. However he went to Berlin as a pastoral worker from 1934-1940. Pastoral workers are lay people who exercise a vital ministry in a church. Then he went to Dominican and worked in the district of Leipzig-Warren till the war ended. He finally stopped being on the Nazis' side when he saw a Jew being shipped to the east so he worked with people against Nazis and he helped save a lot of Jews, communists, and army deserters. "One of the Jewish survivors, Käthe Sackamdt, testified how she had been ordered by the Gestapo to report to an assembly point together with her young son, Joachim Leibel. In her despair, she confided in Johanna Landgraf, who sent her to Father Aurelius. (The Righteous Among The Nations, page 1)." When, where they were staying wasn't safe anymore Aurelius got an Aryan identity card that made it so she could stay with her kid till the war ended. In a sad part a Jewish women doctor swallowed poison while in the house she was hiding in for months. To get rid of the body without getting Gestapo's suspicion, Aurelius buried her. Aurelius Arkenau saved a lot of lives and a lot of Jews were thankful of him.

Aurelius Arkenau was an upstander in the Holocaust. Aurelius Arkenau was an upstander in the Holocaust because he gave Jews water, food, and shelter. The Holocaust was the murder of 6 million Jews. This is scary that this could happen to African Americans, women, or Mexicans, etc. It could happen anywhere, anytime, to anyone. Everybody should be an upstander so another Holocaust won't happen again. It was a hard time for the Jews and most of the Nazis didn't care. During World War II, after the Allies defeated the Nazis, the Jews tried to forget about what happened. I am studying the Holocaust because it was scary because the Nazis were killing the Jews. Also, don't tease or hurt someone who is a victim. The Holocaust was a terrible thing, but I did learn a lot of information about it. I also learned that we should be an upstander to make sure another Holocaust won't happen again.

Works Cited

"The Holocaust Overview." Yad Vashem site. 2016. Web. 12 Feb. 2016

"The Righteous Among the Nations, Arkenau Family." Yad Vashem site. 2016. Web. 12 Feb.

2016.

Johannes & Kathe Bottcher: Holocaust Upstanders

Isaiah Brown McCoy

 "The Holocaust was the systematic, bureaucratic, state-sponsored persecution and murder of 6 million Jews by the Nazi regime and its collaborators. (Introduction to the Holocaust, page 1)." This all happened in World War II when a man named Adolf Hitler was leader of the Nazi regime and killed six million Jews. It only took four and a half years to kill 6 million jews. They didn't just start killing jews, they persecuted them before World War II happened. All the persecution started in 1933 and the murdering of the Jews started in World War II. They never showed any restraint, they only slowed down because they were running out of jews to kill and they stopped when the Allies defeated them. No Jew was safe from the Nazis. They destroyed communites and tracked every Jew. The crime of being a Jew was so great that you had to be put to death. Most of the Jews were dead by 1945. The survivors were lost and had no where to go to. All they had were each other to rebuild their lives. They never meted out justice from all of their tormentors-for what justice could ever be achieved after such a crime? They had so much work to do, they had to rebuild their communities, new families, new lives, and they were forever sad and haunted by their loss. During the time of the Holocaust there was a family that looked over Jews who seemed to be hidden in a church. They were the Bottcher family.

Johannes and his wife Kathe Bottcher were upstanders during the Holocaust because they looked over Jews who were hidden in the abandoned church. Johannes was born in 1895 in Germany and was a minister from 1931 and further on. While the war was happening , Johannes's apartment was destroyed in the summer of 1944, then he moved in with his wife Kathe. Seven Jews were hidden in a destroyed Reformation Church next to Johannes's apartment building. They moved into their apartment and looked over the seven Jews who were hidden in the church. Some of the Jews were hidden in the cellar of the church and others were in the boiler room. All these Jews were "privileged" Jews and they had non-Jewish spouses. Joseph Anschel was one of the

Jews and when he was ordered to go to the Gestapo he went into hiding with his "Aryan" wife and two daughters. Joseph came to Johannes and asked him to hide him, his family, and the other Jews. If anyone found out that Johannes was hiding Jews, Johannes could be in serious danger. The Gestapo were in immediate vicinity of the church where they were hiding. The son of minister Bottcher (who had not been conscripted because of a serious illness) took electricity from the Gestapo to give to the people in hiding. When the air-raid warning sounded, the public air-raid shelter is where they took place next. Johannes asked people for food to give to the people in hiding, and everyone he asked gave him food. When Johannes came back his friend minister Heinrich Held was looking over the Jews. The world war ended and the Jews were set free. Anschel re-establish the Jewish community in Essen. Then sadly after that, minister Bottcher passed away on November 23, 1949. Anschel took place in his funeral to thank him for saving his life. Johannes was keeping his family and himself in danger to save others. And he is a role model for all to be an upstander to anyone who is being bullied. No one likes being bullied so the bible gave an inspiring quote. "And to them will I give in my house and within my walls a memorial and a name (a "Yad Vashem")... that shall not be cut off (About Yad Vashem, page 1)". Be an upstander.

The Bottcher familly were upstanders during the Holocaust. They hid Jews in a church and put their lives in danger to keep others safe and alive. These people are the reason why I study the Holocaust. They teach us how to react in these situations just if it happens again. It also teaches us how to be an upstander to bullying. We can not let what happen to the Jews and what the Nazis did to them ever happen again if we become upstanders. I learned a lot of information about the Holocaust and that it can happen to to anyone like woman, African-Americans, Mexicans, Muslims, etc. So don't let the evil come to you and attack like the Nazis did to the Jews. You should always stick up for someone who can't fight back like how Johannes helped all those Jews, that could not fight back even if they tried , and put them under floors and in cellars to keep them safe. All you need to do is be an upstander to bullies, and help someone in need.

Works Cited

"The Holocaust Overview." Yad Vashem site. 2016. Web. 12 Feb. 2016.

"The Righteous Among The Nations, Bottcher family." Yad Vashem site. 2016. Web. 12 Feb.   2016.

"About Yad Vashem." Yad Vashem site. 2016. Web. 12 Feb. 2016.

Martha Maria-Driessen-Holocaust Upstander

Jahanna Oakes

 "It took the Germans and their accomplices four-and-a-half years to murder 6 million Jews (Holocaust Overview, Page 1)." The Holocaust was the murder of 6 million Jews by the Nazis. The Nazi persecution of Jews began in 1933. The mass murder happened during World War II. They killed most of the Jews from April to November 1942. It's really sad that they killed so many Jews for no reason. They stopped only when the Allies finally defeated them. It's also sad because all Jews were meant to suffer and die. The Nazis would destroy whole communities and hunt and kill all of the Jews they could find. Almost all Jews in Europe were dead by 1945. It took them 250 days to kill 2.5 million Jews. Most of the Jews had no hope. It is very sad that all of those people died for no reason, but luckily there were upstanders. Martha-Maria Driessen was an upstander in the Holocaust.

Martha-Maria Driessen was an upstander in the Holocaust because she was one of the three women rescuers who helped Lilli Wolff. Martha helped by bringing food-ration cards, clothes, and other items while Lilli was living in Dorthea Neff's apartment. "Neff only received help from a few individuals. Two friends from Köln- Meta Schmitt and Martha-Maria Driessen visited occasionally, bringing food-ration cards, clothes and other items (The Righteous Among the Nations, Driessen Family, Page 1)." Martha had three other friends two of them were a part of the three women rescuers. Their names were Lilli Wolff, Antonie Schmid, and Meta Schmitt. Meta Schmitt helped Martha give Lilli Wolff the things. Martha-Maria Driessen was born on January 6, 1908 in Leiden, Holland. All four women were in the clothing business. Martha came into business in 1932. That means she was in her 20's when she came into business. Martha died in 1979

Martha-Maria Driessen was an upstander from the Holocaust from Germany because she helped Dorthea Neff hide Lilli Wolff in her apartment. It was hard being an upstander because all of the Nazis would try to kill you if you were an upstander. Martha was still an upstander even though it was really dangerous. All of the upstanders took a huge risk because they were all determined to end the Holocaust. The Holocaust was a very tragic event. It was very sad to see so many people die for no reason. No one deserves to be starved, no one deserves to suffer, and no one deserves to die. One of the worst parts of the Holocaust is that most of the Nazis felt no remorse for all of the men, women, children, and infants they killed. The Holocaust was one of those things that could have been easily avoided and no one had to die. Upstanders are needed in this world so things like the Holocaust won't happen again. There was no reason to kill all of those Jews. No one should have to witness all of those people being killed because none of those people should have been killed. Studying the Holocaust helped me learn a lot of things. I learned how to avoid unnecessary situations. I also learned why I should be an upstander. I should be an upstander because upstanders make a huge difference. If upstanders helped stop the Holocaust then upstanders can help solve problems that we have in the world today. Another Holocaust doesn't have in order to get upstanders to take action. All of the good people in the world will always try to be an upstander. No one wants another Holocaust to happen and to prevent that from happening we need to be upstanders. After the Holocaust, the survivors set out to rebuild their community. Though the survivors rebuilt their community, they will never forget their major loss.

Works Cited

"The Holocaust Overview." Yad Vashem site. 2016. Web. 12 Feb. 2016

The Righteous Among the Nations, Driessen Family." Yad Vashem site. 2016. Web. 12 Feb   2016

Leonard Bartlakowski – Holocaust Upstander

James Cahayag Jr

"They were at there most efficient from April to November 1942 – 250 days in which they murdered some 2.5 million Jews. They never showed any restraint (The Holocaust Overview, page 1)." This is shocking to know that in just 250 days, the Nazis slayed 2.5 million Jews without mercy. The Holocaust was when the Nazis of Germany murdered 6 million Jews. The Holocaust began in 1933 during World War II, and took four-and-a-half years to complete. The Nazis only slowed down vanquishing the Jews when the Allies were defeating them. There was no escape for the Jews. Nazis were never satisfied with just ending the community for the Jews, they hunted each Jew as if they were fugitives. Every Jew had to be killed because of their crime of being Jewish, for example, "the men, the woman the children; the committed the disinterested the apostates; the healthy and creative the sickly and the lazy – all were all were meant to suffer and die with no reprieve, no hope, no possible amnesty, nor chance for alleviation (Holocaust Overview page 1)." Knowing that that the Nazis were trying to get rid of the Jews is ridiculous. In Europe, most of the Jews were already dead by 1945. Instead of the Jews getting depressed, they decided to rebuild a new community, but will be haunted by the loss of their people forever. Bartlakowski was an upstander in the Holocaust.

Leonard Bartlakowski was an upstander in the Holocaust because he helped hide three people in his home, Romana Kesslar and Dr. Stephanie Reicher, later hiding Abraham Weidenfield and himself. "He offered to shelter his friend and his wife in his home, but Weidenfield, who still had an alternative hiding place in the pharmacy, refused and asked him to hide his sister-in-law, Romana Kessler, and Dr. Stephanie Reicher instead. It was only a few months later, in mid-June 1943, that Weidenfield joined them (Holocaust Overview, page 1)." It's pleasant to know that people would help Jews in this time of grief. Leonard Bartlakowski was a Berlin-born of a Polish family and grew up in Germany. Leonard Bartlakowski was in the middle of a mission with his air squadron on the way to bombard Warsaw in a disguise. Leonard managed to reach Lwow, a Ukraine city later being imprisoned. Leonard Bartlakowski followed the German invasion in June 1941. Lwow was occupied by the Germans. While Lwow was covered with the Germans, political prisoners were being released from prison. Bartlakowski took the power of Robert Kyrinski later being announced at Rawa Ruska, a city at the border of Ukraine and Poland, by a German-Polish interpreter for the local Gestapo. There Leonard Bartlakowski and Alias Kyrinski first met the German-Polish interpreter. The next day the German interpreter went into to Weidenfield's pharmacy for some razor blades. Weidenfield offered a free pack of razor blades therefore a great friendship was born. Rawa Ruska was near the course that transports the polish Jews to the Belzec death camp, which was 30 kilometers away. Leonard Bartlakowski's office was conveniently placed so he could easily gather important information about raids or transports. Any information Bartlakowski gained was then sent to Weidenfiled immediately which was then translated into code and given to specific Jewish councils. Leonard Bartlakowski learned that the local Gestapo were going to empty cattle trucks at Rawa Ruska from Belzec. In the night, Bartlakowski entered the ghetto himself to warn civilians about the cattle trucks. Leonard insisted to shelter his wife and Weidenfield, but Weidenfield still had a hiding place in his pharmacy. Weidenfield wanted Leonard to shelter Roma Kesslar, Weidenfield's sister in law and Dr. Stephanie Reicher instead. A few months later, mid June 1943, Weidenfield joined them in a small apartment which now had 4 people until the liberation of Rawa Ruska on July 27, 1944. Their hiding place was 3 cubic feet in Bartlakowski's bed under his home. While they were hiding, food was very hard to obtain, thus leading to Leonard stealing food from work, which was at the railway station. Food was hard to obtain because he could not buy enough food for four people without arousing suspicion. There were lots of rumors of Leonard Bartlakowski hiding Jews. There was so much that the Gestapo had to investigate Leonard's home with a dog. Leonard managed to lure the Gestapo out of his house with liquor. After the war, Leonard went back to Germany and joined his sister and mother in Berlin. Leonard Bartlakowski died early at the age of 36 by tuberculosis he had caught in Lwow at a Soviet prison. This is great to know people like Leonard would risk something a valuable as his life for other people, like Weidenfield's sister in law, Dr. Stephanie Reicher and Abraham Weidenfield.

 Leonard Bartlakowski was an upstander because he helped hide four people in his home, including himself for about a year under his bed. From the Holocaust I learned that you shouldn't tease or harm someone because of there religion or race because they are different from other people. I also learned why to b an upstander because it's a scary possibility that history could repeat another Holocaust. It's fascinating that Leonard Bartlakowski hid four people under his bed for about a year including him.

Works Cited

"The Holocaust Overview." Yad Vashem site. 2016. Web. 12 Feb. 2016

" The Righteous Among Nations, Leonard Bartlakowski." Yad Vashem site. 2016 Web 12 Feb. 2016

The Courageous Heroes of the Holocaust

Jasmine McWilliams

Before meeting Holocaust survivor, Bernie Marks, I was unaware of what the Holocaust really was. His story inspired me to want to learn more about it. I learned that the Holocaust was a traumatic and devastating time. But, I also learned that there were some remarkable men and women who put their lives at risk to help others.

One of these people was German industrialist, Oskar Schindler. Schindler was an unexpected hero of the Jews, mainly because he was a Nazi. He was also a businessman. Originally, he was hoping to make a profit from the German invasion of Poland in 1939. He hoped to do this by hiding the wealthier Jews and hiring about one thousand cheap slave workers to work in his ammunition factory. But he soon became alarmed by the way the Jews were being treated. So, he started to protect them, with no regard for the profit. He also secretly moved children out the ghettos and requested for hundreds of Jews to be moved to an adjoining factory. He would use his charm and persuasive skills to get the Jews out of challenging situations. He would claim that women, handicapped and unskilled workers were crucial to his business. Oskar Schindler died a poor man at the age of 66. But he gained the everlasting gratitude of his "Schindlerjuden," or "Schindler Jews." Oskar Schindler is the only Nazi to ever be buried in a Jerusalem cemetery.

The next hero is a man named Anton Sukhinski. When the Nazis invaded Poland, he was the only man in the town of Zborow to help the Jews. The first person he helped was a 16-year-old girl who he hid in his cellar. The next thing he did was help a family he knew before the war named the Zeigers. Sukhinski's neighbors eventually learned that he was harboring Jews, and he had to blackmail them so they wouldn't say anything. Things got worse and the Zeigers had nowhere else to go, so Sukhinski, being the selfless person he was, dug a small hole in his cellar and hid them in there. The Zeigers spent the next nine months in this cramped hole, unable to move, and Sukhinski gave them the food he could scavenge. When the Nazis had at last left Poland, the Zeigers could barely walk, but fortunately, they were alive. The Zeigers never forgot Sukhinski's bold and courageous sacrifice.

The following hero is Maximilian Kolbe. Kolbe was a Franciscan priest who established the Militia Immaculata, which is a missionary group that spread the Catholic faith across the world. This all started in 1939 when the Third Reich, invaded Poland. Kolbe took action by hiding 2,000 Jews into his monastery. Unfortunately, the Germans found out about this and arrested him in 1941. Kolbe was taken to Auschwitz, where he did something even more incredible. When he first arrived there, a man had escaped which angered the Nazis. As a result, ten men were to be killed. One of the men was Francis Gajowniczek. When Kolbe found out that this man had a wife and kids, he heroically offered to take his place. Kolbe's body was burned after being injected with a syringe filled with carbolic acid. Francis spread Kolbe's story far and wide before his death in 1995.

The next hero was quite rebellious. His name is Albert Goering. Albert had a brother named Hermann who happened to be second in command of the Nazis. But Albert was the complete opposite of his brother; he hated the Nazis more than anything and he preferred to save lives rather than destroy them. And he did just that. Albert was an export director for a weapons manufacturing company. He would pretend that he didn't see when his workers stole weapons to protect themselves from the Nazis. He even donated large amounts of money to the resistance movement against the Nazis. But he didn't just provide them with money, he also snuck Jews and non-Jews out of the Nazis' reach. He continued to help many others in their search for freedom. The crazy thing about Albert's story is that the Gestapo, the secret police of Nazi Germany, had known about Albert's behavior and kept files on it, arresting him several times. But every time he did get arrested, Hermann would have him ordered out of jail. After the war, the Allies didn't believe Albert's incredible story, so he made a list of all the people he saved from the Nazis. He was finally released, but the Czechs put him in jail again. Albert was officially cleared in 1947. Sadly, because of his brother's position as Nazi second in command, he was never able to move on and start a new life. Albert died as a penniless and miserable man in 1966.

Our final Holocaust hero is Eugene Lazowski. Lazowski was a doctor who was a member of the Polish Red Cross. He lived directly next to a Jewish ghetto, and he would sometimes go over and help people who were ill or wounded. But this wasn't all he did. The most magnificent thing he did was fool the Nazis into thinking that his town, Razwadow, was disease ridden. One of Lazowski's colleagues, Stanislaw Matulewicz, discovered that injecting a healthy patient with a dead typhus bacteria, they would test positive for the disease, even though they didn't have it, and were perfectly healthy. Lazowski and Matulewicz used this opportunity to infect the people of Razwadow, and convince the Nazis that everyone was infected. When Nazi doctors found out about the "epidemic," they went ballistic and quarantined the town. Eugene's scheme saved over 8,000 people. But soon enough the Nazis did find out about the fake epidemic, and Lazowski had to escape. In the late fifties, he ran away to Chicago and became a pediatrician. He was later honored by the AMA (American Medical Association) Seniors Physicians Group.

These are just some of the many heroes of the Holocaust. Unfortunately, a lot of their deeds had gone unnoticed, but I'm sure they weren't any less appreciated by the Jews. But quite a few of these people were honored by Israel's Yad Vashem memorial. They were given the title of "Righteous Gentiles" or "Righteous among the Nations". The valor of these men and women inspires me to do something great for someone. I think more people should learn about the Holocaust and the people who helped make things a little better.

Works Cited

shalomshow.com/stations_&_info.htm

http://www.toptenz.net/10-little-known-heroes-holocaust.php

The Holocaust – Housing a Fugitive: Wanda Dombrowski

Jasmine McWilliams

 "The Holocaust was the murder by Nazi Germany of 6 million Jews (Holocaust Overview, page 1)." All around Europe the Nazis were persecuting people of Jewish belief in 1933 but the killing had started during World War II. This marked the start of the horror that is the Holocaust. The Germans killed with no restraint and reached the peak of their deadly efficiency in April of 1942 when 2.5 million Jews were killed in the period of 250 days lasting until November of that year. In four and a half years 6 million Jews were killed by the wrath of Nazi Germany. With most of the Jews executed by the end of the war there was no escape for those who lived through the horror shadowed by such atrocious methods of warfare. Most were traced by their heritage and hunted regardless of any disabilities, illnesses, age, or gender and killed with no reprieve. Although some survived they still try to rebuild what they lost in the war. A great civilization had been destroyed by tormentors who will not be given justice for their crimes due their crime being too terrible and vast. They would have kept killing if not for the Allies who stopped them but the losses in the war were tremendous resulting in one of the biggest and bloodiest wars in history. Some people during the war chose to help those in need with the risk of death or exile, sheltering those lost in streets covered in broken glass or giving supplies to the Allies as they walk through fields of artillery shells. These small acts gave these devastated people something you'd call hope in a place where it's often scarce in time of war. People responsible for saving and helping fugitives are the reason that not all of the Jewish civilization was destroyed in the midst of war giving hope to those who need it. These people are what we call upstanders in the present day. One such person is a woman named Wanda Dombrowski.

German born Wanda Dombrowski was what you would call an upstander who had housed a fugitive named Herbert Strauss during the war. Strauss had met his future wife in Berlin and had to hide so they had become separated. Due to Wanda's Jewish husband being good friends with Strauss's future wife's uncle, she agreed to help Herbert forge ID papers. Wanda was only one of many people to have housed Mr. Strauss in the war. Although Wanda helped Strauss with the task of ID papers she wasn't the only one to have helped Herbert in a large way. Before, he was housed by Freidrich Wedekind-Strindberg and Utje Strindberg. Friedrich worked as a correspondent for Swedish newspapers so he'd helped Strauss by supplying him with information about the war. Another person to have housed Herbert Strauss was Felicia Pauselius who was a frail elderly woman who had kept Strauss in a spacious apartment and had led people to believe Strauss was her long lost son who she'd given away a long time ago. She'd kept this up for four weeks before Strauss went to Wanda for his ID papers as his last stop.

All of these people are examples of how kindness can still be found in a place of war. These people were not afraid of men with power and chose to hide those who were to be executed. They even chose to house people when they knew they'd be killed if they were found. Thanks to these people Herbert Strauss survived the war and became the director of the Center of Research on Antisemitism at the Technical University of Berlin. Wanda Dombrowski, Freidrich Wedekind-Strindberg, Utje Strindberg, and Felicia Pauselius were all recognized and honored as upstanders during the war giving them the title of Righteous Among Nations for their righteous acts in harsh times. Getting to know more of history is always an opportunity for me even if it is about the devastation of war. It had been an experience getting to learn about the terrible event known as the Holocaust and learning firsthand from the great Bernard Marks and hearing his testimony about his time as a child in the war. Bernard Marks was a survivor of the Holocaust who'd told me about his experience. There was so much I had learned from Mr. Marks involving the Holocaust. One example is when he told us how terribly they treated Jews at ghettos and how his father lied to the Nazis to keep him alive. What I took from this lesson is that, learning from the past, we can prevent this horror from repeating again as individuals in the future and stand up for what you think is right even if it means fighting and dying for your country, people, religion, or rights to give hope to your belief. We may all think differently but in the time of war but we can all fight for a side we think is right. But its best to think of a world without war than to thinking of one riddled with it for the time being. The last thing we want is history repeating the horror of another Holocaust.

Works Cited

"The Holocaust Overview." Yad Vashem site. 2016. Web. 12 Feb. 2016
"The Righteous Among the Nations, Wanda Dombrowski." Yad Vashem site. 2016. Web. 12   Feb. 2016

Luise and Liesel Gansz -- Holocaust Upstander

Jeemin Kim

"The Holocaust was the murder by Nazi Germans of 6 million Jews. While the Nazi persecution of Jews began in 1933, the mass murder was committed during World War II (Yad Vashem, The Holocaust)." This is only a shallow piece of information about the Holocaust. The word Holocaust is made up of the two Greek words holokauston and kaustos. Holokauston means whole and kaustos means burn or burned. Holocaust means sacrifice by fire. The Holocaust was the murder of millions of Jews that happened during World War II. The persecution of

Jews started in 1933, but the Nazis and their partners did the murdering during World War II. The 250 days between April and November 1945 were the most horrific because the Nazis killed about 2.5 million Jews. The Nazis and their partners killed 6.5 million Jews in only four-and-a-half years. The Nazis did not apply any limitations or constraints on killing Jews. They slowed down when they had begun to run out of Jews to kill and only stopped when the Allies defeated them. There was no time to flee or hide for the Jews. The killings were not only set to destroy communities but to trace every single hiding Jew and hunt them down town to town. Being a Jew was so big of a crime that every single one had to be killed including children, women, men, and elderly. They were all meant to suffer and die without hope, no chance to be spared, and neither a chance for comfort. The Jews in Europe were almost wiped out by the year 1945, leaving a few survivors scattered throughout Europe. A society that had lived on for 2,000 years was almost wiped out. The survivors rebuilt neighborhoods with other survivors instead of going out for revenge. The survivors were forever haunted by their loss and memories of their loved ones and the cruelness of the Nazis. Luise and Liesel Gansz were upstanders during the Holocaust. Be an upstander and help stop the next Holocaust. Here is the story of Luise and Liesel.

Luise the mother, and Liesel the daughter were upstanders during the Holocaust. Luise Gansz was born on January 1, 1881 and her death was unconfirmed. Liesel Gansz was born in 1913 and died on November 5, 1971. They both lived in Berlin, Germany. Luise and Liesel helped by hiding the Jews, supplying them the basic goods, and arranging shelters. Liesel was the rescuer of Charlotte Herzfeld. Liesel and Charlotte were friends for many years before the Holocaust. When most Germans cut former friendships with Jews, Liesel tried harder to make a closer friendship with Charlotte. Liesel visited Charlotte at her parent's apartment. It was an activity that could have captured the neighbors' attention without difficulty. When Charlotte knocked on the door of the apartment where Liesel lived in with her mother, Luise, Liesel didn't hesitate and took her in regardless of the danger. Charlotte lived with the Ganszes for several days before Liesel and her friends arranged a shelter for Charlotte. Therefore Charlotte began a life in hiding, moving from place to place, and dependent on her friend to find a safe place where she could stay, and on the food provided for her. Charlotte didn't have identification papers or ration cards with her so; she couldn't buy her own provisions. From time to time, Charlotte came back to her supporter to hide with them for many days until another safe place could be found. Charlotte survived by hiding until the end of the war. After being freed, the ties between rescuer and rescued continued. Surprisingly the two women even lived in the same apartment for a couple of years. Liesel died in 1971, and ten years later, Charlotte died too. Charlotte asked to be buried next to her rescuer, and to her wish, the two graves stand side by side. "Herzfeld hid with the Ganszes for several days, and then Liesel arranged a shelter for her with friends. Thus Herzfeld began a life in hiding, moving from one place to another, dependent on her friend to find her safe place where she could hide, and on the food provided for her (The Righteous Among the Nations, Luise and Liesel)."

Be an upstander and help stop the next Holocaust. Luise and Liesel were upstanders during the Holocaust. Luise helped victims by hiding them and Liesel helped victims by not only hiding them, but with supplying the basic goods and arranging shelters. Even if that was a big thing, even small things such as making a new or bullied person feel welcome can help. I learned why we all need to stop small problems before they become too big to stop by ourselves. It could stop another Holocaust and it can be much simpler than that. It could be fixing a crack in a clay model before the crack gets bigger or adding an extra nail to stabilize a photo on the wall before it falls off the wall. I also learned no matter what someone believes, what race they are, and what you think they are everyone should be treated fairly. I was very interested and grossed out by the Holocaust. It was a meaningful testimony I heard that captured my heart making me want to learn more about it to help not make the same decision and not murder millions of people. Knowing about the Holocaust brings bullying to light. I learned some new facts about the Holocaust that I had never known about such as how many concentration camps that were used in the Holocaust. Another fact that I learned is that the concentration camps had crematories in the camps. I learned that the Jews were moved in cramped trains in which many died because of the lack of food and water, the intense heat, the freezing cold, and the stench of urine. It is unbelievable to imagine such thing could have happened.

Works Cited
"The Holocaust Overview." Yad Vashem site. 2016. Web. 12 Feb. 2016
"The Righteous Among the Nations, Luise and Liesel." Yad Vashem site. 2016. Web. 12 Feb. 2016
"United States Holocaust Memorial Museum, Nazi Camps." USHMM site. 2016. Web. 12 Feb. 2016
"United States Holocaust Memorial Museum, Deportations to Killing Centers." USHMM site. 2016. Web. 12 Feb. 2016

Holocaust Hero -- Hans von Dohnanyi

Kevin N. Tan

 Have you ever been an upstander? Upstanders are people who stand up for others. World War II was just like that. There was the Holocaust, a horrific and terrible event. It was the mass murder of more than 6 million Jews. Adolf Hitler and his Nazi regime slaughtered more than 6 million Jews, in a number of violent and brutal ways. There were some upstanders during this horrible time period. They helped Jews escape from the terrible hands of the Nazis. They hid Jews in basements, attics, and even behind walls. Some people even tried to kill Hitler and his Nazis. But whatever they did, it helped and saved some Jews. Most of these people were known as Holocaust Heroes. One of these heroes was Hans von Dohnanyi.

The Holocaust was a mass genocide of more than 6 million Jews, led by Adolf Hitler and his evil group of Nazis. They rounded up millions of Jews from different cities and towns. They then took the Jews to the many brutal concentration camps around Europe. The Nazis used different methods of killing Jews. The methods were gas chambers, hangings, mass shootings, and many other fatal killing methods. They also made Jews endure very harsh conditions, etc. Luckily, American armies and soldiers came and eradicated the concentration camps. Unfortunately, most Jews didn't survive.

Hans von Dohnanyi was born in Vienna, Austria, on January 1, 1902. But after his parents divorced, he grew up in Berlin. He was executed and hung in the brutal Sachsenhausen concentration camp on April 8, 1945, in suspicion of anti-Nazi activity. What he did to save Jews was he smuggled Jews from many different concentration camps and put them in safe harbors in Switzerland. Another brave feat he did was put a time bomb on one of Hitler's flights. Unfortunately, the operation to assassinate Hitler failed. He also became very disillusioned with the Nazi regime after the Night of Long Knives in 1934 where a party of Nazis killed political opponents and purged the government. He was imprisoned for two years before he was executed and hung. Yad Vashem recognized Hans von Dohnanyi as Righteous Among the Nations on October 26, 2003.

Hans von Dohnanyi was a very brave person who tried to stop the Holocaust along with other people. He has inspired me to resolve and stop the problem if there is one. Hans von Dohnanyi was so determined to stop Hitler that he tried to assassinate him. That act inspired me to stay determined when I am doing something difficult or hard. Though Hans von Dohnanyi was only able to save a dozen Jews and a couple more, he still made a change. That tells me that even the littlest act can have a big impact. So Hans von Dohnanyi has inspired me and other people to keep going and never give up. I will make a difference and help my community.

Hans von Dohnanyi was one of the most determined Holocaust Heroes. Along with many other people, he saved dozens of Jews taken by the Nazis. Overall, he was a very brave man who risked his own life for innocent people who he didn't even know. Hans von Dohnanyi will be remembered as one of the brave and courageous Holocaust Heroes.

Charlotte Salomon – Holocaust Upstander

Kylie Uilani

"And so, within seven months, I lost my father, my brother, and my mother. I am the only one who survived. This is what the Germans did to us, and these are things that should never be forgotten. On the other hand, we had our revenge: the survivors were able to raise magnificent families – among them myself. This is the revenge and the consolation. (Zvi Kopolovich page 1)." Zvi Kopolovich was a brave survivor in the Holocaust. The Holocaust was an awful, atrocious, dreadful, scandalous event during

January 30, 1933 through May 8, 1945. It took place during another despicable event, World War II. The Holocaust was a murder of around 6 million Jews by Nazi Germany. The Nazi persecution of the Jews began in 1933. To murder all 6 million Jews, it took the Germans and their accomplices four-and-a-half years. Their most efficient time of murdering Jews was between the months of April to November 1942. During that time of 250 days, they murdered about 2.5 million Jews. The Germans showed no mercy, until there was an inadequate amount of Jews to slaughter, then started to show mercy when the Allies defeated them. The murderers traced every other hidden Jew and executed them in secrecy. The crime of being a Jew was so bad, that each and every one had to be put to death – men, women, children, the committed, the disinterested, the traitors, the lively and creative, the sluggish and the sickly – all meant to perish and suffer, with no remission, no hope, no amnesty, nor chance for alleviation. Most Jews of Europe perished by 1945. A civilization of almost 2,000 years that had flourished disappeared. There were only a few survivors – one from a town, two from a host – flabbergasted, emaciated, bereaved beyond measure, gathered the components of their vitality and the remaining parts of their humanity, and rebuilt. The survivors never delivered justice to their tormentors. One of the people who witnessed part of the Holocaust was Charlotte Salomon. Charlotte Salomon is one of the many German upstanders.

Charlotte was born in April 16, 1917 in Berlin, Germany. She was a German-Jewish artist. Her parents were Albert Salomon, a surgeon, and Francisca Grunwald. The Salomon's were an enlightened family that defined themselves as "Germans of the Mosaic persuasion." Charlotte made a major impact on our lives as people see it. The reason may not sound important, but it was extraordinary. Charlotte's art was a major impact. Her 769 individual works all put together resulting in the magnificent autobiographical series of paintings "Life or Theatre?" Every single painting has a meaning; even the same of the whole series has a meaning. The title "Life or Theatre?" means "Reality or Fiction?" The events during Charlotte's overall life were so tragic and dreadful that it was unbelievable, which creates the title "Reality or Fiction?" Charlotte's series of paintings is an autobiography. Each painting depicts an event that Charlotte witnessed. The autobiography teaches what has happened during the Holocaust. In her works, it tells a complicated familial story; eight relatives who Charlotte believed were lost, and about whose fates she never told. One family member is her aunt, who drowned herself in a river. In the autobiography, Charlotte explains the story retrospectively, from the time her aunt passed, to when her parents met during World War II, their engagement and marriage, her own birth, and the loss of her mother. Each aspect in Charlotte's work has their own name to highlight their specific features. For example, she nicknames herself as "Charlotte Kann" (the German word for 'Can'), and her parental grandparents the "Knarres" (literally meaning 'mumblers'). When Charlotte was eight years old, her mother leaped out of a window, though she was convinced that her mother passed from influenza. When first introduced the window in

Charlotte's work, it became a symbol of her own family's fate – suggesting that they chose their own destruction.

Charlotte Salomon was an upstander in the horrifying event, the Holocaust. Charlotte made an impact with her fantastic art and autobiography, "Life or Theatre?" Charlotte was an amazing individual who made beautiful works of art. I learned lots of information about Charlotte Salomon. Charlotte was born in April 16, 1917. By September 1943, Charlotte and her husband, Alexander Nagler, were dragged onto a train and was taken to a concentration camp from Nice to the Nazi 'processing centre' at Drancy near Paris. She then was gassed to death at the concentration camp on the date of October 10, 1943. Charlotte was pregnant at the time of death. When Charlotte was deceased, the Holocaust was still present. The Holocaust started January 30, 1933 and ended May 8 1945. The Holocaust was a scary but fascinating event. It taught me how bullying was in the past and how to prevent bullying. The Germans and their accomplices would judge people and Jews specifically on their differences and specialties. I've learned that you shouldn't judge someone on how they choose to live. You shouldn't judge someone for their differences. You shouldn't judge a book by its cover. As the golden rule states: Treat people the way you want to be treated. "And with dream-awakened eyes, she saw all the beauty around her, saw the sea, felt the sun, and knew she had to vanish for a while from the human plane and make every sacrifice in order to create her world anew out of the depths." –From "Life or Theatre", Charlotte Salomon, 1940-42.

Works Cited
"The Holocaust Overview." Yad Vashem site. 2016. Web. 12 Feb. 2016
The International School For Holocaust Studies, Charlotte Salomon." Yad Vashem site. 2016.   Web. 12 Feb. 2016

Hans Fittko - Holocaust Upstander
LC Fuller

"The Holocaust was the murder by Nazis in Germany of 6 million Jews. While the Nazi persecution of the Jews began in 1933, the mass murder was committed during World War II. (The Holocaust overview page1)" The Holocaust was an evil plan to eradicate anyone different. These malicious crimes committed by Nazis brought countries to its knees with sadness. The Nazis nearly killed all of the Jews by the year 1945. The Nazis tried hard to kill the Jews. They used many contraptions to kill the Jews. They either put them in gas chambers or lined them up and shot them. After they were dead they either put them in the crematorium or in ditches where there were heaps of dead bodies or in the back of trucks stacked up high. The Holocaust could easily be the worst crime in history and this began in World War II. This set off a chain of events where bombings killed more innocent people and this was a catastrophic outcome that the world would remember as the Holocaust.

Hans Fittko was born into a blue collar family. But oddly at a young age of twelve he dropped out of school but he continued to educate himself and became a known journalist. Fittko then moved in Berlin's literary and socialist circle. At the end of 1933 Hans was threatened with arrest because of his political activities and this is why he fled Prague, however before fleeing he met his partner and future wife Lisa Eckstein. Together Hans and Lisa would lead many refugees across the border to safety. A short time after their marriage the couple left Prague by an extreme roundabout route that finally reached Paris. The couple was still in danger because they could still be reached by the Germans occupation of France of the Armistice between the third reach Vichy government. So they went to the unoccupied south in the month of August 1934 and they were in Banyuls-Sur-Mer not to close to the border going to Lisbon. During this time they met an American journalist by the name of Varian Fry who was also helping refugees flee to safety. At this time Fry was in need of help and the Fittkos joined in and didn't care about the risk. The group then met a socialist mayor of Banyuls who helped them to an old smuggling path across Pyrenes so they could cross the border without being bothered. From September onwards the Fittkos and Fry led a large number of refugees to safety. Among the refugees there were Jews who were wrongly accused of crimes as well as intellectuals, writers and artists. The secret route that was taken was known as route f. One of the first refugees that were helped over the border by the Fittkos and Fry was a famous essayist and literary critic named Walter Benjamin. The group crossed over the border on September 26, 1940. Once in Spain, the Spanish police threatened to expel Walter Benjamin and because of that he committed suicide. The other fugitives survived as well as many others did in 1941. Even the Fittkos left Vichy France which became dangerous for refuges then they left Cuba where they lived a couple years before settling in the U.S.A on February 8, 2009 (yad Hashem Hans Fittko as righteous among nations).

"In 250 days in which they murdered some two and a half million Jews yad Vashem the righteous among nations)" One reason we should never have another is because for future generations we shouldn't put them through the horror of our past mistakes. This is only one of the many reasons we should better our selves now and in the future do you really want innocent children die because of our mistakes. We need do better our selves for them in my opinion there is a 50 percent chance everybody in my class maybe this school that they will have a least one child. You may say it's not your fault your but you don't even vote but that's exactly right you should vote by not doing any thing you effetely did everything. In my opinion people who are of age to vote should definitely vote because only 19 percent of young people actually take the time to go and vote. For that reason I feel like we should aim higher, in 2 to 4 years it should be raised by 5 percent. I want to see America's youth shape America. In my opinion just by voting you can help America in the long run because voting brings changes in the world. By voting we can effectively prevent another Holocaust from happening. Take these words in mind and better yourself for the future of America. The second thing is about a Holocaust upstander named Hans Fittko was born into a blue collar family he became a respectful man in the literary and social circle and was a victim of you could say a type of profiling because of his political activies so he fled Prague where he met his wife named Lisa Eckstein who was just as brave and courageous. As he was the reason they were brave is because they helped an American journalist who was helping refuges cross the border on this secret path in pyrenes known as route f, a secret route where they would not be bothered as they traveled through there because they led a large amount of refuges who were wrongly prosecuted. But in the end these two great people finally settled down in America. This is also one of the only great people upstanders in this world. You should learn from these people take in account what these people did and do the same. Help other people, better your self and other people. You don't have to smuggle people across the border but try and help any way you can.

Works Cited
"The Holocaust Overview." Yad Vashem 2016. Web. 12 Feb. 2016
"The Righteous Among The Nations, Fittko Hans" Yad Vashem site. 2016 web. 12 Feb. 2016

Hans von Dohnanvi – Holocaust Upstander

Rickeyia Jackson

"The Holocaust was the murder by Nazi Germany of 6 million Jews (The Holocaust Overview, page 1)." The Holocaust started 1933 and ended 1945. During the Holocaust all of the Jews were fugitives to the Germans and hated by most Germans because they were different than others. Jews were not allowed to sit on the same benches or drink from the same water fountains. Kids were sent to a death camp if they couldn't work for Germans. A death camp is a place were Nazis sent Jews and others off to go to a place that was poorly built with a fenced area like a big chicken coop. The camp was very little and the food was a piece of bread and soup, sometimes the soup was just grass and water, and the bread would just be hay blended together.   There were at least 1.1 million Jewish kids killed. Germans boycotted Jews' businesses and looted stores and put out of businesses by Nazi for no reason. The Jews had to sew a star to their jacket and paint one star on ever window of their business. The Gestapo tortured and killed Jews just as a joke. They thought that killing Jews was funny; they would hang them and laugh. The Gestapos were basically Nazi cops. Jews were banned from having jobs unless they were forced and weren't paid or paid with very little food; they were also under paid. Some Germans helped the Jews hide from the Nazis, but some Jew were found. The Nazis only slowed down when they ran out of Jews to kill. There were also more than just Jews killed. There were also gypsies homosexual, disabled people and many more kinds of people whowere different. It's dumb that people did that to each other. There was no reason for those people to be treated so badly. People shouldn't treat each other like they're hunted animals. If any one were to treat anyone like they shouldn't be treated you should stand up for them. Or if anyone was different they shouldn't be harmed because they are different. Do not judge people because there different.

My upstander is Hans Von Donhanyi. He was born in January 1, 1903 in Austria. His parents' names were Elisabeth and Enro. His wife's name was Christer; their kids named Klaus, Christoph and Barbara. Han was an upstander of the Holocaust during World War II. He worked in the intelligence part of the war, and that was how he found out everything that was going on. He was an upstander because in 1942 of September he saved 13 Jews in risk of his own life. Hans went to many secret meetings to plan an escape plan so that he could take the elders, kids, and crippled Jews to Switzerland. But The SS suspected that Hans was helping the Jews. "He was initially charged with foreign currency violations, which he performed in order to transfer the rescued Jews' funds to a Swiss bank. (The Righteous Among the Nation)." Hans's goal was to save the Jews from the camp. Sadly later on was caught by the Gestapo and arrested. He was sent to a death camp and hang in April 1943.

Hans was an upstander because he stood up for someone in need of help and he helped the Jews escape from the Holocaust. Before, I didn't know much about the Holocaust but now that I know what bad things happened during that time it helped me realize to stand up for people more. Be an upstander and help someone no matter who they are. I feel if that if there were more people who can stand up for someone and not judge people, the world would have less hate in it. We can take this experience and make sure this doesn't happen again. Be an upstander and speak up. As part of Nazi final purge of ant-Reich suspect, Von Han Donhayi was an executed in April 1945.

Work Cited

'The Holocaust Overview." Yad Vashem site. 2016. Web. 12 Feb 2016

"The Righteous Among The Nation words document" Yad Vashem site 2016 Web. 12   Feb 2016

Else Blochwitz – Holocaust Upstander

Riley Rulo

"The Nazis were at their most efficient from April – November 1942 – 250 days in which they murdered some 2.5 million Jews (The Holocaust Overview, page 1)." It's sad to realize that 2.5 million Jews were dead in only 250 days, even having 6 million Jews murdered in four-and-a-half years is so sad to think about. The Holocaust was the death of 6 million Jews, murdered by the German Nazis. The Nazi exile of the Jews began in 1933. The murder of the Jews was committed during

World War II. When the Germans started to run out of Jews to kill, they slowed down on killing the Jews. When the Allies defeated the Germans they stopped killing the Jews. There was no escape for the Jews. The German Nazis traced and hunted down the hidden Jews. The Germans thought being a Jew was a crime, so all Jews had to be put to death. The Nazis thought that every Jew, the men, the women, the children, were all brought to concentration camps to suffer and die, with no responsibility, no hope, and had a slight chance of living. Most of the Jews from Europe died in 1945. There was no more of the civilization that developed over 2,000 years. The survivors came from all over. They were in very bad shape after the Holocaust. They were skin and bones, sick, starving, and tired. After the Holocaust they didn't give up on living, they decided to rebuild their families and communities. The Jews never gave revenge to the Nazis. The Jews and everybody were puzzled. The Jews did not know what to do to the Nazis who did these horrific crimes. Instead of seeking revenge to the German Nazis, the surviving Jews decided to rebuild. The Jews made new families and new communities. Forever under the shadows of those who died in the horrible times of the Holocaust are new families. The Jews who survived the Holocaust were near death, but still had to make new life stories. The survived Jews had memories that affected them all through life. It's hard to think about the horrible things that the German Nazis did to the Jews. It's nice to know that Else Blochwitz was an upstander and tried her vey best to help some Jews during the Holocaust. Else Blochwitz was an upstander during the Holocaust.

Else Blochwitz was an upstander during the Holocaust because she hid and took care of the Jews in her house and other places. She used her job, being an air-warden, to hide Jews in the abandoned apartments and cellars. Blochwitz gave shelter to a half - Jewish woman, Rita Grabowski, during the Holocaust. It's great to know the good things that my upstander, Else Blochwitz did to help Jews. Else Blochwitz was born in 1899. Else Blochwitz was German. She worked as an air warden of a large apartment building in Berlin. Blochwitz had an entry way to abandoned apartments and cellars. These abandoned places were used to hide Jews. The Jews were taken care of in her home and other places. Blochwitz was known by her underground alias. She was in charge of having a group of people who donated food, illegal packages, clothing, and letters to the displaced Jews. Else Blochwitz also sent food and toys to children in the Minsk ghetto. The Jewish children gave thanks by sending friendly pictures and letters before they all died in the Holocaust. Else Blochwitz had a deported friend named Herta Arndt, and former lodger. Herta was a doomed inmate in the Minsk ghetto who was murdered in Lublin on October 10, 1943. Else had a very kind heart to do such great things to help the Jews. "Else Blochwitz took advantage of this position to hide and maintain Jews 'on the run' both in her own and in other places (The Righteous Among the Nations, Blochwitz Family Rescue Story, page 1)."

Else Blochwitz was an upstander during the Holocaust because she hid Jews in her house and other places. She used her job, being an air-warden to hide Jews in the abandoned apartments and cellars. After studying the Holocaust I learned how to be an upstander, and how to act in the right times. The Holocaust was a horrible time in history, filled with horrific things that the German Nazis did to the Jews. I learned a lot of information about the Holocaust. We should all be upstanders so another Holocaust will not happen. The Holocaust was a very scary time to learn about. You should not tease or hurt anyone, but especially people who are victims of bullying or Holocaust. It's scary to think that the Holocaust could happen again. The Holocaust can happen to African Americans, Mexicans, Muslims, etc. The Holocaust was a terrible time in history that I don't want to be repeated. If everybody is an upstander and stay and upstander then the Holocaust will not happen again. If one person is an upstander and tries to make a change, then other people might want to be an upstander and make a change too. After learning about the Holocaust I decided I want to be an upstander.

Works Cited

"The Holocaust Overview." Yad Vashem site. 2016. 9 Feb. 2016

"The Righteous Among the Nations, Blochwitz Family Rescue Story." Yad Vashem site. 2016.. 10 Feb. 2016.

The Krebs Family – Holocaust Upstander

Rosemary Bauzon

 "And so, within seven months, I lost my father, my brother, and my mother. I am the only one who survived. This is what the Germans did to us, and these are things that should never be forgotten. On the other hand, we had our revenge: the survivors were able to raise magnificent families– among them myself. This is the revenge and the consolation. (The Holocaust Overview How Vast Was the Crime, page 1)." The Holocaust was when the German Nazis slaughtered 6 million Jews. Although the killing of the Jewish people began in 1933 the majority of the death was accomplished during World War II. In four-and-a-half years the Nazis executed the Jews. During their most powerful time (April –November 1942) that lasted 250 days the Nazis exterminated 2.5 million Jews. The Nazis never held back. When there were no more Jewish people to assassinate that's when they would slow down, and when their colleagues conquered them that's when they stopped. There was no freedom and no hope for the Jewish people. The Nazis were not satisfied with just the destruction of communities. They began to track down hidden Jews and Jews who were fugitives were hunted down one by one. By being a Jew the crime was so abundant that every Jew had to be killed. The women, men, kids, the devoted, the dispassionate, the traitors, the healthful, the gifted, the sick, and the passive. Jewish people died with no mercy, no pardon, no remission nor either comfort. A great amount of Jews died in Europe in 1945. The Jewish society that had thrived for 2,000 years was now gone. There were three survivors of the Holocaust (one from a town, and two from the host) who were disoriented, famished, deprived at a great measure. They collected the remains of their strength and the remains

of their humanity and started over. They never did give justice to the people that had caused their great misery. Instead they started a new life which include new families, (still crying over the ones that have died) new stories to tell, (still hurting with the wounds that were left by the devastating disaster) and new communities. (Left remembering the communities lost in the Holocaust). Even through the disaster killed millions of innocent lives, there were people who became upstanders and stood up for what they believed and that people shouldn't be killed for being who they are. The Krebs family was among those people.

The reason that the Krebs family (Paul Krebs and Helene Krebs) was a German upstander during the Holocaust was because they let fugitives stay in their home. Those fugitives were Edith Meyer and Herbert Heinen. The reason they were fugitives was because the Nazi law didn't allow relationships or marriages between Aryans and Jews. Herbert was an Aryan and Edith was a Jew, and they were engaged. Helene was also a Jew but was luckily protected from being deported since she was married to a man who was not Jewish so they didn't have to be separated from each other. Unfortunately, when Edith visited her friend Paula Berntgen, the person she shipped her belongings to, Paula refused to give Edith back her things and instead told the authorities they were a couple and gave them their address of the Krebs apartment. Luckily Edith and Herbert already left but sadly Paul and Helene were arrested. At the beginning they denied the fact that they would ever let fugitives in their home but they later then admitted that they let them stay for 8 days. The police and the SS authorities had to make sure that Helene would be okay to be deported since she was pregnant. Helene was deported to Auschwitz in 1942 in December when she was 7 months pregnant but Paul was released since his employers said he was a valued worker at the industry of armaments. Paul felt lonely without his beloved wife so to free her he wrote many letters to the Gestapo begging for his wife to be free. "My life has lost its value after my wife has been taken from me. Her family has been living in Germany for over 400 years. . . I ask to spare me, a German who fulfilled his duty during the World War, who today is fulfilling his duty working for the fatherland, expecting the birth of my child, which is carried by my wife... My wife deserves not only compassion but also her rights as the daughter of a German soldier who fell in the World War in Germany. I therefore ask: return my wife to me". The request was then sent to Berlin, and then in 1942 in January 10th he got a response stating that Helene Sara Krebs arrived in Auschwitz on the 10th of December, but unfortunately died in the camp's hospital. She was then cremated and her ashes were preserved in the local crematorium. Paul Krebs did survive the World War, but sadly died in 1955. "They first took a truck to Koenigsberg (today Kaliningrad, Russia), then traveled by train to Berlin, and from there to Solingen, where they arrived on April 30, 1942, at the home of their friends, Paul and Helene Krebs, who hid them in their apartment. (Krebs Family, The Righteous Among the Nations, page 1)." The Krebs family may have died, but we still remember them for being an upstander and for standing up for what they believe in.

The Krebs family was an upstander during the Holocaust. The reason they are upstanders is because they let fugitives stay in their home. The Holocaust and the Krebs family helped me learn life's lesson. The Holocaust taught me that it wasn't just a dark disastrous time that there could be light to the story and that we shouldn't judge people who are different. Just imagine if the whole world was the same just think about how boring it would be. Learning about the Holocaust has inspired me to help our generation prevent another Holocaust and instead except people for who they are. The Krebs family has taught me to stand up for the people who are being picked on and try to make them feel like they belong. They have encouraged me to be an upstander and to stand up for what is right and to teach others to do the same.

Works Cited

"The Righteous Among The Nations, Krebs Family." Yad Vashem site. 2016. Web. 11 Feb.   2016

"The Holocaust Overview How Vast Was the Crime." Yad Vashem site. 2016. Web. 11 Feb.   2016

Otto Berger – Holocaust Upstander

Saray Brown

"The Holocaust was the murder by Nazi Germany of 6 million Jews (The Holocaust Overview, page 1). The persecution of the Jews began after 1933, during World War II the mass murder. It took four-and-a-half years to murder 6 million by Germans and their accomplices. The Nazis were at their best from April to November in 1942 and within those 250 days 2.5 million Jews were killed. There was no escape from the Nazis. The murderers were not satisfied with destroying the communities; they traced and hunted down each Jew and fugitive. The crime of being a Jew was so significant that every single Jew had to be put to death. The men, women And children; the committed, the traitors, the sickly and the weary all were meant to suffer and succumb, with no reprieve, no prospect, no possible forgiveness, no chance for solving. In 1945 most of the Jews of Europe were dead. A civilization that flourished for 2,000 years. The survivors one from a town, two from a host dazed, emaciated, sad beyond measure their vitality and their remaining sparks of their humanity, and rebuilt. Jews never meted out justice for their tormentors. The fact that the Nazis killed and hurt the Jews is just a horrible crime and thing to do. Jews are survivors and they will always be that. Their loyalty and pride will always stay intact. Their sacrifice will forever be in people's hearts and it will go on. Otto Berger was an upstander in the Holocaust.

My upstander is Otto Berger he is an upstander because he helped take care of a Jew, Fedur Bruck. Fedur Bruck's family lived in Upper Silesia where they owned a hotel. Otto Berger's friend Brucks served in German army in World War II, studied dental medicine and worked as a dentist in the schools of Liegnite. Nazi activity elevating even before 1933, Bruck was fired and moved to Berlin. He worked as a dentist for the school system but not for long. In 1933, all Jews were removed from government position, he too lost his Job. He was authorized to treat only Jews patients. On 12 October 1942, Bruck received information that he is going to be deported to the east. He did not present himself and went into hiding. He found shelter with his Berlin associates, and finally reached the home of another dentist Otto Berger. After the war Bruck relates on how the contact was made; "I met Otto at the beginning of 1943 through a mutual friend. When he learned that I was living as an illegal because of my being persecuted on racial grounds, he immediately on our first meeting, supplied me with food and offered to hide me if I had to leave my present hideout, (The Righteous Among Nations, Berger Family Rescue story, page 1)." Otto continued to hide Bruck for 21 months, he had to move twice, his home had been bombed by Allied airplanes, and a second time when the apartment became high-risk. Bruck had no racial card or official ID, Berger not only protected him and sheltered him, but also provided food and all his needs. He finally managed to get Bruck false ID, but continued to shelter him until the war was over. Bruck began to search for his pre-war friends. From Upper Silesia Bruck's former assistant who too had moved to Berlin, where she worked for Driblascke, Adolf Hitler's dentist is Blaske. When the war was over, she was called by the Russian commander to help identify Hitlers remains with the help of his dental records. Bruck showed her and provided some of his expertise. Even though the Soviets offered him to take over the Blascke clinic, Bruck moved to the American zone of Berlin and in 1947 emigrated to the USA. Bruck settled in New York, where he lived until his death in 1982. From Upper Silesia where Otto was also from. He was born in Oppland in 1900. In 1930 he joined Nazi Party and the SA. On August 2009 Otto Berger was recognized as Righteous among Nations. Otto Berger was a kind enough man to help somebody who he didn't even know. He provided for Fedur Bruck for months and protected him and kept him safe until it was safe to go.

Otto Berger was an upstander in the Holocaust. He was an upstander because he helped Fedur Bruck, a Jew, let him hide in his own home and provided for him. Fedur Bruck ran so many times until he found Otto Berger. Otto Berger and Fedur Bruck were survivors of the Holocaust. What I have learned while reading the Holocaust and reading about my upstander is learning how to act certain times and working on knowing how to act. I learned that the Holocaust was a bad thing. I also learned a lot of information. I learned that we should be an upstander so another Holocaust won't happen again. The Holocaust was scary because the Nazis were killing the Jews. Don't tease or hurt someone who is a victim. It's scary to think that the Holocaust could happen again. Scary things can happen to women, African Americans, Mexicans, etc. But the most important thing that I've learned is that be the best person you can be. Don't let evil consume you like evil consumed the Nazis. Be the better person. Be an upstander.

Works Cited

"The Holocaust Overview, page 1." Yad Vashem site. 2016. Web. 9 Feb. 2016

"The Righteous Among Nations, Berger Family Rescue story, page 1." Yad Vashem site. 2016. Web. 9 Feb. 2016

Frieda Adam – Holocaust Upstander

Shantalle Saavedra

 "There was no escape. The murders were not content with destroying the communities; they also traced each hidden Jew and hunted down each fugitive. The crime of being a Jew was so big that every single one had to be put to death – the men, the women, the children; the committed, the disinterested, the apostates; the healthy, and creative, the sickly and the lazy – all were meant to suffer and die, with no reprieve, no hope, no possible amnesty, nor chance for alleviation (Holocaust, Overview, page 1)." The Holocaust was a tragedy because being Jewish was a crime so big. In 1933, the Nazis abused the Jews; mass murder was committed during World War II. In 1945, most Jews of Europe were dead. The Nazis killed 2.5 million Jews in 250 days. The Nazis killed 6 million Jews in total. Once the Holocaust was over everyone came out from hiding or came back from where they were sent. They made new families and forever remembered the people who died, new life testimony, forever scarred from their wounds; new houses, forever haunted by the loss. It is sad knowing that many people died, but thanks to certain upstanders, some people were able to survive. Frieda Adam was an upstander of the Holocaust.

Frieda Adam was a German upstander because in 1942, Erna's mom, Frieda Adam's friend, was sent away to Auschwitz because they were Jewish, leaving Erna Puterman to take care of her deaf brother alone. Erna Puterman did not know how to take care of her brother, so Erna went to Frieda Adam for help and advice because they had been friends for a very long time so Erna trusted Frieda. Frieda said immediately "As long as there is food for us, there will be food for you, too, (Frieda Adam | Germany, page 1)." Frieda Adam did not allow the Jewish laws to affect her friendship. Erna and her brother went under Frieda Adam's protection. Erna Puterman and her deaf brother stayed for two years in her house and continued to arrange her security. When Frieda's husband came back from the Army and found out that Frieda was hiding two Jews, he then started to blackmail her. After that, Frieda was forced to find a new spot for them to hide. After the Holocaust was over Frieda Adam went to the spot where she hid Erna Puterman and Erna's brother to tell them they could go to their house because the Holocaust was over. Frieda, Frieda's three little children, Erna and Erna's brother all survived the Holocaust. I think that it was super hard on Frieda because Frieda had to take care of Erna and Erna's brother for almost half of the Holocaust, she also took care of Frieda's three children at ages 2, 4, and 6, not only them but Frieda also had to take care of herself, too. I think Frieda was scared because of her husband. Frieda said, "My husband was really mean and he was very tough on her and the kids." Frieda's husband was still blackmailing her so Frieda thought that her husband was going to tell the Nazis that she was hiding two Jews in her house, and that the Nazis were going to kill her entire family.

Frieda was an upstander during the Holocaust. Frieda Adam was an upstander because Frieda protected Erna and Erna's brother from the Nazis. What I learned from my upstander and the Holocaust was how to act during the Holocaust and how to be an upstander so another Holocaust will not happen again. It is very terrifying to think that the Holocaust could happen again because nobody should tease or hurt a victim. Horrifying stuff can happen to a woman, African Americans, Mexicans, etc. I am learning how to be an upstander so if another Holocaust really does happen again I will know exactly what to do. I am also working on knowing when to act. The Holocaust was a tragedy because many people died. I think that the Holocaust was a very sad and horrifying moment for many people because many people died some died at a very young age, like maybe a newborn or an infant probably or maybe some died at an old age. I think that Frieda was a very good upstander because she risked her life and her three children's lives because she wanted to help her best friend Erna Puterman and her brother. Frieda helped because she also felt bad for Erna so she tried to help her and her brother from being killed by the Nazis because it was sad to lose a friend that you knew almost your whole life.

Work Cited

"The Holocaust Overview." Yad Vashem site. 2016. Web. 12 Feb. 2016

"The Righteous Among the Nations, Frieda Adam." Yad Vashem site 2016. Web. 11 Feb.   2016

"Frieda Adam | Germany." JFR site.2016. Web. 18 February 2016

Holocaust Essay: Oskar Schindler

Victoria Durunna

The Holocaust caused approximately 6 million out of the 9 million Jews who lived in Europe their lives between 1933 and 1945. A tiny fraction of Jews were prosecuted in Germany, Poland, and Romania. The Nazis were the leading power in Germany and believed that the Germans were "racially superior" and the Jews were "inferior" along with the gypsies, people with physical and mental disabilities, and Poles. All of these people were placed for the "Final Solution" which was the plan to murder all of the people who were considered "racially inferior" (projetaladin.org). Former member of the Nazi Party, Oskar Schindler saved approximately 1,200 Jews during the Holocaust (Oskar Schindler).

One must not judge without knowing one's true nature, much like in the case of Oskar Schindler. Oskar Schindler was a German who was born on April 28, 1908, in

Zwittau of Austria-Hungary, which is currently the Moravia in the Czech Republic. Schindler was born in a family honored with money. He grew up Catholic but lavage in the many sins like gambling, adultery, and drinking. At the age of nineteen Schindler married his wife Emilie Schindler. Though he was married he always had a mistress or two around. His family business eventually failed and Schindler became a salesman with a great opportunity that disguised itself in the name of the war. Schindler came into Poland with the SS and became active in the black-market and became acquainted with the local Gestapo, entrapping them with women, money and alcohol. With these new connections, Schindler got himself a factory which was appropriated by Jewish people which was considered the cheapest labor around (Oskar Schindler). At first, Schindler was a lot like many other German industrialist, motivated by profit and not caring about how he got it. But something changed in him and he began to falter from the Nazism view. Poland used to be a place of heaven for nearly 500,000 Jews but with the Nazi regime the Jewish community were pushed into the ghettos. Not soon after the Nazis took the belongings and selling them to the German industrialist. Eventually, the Nazis did a raid on many ghettos and Schindler saw one of them which became the catalyst to helping out as many Jews as he can. Not soon after getting the Emalia factory, which produced enamel goods and munitions to supply the German front this is where the removal of Jews to death camps began in earnest it started with himself getting permission to keep Jewish people working in his factory. The ones who worked in the factory were the Jews that had some kind of wealth left and invested them into the factory (Oskar Schindler). After witnessing the brutality towards the Jews first hand Schindler's activity in keeping the Jews that work in his factory, who he called his "children," greatly increased. "Beyond this day, no thinking person could fail to see what would happen," he said later. "I was now resolved to do everything in my power to defeat the system." (Oskar Schindler).

Eventually, the Russians finally found themselves into Poland, weakening Germany's hold on the country. With this threat, the Nazi regime now wanted to quickly bring the rest of the Jews through the camps. Schindler used his resources to get 900 Jewish workers from a concentration camp into his factory, which was in Zablocie. The factory operated for a year making defective bullets for German guns (Oskar Schindler). Schindler fled to Argentina after the war ended with his wife and many of his workers and bought a farm there as well. Not soon after Schindler abandoned his wife and the rest of the people he brought along and went back to dividing his time between Germany and Israel where he was taken care of and celebrated by his "Schindlerjuden," who are some of the Jewish people he liberated from many of the Nazi raids (Oskar Schindler). Schindler dies in the city of Hildesheim in 1974.

My upstander influenced me because when he was younger he made mistakes and did a lot of things he shouldn't have done, but as he saw the horrible acts happening around him, he learned that saving thousands of lives was a lot better in the end. It also makes me think that it doesn't really matter about your past as long as you are doing better things in the future and letting go of the foolish things. I think upstanding is important because it can help a lot of people. It also gives others who don't usually speak up a voice and make them feel like they are being heard and listened to. What I hope to do is to be a voice that will impact others in a positive way, and I hope to make a change and difference in this world on how we perceive color people and hopefully it will last for generations to come. First I would make a speech that will possibly get through the minds of everyone to understand. Secondly, I will provide examples of situations, pictures to support it, and illustrations to make it more interesting to people so they would want to learn more about it. Being an upstander is probably one of the greatest things you can do because you are standing up and taking action and not just watching the problem become larger.

The Holocaust cost millions of people their lives, but despite the awfulness that was happening there were still heroes among the many people do evil deeds. It was previously said that we should not judge others before knowing one's true nature. Schindler was a man who was at one point siding with the Nazis because he found it as a good way to make money no matter what wrong it may bring about. Eventually Schindler changed to saving thousands of Jewish people. We and the survivors do not know why he did it and many don't care, after all actions speak louder than word and Schindler actions surely proved that he cared about and understood the wrong that was happening around him.

Josef and Maria Dinzinger- Holocaust Upstander

Zachary Harbaugh (Runner-up)

 "The Holocaust was the murder by Nazi Germany of 6 million Jews. While the Nazi persecution of the Jews began in 1933, the mass murder was committed during World War II. It took the Germans and their accomplices four-and-a half years to murder 6 million Jews (Holocaust Overview, page 1)." The Holocaust was a horrible event in history for the Jews. The Holocaust was where Nazi Germany executed nearly 6 million Jews. Nazi Germany killed most Jews in the timeline of 250 days where they had murdered 2.5 million Jews. When World War II was over that's the first time Nazi Germany stopped killing Jews. When most Jews were dead and the Nazis did not find anymore that's when the Nazis would slow down. There was no escape for the Jews. When the Nazis ran out of Jews to kill they would track down all who were hiding. No matter what age or gender the Nazis would kill them or send them away to concentration camps all around German territory. All the Jews had little to no chance to live. No matter what gender or gender Nazis would kill. The Nazis would kill them all no matter what. If they did not kill the Jews they would send them away to concentration camps and make them work like slaves only if while the rest were killed. In 1945 almost all the Jewish fugitives in Europe had been executed by Nazi Germany. A civilization grew for around 2,000 years had been destroyed by Germany. There were

approximately three Jewish survivors after World War II ended. Together all three rebuilt the Jewish community and made hope. Many were haunted by the past, all the Jews making new life stories. Some Germans were also upstanders who helped the Jews who had escaped from concentration camps or foot marches. Very little Germans had helped the Jewish people who had escaped. While some Jews who escaped got lucky not all them were helped. Most had been gotten caught or had been tattled on by German civilians. An example of one upstander was Josef Dinzinger.

Josef Dinzinger was an example of a German Holocaust upstander. He hid two Jewish concentration camp inmates. When Josef saw the two walk up to his farm called Waldhof located near the moor land of the Bavarian village of Parnkofen he instantly knew that they were Jewish concentration camp inmates. One of the inmates, Yerucham Apfel from Mielec, Poland was an electrician and his friend who is unnamed who managed to slip away from one of the foot marches. Josef had taken them and hid them in his Silo at his farm. It was tough for Josef to hide the inmates because he hid them while a German officer and two of his nephews, who were part of the Hitler youth organization, were also living at Dinzinger's farm. While the inmates were hiding in Josef's silo at his farm, Josef had just acted like they were not there and acted normal. Josef had given the inmates plenty of food, water to drink, and soft blankets. After a week or two of hiding the Jews, Josef's farm was declared headquarters for Nazi Germany. As well as sending the Jews away somewhere Josef also bribed village officials to make their existence legal. "When a few days later the farm was requisitioned by the army as its headquarters, Dinzinger did not just send his illegal visitors away. He bribed some village officials and arranged for Apfel and his friend to receive false papers that legalized their existence (Dinzinger family page, 1)." In 1957, Yerucham Apfel had returned to his savior and paid his respects to Josef Dinzinger who had died in 1948 at age 54. Before he helped the inmates escape, Josef was just working on his farm and doing nothing until he saw and rescued Yerucham Apfel and his friend. Later on, Josef Dinzinger was recognized by Yad Vashem's site in honor of being a Holocaust upstander.

Josef Dinzinger was one of many Holocaust upstanders. Josef was a Holocaust upstander because he hid two Jews in a silo then after his farm was declared headquarters for Nazi Germany he bribed village officials to make the two survivors existence legal and not illegal while sending them away. There were lots of things that people could learn about while studying the Holocaust. You can prevent a lot of things like another Holocaust if you become an upstander stand up for other races that are targeted by armies and other governments. What I learned from the Holocaust is that you shouldn't be offensive to a race or you could probably start a war. So you should just act like there is no such thing as race and treat everybody the same way you do with your friend and family. Now since I learned a lot about the Holocaust it makes me want to learn more historic events that happened in the past way before the Holocaust even started and even a little bit after it ended. I also want to treat people how I want to be treated and be an

144

upstander whenever I see bullying whether someone is bullying me, my friend, or a random person so we could stop bullying and be one step closer to world peace

Works Cited

"The Holocaust Overview." Yad Vashem site. 2016. Web. 12 Feb. 2016

"The Righteous Among The Nations, Dinzinger family." Yad Vashem site. 2016. Web. 12 Feb.   2016

Anna Altynnikova - Holocaust Upstander

Tyler Johnson (Special Award)

"And so, within seven months, I lost my father, my brother, and my mother. I am the only one who survived. This is what the Germans did to us, and these are things that should never be forgotten. On the other hand, we had our revenge: the survivors were able to raise magnificent families – among them myself. This is the revenge and the consolation (Kopolovich, page 1)." Think about what this person went through. It must have been horrible to be a part of this. How can such a thing like this ever happen? Families killed, hearts broken, loved ones lost, and all hope lost. Even after all the torture, death, and misery their revenge was rebuilding. They were peaceful. Kopolovich is saying that after every thing that happened to them, the Jews still continued peacefully.   The holocaust began in 1933, during World War II, and is the killing of six million Jews by the Germans, or Nazis. It took the Germans 4.5 years to kill all of those Jews. The Germans got a lot of killing done in April-November 1942; in 250 days, they killed 2.5 million Jews. The killing started to slow down when the Jew population was running dry, and then the killing stopped when the allies took over. There was no escape, the Germans tried to hunt down every last Jew. The men, women, children, the ones who were trying hard to succeed in life , the disinterested, the betrayers who left others, the healthy and creative, the unhealthy and the careless were all meant to take in all the pain they could and rot away with nothing to live for anymore. No forgiveness, no hope, no possible pardon, and not even a chance to be cheered up or to feel better. By 1945, almost all of the Jews of Europe were deceased. A community that lived for about 2,000 years was no more. The survivors from towns all over the area and the ones who were not even prepared for such an end to their daily lives, they were affected by all of this. Every death that happened throughout those years was dearly missed. The Jewish communities were deleted from the planet by the Nazis. They never brought justice to their tormentors, but what justice could be gained after such a crime? All the killing that happened over the years, the destruction that was caused could all just come right back again if they tried to get justice. So they turned to rebuilding: new families that will always be under the shade of those gone; new life stories, broken from the Holocaust; new communities, forever tuned upside down by the loss. Altynnikova Anna, during all of this killing, was an upstander during the Holocaust.

Anna Altynnikova was an Upstander because she saved the lives of two Jewish girls by getting them fake identity papers. "In tears, the two girls told the tragic fate of their family and how they managed to escape the massacre (The Righteous Among The Nations, Altynnikova Anna, page 1)." Anna Altynnikova was born in 1886 and her death date is unknown. Her Nationality is Ukrainian. Her family members were Anna Lushcheyeva, Anna Altynnikova, and Olga Rozhchenko (the daughter). They all lived in Kiev when the Holocaust came upon them. On September 29, 1941, the Jews that were following a German order went to an assembly near Babi Yar at night. During that night, Anna Lushcheyeva heard a knocking sound on her house's window. When she opened the window, two Jewish daughters climbed into the bedroom. The girls cried as they told the fate of their family and how they escaped the slaughter. The family was kind to them and got the daughters shelter for one month in the house, hiding in the basement when needed. They also got help from a neighbor who was a member of the underground association. The neighbor helped two girls get fake identity papers which allowed them to walk through Ukraine for the time of the occupation. After all of that trouble, the girls survived the war and later immigrated to Israel.

Altynnikova Anna was an upstander during the Holocaust. She was an upstander because she saved the lives of two Jewish girls by hiding them in the basement and by getting them fake identity papers so they wouldn't get caught by the Germans as Jews. After learning a lot of information about the Holocaust, I have realized that we should all be upstanders when it comes to bullying or any kind of harm because it can become a threat if not stopped early on. For example, some people hate Muslims and want them out of some states or even dead; this could possibly start another Holocaust. If another Holocaust were to happen, it could be against any race or religion Mexicans, African-Americans, etc. If we could all be upstanders, another Holocaust most likely wouldn't happen again. So stand up and stop bullying so we can prevent the Holocaust from taking over. I learned all of this from Mr. Marks. Mr. Marks was a Holocaust survivor who came to our school to give his testimony about the Holocaust and what he went through. He also talked about how we could stop another holocaust from happening. In other words, I am glad Mr. Marks came to our school to help us really understand what the holocaust did.

Works Cited
"The Holocaust Overview." Yad Vashem site. 2016. Web. 12 Feb. 2016
"The Righteous Among The Nations, Altynnikova Anna." Yad Vashem site. 2016. Web. 12   Feb. 2016

Dr. Rudolf Bertram Holocaust Upstander

Nathan A Killian (Special Award)

Doctor Bertram risked his life on a daily basis to save the lives of his Jewish patients. The Nazi Germany persecution of Jews began in 1933. In the 1920s to the 1930s Europe saw racial claims, that said, Jews are dangerous and inferior. In 1938 the Nazi party embarked on a campaign against the Jews. This included destroying Synagogues, mass arrests, looting and destruction of Jewish-owned businesses. Jews were soon forced to the ghettos and were only allowed to take very few personal items with them. The Ghettos were parts of the cities and towns that were walled off by Nazis. Jews were forced to work and had almost no food. 14 million Jews were soon moved to concentration camps for labor when during WWII. About 2.5 million allied Prisoners of War were also forced to do labor in concentration camps. Concentration camps were the Nazis final solution for Jews and Prisoners of War. Part of the Nazi torture of Jews included cruel medical experiments. Almost all the Jews that died during WWII were in concentration camps. If Jews did not die in the ghetto or get killed by gas chambers, they were enslaved in concentration camps. In the end about six million Jews were murdered in four and a half years. Just from April to November 1942, in 250 days they murdered two and a half million Jews. The Holocaust was a horrific and brutal time of murder, slavery, torture, and sickness. It showed the worst humanity could do to itself but it also showed the best people could do for each other.

Dr. Rudolf Bertram was a German Doctor that helped save Jews in his care from Nazi authorities. He was one of many German upstanders during the Holocaust helped Jews. Dr. Rudolf Bertram was born in 1893 in Olpe in Westphalial. Dr. Bertram was the Chief Surgeon at the Catholic hospital of St. Joseph and Marine hospital in Gelsenkirchen-Horst and Rotthausen. Nearby was the Gelsenkirchen concentration camp were about 112,000 Hungarian-Jewish women deports were forced into labor at Krupp armament plant. On September 11, 1944 a massive air raid, killed or wounded many exposed Jewish women. After the air raid had ended, Dr. Bertram had to treat the wounded Hungarian-Jewish women in person. Dr. Bertram had a large risk to take, he could administered them doses of precious penicillin (which was forbidden medication for Jewish patients.) and possibly get killed by Gestapo officers. He decided to give them doses of penicillin. He had another risk to take. A patient by the name of Ermine Festinger, who was one of 17 Hungarian-Jewish women hospitalized at Marine Hospital. She had her leg amputated. He had a risk of saving. Dr. Bertram had threated to resign, when Gestapo officials exerted pressure for her early release from Marine Hospital. That when he decided to save her. When the Gestapo officers returned one month later, Dr. Bertram, acting with the rest of the medical staff, hid Festinger in one of the storerooms. They pretended that she had disappeared. When the Holocaust came to an end, Festinger had survived the Holocaust Thanks to Dr. Rudolf Bertram.

Festinger later testified about her rescuers conduct and probably lived a great life knowing that she survived brutal time in history.

The Nazi persecution of Jews was the one of the most brutal times in modern history. About six million Jews were murdered, during the Holocaust. A few German citizens like Doctor Bertram hated the brutal torture on these innocent souls and did something about it. These people would become some of the many German upstanders during the holocaust. Dr. Rudolf Bertram was one of these people. He gave doses of precious penicillin to Hungarian-Jewish patients after a mass air raid. He saved a Hungarian-Jewish patient named Fastinger, who had her leg amputated. By hiding her in the hospital storerooms, she survived the Holocaust. One thing that I or anyone can learn from this paper is to learn about the past so that no one will repeat what Adolf Hitler did to Jewish people. When someone repeats something brutal from the past no good will ever come out of it. A second thing that I/anyone can learn from this paper is to be an upstander. Whenever I see bullying it's kind of what Adolf Hitler did to Germany. You may think it's hard to stand up to bullying but, people like Dr. Rudolf Bertram were upstanders during the Holocaust. They could have been murdered for helping or saving Jews. Learning about the holocaust makes me inspired to stand up for people and be an upstander not a bystander. The people that risked their lives to help and save Jews during the Holocaust were upstanders. They knew that they had to help these people before they were killed. Long story short what I have learned is in this is to never repeat what Hitler did and to be an upstander. For some unknown reason "Bertram FAIMLY-The Righteous Among the Nations." Only works on DRMS computers. I hive tried to find it on my own computer and family computer and I can not find the site I got my info about Dr. Rudolf Bertram.

Works cited

"The Holocaust Overview." Yad Vashon site. 2016. Web. 12 Feb. 2016

"Bertram FAIMLY-The Righteous Among the Nations." Yad Vashon site. Web. 12 Feb. 2016

Holmes Jr. High School, Davis, CA

Jeanne Reeve is an English teacher at O.W. Holmes Junior High school in Davis, California where she has been teaching English for over fifteen years. Social justice and human dignity are at the heart of her Tolerance unit that all her eighth grade students experience on an annual basis. Using historical non-fiction, Mrs. Reeve encourages students to learn about the past in order to create a more peaceful future. As a 2008 co-recipient of the Thong Hy Huynh award, the Davis community has recognized her on-going commitment to students and tolerance. Mr. Bernard Marks is a key part of the Holmes community as he has inspired hundreds of students year after year to "never forget" the injustices of the past with his sobering story of survival.

Mrs. Lisa Mowry

Mrs. Mowry has taught at Holmes Junior High for 23 years. She enjoys traveling and incorporating those travel experiences into her US History curriculum.

True Bravery

Anna Seahill (Co-Winner)

What is bravery? I think that many people might argue that to be brave you must let go of your fears and do what you think is right or what you believe in, but I don't think that that is quite right. In order for a person to be brave, they must embrace their fears and then they must decide that instead of letting those fears take over their lives, they are going to go out into the world, face their fears, and put on a brave face. Bravery is being strong even when the consequences of doing so are deadly.

I think that an amazing example of someone who put on a brave face during the horrific time of the Holocaust is Elisabeth Abegg. She is a woman who demonstrated the qualities needed to be a hero: bravery, stubbornness, and faith in her beliefs. Elisabeth was born in Strasbourg, which is in current-day France, on May 3, 1882. Even though Elisabeth was born more than a century ago, she had the modern belief in equality for all and that kindness toward all ethnicities and nationalities was important. While she was growing up, Elisabeth was able to find a sort of mentor in Albert Schweitzer, who was a famous humanist and theologian among other professions. Although Elisabeth didn't know him personally, he had a huge impact on the way she viewed the world and the way she viewed humans in general. Albert had a strong belief in equality of all human beings, and the holiness and importance of life. These teachings of his helped to shape and mold Elisabeth's ideals and morals while she was growing up in Strasbourg. Without the moral compass that Albert Schweitzer gave to Elisabeth's life, she may have never had the same courage and bravery to help Jews that she demonstrated later on in her life.

After childhood, Elisabeth decided to become a history teacher and moved to Berlin, Germany, in order to pursue her dream. She took up a teaching position at the respected Luisen Madchenschule, an all-girls school where the majority of the students were Jewish. It was there that she passed on all of her beliefs about the necessity of equality to her students. She used Albert Schweitzer's values as a basic foundation for her own style of teaching, and it became her mission that her students learn about how kindness and equal opportunities for everyone are a huge part of making sure the human race lives on and doesn't destroy itself. Elisabeth first began her fight against Hitler and all Nazis when the old director of the Luisen Madchenschule was replaced with a Nazi to govern over the school. To say the least, Elisabeth didn't get along with the new director because her beliefs revolved around equal rights, and the whole idea of Nazis revolved around the belief that some humans are better than others. Because of the moral disagreements, Elisabeth was forced to transfer to a different and less respected school. This eventually led to an early retirement in 1940 because of her refusal to teach students about Nazis. Even though Elisabeth's career ended early, the real work she was going to do for the world was just beginning.

The reason for Elisabeth being forced into retirement is sadly quite simple: she was considered "politically unreliable," and the fact that she didn't agree with Nazi ideals made her a topic of interest for the authorities. At one point in time she was called forth by the Gestapo for questioning, but was released. Although Elisabeth was being watched by the authorities for any rebellious activity, it didn't stop her from remaining in contact with all of her Jewish friends and some of her old students from Luisen Madchenschule. Some people would have not wanted to risk getting into trouble and would have instead decided that cutting ties with all their Jewish friends was the safest thing to do, but Elisabeth proved that she wasn't going to let go of her friends and her past based on ethnicity. Even though Elisabeth could obviously see what the Nazis were doing around her and how they were treating Jewish people, it didn't fully resonate in her mind until it hit home with the deportation of Anna Hirschenberg, one of her best friends who she had known for forty years. This was the seminal event that led to Elisabeth deciding that she was going to help as many Jews as she could from being deported or harmed by the Gestapo. The deportation of Anna was a sad event for Elisabeth, but it was also an inspirational one that started her on the path towards helping Jews stay safe and alive.

The first step that Elisabeth took towards helping Jews was actually more like a bound. She made the bold and life-changing decision to transform her small, three-and-a-half-room apartment that she had been living in with her mother and her sister, Julie, into a makeshift housing center for Jews who were on the run from the Gestapo. Her apartment was utilized as a place for Jews to safely congregate and hide until they could find cover in other locations. Elisabeth was able to operate the shelter she had created by receiving help from members of the Quaker movement, which provided major aid during the Holocaust for Jews who were in need of shelter. Elisabeth was a very caring and passionate woman, which is demonstrated by her changing her entire home into a temporary save haven, even though she didn't have a big home to begin with or a ton of money to spend on the refugees, much less herself. She didn't seem to mind that some of the Jews she took in were strangers to her, but instead she cared about keeping everyone safe and alive. The sad thing is that there were so many people in Germany who could have decided to help Jews if they wanted to, but those people let their fear of being arrested or killed for doing so get in the way of the morally correct thing to do. Elisabeth, however, decided that the risk she was taking was worth it because she was literally saving people from what could have been horrible endings. I'm positive that there were times that Elisabeth was scared or fearful of being caught housing Jews, and being scared is okay as long as you don't let it stop you from doing what is right.

Although Elisabeth could have stopped there with providing safe housing, she was such a dedicated woman that she also gave away some of her food and her sister's food to the Jews seeking refuge within her home. This was a woman who was forced to retire early and then take care of her elderly mother while still providing a place for her sister to live. Elisabeth obviously didn't come from a rich background, and yet she was willing to give up what food she did have to complete strangers that she was letting live in her house. What kind of a person does that? A person who has so much respect for all human life, and a deep caring and understanding for what Jews were going through during the rule of Hitler. Elisabeth provided even more care to the people hiding in her home by handing out food-ration cards to ensure that nobody went hungry. I'm sure that many Jews during this time were extremely worried about what could happen to them or their family, but Elisabeth was able to lessen the stress by making sure that going hungry wasn't an issue. She hosted special dinners in her home every Friday for Jews who needed it, and the point of the dinners extended beyond just simply putting food in people's mouths. They were a time for people to congregate and hopefully forget about everything that was going on outside the comfort of shelter. Even if people were only distracted from the tragedies surrounding them once a week for the short span of dinner, it was much better than living in constant terror. Elisabeth truly cared about the individuals she took in because she not only provided them with housing, but also with food and a chance to forget about how cruel the world had become.

A quality that Elisabeth had to possess throughout her entire time working to keep Jews safe was secrecy. If the Gestapo or anyone else discovered that she was hiding Jews in her home, she could be arrested or worse killed. Not only did she have to worry about being caught herself, but the thought of any of the refugees in her house being found was even more horrifying. If she or anyone else was caught, then everything would have been for nothing. Luckily, this didn't happen. Elisabeth was able to successfully hide many people in her home without ever being caught, which is remarkable enough, but it is even more so because there were some people living nearby that were Nazis. The fact that Elisabeth even decided to house Jews in the first place when she knew that there were Nazis right under her nose was incredibly brave and further demonstrates the lengths she was willing to go to in order to save complete strangers' lives. Not only was there a risk of her Nazi neighbors discovering her shelter, but it was also a concern that any one of her neighbors could report suspicious behavior on her part so as to protect themselves from getting into trouble. The planning and time it took for Elisabeth to ensure that neither she nor any of the hiding Jews was caught is extremely honorable and again shows her commitment to the cause.

Over the course of time that Elisabeth sheltered Jews in her home, it is estimated that she kept about 80 Jews safe from the Gestapo and from Hitler. That is amazing by itself, but Elisabeth went to special lengths to make sure that some specific people were kept out of harm's way as well. Elisabeth decided to help a woman named Liselottte Perles, who was in charge of the Berlin day-care center. Liselottte could not make up her mind about whether or not she should find shelter from the Nazis with her niece, Susie, who was nine years old at the time. Elisabeth strongly believed that the two of them should go into hiding as quickly as possible because they had been living in the "Jews' House." People living in the house were being deported, and therefore rooms were becoming deserted and barren. Elisabeth was able to convince Liselottte that she needed to seek shelter with her niece, and it turns out that Elisabeth had just barely made it because she talked Liselottte into going into hiding the night before the final mass capturing of Jews in Berlin by the Gestapo, which occurred in the beginning of 1943.

By going out of her way to help get two Jewish women to safety, Elisabeth didn't only demonstrate her care for people, but also her patience. If Elisabeth hadn't persevered and convinced Liselottte to hide with her niece, they both could have ended up captured or dead. Some Jewish people didn't want to go into hiding because they thought that it would only make things worse and would lead to harsh consequences, when in actuality it was worth the risk to take cover in hopes of making it through the war.

Another person who Elisabeth was set on helping was a man named Jizchak Schwerzenz. He needed help being secretly transferred into Switzerland, which led Elisabeth to sell some of her own jewelry so it could happen. If it wasn't for the money Elisabeth was able to donate from selling her jewelry, who knows if Jizchak would have ever made it to Switzerland and ultimately to safety.

Elisabeth Abegg was an extraordinarily caring and selfless woman who devoted a major part of her life to helping Jews stay safe and out of reach from the Nazis. Without her help, dozens of Jews could have been put in concentration camps or killed. She was truly selfless because she had absolutely no ulterior motives for doing what she did. In fact, everything she did put her at a higher and higher risk of being caught, but she decided to help nonetheless. She knew that what Hitler and the Nazis were doing was truly awful and she knew that in the end, she would be repaid for all the good she did during her important time on Earth.

Works Cited

"Elisabeth Abegg." Hero Miss. Elisabeth Abegg. About, n.d. Web. 05 Mar. 2016. <http://heroelisabethabegg.weebly.com/about.html>.

"Elisabeth Abegg - The Righteous Among The Nations - Yad Vashem."Elisabeth Abegg - The Righteous Among The Nations - Yad Vashem. Yad Vashem, n.d. Web. 05 Mar. 2016. <http://www.yadvashem.org/yv/en/righteous/stories/abegg.asp>.

"Teachers Who Rescued Jews During the Holocaust." Elisabeth Abegg. Yad Vashem, n.d. Web. 05 Mar. 2016. <http://www.yadvashem.org/yv/en/exhibitions/righteous-teachers/abegg.asp>.

Anton Schmid, a German Hero

Astha Sahoo

The Holocaust was a horrendous and devastating act of Germany toward Jewish citizens; a result of democracy in action. Adolf Hitler, the leader of the Democratic Party instituting the scapegoat for Germany's loss as the fault of the Jews, led this gruesome act that wiped out over 10 million people. Most non-Jews complied with Hitler's theory; but not all. A minority of Germans helped the Jews by hiding them in their houses, apartments, and offices. Others appeared as being loyal to the Nazis and gave the Jews good treatment at the concentration camps. Some Germans smuggled Jews to places with higher chances of survival, risking their own lives in the process. Others, after being warned, kept on helping Jews and were caught and executed; Anton Schmid was one of these great heroes.

Anton Schmid, a man of German ancestry but born in Vienna in 1900, had a serene life. He was an electrician, and owned a small radio shop on the busy streets of Vienna. He was married to Steffi, the love of his life, and had just started a family with one daughter. Unexpectedly, in 1938, Austria was conquered by the Germans and all Austrians were German citizens. At the age of 41, Schmid was forcefully drafted into the German army. However, Schmid was intensely averse to the extermination of Jews. He was compassionate toward the Jews and thought it was inhumane and atrocious to annihilate millions of innocent citizens mercilessly. When he first joined the Nazis, he was posted near Vilnius in the late summer, where he witnessed the herding of thousands of Jews into two ghettos and being led to Ponary to be murdered. This sight touched Schmid's heart in all the sensitive places. He had never seen such a ghastly situation. Whatever loyalty he had for Hitler was gone. He concluded that he would not tolerate such heinous acts anymore, and do what he could to help the innocent victims of the Holocaust.

Soon after, he started helping out the Jews that were being led to the ghettos. He would smuggle Jews to safer places and provide them with edible food to help them survive. Sometimes, he would sneak in food meant for the SS officers inside the jail cells so they had a lower chance of dying. Other times, he would forge their legal papers so that they appeared to be American born citizens. He would not make the Jews work, rather he would let them rest and do the work himself with the help of voluntary Jews. He was never heard to beat, whip, or punish the Jews in any way, shape, or form.

In one letter to his wife, he wrote about the maltreatment of the Jews and how he couldn't abide with the cruelty of the SS soldiers. "You know how it is with my soft heart. I could not think and had to help them," he wrote. After hearing about this activity, his wife disapproved at first. She worried about their only child, the risks of doing so; his death would have a significant impact on the family. Nevertheless, his wife acquiesced as the lives of so many other Jews were more important than two. The decision she took was very painful but selfless; she was sacrificing her husband's life and the idea of a "happy family" for the sake of others' lives.

Although Schmid's acts were humane and benevolent, citizens believed that he was a traitor to his country. After his conviction, Schmid's wife, Steffi, was looked down upon as a supporter of a traitor. She and her daughter were often harassed for this reason; they eventually stayed at home and hired a servant to bring necessary items from the market. Once, while returning from an important errand, Steffi found the window panes of her house smashed and vandalized with graffiti accusing her of heinous crimes that she didn't commit. Nonetheless, time proved her bravery and righteousness.

In addition, Schmid did not think of his acts to be extraordinary or selfless; he wasn't proud of his altruistic actions. At the end of his letter to his wife, he said "I merely behaved as a human being." He was a humble man; even in his execution letter, he wrote that it was God's will that he was being taken. He had been trying to stop something inhumane, but perhaps God didn't want it to stop. He professed that maybe he had been doing something wrong. Although these statements were all false, one can infer that he was a modest gentleman.

Although Anton Schmid tried his best in keeping his behavior a secret, he was caught and executed on April 13th, 1942. He lived until his early 40s and is buried in the Antalkalis Cemetery in Vilnius, Lithuania. Although Anton Schmid left the world, his legacy still remains. In 2000, the federal government named a military base in Rendsburg "Feldwebel-Schmid-Kaserne" in honor of his courage. In addition, the entry to the town of Haifa, Israel is named "Anton Schmid Circus" for his courage to stand up for Jews. Furthermore, on May 16th, 1967 the Israeli government paid tribute to Schmid, and Yad Vashem granted him recognition as "Righteous among Nations" and presented a medal to his widow with the words "Whoever saves one life - saves the world entire" inscribed on it.

Oskar Schindler

Emily Miller

This is a story of a man who risked everything to save Jews from certain death in the Nazi concentration camps of World War II, a man with the generosity and courage to step up and do what was right at any cost.

Oskar Schindler was born on April 28, 1908 in a province of Germany called the Austro-Hungarian Empire. He was raised and attended German-language school in a region called Sudetenland. Schindler had the mindset of a businessman from a very young age and at 12 he got himself a job selling farm equipment with his father. They were very close until Schindler made the terrible mistake of falling in love with a woman. Her name was Emilie and she caused problems in the relationship of the two and Schindler soon left his father's company to work as a sales manager for a Moravian electric company.

By this time Germany's political landscape was changing as Adolf Hitler began to gain power. Hitler started preaching that Sudeten Germans' rightful roots belonged with Germany and not Czechoslovakia. By 1935, many Sudeten Germans had conformed to this idea and joined the Nazi Party. Schindler did as well, but not because he was he was for Nazism. He was a businessman, and he knew that if he did not go with the majority, it would be bad for business. On September 1, 1939, Hitler invaded Poland and prompted a declaration of war from France and Great Britain. Once again Schindler's inner businessman kicked in and he knew he could somehow profit from this conflict. He took action and started making friends with important people in the Wehrmacht (the German army) and the SS (the special armed Nazi unit) who he sold illegal merchandise to such as cognac (brandy) and cigars. He later met a Jewish accountant, Itzhak Stern. They purchased a bankrupt kitchenware factory and soon Stern and

Schindler were very close. Schindler was skilled at knowing what ropes to pull to get what he wanted and he soon had many contracts from the German army for his kitchenware. Schindler still needed workers for his factory to run and he knew just where to get them. There were almost 60,000 Jews living In Krakow, Poland at the time and most were in ghettos.

In the spring of 1940, the Nazis put up a new regulation saying that all but "work-essential" Jews had to leave the city. Soon, Nazi officers started sending Jews to labor camps and some of Schindler's workers, including Stern were the first to be relocated. Schindler managed to keep his workers by bargaining with SS officers, mentioning high powered people, threats, and bribes. Now one may think that Schindler did this because he needed the workers for his factory, but it is more. Schindler knew what would happen to his workers if they got relocated and he knew they had done nothing to deserve it. He was risking a lot by mentioning some connections he had and risking more by standing up for the Jews at all. Most people at the time just shrugged it off because they weren't Jewish so it wasn't their problem. It wouldn't affect them and it couldn't be stopped so why say anything? Schindler knew that the way the Jewish people were being treated was wrong, and even if it didn't affect him he should still say something if he knew it was right.

In 1943 the final liquidation of the Krakow ghetto was ordered. People who were healthy and could work would be sent off to Plaszow to labor camps, and the others were sent to death camps or executed on the spot. Schindler then proposed, to the young SS officer put in charge of the operation, Amon Goeth, that he set up a mini labor camp and keep his factory that employed his workers. Amon agreed after Schindler bribed him, risking his life once again. In 1944 word got out that the destination for the workers being taken out during the final liquidation was changed to a death camp, not a labor camp as was said. Soon after, Schindler heard that the main labor camp and his factory were to be closed. At this point, Schindler mustered up the bravery and courage to approach Goeth again asking about moving his camp to Czechoslovakia so they could "continue to provide war supply for Hitler's army," and after bribing him again. Goeth said to make a list of the people he wanted to take with him since not all of his workers could come. Schindler held life and death in his hands at this point. If he didn't write someone's name, it was guaranteed they would die. Many people would have trouble even imagining being in a situation like that. Having the lives of thousands of people in your hands and whether they lived or died depended on you alone.

In the fall Schindler made the proper arrangements to start moving his factory and workers to Brunnlitz, Czechoslovakia. Soon he had eight hundred men and 300 women whose names he listed were being shipped in boxcars to Brunnlitz. Somehow, the cars with the women and children were mistakenly routed to Auschwitz instead. Schindler immediately stopped this and sent them to Brunnlitz. His factory never made a useful shell for Hitler's army. Schindler blamed it on "start up issues" when in reality he made them specifically so they wouldn't pass quality control.

On May 8, 1945 the war ended. Schindler gathered his workers to one floor of the factory to pass on the good news. He asked them to not seek revenge for what had been done and thanked SS officers who avoided further bloodshed when sending the workers home. Schindler and his wife took their chances and approached U.S. forces instead of risking capture from the Russians. After the war, Schindler went back to his old self and started drinking and living off the donations of the Jewish organization B'nai B'rith. He tried to start many businesses over the years but none of them turned out. He was nobody again, and very few knew what he had done. When he lost his cement business in Frankfurt, Germany he was invited to Israel for the first time. Their warm welcome was completely different from the treatment he got when he showed his face in Germany. People knew what he had done and thanked him for it. Many people in Germany were angry that he "betrayed" his country and helped the Jews, when all he did was show some humanity to people who needed it the most. Schindler returned to Israel every spring for the rest of his life to "bask" in the appreciation of the people there. They were almost like family to him. In 1962 he was officially named a Righteous Gentile and he was invited to plant a tree on the avenue leading up to Jerusalem's Yad Vashem Museum. Schindler was buried in Israel and over five hundred people, both Jews and non-Jews, attended his funeral.

Sol Urbach, a Jewish survivor of the Holocaust, remembers the day when Schindler was picking who to bring with him to Czechoslovakia. When Schindler came close to him he stepped forward out of formation and said, "Mr. Schindler, no carpenter was left". Then Schindler grabbed him by the arm and separated him into a group. At the time Urbach didn't have any idea which group was which, but he later knew that Schindler had saved him. Urbach said that when he was working for Schindler, there was an unspoken knowledge that if anything happened to him they would all be in trouble. Schindler was their hero and protector, and all out of the goodness of his heart. Urbach is not the only one though. There are more people who were saved by Schindler so they could tell his story, and more people that will be remembered because they had the chance to tell theirs.

Works Cited

"Oskar Schindler Biography." Encyclopedia of World Biography. N.p., n.d. Web. 24 Feb. 2016. < http://www.notablebiographies.com/Ro-Sc/Schindler-Oskar.html >.

Saved by Oskar Schindler: Testimony of Holocaust Survivor Sol Urbach. Perf. Sol Urbach. Yadvashem.org. N.p., n.d. Web. 23 Feb. 2016. < https://www.youtube.com/watch?v=rFpLP9_sXdo >.

The Legacy of Oskar Schindler

Erin Cheng

 Oskar Schindler was just a wealthy business man; an unlikely candidate to become one of the greatest wartime heroes of all time. Born of German decent, a man named Oskar Schindler was born in April 28, 1908 in the industrial city of Zwittau, Moravia. In the 1920s, Schindler worked with his father selling farm equipment. After leaving his father, in 1928, Schindler began working as a sales manager for the Moravian electric company. By 1935, Schindler joined the pro-Nazi Sudeten German Party. However, he did not join out of the love for the Nazis, but because he believed it made business sense to go against the current at that time.

It was only within a week when Schindler arrived in Krakow, Poland, after discovering Hitler invaded Poland, Great Britain and France. This caused France and Great Britain to declared war on Germany. Oskar Schindler came in search to profit out of this situation either way. Krakow quickly became the new central location of government for all of Nazi-occupied Poland. Schindler took this opportunity and quickly made friendships with high ranking officers in both the German army and the SS (the special armed Nazi unit), and offering them black-market goods such as cognac and cigars. This was around the time he met Itzhak Stern. The two developed a strong relationship. Later, Schindler purchased a bankrupt factory and re-opened it to hire Jews to work in it.

By 1940, the Nazi persecution against Jews had begun. Schindler was ordered to pay the SS money that would have been wages paid to his Jewish employees. Panic started to spread among the Jews as the news spread.

In June, 1942, the Nazis began to send Krakow's Jews to concentration camps. Some of Schindler's employees, including his manager, were among the first group to report the train station. In panic, Schindler rushed to the train station and agued with an SS officer. He argued how essential his workers were to the war effort. After using the names of some of his Nazi friends and threatening the officer, he was finally able to rescue the workers and escort them safely to the factory. This was only the beginning of his heroic actions.

Another time when he saved Jews was in early 1943. It was this time that the Nazis ordered the final "liquidation" of the Krakow ghetto. A young SS officer named Amon Goeth, the commandant of the Plaszow Forced Labor Camp just out outside of the city, led this operation. Jews who were healthy and could work were sent to Plaszow and the rest would be sent to death camps or executed on the spot without any question. Schindler immediately acted on this and proposed establishing a mini- camp within his factory that would continue to employ his own workers when Goeth announced that local industries such as Schindler's factory would have to be moved inside Plaszow. Goeth agreed to the change after Schindler bribed him.

Things changed in 1944. Plaszow destination was changed from a labor camp to a concentration camp. This meant its prisoners were scheduled for transport to deaths camps. When the word finally came the main camp was going to be closed including Schindler's factory, Schindler approached Goeth to discuss moving his factory and his workers to Czechoslovakia. He claimed he wanted to continue supplying Hitler's army with vital war supplies. Schindler succeeded this with another bribe. Goeth agreed to lend his support behind the plan. He told Schindler to make a list of his people he wanted to take with him. Schindler was forced to face the task of choosing who he wanted to save-literally, a matter of life and death. With this, Schindler came up with a list containing about eleven hundred names, including all the employees from Emalia camp and a number of others as well. This list was known as Schindler's list.

During the fall of 1944, Schindler began the process of moving his factory to the town of Brunnlitz, Czechoslovakia. The liquidation of the Plaszow camp began in October. Shortly after when 800 of Schindler's workers were shipped out in boxcars for Brunnilitz, 300 women and children were mistakenly routed to Auschwitz instead of Brunnlitz. Schindler immediately rescued these women and children and they were sent to Brunnlitz.

Over the next seven months, Schindler's factory never produced a single useful shell (the outer part of the casing of a bullet). He used the excuse as "start-up difficulties" to cover up for his manufacturing errors but in reality, he had done this on purpose. He even made sure they failed at the quality control tests.

After the war, Schindler lived a life full of failed business ventures, drinking, and overspending. He eventually went bankrupt and relied on the charity of a Jewish organization. Schindler was granted the request to be buried in Israel. On the day of his funeral, 500 Jews came to attend to this event.

Oskar Schindler was a great hero and a great human being. He was clever and selfless. His actions tell us he values every single human being. Through his selflessness, he worked tirelessly and meticulously to save the precious lives of Jew and general humanity even if it meant sacrificing everything he had and at risk of his own life. Thanks to Oskar Schindler he was able to preserve the lives of about 1,200 Jews. He was justly being named Righteous of Among the Nations by the Israeli government. The heroic deed of Oskar Schindler cannot and will never be forgotten. His heroic deed will live on for eternity.

Works Cited

"Oskar Schindler Biography." - Life, Family, Childhood, Children, Name, Story, Death, Wife, ...School. N.p., n.d. Web. 26 Feb. 2016.

"Oskar Schindler, Rescuer of Jews during the Holocaust." Oskar Schindler, Rescuer of Jews ....during the Holocaust. N.p., n.d. Web. 26 Feb. 2016.

The Price of Character - Vasiuta Wegrzynowska

Georgia Eastham (Co-Winner)

 One of my friends said she was tortured. What she meant was that she had to stay home and practice her cello instead of biking to the movies with us. My life is so safe and full of opportunity that reading about the suffering of the Jewish family, the Helpers, jarred me. As I learned more about their story, I discovered the bravery of another family, the Wegrzynowskas who stepped out of their own safe zone and paid a great price for sheltering the Helper family from evil.

After liberation of the Ukrainians from the German occupation in late March, 1944 survivors began to emerge and families reunited with the hope of rebuilding their lives. The Helper family came out of hiding for the first time in 18 months and met with the region's other surviving Jews in nearby Kołomyja, Ukraine. Vasiuta Wegrzynowska had suffered, along with the rest of Ukrainians, through both world wars and fights for Ukrainian independence. But despite that she still had a sense of morality and love. She had chosen to hide the Helper family from the brutal Soviet police. It took enormous strength, courage, and belief to harbor three Jews in a time of darkness when anti-Semitism ran deep. In Ukraine, where citizens' loyalty lay with all different sides, people often appeared callous to others' suffering after enduring nearly a lifetime of famine and fighting. Few were sympathetic to the Jews and many blamed them for the war and its costs. The Wegrzynowskas were not Jewish, but they were sympathetic and saved a vulnerable Jewish family and hid them throughout the war. For this humanitarian act, they paid the ultimate price: Vasiuta and her three children: Docia, Michal, and Yan were murdered by a Ukrainian nationalist gang seeking revenge against those who saved Jews.

In 1921 the Soviet Union took control of Ukraine except for the northwest region that Poland held. Ukraine, known for its extremely fertile soil, was used as a food provider for the rest of the Soviet Union. Starting in the 1930's Josef Stalin ordered the industrialization and collectivization of grain and agriculture as part of his scheme to improve productivity by eliminating privately held farms and forcing workers onto state-owned farms. Collective farming did not prove more productive and other factors including natural disasters led to a widespread famine, called Holodomer (Ukrainian for 'extermination by hunger'), killing nearly five million. In 1939 the German-Soviet Treaty of Nonaggression was signed that left Poland under German control and gave the northwest part of former Ukraine to the USSR. By 1941, the Germans, in their plan to attack and control Moscow, invaded Ukraine and occupied it. Ukrainian nationalists and officials initially welcomed the Germans as liberators from the Soviets, but the Germans demanded hard labor and exploitation of resources that led to protests of German rule.

In the 1930's the widowed and poor Vasiuta Wegrzynowska and her children worked on the Helper's farm. Maks and Henia Helper treated the Wegrzynowskas kindly. When all the Jews were ordered by Ukrainian police to report, Henia and her three year-old daughter, Janina, ran to Kolomyja. Henia didn't know where Maks, her husband was, so they doubled back to the opposite side of Zahajpol, their village, where the Wegrzynowskas lived. When they arrived Vasiuta opened the door to her one-room home and said: "Come in, come in. Your husband is here." Vasiuta fed them and offered to let them stay for a night until Maks could build a structure for them to hide in. Vasiuta took Janina and gave her warm milk to help her fall asleep. They slept together in Vasiuta's bed. Maks and Henia stayed right outside on the porch. The next morning, before the sun rose, Maks and Henia heard footsteps along the path. It was one of their neighbors patrolling the village. The neighborhood was dark and quiet and so the patrolman went back to sleep outside someone else's house on a wood plank. After they were sure he was asleep Maks and Henia snuck back into the house and hid under the bed.

The Ukrainian police would collect the Jews and give them to the Einsatzgruppen or the SD to "eliminate the undesirables". Both the Einsatzgruppen and the SD were elite branches of the SS. The Einsatzgruppen were a mobile execution squad that shot Jews in areas that Germany occupied. The SD were more educated and stuck to the beliefs of Nazism to the upmost degree. They were known for their ruthlessness. The Wegrzynowskas were risking everything to save the Helpers's lives; if the Helpers had been discovered by anyone, all seven occupants of the household would have been brutally murdered.

Maks and Henia and their three-year-old daughter Janina hid in a pit below the cowshed for 18. Every day the Wegrzynowskas would give whatever meager offering they had to the Helpers for nothing in return. Sometimes the Wegrzynowskas would give their last piece of bread. Times were tough and food was very scarce. The Helpers's hiding place was tight; it was impossible to sit up or move. The only source of light was a small hole Maks carved through one of the walls. Ukrainian police searched the Wegrzynowska's house often but the Helpers's hiding place was too well-concealed for them to find.

One Sunday, Vasiuta told the Helpers they could come out for a while and she would be standing guard outside. The Helpers went to look out the window. Janina saw the local children playing and begged her mother to let her go out and play with the children. Henia told her she couldn't "Because you're Jewish. Jews aren't allowed to. You have to wait until another army comes and they'll let us go out and then we'll have fun and go see Grandpa and eat and drink and dance and be happy." Janina accepted this and went back into the pit to wait.

The Wegrzynowskas were murdered not far from where they selflessly saved the lives of three Jews, the Helper family. Trees now grow there; a reminder of the cycle of life. On March 25, 1981 Yad Vashem honored the Wegrzynowskas as "Righteous Among Nations". By sheltering a hunted family, ultimately at the cost of their very lives, the Wegrzynowskas had lit and sheltered a candle in a time of darkness, when light was forbidden.

It is difficult to maintain your character when the world is run by hate, but the Wegrzynowskas, along with many other people, stuck with what they considered morally correct, and saved lives. A story such as theirs is a reminder true character can endure even the harshest tests. Wherever you go, your choices and past deeds follow you. It is not possible to be perfect, but to always try to do right. As I reflect on the comforts of my own life, I realize that maybe the world seemed peaceful and good to the Helpers and the Wegrzynowskas before the invasion of Ukraine. It made me realize how important it is to stand up for what is right and not passively allow evil to rule. I hope to be a voice of tolerance and if ever faced with such evil, to have the courage to act with the compassion the Wegrzynowskas showed the Helpers, and the world.

Works Cited:

"History of Ukraine - the Soviet Union Period." History of Ukraine - the Soviet Union Period. UkraineTrek.com, 2007. Web. 22 Feb. 2016.

"Murdered By Their Neighbors." Yad Vashem. Yad Vashem, 2016. Web. 20 Feb. 2016.

"The Righteous Among the Nations." Yad Vashem. Yad Vashem, 2016. Web. 20 Feb.   2016.

"Ukraine. Historical Background - The Righteous Among The Nations - Yad Vashem." Ukraine.   Historical Background - The Righteous Among The Nations - Yad Vashem. Yad Vashem,   2016. Web. 22 Feb. 2016.

Two Heroes of the Holocaust: Oskar Schindler and George Ferdinad Duckwith

Vinita Saxena (Special Award)

The Holocaust was a horrible, grief-filled time for everyone who was involved in it. But because of the Holocaust, many heroes emerged. Some of these heroes were known, but many were unknown. These heroes risked their lives to help others. They provided Jews with food, water, shelter and a place to hide. Because of them, the lives of many Jews were saved from the Nazis. These heroes were very brave in helping others, but it was well worth the danger and risks they had taken to help innocent people suffering from injustice.

Even though Hitler and the Nazis were German, there were many Germans who were very helpful in saving thousands of innocent Jewish lives. These heroes had to be brave, cautious, and alert to make sure that no one knew that Jews were around. They had to be secretive so that they wouldn't be caught, because providing shelter to a Jew

162

could be punishable by death. It was very hard, but these heroes succeeded in hiding Jews and therefore saving their lives.

One of these heroes was Oskar Schindler. In the 1930s, Schindler started working for the local pro-Nazi organization and started collecting intelligence for the German military. In 1939 he was arrested by Czech authorities for spying and was sentenced to death. He ended up being released soon after he was arrested when Germany annexed Sudetenland.

In September of 1939, Schindler, at age 31, went to Krakow after Germany had invaded Poland. This city was the seat of the German occupation administration, Generalgouvernement, and was home to about 60,000 Jews. Many German entrepreneurs, such as Schindler, went there to see if they could make money off of the country. Schindler used the black market to his advantage, because he wanted a way to quickly make money. In October 1939, Oskar Schindler took over a former Jewish enamelware factory that produced kitchenware and armaments for the German military. In November of 1939 he renamed the factory Deutsche Emaillewaren-Fabrik (German Enamelware Factory) and with a small task force of 45 employees, the company started production. Schindler then secured many German army contracts for kitchenware and armaments, so he could send his products to the army to help the cause. After that, he met with Isaak Stern, a Polish-Jewish accountant who connected him to Krakow's Jewish community, with whom Schindler could staff his factory.

Schindler's business grew incredibly, and in three months there were 250 staff members. Soon, Schindler had multiple factories in different places, one of them being in Brünnlitz, in his home country of Sudetenland. In three years, the original Krakow factory had grown into a huge enamelware and ammunitions production center that employed about 800 people, 370 of them being Jews from the Krakow ghetto that the Germans had established when they invaded Poland. At its peak in 1944, there were 1,700 employees, with at least 1,000 of them being Jewish. Oskar Schindler was no different from any other entrepreneur, except that he treated his workers humanely, especially the Jews.

Schindler had known what the Nazis were doing to the Jews, but he had never taken a large stand against them. Soon, though, he began to be repulsed at the thought of the horrible things they were doing and decided to do something to help as many Jews as he could. Slowly, the idea of making as much money as possible began to lessen and the idea of rescuing as many Jews as possible increased and became his goal. He knew that he would use as much money as needed to save Jews from the Nazi executions. By 1942, almost half of Schindler's employees were Jews.

Because Schindler was a wealthy businessman, he could use his status to help Jews who were powerless under the SS. When his Jewish workers were threatened to be taken to labor camps, he claimed that all of his employees were necessary to the war effort and made them exempt from being taken away. Schindler also forged records, saying that everyone, including women and children, was an expert in their field of work, so they were necessary for the factory to continue operation. He also covered up for unqualified and impaired workers, and personally went to rescue any Jews from being taken to concentration camps. One incident of when this happened was when several hundred of his employees were to be taken by train to labor camps. Oskar Schindler rushed to the train station and confronted the SS officer, saying that each person was crucial to the war effort. Soon, after several anxious minutes, Schindler's employees were released and he was allowed to take them back to the factory.

Oskar Schindler had been arrested many times by the Gestapo, and he was charged with irregularities and favoring Jews. None of this could be proved, so nothing happened to him. Even though he had been arrested, Schindler did not stop helping as many Jews as he could. In March 1943, The Nazis enforced a liquidation of the Jewish population in Krakow. Everyone was to be relocated to the labor camp in Plaszow, which was outside of Krakow. Schindler talked to Amon Göth, a fellow drinking partner who was also the camp commandant, and asked him to let Schindler to set up a sub-camp in Zablocie where his employees could work. He also had a relationship with Göth where Schindler could bribe or blackmail him whenever a Jew was to be sent away or executed and Göth could intervene. The sub-camp had slightly better conditions and Schindler could give the Jews the food they needed. The factory area was also an out of bounds area from the SS guards who were at the sub-camp.

In 1944, the Russian advance called for the Plaszow camp and all of its sub-camps to be evacuated. Many of the men, women and children living in the Plaszow camp were sent to the extermination camps in Auschwitz. There were about 200,000 Jews sent. When Schindler heard about this, he asked for and received authorization to continue production of kitchenware and armaments in his Brünnlitz factory. Oskar Schindler made a list of every Jewish worker he had, and secretively added some others from the Plaszow camp. This was the list of workers who would go the factory in Brünnlitz. There were 1,200 Jews on the list. The men on the list were taken to the Gross-Rosen concentration camp and the women were taken to Auschwitz, instead of both groups being taken to Brünnlitz. When Schindler heard about this, he made sure that the men at the Gross-Rosen camp were released. He then sent his secretary to Auschwitz to discuss releasing the women. He ended up getting them out by bribing the workers.

All of the workers safely got to Brünnlitz and continued working there. Schindler got the factory classified as a sub-camp of the Gross-Rosen concentration camp. He also made the factory produce only armaments, and not kitchenware. Since Schindler didn't want to contribute to the war effort, he had his employees make broken and defective products that would fail their inspection. In eight months of production, only one wagonload of live ammunition was produced. Schindler showed the Gross-Rosen camp fake production totals, which supported the reason for the camp's being there.

Oskar Schindler saved the lives of over 1,000 Jews with his work. Schindler was a true hero in helping 1,200 Jews stay alive in his factory and personally going to do whatever he could to make sure that nothing happened to them, be it pleading begging or blackmailing. Schindler's List is a well-known part of his work and Schindler will be forever known as a hero of the Holocaust.

Another Holocaust hero was a man named Georg Ferdinand Duckwitz. Duckwitz was a German diplomat who had been assigned by the foreign ministry to the German embassy in Copenhagen as an expert in maritime affairs in 1939. Because he already knew the area, Duckwitz had established good connections with Danish leaders. One of these leaders was Werner Best, the Reichsbevollmächtigter, or Nazi Reich Representative of Denmark. From 1942 onwards, Duckwitz and Best had a close relationship and were close confidants to each other. Even though Best had formerly been a deputy of the chief of the Gestapo and completely followed the Nazi ideology, he decided to maintain the more moderate policies of his predecessors, which were used to govern Denmark. Hitler, though, demanded an iron-fist policy towards the country rather than the moderate one Best was using. Hitler also wanted the "Final Solution," a plan to exterminate Jews, be put into action immediately.

Germany occupied Denmark on April 9, 1940. When this happened, there were no immediate threats to the Danish Jewish population, because the two countries had an agreement that stated that the Danish government could keep their army as long as the Danish people didn't resist. Over time, there was in increase in resistance activity in the form of strikes and sabotage. This caused tensions between the German forces occupying Denmark and the Danish government. In August 1943, The Germans told the Danish government to stop the resistance actions, but the Danish government refused and resigned. The Germans took over the government and decided that the Danish Jews were to be deported to Theresienstadt, Bohemia, now the Czech Republic.

Werner Best was informed of the plan and told Duckwitz on September 28, 1943. When he heard the news, Georg Duckwitz flew to Berlin to try to stop the Nazi plans. When that didn't work, Duckwitz flew to Stockholm to discuss and consider the idea of smuggling Danish Jews into Sweden with Prime Minister Hasson. Duckwitz also told the leading Danish Social Democrat, Hans Hedtoft, who in turn, informed the leaders of the Danish Jewish Community, C.B. Henriques and Dr. Marcus Melchior of the imminent deportation of the Jews in Denmark. The deportation was going to begin on the Jewish holiday Rosh Hashanah.

The leaders of the Danish Jewish Community spread the word of the deportation, and the news of the Nazi plan was now known by Jews throughout Denmark. Because the persecution of a minority was against Danish ethics and their culture, they quickly organized a nationwide effort to help as many Jews as possible. The Danes helped hide Jews in hospitals, homes and churches. Many Jews went across the Øresund and into Sweden, a neutral country. Over a two-week period, fishermen helped to take about 7,200 Danish Jews and about 700 non-Jewish family members across the Øresund. While the Jews were taking refuge in Sweden, their non-Jewish neighbors kept an eye on their property.

Denmark was the only country to actively resist the Nazis's attempts to deport its Jewish population. Even though the effort was nationwide, it was not a complete success. By October 2, when the Gestapo started to put their plan into action, most of the Jewish population was gone, but about 500 Danish Jews remained. They were taken and deported to Theresienstadt. Even though they were in a concentration camp, everyone except 51 Jews survived. This was due in large part to the Danish government pressuring the Germans to make sure that the Danish Jews were doing well. The country of Denmark proved that it was possible to save lives by supporting the Jews and resisting the Nazi regime.

Because of what he did, Georg Ferdinand Duckwitz helped save the lives of over 7,000 Jews. He could have just taken the information that Werner Best had given him and ignored it or forgot about it, but Duckwitz decided to do something with the information and, in doing so, he saved over 7,000 lives. Even though it could have cost him his life if he was caught, Duckwitz was a hero in passing on the information he had received and telling the leaders of the Danish Jewish Community. Georg Duckwitz is a true hero of the Holocaust.

Only two heroes were mentioned by name in this essay, but there are many other heroes of the Holocaust. All of the heroes had a choice to either do what the Nazi regime wanted them to do or to stand up to them. Every hero chose to stand up to the Nazis because they knew that it was wrong to kill innocent people. None of them wanted any Jew to have to go to concentration camps or gas chambers just because they followed a certain religion. These heroes had to be secretive because if anyone found out what they were doing, it could cost them their life. All heroes of the Holocaust were very brave in helping Jews, and everyone is very thankful to them for saving so many lives.

Works Cited:

Biography.com Editors. "Oskar Schindler Biography." Bio.com. A&E Networks Television, n.d. Web. 20 Feb. 2016. <http://www.biography.com/people/oskar-schindler>.

"Duckwitz, Georg Ferdinand." The Jewish Foundation for the Righteous. N.p., n.d. Web. 24 Feb. 2016. <https://jfr.org/rescuer-stories/duckwitz-georg-ferdinand/>.

"Georg Ferdinand Duckwitz." The Righteous Among The Nations - Yad Vashem. Yad Vashem, n.d. Web. 25 Feb. 2016. <http://www.yadvashem.org/yv/en/righteous/stories/duckwitz.asp>.

"Oskar and Emilie Schindler." The Righteous Among The Nations - Yad Vashem. N.p., n.d. Web. 20 Feb. 2016. <http://www.yadvashem.org/yv/en/righteous/stories/schindler.asp>.

"Oskar Schindler." United States Holocaust Memorial Museum. United States Holocaust Memorial Council, 29 Jan. 2016. Web. 23 Feb. 2016. <http://www.ushmm.org/wlc/en/article.php?ModuleId=10005787>.

"Rescue in Denmark." United States Holocaust Memorial Museum. United States Holocaust Memorial Council, n.d. Web. 25 Feb. 2016. <http://www.ushmm.org/outreach/en/article.php?ModuleId=10007740>.

C. K. McClatchy High School, Sacramento, CA

PAMELA RICE

B.A. Scripps College, Claremont,California; International Relations Junior Year Abroad, University of Heidelberg, Germany; Masters in German, CSUS; Credentialed in German and English.

Currently teaching German at C.K. McClatchy High School, Sacramento, CA

Otto Weidt

Alex Costello

Have you ever seen a person who had some sort of medical disability or did you just see a poor person on the edge of the street who was helpless and looked desperate for help and somewhere inside you, you had the wanting urge to help that person? Imagine that you were working at someplace such as a coffee shop and outside the shop's window you see a homeless person who's just sitting there on the sidewalk holding a sign that says 'Spare some Food.' Would you feel content to bringing him a slice of bread? Would you feel the need to let him in for a bite of something to eat or something to drink? How about this, would you have offered him or her a job on the spot just so he can make some money to support himself? That is solely up to us whether we want to help someone in need or not. Now picture living in a society where an ethnicity of people have had their businesses closed down and their homes and even their rights taken from them. The government has just left them on the street to fend for themselves and to make matters worse, you can't even help them because the authorities would have had you arrested. Just to see their poor, helpless expressions in their eyes and you can't do anything to help because it's forbidden. That's kind of like what Otto Weidt, a former wall paper hanger, had to face in his everyday life. Otto Weidt, a working-class man born in 1883, could no longer work as a wallpaper hanger because he was becoming blind and it was forcing himself out of a work. Because of him growing blind, he set up a workshop in Berlin that mainly manufactured brooms and brushes where he worked alongside Jewish workers. He was able to gather a lot of workers but a lot of his employees were Jewish and suffered medical disabilities such as being blind deaf, and mute. Otto Weidt had different means of trying to keep them out of the hands of Gestapo officials and keep them from getting deported to horrible places such as Theresienstadt, Christianstadt, and Auschwitz which were places under the occupation of the Nazis as you will read about later in this essay. After reading his story, in my opinion, I believe the overall theme I learned from this gentleman's story is that life is a gift and not a right and just because someone has a medical disability or is of a certain race or religion does not mean that that person has no purpose or can never have a purpose in life. Otto Weidt didn't let the Nazis take those people who worked for him; they were important to him and he didn't give up hope in the people he saved. Breaking the law and using unlawful means was his way of saving the Jews and the risks he took certainly made him a hero. Throughout this essay you'll read about how he was able to get the Jews out from being deported, the very risks he took in which doing so, and how significant his acts towards saving the Jews were.

However, the blind, deaf, and mute Jews who came to work for Otto Weidt did not come from the streets just like the example I explained in the first paragraph. The

Jews who came to work for Otto Weidt were assigned to him by the German authorities from the Jewish Home for the Blind in Berlin-Stegliz. As I explained before, sometimes we force ourselves to help someone even though it's forbidden to do so. We do this because we know what is morally correct and not go by what others say is correct when it's not. Otto Weidt was brave enough to help the Jews, especially when the deportations began, he was brave enough to argue with Gestapo officials over the lives of every single Jew who worked for him. Although he didn't use violence to tackle the Gestapo officials and defend the very Jews who worked for him, he tried to persuade the Gestapo officials by using bribery to let him keep the Jews or argue with them on the fact that those Jewish employees were important for him to fulfill the orders that were commissioned to him by the German military. As you're probably wondering what might be driving him to do this just to save his Jewish workers even though he's not a Jew is because they're regular, innocent people just like any other person and he knows it.

However, after Otto Weidt's struggle to keep the Gestapo officials from arresting his fellow workers, they still went on and arrested them. Weidt still didn't let the Gestapo officials get in his way to free his fellow workers. He marched himself down to the assembly camp at the Grosse Hamburger Strasse where his workers were imprisoned waiting for their time to be deported. Right at the very last minute, Otto Weidt was able to secure their release and prevent them from becoming victims under the hands of the Nazis. Otto Weidt was determined to keep his fellow workers from being deported and he succeeded. He didn't give up and had achieved his goal in saving his workers from the deadly hands of the Nazis. You may be wondering what else he could have done to help the Jews escape from deportation.

Besides helping the deaf, the blind, and as well as the mute, Otto Weidt also helped employ healthy Jewish workers to his workshop. This was a risky thing for him to do for this was strictly forbidden under Nazi authority but Otto Weidt didn't care if it was illegal. All workers that were of Jewish origin had to be accepted by the labor employment office which was usually posts Jewish workers to forceful labor conditions. Otto Weidt made sure the healthy Jewish workers evaded having to be checked out by the employment office so they wouldn't have to harm themselves by the Nazis slave-like working conditions. By any means necessary, Otto Weidt helped the Jews get out of the hands of the Nazis. It didn't really matter to Otto Weidt if the Jews had a medical disability or not. Deaf, blind, mute, injured, or even healthy, he accepted all Jews into working for him at his workshop and disability or not he helped them out of danger whenever he and his Jewish employees ran into trouble with the Gestapo officials. Are there any situations that were so risky that Otto Weidt nearly got in trouble by the law?

By using bribery and deceit, Otto Weidt was able to achieve in pushing aside the objections of the employment office. Using these forms of persuasion, Otto Weidt was able to save many medically disabled Jews and even healthy Jews from forced labor by the Nazis. One of the eight healthy Jewish workers who worked with Weidt at his workshop was a girl by the name of Inge Deutschkron, for she and her mother had to live illegally in order to prevent themselves from being deported. Otto Weidt however, was able to arrange an Aryan work permit that he got from a prostitute who no longer had a use for it. With the permit given to Inge, she was able to work at Otto Weidt's workshop and was able to support herself and her mother. Otto Weidt was always able to find a loop hole in the Nazi deportation system Whenever they tried to deport one or some of his workers or even deport someone whom he would consider in hiring for his workshop, he would always find a way to get them out of getting deported to the concentration camps. This goes to show how far he's able to go to be able to save his fellow workers from falling into the hands of the Nazis. One of Weidt's most outstanding rescues was the rescue of a Jewish girl who was deported to Poland.

To recall, from the last paragraph, one of Otto Weidt's most outstanding rescues was of the Jewish girl known as Alice Licht who was deported to a concentration camp in Poland. She and her parents were provided with lodging and work in a secondary site of the workshop that was hidden behind a row of already made brushes and brooms. Sadly though, the Gestapo officials were tipped off by a Jewish informer who revealed Alice and her family's secret hiding place. Alice Licht and her family were them taken by Gestapo officials and then deported to camps such as Theresienstadt and then Auschwitz and later to a sub-camp known as Gross Rosen in Christianstadt. Otto Weidt was able to travel to the camp to look for her to help her and her family escape. Alice Licht and Otto Weidt had made their plans for their escape but their plans didn't go as expected. Luckily, Licht and Weidt were able to make their escape when the inmates of Christianstadt were lead on a death march and they were able to get back to Berlin but sadly her family didn't make it out. To make matters worse, when they got back to Berlin, Otto Weidt's apartment had become destroyed by a bombing but nonetheless, Weidt was able to shelter her until the war was over. This is another fantastic example of how Otto Weidt was willing to go to save Jews from Nazi hands. If Otto Weidt's plan had back fired, he probably would have never have made it out of the camp with Alice Licht. He probably would also have been founded out about by the authorities, have been arrested, and maybe have suffered the death penalty for bribery, his means of persuasion, and even sneaking the Jews past Gestapo officials. Otto Weidt had no other choice, this was the only way to help the Jews escape and lead them to a wonderful life of freedom without suffering under the forceful hardship labor, mistreatment by the Nazis, and even death in the concentration camps.

Throughout this essay, you've read about how Otto Weidt was able to get Jews out from getting deported by means such as persuasion, bribery, or thinking up a good excuse to get them out of trouble, the very risks he took such as letting a Jewish family lodge in his workshop or helping Alice Licht escape Christianstadt while Jews were being lead on a death march, and you've also read about how significant these acts were. By helping the Jews find work to support their families and escape deportation I can tell he is very generous. The overall theme of Otto Weidt's story is that life is a gift, not a right and also that just because someone has a medical disability or is of a certain religion or ethnicity does not mean that that person does not has no purpose in life and that he or she will never have a purpose. It was not moral of the Nazis to be able to choose who should die, especially basing that on who's Jew and who's not. To recall the question from the very first part of the essay; have you ever seen a person who had some sort of medical disability or did you just see a poor person on the edge of the street and somewhere inside you, you had the wanting urge to help that person? Otto Weidt had that wanting urge to help those poor, innocent Jews by helping them get jobs at his workshop. That right there is a generous deed if you can recall from the first paragraph about how if you were to help a poor person by hiring them on the spot to be able to earn money to support themselves. Instead of resisting in helping the Jews, he helped them regardless of every racial slur or rumor he heard about the Jews. He didn't even let the government influence him on what was right or what was wrong. Otto Weidt listened to his heart, about what he thought was morally correct and not listen to what others said just because the law said so. After hearing Otto Weidt's story, I think the thing we should get from his story is that generosity comes from the heart and no one can be able to tell you to treat someone improperly just because of his or her race, gender, or religion. If there's one thing we should consider, it's that we should treat everyone how they would like to be treated. We maybe of different races, genders, religions, and countries, but if there's one thing we all have in common, it's that we're all human. I think this statement is what went through his mind when the Gestapo officials tried to take away his Jewish employees. I even bet he didn't just see them as workers. The fact that he expected both medically disabled Jews and healthy Jews and didn't' let them fall into the hands of Gestapo officials shows that his fellow Jewish workers to him, were family.

Works Cited
"OttoWeidt."YadVashem.YadVashemTheHolocaustMartyrs'andHeroes'Remembr anceAuthority,
2016.Web.6Jan2016.www.yadvashem.org/yv/en/righteous/stories/weidt.asp.

A Heartwarming Brave Story of the Rescue

Amani Peer-Baadqir

The Holocaust was a world changing tragic event that occurred from 1939-1945. An overview of the Holocaust is it began as Hitler rose to power because Germany was in a depression. He was in power in German politics as the leader of the national Socialist German Workers Party, known as the Nazi Party. He then became chancellor of Germany. Hitler was a demagogue who came to power unfortunately. When he came to power he promised the Germans a better future. During his dictatorship he started blaming the Jewish people for what happened to Germany. This resulted in 6 million Jews deaths, a genocide that can't be undone. However, there were some good people left in Germany who helped and risked their lives for helping the Jewish people such as Aurlieus Arkenau, a German priest who rescued two Jews. The names he went by are Aurelius and Josef. Josef was born in 1900 in Essen/Oldenburg and his parents were farmers. He had five siblings and he was the fourth child. During his childhood he grew up with strict parents who were religious Catholics who influenced Josef's decision to become a priest. Josef passed his examinations at a young age in 1921. Josef wanted to follow in his elder brother's footsteps and joined the Dominican Order as a novice. In 1929 he became a priest and received the name Aurelius. When Hitler became known and chosen leader Josef resisted Hitler and his beliefs. At first he was ok with Hitler because of the promises Hitler made for Germany becoming strong again, just not with what he ended up doing to the Jewish people. However, in April 1934 he was sent to Berlin as a pastoral worker. Soon he saw the realities of what Hitler was doing with the Nazis terrorizing people and killing anyone against them. This soon erased the Christian patriotic revival. During the year 1940, Josef was transferred from Berlin to the Dominican chapel of Leipzig. He served there until the war ended. Josef already gained hatred toward the Nazi regime and when he would make trips home to Oldenburg he would witness inhumane treatment toward the Jews. As an example he passed through Magdeburg and he saw unfair and cruel treatment toward the Jews who were being transported east. Father Aurelius worked with other anti-Nazis who benefited him to help save dozens of Jews, Communist, and army deserters. Käthe Sackarndt was a Jewish survivor who was demanded to testify by the Gestapo to report a meeting with her son Joachim Leibel. In her desperation she discreetly spoke with Johanna Landgraf who told her to go to father Aurelius. He found Christian families for the mother and child to hide them while he remained to support them with money and food ration cards. Their first hiding place in Leipzig became insecure they took an Aryan identity card that made it possible for her to stay with her child in Halle until the end of the war. In a devastating case a Jewish woman who was a doctor swallowed poison in the house she had been hiding in for a few months. Father Aurelius arranged a ceremonial Christian burial under an assumed name. Even though this happened in the past we shouldn't let this happen in the future. As a current event going on there are many candidates running for president within the Republican Party however by contrast there has been a dearth of candidates in the Democratic Party. One significant group that I feel has been harmed the most are Muslims because Muslims have been under fire recently as a result of ISIS and the acts of terrorism they committed. To clarify the term terrorism means the use of violence and intimidation in the pursuit of political aims. With this in mind anyone could be a terrorist, however with the recent devastating attacks such as the Paris attack last year in November labeling all Muslim immigrants as terrorists. This influenced Donald Trump to make statements to persuade his supporters and others that all Muslims are terrorists or are a part of ISIS. I am a young American Muslim and feel offended by Donald Trump's remarks. I saw the news where Donald Trump claimed many American Muslims were celebrating after the 9/11attacks, which is incorrect to the facts. Muslims were frustrated toward the people who committed the crime of horror and some Muslims were the innocent people killed.

In addition, it's statistically proven that there are 1.6 billion Muslims in the world and a very small percent of Muslims are a part of ISIS. With this substantial evidence, Muslims are not all terrorists and disagree with what ISIS has been doing. The relevance that this has to immigration is Trump has proposed a plan if he wins the presidency to ban all Muslims from entering the country and register all Muslims living in the U.S. I think this is outrageous because it violates our First Amendment right as it limits our freedom of religion. This is a clear bias since no other people of religion have to register or be banned from entering the U.S.A. Donald Trump imposes great fear on Americans to win the presidency. Perhaps a group who has been affected by the most is Syrian refugees who are seeking a better life and safety from war. I understand that many people think a terrorist could pretend to be a refugee and whoever does this isn't a good person. However, the process of going to America or Europe and escaping the gruesome life back home is long and difficult. To support my statement there is a family who lived in Syria and had a home, the father worked, the children attended school, and they visited friends. One day it all came to an end when ISIS militia came and threatened to burn their house with them in it if they didn't leave. They went to the mother's brother's home and stayed there for a while, but his house was going to be bombed also so they fled to go on a long trip through a desert struggling to survive, going through many checkpoints. Unfortunately the brother stayed at his home and got killed. All of their friends and family have been killed because of ISIS. This family went to Jordan and was poor with nothing and the eldest son had to find work and the mother too. They struggled to provide enough for their family of six including them. They lived in Amman, Jordan without legal documentation for a year. Statistically its stated more than 200,000 Syrians have been killed and nearly 12 million have been displaced from their homes. With this information in mind it is very difficult for a terrorist to go through this process and it's illogical to prevent helping these refugees who end up targeted because of attacks occurring and people wanted to blame a group who has nothing. This issue violates the First Amendment because the majority of them are Muslims and because of that Donald Trump wants to restrict them from entering. I can understand for security reasons, but on the other hand the process is already long and security is efficient when the refugees come to America and Europe. So there is not much of a reason to ban them or prevent them from entering for religious differences. In conclusion, Donald Trump's proposed policies on immigration that are un-American go against the values of this country that is made upon immigrants. My mother is an immigrant from Germany, and she is the best example I could have of what it means to be American because she has accomplished so much and contributed to this country by working hard like many immigrants have done. The plans he proposes are irrational and don't help the fact that the terrorist attacks that have occurred are by people from the U.S. A man went into a church in South Caroline and killed 9 innocent people and no one was reporting him a terrorist, specifically Donald Trump. Overall, I believe Donald Trump's suggestions are in violation and should be prevented. In addition, I feel that the Jewish people's rights have been violated too. A horrific genocide like the Holocaust should not have happen again. This is why the history is very important for us learn and understand so the new leaders in the future and currently don't make the same mistakes. It's important to bring awareness to the sensitive topic because the rights of people get violated when you allow the government to. This year we have many Republican candidates who are running for president who I feel have strong views against immigration and certain groups of people. With our knowledge of the Holocaust that occurred in the past we should not allow our "American values" to adjust to preventing others entering the U.S and hurting or separating a group from the others. By doing this action people don't realize there are consequences with this. There are many stories that should be told about the survivors and what they went through to survive. It will impact the readers tremendously because after I read the story of Aurelius I felt that we need more people especially the youth to speak against this happening to any group. Currently it's the Muslims being attacked because of their religion and other powerful people creating a greater fear in people of Muslims than what it is. When we think that we would never vote for someone like Hitler anything can happen. I saw this movie called "The Wave." It was a great movie, the description of the movie included a teacher and high school students who never understood why Germans would vote for Hitler. The teacher started a game of forming a group called the wave with his students. Unfortunately it got serious and ended with a death and an injured person. This movie represents the impact one person can have when you constantly hear the same thing and when it makes people feel united. Also no one feels the outsider because everyone has power and feels like they're not left out. In conclusion, I felt appreciative of being able to read the moving story of Aurelius and learning how important the event was. I learned that helping others could put your life in danger. That no matter what race, religion, or background the person came from we are all equal and should be treated fairly. In fact people who have different beliefs help people stay open minded. Even though, we may be in desperate times where we make terrible mistakes we shouldn't let that impact our decision when picking a leader. For example, Hitler was in an anti-Semitic group, which would soon lead Germany to kill 6 million Jews. The point would be to choose carefully of who the future leader is and what they were associated with. Overall, I believe in change in the way that people think of others and for us not making the same mistakes.

Works Cited

"Holocaust Timeline: The Rise of the Nazi Party." Holocaust Timeline: The Rise of the Nazi Party. N.p., n.d. Web. 28 Feb. 2016.

"The Righteous Among The Nations." N.p., n.d. Web. 28 Feb. 2016.

"Aurelius Arkenau." Wikipedia. Wikimedia Foundation, n.d. Web. 28 Feb. 2016.

"Tabelle." Tabelle. N.p., n.d. Web. 28 Feb. 2016.

A Brief Herstory of Johanna Eck

Annabelle Long

 History seems to be exactly that. His story. Rarely do we hear of the brave feats of female heroes around the world, and rarely are they truly celebrated in the way that many men are. History seems so centered on the stories of men, and the powerful things that they have done, and it often leaves the amazing feats of brave and courageous women in the dust. Johanna Eck opened her home to several people, including Jews, escaping persecution during the second world war yet we still don't know much about her. This tragic gap in history must be recognized, but we must still tell her story. Ms. Eck acted because she said it was her duty to, and she felt that it was her responsibility to help those in need. Johanna Eck was a strong, independent, and gracious woman who acted boldly and bravely in a time when many were afraid to, and it is about time that her story is told and that she is celebrated. It is high time that there is a story that remembers heroes of the Holocaust that is not just his story, but her story as well, and it is time that we recognize the achievements of a great woman who acted out of the goodness and fearlessness of her own heart.

Johanna Eck's life before the war began remains somewhat of a mystery, and it has been said that much of what her life was like before the war has been lost to time. What is known, however, is that she was widowed during the war. Her husband was killed while he was fighting, and after his death, Johanna was forced to be dependent only on herself, something that likely contributed to her bravery and willingness to help those in need. She could no longer hide in the shadow of her husband and look to him to be the problem solver of the relationship; instead, she had to act for herself and take things in to her own hands. This independence she was forced into following the death of her husband was likely a driving force in her ability to save so many people. If she hadn't had the strength that she did, it would definitely not have been any easier to work against the brutal Nazi regime in the way that she did. While it was most definitely not a good thing that she was widowed, she was forced to come into her own and develop a sense of independence and utter self-reliance that she might not have found otherwise. Johanna Eck was admirably independent, and had an aura of strength and courage about her that was necessary in acting against such a brutal order.

When we hear stories of success and triumph, not only are they typically stories of men and masculine figures, but they typically focus on the physical strength and prowess of the hero, and not the mental toughness or strength, which is often more significant. Johanna Eck exhibited great mental strength in the face of great danger, and it is time that this is recognized. Too often, we overlook to great and notable feats that aren't as on-face phenomenal or dramatic. We often find ourselves distracted by things that are action-packed and large scale and super dramatic and turn away from things like the bravery it took to hide Holocaust victims. It's easy to say that these feats aren't as great because they aren't as flashy or showy or dramatic, and that fact really takes away from how impressive and important those feats really are. Without people like Johanna Eck, who help others not for the recognition or the fame, but out of the goodness of their hearts, the world would be a much colder and crueler place, and quite frankly, I would not be so inclined to live in that world. It is important to recognize the importance of feats of mental strength with the same reverence that we do feats of great physical strength, and it is important to understand that secretly working against something can be just as scary as standing right in someone's face and threatening them.

Johanna Eck's work to save and shelter Holocaust victims began in 1942, when she offered up her home to Heinz Guttmann. Heinz's father, Jakob Guttmann, and Eck's husband had been colleagues in the war together, so they did have some prior relationship, but unlike most of Heinz's close friends, Eck actually stood by him in his time of need and offered to help him when he needed it most. Heinz's father, mother, and siblings were all deported and virtually banished from Germany, and were told never to return. Heinz was left all by himself, with no one to look out for him. He was homeless, with no means of getting food and no way to sustain himself. Everyone he turned to turned him away for fear of being caught with a Jewish criminal on their hands. Johanna Eck was the only one out of all of the Guttmann's non-Jewish family friends to offer up what she had to him. While she really didn't have much to offer him, she gave him a roof over his head and a portion of her small food rations, enough to keep both of them alive. He stayed, hidden away in her home until November of 1943, when there were airstrikes and Eck's home was destroyed. Eck prioritized finding him a new home, and found him a new place of refuge, where she still kept an eye on him. Heinz then stayed with a woman called Ms. M. Even after he was out of her direct care, she made sure he was comfortable in his place of shelter and had sufficient amounts of food and water. She would often offer him more food from her food rations, despite her not having much food to herself to begin with. Heinz Guttmann's encounter with Johanna Eck, and her utter selflessness and willing to help a young man who many would deem a criminal shows her sheer mental strength, along with her heart of gold and true hero qualities.

The next person who Johanna Eck helped was a young girl named Elfriede Guttmann (despite having the same last name, she was not related to Heinz). Elfriede had been staying with Ms. M, the same woman who opened her home to Heinz after Eck's was bombed. In December of 1943, Elfriede was traumatized when the Gestapo burst into and raided Ms. M's home. She narrowly missed arrest by hiding under a bed, and was truly shaken by what had happened to her. She no longer really felt safe within Ms. M's home, and sought out Eck for help. At this time, Johanna Eck was living by herself in a one-room apartment that had been assigned to her. When Elfriede finally reached Johanna and told her of her experiences, Johanna did not hesitate to offer up what little space she had to the girl. The two of them lived in very close quarters then, but neither of them seemed to mind: one, because she knew she was doing the right thing by helping someone in need, and the other, because she felt safe from the raids that had almost cost her her life and the little freedom she had left.

Johanna Eck and Elfriede Guttmann had a great relationship with one another. One day Johanna took Elfriede to a bakery, and as they waited in line, a young girl around the age of Elfriede approached them and excitedly greeted Elfriede. It turned out to be a former classmate of hers from when she attended school in East Prussia (now Poland). The girl was named Erika Hartmann. Erika sat with Johanna and Elfriede for a while, and listened to Elfriede's traumatic tale. She was very deeply affected by it, and was willing to do anything to help her out. She offered Elfriede some of her own personal Aryan documents, including one that said that she had done work for the Labor Service. It was these seemingly small acts of generosity and kindness that meant so much to people like Elfriede, and ultimately made a huge difference in her life, as well as in the lives of many others.

It was truly lucky that Erika Hartmann was in that bakery that day, as it was her documents that likely allowed for Elfriede's survival through the war. There was one particular instance where Elfriede probably would not have survived without those documents. It was January 30 of 1944, the night of an Allied airstrike in Berlin. Berlin was in a state of true chaos, and police authorities were patrolling the city relentlessly. Several of them showed up at the door of Johanna and Elfriede, and demanded to know the residents of the apartment. Johanna used a bit of trickery and deceit to fool the authorities in to believing that Elfriede was actually a girl named Erika Hartmann, whose original records had been lost in a house fire as a result of an air raid. The authorities bought it, and it was in that way that Elfriede was allowed to stay with Johanna, just under the pseudonym of Erika Hartmann.

The two of them lived together as peacefully as they could in this time of chaos and conflict, and both of them escaped the war alive and physically well, although both fairly traumatized by the tragedies that the war had brought to them. Elfriede died shortly after her liberation. She died of a stomach constriction that came out of nowhere. The day following her death was supposed to be the day that she immigrated to the United States. Johanna Eck was by her side and supported her until she passed away. Eck was a registered and fully trained nurse, and sat at Elfriede's bedside in her final moments. She paid for Elfriede's burial and gravestone, and searched throughout the Jewish community to find information about Elfriede's family. Once she found who they were, and found out that they were all deceased as well, she paid more money to have their names etched with Elfriede's on her gravestone. The kindness shown by Eck is a very unique one. It is all too rare that people have the courage to see the ones they love in a less than optimal state, and Johanna did her best to put on a brave face and support Elfriede in her last moments on Earth. Eck is the epitome of goodness and kindness, and her support for Elfriede is truly admirable. Even after Elfriede's death, Johanna wanted only the best for her, and wanted her to be as close to her family as possible.

Even if she didn't save the most lives, Johanna Eck made an enormous impact on those that she did. The impact on Heinz and Elfriede's value to life is nearly immeasurable, and without Johanna, the two of them would not have had the lives that they did. Johanna Eck's imprint on their lives is without a doubt positive, as it allowed for both of them to live longer and have ultimately more happiness throughout their lives than they would have without her. Eck's impact on the lives of Heinz and Elfriede Guttmann was huge – if she hadn't offered them help, Heinz would have remained out on the streets, with no way to get food and nowhere to go, and Elfriede would have had shelter, but she would have been forced to stay in the place that constantly reminded her of her near miss with arrest and detention.

This was a glimpse back in to herstory, not history. This was an important insight on the feats of a strong, independent and self-reliant woman that acted not for herself, but to help those that needed it more than she did. This was a story of selflessness and giving, and of giving all you have to those that need it more. This was a celebration of a woman who has never received the recognition that she deserves, and this was an honoring of the lives of those that she worked tirelessly to save. Johanna Eck was an independent woman in a time when a man was something that a woman was supposed to be tied to, and she was a fearless woman in a time when women were supposed to be doubtful, insecure, and submissive. Johanna Eck was a rebel in a time and place where people like her were supposed to go with the flow, and play along with the regime that many of them knew was wrong. Johanna Eck used her little power to swim upstream and work against what she had been taught to support. Johanna Eck was a hero, and it is about time that she gets that recognition and that ultimate celebration.

Semyon and Yelena Krivoruchko

Ben Schwartz

I once heard a story about starfish. The story went that there was a beach, and on the beach were dozens, even hundreds of starfish washed up on the shore. A little girl had come to the beach, and had seen the starfish. She immediately got down on her knees and began picking up the starfish one by one and flinging them into the ocean. She had been at this for a little while when a man passing by saw this girl methodically and deliberately picking up starfish and tossing them into the sea. He found this rather strange so he approached her. "Little girl," he asked, "Why are you doing this? There are so many starfish and just one of you. You can't possibly hope to rescue them all!" The girl simply picked up another starfish and tossed it in, and she said, "It made a difference for that one." This story, though simple, carries wisdom that we can all learn from. It reveals the idea that every little thing makes a difference, and that you don't need to solve every problem the world has to have a tangible impact on someone's life. In 1941, Semyon Krivoruchko and his wife, Yelena, took in Vera Viron, a Ukrainian Jew, and her daughter to save them from the Nazis. They hid them with relatives in a nearby village and made sure they were taken care of for the duration of

Nazi occupation. They, with righteousness and bravery, saved two humans from certain death. They, like the little girl on the beach, recognized the difference they could make by saving even two people. The Krivoruchkos are true heroes, risking everything to save a woman and her child. They should be remembered for their righteousness and as symbols of the attitude that any good is worth it, for which we should strive.

The portion Mishnah Sanhedrin 4:9 of the Talmud states that "Whoever destroys a [life], it is considered as if he destroyed an entire world. And whoever saves a life, it is considered as if he saved an entire world." The Talmud teaches that every life can have a profound effect on the world, that everyone's life is essentially a world because without him or her, the world wouldn't be the same. On September 16, 1941, Nazi soldiers began the murder of Jews and gentiles in the city of Mykloaiv in Ukraine, killing 35,782 by September 30. On September 29 and 30, 33,771 Jews were massacred at the Babi Yar ravine near Kiev, the largest single massacre in the whole Holocaust. Between the days of September 16 and September 30, Nazi officers destroyed 69,553 or more worlds in Ukraine. The Nazis established ghettos, notably at L'vov and Tarnopol. They created concentration camps at Bogdanovka and Janowska, where at least another 80,000 were murdered. Possibly the most tragic part, however, was that many Ukrainian gentiles collaborated. Estimates place the numbers of Ukrainian collaborators over 100,000. Some of them ratted on Jews they knew. Some joined police units that aided the Nazis in hunting down Jews. Some even went so far as to participate in mass shootings of Jews like the ones at Mykloaiv and Babi Yar, or staff the concentration camps in Ukraine. In the end, over 900,000 Jews were killed. Between the years of 1941 and 1945, Nazi soldiers and Ukrainian collaborators in Ukraine destroyed over 900,000 worlds. 900,000. For every 9 Jews murdered, 1 of their fellow humans was a collaborator. Nine-hundred-thousand is nearly one-sixth of all Jews killed in the Holocaust and one-eleventh of all people killed. Not only that but countless children were never conceived, never had the chance to experience this world, because of the actions of the Nazis. The Ukrainian Holocaust was the second largest of all countries, second to Poland with 3.3 million casualties, yet it is sometimes forgotten. Most of the time we hear about the Holocaust in Germany and Poland, yet a large portion took place in Ukraine. In fact, it seems it is being forgotten even in Ukraine, where neither a Holocaust perpetrator nor even one Nazi war criminal has ever been prosecuted. In postwar Ukraine, Jews were considered allies of the West and were discriminated against by the Soviets. Why is it that so many people are seldom discussed, never looked back on? Ukrainian textbooks emphasize the tyranny of Nazis and Soviets toward the general population, not the mass murder of Jews, but how is it that those 900,000 who lost their lives are glanced over in classrooms and other settings, even in Ukraine? I, for one, had only really heard and read about the atrocities committed in Poland and Germany until this project. The Ukrainian Holocaust needs to be remembered, to be mourned, because of the 900,000 ways our world would be different, would be better, if it hadn't happened.

In September 1941, the Nazis established the first ghettos across Ukraine. Following the massacres, Jews were rounded up and shoved into these ghettos, eventually on trains to concentration camps. Vera Viron, a Jew, lived with her daughter Yevgeniya, who was four years old, in the town of Nemirov. When the Nazis came to Nemirov to round up Jews for the ghetto, Vera sensed something was amiss, that the ghetto would not be a safe place for her and her daughter. They began wandering the countryside, going from village to village seeking refuge in a village where the inhabitants would not recognize them. After some time of this, days or weeks, they came to the village of Kudlai. They were acquainted with some people living there, and there was one family they knew relatively well (not so well that they were friends, but well acquainted). This family was that of Semyon and Yelena Krivoruchko, moderately well-off farmers. Vera and Yevgeniya were exhausted after days of this, and Vera had a decision to make: would she ask the Krivoruchkos for help and risk being turned in, or would they continue to wander for an unknown destiny? She decided to approach the Krivoruchkos, and she went to them asking for refuge. Semyon let them in, promising to help them. Vera didn't wish to stay in Kudlai, for she feared being recognized by the people of the town. Yelena hid them and took care of them for a few days while Semyon visited the nearby village of Bayrakovka, where his sister Solomiya and her husband Safron Derun lived with their 17-year-old-daughter Tatyana. Vera did not know anyone in Bayrakovka, so it would be a good place to hide. The Deruns agreed, and Semyon brought Vera and Yevgeniya to the Deruns' home in Bayrakovka. Luckily, Safron, a highly respected member of his village, had been appointed village headman after the Nazi occupation. He said that Vera and Yevgeniya were his wife's cousins who had come to stay with them, and no one questioned him due to his respected and trusted status. Vera and Yevgeniya lived openly in the village; Vera farmed with the other adults and Yevgeniya interacted with the other children her age. Semyon visited regularly to see his sister and check on Vera and her daughter. When searches were conducted or Nazi officers were coming, Vera and Yevgeniya, assisted by the Derun daughter Tatyana, fled to the forest and took refuge there until the Nazis or Ukrainian authorities left. Two years later, in October 1943, Solomiya had another daughter, Antonia, and Yevgeniya, now six or seven, helped take care of the child. Finally, in March 1944, Soviet forces liberated Ukraine, and Vera and Yevgeniya returned to Nemirov, eternally grateful to their rescuers. Semyon, feeling a duty to the Soviets for liberating them, enlisted in the Red Army, and unfortunately lost his life in combat. The Virons kept in touch with the Krivoruchkos and the Deruns for many years afterward. They helped two people, saved them from certain death, and saved two whole worlds in doing so.

The story of the Virons, the Krivoruchkos, and the Deruns has changed the way I look at the world. I have learned about the atrocities committed in Ukraine and the worlds that were ended. I learned about a woman and her child, given safe haven by righteous souls. I learned about the value of each and every life, and the devastation that comes with taking one away. I, in writing this essay, will forever remember the Ukrainian Holocaust, and the heroism of Semyon, Yelena, Solomiya, Safron, and Tatyana. I feel this story applies quite directly to a situation today. Firstly is the Syrian refugee crisis. When we look at the refugee crisis, Germany stands out as a leader in acceptance rates, having accepted around 350,000 refugees last year. Germany is, of course, the best equipped to handle an influx of immigrants, and it was good to see that Angela Merkel was taking such a firm stance on the issue. I say "was" because Merkel has recently said that reduction of acceptance is pertinent. This is due, unfortunately, to the uproar of the German people and members of Merkel's party against the influx of refugees seen over the past years. It saddens me that the German population is so scared of the immigrants, so determined to stop them from entering because of racism or fear of their impact on the economy, especially considering that immigrants seem to have a net positive or net neutral impact on economies. The reactions of Germans and Merkel's recent statements, since Germany is a leader, have an effect on immigration policy throughout Europe, so the decisions made in Germany carry throughout the European Union. It seems rather like the situation in Ukraine. These peoples' (Jews or Syrians) lives are threatened daily, and the decision is whether to risk your own well-being (being caught by the Nazis or the economy suffering) to save these people from misery (civil war or labor camps) or death. In my eyes, the decision is clear. I, however, am not actually in that position, so I can understand how the Germans would be scared; I probably would be too were I in that situation. That being said, I hope they can weigh the options and come to what I feel is the right decision, the decision to risk some of your well-being for the life of another. This is the choice that the Krivoruchkos and the Deruns made, and this is the choice that saves worlds from certain destruction. This choice needs to be made for the good of the refugees, for the good of Germany, and for the good of Europe. It can be made on a small level, by choosing to embrace Syrian neighbors and make them feel welcome, offering them not only work but a place in the community. It can be done on a large level, by choosing not to lower the cap on refugees, or to raise it, sending the message to the rest of Europe that it is necessary and for the good of all. Don't think, however, that this must be done individually. The Krivoruchkos and the Deruns show us that working together allows us to accomplish what we couldn't individually. Only together could they save the Virons; individually they would have failed. Germany must not do what countless did in the Holocaust and say, "let someone else handle it, we have our own problems," for when everyone says that, no one handles it. We must remember what happened, remember the obscenities, so we do not fall into this mindset and unwittingly let it happen again. We must work together to solve the problem, and set an example for others to follow, such that we prevent the problem everywhere and not just in our backyard. We must not stop until this has happened, and only then will our work be complete.

The Krivoruchkos as well as the Deruns exemplified values that we should all strive for. They unhesitatingly helped those in need and did what was right, not what was easy. They saved a woman and her child, and their entire line of descendants, and, in doing so, saved countless worlds. They certainly affected the lives of Vera and Yevgeniya, but they should also have an effect on the rest of the world too. Let them be examples for all of us to look up to, to think of, when we have to choose between upholding what is just and doing what is simple or selfish. They are truly righteous among the nations, and deserve to be honored and remembered by people across the world. We learn from them what it means to save a world. We learn from them to work together to tackle issues we couldn't solve alone. We learn from them that we shouldn't give up because we can't do everything. Their story teaches us, above all, that on a beach covered in starfish, helping even one makes all the difference.

Bibliography

"Angela Merkel Wants to 'drastically Reduce' Refugee Arrivals in Germany." The Guardian. Guardian News and Media, 13 Dec. 2015. Web. 26 Feb. 2016. <http://www.theguardian.com/world/2015/dec/14/angela-merkel-wants-to-drastically-reduce-refugee-arrivals-in-germany>.

Gregorovich, Andrew. "Ukrainian History -- World War II in Ukraine." InfoUkes. InfoUkes, n.d. Web. 23 Feb. 2016. <http://www.infoukes.com/history/ww2/page-28.html>.

"Holocaust." Encyclopedia of Ukraine. Encyclopedia of Ukraine, n.d. Web. 21 Feb. 2016. <http://www.encyclopediaofukraine.com/display.asp?linkpath=pages%5CH%5CO%5CHolocaust.htm>.

"Is Migration Good for the Economy?" Migration Policy Debates May 2014 (2014): 1-4. OECD. OECD, May 2014. Web. 27 Feb. 2016. <http://www.oecd.org/migration/OECD%20Migration%20Policy%20Debates%20Numero%202.pdf>.

"List of Major Jewish Ghettos." Jewish Virtual Library. American-Israeli Cooperative Enterprise, n.d. Web. 21 Feb. 2016. <https://www.jewishvirtuallibrary.org/jsource/Holocaust/ghettolist.html>.

"List of Nazi Concentration Camps." Wayback Machine. Internet Archive, n.d. Web. 21 Feb. 2016. <https://web.archive.org/web/20121103180512/http://www.gesetze-im-internet.de/begdv_6/anlage_6.html>.

Martinez, Michael. "Syrian Refugees: Which Countries Welcome Them." CNN. Cable News Network, 10 Sept. 2015. Wcb. 26 Feb. 2016. <http://www.cnn.com/2015/09/09/world/welcome-syrian-refugees-countries/>.

"Migrant Crisis: Migration to Europe Explained in Seven Charts - BBC News." BBC News. BBC News, 18 Feb. 2016. Web. 26 Feb. 2016. <http://www.bbc.com/news/world-europe-34131911>.

Oldberg, Ingmar. "UKRAINE'S PROBLEMATIC RELATIONSHIP TO THE HOLOCAUST." Baltic Worlds. Centre for Baltic and East European Studies, 1 Aug. 2011. Web. 23 Feb. 2016. <http://balticworlds.com/ukraine's-problematic-relationship-to-the-holocaust/>.

"Semyon Krivoruchko." Yad Vashem. Yad Vashem, n.d. Web. 21 Feb. 2016. <http://db.yadvashem.org/righteous/family.html?language=en&itemId=4035622>.

Johanna Eck

Christian Barajas

"In principle, what I think is this: If a fellow human being is in distress and I can help him, then it becomes my duty and responsibility." – Johanna Eck. This righteous woman, being German, went against her own country to save two Jewish individuals under Nazi persecution. Being an American teenager of the 21st century, I have always had a negative view on all Germans of the Nazi era. After gathering research I feel that everyone who did the right thing, including Johanna Eck, is noteworthy and should be recognizable in today's society. That's enough about "now," let's talk about "then." Johanna Eck became a widow after she lost her husband, as many other wives did during the First World War. During the war, her husband befriended a Jewish fellow named Jakob. After the bloodshed of World War I, Jakob and his family were deported to the East, never to return. In doing so, they left behind their youngest son, Heinz. Having been acquainted with the family in the past, Johanna offered refuge to the poor boy. Although Mrs. Eck received a meager amount of food rations, she managed to share as much as she could with the son of her beloved husband's best friend. She would spend weeks at a time away from home in effort to obtain extra rations for Heinz. Sadly, on a gloomy day in November, Johanna's house was obliterated by an enemy air raid, leaving herself and Heinz homeless. Before she relocated herself, she first made sure that Heinz maintained a hiding place. Although they no longer lived in the same home, Eck preserved their relationship by sending him food rations and vital contacts, as the need arose. Johanna's level of perseverance showed that she was a bona fide hero of the Holocaust. Knowing that she could easily be killed for being a traitor of the German government, she found the righteousness within herself to house an innocent victim of the Holocaust. If she would have been caught, she would have been viewed as a traitor, which was in Nazi Ideology, worse than a Jew. She put absolutely everything on the line for young Heinz.

Through Heinz's new landlady, Ms. M, Johanna subsequently met a Jewish girl who went by the name of Elfriede Guttmann. In 1943, the Gestapo (secret state police of the Nazi Association) raided Ms. M's house. Poor Elfriede hid under her bed, uneasily watching the Nazi feet pass her by. Being mentally shattered by the recent events, Elfriede ran to Eck for comfort. Eck, who in the meantime had been staying in a small one bedroom apartment, immediately offered the unstable girl refuge. Elfriede agreed with haste and the 55-year-old woman once again prevailed as a hero in a victim's life. Like before, Johanna selflessly accepted a refugee of the German government, but this time it was truly because of Eck's warm and compassionate heart.

One day, as the pair was standing in line at a local bakery, Elfriede was unexpectedly reunited with her childhood friend, Erika Hartmann. Finding the Jewish girl charming and kind, Erika gave her some of her personal Aryan documents, including a piece of evidence that proved she had done work for the labor service. Using this newly acquired documentation, Johanna attempted to register Elfriede as Erika Hartmann. Unfortunately, allied planes wreaked havoc over Berlin and once again, the poor woman's house was destroyed by the major effects of war. Along with Eck's house, Erika's certification was also incinerated in the explosion. Although these regrettable mishaps set the duo back, they were still motivated to keep going on. In 1946, on the day before she left for the Americas, Elfriede met her abrupt and bitter fate. After all of the cataclysmic discrimination that the young lady survived, she was suddenly taken by an unlikely stomach constriction. On her last night on Earth, the dying 24-year-old was accompanied by the soul that saved her from the violent ways of war, Johanna Eck. After Elfriede's untimely passing, Johanna took the time to inquire with the Jewish communities in an attempt to find the girl's parents so their names could be engraved on the young girl's headstone. After a couple months of inquiry, she learned that Elfriede's parents and siblings had all perished. Fortunately, Eck could still do what she set out to do and inscribe their names on the 24-year-old's final resting place.

Later on in Johanna's purposeful life, she was recognized for her heroic acts of kindness. At an interview, she was asked about her motives. This was her reply, "The motives for my help? Nothing special in a particular case. In principle, what I think is this: If a fellow human being is in distress and I can help him, then it becomes my duty and responsibility. Were I to refrain from doing so, than I would betray the task that life – or perhaps God? – demands from me. Human beings – so it seems to me – make up a big unity; they strike themselves and all in the face when they do injustice to each other. These are my motives." Personally, this single string of words tells me so much about Johanna's complete outlook on life, and the fact that she was able to see the good within herself, makes her one of the many German Heroes that overcame Nazi influences.

Although some Germans did do the right thing, we can't ever forget about the terrible misdeeds of the infamous German Nazis. Adolf Hitler and his army deliberately executed about one third of the Jewish population, along with many other ethnic groups, in order to start a new world that only contained the "superior" race. The Holocaust made some German people turn into horrible monsters all because of the sick persuasion of one man. How could one man do this? How could one man convince a whole country that the German Race ranked higher in the eyes of God? This is why I'm writing. This is exactly what lured me into composing this essay. It brings a certain warmness to my heart to know that there were many Germans who conquered the abstract and obscure ideas of Hitler.

"Darwinism by itself did not produce the Holocaust, but without Darwinism... neither Hitler nor his Nazi followers would have had the necessary scientific underpinnings to convince themselves and their collaborators that one of the world's greatest atrocities was really morally praiseworthy." - Richard Weikart. As we know, Darwinism (the theory of the evolution of species by natural selection advanced by Charles Darwin) was one of the main things that drove Hitler. This scientific theory

184

gave Hitler the deadly spark he needed to come up with the idea that all inferior races must die, similar to how some species die out in nature. But like in many other cases, the human race cannot be compared to the animal kingdom. Adolf Hitler wasn't even justified in believing in Darwinism because he wanted to knowingly annihilate the Jewish population, when in Darwinism; nature would've done that for him. Knowing that some people actually believed in Hitler's twisted theory disgusts me on so many levels.

Fortunately, there were many people like Johanna Eck, whose morals weren't warped by Hitler's ignorant ideas, which leads me to wonder why so many people fell for Hitler's persuasion. Was it because they actually agreed with Adolf, or was it merely because people were terrified of the power that Hitler possessed? It was most likely a mix of the two, considering the fact that everyone felt differently about the Holocaust during this time. Either way, I think that Johanna Eck along with all other German saviors of the Jewish people deserves gratitude across all four corners of the world. Using their innate ability to see the good in mankind; they accepted Jewish refugees into their lives.

If another Holocaustic situation were ever to occur again, I would beg on my hands and knees that our world would be blessed with more people with the same morality as Johanna Eck.

Sources
""Women of Valor"" Johanna Eck. N.p., 2016. Web. 24 Feb. 2016.
"Quotes About Holocaust." (225 Quotes). N.p., n.d. Web. 28 Feb. 2016.
"Holocaust | Basic Questions about the Holocaust." Holocaust | Basic Questions about the Holocaust. N.p., 2009. Web. 28 Feb. 2016.
Grieshaber, Kirsten. "Museum Created for Germans Who Hid Jews."Washington Post. The Washington Post, 08 May 2007. Web. 28 Feb. 2016.

Elisabeth Abegg
Claire Fetros (Special Award)

Six million. That number is overwhelming by itself. When that number is related to the number of Jewish people who were horribly slaughtered during the Holocaust, it is outright frightening and unfortunately true. The mind boggling slaughter of Jews began with Adolf Hitler. In his obviously demented mind, Hitler blamed Jews for much of what was wrong with Germany, and the world. He even believed that Jewish people were somehow responsible for Germany's loss in World War II. What made Hitler's anti-Semitism worse was the fact that thousands of others in Germany shared his beliefs. With them rallying behind him, Hitler transformed the Nazi party from a group of less than ten men to the leading power in Germany. He rebuilt the military that the Treaty of Versailles prohibited and began forcing Jewish people to wear the Star of David to identify themselves as Jewish. What made matters worse was how no one stopped him. The majority of Europe and Britain had a policy of appeasement, letting Hitler go on to avoid conflict. The United States was primarily isolationists so they too did nothing to stop Hitler; after World War I they wanted nothing to do with foreign affairs. With almost nothing standing in his way, Hitler rose up and as he rose to power in Germany, the dangers of being Jewish rose as well. Hitler, along with the thousands who helped him rise to power, brought the whole world to war while at the same time bringing Jews to concentration camps where most were killed unbeknownst to most. However, not all of Germany backed up that horrible tyrant. There were many righteous Germans who realized Jewish people were innocent of everything Hitler and his followers blamed them for. These Germans risked everything, even their lives, to help Jews escape the death Hitler had planned for them all. Elisabeth Abegg was one of these Germans that helped save Jews lives during World War II.

Elisabeth Abegg was born on May 3, 1882. She was born in Strasbourg, which at the time was a part of the German Empire. Not much is known about her childhood but it can be assumed that her parents, Johann and Marie, were kind, giving people since they raised such a selfless child. Her cousin, William Abegg, was a well-known Social Democratic statesman who also contributed to the woman Elisabeth Abegg became. Another huge influence in her life was Albert Schweitzer, who grew up in Strasbourg as well. He was a theologian, organist, doctor, and humanist. His teachings, mainly those concerning equality for all, had a lifelong impact on Elisabeth Abegg. The fact that the French-German Schweitzer considered himself to be French instead of German may have also shaped Abegg's view of Germany early on. If her idol had seen flaws in Germany and decided to not be seen as German, it is likely that Abegg never was a nationalist. Elisabeth Abegg was undoubtedly a good person but without these major influences in her life she probably would not have had the courage to rescue Jewish people as she had done.

Even before the war began, Elisabeth Abegg led a very respectable and giving life as a teacher. To be a teacher implies that she cared about others. The whole profession is about helping children understand the world they are living in. It was a perfect job for her. She taught at Luisen Madchenschule, which was a very fashionable all-girls school in Berlin. Her students remember her being a very caring teacher and she was well liked. As she taught at this school, she passed on many of Schweitzer's humanist beliefs. She wanted her students to realize like she had at an early age that everyone is equal. This was especially comforting to her Jewish students who felt some discrimination, and many of her students did come from Jewish homes. Her strong humanist beliefs and how unashamed of them she was later got her into trouble.

After Hitler rose to power, her school was appointed a new director by Nazis. Obviously, this new director shared the same beliefs as the Nazis who appointed him. With his anti-Semitism and Elisabeth's humanist beliefs it was no surprise there were many conflicts between them. She refused to sit by and do nothing while he made his dislike for Jews known. Therefore, not long after the new director started working at her school was she forced to leave. She was moved to a much less fashionable school. However, that did not discourage her. She kept teaching with the same passion as she had before and she kept enforcing her humanist beliefs. Unfortunately, she was forced to retire in 1940, only a year after the war had begun. She still kept contact with many of her friends and former students, from both schools, who were Jewish.

Elisabeth Abegg was deemed "politically unreliable" very soon after being forced to retire. This was the government's way of saying she liked Jewish people and was proud of it. This was thought to be such a serious threat that she was summoned by the Gestapo for interrogation. The Gestapo, a nickname for Geheime Staatspolizei, was the official secret police of Germany and German-occupied Europe. Stated plainly, they were the secret state police, the bad guys. Being interrogated by them was a very intimidating thing and many people would have left there scared. Elisabeth Abegg, however, couldn't be persuaded by the Gestapo, nor did she give them any reason to detain her. She left them even more faithful to her humanist beliefs.

Elisabeth Abegg's decision to help Jewish people escape persecution began with one of her close friends. Anna Hirschberg, a Jew, had been Elisabeth's friend for over forty long years. Since they were young adults, Elisabeth and Anna had shared their lives. There were like family. And then, sadly, Anna was deported to the East. It was when she was deported that Elisabeth realized the severity of Nazi persecution of Jewish people. Losing a friend that close to her obviously hurt her a lot. Even though it was too late to save Anna, Elisabeth Abegg decided to save others from having the same fate.

Elisabeth lived in a three-and-a-half room apartment with her eighty-six-year-old mother and her invalid sister, Julie. To many people in the modern world, that seems fairly small for three grown adults. More than a few would have trouble not going crazy living so close to others. Elisabeth herself probably felt cramped sometimes. But that didn't stop her from opening her house up to others who needed it. She turned her home into a temporary shelter and assembly point for Jewish people. It was a place for "underground Jews" to meet and hide for a short amount of time. These were the Jews who had decided to go into hiding after seeing or hearing about what their fate would be if they did not. She provided the underground Jews with temporary accommodations while she found other permanent hiding places for them. Her friends in the Quaker movement worked with her to find places for them to stay. In addition, she procured forged papers for those who were hiding in her home. This allowed them to leave the country and find permanent and less dangerous hiding places. Elisabeth even skimped on her food as well as her sister's. They gave their extra food-ration cards to Jews. Also, every Friday, she had a special meal in her house where everyone ate together. This helped bring unite everyone and become quite close. She did whatever she could to make the Jews escape as comfortable and successful as possible. In one case she even sold her own jewelry to organize the smuggling of Jizchak Schwersenz into Switzerland, which was a desirable place to go since it was neutral in the war.

In the beginning, many of the Jews who came to her for help were former students and their families. They remembered what a kind person she was and knew she would help them somehow, even if it was just with encouragement. And after knowing each other so well, Elisabeth couldn't turn them away to what would inevitably be their death. She also gave them a lot more than encouragement. But soon after she began helping them, word got around the Jewish community. Before long there were complete strangers coming to her home to ask for help. The way she treated them was no different than how she treated those she knew very well. That alone shows what an amazing person she was. To give up so much for a stranger was remarkable. Many people now wouldn't even spare a dollar for someone they did not know.

What was even more impressive was that no one ever found out what she was doing. In her building, she had many Nazi neighbors. Obviously, they would've turned her in the second they found out given that they believed Jewish people deserved what Hitler had planned for them. Her kind heart and humanists beliefs that led her to want to save Jewish people were amazing. What was just as amazing was her brains that allowed her to do that. She was able to keep her mother and sister quiet while also having over many Jews without any suspicion. Tricking so many Nazis was just icing on the cake.

One of the most memorable success stories of the Jews she helped was the one of Liselotte Perles and her nine-year-old niece Susie. Elisabeth Abegg had met Liselotte through her teaching career; Liselotte was a director of a day care center in Berlin. The two had become quick friends because of their similar jobs and beliefs. Liselotte and her niece Susie had definitely felt the antisemitism that was in Germany. They were forcibly moved into a place called the "Jews' House" in 1943. Three of the apartments were mysteriously closed off after the Jews living in them were deported to the East. They were still living in that awful place when Elisabeth came to the rescue. Despite the anti-Semitism, Liselotte still wasn't sure if she and her niece should go into hiding like many of her friends and family had. She could not be sure if the horrible rumors she heard were true and that kept her from leaving the Jews House with her niece. Fortunately for them, Elisabeth had convinced them to leave the Jews House and go underground. The day she convinced them happened to be an eve of the last large Gestapo round-up of Jews in Berlin. Any later and Liselotte and Susie would have been dead within a month. Elisabeth's constant persuasion and effort to save them paid off. Liselotte and Susie, without a doubt, never forgot what Elisabeth did for them.

Elisabeth Abegg certainly was a righteous person from World War II. Without her selfless act to save Jewish people, hundreds more would have been horribly slaughtered but the Nazis. If she could have helped the six million Jews who were put to death she would have without hesitation. Through her countless efforts to safely bring Jews into hiding she proved she would risk her life for others. The thought of what the Nazis would have done to her if she had been caught is frightening. But despite that frightening image she still helped those who were unfairly blamed for Germany's problems. She was also proof that not all Germans were bad people. The antisemitism that swept through the country showed how awful humans could be. People like Elisabeth Abegg, however,

188

proved that there was still also a lot of hope for the human race. In times of complete and utter destruction, Elisabeth Abegg was one of the minority of righteous Germans that kept everything from completely collapsing. Her efforts were so helpful and influential that the people who were saved by her created a collection of memoirs titled "When One Light Pierced the Darkness." That title says it all.

www.yadvashem.org/yv/en/righteous/stories/abegg.asp
www.holocaustcenter.org/page.aspx?pid=514
www.encyclopedia.com/article-1G2.../abegg-elisabeth-18821974.html
www.history.com/topics/world-war-ii/the-holocaust

Look Past the Title

Clarissa Nowag-Nelson

 When mentioned, the name Goering perhaps entails the second most hatred and anger of any other name of the Holocaust, besides Hitler. Hermann Goering was second in command in the Nazi regime, and he commanded the air war against Britain, prepared the German economy for war, and in 1941, he ordered, "make all necessary preparations for a final solution of the Jewish question in Europe." There is no question that Hermann Goering was an embodiment of all the evil that was the Nazi regime during and before the Second World War. However, as one wise person once said, "Jumping to conclusions is not actually exercise." This could not be more applicable than in the story of Albert Goering's younger brother, Albert, otherwise known as the "good brother." Albert hated the Nazis because of his strong moral convictions, which led him to do all that he could to fight and disrespect the Nazi regime, while also attempting to save as many Jewish or other endangered people as possible. The Holocaust was an enormous crime brought not only against the Jews (6 million killed), Soviet Prisoners of War (2-3 million killed), ethnic Poles (1.8-2 million killed), Serbs (300,000-500,000 killed), disabled (270,000 killed), Romani (90,000-220,000 killed), Freemasons (80,000-200,000 killed), Slovenes (20,000-25,000 killed), homosexuals (5,000-15,000 killed), Jehovah's Witness (2,500-5,000 killed), and Spanish Republicans (7,000 killed), but all of humanity because it made us wonder if there really was any of it left. Those brave souls, like Albert Goering, reminded people that there certainly was and is. Yet, when the Holocaust finally did end, crimes were still being committed, specifically against Albert Goering. Even after all of the good that Albert did, the name Goering left him with an evil reputation and even years of imprisonment, all of which he did not deserve. All of that could have been avoided if people had been responsible and recognized and spread the true story of Albert Goering, instead of assuming that he was a Nazi, just because his brother was, hence the quote, "Jumping to conclusions is not

always exercise." Fortunately, the situation can still be rectified by telling the real story of Albert Goering, so here it is.

His story begins on March 9, 1895, when his Mother, Franziska Tieffenbrunn gave birth to him in a hospital in Berlin. Who his father was is still up to debate. The husband of his mother was Heinrich Ernst Goering, but about a year before Albert was born his mother and a man with the last name of Von Eppenstein were having a sexual affair, so it is quite possible that Albert was actually a half-brother to the rest of his siblings. Von Eppenstein was an aristocrat doubling as a Godfather to the Goering children. It has been reported that Von Eppenstein took a liking to Albert when Albert was still very young, and were strikingly similar in appearance. This may seem inconsequential, but if Von Eppenstein was truly Albert's father then that would make Albert half-Jewish, since Von Eppenstein came from a Jewish heritage. Even so, Albert considered Heinrich Goering his father, as far as it is known, therefore Albert also considered himself non-Jewish. Albert came from a well-known, wealthy family due to his father's work as Reichskommissar to German Southwest Africa and as the German Consul General to Haiti. The family was well connected with friends including the aviation pioneer Ferdinand Von Zeppelin, the German nationalist art historian Hermann Grimm, and the Merck family, owners of the enormous German pharmaceutical corporation Merck. From a young age, Hermann and Albert had a very close relationship, and even when the Nazis rose to power they maintained this fondness of each other by never discussing their political views with each other. This may have been strategy on Albert's behalf because without his brother's help, it would have been very difficult to help as many people as he did escape from Germany. As the Nazi era of Germany began, Albert openly criticized the government and moved away from Germany to Austria. There, he worked to become a filmmaker on a small allowance from Von Eppenstein. This was very noble of Albert, considering he could have taken the easy way out by simply accepting the Nazi regime, and living in the lap of luxury for the rest of his life. However, as will soon be revealed Albert was not the type to accept injustice on other because it was the easy way out.

If one happened to see Albert on the street, that certain someone would see a well-groomed, elegant man with a pencil mustache, cigarette holder, and a melancholy demeanor. He was a lady's man, a musician talented on the piano, and most of all he had the carefree nature of someone who didn't feel any real loyalty to anyone. He was the definition of bourgeois. Yet, according to George Pilzer, the son of one of the victims who Albert valiantly rescued, at his core he was a downright good person who had strong moral convictions to which he always stayed loyal.

Now the story of Albert Goering can properly begin. He threw himself into helping the victims of the Holocaust and speaking out against the Nazi regime, giving up his past ambitions to become a filmmaker. There are an innumerable amount of stories that have been reported detailing how he helped someone in need, or how he showed solidarity with the victims of the Holocaust. One of the best ones describes someone old Jewish women who were forced to get down on their hands and knees by some SS officers to scrub the streets beneath their feet with their jackets. While people gathered around to watch the horrific scene unfold, jeering at and shaming the older women, Albert Goering pressed past the crowds to take off his jacket and start scrubbing the streets as well. As everyone looked around in surprise, the SS officers recognized him as Hermann Georing's brother. Knowing that if any of their superiors were to find out how Albert Goering had publicly shamed himself as a result of their doing they would be severely punished, they demanded he stop immediately. Albert responded that he would not stop until all the old ladies were allowed to stop as well. With this ultimatum, the officers decided to dismiss the ladies as to not bring further punishment to themselves. This demonstrates Albert's willfulness to help others, even if there is no personal gain of his own involved. In this instance, Albert did not save anyone on a life or death situation, but he did that plenty of times, too. In the autumn of 1943, he signed the papers of Czech family so the family members could escape the persecution they were currently experiencing in Czechoslovakia due to the Nazis seizing control of the country. By putting his own name on the document, if the situation had been discovered, he could have faced imprisonment or worse, for allowing them to escape. Ernst Neubach, a well-known writer who Albert helped in his escape from Germany to France in 1938, reported of many other good deeds Albert did. This includes his aid in rescuing his personal doctor, Max Wolf, and many others from being sent to the Dachau concentration camp by obtaining exit permits. Afterward, he would transfer all of the confiscated possessions of these victims to a bank in Zurich, where the victims could reclaim them. One of his bravest endeavors was personally driving the film producer and president of Austria's largest film production company, Oscar Pilzer, to the border, releasing him from the fate of certain death. Undoubtedly, Albert Goering had no fear of risking his own life to help others.

Albert was not only incredibly brave, but he was also clever. A large part of Albert's success came from manipulating his brother and his brother's power to rescue people. One of his common strategies was visiting Hermann and saying that such and such was a very good Jew, and was very deserving of release. Hermann would sign the papers for the Jew to be released and tell his younger brother this was the last time, until one month later when Albert would come begin again. Albert capitalized on Hermann's joy of showing off to him because it took a lot of power for a Jew to be released from a concentration/death camp and Hermann wanted to show Albert he had that power. It is believed that this technique freed over 100 people, including the wife of Franz Lehar, the famous German composer. Another way in which Albert used his brother was in protection. Albert was imprisoned several times, but he was always able to persuade the officers to release him after explaining he was Hermann Goering's brother. Albert showed his tactfulness again while in Prague. A doctor and resistance fighter named Josef Charvat was being kept at Dachau. Albert obtained a letterhead featuring the name "Goering" and wrote to the commandant of the camp to let Charvat go. Two men at the camp happened to have that last name, and since Albert had not specified which one to release, the commandant released both. This cleverness that Albert exercised to fight the Nazis from the inside was a crucial part in Albert's success in saving so many people from the murder and torture of the Holocaust.

As the Nazi regime kept on, Albert was able to find a job as the export director at the Skoda Works in Czechoslovakia. Here, Albert was able to instigate his genius in passive resistance to the Nazis. He would forge his brother's signature on documents so prisoners could escape. He would request laborers from other concentration camps and then have the trucks that were responsible for picking up the prisoners stop in isolated areas so all the workers could escape. Karel Sobota, the assistant to Albert at Skoda told of how Goering would look the other way when Czech workers took longer to do work than expected, incorrectly translated catalogs, "forgot" to do assigned tasks, left work unfinished, and "lost" important documents. At Skoda, Albert was extremely kind to all of the Czech workers and when the time came for Albert's trial in Czechoslovakia, so many people showed up to support him with testimonies to his kindness, they could do nothing other than release him, despite his last name.

Although Albert was intelligent. as we can tell by the way he took advantage of his brother and tactfully helped people escape, often his morals were so against all the persecution and discrimination of the Nazi regime that he could not help but draw attention to himself just to show how much he hated and disrespected Hitler and his regime. A woman named Tatiana Otzoup Guliaeff, who was a young girl of only about six at the time, recounted an amusing memory of Goering. She told of how whenever he would walk into grocery stores, if he found the item he was looking for he would say, "Gruess Got," (God greet you). However, if he could not find the item he wanted, he would say, "Heil Hitler." While stationed in Bucharest, Albert was spotted by some SS officers who were passing by, and they did the Heil Hitler salute. Albert responded by saying, "You can kiss my ass." SS officer disrespect seemed to come naturally to Albert. One day, while working at Skoda, a high-ranking SS officer burst into his office unannounced. Albert required that everyone be announced before they enter his office, so he told his assistant Sobota to lead the man out, and leave him there, while Sobota and he conversed about the weather and their families for over half an hour, until Albert decided to let the SS officer enter. Albert's natural response to anything Nazi was full of sass and rudeness, which is another attribution to his willingness to oppose anything that he thought was wrong wholeheartedly. He never pretended that he supported the Nazi regime because he was a downright sincere person, and to pretend was not a part of his vocabulary.

Some people may consider Albert Goering less courageous than other heroes of the Holocaust because he had this constant umbrella of protection from his brother, but this is an unfair thought. The Gestapo had Goering under constant surveillance due to his dealings with "Jewish circles." They also watched him due to his refusal to participate in Nazi conventions, such as not returning the Heil Hitler sign when prompted--a very common practice of Albert. These observed behaviors resulted in three Gestapo arrest warrants. Finally, on August 24, 1944 the Nazi governor in Prague wrote this official letter to Berlin: "Mr. Albert Goering, who in my opinion is a defeatist of the worst sort, arrived n Prague from Budapest yesterday, bringing news of atrocities. Because he entertains relationships with unreliable Czech industrialists, I consider his unrestricted mobility to be dangerous and therefore request permission to transfer him to the Reich Security Head Office in Berlin for interrogation and clarification of serious suspicions." Although Albert was never brought in, it is clear that the Nazis were planning a way to surpass Hermann's power to incriminate Albert and dispose of him for good. With that kind of threat lurking in his mind, he still continued protesting against the Nazi regime and saving people, who were threatened by the Nazis. How could he not have been brave?

When the war ended, and the Nuremberg Trials ensued, Albert Goering was barely recognized for all of the good that he did. He was immediately imprisoned due to his last name, but after several people testifying for him, he was released. However, not for good. The Americans decided instead to send him to Pankrac Prison in Czechoslovakia with German war criminals, looters, and murderers where he was put on trial again. His trial was held in March 1947, and at the time any person with the last name of Goering was going to be given a death sentence. But, as a testimony to all that he had done for them, the Skoda plant workers and resistance fighters showed up to praise him for everything that he had done to save them and their families. Albert then returned to Germany, but could not find work due to his last name, and was forced to live out the rest of his life quietly in a modest flat. For almost three decades after his death, nothing was published about him, nor was anything published recognizing all of the good deeds he did. A sad example of how the crimes cause by the Holocaust persist today. Albert was such a kind man, in fact, that a week before he died, he married his housekeeper, so that she would receive his pension after his death.

Upon reflection of Albert Goering, one cannot help but see a man of great courage, intelligence, and strong moral convictions. He stood up for others, even though it resulted in no personal gain, simply because it was the right thing to do. He put his life on the line for people he barely knew for no reward, which of course he didn't oppose the Nazis because he thought he was going to be rewarded. The way he was treated after World War II shows how crimes against humanity will continue to be committed if people fail to recognize the true heroes of the Holocaust. It is downright depressing that in 1962, when Ernst Neubach attempted to bring the nobleness and courage of his friend to light, the Germans hushed him up simply because of Albert's namesake. Even worse, is that 20 years after the Holocaust, biographies were being written about Hermann Goering with no reference or appraisal of all the good deeds of his younger brother. Unfortunately, Albert is dead, so he can no longer be thanked or celebrated for the invaluable service he committed to saving those unfortunate victims of the Holocaust, but at least his memory can be spread and recognized so people know what a true hero is.

Goering was an incredibly courageous, intelligent, and even a little humorous man. He avoided the greed trap he could have easily fallen into by simply accepting the ideology and turning a blind eye to all the struggles of the victims of the Holocaust, so he could potentially live out a life of wealth and splendor. Instead, he took the difficult and dangerous path of doing what he knew was best. Even today, after all of his good deeds are available for public knowledge, he is still overlooked by many simply because of his title. Do not jump to conclusions like so many misinformed people have done and recognize Albert Goering for the great man and hero that he truly was.

Works Cited

"Albert Goering." Wikipedia. Wikimedia Foundation, 23 Feb. 2016. Web. 28 Feb. 2016. <https://en.wikipedia.org/wiki/Albert_G%C3%B6ring>.

Bulow, Louis. "Albert Goering, the Good Brother." Albert Goering, the Good Brother. Dk, 2013. Web. 28 Feb. 2016. <http://www.auschwitz.dk/albert.htm>.

Green, David B. "This Day in Jewish History: The Goering Brother Who Would save Jews Is Born - This Day in Jewish History." Haaretz.com. Haaretz, 9 Mar. 2015. Web. 28 Feb. 2016. <http://www.haaretz.com/jewish/features/.premium-1.645880>.

Sporl, Gerhard. "Göring's List: Should Israel Honor a Leading Nazi's Brother?" Spiegel.de. Spiegel Online International, 7 Mar. 2013. Web. 28 Feb. 2016. <http://www.spiegel.de/international/germany/israel-weighs-whether-to-honor-brother-of-leading-nazi-hermann-goering-a-887032.html>.

What Were The Odds?

Cloey Birkmann

"A destruction, an annihilation that only man can provoke, only man can prevent." The concept Elie Wiesel models in his words are not only representative of grand heroism, but the honorable deeds done by the individual. The power of an individual could not stop the destruction that occurred in the years of the Holocaust, it simply was not possible. However, it was the individuals who prevented tragedies and protected wavering hearts from these perils created by man. But what were the odds of a German becoming one of these righteous folk? From a psychological stand point, the chances of a German going against the grain of his or her own people is very low. One of the reasons is because of a concept called the in-group bias. The in-group bias is a human tendency to favor the group that they associate with, and the Nazi Party utilized propaganda to manipulate this tendency. Propaganda drew the picture that Germany was the in-group, while everyone else, specifically the Jews, was the out-group. With the us-and-them concept floating throughout Germany, it made it very easy for members of the Nazi Party to do as they pleased. People either joined in on the activities of the in-group willingly, turned a blind eye to it, or were threatened that going against the grain could cost them their life.

The use of Nazi propaganda went even deeper into manipulating the collective German psyche by mixing the implications of the in-group bias with the scapegoat theory. By creating an us versus them, Germans versus Jews, concept, they also blamed the problems of Germany as a whole on the Jewish people in the country. This created an atmosphere in Germany that allowed perfectly sensible people to turn against anyone who was not a part of their perception of "us" and had now been convicted as the source of Germany's state wide economic dilemmas. However, even with Nazi manipulation of human nature sucking Germans into the destructive Nazi Party, some people still, against all odds, silently rebelled and shattered the shackles of their psychological predisposition. One of these normative outliers was a man by the name of Walter Groos.

Walter Groos grew from humble beginnings. He was born in the year 1898, allowing him to grow to maturity before World War II even began. In his early life he was said to have an aptitude for mathematics and problem solving. Working upon his natural skill, Groos studied at the Technical University of Munich to become an engineer and began working as a civil engineer. Through his work, Groos landed a job as the site manager in a site at one of the sub- camps for Dachau. Thousands of Jews were imprisoned here and forced to work in extreme conditions. The conditions caused so many deaths that inmates called it the "cold crematorium." Now, in the circumstances of Mr. Groos, statistically he would have just done his job and left the imprisoned Jews alone. He was in a position where the easy decision would be to go with the tides of his in group. He could blame the problems of the Germans on these inmates like the others and go on with his work, but he did neither. Groos took advantage of his position to assist the Jews imprisoned here. He brought warm gloves to help protect them from the harsh cold, food to supplement the lack of it provided by the camp, and he also provided much needed medication to help cure the illnesses that were rampant in the camp.

With all of the assistance he provided to the members of the camp, Groos most definitely put himself in danger which, again, goes against his psychological predisposition for self- preservation. Not only did Groos put himself in danger, but he also put his family in danger, but perhaps the answer to Groos' ability to defy predisposition lies in his family dynamic.

Groos was married to a woman whom would be considered half-Jewish by the Nazi regime. She was on the Nazis' radar, however, their family was intentionally looked over due to Groos being a German, and the fact that their children were raised as German Christians. However, if Groos was found out by the Gestapo of the camp he was assisting and reported, his wife would without a doubt face consequences as well. The situation of getting caught grew in potential severity when Groos began hiding his mother-in-law who was half-Jewish like his wife, and two of the boys from the camp by the names of Alexander Rothschild and Mendel Thomas. With the newly developed offenses against the Nazi Party, Groos pushed the limits of his psychological disposition even further. In the face of authority, humans are generally rendered morally impaired at said authority's command, and even more so in the presence of severe punishment for disobedience. This is the reason that after the end of World War II, people who were critical to the Nazi Party and were facing conviction on the world stage claimed that they were "simply following orders." These individuals were the ones who fell to the mind manipulation of the Nazi Party. Numerous psychological studies have delved into this type of authoritative pressure, and have found results that show 90 percent of participants following morally questionable orders in the face of authority even in the absence of punishment. The participants of those experiments had nothing to lose because there was simply no threat, however Groos had everything to lose, and despite that he chose to follow the morally sound path.

Groos was well aware of the consequences that would come with being caught, and yet under every circumstance he stayed true to his personal moral code. With thousands of Nazi Germans being the example of what happens when one doesn't stick to his or her morality and caves in to self-preservative tendencies, Groos still may not be considered a special case. Even if the majority of humans are inclined to crumble to their natural weaknesses, the behavior of Walter Groos is still very much human.

There is a phenomenon that is known in the psychology community as altruism. Altruism is the unselfish regard for the welfare of others, and it is generally seen in abundance where great negativity is present. One may consider it the shining light in a seemingly endless sea of darkness. This is the duality of human nature, and the essence of Elie Wiesel's quote. Groos' actions are most definitely a highly improbable case of altruism. This concept goes against the general truths of human selfish tendencies that manifested in the majority of Germans during this time. So, the question of why Groos, as an individual, ended up taking such actions is till very much unanswered.

From a psychological stand point, this case of duality can be summed up to morality versus authority. Unlike many others, Walter Groos chose to stay true to his morality, and go against the reigning, oppressive authority of the Nazi Party. One reason could be the previously discussed in-group bias. It may seem at first glance that Groos' in-group was the Germans, however when it is taken into account that Groos married a woman with Jewish heritage, he had to have been faced with the subconscious decision between identifying with either the Germans or his wife when the Nazis turned against the Jewish population. Assuming that he claimed his wife as a superior in-group in contrast to the Germans, there are definitely reasons as to how he would've decided upon this.

As Hitler began his rise to power in Germany, Groos did not hide his disdain for the party's politics. In fact, Groos rejected participation in the political world of the twenties and thirties because he claimed that it was too chaotic. The rift between Groos and the Germans was most likely widened even further when the Nazi Party attempted to get him to abandon his wife so that they could persecute her for being a Jew. Groos adamantly refused their requests and stayed with his wife, leading to the unspoken deal that the Nazis would overlook their family. The tension between Groos and the Nazis was definitely visible, but this was a case of protecting someone close to him, unlike his later assistance to the people in the labor camp. With this small battle with the Nazis resolved, Groos most likely solidified his banishment of Germany, as a whole, being his in-group.

With his wife as a living contradiction to the Nazi propaganda campaigns, Groos was, for lack of a better word, immune to the lies being spread about the Jews. Without a doubt, it can be said that Walter Groos was a hero, however it is even more important to recognize that this man was an average human being. Given the correct circumstances, Groos could have very well become a member of the Nazi Party while someone who served as a Nazi could have done something to become a hero as well. Average people that become heroes do not have a sole predisposition for heroism, and those average people that become villainous do not have a sole predisposition for being villainous. It is the duality of human nature that gifts us with the potential for greatness, and curses us with the potential for destruction.

Individuals like Walter Groos are who give humanity guidance in the face of disaster. If man was to disregard the Holocaust as an event brought about by evil, no one would learn that this event was not some inhuman event. The Holocaust was, unfortunately, very human. The actions of Mr. Groos highlight this fact more than one may care to see. Groos' humanity shines through the most in his relationship with the two young boys from Dachau.

Groos helped out more people than just Alexander Rothschild and Mendel Thomas, but unlike the others, he created a very strong bond with those two boys. Groos hid them both alongside his mother-in-law, and showed them the first bit of human compassion they had seen since being enslaved in the camps. Like the others, Groos provided them with luxuries that were not provided in the camp, but he also welcomed them into his family. After the liberation of Dachau, the Groos family took the boys in until they could build up a new life for themselves. Once the boys had moved on in their lives, they continued to keep in close contact with Groos as if they were family.

Groos' relationship with Alexander and Mendel was a prime showcase of altruism. Groos did not have to get close to any of the inmates at Dachau, and it would probably have been safer for him not to. Groos continued to put himself in perilous danger on behalf of the people suffering in Dachau, especially these two boys. It is a huge possibility that if Groos had not grown fond of those two, they would not have made it out of Dachau alive. Even after saving their lives, Groos continued to nurture them. The compassion that saved Alexander and Mendel was just as human as the hatred that put them in the situation that made it so that they needed to be saved.

"A destruction, an annihilation that only man can provoke, only man can prevent." These words were spoken by a man who experienced life as a Jew in a Nazi ruled Germany, so it makes sense as to why it would apply to Walter Groos. But it isn't just about Walter Groos. It is about every average human being. Every person has to decide what side of the coin they will choose. Humanity is the duality created by the conflicting potential to do good or bad, and in the Holocaust it was no different. Every single person had their time to choose what path they would lead. Every single person had equal potential to take either path. In Walter Groos' case, he chose the righteous path. He chose to exercise his power to prevent even greater tragedy in the lives of those imprisoned in Dachau. Walter Groos is a hero, but he is even more so a human.

Works Cited

"Alexander Rothschild." Sunday News. N.p., n.d. Web. 25 Feb. 2016.
< http://sunday-news.wider-des-vergessens.de/?tag=alexander-rothschild >.

"Elie Wiesel Quotes." brainy quotes. N.p., n.d. Web. 25 Feb. 2016.
< http://www.brainyquote.com/quotes/authors/e/elie_wiesel_2.html >.

"Ingroup Bias." AlleyDog.com. N.p., n.d. Web. 25 Feb. 2016.
< http://www.alleydog.com/glossary/definition.php?term=Ingroup%20Bias >.

"Nazi Propaganda." Holocaust Encyclopedia. N.p., n.d. Web. 25 Feb. 2016.
< http://www.ushmm.org/wlc/en/article.php?ModuleId=10005202 >.

"The Righteous Among Nations." YadVashem. N.p., n.d. Web. 25 Feb. 2016.
< http://db.yadvashem.org/righteous/family.html?language=en&itemId=4015126 >.

Ukrainian Hero of the Holocaust: Aleksei Glagolev

Erica Noe

The Holocaust is an event in which we look back and reflect. We look at not only the individual countries, but as humankind as a whole. And we wonder: how could something as small and uncontrollable as culture cause humans to mercilessly and coldly kill millions of their own kind? We look back on the Holocaust and we remember, and try to imagine the pain each and every one of those 6 million Jewish and many other minorities felt every day the Holocaust went on. Although the Holocaust is remembered for its endless hardships and horrors, it should also be remembered for its many heroes who helped to save the lives of these oppressed Jews. These people demonstrated true selflessness and bravery, risking, and some ultimately losing, their lives for the sake of others.

One of these brave heroes was Aleksei Glagolev. Aleksei Glagolev was a Ukrainian Orthodox priest. He was born on July 2nd, 1901, and unfortunately passed away on January 23rd, 1972. However before his death, he was honored as one of the "Righteous Among the Nations." This is a title given to non-Jews who risked their life in the Holocaust to harbor and/or save Jews from the Nazis by the State of Israel. Aleksei's father, Alexander Glagolev, was the priest and professor of Kiev Theological Academy. However, his father died in prison in 1937. His grandmother was the head librarian of the Kiev Theological Academy. His mother's name was Zinaida Petrovna. He had two siblings, a brother and a sister. His brother's name was Sergei and his sister's name was Varavara. He graduated from a high school in Kiev (the capital of Ukraine). He then went on to follow is his family's footsteps and study at the Kiev Theological Academy. This was from 1919 to 1923 (four years). In 1926 he married Tatiana Pavlovna, née Bulashevich. Her family occupation was sugar farming, which influenced her status

198

in the community and their marriage. They were both members of the Kiev religious community of the priest Anatole Zhurakovsky. They had two little girls. The first born was Magdalina, and she was born in 1926. The second born was Maria, and she was born in 1943. He was arrested in 1932 for supposedly acting against the government, however he was released shortly after that. It was only about a week's time. He was set free, but was given no voting rights as a priest. He was allowed no input on important religious matters. Then, he decided to take on a new temporary occupation for the time being. He worked at the constructions side, security in the nursery at the jam factory. In 1936, he went back to school to earn a degree in physics and mathematics at the Kiev Pedagogy Institute. He graduated four years later (in 1940). But throughout all this time, he continued secretly working in an underground church.

In 1942, the Nazis occupied Ukraine. This gave them control over the Ukrainian people, meaning all of their strict laws and fear tactics applied to the people of Ukraine as well. This meant no one was safe. Glagolev and his family risked their lives and harbored Jews in their home. He and his family would not have even been targeted before, due to the fact that they were white Ukrainian Orthodox, with the main job of the household being a priest. If they were to be caught, they would be tortured and executed along with the 6 million other victims of the Holocaust.

Glagolev hid Jews in his own home, and in the homes of other friends and family members. He also tried to make sure that these people had the lowest chance of being searched by Hitler and his Nazi officers. This would ultimately result in the death of the Jews found, and the death of the owners of the home. Glagolev also gave Jews fake christening birth certificates. He got these leftover from his father Alexander Glagolev, who was a priest. His wife Tatiana even changed the photo in her own passport and gave it to a Jewish woman once. This allowed her to leave to a neutral country before the Nazis could get to her. Aleksei Glagolev described this event by saying: "My wife almost paid with her own life for her reckless action. Gestapo walked flat to flat for requisitions. They asked for her papers and when they found out that she did not have a passport, they were going to arrest her and take to Gestapo. Very few people returned to their homes after such arrests. We begged and just about managed to persuade them to leave her alone, a few witnesses having identified her identity." Because Glagolev's wife had given her passport to a refugee Jewish woman, she was almost caught by the authorities. When she was stopped and asked for her passport, she didn't have one. They tried to take her into custody, however they had friends confirm her identity to the authorities. This persuaded them to let her off with a warning. However if they had decided not to listen to the witnesses, she could have been found out and immediately put to death. They also managed to save a family of a Jewish Russian Red Army lieutenant colonel. He had a wife and six kids. The Glagolev family took a huge risk because hiding Jews was punished by execution. Hiding eight Jews together would also be much more difficult. Tatianna was also pregnant at the time.

The stories of the ways Tatiana Pavlovna, Aleksei's wife, helped shows that it was not only Aleksei, a white male, who had the power and bravery to help Jewish victims. Many women took initiative and helped protect and ultimately save the lives of many Jews. Women can also risk their lives and do these heroic things. It shows the power of the women and demonstrates feminism, which is starting to emerge in this era, where women are still thought of as unequal and inferior to men.

There are many methods heroes of the Holocaust used in an attempt to hide and save Jews from being sent to the concentration camps. There were also several risks for discovery of hidden Jews. Jews trying to hide in Christian society was a daunting task.

For example, access-reaching the Christian world required an illegal departure from a ghetto, a transport or a camp, and abandonment-hiding often meant breaking up a family unit. Trying to change, or create new and fake, legal government documents required several types of official documents or forgeries. Jews had to pretend to be Christians, however majority of them had no knowledge of the faith and its core and basic beliefs.

Many Jews had the stereotypical physical characteristics of curly black hair, dark eyes, dark complexion, and a long nose, which made them even more of a target.

Majority of Jewish men were circumcised whereas Christians usually were not. This created a new way of identifying Jewish males. Majority of Jewish people had Yiddish accents and/or used many Yiddish terms. The rescuers were risking their lives in this process. Money or items of value were needed to pay those rescuers who required payment, to purchase food on the black market (hidden Jews did not have ration books), to purchase counterfeit documents. There were also many people who would blackmail rescuers of Jews into giving them money or else they would tell the Nazi officers that they were harboring Jews. This would get not only the Jews killed, but the rescuers as well. Some people even went as far as turning this blackmailing into a profession.

In Autumn of 1943, Aleksei Glagolev was taken into custody by German authorities. He was beaten twice and later deported to Germany along with his son. However, they managed to escape. In 1945 he wrote a detailed letter about the Jews he had saved to the First Secretary of the Central Committee of Ukraine, Nikita Khrushchev. After the war, Glagolev continued working as a priest at Pokrov church until it closed. Afterward, he worked at a few other churches, keeping his same occupation. Toward the end of his life, he fell very ill and physically strained due to his major beatings by Nazi generals while in custody. He had a couple invasive surgeries. The journalist Sergei Kokurin described Aleksei Glagolev and his bravery by saying:

"It is hard to understand to an average man the determination with which Glagolev went against the tide. In 1936 this fragile-looking intellectual was publicly carrying the cross taken off a Church of Nikola the Kind and despite the threats from Komsomol members kept it in his flat. He was the only priest in Kiev that refused in April 1942 to hold a church service to celebrate Hitler's birthday. He was not afraid in 1946 to host in the church the family ordered by Court to leave Kiev within 24 hours, because NKVD officer occupied their flat."

On September 12, 1991, Yad Vashem recognized Aleksei Glagolev and his wife and daughter as Righteous Among the Nations. Harboring Jews was a scary, yet brave thing to do. If one was caught harboring a Jew, it was punishable by death. By saving these Jews, Glagolev was risking not only himself but his entire family as well. People and families who were willing to do this were a very small minority. It demonstrates extreme bravery and it also shows that among the terrors and extreme evil that the Holocaust brings, there were still some good people that were willing to go against the majority to fight for what was right, no matter how scary it may be. People like this are what give me hope for humankind. They help me believe that we as humans have learned from an event as tragic as the Holocaust. Our teachers always say, "We learn about history so that history does not repeat itself." People like Aleksei Glagolev, his family, and other heroes of the Holocaust give me hope that a tragic event like this will hopefully never repeat itself, no matter how many cruel and ignorant people are in this world.

Works Cited

"Holocaust Survivors: Encyclopedia - "Hidden Jews"" Holocaust Survivors: Encyclopedia - "Hidden Jews" N.p., n.d. Web. 28 Feb. 2016.
< http://www.holocaustsurvivors.org/data.show.php?di = record&da = encyclopedia& ke = 98 >.
"I Am My Brother's Keeper." Russian Orthodox Father Aleksey Glagolev. N.p., n.d. Web. 21 Feb. 2016.
< http://www.yadvashem.org/yv/en/exhibitions/righteous/glagolev.asp >.
"Righteous Among the Nations." Wikipedia. Wikimedia Foundation, n.d. Web. 21 Feb. 2016. < https://en.wikipedia.org/wiki/Righteous_Among_the_Nations >.

George Ferdinand Duckwitz

Erykah Erickson

"If we wish to live and to bequeath life to our offspring, if we believe that we are to pave the way to the future, then we must first of all not forget" –Prof. Ben Zion Dinur. In the beginning of World War II, September 1, 1939, was the day that was marked a new phase in the German policy toward Jews. In south-eastern European countries, Jews were drafted into forced labor by governments. Tens of thousands were perished. World War II had transformed Europe and the entire world that resulted in the killing of millions of civilizations and the evolution of satanic scheme of genocide. Hiding Jews in the rescuers home or their property in hideouts and bunkers under houses, cowsheds, and barns, where the Jews could be hidden from the Nazis. With the threat that Jews held over their head, the physical conditions in dark, cold, airless, and crowded places over long periods of time. The rescuers who were putting their life on the line as well would undertake food for the Jews. They would provide false papers and false identities to preserve Jews as non-Jews. The clergy would also fake a baptism certificates. Diplomats in Budapest in 1944 issued protective papers and hung their flag representing their country over whole buildings. Smuggling and assisting Jews to escape was also a very high risk. After completing their immensely successful military campaign in the west, the Germans tightened their grip on European Jewry. South-eastern Europe willingly accepted the German dictate and was incorporated into the Nazi sphere of influence. Through the Nazi ideology prescribed the same fate for all the European Jewry, different methods of implementation of anti-Jewish policy were employed in the conquered countries. Western Europe didn't ghettoize the Jews. The Jews were imprisoned behind fences and walls with the assistance of members of the population. As Nazi tyranny spread across Europe, the Germans and their collaborators persecuted and murdered millions of other people. Between two and three million Soviet prisoners of war were murdered or died of starvation, disease, neglect, or maltreatment. In the early years of the Nazi regime, the National Socialist government established concentration camps to detain real and imagined political and ideological opponents. Increasingly in the years before the outbreak of war, SS and police officials incarcerated Jews, Roma, and other victims of ethnic and racial hatred in these camps. To concentrate and monitor the Jewish population as well as to facilitate later deportation of the Jews, the Germans and their collaborators created ghettos, transit camps, and forced-labor camps for Jews during the war years. The German authorities also established numerous forced-labor camps, both in the so-called Greater German Reich and in German-occupied territory, for non-Jews whose labor the Germans sought to exploit. Following the invasion of the Soviet Union in June 1941, Einsatzgruppen and, later, militarized battalions of Order Police officials, moved behind German lines to carry out mass-murder operations against Jews, Roma, and Soviet state and Communist Party officials. German SS and police units, supported by units of the Wehrmacht and the Waffen SS, murdered more than a million Jewish men, women, and children, and hundreds of thousands of others. Germans targeted the non-Jewish Polish intelligentsia for killing, and deported millions of Polish and Soviet civilians for forced labor in Germany or in occupied Poland, where these individuals worked and often died under deplorable conditions, From the earliest years of the Nazi regime, German authorities persecuted homosexuals and others whose behavior did not match prescribed social norms. German police officials targeted thousands of political opponents and religious dissidents. Many of these individuals died as a result of incarceration and maltreatment. In the final months of the war, SS guards moved camp inmates by train or on forced marches, often called death marches in an attempt to prevent the Allied liberation of large numbers of prisoners. As Allied forces moved across Europe in a series of offensives against Germany, they began to encounter and liberate concentration camp prisoners, as well as prisoners en route by forced march from one camp to another. The marches continued until May 7, 1945, the day the German armed forces surrendered unconditionally to the Allies. For the western Allies, World War II officially ended in Europe on the next day, May 8, while Soviet forces announced their "Victory Day" on May 9, 1945. In the aftermath of the Holocaust, many of the survivors found shelter in displaced persons (DP) camps administered by the Allied powers. Between 1948 and 1951, almost 700,000 Jews immigrated to Israel, including 136,000 Jewish displaced persons from Europe. Other Jewish DPs emigrated to the United States and other nations. The last DP camp closed in 1957. The crimes committed during the Holocaust devastated most European Jewish communities and eliminated hundreds of Jewish communities in occupied Eastern Europe entirely.

Georg Ferdinand Duckwitz was born on September 29, 1904 in Breman, Germany. He grew up in an old patrician family in the city. Even though there isn't a lot about his younger life he attended college and afterward he began his career in the international coffee trade. Duckwitz was a businessman trading with the Scandinavian countries. Soon later he joined the Nazi party in 1932 and worked for a man named Alfred Rosenbergs and his foreign policy office. Eventually left to work for the Hamburg America line shipping company. In 1939 the third Reich assigned him to the German embassy in Copenhagen. Soon later he began working with the Nazi Reich representative Werner best. On September 11th 1943 this had changed his life he was ordered to round-up all the Danish Jews. He traveled to Berlin in attempt to stop the deportation through official channels. But sadly it failed and he had flew to Stockholm two weeks later, ostensibly to discuss the passage of the German merchant ships. While he was in contact with the prime minister he asked if Sweden would be willing to receive Danish Jewish refugees. A couple days later Hansson promised them a more favorable reception. In Denmark on September 9, Duckwitz contacted Danish social democrat Hans Hertfort and notified him of the intended deportation. Hertfort warned the head of the Jewish community and the acting chief Rabbi Marcus Melchior, who helped spread the warning. Sympathetic Danes in all walks of life organized a mass escape of over 7,200 Jews and 700 of their non-Jewish relatives by sea to Sweden. Duckwitz had assumed that he had done everything he could and possibly fearing exposure to the Gestapo he had went back to his official duties. Hitler demanded a new iron-fist policy toward the increasingly rebellious country and an immediate implementation of the "Final Solution." With his help the Jews were transported overnight in ships and boats across the sea to the safety of neighboring Sweden. But sadly only 500 Jews were caught and deported to the camp of Theresienstadt. The persecution of a minority was against the ethos of Danish culture the Danes galvanized themselves to assist the Jews in whatever ways possible. While the Jews enjoyed temporary refuge in Sweden, their Danish neighbors oversaw the protection of their property. Because of the actions of Duckwitz and the Danish people, nearly the entire population of Danish Jews weren't killed.

In conclusion because of this man, many of the Danish Jews were saved and continued to live their life.

Willi Garbrecht: The Everyday Hero

Evan Drukker-Schardl

Trembling and afraid, the Jews of Zawiercie, Poland stood in lines in the square. Gestapo officers strode past, eying each person coldly. They pointed at individuals, sometimes, or families. Women, children, and old men were pulled out by Nazi soldiers carrying rifles and shoved into a shivering huddle at the train platform.

A pair of Luftwaffe officers arrived in the square. "We need workers in our factory," one told a Gestapo officer. They began pulling people from the lines. The Gestapo officers stood by. The officers grouped the people they selected in a corner of the square. They worked quickly, gesturing to whole families to join the group. The Jews whom the two officers selected stood to the side in the square, huddled and not daring to question their fate—they could neither bring themselves to expect death, nor expect life. As the group in the square grew, a Gestapo officer stepped toward the two errant officers. One of the officers took the sidearm from his belt, fired it once into the air, and gestured towards the huddled Jews. The Gestapo officer nodded once and returned to his own selection. The two Luftwaffe officers watched as the Gestapo drove almost 2,000 of the occupants of the Zawiercie Ghetto into the cattle cars of a waiting train. They knew the fate of those people, but they could do nothing. They had already assembled a group of about 40 Jews, to whom they issued factory work cards.

The two officers were Lieutenant Willi Garbrecht, who worked in the local factory; and his coworker, a man named Teichert.

We do not know very much about Lieutenant Garbrecht's background. He was born in 1903 in Germany, though the exact location has never been published. We know nothing of his childhood, family background, or education. We do not know exactly how he came to be stationed at a Luftwaffe factory in a medium sized, rural village in southern Poland. We do know that Lieutenant Willi Garbrecht of the Luftwaffe was the manager of the sewing workshop at a uniform factory in Zawiercie, Poland in 1942, when the first group of Jews was sent to Auschwitz from the ghetto.

In 1942, Willi Garbrecht was a tall, slender young man. At first glance, Lieutenant Garbrecht looked not unlike most Nazi officers. He had a round, perfectly clean-shaven face, light eyes. He wore his light brown hair very short and almost always under his peaked officer's cap. Upon closer inspection, the observer noticed that his lips curved down on one end and up on the other. The observer might wonder whether, at any given moment, he intended to scowl or smile. His eyes, when they were visible from under the bill of his peaked officer's cap, were small but complex. They questioned, but exuded a calm assurance of righteousness assaulted by the pain of the war.

Though we know little about Lieutenant Garbrecht's military career, we can assume that it was fairly unremarkable. Though Garbrecht was an air force officer, he was far from taking flight. Someone placed him in charge of a Luftwaffe uniform factory in out-of-the-way southern Poland, certainly not a complimentary appointment. There are no records of Garbrecht ever having won an award in the course of his service. These facts speak to a less-than-stellar career, at least from the German war perspective. From the perspective of this writer, however, Lieutenant Garbrecht made a great name for himself through his military service.

No one has explained why Lieutenant Garbrecht and his coworker, known to history only as Teichert, were in the market square of the Zawiercie one morning at the end of May 1942. For whatever reason, the two officers were there. Seeing a group of Gestapo officers humiliating the Jewish captives in the ghetto before pulling them from the square to be deported to Auschwitz, Garbrecht and Teichert began pulling dozens of people from the lines of Jews. The Gestapo had not instructed them to do so. No higher-ranking officer had requested more workers in the uniform factory. The two officers didn't know if they would be allowed to pull people from the crowd, but they did so anyway. That day, Garbrecht and Teichert intentionally risked their careers—and probably their lives—to save about 40 Jews from the gas chambers of Auschwitz.

It worked. Garbrecht and Teichert fooled the Gestapo, and began to take in more Jews to work at the factory. As many as 500 Jews worked under Garbrecht. Garbrecht began to form ties with some of the Jews. In one of the few pictures of the Lieutenant, he stands next to his Jewish secretary, a woman named Bam. They stand with their arms clasped behind their backs outside the windows of the factory. Bam is a head shorter than Garbrecht. She is wearing a wool skirt and a blouse unbuttoned to the chest. Her frizzy hair is tied behind her head, and she is smiling brightly. Garbrecht is in his bare, undecorated uniform. He leans slightly towards Bam, so that his right arm brushes her shoulder. Garbrecht's eyes are hidden by the shadow of his cap, and his mouth hovers somewhere between happiness and seriousness. They appear to be friends. We do not know if Bam survived the war, or anything about her life other than that she was Garbrecht's friend and secretary.

Garbrecht also befriended a young man in the ghetto named Joel Grinkaut. Grinkaut was a talented Jewish tailor, and was one of the first whom Garbrecht declared "essential to the war effort" with a group of other young men. Grinkaut survived the war, wrote a book in Yiddish about his experiences, and contributed to Garbrecht's recognition as Righteous Among the Nations in 2011. Grinkaut died in 1981, but his son and daughter-in-law live in Pennsylvania.

Before dawn on a June morning in 1942, the Jews incarcerated in the Zawiercie ghetto were awakened by the shouts and stomps of SS men in the streets. "Alle Juden raus!" they yelled. The Nazis were preparing to deport more people. Those with work cards from the factory took them into the street with them. Those cards would keep them safe. The Gestapo officers ordered the assembled Jews to lie on the ground. They lay in the street for two hours without a word. When a Gestapo officer ordered them to stand, they beat those who did not stand quickly enough. The Gestapo proceeded to check every person's papers. Not everyone had worked in the factory, however. Those without cards stood waiting for a Gestapo officer to pull them into the street and drive them to the cattle cars. Suddenly, the seemingly omnipresent Lieutenant Willi Garbrecht ran down the street. He approached groups of Jews without work cards and said, just loud enough to be casually overheard by the SS, "You forgot your work cards! You must return immediately to fetch them. You are essential to the war effort!" Dozens of young men went to the factory, where they had never worked. They were not deported that day.

Garbrecht was not all-powerful in his ability to save the Jews of Zawiercie, and he knew that. When an Aktion occurred in the ghetto, the Lieutenant came up with as many ways as possible to save who he could, but he could not stop the deportation of thousands of the ghetto's inhabitants, many of whom were women and children. In 1943, the Nazis scheduled the ghetto for liquidation. Lieutenant Garbrecht lobbied to keep the ghetto open to provide labor for his uniform factory, but to no avail. On August 26, 1943, roughly almost all of the roughly 5,000 people in the ghetto were deported to Auschwitz. That day, more than 100 people sat on the street and refused to move when the SS directed them towards the cattle cars. In a final assertion of control and humanity, they stared down the soldiers' gun barrels and into the eyes of their murderers and refused to comply. Each was shot on the spot.

About 500 Jews remained for a few months to continue working in the factory, but the factory was closed on October 17, 1943. Most of the Jews who remained there were deported to Auschwitz, where they were murdered.

Though Garbrecht ultimately failed to save the lives of the vast majority of the inhabitants of the ghetto, his story does not stop with the liquidation of the ghetto. The day before the majority of the Jews were deported from Zawiercie, Garbrecht took his friend, Joel Grinkaut, Grinkaut's wife, Priwa, and six other men into the basement of the factory and hid them there until the deportation ended. A Pole named Antoni Jastrzab, a friend of Grinkaut's, had offered to hide Grinkaut if it was ever necessary. Garbrecht contacted Jastrzab and arranged for one of his assistants in the factory to escort Priwa Grinkaut to his hiding place. Priwa arrived unharmed, and Jastrzab procured false papers for her. She worked in the Sudetenland for the remainder of the war with the false Polish papers. Lieutenant Garbrecht remained in charge of the uniform factory after the murder of the Jews of Zawiercie, so Grinkaut and the six other Jewish men remained hidden in the basement of the factory until the war ended.

We do not know what happened to six of the seven men after the war. Joel and Priwa Grinkaut, however, were reunited, and they immigrated to Israel shortly after the war. Though they rarely discussed their experiences in the war, Joel wrote a Yiddish memoir in Israel about his escape from death. They had one son before moving to the United States. Their son, Dr. Abraham Gonen, is now a professor and dean at Salus University in Pennsylvania.

We know little about the fate of Willi Garbrecht following the war. There is a photograph of his West Berliner driver's license dated August 31, 1953, meaning that he lived in Berlin after the war. He was married once more, and he had a son named Christian. Christian still lives in Berlin, and he represented his father at the Israeli

Embassy in Berlin when Yad Vashem listed Willi Garbrecht as one of the Righteous among the Nations. Garbrecht passed away in 1981.

Though there is little information about the life and character of Willi Garbrecht, his story is enormously compelling. He risked his own life to snatch Jews from under the noses of the fearsome Gestapo. He remained loyal to his friends and maintained his sense of morality in the face an act of pure evil. Garbrecht not only refused to assist in the murders, he refused to allow wanton murder to occur in front of him without resisting as much as he could.

Garbrecht's story is a foil to the faceless evil of the Nazis. The Holocaust typified Hannah Arendt's concept of the banality of evil—acts of horrific inhumanity perpetrated by ordinary people whose stories are shrouded in obscurity and whose culpability is shielded by bureaucracy. Garbrecht was banal. He was a minor Nazi functionary without a story. But instead of using his unimportance to justify permitting or perpetrating pure evil, he used his position as much as he could to try to prevent evil. Garbrecht symbolizes the banality of good—and that is what makes his story so irresistibly hopeful.

Garbrecht's character is particularly compelling because it is a blank slate. He could have had any childhood. His parents could have represented a broad spectrum of values. Any number and combination of experiences could have influenced his mind. Garbrecht represents all of us. Garbrecht is the ordinary person. He contradicts the popular idea in our historical narrative that the ordinary person is powerless, that we must leave bold action to the elite and extraordinary. Garbrecht's story teaches us that we are all extraordinary, that we all have a powerful drive to be good. Wherever we come from and whoever we are-regardless of gender, health, wealth, or circumstance, we can and will stand up for righteousness when righteousness needs vigorous defense. When we are faced with the choice to act, watch, or participate, may we always channel Lieutenant Garbrecht and go out of our way to act with determination against the evil bred by hatred and fear.

Ukrainian Heroes of the Holocaust: Klymentiy Sheptytsky

Geraldine Castaneda

Following World War I, the Treaty of Versailles explicitly focused blame on the Germans. The treaty worked to humiliate and impoverish the German people throughout the nation. It called for reparations that would stem from the German economy and also stripped Germany of much of its territory and army. As a result, Germany entered into the 1920's in economic chaos and instability under the Weimar government. Inflation throughout the nation was at an extreme which allowed for the vulnerability of the common people as they were struggling to find some strand of hope to hold onto during the adversity they faced at the time. this vulnerable environment was the perfect breeding ground for Adolf Hitler to rise to power. This demagogue utilized the susceptibility of the German people of the time as a platform to create the socialist Nazi Party. Hitler successfully played on German anti-Semitism, blaming the Jews for the German defeat of World War I. Initially, Hitler was jailed for trying to overthrow the government. Surprisingly, his time in prison worked in his favor as he was able to write his book "Mein Kampf" (My Struggle) while in jail in 1923. However, Hitler soon returned to politics as the Nazi Party began to rapidly ascent to power. Adolf Hitler was appointed chancellor of Germany in 1933 after a fire incident in Reichstag, for which he blamed the communists. It was during this time that Hitler took advantage of the situation and declared a national emergency where he followed to take dictatorial powers. Once in power, Adolf Hitler immediately began to rebuild the German army which effectively broke the rules and regulations stated in the Versailles Treaty. The German economy rebounded under Hitler's rule as he focused on rebuilding the nation's army and their supplies as well as the autobahn system which stimulated the growth of jobs throughout the nation.

For fear of the initiation of another worldwide conflict, the United States and the allies followed a policy of appeasement. This policy called for the allied nations to allow Hitler to, at a certain extent, do as he pleased in order to avoid another war as many of the nations throughout the world were still recovering from the reparations that World War I called for as well as recovering both emotionally and economically as a people. As the allied countries continued to follow this policy of appeasement, Hitler was able to take advantage and he soon began to invade neighboring lands without a second thought. Hitler successfully occupied Austria, the Sudetenland and Czechoslovakia between the two-year span of 1938 and 1939. The appeasement policy continued to be favored by the allied populations, and especially for the United States of America. As the American public and political figures figured that the policy of appeasement had kept stability following the first world war, America proceeded to adopt a policy of isolationism that called for the avoidance of involvement in world relations. They turned into a reluctant power. At the time, this seemed the best option for the American people as America's economy was still suffering from unpaid war debts. Still traumatized by World War I propaganda and soldier's stories and news, the American people held xenophobia, a fear of strangers or outsiders; different people. America was still also striving to recover from the social and economic effects of the Great Depression. Lastly, American people everywhere, especially the up and coming younger generation, strongly advocated pacifism and the notion of non-violence and non-involvement in world affairs.

During the same time, Hitler was following a seemingly similar route of peace, but with the Joseph Stalin. In 1939, Hitler signed the Non-Aggression pact with the Soviet Union. Together, Germany and the Soviet Union invaded Poland on September 1939. Hitler's blitzkrieg tactics dismembered Poland in a matter of two weeks. This attack from the part of Germany and the Soviet Union triggered the declaration of war on Germany from France and England. World War II ensued.

The Republican party lead isolationists. The Nye committee investigated deeper into U.S. armament manufactures during World War I looking into those who profited the most from World War I and later into general wartime profits and misuse. A case that strongly supported the pacifist movement was the question that stemmed from many Americans, "Why go to war when so many people profited from World War I?" The movement triggered the neutrality legislation that banned the sales of arms to belligerent. In other words, the legislation banned loans to those nations in war;for America specifically, that meant no loans to Europe. However, a loophole was soon created where we would be able to give cash to our allied nations. This process was coined "Cash and Carry," which allowed the United States to grant our allies at war cash that would allow them to buy weapons. At this time, England was the only country not under the control of the Soviet Union or Nazi regime. Essentially, the United States was England's only friend.

The United States continued to operate a lend and lease policy to its allies. In response to Japanese aggression in China and Korea the United States imposed an embargo of raw materials to Japan which worked to freeze Japan's assets. Japan, disgruntled, attacked U.S. ships on December 7th, 1941 at Pearl Harbor. The United States wasted no time in declaring war on Japan and Germany followed by those countries declaring war on the United States days later.

After Germany's conquest of Poland. According to Nazis, Ukrainians were deemed sub-human along with the Jews. At this time 40 million Ukrainians lived in the area that was allegedly the land that would form the new perfect German nation. On June 22nd, 1941 Hitler commenced his "Drive to the East" in which he invaded Ukraine on his way to the complete and brutal invasion of Moscow. On the first day of the invasion, the Ukrainian cities of Odessa, Kiev, and L'viv were bombed. The German troops with the full support of the whole German army invaded and captured huge territories of Ukrainian land with little resistance. At first, the Ukrainian people treated Nazi rule as liberation from Russian communist rule. Russian communist rule imposed harsh limitations on the Ukrainian population and the repression was widely rejected throughout the nation. Although the Nazis seem to be at first the liberation of this communist rule, the true Nazi intention soon came to light as the Ukrainian people found that they were treated far worse under German Nazi rule. In accordance to Stalin's earth scorching policy, the Russian army made sure that a large amount of Ukrainian land and resources were destroyed before they were finally to be taken over by the German army. Since the government of the Ukrainian SSR fled the country, it was not able to be considered a collaborating partner of Germany. Ukraine then was occupied by a variety of national forces. Though there were many attempts to establish an independent Ukrainian nation, the German army was quick to put down these "rebellions" and arrest their leaders. The Ukrainian Insurgent Army (UPA), was founded in 1942 and consisted of over 200,00 men and women who fought and stood up against the German and Russian armies in attempts to win their independence.

The initial plan of the German army was to kill all Ukrainian men over the age of 15. However, they decided to instead work them to death so as to have these men help the German war effort. Throughout their own homeland, Ukrainians were forced to wear badges like prisoners in order to make them easily recognizable by any German that was more than willing to abuse a Ukrainian citizen. Ukrainian citizens were allowed only the most primitive accommodations and still many died of starvation because of their extremely limited food rations. Many Ukrainians were sent to Germany to work in slave laborer camps. Others were killed by allied bombings and only a scarce amount of survivors were successfully allowed back to their homeland.

The German invasion of the Soviet Union in the summer of 1941 triggered the rise of pogroms in virtually every town or village where large Jewish populations resided, including Ukraine. The pogroms employed brutal violence against Jewish communities in several harsh ways. Though in some areas only professionals such as lawyers and doctors were targeted, the common Jewish populace such as women, elderly people, and even children were often times attacked without a warning. Those participating in the pogroms were known to use agricultural tools as well as household items such as axes, sticks with razor blades, and bats to harm, and many times kill, Jews they encountered. The "Petliura Days" were also an enticing motive for the excessive brutality against Jewish Communities. During these days, the Nazis offered the Ukranian people an opportunity to avenge the assassination of their leader, Symon Petliura by a young Jew in 1926. These acts of violence and murder were largely associated with the looting of Jewish homes, the abuse of Jewish women, and the burning down of synagogues. In many pogroms, Jews were randomly selected to dig up the graves of NKVD officers whom had evidently been assassinated by the Ukrainian people. These unfortunate select Jews had to dig up the mass graves, retrieve and clean the corpses- sometimes even forced to lick the corpses- and then beaten to death and later thrown in the same grave they had just emptied.

These merciless acts against Jews in Ukraine were much too common. However, there was bound to be some exception to this brutal hatred towards Jews. In his time, Klymentiy Sheptytsky was the exception. Sheptytsky was born in a village near L'viv in 1869 to a noble Polish family. He was fortunate enough to have received his education at home. He went on to study in Munich as well as in Paris and became a doctor of law at Jagiellonian University at the age of 23. After studying, he returned to his village in order to care for his parents and manage the family estates. In 1911, Sheptytsky decided upon being a monk and entered the Benedictine monastery in Beuron, Germany. After a year, he followed in his brother's footsteps and returned to the Ukrainian Greek Catholic Church. There, he took the religious name Clement after Pope Saint Clement I. In 1937, he traveled to L'viv to aid his ill brother. In 1939, the area was occupied by communists, however, the Soviet "liberators" quickly adopted a plan to get rid of Ukrainian intellectual elites and the church. Their army murdered his brother along with his family. In 1941, the persecution of Christians was halted due to the Nazi-Soviet War and the German occupation of Ukraine. During that time, Father Clement helped rescue a numerous amount of Jews, harboring them in Studite monasteries, and organizing groups of people who were willing to help the Jews escape. Because of the large community of monks at the Studite monastery, many of the Jewish boys would go unnoticed by German authorities. As the Soviets returned in 1941, an order to destroy the church and subject it to Moscow Patriarchate was implemented as Father Clement was named the Archimandrite of the Studite Order which placed him as one of the highest ranking clergymen. In this position, he soon became an informal leader of the church and regularly met with monks and priests in order to strengthen their resolve. On June 5th, 1947 he was arrested by the Soviet authorities and held initially in an NKVD prison in L'viv and was later taken to a prison in Kiev. He refused to renounce his faith and serve the Moscow Patriarchate and was consequently sentenced to eight years of imprisonment. Father Klymentiy was remembered as being tall, thin, and having a rather long white beard. He unfortunately died on March 1st, 1951.

Works Cited

http://www.history.ucsb.edu/projects/holocaust/Resources/BookReviews/rebecca.htm

http://www.ushmm.org/m/pdfs/20130500-holocaust-in-ukraine.pdf

https://en.wikipedia.org/wiki/Klymentiy_Sheptytsky

Albert Goering

Ginger Harris

 We like to believe that right now the Holocaust has ended. However, our world today is living in a time period of another Holocaust. The Islamic State of Iraq and Syria (ISIS) and their efforts to drive out Christians have an unparalleled connection to the same principles of the Holocaust. Yes, it is in a different place, at a different time, and is happening to a different group of people, but it is still genocide. The major difference in what is happening now and what happened then is the influence of western media. We all are witnesses to ISIS and what they are doing. Many people were not aware of what was going on during the Holocaust until the damage had already been done. As we evaluate the unsung German heroes of the Holocaust, let it inspire bravery in all of us to stand up to the genocide that is taking place in our world today.

The Holocaust was the systematic killing of 6 million Jews by the Nazi regime. When the Nazis came to power in Germany, they took action believing they were the superior race. Jews were therefore deemed inferior and a threat to the racial well-being of Germany. Many other people were targeted due to their "inferior race" also those who were disabled and homosexual. It is a very dark period of history. This event took a toll on our humanity but it also brought out the best of our humanity. The Holocaust made individuals step up to the challenge being presented to them. Many had to make ethical decisions that in the end saved people lives. The amount of bravery brought out in people is extremely remarkable. I will be focusing on one man in particular, Albert Göering. He, along with many others, risked his life to save the lives of others.

Albert Göering was the brother of Hermann Göering, a very high up Nazi, who worked closely with Hitler. The two brothers had a very messy childhood. They had three other siblings. Their father had a career that forced him to travel greatly, and in turn be away from home quite often. Their mother had an affair with Dr. Hermann von Epenstein. He was at their mother's side at the birth of both of the boys. He then became the godfather of the children and housed them. He took them to a beautiful castle to spend the summers in. Hermann had bright blue eyes and blond hair. Albert had dark features like brown eyes. Most people suspected that Albert was the love child of Dr. Hermann and not the child of Hermann's father. Hermann was very outgoing as a child, whereas Albert was far more quiet and reserved. Hermann showed a great interest in politics, whereas Albert showed hardly any.

Albert took an education path far away from politics. He served as a communication engineer in the First World War. He then enrolled at a technical school in Munich to study mechanical engineering. The college was full of political activists. Albert interacted with many leaders of the Third Reich. He, however, was extremely uninterested when it came to politics and stayed away from it. He was a very smart, but reserved boy. He was often referred to as sad and distant.

Hermann Göering was having a much different experience than Albert at this time in his life. He was going around blond hair and blue eyed having a blast in college. He really took these years to dig into politics. He got along well with many people. He fell into Hitler's bait to have a strong group of young nationalists. He was passionate and very involved in what he was doing. Following this period of Hermann's life he went into four depressing years. He became addicted to morphine. It was at this time that extreme years of silence between the brothers began. Albert strongly opposed the actions Hermann was taking and urged him to draw away from it. He told his peers that if his brother didn't get out now he would travel on the completely wrong path. This continued for twelve years to come.

Hermann Göering went off the grid for four years and came back to Hitler only to become one of his most trusted Nazi leaders. When he returned he climbed the ranks, eventually becoming one of the most powerful German leaders practically controlling the economy. In 1938, when the Germans annexed Austria, the brothers were reunited and began speaking to each other again. As noted before, Hermann was addicted to drugs. His actions were at times odd and unexplainable. On drugs or not, many of his actions are unjustifiable. In 1933, he became head of the air force in Germany. Albert would use his closeness to his brother and his insecurities to get what he needed to save Jews lives.

Albert often went to his brother to sign papers to approve the movement of people, not to mention him. Hermann Göering went through a very hard phase in his life. He was depressed and addicted to drugs. He was insecure about himself and the way he was presented. When Hermann came to be the head Nazi he was, Albert used his past and his emotional connection to manipulate him into doing things he otherwise wouldn't have. Albert would go to his brother to get papers signed to let Jews out of Germany. Albert would deceive his brother, especially appealing to his ego. Albert would say to Hermann that he needed to prove his power to him. Hermann, having the past experiences that he did gave into this. Every time Albert went to Hermann for help he would claim it was his last. However, Albert kept coming back for to receive help for others. Albert also in trouble with the Nazis many times, had to use his last name to his advantage.

There are some incredible stories of how Albert saved Jews. He once managed to convince a number of guards to load Jews up onto these trucks before driving away into free land. He saved many people from humiliation in the streets. He put his life on the line day in and day out to fight something he thought was wrong. Albert hated the idea of this genocide happening. He absolutely despised it. It didn't matter where his brother stood or what he believed in; Albert fought the system. Once in Vienna, Albert came across a mob mocking these women being forced to scrub the streets. He stopped and very heroically took off his jacket and took the womens' place. He managed to diffuse the crowd by showing his papers with the name Göering. Albert was arrested by the Gestapo when he punched two of the officers to help save a 75 year old woman. He helped many of his friends escape from Austria into a safer land. When Hermann captured an important Jew in Austria he was so proud of his triumph that he offered his sibling one wish. Albert had him release one of his friends from jail. Hermann had to live up to this wish as to not damage his reputation with his brother.

Albert kept a list of all the people he directly managed to save from execution. This list had 34 people on it. That is 34 lives that otherwise would have been taken. Think of it like a class of students. If you were to die, think of the amount of people it would affect. Think about the amount of people who would feel loss and pain from your death. Now multiply all those people by 34. The amount of pain the Holocaust caused among the human race altogether is unbelievable. Albert managed to save the lives he could. If I was in his position, or if any of us were in his position would you have done the same? The courage brought out in people gives the inhumanness of the Holocaust a good fight. Albert kept record of the people he saved because he knew that the rest of the world would punish those who supported this genocide. He had faith that Hitler and the Nazi regime would fail. He was right. Albert, by keeping that list, managed to save his own life when the world finally cracked down with justice. The world is supposed to contain all different kinds of people. That is what makes it interesting. What would life be like if everyone looked and acted the same as everyone else. All of us being different, allows us to challenge and push each other to strive for a better world as a whole.

In 1944, Albert was sentenced to execution for fighting the Nazi regime. At this point in time, Hermann put out all his resources into saving his brother. Hermann's position was weak at the time due to past helpings for his brother. Hermann explained it was the last time he could help his brother, that this was really it. Albert's life was saved and he was able to testify at the Nuremburg trials. The last time the brothers saw he each was in 1945. The Allies caught Hermann; this was a huge victory for them. Albert was also detained for being his brother, in close ties with Hermann. Hermann told Albert that he would be free soon enough. It amazes me how these two brothers were able to keep a good friendship even with such extreme opposite political views.

Two years after the brothers' final interaction Hermann was imprisoned for crimes against humanity. Hermann committed suicide in his cell before they could execute him. Albert also was in prison for two years. He was unable to convince his interrogators that he was innocent in the process. I can completely understand that it would be hard to find a close brother of one of the head Nazis innocent. The testimonies of the people Albert saved, accessible through his list, were the reason he was set free. While free, the burden of Albert's last name was one he would never be able to run away from. When free, Albert had an extremely difficult time interacting with anyone. He was often shunned everywhere he went throughout Germany. He fell into a dark period of depression, drinking heavily. His wife divorced him and took their daughter away to Peru. Albert was very lonely and unhappy.

Albert lived off of food sent to him by the people he had saved. Their support came at a time when he needed it most. He had saved these people's lives and it was up to them to return the favor. Albert died in 1966 due to pancreatic cancer. He did, however, die an honorable man.

Albert's amazing actions were only discovered and made public in the very recent past. If Albert's story took so long to reveal, imagine how many more are still out there. There are so many people who we don't know about. So many people had the valor to stand up for what they believed was right. Learning about all these heroes allows us to gain some motivation to stand up for what we believe in. Never let someone push you down without a fight. Learning all about the German heroes of the Holocaust restores my faith in humanity that otherwise might have been lost from the Holocaust. Albert Göering was strong enough to go against his brother's political beliefs. He was very close with his brother despise their difference. He saved thirty-four lives that otherwise would have been lost. Anne Frank once said, "I don't think of all the misery, but rather the beauty that still remains." I believe reflecting on the Holocaust we should have this perspective in mind. It is important to remember all these beautiful people that show off that people have compassion inside of them. Let the bravery of the people before us; encourage us to face all of our world's harsh realities with the same might and a desire to fix what has been broken.

Works Cited

"Albert Goering." Albert Goering. Web. 25 Feb. 2016. <http://www.hitlerschildren.com/article/647-albert-goering>.

Bulow, Louis. "Albert Goering, the Good Brother." Albert Goering, the Good Brother. 203. Web. 25 Feb. 2016. <http://www.auschwitz.dk/Albert.htm>.

Bulow, Louis. "Albert Goering." Albert Goering. 2013. Web. 25 Feb. 2016. <http://www.goering.dk/>.

Burke, William H. "Albert Göering, Hermann's Anti-Nazi Brother." The Guardian. Guardian News and Media, 19 Feb. 2010. Web. 25 Feb. 2016. <http://www.theguardian.com/lifeandstyle/2010/feb/20/albert-goering-hermann-goering-brothers>.

On the Sacrifices of a Righteous Soul

Henry Genus

World War II was a trying time for a large percentage of the world's population. Through the duration of this period of suffering, some of the world's worst atrocities were seen. The circumstances that led up to this suffering involved a continual storm of suffering, specifically for the people of Germany. World War I left the country in shambles, laying the path for the rise of the Nazi Party, and the eventual need for righteous souls to save the Hebrews from their wrath.

The end of World War I in 1918 destroyed the German morale. Due to the parameters set by the Treaty of Versailles, economic and military growth in the country was limited. The country lived in relative poverty. The people searched high and low for someone to take the blame, and this allowed for perhaps the world's best known demagogue, Adolph Hitler.

Hitler and his Nazi Party turned directly towards the Jewish community as a scapegoat for their problems. They looked toward the economic success of the Jews and out of frustration, blamed the loss of World War I on them. Because of the vulnerable state of the nation, people largely accepted these ridiculous remarks. They grew to a fanatical support of Hitler, which allowed for him to violate the Treaty of Versailles with little to no opposition from the German community. His actions in this trying time led at least in part to the conflict now known as World War II.

Hitler kept his true motives in relative darkness in the early parts of his campaign, but his plans all came to fruition November 9, 1938. On a night that ultimately became the beginning of the end for the safety of German Jews, German soldiers smashed windows and destroyed property owned by Jewish citizens, which led to the date being remembered as Kristallnacht, or the "Night of Broken Glass."

Anti-Semitism only became worse from there. Following the trend set on that infamous date in November, people began to abuse, both verbally and physically, Jewish citizens. Very soon they were required to wear Stars of David on their clothes as identification of their religion. Special laws, the least of which being a curfew, were put in place regarding these people. German officers, known as the gestapo, soon began arresting Jewish people and taking them away to a location unbeknownst to the population.

At this time, the majority of German citizens saw the disappearance of Jewish civilians as not the main problem on their minds; instead, war issues were in the forefront of their imagination. Hitler faced a constant fear of betrayal from his tentative ally Russia to the east. They attempted to battle west to quickly remove the possibility of a war on two fronts, and moved forward relatively easily through the French countryside, by route of the Ardennes Forest. Ally troops were not expecting penetration of this haven for foliage; therefore, the Germans faced low casualties in their march toward the Atlantic Ocean.

Another reason for the relative ease with which German forces tore through enemy lines was their military strategy. They came first with bombing, followed by a quick assault by way of panzer, or armored, tanks. This tactic became known as Blitzkrieg, or "lightning war," because of its quick but effective nature. The people of Germany, in this phase, were concerned with the disappearance of the Jewish people because of the relative lack of war-based fear, but this all changed very quickly on June 6, 1944.

June 6 saw a quick reversal in the mental and military state of the German population. Ally forces landed on multiple beaches in Normandy, northern France. The Germans mowed them down early, but because the invasion caught the Germans off guard, the allies were able to battle their way into German territory. They pushed the German forces to the east, and proceeded to prepare for a final strike, when German forces quickly pushed through ally lines and "bulged" into ally territory. General Patton of the American army quickly and efficiently put a stop to what later became known as the Battle of the Bulge, effectively ending the German war effort. From then on it was a quick and simple effort to invade the German capital of Berlin. Upon arrival at Hitler's bunker, Soviet forces, coming from the opposite direction, found Hitler dead of apparent suicide.

This quick downfall of the German war effort frustrated the German people. They began frustration with their government, especially after hearing about Hitler's "Final Solution," which was the codename for the horror-filled episode known now as the Holocaust. When the German people heard of this tragedy, they protested, and Hitler claimed he stopped; however, he did not. He continued the Holocaust until his death, even ramping it up as the Germans came closer and closer to defeat.

The horrors of the Holocaust were unbeknownst to the majority of the world until ally forces swept through the western front and began to share stories with the Russians. Upon traveling in the war effort, allied forces stumbled upon remnants of the horrible tragedies that had occurred. The full scale of the horrors was not understood until later, but the American soldiers essentially saw work camps where Jewish people were taken when they were taken from their homes.

We now know that many of these camps were much worse than work camps, however. Many of the camps served a much more sinister purpose. Able-bodied men were sent to the work camps, but women and children faced a much more horrible fate. They were sent to death camps, to be killed with cold efficiency in poisonous gas showers. German scientists did much worse with many of them though. Secret tests were run on living human subjects into the most efficient and painful ways to kill a man, as well as tests which actually served a positive purpose for the scientific community, but were crueler than anything that should have been attempted. When the German war effort began to go downhill, Hitler sent orders to begin killing everyone. They flushed everyone into the showers and gassed and cremated them with dark, evil resolve. These camps killed a sum of approximately 11 million people over a span of within five years, 6 million of which were of the Jewish faith. This was one of the darkest and most horrible times in recent history for the human race.

These dark and trying times for the world developed perfect circumstances for the righteous to prosper. One such of these was a man named Hans Georg Calmeyer.

Hans was born in Osnabrück. His father was a powerful judge in the area, so all throughout his childhood he knew he wanted to be a lawyer, and become one he did—he was known as one of the most effective lawyers in the area. His practice, which was very small, employed one Jewish woman, so when the Nazis came to power he was banned from practicing because his allegiance was in question. Calmeyer decided to join the army instead of attempting to fight it.

Because he was fluent in Dutch, he was assigned to intelligence during the 1940 German invasion of the Netherlands. There he met Dr. Stuler, director of the Department of the Interior of the Generalkomissariat für Verwaltung und Justiz, or department for administration and justice, a man who would permanently alter the course of his life. He offered Calmeyer a position identifying the Jews in Holland and overseeing appeals.

Calmeyer was appalled by the sheer number of people essentially sentenced by the state due to their perceived heritage, so he worked hard to overturn as many appeals as he could. He chose coworkers who he knew he could trust with his life, so that his cell could effectively free as many Jews as possible from the death sentence of the Nazis. He then worked diligently analyzing the Nuremberg Laws, which set forth the laws with which Jewish people were captured. He found a loophole, and his department quickly overflowed with appeals requesting he help them escape from the trap set forth by the Nazis. People wanted him to change the status of their grandparents to half-Jewish, which would dilute the religion enough in the genealogy to clear them of any suspicion from the Nazi government.

Calmeyer's department often worked in ways he would not personally be a part of, but which he would oversee, and which he was responsible for by proxy in appointing these staff members. His employees appointed certificates of Jewish citizens, which established them as Christian and removed all suspicion from their shoulders. In the cases where a certificate could not be awarded, they aged paper and forged the writing and seal, saving the lives of those who were given these.

Hans Calmeyer, while his department was forging papers, worked on an equally important task. He dealt with cases based purely on suspicion, which people appealed on the grounds of insignificant evidence. He was to order anthropological investigations, performed by Professor Dr. Hans Weinert of Keil. This man was in conjunction with Calmeyer, so he constantly produced reports claiming the accused were in fact not of Jewish heritage, and sparing their lives. Calmeyer then made the decision of whether or not to help a person based on how much suspicion it would bring to his department—if he were found out it would jeopardize the lives of everyone he could have saved later, as well as the many he had already saved.

Along with ancestry, Calmeyer went in another direction to save the lives of many Jewish people. Clammer worked diligently to save the lives of those involved in mixed Aryan-Jewihs marriages by claiming the children had not been brought up in the Jewish faith.

Calmeyer became more and more gracious with who he would save as the war went on, so the Nazis began to take note of him. They accused him of abbstammunsschwindel, or genealogical fraud. When the people he had saved came back to try to claim the possessions that had been unfairly taken from them by the state, even more suspicion fell on Calmeyer.

In this state of suspicion, the Nazi secret police acquired a spy named Ludo ten Cate, who stole and relayed information on spared Jews and even the colony of Surenham, where many of them had been hiding. Zimmer caused a 1944 ruling that the state should look closely into all cases overseen by Hans Calmeyer, but it was never enacted due to ten Cate's rabid anti-Semitism.

Calmeyer's most impressive feat, however was a collective appeal by a sum of 4,787 Jewish people currently residing in Portugal. All of those who appealed could not be deported, so their lives literally fell into the hands of Calmeyer in the form of these petitions on paper. Calmeyer was able to spare 2,019 of these people, a feat which should not be taken lightly in any sense. To the ones whom he rejected he provided detailed information on how to disappear and tips on the fact that the Gestapo was coming for them, saving many of their lives as well. Calmeyer, through this one collective appeal, saved the lives of approximately 3,000 people.

Calmeyer's actions should not be taken lightly. He risked life and limb in this trying time in world history to save the lives of many people whom he had never even met. With all the tragedy he saw around him in his service, he still found it in his heart to save an incredible sum of Jewish people from the horrors of Hitler's final solution, for a large stretch of the time without knowledge of the exact details of the Nazi actions. When he learned of the horrors and risks involved in this horrid plan, he was not deterred, in fact, this is when he began to sporadically approve more and more petitions, risking himself further for the lives of complete strangers. By the heroic nature of his actions, it is no wonder why this amazing man is recognized as one of the righteous Gentiles of this horrendous era.

Hermann F. Graebe's Employment

Hunter Hill

There are some who believe that with every evil there is a balancing kindness in response, that when there is a great darkness that a balancing light will come out of it. The Holocaust was a time of mass murder and enslavement for the Jews, and while it was a time of many evils, it was also a time where the depths of human altruism shined through. An example of this is the German construction worker Hermann Friedrich Graebe, who single-handedly saved dozens of Jewish people, even though he was initially interested in the Nazi Party. He was not Jewish and could have been as easily swept up by the Nazi Party's words as many German people were, but instead he fought for the side of the victims, saving as many as he could. Hermann Graebe was a single man who had a large hand in helping the Jewish people of Germany, and deserves the title of "Righteous Among the Nations."

Graebe was a German man who, despite his situation in life, was still able to make the right decision in the end. Hermann Friedrich Graebe was born on June 18, 1900 to a poor family in Rhineland, Germany. (Yadvashem.org) At the time, Rhineland was an area that housed mostly Roman Catholics, which meant even more hardship for Graebe as his family was Protestant and the relations between the two were tense at minimum. He grew up living with an unfortunate situation, and only got worse when World War I started. From the age of 14 he had to live with the effects that the war and its aftermath had on Germany, on top of already being poor to begin with. In 1931, he joined the Nazi Party, initially taken by their words as many Germans were. (Yadvashem.org) His initial decision was one he soon realized was not correct, for in 1934 he openly criticized its campaign of Anti-Semitism at a Nazi Party meeting. (Yadvashem.org) He was jailed for this "offense" for several months. (Yadvashem.org) This event is impressive to say the least because Graebe lived a hard life in his younger years, and he could have been one of those who blamed the Jews for his hardships. Being not only born into an unfortunate life, but also raised Protestant, it would have been easy for him to blindly hate Jewish people, to blame them for all of his problems in life. Yet despite all of his hardships, he was still able to make the correct choice, which led him down the path of the savior. This one action of speaking against the Nazi Party led him down a path of saving Jews, which was helped by his position in a certain construction company.

From 1941 to the end of World War II, Hermann Friedrich Graebe spent his life in an effort to save as many Jewish people as he could from enslavement/execution by the Nazis. In 1924, Graebe managed to successfully become an engineer, which gave him the opportunity to work for the Josef Jung Construction Company. (Yadvashem.org) In 1941, he was assigned to Volhynia, Ukraine in order to keep maintenance on buildings that were necessary for railroad communications there. (Yadvashem.org) He was given a workforce of 5,000 men and women of Jewish faith. (Yadvashem.org)

Throughout the next few years, he would try to make this number rise in order to save as many Jewish people as possible. The following year (1942) he witnessed the mass execution of another group of 5,000 Jewish men, women, and children near a city in Ukraine called Dubno. (Poliakov, Leon 125-126) This is what enforced his goal to save the Jewish people from the Nazis, by any means necessary. He took more contracts than he could handle, therefore rising the need for employees, and with every Jewish person he hired he made a promise to protect them as well as their families. (Yadvashem.org) In July of 1942 he came into a ghetto of Ukraine called Rovno, and "gun in hand" rescued 150 Jewish people from execution. (Yadvashem.org) Later, when the location he had put his main office, Zdolbuniv, was turned into a ghetto he managed to give 25 of his workers fake papers identifying them as Aryan. (Yadvashem.org) He transported them to a branch of his project in Poltava, which was not authorized and funded by Graebe's personal funds. (Yadvashem.org) All of this was an effort to get them over to the Russian side so they could at least be safe from execution by the SS. Hermann Graebe spent his entire time in Ukraine fulfilling his purpose of saving as many people as he could from the deaths they would have surely been given otherwise. He risked his life, his career, and any semblance of freedom he had by preforming these tasks. Even knowing that, he still felt something had to be done about the awful events taking place in front of his eyes. His sense of moral duty took over any fear he could have had, and helped him to make the tough, but correct decisions he needed to make for himself. He couldn't stand aside and do nothing while his own people were killing each other, so he helped the victims as much as he possibly could, even after the war was over he still spent his life trying to bring those of evil to justice.

After he saved as many people as he could using his profession, Hermann Graebe defected to the U.S to help in the ending of the war, the ultimate completion of his goal. During the years of 1938-41, Graebe was assigned by the Josef Jung Construction Company to make fortifications to the Western Border of Germany. (Yadvashem.org) In September 1994, Graebe went to the U.S. and informed them of strategic weaknesses in the walls there. (Yadvashem.org) After doing so, he went even further with the aid he gave the U.S. from February of 1945 to autumn of the following year he helped with the preparations of the Nuremberg Trials, the thirteen trials done to bring Nazi war criminals to justice. (Yadvashem.org) Hermann "was the only German to testify for the prosecution at the Nuremberg Trials." (Yadvashem.org) This caused him to be threatened in his own country, and in 1948 he emigrated to the U.S. (Yadvashem.org) Afterwards he spent much of his time hunting down war criminals and bringing them to justice. (Yadvashem.org) Graebe was a free man, the war was over, and for many that was it, but not him. He still felt that there was some justice that had not been created that needed to be. Through the Nuremberg Trials he tried to bring as many to justice as he possibly could.

Graebe was one of the most helpful Germans when it came to the events of the Nuremberg Trials. He helped prepare for the introduction and other facets of the Nuremberg Trials, and was the only German to testify for the prosecution in the years they took place, 1945 through 1949. (Yadvashem.org) His testament was his own eyewitness account of the mass execution he saw take place near Dubno, Ukraine. "I looked at the pit and saw the bodies were twitching or the heads lying motionless on top of the bodies that lay beneath them... The next batch was approaching already. They went down into the pit, lined themselves up against the previous victims and were shot." (Poliakov 125-126) This was one of the many moving things he saw, the people dying without a single complaint, along with the families before they died, the crying parents of a small child who had no idea what was about to happen to him, and a man possibly explaining to his son what heaven was like. (Poliakov 125-126) These are the events Hermann Friedrich Graebe had to witness, the death of an enormous group of Jews, unable to do anything to save them. This is what moved him to not only save as many people as he could from the Nazis, but also hunt down and bring war criminals to the justice they deserved. This horrible event was the second catalyst that set the events for the next few years of his life in motion, saving those who were persecuted, and bringing the persecutors to the fate that was right for people like them. It is awful that he had to see such events, it is awful that they happened in the first place. But these events happened, and it was necessary for Graebe to see them in order for him to make the decisions he did in his life.

Hermann Friedrich Graebe deserves the title given to him by Yad Vashem as Righteous Among the Nations. As evidenced before, he lived in a world of poverty and torment growing up as a child, which was only furthered by the horrible event of World War I and the ensuing aftermath of it all. He grew up being an unfortunate German, which almost made him take the decision to join a side that would only harbor evil in the following years. What makes him special is not only the fact that he realized the possible horrors while he was inside the Nazi Party, but also the many things he did afterwards. He saw the temptation, realized the awfulness that would come with it, and then witnessed the horrors first-hand, and did something about it. He saved so many people within the short span of a few years, all by himself with no one else's help. This is what is remarkable about him, his ability and his strength that was needed to be able to protect that many people from the death they all could have possibly faced. His sense of moral duty was so overwhelming that instead of cowering in fear and doing nothing like he could have done, he stood up for the those that had become unable to help themselves, and sometimes unwilling to help themselves as seen by Graebe's testimony. Hermann Friedrich Graebe was a remarkable man, and an even more remarkable German for the time period. His actions in the Second World War are completely and absolutely deserving of the title given to him as Righteous Among the Nations.

World War II was one of the worst events in history. The destruction of homes, the mass slaughtering of the Jewish people, and the amount of lives lost, it was all a greatly horrific scene to unfold. So much hatred, so much darkness, so little room to hope and too much evil trying to extinguish what was left. This is a sentiment shared by many people, anywhere from the start of the event to the current times, no matter what your race or creed. Everyone remembers the World War II and the Holocaust as one, if not the worst event in history up to this point. But even though this war was so awful and long-fought, there were those who gave hope to those who had none. Hermann F. Graebe was one of those kinds of people, who helped anyone he could even though it was not required for him to do so. Those that are able to not only survive the darkest of times, but also help others survive it as well, are those who are truly strong in this world. That is the legacy Hermann Graebe has left behind, and it is not one that will soon be easily forgotten. The saving of dozens of people in any situation, of any color or creed, is noteworthy enough, but the saving of Jewish people during the Holocaust is a great achievement. Graebe deserves to be remembered for as long as World War II and the Holocaust are taught by school systems and remembered among the masses. He was a true hero in those times of darkness.

Works Cited:
Poliakov, Leon. Harvest of Hate. Syracuse, N.Y.: Syracuse University Press, 1954. Print.
"The Witness to Murder Who Decided to Act." Yadvashem.org. Yadvashem.org, n.d. Web. 21 February 2016.

The Story of Karl Plagge

Hunter (Jesse) Brown

 The Holocaust was a horrible event in history that should not have happened, but because it did it is our duty to remember it and not let it happen again. Though this event was horrible for the Jewish people, and whoever else Hitler saw as imperfect, within the territories conquered by Germany in World War II there were some kind people that helped to make a difference by saving the lives of these people. These people ranged from simple civilians doing all they were capable of to German officers who saw what they were doing wasn't right. To sum it up during this time many risked their lives in order to save the lives of other during the Holocaust.

The Holocaust occurred throughout World War II as Nazi Germany conquered more and more territories. In total between 5 to 6 million Jews were killed. In addition to this there were also 5 million non-Jewish civilians who were killed in the Holocaust. Why was this terrible genocide that took the lives of so many allowed though? Hitler seemed to hate the Jewish people almost like it was an obsession of his, and as some of his subordinates have stated it may have been. He wanted to get rid of all the Jewish people and his plan consisted of multiple stages that ended with his "Final Solution." At first there were things like the Nuremberg Laws that excluded the Jewish people from society. These laws forbade marriages between Jews and Germans and forbade employment of German females under 45 in Jewish households, and it also stated that only those of German blood were Reich citizens. They created concentration camps in

1933 and ghettos in 1939. The concentration camps were forced labor camps that exploited slave labor for Germany's war effort, and had terrible conditions. Ghettos were areas sectioned off as "Jewish" that the Nazis would put Jews and Gypsies inside of. Next was the Einsatzgruppen's murder of around 2 million Jews. Finally, there were the extermination camps that were used by the end of 1942. People were transported on freight trains and then sent to gas chambers if they managed to survive the train ride until the end of the war. This genocide was atrocious and should have been prevented, but most European countries took up a policy of ignorance because they thought Germany deserved to take some more land after World War I.

All we ever hear about who was behind of the Holocaust is Hitler, but there were other people involved. In the camps the prisoners were either killed or put to work, but a man named Josef Mengele took up human experimentation as a hobby. While he was in Auschwitz he chose twins for his experiments. While those he chose had better living conditions than the rest of the prisoners and temporary safety from the gas chambers, the experiments he performed typically would kill them. For the children he had a playground made and they often adored him despite the fact he could kill them in the next hour. Sometimes he'd infect a twin with a disease and when it died he'd kill the other for comparative results. Another experiment of his was the forced conjoining of twins. He took a pair and sewed them together, back to back. The worst thing about this was that they lived for a few days after suffering constantly until they died of gangrene. As I have written Hitler was the start of all these crimes against humanity, but he was not the only one that took part in these.

On a lighter note a man who fit the role of a savior during this time was named Karl Plagge. Karl was a Wehrmacht officer, engineer and member of the Nazi Party in World War II. Because Karl was a staff officer at the time he used his position to employ 1,250 Jews. Of these 1,250 there were about 500 men and the others were women and children. This gave them a better chance of survival as opposed to the very little amount that survived total annihilation in Lithuania. Basically what he did was he just gave them any job that could've been considered as slave labor whether or not it was actually useful to save them from being killed. He gave them work certificates that certified them as skilled workers that were essential. These certificates would save the worker, his wife, and 2 of his children from the SS sweeps that went through the Vilna Ghetto. The HKP camp that they worked at was much nicer than the Ghetto and the people there wouldn't starve to death either. Eventually however, Karl was forced to retreat which destroyed the slave labor framework that protected those that he hired. Nearly 78 percent of those who he hired died, but it was a better survival rate than the 96 percent death rate of the rest of Lithuania's Jewish population. Karl did all that he could to save the Jewish people who he hired, but even after the war he went on to blame himself for not saving more.

The big question now is, why did Karl do what he did to save the Jews in Lithuania? Well, he was a German who had pride in his country and witnessed genocide in Vilnius and couldn't help but feel responsible and wanted to work against this genocidal machine. As a result he used position as commander of engineering unit HKP 562 to hire only Jewish workers to attempt to save them from the genocide. He hired 1,250 Jewish workers, but only 250-300 survived after he had to retreat. Before he had to retreat he knew it was going to happen soon so he tried to create a freestanding slave labor camp to try to save as many people as he could, but he was unable to sadly. Instead of this, he tried to give the workers a hidden warning in a speech he made to them saying that he and his men would be relocated. The workers all knew what this would mean for them of course and they acted on this. Over half of the work camps prisoners went into hiding following this. On July 3, 1944 the SS death squads arrived at the camp and when 500 people showed up to roll call they were taken and shot shortly later. The SS would go on to search for the rest three days later and find 250 more who would be killed later, however 250 others were not found and managed to survive. Karl went on to compare himself to a character from a book called The Plague in which he was in a hopeless struggle against the plague of death that slowly envelops the inhabitants of the city. After the war he returned to Darmstadt, Germany and was tried as a result of the de-Nazification process, and during the trial a group of his prisoners was nearby and sent a representative to the court. This unannounced visit turned the trial in Karl's favor and would lead the court to offer him the title of an exonerated person, but he decided to take the title of follower since he still blamed himself. Karl would go on to live the last decade of his life in peace.

Of the people Karl saved many went on to tell their children how he saved their lives. Many of his workers wanted to thank Karl over 50 years after the Holocaust, but he died within a decade after the fact. One survivor of his was named Pearl Good. Pearl talked about how Karl had given her father a skilled worker certificate in order to protect them from being killed. Apparently before the camp was set up she stated that they were all to be put on a train that went to the slate mines and that Karl had a big conflict with an SD officer trying to prevent them from getting on. A rumor that went around was that he went to Berlin and lied about how his skilled Jewish workers were indispensable for the war effort, which if discovered could lead to him being executed. Another set of survivors, Mark and Anna Balber, also had good things to say about the efforts of Karl. They said that they knew he would do everything within his power to help them and alleviate the suffering they were going through. When the SS commander Kitel decided to pick out the young and pretty girls of the camp at role call one of the workers appealed to Karl and they were released the same day. Another incident that arose happened when Karl was on leave to Germany. An SS officer named Weiss took all the small children of the camp to Ponary where they were killed. The only reason this was successful was because Karl was not present to object to this. As the survivors stated, they were very grateful to Karl for everything that he did, and when he got the title of "Righteous Among the Nations" Pearl Good visited the memorial to show her gratitude.

Karl wrote a few letters while he was managing the camp. He used one to justify using Jewish workers as laborers, and the other was to his wife. The letter about the laborers talked about how following disbandment of the ghetto his work camp was to have 500 Jewish laborers reserved. He went on to add that it was necessary for their wives and children to be there with them to be productive which brought the amount of Jewish to 1,243. Obviously this was not required, but Karl was trying to save as many people as he possibly could from being killed. Without doing this everyone who he saved by employing would have been executed in no time. The letter to his wife talked about how the situation was taking a toll on him, and how difficult it was to maintain with new problems arising. He stated that their German reputation was suffering so much as a result of everything happening, but that it was in his nature to help the people in the camp. Clearly, Karl worked hard in order to save the people in the camp and seemed to have also seen it as his duty to try and make up for all the atrocities that were happening by saving as many as he could.

In all, Karl's efforts saved the lives of many Jews during the Holocaust at the risk of his own life. He didn't have to, but he went out of his way to help them and although he was not able to save everyone that he hired he tried his best and that's saying a lot for someone that was actually a part of the Nazi Party. After seeing what the party was doing he decided he was also responsible and wanted to make up for it in some way, and that's why he worked to save his workers. He constantly risked his own life with to save so many others by doing things like only employing Jewish workers which could have led to him being executed, and warning them beforehand that they would be killed if they didn't leave the camp after he was relocated. For all his work many survivors ended up being in his debt because without him they would not have lived through the Holocaust.

Works Cited

"Holocaust | Basic Questions about the Holocaust." Holocaust | Basic Questions about the Holocaust. N.p., n.d. Web. 26 Feb. 2016. <http://www.projetaladin.org/holocaust/en/40-questions-40-answers/basic-questions-about-the-holocaust.html>.

"Karl Plagge. Survivors Stories Www.HolocaustResearchProject.org." Karl Plagge. Survivors Stories Www.HolocaustResearchProject.org. N.p., n.d. Web. 25 Feb. 2016. http://www.holocaustresearchproject.org/survivor/Karl.html>.

Schwartz, Terese Pencak. "The Holocaust: Non-Jewish Victims." Jewish Virtual Library. N.p., n.d. Web. 26 Feb. 2016. <https://www.jewishvirtuallibrary.org/jsource/Holocaust/NonJewishVictims.html>.

"Karl Plaggel - The Righteous Among The Nations - Yad Vashem." Karl Plagge - The Righteous Among The Nations - Yad Vashem. N.p., n.d. Web. 25 Feb. 2016. <http://www.yadvashem.org/yv/en/righteous/stories/Karl.asp>.

United States Holocaust Memorial Museum. United States Holocaust Memorial Council, 29 Jan. 2016. Web. 26 Feb. 2016.

Albert Goering: Remember the Name

Jonah Wiener-Brodkey

 To quote English writer William Shakespeare, "What's in a name? A rose by any other name would smell as sweet." Shakespeare's message is clear: a name does not always have an implicit meaning. According to Shakespeare, if roses were renamed "thorns," their smell would remain unchanged. The same applies to people. Over 4,000 men in the United States are named Jerry Brown – not all of them are the governor of California. If Adolf Hitler's name had been Jerry Brown, his role in the Holocaust would not have changed. Essentially, one's name does not determine the life he or she lives. However, it is our tendency to make generalizations. It was this tendency, in fact, that enabled Hitler to gain power by convincing Germany that the title "Jew" suggests something subhuman; it was this generalization that led the way to the Holocaust. Are names, in fact, meaningful? For many, the name "Goering" evokes fear, hatred, and disgust. For a rare but significant few, it is a reminder of empathy, sacrifice, and heroism. Though the name of Hermann Goering is well known in the history of the Holocaust, the name of his brother, Albert, has been overshadowed. Through his heroic acts during the Holocaust and ceaseless concern for the lives and wellbeing of Jews, Albert Goering demonstrated that names do not define people, while proving himself to be a hero of the Holocaust.

Goering began a life of politics simply by being born into a politically active family. He was born on March 9th, 1895 and was the fifth child of Reichskommissar Heinrich Ernst Goering, a German diplomat of then South-West Africa (now Namibia), and Franziska Tiefenbrunn. The Goering family lived in the Friedenau, a suburb outside of Berlin. Because his father's position required constant travel, Albert and his siblings were primarily raised by their wealthy godfather, Hermann von Epenstein, a physician and formerly Jewish convert to Catholicism. When it became clear that Heinrich Goering would continue to be an absentee father, von Epenstein became the children's de facto father, inviting Tiefenbrunn and her children to live with him in two of his southern castles. In fact, an affair between von Epenstein and Tiefenbrunn shortly after Albert's birth, paired with Albert's close resemblance to von Epenstein, led many to believe that von Epenstein was the true father of Albert Goering. Though this was later disproven, von Epenstein continued to play an integral role in the lives of the Goerings.

As Albert Goering grew, it became increasingly apparent that he and his older brother, Hermann, were vastly dissimilar. On the surface, they hardly resembled one another at all; Albert appeared central European with dark brown eyes while Hermann's blue eyes and blond hair were the epitome of Aryan features. Their personalities differed as well. As a boy, Albert was said to be quiet and introverted, occupying his time with reading indoors. Hermann, on the other hand, was not only extroverted but rebellious. His childhood was characterized by the many boarding schools his mother forced him to attend. Some have told of an instance at Hermann's final boarding school in which he cut the strings off all of the school's violins and cellos. This act of rebellion landed him in military school. The disparity between the melancholy Albert and exuberant Hermann only widened as they aged, eventually developing into differences in political ideology.

Both Goering brothers served in the First World War, Hermann as a fighter pilot and Albert in communications. When they once again went their separate ways, Albert chose to stray from politics and attended the Technical University of Munich in 1919 to study mechanical engineering. Hermann, on the other hand, began frequenting Munich beer halls, where he developed a growing resentment for Germany's failure in World War I and the economic consequences. He became fascinated with German nationalism and the speeches of Adolf Hitler, and even participated in Hitler's 1923 Beer Hall Putsch, a failed coup to seize power from the German government. He fled to Sweden, marking the beginning of 12-year silence between the Goering brothers. While Hermann's fascination for Nazism became greater, Albert developed a hatred for the movement. As soon as anti-Jewish laws were passed in Germany, he moved to Austria and began fighting anti-Semitism in Vienna. Some tell of a case in which Goering joined a group of elderly Jewish women who had been ordered to scrub a cobblestone street. Until 1938, he remained in Vienna writing visas for fleeing Jews and assisting them in escaping to non-occupied countries.

Following the 1938 German annexation of Austria, Albert and Hermann reunited, leading to Albert's realization that he could benefit from Hermann's newly earned power. Hermann, now a high-ranking member of the Nazi Party, had arrived in Austria and given a successful speech on Nazism and anti-Semitism. In a positive mood, he came to grant a wish to his younger brother. Much to his surprise, Albert wished for the liberation of Austria's Archduke Josef Ferdinand from Dachau. Despite the brothers' ideological differences, their bond as brothers prevailed and Hermann ordered for the Archduke's release. This was merely the beginning of Albert Goering's heroism during the Holocaust at the expense of his brother's position.

To continue to escape Nazi advances, Goering moved to Czechoslovakia in 1939, where he became the export manager at the Skoda automotive factory. Even through his occupation he continued striving for heroism. On multiple occasions, Goering forged his brother's name on documents for Jews or dissidents who worked at the factory. He also allowed his factory workers to sabotage exports being sold to Germany. It is reported that Goering often forged his brother's signature on documents requesting Jewish laborers from prison camps. After the trucks arrived with Jewish prisoners, Goering would release the Jews in an isolated area and allow them to escape. When he encountered Jews he could not help on his own, he capitalized on his brother's sense of familial responsibility. Many times a year, Goering would travel to Hermann's Berlin office and request assistance in his ant-Nazi projects. Hermann, feeling a duty to help his younger brother, allegedly signed hundreds of documents, citizenship papers, and visas for Jews whom Albert hoped to assist. Despite Hermann's increasing reluctance to help, Goering continued to exploit his brother's position of power for the purpose of fighting Nazi influence and helping Jews flee.

The more he assisted Jews in their escapes, the more attention he drew from the Nazi regime. Though he was arrested multiple times, his brother's status was always enough to vindicate him. Even when four warrants for his arrest were issued, Hermann guaranteed his safety. Only when World War II ended in 1944 was Albert arrested and by American troops and later tried at the Nuremberg Trials. Hermann had been accused of war crimes while Albert had been arrested for bearing the Goering name. In an Augsburg jail, Albert thanked his brother for his ceaseless loyalty and apologized that he would suffer on his behalf. This was the Goering brothers' last exchange before Hermann was found guilty of crimes against humanity and sentenced to hanging. He ingested cyanide just hours before his execution. Albert, on the other hand, spent two years in prison, unable to relieve himself of the connotation of his notorious surname. Only after Jews and other dissidents spoke on his behalf was he cleared of his alleged crimes and released.

After his release in 1947, he was ostracized on account of his last name. Employers refused to hire a Goering despite his heroic acts during the Holocaust. He slipped into depression and alcoholism, leading his wife to divorce and take his only daughter. The remainder of his life was spent largely unemployed, weighed down by the Goering name and surviving only off of a state pension. As he approached his death in 1966, he realized his pension would be transferred to his wife upon his death. In a sign of gratitude, he married his housekeeper the week before his death in order to secure her financial wellbeing. Despite his unfortunate circumstances following the Holocaust, Goering remained a selfless hero.

The name is not one that should live in infamy. Though Albert Goering's achievements went unrecognized in his lifetime, his story should now be well known. Goering is not a name that should live entirely in infamy, but should rather be a reminder of sacrifice and the importance of answering the cries of those in need. After his death on December 20, 1966, Albert Goering was buried in his family plot beneath a tombstone that read, "Wir sind nicht von denen die da weichen sondern von denen die da glauben" – "We are not among those who yield, but among those who believe." Truthfully, Albert Goering was not one who yielded as so many did during the Holocaust, but rather one who believed; for this reason, Goering is undeniably a hero of the Holocaust.

Works Cited

Burke, William Hastings. "Albert Goering, Hermann's anti-Nazi brother." http://www.theguardian.com/lifeandstyle/2010/feb/20/albert-goering-hermann-goering-brothers, 19 Feb, 2010.

Green, David B. "This Day in Jewish History: the Goering Brother Who Would Save Jews Is Born." http://www.haaretz.com/jewish/features/.premium-1.645880, 9 Mar, 2015.

Johanna Eck

Katie Paul

 The song "Frensei" by artist Artie Shaw and His Orchestra was at the top at number one on the Billboard charts for three months in the year 1941. In 1940, Winston Churchill was declared Time Magazine's Man of the Year. In October 1941, after 14 years of carving, Mount Rushmore was finally completed. Walt Disney won an Academy Award in 1943 for his animated short film "Der Fuehrer's Face." The famous signing of Jackie Robinson to a player's contract by general manager of the Brooklyn Dodgers occurred in 1945. And famous marvel superhero Captain America was brought to life in 1941.When just hearing these events the 1940's seems like a time of growing culture, yet that was not the case at all. On September 1, 1939 through September 2, 1945 millions of lives were lost in the violent fight known as World War II. Hitler was a politician in Germany at the time and head of the Nazi Party, and also he was responsible for the genocide of 6 million Jews in Europe. Hitler had believed in the Aryan race, white, blonde hair, and blue eyes, and thought Jews threatened the spread of this race. Due to this belief he established concentration camps where Jews were crammed together as if they were sardines, brutally murdered, and overall dehumanized. This was known as the "Final Solution," two out of every three Jews in Europe were being found and thrown in concentration camps, which for most usually ended in death. However that means that one out of every the three lived through this time barbaric persecution thanks to enlightened heroes and heroines across Europe who put their lives on the line and disobey their powerful leader, Adolf Hitler.

"We could never learn to be brave and patient, if there were only joy in the world," said Helen Keller, a heroine in her very own way. Heroes come in all different shapes and sizes. The formal definition of a hero/heroine from dictionary.com is a man or woman of distinguished courage or ability, admired for his or her brave deeds and noble qualities. Sadly it takes violence and mistreating of others to bring forth these heroes/ heroines. One of these violent mistreating of others that shed light on hundreds of brave souls was the Holocaust. The heroine who inspired me the most who showed her true colors in such a dark time was Johanna Eck. Through further research on her I found myself further and further intrigued and jaw dropped by her actions. Her determination to help the most helpless at the time is what made her stand out to me.

Johanna Eck was born January 4, 1888 in Berlin, Germany. She had been married but her husband was killed in World War I. Her husband had been close acquaintances with a man named Jakob Heniz who later became close with the Eck family.In 1942 in the midst of war Jakob Heinz, his wife, and his kids were deported to East Berlin. Jakob was just barely able to escape arrest due to the fact that he and his family were Jewish. Once he escaped he had not a single plan and it seemed people he was once friends with turned their backs on him. Every person he asked for help turned a blind eye because they wanted nothing to do with a Jewish fugitive in fear of being caught and killed themselves. Johanna was the only non-Jewish acquaintance who offered up her help and gave him refuge in her home. At this time during the war food rations were extremely scarce, despite this she still shared the little food she had with him. Sometimes she would spend days at a time out looking for extra food rations from close friends to share between the two of them. However, in November of 1943 Eck's home was destroyed in an air raid. Eck felt as if it was her responsibility to find a safe place to relocate Heinz. Even while Heinz lived away from her Eck still kept in good contact with him. When necessary she would provide him with food ration cards and vital contacts.

In December 1943 the brutal Gestapo raided the home of Ms..M, Heinz's landlady. Ms. M had been hiding a Jewish girl named Elfriede Guttman, who had been under a bed and just barely managed to escape detection. Following this event the traumatized girl payed a visit to Eck and told her everything that had happened her. Even though Eck had just recently been relocated to a single room apartment she gave the idea no thought and immediately offered Elfriede refuge in her home.

One day Eck and Elfriede were in line at a bakery when Elfriede was greeted by another young girl. This girl turned out to be Erika Hartmann, an old classmate of hers from a school she had attended in East Prussia, now Poland. The kind-hearted Erika Hartmann was enticed by Elfriede and was more than eager to help her. She gave Elfriede her own personal Aryan documents that had said she had done work for the labor service.

On the night of January 30, 1944 planes flew over Berlin and destroyed quite a lot and caused lots of confusion. Eck decided to take advantage of this confusion that lay over everyone and register Elfriede as Erika Hartmann. Eck claimed that the new Erika Hartmann's house and personal documents had been downed in the recent air raid. It all paid off because Eck was able to legalize her resistance and register her as a lodger in her apartment.

Sadly after surviving the violent war Elfriede's young life came to a sudden end. She fell to her death due to a stomach constriction shortly after the liberation. She passed away in June 1946 and Eck was by her side the through it all. As a registered nurse Eck cared for her till death and in her hour of passing Eck was by her bedside. After the passing Eck provided the Jewish community with the names of Elfriede, her parents, and her brother. Even though all of them had died at the hands of the final solution. She had all of the families names inscribed on Elfriede's gravestone which she had paid for at her own expense.

Later on, when Johanna Eck was questioned as to why she put her life on the line to help, she said, "The motives for my help? Nothing special in a particular case. In principle, what I think is this: If a fellow human being is in distress and I can help him, then it becomes my duty and responsibility. Were I to refrain from doing so, than I would betray the task that life – or perhaps God? – demands from me. Human beings –

so it seems to me – make up a big unity; they strike themselves and all in the face when they do injustice to each other. These are my motives."

It's vital to recognize heroes and heroines of the past like this as well as the madness which these heroes arise from. There are people that deny the genocide of 6 million Jews, deny the concentration and death camps, and even deny that the Nazis aimed to eliminate Jews. It is even believed that the diary of Anne Frank is a forgery and that the figure of 6 million Jews who died is an exaggeration. Most believe that the Holocaust is exaggerated by the Jews to evoke sympathy for them. However it's essential for kids to learn about horrific events such as the Holocaust so history doesn't repeat itself. We must learn from our mistakes in order to ensure things like this don't happen. Sadly however genocide happens all around the world, and still is constantly a problem.

Johanna Eck's story also opens the minds of people who might believe that all German citizens during World War II were at fault and did nothing to help the Jews. This is the power of a single story, a single story can create segregation and close minded people. This is not true however, there were plenty of German heroes and heroines who put their lives on the line to save helpless Jews.

Johanna Eck inspired me greatly; she showed the world the strengths and capabilities of a woman. Having lost her husband early on in the war the widowed Johanna dealt with the hard times by herself and had to take on jobs most woman didn't. Johanna Eck lived through many challenges as a woman and during the time period she lived in. Even though woman won the right during World War I women still were not viewed as equal. Also woman were very reliant on men. Women were expected to work until married, then they would become housewives for their husbands. As a young woman the thought of such inequality and have to live in another man's shadow is not right. Woman are just as qualified as men are in most jobs. Another example of inequality women faced in the 1920's was that men were involved in many kinds of organizations where women were only allowed to participate in very limited ways. Woman doctors and lawyers were scarce and no man would put his life in the hands of a woman doctor or put his business career in the hands of a woman lawyer, it was such a taboo thought at the time. As time went on more and more women began to be hired as sales clerks, nurses, secretaries, etc. however they earned $8 a week, which was 54 percent to 60 percent of what men earned. Most employers discriminated against woman and refused to hire them because it was universally known that a woman's place was at home. Johanna had also lived through an era known as the flapper era. Woman dancers known as flappers wore short skirts, cut their hair short, listened to jazz, and flaunted their displeasure for the sexist views that they faced each and every day. It is a great possibility that the discrimination Johanna faced as a woman living in the early 20th century could have contributed to her feeling the need to step up above others and help hide out several people in her home. Her story continues to amaze me every time I read it. Reading her story should be empowering to women and prove the power, strengths, and capability of women across the world. You always hear about super heroes, so much so that I had no idea what a heroine even was. It was nice to read and research a heroine, a female hero, for a change.

I'm glad I was able to have this experience and research such an honorable person. As a member of the general population I was lead to the misconception that all German people during the Holocaust were at fault for not lending help and turning a blind eye. I'm glad I know different now. Johanna really opened my eyes. I feel empowered not only as a woman but as an average member of society. She was just like everyone else around her, she was a "normal" citizen who made a difference in multiple people's lives. Next time I find myself saying "What can I do? There's nothing I can do to make a change," I'll know that that statement is false. There's always something a person can do to help a situation. For example. bullying is a common problem in today's schools. Tell a teacher or get an adult. Even after death Johanna Eck is still making an imprint and her legacy lives on.

Bibliography
"Adolf Hitler." History.com. A&E Television Networks, n.d. Web. 25 Feb. 2016.
"Timeline of Events." United States Holocaust Memorial Museum. United States Holocaust Memorial Council, n.d. Web. 25 Feb. 2016.
Wikipedia. Wikimedia Foundation, n.d. Web. 25 Feb. 2016.
Wikipedia. Wikimedia Foundation, n.d. Web. 25 Feb. 2016.
"Women in the 1920s." Women in the 1920s. N.p., n.d. Web. 25 Feb. 2016.
""Women of Valor"" Johanna Eck. N.p., n.d. Web. 25 Feb. 2016.

Oskar Schindler

Kyle Wiesenthal

1200. This is the number of Jews who, thanks to Oskar Schindler, survived the Holocaust. Schindler was one of the more unlikely heroes of the Holocaust. Living in Germany, he began his work for the Nazi Party. However, he was able to rise from the chaos and madness of the Nazi Party and became the man to save more Jews from the gas chambers than anyone else. The Holocaust, as many of us are quite aware, was a very dark time for much of Europe, making it difficult for millions to reach down and access their sense of humanity. Oskar was different though. He turned his life completely around and used the same skills he had becoming a war profiteer to progress in other directions. These included, his talent through presentation, bribery and grand gestures. Later, it was the money he earned while working earlier on in life that was ultimately used for the protection and rescue for hundreds of Jews.

Initially, Oskar desired to make a profit by hiding and then employing Jews as laborers in a factory in Poland during the time of the invasion. Suddenly the rise of

Hitler and his party surfaced and Schindler realized that the Jews who worked for him needed protection more than jobs. From there, he began smuggling children out of the ghettos where many of the Jews had been relocated to and requested from his superiors that the Jewish children be moved to a factory nearby. Eventually, Oskar used his skills to continue helping Jews in need. This group of people was later known as "Schindlerjuden," meaning "Schindler Jews." He helped them out of their difficult situations and provided as many as jobs as possible and eventually hiding spots.

Oskar also had help along the way from his wife, Emilie Schindler. Emilie was not only a strong counterpart next to her husband, but also established a name for herself. She worked just as hard as her husband to save the Jews, and together they created a safe place and later a legacy together – willing to spend whatever it took to save this group of people.

Looking back at the number of the people who were saved, this is almost half of my high school population. To imagine the steps and decisions taken and made to achieve such a goal is incredible. Having a history in the Nazi Party and then making a complete 360 and helping those that he used to be totally against is such a large turnaround. I believe it's sacrifices like these that come with loyalty – what started out as simple factory jobs unknowingly lead to what saved the Jews who worked for him. Spending the money Schindler had earned all ended up going toward this amazing deed, making it an even more selfless act.

None of us really know exactly what made this complex man do what no German had the courage to do. There has been continuous fascination with Schindler because not even those who admire and know about him most can figure out his motives. But Oscar Schindler rose to the highest level of humanity and walked through the difficult realm of the Holocaust without damaging his character. His compassion and his respect for human life gave his Jews a second chance. He miraculously managed to muster up the will to do it and then found a way to pull it off. Oscar Schindler was a sentimentalist who took pride in the simple and yet beautiful act(s) of doing good. A man full of flaws like the rest of us – an ordinary man but became someone who even in the worst of circumstances did extraordinary things, matched by no one. The unlikeliest of all role models who started by earning millions as a war profiteer ended his life using his last bits of money and risking his life to save his 1,200 "Schindlerjews." Oscar Schindler not only saved their lives, but helped salvage their and our hope for more acts of human kindness.

Researchers discovered some of the stories recorded from some of the Jews he saved and even some words from Schindler himself. Twenty years after the war, Moshe Bejski, a Schindlerjew who later became a Supreme Court justice in Israel, asked Schindler why he did it. Schindler replied, "I knew the people who worked for me. When you know people, you have to behave towards them like human beings".

Poldek Pfefferberg, another Schindlerjew, recalled how Schindler in 1944 was a very wealthy man, a multimillionaire, and acknowledged a large amount of gratitude toward the man: "He could have taken the money and gone to Switzerland ... he could have bought Beverly Hills. But instead, he gambled his life and all of his money to save us..." When Pfefferberg asked him the same question 'WHY?' Schindler answered, "There was no choice. If you saw a dog going to be crushed under a car, wouldn't you help him?"

Even during the darkest days of the Holocaust and people seemed to be dropping like flies, there was hope in Krakow, which became the capital of Germany's General Government during the time. The Jewish population of the city was forced into a walled zone known as the Kraków Ghetto from which they were sent to German extermination camps such as the nearby Auschwitz, never to return, along with other camps. But because Oscar Schindler was there, there was hope for a large amount of Jews in the area. Helen Beck, a Schindler survivor, recalls, "We gave up many times, but he always lifted our spirits ... Schindler tried to help people however he could. That is what we remember".

Rena Ferber, now known as Rena Finder, was only 10 years old when the Nazis invaded Poland. She was saved by Oscar Schindler and later stated, "He was a gambler, who loved living on the edge. He loved outsmarting the SS. I would not be alive today if it wasn't for Oscar Schindler. To us he was our God, our Father, our protector".

Roman Ferber's name also was on 'Schindler's List'. He was one of the youngest 'Schindlerjews' and later told how Oscar Schindler underwent a transformation when he witnessed the true evil of the Nazis and gave up everything to save as many lives as he could. "I thank God for Oscar Schindler. If not for him, I would not be here and not have any family."

As an 11-year-old boy, Zev Kedem was another Schindlerjew whose life was saved and changed by Schindler. He believed that only someone like Schindler, with his smarts and sense of good could have pulled this off. Kedem says, "If he was a virtuous, honest guy, no one in a corrupt, greedy system like the SS would accept him. In a weird world that celebrated death, he recognized the Jews as humans. Schindler used the corrupt ways, creativity and ingenuity against the monster machine dedicated to death."

Abraham Zuckerman spent five of his teenage years in Nazi camps. He later discussed Oscar Schindler this way, "There were SS guards but he would say 'Good morning' to you. He was a chain smoker and he'd throw the cigarette on the floor after only two puffs, because he knew the workers would pick it up after him. To me he was an angel. Because of him I was treated like a human being. And because of him I survived." Oscar Schindler also managed to get 300 Schindler-women released from the death camp Auschwitz. "What people don't understand about Oscar is the power of the man, his strength, his determination. Everything he did he did to save the Jews. Can you imagine what power it took for him to pull out from Auschwitz 300 people? At Auschwitz, there was only one way you got out, we used to say. Through the chimney! Understand? Nobody ever got out of Auschwitz. But Schindler got out 300!"

The 300 Schindler-women were accidentally sent on a train to Auschwitz – death awaited them at their final destination. A Schindler survivor, Anna Duklauer Perl, later discussed, "I knew something had gone terribly wrong .. they cut our hair real short and sent us to the shower. Our only hope was Schindler would find us".

The Schindler-women were being herded off toward the showers – their fate unknown – would it be water or gas that they would be exposed to? Then they heard a voice, "What are you doing with these people ? These are my people". It was Schindler coming to rescue them from certain death. He bribed the Nazis to retrieve the women on his list and bring them back. As a result, the women were released.

They returned to his factory, barely human – lacking strength and balanced body heat. Schindler met them – standing in the doorway, a memory the women would never forget. His raspy voice made them an unforgettable guarantee, "Now you are finally with me, you are safe now. Don't be afraid of anything. You don't have to worry anymore".

Jonathan Dresner, another Schindlerjew's mother and sister were among the 300 Schindler-women. "That was something nobody else did," Dresner eventually mentioned. "Schindler was an adventurer. He was like an actor who always wanted to be centre stage."

Another Schindler survivor, Ludwik Feigenbaum, gave this description of Schindler, "I don't know what his motives were, even though I knew him very well. I asked him and I never got a clear answer and the film doesn't make it clear, either. But I don't give a damn. What's important is that he saved our lives".

Poldek Pfefferberg, a Schindlerjew who spent 40 years with immense interest in the Schindler story, had no doubt about the nobility of Schindler's goals. He was convinced that Oscar Schindler only had good intentions, "He risked his life" and "He was doing it from the first day".

Similar commentary came from Irving Glovin who was Schindler's attorney. "The man rose to an occasion," Glovin said. "Why the story is remarkable is that he did something when it appeared that the Germans were winning, and he did it over a long period of time, about four years, and he did it in the worst area, Poland, and he did it openly ... He did it for strangers."

Oscar Schindler earned the everlasting gratitude of his Schindlerjews. No matter his intentions and no matter his history and flaws. The only thing that matters to his Jews is that he rose from the madness of the war and risked everything to save them. Generations of Jews/people will remember him for his noble deed.

After this immense goal was achieved, Schindler created another business, hoping to earn back the money he had spent in the past. However, Schindler died at the age of 66, penniless, but remembered for more important things. The value of his actions are of far more value than any amount of money will be.

Eventually, as many of us know, the movie Schindler's List was released in 1994 and won seven different Academy Awards and one Golden Globe for its production. From this, this man's story was spread beyond Europe and thousands of people were now made aware of his heroic gesture. Schindler was a simple man who took on an immense action and was incredibly successful. Having saved more than a thousand Jews, he has received many great words and appreciation from these people for the actions that allowed them to create families and lives of their own. No one expected a man who was previously associated with a political party who wanted nothing more than the Jewish population dead, to find a desire to save the Jews.

So what is a hero? For some, it is a doctor who has cured a disease and for some it is a musical artist who affected them in either or both small and large proportions and for some it could even be their pet. But, for 1,200 Jews in a time when things seemed hopeless and for some on a direct route to certain death, Schindler was their hero. As mentioned before, Schindler was a simple man with basic desires, but what made him different was his love for actions of basic human kindness. He was a man once compelled by an evil group of people, but changed for the common good of people who had only been loyal to him. Schindler's actions took courage, large amounts of strength and ability to give up something that was rightfully his to help those who everyone in your community is fighting to get rid of. Schindler was a hero then and a hero now because he allowed Jews to continue their lives and regain hope for human kindness, in a time when they thought it no longer existed.

Works Cited

"Oscar Schindler – His List Of Life" http://www.oskarschindler.com
    2015-17. Web.

"The   Shalom   Show   on   TV   –   Holocaust   Heroes"
http://www.shalomshow.com/holocaust_heroes.htm   2002. Web.

"Schindler – Why did he do it?" http://www.auschwitz.dk/why/why.htm
    2008-2010. Web.

"Why? Why? Why?" http://www.oskarschindler.com/11.htm   2015-17. Web.

How Far Would You Go To Save A Life?

Lyric Morales

Many people define a hero as someone who does these incredible, noticeable things in life, but oversee those who do small but great things. The women who struggle to feed their children in scarcity are heroes. The men who put their lives at risk to save their children are heroes. The greatest heroes are those who try to do what they know are right in spite of how difficult the circumstances are.

In history's darkest moment many innocent people died. There is no one answer to why the Holocaust began. It was a very slow process, and one that was made up of many different aspects. All of them came together to build a series of horrible misery. For many centuries there were many anti-Jewish sentiments. People felt that Jews were inferior for religious reasons. Many things happened in which Jews would be killed by mobs or their houses burned down. By the 1900s, acts of assault began, but the global feeling of fear and conjecture remained. The Holocaust is said to have really begun when soldiers returned from World War I, they began spreading rumors, saying that Jewish assistants had "stabbed them in the back" in combat. But the Holocaust was first not meant to represent violence but by slow oppression and the contraction of rights. That's when Jews progressively lost rights to travel, operate businesses and so on. There is on one group to blame for the Holocaust; Hitler clearly takes full authority, but the people to blame are the ones who went with his aid to power, using the extensive genocide as a way to gain themselves but we owe it to the very few who had the courage to stand up for their beliefs. Those people created hope in the face of desperation. The story of Albert Goering is almost unknown. For most people, hearing the name 'Goering,' they think of the disgraceful Hermann Goering; appointee of Nazi Germany. But Hermann wasn't the only member of his family associated with the Holocaust. His youthful brother, Albert, was massively involved, only Albert saved lives instead of wrecking them.

Albert abhorred the Nazi Party. Being a director of a weapon manufacturing plant, he turned an unsighted eye when his co-workers stole guns to fight the Nazis. He also contributed huge amounts of money to the resistance movement, abating their war against Hitler's administration.

Albert's additions go far more than financial stability. He was responsible for sneaking Jews out of the Third Reich's reach. One night, Albert bamboozled the commandant of Dachau into discharging a resistance fighter by sending him an order on a card bearing the Goering name. Additionally, he directly drove an Austrian producer to opportunity, helping him escape, just in time.

Albert helped plentiful others find freedom. From setting up Swiss bank accounts so they could survive away from home, to getting exit permits. No one will truly know what made this complex man do what not many German man had the audacity to do.

Albert saved hundreds of Jews and political dissidents during the Second World War. But he not only saved Jews, he put his life in danger doing it and risked his relationship with his brother. Albert showed fearless benevolence on many occasions. In Vienna, he joined a group of Jewish women who had been forced to scrub a street clean, giving the officer no alternative but to release the entire group. He helped save his Jewish friends and friends who were married to Jews break out to Europe or go into hiding.

A man in the Gestapo knew exactly what Albert was doing. He kept a file on him and had him arrested on several occasions. But of course, bigger brother, Hermann ordered Albert's release. He was definitely Albert's get out of jail free card. After the war, many people didn't believe Albert's story. He hoped to prove his chastity, by making a list of thirty four figures he had saved during Hitler's decree. Being released only to get arrested again but this time by the Czechs. After weeks, he was certainly cleared of any false doing. But because the recognition to his brother's legacy, Albert was unable to start a new life. He was definitely a survivor and determined. He would get arrested and as soon as he got out he would go right back to what he was doing; saving people.

Albert died on December 20th, 1966 at age 71, in Munich. He died impoverished and gloomy. His last act was also of compassion; he married his housekeeper so she could inherit his state pension.

I choose Albert for many reasons. One is because I love how he gave his all because of how he felt. Gave all his money, risked his life, and risked the relationships of family members. He was willing to do anything and everything to save lives and I very much respect that because I believe if I was put to the task, I would have done the same thing. I wouldn't say I would risk my life for someone because that was how I was raised because I asked my parents and siblings if they would risk there life and they said "not for a stranger, but definitely my family". If you asked me why I would risk my life for a stranger, I couldn't give you an answer because truthfully I don't know why I would. Think of it this way: would you want someone to risk their life for you? You can't expect something in life if you're not willing to do it yourself. My point being is, I would risk my life for someone even if I was guaranteed to die right then and there because even if I died I would have saved someone else's life, and even if I grow up to be a not so extraordinary person, I would be a hero to that person and his or her family and that is all the greatness I need in life. I will be that 1 percent, to risk my life just like Albert Goering was that 1 percent.

Albert Goering was just a man. His story was almost unknown and his actions almost faded into oblivion and now I chose him to be my true hero of the Holocaust. Many people didn't think of Albert as a good guy because of his brother but I know he changed so many people's lives. Albert Goering's legacy will forever live on.

Works Cited

Bulow, Louis "Albert Goering" http://www.auschwitz.dk/albert.htm

History.com "The Holocaust" http://www.history.com/topics/world-war-ii/the-holocaust

Meriam-Webster "Holocaust" http://www.merriam-webster.com/dictionary/holocaust

Wikipedia "Albert Goering" http://www.auschwitz.dk/albert.htm

Wikipedia "The Holocaust" https://en.wikipedia.org/wiki/The_Holocaust

Heroic Impact in an Atrocious Time

Max Zoglio

From 1941-1945, perhaps the most atrocious event in all of history occurred. In Nazi-run Germany during World War II, around 6 million Jews were murdered, making up the monumental genocide known as the Holocaust. In addition to the 6 million Jews who were murdered, 5 million non-Jews comprised of "unordinary" groups of people like homosexuals and gypsies or people who spoke against the government or disagreed with its policies were murdered. Astoundingly, the crime against humanity experienced by the Jews all expanded from one demagogue's power: Adolf Hitler.

Historians are still unclear on the origins of Adolf Hitler's raging anti-Semitism. Some believe that Hitler blamed the Jews for the World War I German defeat in 1918. An additional speculation is that the doctor who treated his ill mother, a Jewish man, couldn't revive her and he blamed the man for failing because he was Jewish. Preceding his period of rule, Hitler was imprisoned in 1923 for treason in correlation with the Beer Hall Putsch, the failed coup of the Bavarian government. While in jail, he wrote a memoir: "Mein Kampf." Translated into English it means "my struggle." In it, he wrote about how the Jewish population in Germany would be exterminated in a future European war. Unfortunately, Hitler was able to make his ludacris prediction into a reality.

Germany was forced to sign the Treaty of Versailles after World War I. The document humiliated and impoverished Germans. Germany entered the 1920s in economic chaos under the Weimar government. Hitler took advantage of Germany's poverty and used it to come to power. After he served his time in jail, he was appointed as chancellor of Germany in 1933 after the fire at Reichstag. He then declared national emergency so he could assume a position as dictator. He immediately broke the Treaty of Versailles and rebuilt the German army. The German economy therefore rebounded under Hitler, but Hitler would bring so much negativity to the world thereafter.

In the beginning of the Nazi Revolution, Hitler really only had two goals. First and foremost, he wanted to initiate a "racial purification" to wipe out those who were inferior to Aryans, the so-called German master race. In addition, he wanted to expand the borders of Germany. Hitler began to scratch the surface on his plan around the year 1933, and by the time World War II officially began in 1939, he had begun to propel his devious, immoral plans into high gear. In 1939, Nazi Germany seized Poland's western half and began to mass murder those with mental illnesses and physical disabilities. Hitler called it a "program" and named it the Euthanasia Program. This program strongly foreshadowed the Holocaust.

The notoriously inhumane death camps of the Holocaust became prevalent in 1941. People who were viewed as not useful to German society like old and sick people were the first to be gassed to death. Six death camps were soon built in western, German-occupied Poland; the first of which was Belzec and the largest and most historically notorious of which was Auschwitz-Birkenau. Starting in 1942, Jews started to be rounded up in massive numbers from the ghettos they were previously placed in and from various places throughout the European continent. Over the course of four years, thousands of Jews were gassed per day at the death camps.

The fact that Hitler and his accomplices somehow convinced German people that all minority groups, disabled groups, and Jews should be placed in concentration camps is simply astounding. It is hard to imagine the thought process that caused that aforementioned decision. It is completely irrational that one would resort to mass murdering, and it is even more irrational how one could get away with it for four years like Hitler did. There is nothing permissible or beneficial to imprisoning innocent people because of their faith, starving them, making them work constantly in filthy conditions, separating them from their family members, and killing them in massive proportions.

The Germans kept killing Jews up until the very end of the war. After D-day, 12,000 Jews were murdered every day at Auschwitz. Inmates were sent on death marches during the fall of 1944. The marches killed hundreds of thousands of people. Germany soon surrendered on May 8, 1945. Decades of hate by many would be directed at the Germans from this point forward.

There were very few survivors from the concentration and death camps. Those who managed to survive were forever scarred and the vast majority of them were returning to their homes without some or all family members who were captured and initially transported to camps with them. However, justice was served at the Nuremberg trials during 1945 and 1946, where the Nazis who had roles in promoting the extermination of Jews and Nazis who killed Jews themselves were tried and given heavy punishments for their inhumane actions.

Needless to say, the Holocaust was an awful event in history with a monumental negative impact on the European Jewish population as well as the mentally disabled, gypsies, physically disabled, and other such groups of people. Pre-existing anti-Semitism became exponentially more prevalent in Germany and the rest of Europe as a result of the Holocaust. This, in turn, resulted in the survivors returning home to their very anti-Semitic neighbors. The remaining Jewish population received financial compensation from the German government beginning in 1953. In addition, Israel was created in 1948 as a homeland for the few Jews who survived the Holocaust.

The Holocaust signified the potential we as humans have to be cruel. It showed that such an unimaginable genocide could become a reality through utter ignorance and carelessness of a vast demographic. Delegating a religious group of people to blame for a war loss, discriminating strongly against them for years, and supporting a war revolving around mass genocide of them is a horrific representation of who we are as members of the human race.

It is important to note that such horrible feats have the potential to rise in our world once again. The human race has thoroughly exemplified the amount of sheer cruelty and hate that can possibly exist. Who is to say that some places in the world either now or in the future, there couldn't be another demagogue like Hitler to emerge as dictator and order the killing of millions of people. The Holocaust additionally exemplified how much power a given individual or a few individuals can acquire over the course of time and the influence they are capable of spreading to the people they govern. It is simply remarkable that so many German citizens would comply with the regulations and policies of Adolf Hitler. It goes to show that when someone like Hitler comes to power, powerful countries like the United States should intervene immediately to prevent as much power from being gained and as many people from being killed as possible.

The main reason the Holocaust wasn't halted in the beginning was that the Allies followed a policy of appeasement. They left Germany alone and gave Hitler what he wanted and hoped Germany would be satisfied. After Hitler started invading neighboring countries like Poland, the Allies continued to follow a policy of appeasement. It wasn't until 1939 that the Allies decided to intervene. So much suffering could have been prevented had the Allies intervened sooner.

Despite the fact that many Germans were on board with the ways of the Nazis, there were definitely some Germans who weren't anti-Semitic and wanted to help their Jewish friends and neighbors by any means they could. Their help would usually consist of tasks like hiding Jewish families in their homes, which unfortunately the Nazis came to realize and began conducting more thorough searches of homes. However, the ways people helped were sometimes creative and unique.

There are hundreds of people who strongly opposed the Nazis and made a difference in the lives of many Jews. We have all heard stories like those of the famous Anne Frank. She and her family were shielded for quite a long while by business owners until she and her family were eventually discovered by the Nazis and taken to a concentration camp. The people who helped them were good-hearted and became noted historically because of Anne Frank's diary's fame. Not very many people have heard of other noteworthy people who helped Jews like Hans von Dohnanyi.

Hans von Dohnanyi came from a very interesting background. He was born to two Hungarian musicians, one of whom was a composer and the other a pianist. When they divorced, he moved to the city of Berlin, Germany, and proceeded to continue to grow up there. He decided on studying to become a lawyer. Toward the end of his studying, he married a woman named Christel Bohnhoeffer and had three children, one of whom would eventually become mayor of Hamburg in the 1980s. Dohnanyi's career following the establishment of his family life would prove to be very significant.

Dohnanyi's career eventually placed him in a prime position to help Jewish victims of the Holocaust. In 1929, he started working at the senate of Hamburg, then transitioned to work at the Reich Ministry of Justice. While working there, his primary job was to consult with justice ministers. Dohnanyi became an adviser to a man by the name of Franz Gürtner starting in the year 1934. Advising Gürtner put him in a prime position because it lead to him receiving access to classified documents of the justice ministry. It also lead to him becoming acquaintances with Joseph Goebbels, Heinrich Himmler, Herman Göring, and lastly Adolf Hitler.

Dohnanyi strongly opposed "legitimized" murders ordered by the government, so he began to associate himself with German resistance circles. He wanted to be prepared for the collapse of the Third Reich, so he recorded as many crimes against humanity he could keep track of that the Nazi regime committed, in a personal effort. He wanted to make sure justice was served in the end, should there be one. Directly before World War II began, Dohnanyi became a part of the Abwehr of the Oberkommando der Wermacht. This was the center where resistance against the wrongdoings of Hitler was the most saturated. While a part of the Abwehr, he ensured that his childhood friend, Dietrich Bohnhoeffer, whom he met at the gymnasium he attended, wouldn't be drafted into the German military. Dohnanyi said that Dietrich had many useful ecumenical contacts that could serve as assets to Germany. Aiding Dietrich in not being conscripted was just the starting point of Dohnanyi's impact.

The next maneuver Dohnanyi executed was the emancipation of Jewish lawyers Friedrich Arnold and Julius Fliess along with each of their families from Nazi Germany to Switzerland. Not only did he forge many signatures and help disguise them as Abwehr agents, but he also travelled to Switzerland himself to ensure that his plan to get them there went smoothly. Dohnanyi's deed emphasizes how good-hearted and rational-minded he was during this dreadful period of time.

Dohnanyi's next endeavor was in 1943 when he aided in an assassination attempt against Hitler, headed by Tresckow. He smuggled a bomb onto Hitler's plane but it did not detonate, making the attempt unsuccessful. A couple months later, the Gestapo unfortunately arrested Dohnanyi. The reason for his arrest was that he placed money in Swiss bank accounts for the Jews he helped transport there. The Gestapo transported him to a concentration camp by the name of Sachsenhausen. The Gestapo discovered documents that he had previously set aside as well. Hitler personally ordered that he be executed, and he was indeed.

Hans von Dohnanyi was certainly a righteous hero during the Holocaust. His accomplishment of transporting the two Jewish lawyers and their families safely to Switzerland emphasizes how his attitude and charisma had an effect on the Jewish population. Though unsuccessful, his aid in the assassination attempt against Hitler exemplified his persistence and genuine hatred for Hitler and the ways of the Nazi regime. Even though Dohnanyi was eventually caught in the end, he lived an honorable life. He made a difference. He deserves remembrance. Dohnanyi is one of the heroes who passionately helped Jews and put others before himself, which made him immensely influential.

Work Cited

http://www.ushmm.org/wlc/en/article.php?ModuleId=10005143

http://www.history.com/topics/world-war-ii/the-holocaust

https://www.jewishvirtuallibrary.org/jsource/Holocaust/history.html

http://www.nybooks.com/articles/2012/10/25/tragedy-dietrich-bonhoeffer-and-hans-von-dohnanyi/

https://www.bostonglobe.com/arts/music/2013/10/12/legacy-resisitance-recalling-life-and-struggle-hans-von-dohnanyi/s30Pu3ftHhz7AWYOMl4yNN/story.html

http://ww2db.com/person_bio.php?person_id=188

Helmuth Groscurth – The Loser
Nathan K. Fleming

 While speaking to a survivor of World War II, philosopher Jeremy Fernando remarked that, upon asking the woman what the difference between being a free and non-free citizen was, she responded that it was entirely contingent on the capacity and luxury to say no. As he puts it, "Every question put to her was never a true question—it was only a question in form; a question to which an answer was already known." This imperative, as he puts it, marks the dichotomy between captor and captive that defines the violence of all war. Unsurprisingly, that is particularly striking in the case of the war to end all wars, where those most charged with heroism often found themselves on the receiving end of a pistol.

This will not be a story of super-human feats of military brilliance or cinematic grandeur. Often the narrative triumphs of times of hardship are clouded by the heroic achievements of the few and fleeting, folks like Schindler. These are the heroes of film and fiction, the household names treasured by families long after the war, because they succeeded, and did so in a way that exceeds the constraints of the everyday human condition. This will not be about those people. The tragedy of such narration is its attribution of success with heroism. The litmus test for grandeur is lives saved, not actions taken. It seems unfair that, purely as victims of circumstance, those who say no and fail are often abolished from the history books in favor over silver-screen stories with happy endings and a love interest. This will not be one of those stories. Helmuth Groscurth was not a hero who won. He was a hero who tried, said no, and failed; all with the grandeur and enthusiasm of as true a hero as one can hope to find in the inhuman wasteland of the greatest conflict in modern history.

Helmuth Groscurth was a German military man who rose to considerable esteem during the beginning years of the Second World War. Born in Ludenscheid in 1898, Groscurth entered his military post during the war already a well-aged man. Raised Protestant and quite conservative, Groscurth's grievances with the National Socialist movement were lengthy and fervent. He despised the Nazi campaign against the Jews, even to the extent of telling his wife, "We cannot be allowed to win this war," shortly before leaving for his new post leading the 295th Infantry Division into Russia. His grievances with the party did not stop there. A proud German, Groscurth held a relatively common opinion among a great many conservative Germans during the era, that the legacy of the campaign would remain a black mark on German heritage and ultimately damage the reputation of the nation in the international community. His fears, as we now know, were more than justified. As his diaries would later come to indicate, Groscurth's disdain for the Nazi Party, and Hitler in particular, became one of the predominant forces to structure his political life, military career, and posthumous legacy.

After several months of constant fighting in 1941, the 295th Infantry Unit stopped in the small Ukrainian town of Byelaya Tserkov. The village, already overrun by S.S., had been taken several days prior in a short but bloody massacre subjecting a large portion of the town's Jewish and Russian population to slaughter. The estimates, while rough, believe the body count upon his arrival was something around 800 people. Shortly after the division made camp at the scene, on August 20th, a small assemblage of the town's children were found by S.S. members in a dilapidated house on the fringes of the town. Ranging from only a few months old to around age seven, the group had been abandoned by their parents to hide for safety several days prior, largely without the food or water necessary for any extended secrecy. The description of their reveal is haunting, as they were reported to have been found "without water, covered with flies, and reduced to eating mortar pried from the brickwork, [they] cried and screamed throughout the night," only to be found in the morning by a small group of German soldiers on the command of Colonel Helmuth Groscurth. Upon receiving the report, Groscurth reported immediately to the commanding S.S. official on site, who ordered Groscurth continue with standard procedure for the mission: shoot all survivors. On the Eastern Front, the practice was exceedingly commonplace. The estimates of casualties of captured Russian soldiers alone are estimated to surpass 3.5 million, all before even considering the nearly-unquantifiable number of civilians who died from slaughter, famine, weather, or disease while being subjected to the cruelty of German captivity.

Thus, Groscurth found himself in the same position a great many other leaders and soldiers who resented the German conquest faced – executioner of the innocent. The action that sets Groscurth apart from the others is his reaction to such an ultimatum. Groscurth refused, adamantly. He insisted on relaying the situation directly to High Command, despite the explicit orders of his commanding officer. Upon making such an ultimatum, an S.S. official threatened to send some of his men to do the task instead, if Groscurth refused. His response bordered on insanity for those in his position. Without batting an eye, Helmuth Groscurth announced that if a single gesture was made to harm the children before high command had been spoken to and consulted on the official fate of their captives, he would order the 295th to protect them as if they were German soldiers and turn their guns back on the S.S. without a moment's hesitation. For a German officer to go rogue this way was a nearly unheard of event, especially amidst the brutality and harshness of the Eastern Front.

Tragically, Groscurth's attempts were ultimately futile. Upon reaching High Command and making his plea for mercy, the colonel received a nearly identical order to that which he had been given only a few days prior, and was thus ordered to relinquish his refugee hostages to the commanding unit of the S.S., where they were slaughtered only a few hours later. Groscurth's action yielded a few hours of survival and consideration to those who were all but lost in the horrors of the war. His actions presented a small glimmer of humanity amidst a campaign defined by gratuitous casualties, grotesque cruelty on both sides, and death beyond that which had ever been witnessed by the modern world. Groscurth's heroism is not that of a normal hero, filled with righteousness, a superman-like ethical code, or a built-for-cinema storyline. His story is one of trial, failure, and, without a doubt, bravery in the face of authority. Stanley Milgram, a famous Yale psychologist, conducted an experiment to gauge the effect of authority on decision making. Over the course of several weeks, Milgram found that, in the presence of a seemingly authoritative and knowledgeable superior, 68 percent of people are willing to deliver a deadly shock to a complete stranger under only slight duress by a superior. For Groscurth to say no to a higher-up in the face of atrocity at all is impressive, and to do so while staring down the metaphorical gun-barrel of the Nazi military hierarchy makes his stand one of incredible valor and intrigue. Astoundingly, Groscurth's dissent within the Nazi Party did not begin with his attempt to save those children.

The "September Conspiracy," as it is often referred to, was an exceedingly infamous plot to murder Adolf Hitler and overthrow the Nazi regime in Germany. The plot, it appears from what little primary evidence is left of the event, was an elaborately planned attempt to assassinate the German leader facilitated by a number of American spies and German military officials in secrecy from within the regime. Groscurth's role in the movement was twofold. The first was the necessity of his position in the military, which served to give the movement a pipeline of information to wield against the Nazis both through leakages to the allies and in the planning and organizing of plots and attacks on Nazi leaders. Groscurth's second, and arguably more significant role, was his position as head of the "Department of Special Assignments," within their larger coalition against the Nazis. There, Groscurth was responsible for managing a litany of exceedingly enthusiastic recruits. One of his main jobs, while hardly the exclusive task of our protagonist, was explosives manager. His task was, in essence, accumulating large amounts of black powder, blasting caps, and other chemicals necessary for producing large explosive devices, which the coup intended on deploying at a number of major government buildings during their uprising. While little of the operations of the group are known, the bulk of the information now gathered by historians has been largely a product of Groscurth's detailed journals transcribing the events of his lifetime, including the goings-on of the internal workings of the coup.

While little is known of their ultimate downfall, what details we are provided indicate that some security breach in late October of 1939 marked the dissolution of their revolutionary plans. The last mention of it most historians can find is from an entry chronicling the events of November 5, which seems to be the official date of death for Groscurth's revolutionary pursuits. As we understand it, November marked the crescendo of Hilter's long-mounting paranoia, and newly implemented security operations by the S.S. made attempting to gain access to the dictator a lofty and very unlikely proposition. Additionally, heightened surveillance of dissident groups, as well as a number of police raids on the headquarters of the group ultimately compromised the group's larger political ambitions. While most evidence of the raids has since been destroyed, Groscurth does isolate one incident in particular, where blueprints for a number of explosives and military campaigns, already laid out for the resistance, were copied and then destroyed by S.S. soldiers, inducing near-crippling setbacks for the revolutionaries and ultimately compounding into their dissolution in the period between the close of 1939 and early 1940.

Helmuth Groscurth's demise was far less climactic than his rise. In fact, he died in much the same way a great many German soldiers did while fighting on the Eastern Front — in a Russian prison camp. Despite his virulent hatred of the Nazi Party, Groscurth remained an officer in the military until his death in April of 1943. While working as a staff officer on the Eastern Front, Groscurth was captured during one of the many skirmishes at the battle of Stalingrad, where an estimated 800,000 Axis soldiers perished over the course of the four-month-long battle in the dead of winter. Ultimately, Groscurth was captured at some point in the fighting and banished to one of the many infamously horrible Russian POW camps, defined by their lack of sufficient medical care, poor facilities, the absence of food, and ravenous disease. Unfortunately, Groscurth fell victim to the latter, and perished of Typhus, like many other Germans, at some point in April, after the battle itself had settled down.

The tragedy of his death speaks to the odd features of heroism, that often living heroically does not guarantee dying heroically. Groscurth lived, by most standards, quite heroically, but for the outside observer, he died like any other Nazi. Had it not been for the trace historical relics he left behind to chart his lifetime, as well as the stories told by his wife and several insider comrades during the coup, the legacy of Helmuth Groscurth would be not only lost, but reversed in almost its entirety. He would have been remembered not as a rebel or a hero, but as a Nazi mourned by no one. One can only imagine that, amid a pile of half-frozen bodies in a Russia prison, the glimmer of Groscurth's heroism shone only fleetingly amongst the horrors of his surroundings. Fortunately, the one memento left behind in the wake of Groscurth's death was his journal, which has proven an indispensable tool for both history and justice after the war. His accounts of S.S. killings – like the one he intervened in – became primary evidence during the court hearings for a number of high-ranking Nazi officials, and his posthumous testimony helped levy charges against multiple particularly unpleasant relics of the Nazi era. Additionally, his inside-account of German politics and the goings-on of the Wehrmacht during the war has become a vital resource to historians chronicling the conflict. Thus, Groscurth presents a dilemma to the traditional hero story, because he was, by most metrics, a failure. His coup never left the ground, he was unable to stop the S.S., and he remained largely obscured from the grandeur and fame of the famous revolutionaries of the era. Yet Groscurth did what few around him could do — he said no. In the face of authority figures as daunting as the Nazis, that refusal ought to be enough to earn him a place in a history book. So, as we look back at Jeremy Fernando's interview with a survivor, we should once again remember that the difference between a captive and a captor is not chains or shackles, but the privilege of refusal. Groscurth was, in many senses, a captive within the Nazi regime, and his refusal to sit idly by and be captured, play along, and swallow the Kool Aid makes him hero enough for my standards.

Bibliography

Combing, Beach. "The Children of Bjelaja-Zerkow - Beachcombing's Bizarre History Blog." Beachcombing's Bizarre History Blog. N.p., 25 Apr. 2013. Web. 25 Feb. 2016.

Deutsch, Harold C. The Conspiracy against Hitler in the Twilight War. Minneapolis: U of Minnesota, 1968. Print.

Harrison, Edward. "Not Just Hitler | The Spectator." The Spectator. The Spectator, 25 Nov. 2008. Web. 24 Feb. 2016.

"Helmuth Groscurth." Wikipedia. Wikimedia Foundation, 5 June 2015. Web. 24 Feb. 2016.

"Historical Memory and the Power of Documents." CNN IReport. CNN Reports, 18 July 2012. Web. 25 Feb. 2016.

Mc/leod, Saul. "Milgram Experiment | Simply Psychology." Milgram Experiment | Simply Psychology. Simply Psychology, 2007. Web. 22 Feb. 2016.

North, Jonathan. "Soviet Prisoners of War: Forgotten Nazi Victims of World War II | HistoryNet." HistoryNet. World War II Magazine, 12 June 2006. Web. 23 Feb. 2016.

White, Mathew. "Twentieth Century Atlas - Casualty Statistics - Biggest Battles and Massacres." Twentieth Century Atlas - Casualty Statistics - Biggest Battles and Massacres. Necrometrics, Apr. 2014. Web. 24 Feb. 2016.

Lars Berg

Nicholas Ambrosini

In September 1939, Germany, under the awful dictator Adolf Hitler, began its vicious strike on Europe with the Nazi regime's first victim, the country of Poland. Shortly thereafter, the two countries of Britain and France responded by inciting war, however, in the next following couple of months, the two countries did not take any action towards Germany. Hitler used this time to launch his next initiative and in 1940 he attacked the countries of Denmark and Norway, and then shortly after that he began attacks on Belgium, the Netherlands, and the country of France itself.

Germany was able to rapidly conquer these countries because of its military might at the time. And then again in 1940 Hitler pushed for Germany to launch another attack this time on the great country of Britain, but this attack was different, Hitler did not employ all-out war on the country of Britain, he simply bombarded it from the air mercilessly. However, on the bright side this was also Germany's first military failure at the time, in this campaign, the German Air Force was overtaken by the British Royal Air Force.

Meanwhile in Italy, Hitler's ally Mussolini, expanded the war effort by invading Greece and North Africa, however the Greek campaign was a failure and Germany had to come to Italy's assistance in the year of 1941. This was because the Greek people put up too much of a fight for the Italians' military prowess.

And then Germany decided to try to overtake the Union of Soviet Socialist Republics. That was when Germany began its most ambitious war effort to date. Trying to invade the Soviet Union was a huge undertaking and although the Germans at first seemed to make a lot of really good progress and they got deep into the Russian land. This attempted invasion of the USSR would prove to be the very downfall of Hitler's Third Reich. The country was far too large, and even though Russia's initial fight was weak the nation's strength gained over time and that combined with the brutal winters was what completely shattered the Germans' will to fight in 1943. The front began to become a death march and/or a death sentence and the military's eyes or at least in the soldiers' eyes. In 1944, after the battles of Stalingrad in Kursk, Germany had to actually start its full-scale retreat.

After that, the Allied forces then pushed Germany through Europe back into its own borders in 1945, and this was happening all the while that the Normandy invasion was as well. In the month of June 1944, the British and American forces launched what became to be known as the D-Day invasion. They landed in the German-occupied France on the coast of Normandy, and soon after the bloodied battle the German army was forced to retreat from that side as well. Then at last by 1945 the Allies began to close in on Germany, the Nazi army had to admit defeat and Adolf Hitler committed suicide. And this is to speak nothing of the Japanese campaign, but that has less to do with the movement and the setting for the Holocaust, arguably the worst part of World War II.

The Holocaust was a ghastly affair, a terrifying show of bullying on a national scale. Millions of Jewish people were imprisoned and killed simply because of their beliefs, and because one man did not like them. The word Holocaust has historically been used to showcase a sacrificial offering burned on some sort of altar, however since 1945, the word has taken on a whole new, and darker meaning. Gypsies and homosexuals were also persecuted during this time.

During the beginning of the war Germany occupied the western part of Poland, the Germans soon forced thousands of Polish Jews from their houses and into places called ghettos. The German army then gave the confiscated property to people of German ethnicity, usually people from the Reich or Polish gentiles. Surrounded by high walls and barbed wire, which means virtually inescapable, the Jewish ghettos occupied like captives. Widespread unemployment, poverty, hunger, overpopulation and disease went rampant in these such ghettos, because there was relatively little to be done inside of them.

Around 1940 to 1941, the final solution, or Hitler's plan to start exterminating Jews, began to really start. This happened after Hitler expanded his empire. He conquered

Denmark, Norway, the Netherlands, Belgium, Luxembourg and France. And so the Jews from all over the continent at that point as well as a bunch of gypsies and many homosexuals were put into these such ghettos as well. They then began forcing Jews into work and death camps, these were under the most unimaginably brutal circumstances that the history of humanity seems to have to offer. And this was truly one of the most despicable and horrible acts of humankind, 6 million some Jews died in the Holocaust, and that is not okay.

However there were a brave few who began their campaign against the Holocaust, even without an army to back them. They were brave men and women who fought as freedom fighters for the Jewish people with either within Germany or within occupied and/or neutral states to provide for the war effort even though they were not part of an army involved directly in the actual war effort. The identities and details of these people are now available on Yad Vashem to be recognized for their heroic deeds and so in keeping I've decided to chronicle the heroic acts of a man from my land.

His name was Lars, Lars Berg. He hailed from the country of Sweden. He was a member of the movement to help the Jewish people in Budapest. He was also a member of the Swedish legation in Budapest and was an ambassador.

One of Lars Berg's most well-known friends at the time was a man named Wallenberg, this man became much more well-known than Lars Berg. Although Lars Berg contributed as much to the cause, and received much less as an outcome. Lars Berg described Wallenberg when he first met him, that he seemed to be somewhat of a blank page, sort of like a tapestry on which things could be etched, and this is not met and a bad way. Lars Berg was also present in the very famous dinner between Wallenberg and Eichmann. This was a very tense and seething moment in history in which he sat and saw them debate and work out a deal. This whole ordeal was made entirely possible by Lars Berg because, at the time Lars Berg lived with a very wealthy nobleman in Budapest. This wealthy nobleman's house served as a location for which the meeting took place because nobleman had the wealth to spare to wine and dine Adolf Eichmann. And in the meeting at Berg's house, he and others witnessed Eichmann threaten Wallenberg that, "accidents do happen, even to a neutral diplomat."

Two noted people Lars Berg also rescued were named Lars Ernster and Hugo Wohl, Lars Berg was finally commemorated with the tree/wall of honor and has been recognized on Yad Vashem. Another story showcasing Lars Berg's nobility and courage in the face of danger comes from his saving of a young child named Peter Zwack.

Peter and his family were hiding in the cellar of a house from the Arrow Cross, a group in affiliation with the Nazi cause. On this particular day, their efforts to hide from the Arrow Cross were in vain. For on this day, they came and they marched up to his house up the stairs and they started taunting Peter's uncle. They then started talking of taking some of them to be shot. This was a moment that Peter remembers because he ate his entire chocolate bar, it was his treat to be saved for the entire time he was hiding, but because he thought he was going to die right then and there, he decided he would want to eat it before he died. And so they began to march out the family of Peter Zwack, and if Lars Berg had not interfered right then and there, that probably would've been the end of all of their stories. Lars Berg on that day showed true courage when he jumped in holding a machine pistol. Lars Berg then claimed right then and there that the house was under Swedish protection and he began a standoff with the Arrow Cross. He won and the Arrow Cross left. I'm sure this is but one of many, many heroic tales that come with the mention of Lars Berg's name to some, but they are from another time, and so we must share his story and the story of others like him -- the ones who saved and helped the Jewish people when no one else would.

Those who stood out and bravely said no. Lars Berg also wrote a novel that chronicled most of his other tales, however I could not find a copy in distribution around Sacramento.

Lars Berg was also in a diplomatic mission to Budapest, and this is a large portion of what his novel is about, titled, "The book that disappeared: what happened in Budapest." This novel also chronicled the gruesome details of Wallenberg's mysterious disappearance. During his time in the Swedish Embassy he ran sector B, which oversaw the interests of foreign nationals and of Hungary. And during World War II, Sweden actually represented Hungary in the Allied countries. During the war, Lars Berg carried out several missions in his lifetime to free Jews, he protected them further and also from being deported. However despite his heroic efforts, after the war, the Soviets took over Budapest and thusly began imprisoning and taking over all the other government officials from before like the people that Lars Berg worked with, in fact, almost all of the people Lars Berg worked with closely, including the people in his own sector that he ran were arrested and shot some of them. But this is where perhaps karma came back for Lars Berg, to pay him back for his many heroic deeds and selfless acts to free the Jewish people and to help them escape tyranny. A kindhearted man who selflessly deserves what happened then because randomly, the man who then took over his position decided instead of what the law was requiring at the time, which would be to have Lars Berg in prison so he could be either executed or imprisoned depending on the severity of his enemy to the state profile, he simply let him go.

Actually, the man offered him some advice on how to conduct himself properly so that he would not be arrested at all or face even worse fate in the case of execution or just random acts of violence that would be justified in their eyes. And so Lars Berg made it to write his book back in his native homeland of Sweden and get married. Lars Berg's widow now lives in Brazil and surely remembers the heroic acts of her husband, if he was even brash enough to share as that's how heroes are.

Bibliography:

"Lars Berg, a Member of the Swedish Legation in Budapest, 1944-45, Poses with His Dog next to a Car." - USHMM Collections Search. N.p., n.d. Web. 28 Feb. 2016.

"Lars Berg." Funkascript ATOM. N.p., n.d. Web. 28 Feb. 2016.

"Possible Reasons for the Arrest." Funkascript ATOM. N.p., n.d. Web. 28 Feb. 2016.

"The Holocaust." History.com. A&E Television Networks, n.d. Web. 28 Feb. 2016.

Wilhelm Hammann

Owen Siden

Life is full of tragedies, however it is also full of heroes who can help in these times of need and distraught. One gargantuan catastrophe that almost everyone on the planet knows about is the mass genocide known as The Holocaust. The Holocaust began in 1933 in Germany with the rise of the Nazi Party and the appointment of Adolf Hitler as the Chancellor of Germany. At the time, the German Nazis saw themselves as the superior race and believed that all inferior races should be eradicated. These "inferior races" included Jews but were not limited to them. The Nazis also categorized Gypsies (Roma), the disabled, homosexuals, many Slavic people, and other groups to be inferior races. This plan to rid Nazi Germany (and Europe) of these "inferior races" was known as the Final Solution. This Final Solution also planned for the containment of Jews in concentration camps (but I'll get into that later). Nazi Germany was attempting to make a "perfect society" where everyone in the community had to meet the Nazi checklist. Basically anyone who did not match this small list of traits that Nazis were looking for, were murdered or persecuted. The ideal human that Nazis were trying to breed, known as the Aryans, were referred to as the "master race" (according to Nazi Germany that is).

During the Nazi rule nearly two out of every three European Jews were killed, which was part of Adolf Hitler's plan to create this "master race" in Germany. During the time period of the Holocaust, over 11 million people were killed and around 1 million of them were children. Six million of those 11 million people were Jewish and the rest were other groups such as Jehovah's Witnesses, homosexuals, the mentally and physically disabled, and Gypsies. However, apparently killing Jews wasn't enough for the Nazis because they also built these dreadful concentration camps in order to separate Jews from society and torture them. Some of the most famous Nazi concentration camps are Auschwitz, Buchenwald, Dachau, Kaiserwald, etc. Some of these Nazi concentration camps were used for forced labor while others were purely used as extermination camps. In forced labor camps the captives were forced to do inhumane tasks such as pulling massive carts full of stones and often times many people would die during this process. However, at extermination camps prisoners were sent into crammed rooms (like gas chambers) to be killed off in mass amounts. In these camps there would be thousands of Jews shoved into miniscule spaces and they were given very little food and water. This is torture. How could someone possibly do this to another human being?

Besides the concentration camps, Nazis also segregated Jews within society by isolating them into areas in the cities called ghettos. Ghettos are small isolated parts of the city that are usually occupied by minority groups (such as Jews) and can also be referred to as slums. Another way that Nazis promoted anti-Semitism was through Kristallnacht, or "the night of broken glass." On the night of November 9th 1938, Nazis flooded the streets and rioted. During these two days, "over 250 synagogues were burned, over 7,000 Jewish businesses were trashed and looted, dozens of Jewish people were killed, and Jewish cemeteries, hospitals, schools, and homes were looted..." according to the United States Holocaust Memorial Museum (USHMM). It is called the "night of broken glass" because of all the glass shards that littered the streets after the riots. One of the worst parts about this is that after all the rioting was over, Jews were the ones who were arrested and sent to concentration camps, not the rioters.

The most common misconception that I hear about Germans today is that all Germans were Nazis and they all took part in the mass genocide during this era, however this is just not the case. In fact there were many Germans who helped Jews during the Holocaust and saved them from Adolf Hitler's mighty wrath. One example of a German hero who helped Jews during the Holocaust is Wilhelm Hammann, who helped to save hundreds of Jews. But before we get into his heroic deeds let's start with some background information.

Wilhelm Hammann was born into a working class family in the year 1897 and was later drafted into the German military. During his time in the military he attended a military pilot school in Halle. While he was in Halle he engaged in communist actions which later lead him to join the Communist Party of Germany. In 1920 Wilhelm passed his teaching exam, retaining a teacher's permit, and in 1922 he began teaching in Wixhausen. Six year later, in 1928, he was elected to town council and to the Landtag of Hesse. A Landtag is a representative assembly, or parliament, for German speaking countries. In 1930, after defying police suppression, Hammann was banned from teaching and imprisoned for one month. Later on Wilhelm was arrested again and spent almost all of 1933 in jail and then in 1935 he was sentenced to three years behind bars. Later on, in 1938, Wilhelm Hammann was transferred to Buchenwald, a Nazi concentration camp.

Buchenwald was built by prisoners of war in the summer of 1937. Nazi commanders forced Jews to use their time and energy to carry very large boulders and pull heavy carts full stones from a nearby quarry to the camp. Some prisoners were too small and weak to do this type of labor, in the eyes of the Nazis, so they were executed on the spot. Buchenwald eventually turned out to be one of the largest Nazi concentration camps of its time. In the beginning of Buchenwald's existence, mostly only political prisoners were sent here. However, after Kristallnacht, almost 10,000 Jews were sent to Buchenwald to be punished. And let me remind you that the Jews were not the ones who were rioting; they were being punished simply because they identified as being Jewish. According to Jewishgen.org, "the official goal of Buchenwald was the destruction of the prisoners by work. Thousands of prisoners were murdered in Buchenwald by work, torture, beatings, or simply starvation and lack of hygiene."

This concentration camp was originally categorized as a forced labor camp yet they were killing off prisoners like they it was an execution camp. This was just another way for Adolf Hitler to speed up the total annihilation of the "inferior races." Nazis tortured the prisoners at Buchenwald in many different ways but by far the most gruesome thing

I have read about is how the Nazis skinned prisoners. Nazi commanders would murder the prisoners and then skin them, like they were deer. After this, they would tan the skin and send it off for it to be used as book covers and other things. As I was reading about this I was completely mortified and couldn't believe that a group of people could be that evil and do such a terrible thing to other human beings. These were living, breathing humans, just like you or me, and the Nazis treated them like they were nothing more than some fresh roadkill they found on the side of the highway. This is sick. Not only were an abounding amount of people killed at this camp, but the ones who lived where treated like dirt. The prisoners only received half-liter of a light soup and one loaf of bread for eight inmates per week. Soup and some bread shared among eight people per week, is that even considered living? And that's not all; the commanders would throw the food onto the muddy, disgusting ground so that the prisoners would have to kneel before them in order to eat their food. This was just another way the Nazis promoted their idea of the social hierarchy. But now let's bring it back to our hero without a cape, Wilhelm Hammann.

Wilhelm Hammann spent several years in the concentration camp Buchenwald, but during his time there he did quite a lot. After a few years at the camp he was put in charge of the barracks, Block 8, where all the children were kept. He gained this rank because there weren't enough commanders at the camp to do all the jobs, so political prisoners took over the open jobs. Originally it was the criminals who fulfilled these untaken jobs but eventually they were caught stealing from the barracks, which caused the commanders to give the positions to the political prisoners. However rather than stealing, Hammann did something very beneficial with this position of power. Before Nazi commanders came around to collect the Jews for the execution chambers, Wilhelm and other men helped the children remove the patch that signified that they were Jewish (a Star of David). He also told all the children to not respond when the commander came by and asked who was Jewish. Then, when the guard came by Hammann simply told him that he had no Jewish children in his block. Because of these noble actions, hundreds of Jewish children's lives were saved. In fact Wilhelm Hammann was the only Buchenwald prison honored by Yad Vashem for his valiant actions to save hundreds of lives. Hammann was by no means the only person who helped to save these children but without him the efforts may not have been as successful. Due to his higher rank at the camp the guards trusted him a bit more than others so if he said there were no Jews, they believed him.

Through researching this topic and typing this essay I feel that I have learned many things and grown as a person. Coming away from this essay I feel that I am much more informed and aware than I was before. Before I wrote this essay I had an idea about how bad the Holocaust was but I never knew specific statistics and things that I know now because of this essay. For example, I knew that Nazis discriminated against Jews during this time period, but when I read that it was Jews who were arrested after Kristallnacht, I was completely appalled. I couldn't believe that all this hate and damage was forced onto the Jewish people and then after all the rioting was over, the people who were being attacked were the one who were arrested. That's like punishing someone and then punishing them for being punished. It just doesn't make sense. Another thing that I learned while writing this essay that blew my mind was that Nazis murdered and skinned prisoners at Buchenwald. Just think about that for a moment, Nazis actually took the skin off of another human being. Honestly while I was reading about this I was at the brink of tears because of how completely awful this is. How can someone have it in them to treat another human being that way? It is completely inhumane and unjust. The term "Holocaust" fits its definition in every way and form. The Holocaust is directly defined as: destruction or slaughter on a mass scale.

In the world that we live in today there is a lot of hate and discrimination that is still live today. Now you would assume that we would learn from our historical mistakes and attempt to not have these tragedies happen again. However lately while looking at all the discrimination in the world, I have heard people pondering, "Could this be the next Holocaust?" Just the thought of this question being brought up sends chills down my spine. The fact that people are even questioning this is terrible and should not be happening. I think that if people knew more about the Holocaust and all of its tragedies then we would be more motivated to prevent a new one. That is why I highly suggest that everyone attempts to write this essay. And if you don't have the time for it then at least research the Holocaust so that you know the whole truth and not just some of it. My question for you is, will we be able to learn from our mistakes in the past, or is history bound to repeat itself?

Works Cited:
"Buchenwald Concentration Camp (Germany)." Buchenwald Concentration Camp (Germany). N.p., n.d. Web. 23 Feb. 2016.

"Buchenwald." United States Holocaust Memorial Museum. United States Holocaust Memorial Council, 29 Jan. 2016. Web. 24 Feb. 2016.

"11 Facts About the Holocaust." 11 Facts About the Holocaust. N.p., n.d. Web. 23 Feb. 2016.

"Introduction to the Holocaust." United States Holocaust Memorial Museum. United States Holocaust Memorial Council, 29 Jan. 2016. Web. 22 Feb. 2016.

"The "Night of Broken Glass"" United States Holocaust Memorial Museum. United States Holocaust Memorial Council, n.d. Web. 24 Feb. 2016.

"Saving Children in Buchenwald." Jewish Currents. N.p., 30 Nov. 2015. Web. 22 Feb. 2016.

"Wilhelm Hammann." Wikipedia. Wikimedia Foundation, 27 Oct. 2015. Web. 20 Feb. 2016.

Albert Goering

Payton Eldridge

It began in January in the year of 1933. Adolf Hitler and the Nazis had completely taken over Germany and slowly were expanding their rule. The Holocaust was 12 years of terror instilled in the lives of many Jews. Nobody who practiced Judaism in Europe was safe; the Nazis' persecution ranged from Germany to Greece and even all the way to Yugoslavia. This endless persecution ultimately resulted in roughly 6 million recorded innocent murders all throughout the continent of Europe. It leaves you thinking if there were 6 million recorded deaths then how many unrecorded lives were taken by the Nazis over the course of those twelve years? This was a time that most people choose to block out of their memories because it is unbelievably disgusting how your prejudices could lead you to doing something this extreme, but we have to learn from history so that nothing like this ever happens again. Even during this horrific time many individuals stepped up and risked their lives to save the lives of countless Jews. These heroes were spread across the world risking everything to help complete strangers survive. Albert Goering was one of these courageous individuals who did all he could to save the lives of many.

Albert Goering was the youngest brother of Hermann Goering and is known as "The Good Brother." As a child he was described as a sad boy with doe-brown eyes, a polar opposite in comparison to his brother. Their mother's name was Fanny and their godfather's name was Baron Hermann von Epenstein. Albert's entire life was full of deep moral principle and he quickly became cynical of the Nazis. He moved to Austria to live with von Epenstein on allowance and he worked at a film studio in Vienna. It was then that he started speaking out against Adolf Hitler and his army of Nazi soldiers.

When the Nazis made their way into Austria, Albert was immediately put into trouble, but his brother Hermann managed to keep him away from the Gestapo. Hermann Goering was Hitler's closest associate in the Third Reich. He was the strongest man in the Nazi ruling circle and he had complete control over the economy in Germany. He also was the founder of the Gestapo and helped to create the very first concentration camps. He was the equivalent to Hitler's wingman and he was the only other Nazi leader who the people could identify with. Hermann's horrific participation in the Holocaust turned out to be it quite useful for Albert. He was also able to help Albert save the lives of Jews because of his constant need to show off his power and also because of his constant search of approval from his younger brother.

It was not until recently that Albert was believed to have saved the lives of Jews. He was automatically deemed as a "bad guy" due to his last name. His brother's participation and actions were grouped along with Albert, even though that was not the case. The severity of his brother's crimes and acts of hate against Jews made it so that his actions of justice were not noticed. Testimonies were discovered in the British archives that cleared Albert Goering's name and shone light upon his actions that defied Hitler and the Nazis.

After he started to speak out against the Nazi party and against Adolf Hitler himself, he quickly became more informed as to what Hitler's plan was. He discovered that they were planning to exterminate women, children, and men to completely rid the continent and in hopes the world of Jewish people. Goering began to loathe Hitler and the inhumanity of the Nazis. He then witnessed the violence and terror that often came around with the Nazis and he decided that it was his turn to take action and do something to put a stop to this insanity.

A new chapter started in Albert Goering's life after he became informed of the cruelty and injustice acts of hate that the Nazis were taking part in. He started off by helping many Jews escape from Vienna by obtaining travel documents for them. He then had his brother Hermann guarantee the safety of the famous composer Franz Lehar's wife, who was Jewish. Albert was always willing to help anyone in need, he even befriended the Otzoup Guliaeff family in 1943 and signed their passports ensuring the parents safety and the safety of their daughter Tatiana. He would often name drop his brother in order to get whatever he needed, so his brother's high rank became extremely useful to him to provide safety for the Jews. Albert would go to his brother and declare that a specific Jew was a "good Jew" and that they do not belong in concentration camps. Hermann would let them go every time because he wanted to prove how powerful he was to his brother, and eventually he freed roughly one hundred Jews that were featured on Albert's list all because of Hermann's constant need of approval. Albert would also forge his brother's signature on documents and gave orders over the phone by imitating his brother's voice. Albert helped a former boss, a Jew named Oskar Pilzer, and his family get out of the country. Henny Porten, the actress, was forced to leave the German film industry because they discovered that she was married to a Jew and they did not want to be accused of having relations with Jews. Goering was requested by Henny to intervene and he arranged a contract for her. Albert gave Laszlo Kovacs, his doctor, money so that he could set up a joint bank account at the Bank Orelli in Bern. This in turn would be used to help Jewish refugees to get to Lisbon. Albert Goering spent much of his time until 1945, doing anything possible that he could to attempt help as many individual Jews as possible to survive, often using his brother and his connections.

Throughout the course of Goering saving many Jews, he was arrested by the Gestapo several times, but again thanks to his high ranking brother, he managed to be freed every time. He later worked as an export director of the Czech arms factory Skoda. There he was able to save the lives of many workers and help protect the Czech resistance members and their actions. It was also there that he put himself in grave danger because he took part in a Czech Resistance movement that was highly against Nazism. This put him under the magnifying glass of many Nazi soldiers. Whenever Nazi officers would visit his office he would refuse to return the Nazi salute every time as a small act of defiance. The refusal of the Nazi salute was enough to land you in jail or possibly even worse.

Albert Goering was always seen as a great man by those he saved and others, but sadly he was not recognized until the records were found in Britain. The workers of Skoda spoke nothing, but highly. They loved him as a boss because he was understand of them and treated like fellow humans rather than inferior beings. He was extremely lenient on forgetfullness, lost work, or wrong translations of catalogs. He knew that they risked their lives every single day because if they were to get caught by the Gestapo of the SS, they would be executed without question or hesitation. Another example of why he is beloved by many is because when he saw the Nazis trying to humiliate the Jews he went and did whatever they did with them. For example they were making the Jews scrub the sidewalk as a way of public humiliation. Instead of walking away or laughing like most people did he took off his jacket, got on his knees, and helped them scrub. He was always considered to have deep moral conviction like I stated earlier and once he saw the horrors of the real world he felt obligated to do soemthing about it.

After the war and the Holocaust were completely over, Albert and his brother had to deal with the consequences of bearing the last name "Goering." Hermann was tried in the Nuremberg Trials, but he could not convince the judges of his innocence. He was sentenced to death by hanging and he pleaded with the court to shoot him instead so that he could "die like a man." Of course the judges denied his request and had him imprisoned until his execution. Somehow he obtained a cyanide pill and managed to hide it during his imprisonment. He then proceeded to take it, which resulted in death, roughly two hours before his execution. Before committing suicide he made Albert promise to take care of his wife and daughter. Because Albert was cursed with the last name of "Goering" he was imprisoned for years and the name became a handicap to him. His relation to his brother was a curse. Luckily his grateful survivors came to his rescue this time. They helped support throughout the years when he was unemployed. When he got back on his feet, he married several times and landed a jobs as a designer in a construction firm in Munich. After a long, selfless and courageous life Albert Goering passed away in 1966.

The Otzoup Guliaeff family that I mentioned earlier, never forgot how Albert managed to save them from the horrors of the Holocaust. The daughter, Tatiana, was born in Berlin with Russian parents. She had a silent movie star for a mom and a movie producer, art collector, and multiple award winner as a father. Their family only managed to escape the Holocaust due to Albert Goering signing their false papers. Goering was the godfather of Tatiana and the last time she saw him was in Vienna when she was six. She grew up to be an actress of 25 years and an amazing writer. Tatiana wrote a letter to Albert Goering speaking of how much she loved and cherished him and everything that he did for her family and her. She talked about all the nights he would sit in his office that was off limits to Tatiana and work endlessly trying to save as many lives as he could. This entire letter is explaining that she did not know all the things that he did and all the things that happened to him in his life, but she is expressing her appreciation and love toward him. Tatiana addresses the letter to "Onkel Baer" which translates to Uncle Bear. This is a very touching letter and it helps give more insight on how much work Goering truly did to save lives.

In 1966 we lost a hero. We lost someone who went under the radar and saved hundreds of lives. We lost someone who saved people from experiencing the Holocaust. We lost someone who prevented hundreds of people and their families from being tortured daily and eventually murdered. Albert Goering was a hero. He spent a huge portion of his life working to help those who could not help themselves. He did almost anything so that he could save many innocent lives. I admire this man. I wish that there were more people that could have done what he did at the time. Thinking about the Holocaust and all the things that happened in it makes me sick to my stomach. I cannot even imagine what that was like to the millions of Jews in Europe. I admire everyone who had to experience this horrific event in history. Not just the Holocaust heroes, but every single Jew because the survivors somehow found the will to keep pushing to survive and even the deceased are admirable for all the time they spent fighting for their lives. Even though this is a hard topic to learn about for everyone, it is critical that we take the time to remember all the lives that were lost so that nothing like this ever happens again. I am so glad that the records were found proving what Albert Goering truly did because if they had not been found I would not have gotten to learn about this amazingly courageous individual.

Noblemen of the Holocaust

Qiera Nixon

Throughout history, a person's worth has been measured by their physical strength. There are myths and folktales written about great heroes and heroines who were physically gifted. The stronger and more capable the person, the more respect and recognition they received from others in their society. Much less often were people recognized for their courage. From 1933 to 1945, Adolf Hitler reigned power in Germany in name of the Nazi regime. His intolerant policies and terrifying, anti-Semitic views have made him one of the most recognized men in History. Committed under Hitler's reign was also the greatest organized mass murder know in history. The Jewish Holocaust. Hitler and his supporters controlled almost all of Western Europe using intimidation and manipulation tactics. Through these tactics many people came under the Nazi Party's control. Hitler gained an overwhelming number of supporters this way. However there were a solemn few who chose otherwise. These righteous few helped to save the lives of those who were outcast by Nazi policies. One distinguished person among these few was Dr. Irena Block, a doctor who helped to hide and ultimately safe the life of one of her Jewish patients at extreme risk to herself. Dr. Irena Block and others like her are considered heroes of the Holocaust.

258

The Nazi Party didn't rise to power overnight, it was a force that had been building in Germany since the end of the First World War. Germany's formal surrender marked the defeat of the central powers and brought an end to the First World War Twenty one nations gathered for peace talks that took place at the Palace of Versailles and as a result the Treaty of Versailles was created. Although Austria-Hungary, the Ottoman Empire and Germany all made up the central powers, Germany took almost all of the blame for what had happened during the war. France, the country most affected by the war, wanted Germany completely disarmed and crippled to the point of never being able to wage war on France again. America and Britain, which were much less affected by the war, wished to focus more on maintaining peace between nations. However France's points could not be ignored when looking at all of the devastation that had been caused by the war. In the end, Germany was stripped of all of its colonies and they were distributed to the Axis powers. Their territories of Eupen-Malmedy and Alsace-Lorraine were given to Belgium and France. And substantial parts of eastern Germany were also taken and given to other countries. Saar was also taken away from Germany for 15 years. This resulted in a huge loss of natural resources that the country desperately needed. The German army was also reduced to a size rendering it not only incapable of waging another war, but incapable of defending the country as well. This displaced almost all army personnel who now had no jobs to return to due to the lack of positions available. The treaty also forced Germany to assume full responsibility for the war and pay war reparations amounting to about $30 million to account for damages and losses sustained by the Allies. In effort to pay the reparations Germany began to print off an exorbitant amounts of marks (German currency), which caused severe hyperinflation in Germany. The hyperinflation combined with the huge loss of jobs brought on by the reduction of army personnel plunged Germany into a great depression. During this time in Germany money became essentially worthless. Children were seen playing with stacks of money in the street and people burned it for fuel rather than attempting to buy anything with it. Many German people starved during this time, yet no assistance was offered from other nations. All of the hardship brought on Germany by the Treaty of Versailles was enough to fuel the start of revolution. The Nazi Party started out as a gang of unemployed soldiers. The group came to call itself the German Workers Party. Hitler joined the group and rose quickly in the ranks through his amazing speaking and rallying abilities. He often spoke of national pride, militarism and the necessity of a pure Aryan race. In many of his speeches, he targeted the Jews of Europe, laying blame on them for all of Germany's problems. He used the Jews as the scapegoat they had often been used as for before as validation for all of his accusations. In its early years the Nazi Party was all but unrecognized among the German people. In 1924 it received only 3 percent of the popular vote. However in 1932 it had up to 33 percent of the popular vote. Many Nazi leaders won seats in the Reichstag house and so began the Nazi Party's rise to power.

Hitler began his reign in February 1933 when he was appointed Chancellor of Germany. In March. shortly following Hitler's appointment as Chancellor, the

Reichstag building, a building that housed the Imperial Diet, was set on fire. Blame for the incident immediately fell on the Communist Party although it is still unknown if it was in fact the Communist Party. There is suspicion that the Nazi Party set the building aflame to create chaos out of which they could emerge as a leader. After the incident the Communist Party was considered a threat to the German state. This made the Nazi Party the only political party left in Germany that could realistically lead the nation. Following the burning of the building, Hitler demanded a declaration of panic so that dictatorial power could be given to him. When he was awarded this power he began administration of his policies. He began by restricting individual freedoms and outlawing all political parties other than the Nazi Party. To eliminate the threat of the Communist Party, Hitler ordered his SA and SS officers to roundup all communists and liberals and put them into SA barracks where they were beaten and tortured into submission. With the Communist Party dismantled, the Nazi party had sole political power in Germany. Hitler immediately began to target Jewish people. In his speeches Jews were given blame for all bad things that had befallen Germany. Within months of Hitler's appointment as chancellor the Dachau concentration camp was opened. Following shortly were the openings of the concentration camps Buchenwald, Sachsenhausen and Ravensbrueck. These acts were followed by the boycott of Jewish-owned shops and businesses. The Nazi stormtroopers lead marches in the streets with signs saying to protect your own people and to not support Jewish business. More and more the necessity of being of pure Aryan race became part of the Nazi Party's platform. Anyone of Jewish heritage or non Aryan was considered impure by the Nazi regime. People found to be carrying or possibly be carrying genes, including already pregnant women, that could lead to genetic defect were forcibly sterilized. Any of these people along with the homeless, beggars, alcoholics, unemployed, disabled and criminal were to be sent to concentration camps. Laws began to be passed against Jewish people, effectively separating them from German society. Jews were prohibited from owning land, from being involved in the arts, from holding government positions or working for the German state, from being the editor of newspapers, being part of the German labor front, from having state insured healthcare, working in the military and receiving legal qualifications. Citizenship rights were taken away from Jewish people. They were not allowed to marry Aryan people and there were forced medical examinations to determine if a person was of any Jewish heritage. The German police force known as the Gestapo was created. The Gestapo were the Nazis' secret police. They worked through intimidation and brutality, seeking out anyone not fitting the idea of the Aryan race and those who were opposed to the leadership of the Nazi state. Germany also began to invade neighboring countries in order to create more room for the Aryan master race to live and grow. On March 7, 1946, Germany occupied the Rhineland. A clear violation of the Treaty of Versailles, yet no preventative action was taken by other nations. Germany then invaded Poland, and Austria-Hungary and was met with little to no protest. Upon learning of the events happening under Hitler's control a League of Nations conference was held to determine what to do and how to give assistance to the

Jews. However. no country was willing to engage in war with Germany and no country was willing to accept such a large number of Jewish refugees so the matter was left alone. Germany's army went on to take over all of Western Europe. By the time other nations decided to get involved and wage war on Germany it was almost too late. At the end of the war when American soldiers went into Germany what they discovered was beyond what any had thought possible. The soldiers saw the concentration camps. They saw the starving people, the mass graves left uncovered and the bodies still burning. While the axis powers had been defeated, knowledge of the atrocities committed by the Nazis made it seem as if the war had been almost for nothing. It is estimated that in total about 5 to 6 million Jews were killed in the Holocaust. Although it is impossible to be sure just how many actually perished. Of all the millions of Jews who were slaughtered or taken to concentration camps, there were a few who managed to survive by hiding from the German state. The people who housed these Jews put themselves as well as their families at incredible risk simply because they knew it was the right thing to do. One among the many heroes who helped to save the life of a Jewish person was Dr. Irena Block.

Dr. Irena Block was a doctor of law. She advised her clients on foreign currency and was one of few who continued to accept and receive Jewish clients. One of her clients was Maria Johanna Fulda, a mentally and physically unstable Jewish woman. Through their professional meetings the two women developed a friendship. Fulda lived in a segregated section of Jewish houses in Frankfurt which endured periodic sweeps from the Gestapo to take Jewish people to concentration camps. Dr. Irena used her status to obtain Fulda's medical records. She used the records to prevent Fulda from being taken away. Time and time again Dr.Irena did this until the day of the final sweep by the Gestapo where every person would be taken to concentration camps. On this day Dr. Irena went to her client's house and took her from her home. Fulda was in a state of utter confusion and her body and mind were on the verge of collapse. The yellow Jewish star was removed from Fulda's clothes and together the two women made their way to a train station where they boarded a train to a farmhouse owned by Dr. Irena where Fulda lay in wait for several days. Several days later Dr. Irena returned to the farm house and brought Fulda back to her apartment in Frankfurt. Here Fulda remained for two years, never venturing outside and hiding in the bedroom when Dr. Irena had clients in her home for business meetings. The apartment was later destroyed by a bomb in an aerial raid. The two women moved to a small town where Fulda with the help of Dr. Irena obtained an Aryan identity card. Dr. Irena displayed amazing bravery in taking in Fulda. Every day she risked the loss of her own life as well her friends and the possible harm and humiliation of her loved ones by the Nazi party. If it had not been for her fearlessness Fulda, like countless others would have been taken to a concentration camp and murdered.

The Holocaust is a scar on the world that will never be healed. It shouldn't be healed. That solemn time must be remembered by the world so as not to make the mistake of repeating it. The world experienced so much loss in the time of war and during the Holocaust. Atrocities as such were committed by the Nazi regime will never be forgotten. Many people lacked the courage to stand up to Nazi Germany because of their overwhelming power and ferocity. The many few who did stand up to the regime deserve to be honored and recognized. People like Irena Block who risked everything they had and would ever become in order to save the lives of others for the simple reason of it being right.

Works cited

"Holocaust Timeline: The Rise of the Nazi Party." Holocaust Timeline: The Rise of the Nazi Party. N.p., n.d. Web. 28 Feb. 2016.

"The History Place - Holocaust Timeline." The History Place - Holocaust Timeline. N.p., n.d. Web. 28 Feb. 2016.

"Nazi Perpetrators. The Gestapo".
https://www.jewishvirtuallibrary.org/jsource/Holocaust/Gestapo.html

Yad Vashem".
http://db.yadvashem.org/righteous/family.html?language=en&itemId=4042975

https://fcit.usf.edu/holocaust/timeline/nazifica.htm

Emilie Schindler: A True Hero of the Holocaust

Rachel Redman (Co-Winner)

H.P. Lovecraft, a renowned horror-fiction novelist and literary analyst, said in his book Supernatural Horror in Literature that, "the oldest and strongest emotion of mankind is fear, and the oldest and strongest kind of fear is fear of the unknown." This truth, that mankind's deepest and most primal emotion is the fear of the unknown, is easily proven through examination of human behavior throughout history. People are afraid of the dark because what is in it is unknown. People are afraid of death because what happens after it is unknown. People are afraid of other people who are not like them because they are unknown. The bottom line is that human beings are afraid of things that they do not understand or things they are not familiar with. Many events throughout human history have displayed this concept, but none quite so well as the Holocaust. One man's fear of something he did not understand leading a whole group of people to fear something they did not understand resulted in the coming of the Second World War and the deaths of over 50 million people, with 6 million of those deaths being Jews who were persecuted for being misunderstood, for being the "unknown." It is chilling to think that real human beings gave into their primal, animalistic fears and allowed themselves to be led into believing that all of their misfortunes must have been the fault of a single group of people, but it is the truth of what happened. Hitler and his army led an entire country to believe that the Jews and other minorities were at fault for Germany's troubles after the First World War, and that eliminating them would allow for German world domination. Although it is important to talk about the crimes committed during the Holocaust, that is not the aim of this essay.

The aim of this essay is to recognize the people who, amidst chaos, destruction, and great evil, did good deeds and saved the lives of as many people as they were given the chance to. Although the Holocaust is history's greatest example of the innate human fear of unknown, misunderstood, and unrecognized things, it is also history's greatest source of proof that humans can overcome these fears, as well as many other obstacles, and do good things in the face of evil. Many examples of brave, selfless, compassionate, and overall heroic people came out of the Holocaust. These righteous, heroic people are often glossed over in the rush to educate people on the Holocaust and other events of World War II, but their stories are just as important as the stories of Hitler and the Nazis because they show examples of hope and heroism in the face of adversity. This essay is an attempt to recognize all of these heroes through the story of just one of them. The heroic deeds of Emilie Schindler will hopefully serve as an example of the selfless bravery of all of the heroes of the Holocaust.

The name Emilie Schindler may sound familiar, as her husband, Oscar Schindler, has garnered fame from the 1993 movie Schindler's List, which tells of her husband's heroic efforts during World War II. The movie showed some of Emilie's story, the parts that involve her working with her husband, but focused mostly on Oscar. Although her husband's name is more famous because of this movie, Emilie's heroic actions, both together with her husband and without him, show her to be just as selfless, brave, and compassionate as Oscar. Emilie's full story deserves to be told, and it will be told through this essay.

Emilie was born on October 22, 1907, in the city of Alt Moletein, a village in the German-populated border region of what was then Austria-Hungary and now the Czech Republic, to German farmers Josef and Marie Pelzl. She had an older brother named Franz. Her early life in Alt Moletein on her parents' farm was idyllic, happy, and peaceful for the most part. Her family was Catholic, like the majority of the people in her village. Even as a young girl, Emilie showed that she valued fairness and equality, and would not be deterred or controlled by a fear of the unknown. She was quite fond of nature and animals and was intrigued by the music, stories, and nomadic lifestyle of the Romani people, as groups of them would often camp near her village for a few days at a time. She made friends with a young Jewish girl in her village named Rita Reif, and they became very close. The local pastor, who was a family friend of the Pelzls, told Emilie that her friendship with Rita was bad because Rita and her family were Jewish. He stated that she must end the interactions immediately, but Emilie defied his instruction. She remained friends with Rita, and the two grew even closer, until Rita was murdered by Nazis in 1942. Still, Emilie showed from a young age that she could overcome the fear of unknown things that prevented so many other people in her community from associating with Rita's family just because they were different. This skill would help her to save the lives of around 1,500 people just a little later in her life.

Emilie first met Oscar Schindler when he came to the door of her family's farmhouse in Alt Moletein in 1928. He was attempting to sell electric motors to her father. She and Oscar began dating, and after six weeks, they were married on March 6, 1928, in an inn on the outskirts of Zwittau, Austria-Hungary, Oscar's hometown. Emilie's father had given Oscar a dowry of 100,000 Czech crowns, a considerable amount of money for that time, and he soon bought a luxury car with it and spent the rest on outings with Emilie. Despite his lack of fiscal responsibility at this time, the marriage was going well. In 1938, Oscar joined the Nazi Party, as many did during that time, and moved to Cracow in Poland, leaving Emilie in Zwittau. Eventually, through some pretty shady dealings, Oscar gained control of a bankrupt enameled-goods factory, Deutsch Emailwaren Fabrik, close to the Jewish ghetto in Cracow. There, he began principally employing Jewish workers because they were the cheapest labor at the time. Soon, though, he realized the true brutality of the Nazis' persecution of the Jews, and began to do things to help and protect his workers. In 1944, he moved his factory, along with all of its workers, to Brünnlitz, Austria-Hungary, preventing all of the workers from being deported from the labor camp they lived in to an extermination camp. Emilie moved to Brünnlitz to be with Oscar again, and when she saw the factory workers and heard about the truth of the Nazi Party, she began to help Oscar to protect the workers.

From 1944 to the liberation in 1945, Emilie worked alongside Oscar doing everything in their power to save the factory workers. Emilie and Oscar even referred to the workers as their children. Through bribery and Oscar's Nazi Party connections, the Schindlers secured the safety and relative well-being of the 1,300 factory workers. By claiming that the factory was manufacturing ammunitions for that Nazi Party and that all of the workers were essential to the workings of the factory, they prevented their workers from being subjected to the labor camps and death camps and the will of other Nazis. In fact, in the seven months that it was running, the factory produced no usable munition shells. Instead, false military travel passes and ration cards were produced and Nazi uniforms, weapons, ammunition and hand-grenades were collected. They spent their own personal money to build barracks on the factory grounds so that their workers would not be subject to conditions in the nearby labor camp. In their factory, no one was mistreated or abused, but it was still hard to keep everyone comfortable on the small budget they had and without making people suspicious of them. To treat the ailing workers, the Schindlers set up a secret medical facility in the factory with equipment purchased on the black market. Emilie worked tirelessly there to try to help the sick workers. Those who did not make it were given respectful, proper Jewish burials in a secret graveyard that the Schindlers set up. Emilie and Oscar spent millions on food, medicine, and clothing for the Jews in their factory. Emilie even sold all of her jewelry to fund the bribery and troubles they had to go through to provide for the workers. Together, the Schindlers protected about 1,300 Jews from persecution, allowing them to survive through the war.

After the war, several surviving factory workers recalled specific events that serve as examples of Emilie's tireless, selfless work to help them survive. One survivor remembered her exceptional kindness, something that had been hard for him to come by at that time. When she heard that his glasses had been broken in the factory, she paid and arranged for a new prescription to be made for him. Then, she traveled all the way to Cracow to pick them up. Another survivor, Feiwel (today Francisco) Wichter, said, "As long as I live, I will always have a sincere and eternal gratitude for dear Emilie. I think she triumphed over danger because of her courage, intelligence and determination to do the right and humane thing. She had immense energy and she was like a mother." Many more of the Schindler factory workers who survived the war recall times she smuggled bread to them, brought apples to sick workers, gave them her own clothing, gave up some material good to fund the operation, or countless other times she acted selflessly to provide for them and protect them. Although the efforts she put in alongside Oscar were extremely valuable and important, her most defining act of heroic selflessness and bravery came at a time when Oscar was not at her side.

In 1945, just before the war ended, Emilie was working tirelessly at the factory while Oscar was in Cracow for business. In one night, she single-handedly saved 250 Jews from impending death. While out on a supplies run from the factory, Emilie ran into Nazis transporting the Jews, crowded into four train cars, from Gollechau to a death camp. She stopped them, and persuaded the Gestapo to send those Jews to her factory camp by telling them that they would be of more use furthering the production of ammunition in the factory than if they were dead. In her A Memoir she recalls unbolting the frozen doors of the railroad cars to find the emaciated people inside. She had seen hungry, tired workers in her factory, but she had never encountered the amount of suffering she saw there. She said:

"We found the railroad car bolts frozen solid... the spectacle I saw was a nightmare almost beyond imagination. It was impossible to distinguish the men from the women: they were all so emaciated - weighing under seventy pounds most of them, they looked like skeletons. Their eyes were shining like glowing coals in the dark..."

Emilie quickly got help from the factory. They had to unload the people from the train cars and carry them, as they were all too weak to walk. They found thirteen already dead. Throughout that night and for many nights following, Emilie worked without stopping to rally the starved skeletons of people she rescued. One large room in the factory was emptied out for the purpose. Three more men died, but with Emilie's hard work and gentle care, the rest of the 250 people were saved. This defining moment of selfless compassion and hard work shows Emilie's worthiness of the status of "hero." Without anyone else by her side, Emilie faced the Gestapo, the embodiment of the oppression she had been fighting against, and faced horrific sights that would make anyone weaker turn around and run, and did the right and humane thing: to help those in need to the best of her ability.

The war ended within two weeks of the rescue. When the Soviets moved into Brünnlitz to liberate it, the Schindlers left the Jews in the factory with a heartfelt goodbye and went into hiding, in fear of being prosecuted because of Oskar's ties with the Nazi Party. Eventually, Emilie moved to Buenos Aires, Argentina, with Oscar and several of the surviving factory workers. She and Oscar were very poor, having spent literally all of their money to protect their Jewish workers. They became farmers, and were supported financially by a local Jewish organization and the thankful Jews they had saved. Emilie and Oscar were divorced when Oscar became bankrupt in 1957, and he traveled back to Germany alone, where he remained estranged from his wife for 17 years before he died in poverty in 1974, at the age of 66. Although they were divorced, Emilie said she would have stayed with him if he had not chosen to leave. She and some of the Jews they had saved together visited his grave in Jerusalem in 1993, during the production of the movie about his life.

Emilie fell at her home in San Vicente, 40 kilometers south of Buenos Aires, in November of 2000. After undergoing a hip replacement operation, Emilie had to enter a home for the elderly in Buenos Aires and her care heavily subsidized by Argentine charities. In July of 2001, while visiting Berlin to give some documents of hers and her husband's to a museum, she told reporters that she had one last wish: to live in Germany again. Immediately, offers came from elderly homes around the country to let her live there. Eventually it was decided that she would move to the Adalbert Founder Home in the Bavarian town of Waldkraiburg. Emilie Schindler died from the effects of a stroke in Märkisch-Oderland Hospital, Strausberg, on the night of October 5, 2001, at the age of 93. She is buried at a cemetery in Waldkraiburg.

Emilie has been recognized by several organizations for her humanitarian work. In May, 1994, Emilie Schindler received the Righteous Amongst the Nations Award by Yad Vashem - along with Miep Gies, who hid Anne Frank's family in the Netherlands and preserved her diary after the family was taken away by the Nazis. In 1995, she was decorated with the Order of May, the highest honor given to foreigners who are not heads of state in Argentina. In November, 2000, Emilie, was named an Illustrious Citizen by Argentina. She surely deserves these awards, but they were not what mattered the most to her before she died. She said she wanted recognition, not for fame or for money or for awards, but so that people may know her story, and understand that there were people who recognized that the persecution of Jews and others that happened during the Holocaust was not okay, that there were people who overcame their fear of the unknown and tried their best to do the right thing. She wanted people to be educated on the truth of the Holocaust, including both the horrific events that took place and the stories of people like her that would give people hope for humans when learning about such a dark topic.

Six million Jewish people died in the Holocaust. Fifty million people died in World War II in total. Emilie Schindler helped save just 1,500. With just the statistic, it could almost seem insignificant, but Emilie's contributions are more than just numbers. One-thousand-five-hundred human lives are invaluable, and their contributions to the world are immeasurable. Those 1,500 people have an estimated 8,500 decedents living around the world today. Emilie saved those lives, and that is better than her sitting idle and doing nothing, or worse, having been one of the persecutors herself. She has shown us the good that human beings are truly capable of. Inscribed on Emilie's tombstone are the words, "Wer einen Menschen rettet, rettet die Ganze Welt," from the Mishnah, Sanhedrin 4:5, meaning "Whoever saves one person, saves the world." Emilie really has saved the world, in a way. By saving the lives of these people, she can save faith in humanity. When learning about the Holocaust, and the atrocities committed by human beings for fear of the unknown, it is easy to lose faith in the fact that humans are anything more than animals, giving into primal fears, but stories like Emilie's can prove to us that humans are also capable of amazing things. Through selflessness, bravery, and compassion, Emilie has shown herself to be a true hero, an example of the righteous, good things that humans can do when they overcome their fear of the unknown.

Bibliography

Bülow, Louis. Emilie Schindler: An Unsung Hero. The Holocaust Project. Web. 20 February 2016. <http://www.auschwitz.dk/Emilie/Emilie.htm>.

Emile Schindler. The Holocaust Project. Web. 20 February 2016. <http://www.emilieschindler.com/>.

Emilie Schindler: Resucuer of Jews. The Holocaust Project. Web. 20 February 2016. <http://www.annefrank.dk/rescuers/new_page_5.htm>.

The Jewish Virtual Library: Emilie Schindler. American-Israeli Cooperative Enterprises. Web. 20 February 2016. <http://www.jewishvirtuallibrary.org/jsource/biography/emilieschindler.html>.

The Heroic Troupe: The Story of Adolf and Maria Althoff

Rebecca Grace Harbison

 The Holocaust. The word Holocaust comes from the Greek word "holokauston," which means sacrifice by fire. It is most associated with the systematic murder of over 6 million Jews (and millions of others) by the German Nazi regime in World War II. But many Jewish scholars prefer to use the term "Shoah" for these events. Shoah means catastrophe in Hebrew. Holocaust or Shoah, this was a nightmarish period of history which should never be forgotten so it will never happen again.

In January 1933, The Nationalsozialistishe Deutsche Arbeiterpartei, or the Nazi Party, rose to power in Germany. The Nazi party was infamously lead by a man named Adolf Hitler. Hitler came to power by promising Germans greatness.

World War I was devastating to Germany. They had to pay large reparations and German money became worthless. Unemployment was very high and most people were barely getting by financially. Also, Germans were looked down on by the rest of the world. Many Germans liked Hitler's ideas about bringing Germany back to its superpower status,

Some Germans saw Hitler as pompous and extreme. They did not take the Nazi Party seriously and underestimated the amount of support it could get. By the time Hitler became chancellor it was too late to stop him and his radical party.

Many intellectuals (both Jews and non-Jews) fled Germany as the Nazis became more powerful, but it was not easy to do as time went on and many lost their lives.

The Nazi belief was that the so-called "German race" was a superior race in humanity. Jewish people, gypsies, and others were considered a threat to their German bloodline. So, the Nazi idea was to wipe out the Jewish race entirely, as well as killing off other "undesirables."

The Nazis called this "Endlösung" or the "Final Solution." This was meant to be a complete genocide of a race of people. Never in history has such an abominable act come close to achieving its evil goals.

The "Final Solution" started gradually so it would not cause alarm in the world and in the Jewish community. Obviously, if they had broadcast that the end goal was to kill all Jews the world would have been horrified and many lives that were lost would have been saved.

The Nazi Party first started out by excluding the Jewish people from the rest of society. They enforced a boycott of Jewish businesses. They established the Nuremberg laws. These laws stripped the Jewish people of their citizenship and banned marriage between Germans and Jews.

Throughout the years that the Nazi Party was in power, they implemented more and more laws that had the Jewish people living less like human beings. On the night of November 9, the Nazi Party began a pogrom (a violent massacre of an ethnic group) against Jewish people in both Germany and Austria. It was later called "Kristallnacht," which means the night of broken glass. On this night, the Nazis were allowed to smash the windows and pillage through the Jewish-owned businesses and stores, burn down synagogues, and physically assault the Jews. About 30,000 Jewish people were arrested that night and sent off to concentration camps.

The majority of those sent to the camps would die.

Every day people mourn and honor the people who had their lives taken from them during this awful time. However, we also give honor to those who persevered through this inhumane time and defied the laws to help the Jewish people find refuge at the risk of their own lives. Sadly, not all of the people who tried to help save the Jewish people survived to tell the tale. Many of these heroes of the Holocaust were very extraordinary and had extraordinary ways to help save the Jewish people from the Nazi regime. However, one story of heroism that sticks out the most of all is the one where the Jewish people went to a circus for help.

What happens in the circus stays in the circus. This was the way it was within the Famous Althoff circus. Although there were many German Holocaust heroes, ones who I think should be recognized are Adolf and Maria Althoff. They took a great risk hiding a family of four Jews within the circus act. If Adolf and Maria were caught hiding them, they would be sent to concentration camps themselves. Adolf and Maria spent 5 years hiding the Danner family within the circus, but the Gestapo never caught them.

Adolf Althoff was born on June 25, 1913 in Sonsbeck, Germany on a family circus wagon while the circus performances were still going on. His older brother and sister took over the family-owned circus while he established his own circus where he was the ringmaster in 1939. His circus consisted approximately 90 performers and their families. They toured all over Europe throughout the years of the war, traveling from one country to the next.

The Althoff circus family is a very long running circus family. One aspect of the circus that was helpful was that no one asked questions about the act's past. Many secrets could be kept. Although some workers in the circus knew about the Danners, they would not speak out against Adolf because they knew if they did, they would be fired for it. Both Adolf and Maria were born into circus families. Adolf was the ringmaster for about 30 years, while his wife was performing with the animals for a long time. According to fellow circus colleges, Adolph was also very good and understanding with animals.

In the summer of 1941, the circus had a round of performances near Darmstadt in Hesse, Germany. A young dancer and artist named Irene Danner attended these performances. Irene used to be with a circus with her mom called the Lorch circus, however, the circus went bankrupt due to the workers leaving, and people stopped attending shows when the indictment of Jews began.

Irene had Jewish heritage from her mother's side, while her father was German and was enlisted in the German Army. She celebrated her German-Jewish circus dynasty and was settled in the small town of Eschollbrücken near Darmstadt in the 19th century. Even though she was only half Jewish, both her and the rest of her family were labeled as Jews by the government and were discriminated against by the public. At school, both the teachers and their fellow students ridiculed both Irene and her sister, Gerda. Irene was excluded from physical education and her teacher turned her fellow students against her. The children called her a "stinking kike," which is a very derogatory term in German. Then after Kristallnacht, they were completely expelled from their school. She also was forced to give up her violin lessons and was barred from fulfilling her dream to go to ballet school.

Everywhere around them, there was nothing but hate toward them, and the regime started deporting the Jews in her area into concentration camps. All that Irene and her sister could see was more and more doors being slammed in their faces. Running out of options, Irene ran to the Althoff family circus desperate for hiding. Adolf felt bad for her, and felt like if he refused her, it would be just as bad as the Gestapo killing her.

So, he let her into the circus as a dancer and under a false identity. After some time, the Gestapo got very suspicious of the Althoff circus due to Adolf's blatant resistance to the regime. However, they never were able to prove that he was harboring Jews since Irene did not have papers. While working at the circus, Irene met Peter Storm-Bento, one of the circus clowns from Belgium. Although they could not marry legally, they had two children together and considered themselves to be married. Maria was very supportive of Irena when she was going through her two pregnancies while she was in hiding. She helped take care of her, and gave her all of the provisions that she needed during her time of pregnancy.

In 1942, the regime started cracking down on deportation of the Jews in Darmstadt to concentration camps. Irena's grandmother ended up deported to Lublin, Poland. Luckily Irena's mother and sister were able to escape and followed Irena's footsteps to the circus. Adolf also let them hide in the circus with Irena. He simply could not separate Irena from her mom and sister again, since the Gestapo would probably have them killed. Eventually, Irena's father joined them in hiding at the circus as well. Although her father was fully German and was in the army, he defied orders by refusing to go home and divorce his wife. He then was listed as a traitor and was forced into hiding. Adolf allowed the family to work at the circus without any papers. Every time the circus made a new stop on the tour, the Nazi control agency inspected the circus group and grounds.

However, all these inspections were planned ahead of time and were alerted to Adolf so he was able to alert the family beforehand to give them time to hide. Adolf created the code words "Go fishing" to use anytime the circus grounds would be inspected, or the Gestapo would stop by. Usually, they would go to the forest to have a picnic, or go on a fishing trip so they would look like a normal family. If they could not do that, they would try to hide in an abandoned circus wagon until they left the circus grounds.

All of the other workers at the circus knew about the family's secret and helped them stay hidden. No one denounced them for being Jewish. However, one performer threatened to exposed the circus to the Gestapo but the problem was quickly resolved with Adolf sharing some drinks with the Gestapo officers and giving the family enough time to disappear for the time being. After the Gestapo officers left them alone, Adolf fired the performer who attempted to expose the Danners without question.

When the war ended, Irene and Peter officially got married and had three more children together. Irena frequently came to visit the couple and performed in the circus for a couple of years after the war. Adolf and Maria received awards for the brave acts for saving Irena and her family during the war. Sadly, in 1965 the circus was sold due to Adolf's declining health issues. Then in 1977, his son Franz founded a new circus based on the old Althoff family circus called the Williams Althoff circus.

Adolf and Maria won an award from the Yad Vashem Holocaust memorial in 1995 for their brave, heroic acts during the war. "We circus people see no difference between races and religion," said Adolf Althoff when he received the Righteous Among Nations award. "Circus people don't ask if you are Christian, Jewish or heathen"

The Althoffs took a huge risk to their personal health for many years by defying Nazi Germany and protecting the Danner family. Their heroism was a rare example of compassion in that dangerous time. If it were not for Adolf's bold decision to help Irena, her sister, mother, and father, none of them would have made it out of the Holocaust safely.

One aspect about the circus that makes them unique is how they never really saw what made them different; all they saw was what the person could do and how they performed on stage. I believe if Adolf Althoff were still alive today, well we would have a lot more people running off to go join the circus.

Sources Cited:

Rescue in a circus; Adolf and Maria Althoff www.yadvashem.org

From the testimony of Adolf Althoff, Der Clown und die Zirkusreitering, Malik 1997 www.yadvashem.org

From the testimony of Irena Danner-Storm www.yadvashem.org

"The testimony of Irena Danner" Der Clown und die Zirkusreitering, YadVasheem, Malik 1997 www.yadvashem.org

Adolf Althoff, 85, Circus chief who hid people from the Nazis. Eric Pace. October 19, 1998 www.nytimes.com

Escaping the holocaust in the circus. Jewniverse, August 24, 2012 www.thejewniverse.com

Georg Ferdinand Duckwitz

Rod Beale

Georg Duckwitz was born in 1904 in Bremen, Germany to a patrician family from the Hanseatic City. After completing his degree at commercial college, he went into the business of the international coffee trade, forcing him to move throughout many different Scandinavian countries for several years. Duckwitz had close ties with German Nazi leaders and experience in the workings of the economic and political relationships between Germany and the bordering European countries, so when the Nazi regime came into power in 1939, Duckwitz was immediately assigned to work in the German embassy in Copenhagen. Through his work for the Nazi government in Denmark, Duckwitz became close business associates and friends with Werner Best, the Nazi representative in Denmark at the time. Best was a true believer in the Nazi fascist movement, but was also well aware of the moderate political environment of Denmark at the time and maintained his own policies accordingly.

Germany began to occupy Denmark in April of 1940, and during this period early on in World War II, no immediate threats had been placed on the more recently formed Jewish Danish community. The first Jewish population came to Denmark in the seventeenth century, when the Danish royalty had invited Jewish merchants to come and work in Denmark to help stimulate their failing economy. By the 1700's, there were around 1,700 Jews residing in different main cities of Denmark, including Copenhagen, with special permission from Denmark's crown. Despite some undercurrents of anti-Semitism and one outburst of violence toward Jews in the 1800s, the Jewish population thrived and prospered within Denmark's economy. By 1930, there were over 6,000 Jews living in Denmark, representing a symbol of integration and procreation, as the Jews were a migrant minority that became a vital part of the Danish nation. Before the outbreak of Nazism and World War II, there was a relatively nonviolent relationship between the Jews and their fellow Danish neighbors.

During the Nazi occupation of Denmark, they used a practice uncommon to the traditional barbaric Nazi way: a policy of cooperation and "negotiation" with the existing Danish government. This allowed ordinary Danes to go about their daily business while the German Nazi troops were given free passage, produce, and some industrial products. Because of this agreement between the two governments, the Danish government had a position to protect the rights of the Jewish community in their country, with the argument that Jews are Danish and have a right to be protected like every other Danish citizen. Denmark downright refused to discriminate against the Jews, even though the Germans had demanded them to. The Danish took an adamant opposition of the Nazi army and their defiance of the rules set in place by Hitler including curfews, a ban on strikes, press censorship and public protest restrictions. Hitler finally decided to end the diplomatic relationship and left Werner Best in charge of fulfilling the implementation of the "Final Solution" in Denmark.

This is the part of the story where a man who understood the workings of Denmark played a remarkable role, Georg Ferdinand Duckwitz. Duckwitz was currently working part time for Best as an economic and political advisor, and, being drawn into the ultranationalist propaganda, had joined the Nazi Party. Duckwitz, however, soon became disillusioned with the party after learning about Hitler's violent intentions. When the Germans had taken over Denmark, Duckwitz sympathized with the plight of the Danish people, especially the persecuted Jews.

As the Germans declared a state of emergency in August, the Danish government fully protested. Best thought that now was the time for the deportation of the Jewish people in Denmark, and proceeded to send an inquiring telegram to Hitler about the matter. Duckwitz received news of this telegram in September of 1943, and immediately expressed his dissent to Best, who dismissed his concerns. Best, however, allowed Duckwitz to go to Germany to try and suppress the telegram, but when Duckwitz arrived, he found out that Hitler had already approved the order. Knowing full well the result of this order, Duckwitz immediately flew to the bordering neutral state of Sweden and met with President Per Albin Hansson. He told President Hansson of Best's plan, and in return received an assurance that the runaway Jews would have warm reception and care provided to them upon arrival on Swedish soil. Duckwitz then got in touch with people in the Danish underground resistance, who began preparing hiding places and arrangements for transportation out of the country through the Øresund strait. A week after, Duckwitz learned of the exact time and place of the round up of the Jews, which was to be held on Friday, Oct. 1 in the country's capitol of Copenhagen. Upon learning this, Duckwitz informed the leaders of the Jewish community around Copenhagen, and suggested for the leaders to instruct their people to go into hiding and prepare to leave their homes.

The massive Danish effort to help move the Jews from hiding place to hiding place, and eventually out of the country into Sweden, culminated to be one of the most historic rescues of the Holocaust. Duckwitz continued to work behind the scenes as the head of the German navy that patrolled the Øresund strait, making it so that "very few German navy patrols were at sea during the [operation of transporting Jews out of Denmark]." In total, 7,200 Jews made it safely to Sweden while only a mere 474 Jews were captured by the Nazis. Duckwitz would end up being the highest-ranking German official directly involved in the rescue of Jews of this proportion, and eventually was given the honor of Righteous Among the Nations in 1971.

The Cheerful Chaplain

Ruby Lindgren (Co-Winner)

It was a dark and ominous night—but the storms that raged around the city of Berlin were not at all of nature's creation. A small couple crouched, huddled, in an air raid shelter, not knowing how long it would be until relief could come from this terrifying barrage. Little did they know that a much more dangerous task awaited them back at their apartment on Afrikanische Strasse. Harald and Dorothee Poelchau were not like many Germans of the World War II time period. They knew that true safety during this war, in this city, was rare if not nonexistent, and it was not worth it to let other people suffer without offering any help or relief. Therefore they had made a wonderful name for themselves among those who were of that same mind, distributing food and finding trusted families to house the many, many people who were forced to hide in order to survive. This was how two young Jews knew to come stumbling to their doorstep, injured and out of breath having run for two and a half hours from a makeshift concentration camp. The Poelchaus had had their share of scares for the night, but still they put their troubles aside and tended to the exhausted pair. American children's writer Judy Blume once said, "Our finger prints don't fade from the lives we touch." Well, the Poelchaus left their finger prints everywhere in World War II era Germany, and always with a positive result.

While there is not a lot of information available about Dorothee's earlier years, we do know about Harald's. Born in Potsdam in 1903, he was raised in a small Silesian town where his father was a Protestant pastor. In 1922 Harald began studying theology in Bethel, and continued with his studies in a variety of other places. In Tübingen, for example, he became the secretary of the Köngener Covenant, and in Marburg he was mentored by Paul Tillich, a prominent twentieth-century theologian and philosopher. Harald was also an assistant to Tillich in Frankfurt, and was strongly influenced and shaped by his views on religious socialism. Then while Harald was studying in Berlin, he met Dorothee Ziegele. She was working as a librarian at the time, and the two married in 1928.

After applying in 1932, Harald Poelchau became the prison chaplain for the Tegel prison in Berlin on April 1, 1933. He also worked in Plötzensee and Moabit, and had admittance to all prisons. As a part of this job, Harald had to be present at the executions of the prisoners—a horrifying experience that he was obligated to go through more than 1,000 times. However, as chaplain he also had the ability to reach out to the prisoners and help them through this trying time. He once said, "It is still with the Bible you can best help the people who must wait for their sentence to be carried out." He helped prisoners in tangible ways as well, bringing food, letters, and news of friends and family. These things were incredibly helpful, because the conditions in all of the prisons were awful.

In the book The Power of Solitude: My Life in the German Resistance, author Marion Yorck von Wartenburg writes about her experience in the Moabit prison:

Then came the air raids, and because people like us were not "worth rescuing," as they said at the time, the women from the conspiracy circle were often moved together to the third floor. There we could see the light spectacle of the impending attacks when the English and when the Americans were approaching. [...] The Gestapo naturally wanted to make us fearful by this transfer.

However, she was always cheerful in her narration of Harald. "Poelchau came with bulging suit pockets, and in them were rock candy and carrots, honey rolls, and I don't know what else. He came every week, and he brought us everything, including letters, which of course was strictly forbidden." She also writes about another way that Harald was able to brighten up her time:

You see we found a very nice way to communicate with each other and be together. The governess of the jail had given us a hymnal and a New Testament with the approval of the Gestapo. Of course, Bärbel knew all the songs much better than I did. And every evening, one, two, three, four, she tapped with her wedding ring on the pipe the number we would sing from the hymnal. And then we sang loudly. The walls in Moabit are tremendously thick. You didn't even hear it when someone went to the window and screamed. But we knew that the other one was singing. Afterwards she would also tap out which Psalm we would read, and so we could communicate wonderfully, without any other person in the jail noticing it. Harald Poelchau taught us the tapping system.

Harald was able to do tremendously great things inside of the prison, but with the help of Dorothee, the pair brought love and kindness to many people throughout their community outside Tegel and Moabit. A friend of the Poelchaus, Freya von Moltka, wrote about this in her book, Memories of Kreisau and the German Resistance, saying: "Almost daily we picked up messages and received consolation from [the Poelchaus] in their apartment[...], exchanged letters, and restored our strength." She added that "Not only did he help political prisoners, but he also helped feed Jews who were hiding in Berlin. At any rate, several times we sent him sacks of dried peas that had been raised on our farm, which he then distributed." Indeed, Harald was a big help to the Jews in hiding. He had information about who would be able to house them in the first place, and would also offer ration tickets, cash, and places where they could work. All of this was infinitely valuable to people who had been through so many trials and owned virtually nothing.

This is where our story of the Neumanns fits in—the two desperate Jews running up to their door. Ralph and Rita had been helped by a woman named Ruth Wendland, but Ralph was found, arrested, and tortured until he had given away the names of his sister and helper. All of them were arrested, and the Neumanns were taken to a makeshift concentration camp in Schulstrasse. The siblings managed to escape during the air raid and they ran until they collapsed in the loving arms of the Poelchaus. They ended up staying in that apartment until the end of the war, which was very unlike Harald's usual mode of giving out addresses for alternate housing. This was also very dangerous, what with Harald already pushing the limits smuggling in letters and food to the prisoners at his work. However, nobody found out, and the Neumanns lived there in safety for as long as they had needed.

The Poelchaus also had the experience of helping a more famous family—the Lattes, in particular Konrad Latte. Harald was forced to split them up and send them to different places (the mother to become a cleaning woman, the father to a job with a formal political prisoner, and Konrad to a temporary address he knew) but he kept them alive. Konrad moved from place to place, always with the new addresses from the Poelchaus, until they were able to find him a job as the air raid warden for a bank which provided a place to sleep.

Amazingly, Harald found a way to push the limits of safety even further. Since its conception, he had been a member of the Kreisauer Kreis, or Kreisau Circle, the anti-Nazi group whose members plotted the failed assassination of Hitler on July 20, 1944. Harald had therefore the dreadful misfortune of having to witness many of his close friends' arrests and executions. However, for those who were not executed he could lessen the discomfort of prison life with food, letters, and cheerful conversation; for those who escaped imprisonment altogether he could comfort them with letters from (and news of) their comrades. Both authors Marion Yorck von Wartenburg and Freya von Moltka were spouses of big members of the resistance. Freya, the wife of Helmuth James Graf von Moltka (the head of the Kreisau Circle) noted:

For almost four months until Helmuth's death we could write each other daily. For four months Harald and Dorothee Poelchau surrounded Helmuth and me with their inexhaustible friendship, at risk to themselves. And until the end of Helmuth's life Harald managed to smuggle in his pockets foodstuff from Kreisau into Helmuth's cell. Besides Helmuth, Eugen Gerstenmaier and Alfred Delp from the Kreisau community were also imprisoned at Tegel at that time. They were also taken care of by the Poelchaus.

Marion, the wife of Peter Yorck von Wartenburg, was imprisoned at Moabit and was ever impressed by the gracious acts that Harald was inclined to accomplish. At one point, she wrote:

Looking back Harald Poelchau appears to me like a bridge between my life with Peter and my later one in the period after the war. He was the first who visited me in jail. Later, here in Berlin, it was he who was always ready with advice and help for all women and widows of the resistance [...] He was a man who was always ready to do something for others, and Dorothee was exactly the same. Their house in Zehlendorf was open to everyone. They had many close friends. He was a person who endeavored to be a Christian without making a show of it.

Although Harald mostly worked in the background in order to lessen the probability of being caught and most likely killed, there were times that it is said he took dramatically precarious actions. New York Times author Peter Schneider wrote that one time, "When he was helping to clear rubble after an air raid, [Harald] discovered that the entrance and windows of a police substation had been damaged. With great presence of mind, he broke into the offices and made off with a variety of official forms and seals." Schneider added that "It's almost a miracle, in fact, that this man of God, who broke nearly every Nazi law in the name of justice and extended a sheltering hand over dozens of persecuted individuals, should have survived the Third Reich unscathed."

Another miracle would probably be that Harald was able to retain his cheerful attitude and positive outlook. He witnessed a thousand people, including his close friends, be murdered right before his eyes. For most people, seeing only a few deaths can be psychologically damaging, yet Harald kept a steady mind and was there for the people that needed him the most. He saw all the negativity, and instead of despairing, he channeled all those feelings into a determination to help all the people that he possibly could. In all the records out there, Harald is depicted as pleasant, positive, good-humored, kindly, and loving—someone who would brighten the atmosphere of a room, and always endeavor to follow the commandment to love one another, and love your neighbor as yourself. He was this way all through his life until he died in 1972, at the age of 69. Dorothee planted a tree in Yad Vashem in his honor. Five years later, she passed as well at the age of 75.

There were few people who did anything to help one another during the treacherous Nazi era, and fewer still who were able to do as much as Harald and Dorothee Poelchau. Harald was a blessing to all those unfortunate enough to have been imprisoned or sentenced to execution, bringing food, letters, God's word, and most important of all, hope. Together the Poelchaus were able to provide food and homes to those in need of a place to hide, and comfort to their friends in the Kreisau Circle who had lost many a loved one after the failed assassination of Hitler. They even took two Jews—the Neumanns—into their home themselves. All of these things prove them to be more than worthy of the title they were awarded: Righteous Among the Nations.

Works Cited

"Harald Poelchau." The International Raoul Wallenberg Foundation. Web.

"Harald Poelchau." Wikipedia, the Free Encyclopedia. 17 Jan. 2016. Web.

Klesmann, Martin. "Courage Should Be Honored." Berliner Zeitung. 18 Jan. 2015. Web.

"Kreisau Circle." Wikipedia, the Free Encyclopedia. 23 Sept. 2016. Web.

Paldiel, Mordecai. Churches and the Holocaust: Unholy Teaching, Good Samaritans, and Reconciliation. N.p.: KTAV Publishing House, Inc., 2006. 61-62. Print.

"Paul Tillich." Wikipedia, the Free Encyclopedia. 24 Feb. 2016. Web.

"Poelchau, Dorothee." Deutsche Biographie. Web.

"Poelchau FAMILY." The Righteous Among the Nations. Yad Vashem. Web.

Schneider, Peter. "Saving Konrad Latte." New York Times 13 Feb. 2000: 4,8. Web. 26 Feb. 2016.

Von Moltke, Freya, Julie M. Winter. Memories of Kreisau and the German Resistance (Errinerungen an Kreisau). Lincoln, NE: University of Nebraska Press, 2003. Print.

Yorck von Wartenburg, Marion, Julie M. Winter. The Power of Solitude: My Life in the German Resistance. Lincoln, NE: University of Nebraska Press, 2000. Print.

Emille Schindler

Samantha Delfino

Oskar Schindler was one of many people who helped save thousands of Jews during World War II. His story is well known and even was made into a movie. He saved thousands of Jews, but the untold hero in his story is his wife, Emilie Schindler. He wouldn't have been able to save all of the Jews in his factory without the help of Emilie Schindler. She saved millions while sacrificing herself. Even throughout her childhood, Emilie Schindler showed signs of perseverance and belief in equality. Instead of just making money off of Jewish people, like other Nazi soldiers and generals, Oskar and Emilie sacrificed themselves and spent all their money to help and rehabilitate Jewish people who were the victims of the Holocaust. When the Jews were liberated at the end of World War II, Emilie and Oskar were very poor and they moved to Argentina, where Emilie stayed and Oskar moved back to Germany. Emilie did not see Oskar until she returned to Germany in 2001 to live out her final days.

Emilie Schindler was born on October 22, 1907, in alt Moletein the then-German-speaking area of the Republic of Czechoslovakia. When Emilie was a young girl, Emilie's pastor told her to stop being friends with her friend, Rita, who was Jewish. Emilie defied her pastor and remained friends with Rita until Rita was killed in front of her father's store in 1942. This is the beginning of Emilie's defiance towards the Nazi rule. This story foreshadowed Emilie's further actions to save and help Jewish people instead of supporting the Nazi party.

Emilie stayed in her town until she met Oskar Schindler in 1928. Oskar was a salesman visiting her town, where he met Emilie. They courted for six weeks and then married. When they married, Emilie's father gave Oskar 10,000 Czech crowns, which was a lot of money at the time. Oskar wasted the dowry on a luxury car and other expensive items. Since they were broke and Oskar did not have a job, Oskar joined the

Nazi regime where he acquired a factory which had Jewish workers in Krakow, Poland. At first, Oskar was more than willing to take advantage of the innocent Jewish people, but when he caught sight of Jewish people being murdered, gassed, burned, and worked to death, he no longer wanted to help the Nazis. Instead, he chose to protect the Jews with the help of his wife, Emilie Schindler.

During World War II, the Nazis had moved into Poland and other areas in Europe and taken over Jewish businesses and their factories and kicked the Jews out of their homes so that Nazi soldiers and generals and Nazi supporters could take over their homes and factories and shops. The Schindlers were part of the Nazi party that occupied Poland and the Jewish homes and factories. Many cities were occupied until liberation in 1945. Jewish people were forced to work in factories or in concentration camps where many died. The Nazis looked at the Jews as either people who would do their dirty work for them or would be killed. There was no in between. Many Jews were killed or they worked them in such bad conditions for so long that they died. The Nazis would make the Jewish people work in crowded work spaces with no ventilation system, very little food or water, little to no breaks, and no form of medical care. Many people died from emaciation, exhaustion, fires, work accidents, and other causes. The Nazis treated the Jewish people terribly. They were very disrespectful, careless, and ignorant of the fact that Jews were human beings just like them. Without people like the Schindlers working to help the Jewish people, there would have been more people killed during the Holocaust.

After witnessing the atrocities caused by the Nazis, Oskar Schindler and his wife decided to change their factory into a safe haven for the people that worked there. They used up all of their money and resources to make sure that their workers had the best working conditions possible. They also made sure that no one was sent to concentration camps or killed. They treated their workers as part of their family, growing attached to a lot of their workers. Emilie sold her jewels to create a medical area for their workers if they were injured or got sick. Emilie bought medical supplies on the black market, so that their workers could have the proper medical treatments if necessary. They tried to house, clothe, and feed their workers as best as possible with the little money they had. They also made sure that all of the Nazi weapons they made did not pass the qualifications to be used in the war.

The Schindlers worked to protect their workers from as much harm as possible. They bribed officials so that no one would be sent to the concentration camps or killed. They were successful in keeping all of their workers from being sent to concentration camps or killed by gas chambers or other ways. They saved more than 1,300 Jews from harm from the Nazi party. Instead of sitting by and watching the Nazi party commit unspeakable crimes against the Jewish people, the Schindler family worked to save Jewish people from all harm possible. It is estimated that Emilie and Oskar Schindler spent more than 4 million German marks to ensure that Jews did not go to the Nazi concentration camps. The Schindlers spent all of their money to make sure these people were safe and kept alive.

Even though Oskar got a lot of the credit for saving thousands of Jews, Emilie saved a lot of Jews, too. She did a lot of work by herself that is not recognized by many people. One day, Emilie was out walking around and came across four train cars with 250 Jews who were emaciated and looked more like skin and bones than human beings. Emilie was horrified that someone could treat people like this. When seeing the car, Emilie said, "We found the railroad car bolts frozen solid ...the spectacle I saw was a nightmare almost beyond imagination. It was impossible to distinguish the men from the women: they were all so emaciated - weighing fewer than seventy pounds most of them, they looked like skeletons. Their eyes were shining like glowing coals in the dark ..." She knew she had to save these people. All on her own, Emilie convinced the Gestapo to send 250 Jews (minus 13 who had died during the trip) to work at her factory where she rehabilitated all but three more men who died of illness. She worked day and night, turning one of the rooms in the factory into a place for the people from the train car to sleep and live. She fed them, treated their illnesses and injuries, and allowed them to work at her factory. Many lived to tell of the kindness and care that Emilie and her husband gave the Jews that worked in their factory. While Oskar has been publicly hailed as the hero in this story, I do not think that he could have saved as many people as he did without the help of his wife Emilie. Emilie worked very hard to save these people, too. She single-handedly ran the medical care for the entire factory and all of the people that worked there. Indeed, Emilie was the savior behind the scenes.

After World War II, all of the Jewish people were freed and Emilie and her husband were broke. They had no job and no money. Oskar and Emilie tried to move to the U.S., but since Oskar was part of the Nazi army, he was not allowed into the U.S. In 1949, he moved to Argentina with Emilie along with other Jewish people freed from their factory. They tried to become farmers and raise chickens and nutrias, but they ended up filing for bankruptcy in 1957. To fix their financial problems, Oskar moved to Germany and Emilie stayed in Buenos Aires. Emilie never saw Oskar again. She received pensions from Israel and $650 pension from Germany. Emilie was barely scraping by with these earnings. Everything changed in May of 1994 when Emilie received the Righteous Amongst the Nations Award for her efforts in World War II to protect and save Jewish people from Nazi control. In 1995, Emilie received the most honorable award a foreigner in Argentina could receive if they are not a head of state. She received the Order of May. Argentina then promised a pension of $1,000 until her financial situation was settled. Emilie was finally recognized, but, unfortunately, it was at the end of her life.

In July of 2001, Emilie returned to Germany to spend her last days. She visited Oskar's grave long after he died upon her return to Germany. Although they separated back in 1957, Oskar and Emilie were still formally married. In A Memoir, Emilie talks about what she thought upon seeing her husband's grave: "At last we meet again... I have received no answer, my dear, I do not know why you abandoned me ... But what not even your death or my old age can change is that we are still married; this is how we are before God. I have forgiven you everything, everything..." Emilie Schindler later died in a hospital in Germany on October 5, 2001. When a memorial was held for her, more than 2,000 people showed up. Thanks to Steven Spielberg's movie, Emilie's story was highly publicized and many supporters, including the survivors and the families of the survivors from her factory, attended her memorial. She was a highly respected, loved, and admired woman.

I see Emilie as a strong, driven, and powerful woman who worked to better the world, especially when she was surrounded by such darkness. Instead of just sitting back and watching the horror and injustice, she worked to change things. She gave up her life so others could live theirs. If that is not inspirational, I do not know what it is. I have the utmost respect for Mrs. Schindler and all the work she did in this world to better other people's lives. Without Mrs. Schindler and her husband, many more Jewish people would have been killed and tortured by the Nazi regime. 1,300 people were saved. Some survivors recount their love for Mrs. Schindler and how she helped them through a very hard time in their lives. Feiwel (Franciso) Wichter, 75, who was number 371 on Schindler's List says, "As long as I live, I will always have a sincere and eternal gratitude for dear Emilie. I think she triumphed over danger because of her courage, intelligence and determination to do the right and humane thing. She had immense energy and she was like a mother." Another survivor, Maurice Markheim, number 142 on Schindler's List recalls his fond memories of Mrs. Schindler, "She got a whole truck of bread from somewhere on the black market. They called me to unload it. She was talking to the SS and because of the way she turned around and talked, I could slip a loaf under my shirt. I saw she did this on purpose. A loaf of bread at that point was gold... There is an old expression: Behind the man, there is the woman, and I believe she was the great human being." These are just a few quotes from the people who Emilie saved and it seems clear that she has greatly impacted their lives and they will forever remember her and her husband as amazing people. I am always inspired by strong, amazing women and Emilie is definitely at the top for being strong, independent and full of love. Rest In Peace, Mrs. Emilie Schindler, you are a real hero for thousands of people around the world.

Work Cited
Link: "Emilie Schindler"
https://www.jewishvirtuallibrary.org/jsource/biography/emilies chindler.html
Article: "Emilie Schindler, 93, Dies; Saved Jews in War" New York Times.
http://www.n ytimes.com/2001 /10/08/world/emilie-schindler-93-dies-saved-jews-in-war.html Website. October 8, 2001
Link: "Emilie Schindler" http://www.emilieschindler.com/
Link: "Schindler's List: Oskar and Emilie Schindler"
http://www.yadvashem.org/yv/en /righteous/stories/schindler.asp
Encyclopedia. "Emilie Petzl Schindler." Encycolpaedia Britannica.
http://www.britann ica.com/biography/Emilie-Pelzl-Schindler

The Righteous Who Stood in the Dark

Sam Carter

Discrimination has been a part of our planet's history no matter where one looks. Everyone's hands are dirty. Whether it be Japanese Internment, the rise of Imperialism, Slavery, or the Holocaust, our planet has truly gone through some fatal events. But in those times of great tragedy, we often hear of tales that shed some light on those dark times. Famous individuals who we often think of for going against the current when everyone else was following it include Abraham Lincoln and the 442nd Infantry Regiment, but often times there are many other individuals who were equally as righteous who have gone much less noticed. The Holocaust, however, was a much darker event than anything the world had seen before it. It began with the rise of the Nazi regime, which was sparked by the inflation and penalties inflicted on Germany after Der Erste Weltkrieg(World War I) from the Treaty of Versailles. While the German people went through the dark days after the war, the people found a false glimmer of hope in Adolf Hitler. Hitler was able to captivate a large quantity of Germany's population through the idea that the Aryan race was the most biologically advanced and that all other individuals whether it be Jews, disabled, or mentally challenged to name a few were to be terminated and eliminated from the world population. This kind of human behavior is what can tear our world apart, and while people do not realize what kind of a system they are actually supporting, an event like this can repeat itself in a matter of days.

The Holocaust itself was a genocide that was based around Adolf Hitler and his men's goal to completely terminate the Jewish population. Hitler was able to kill roughly 6 million Jews, approximately two-thirds of Europe's Jewish population. Of the 6 million, about one million were children. On top of the 6 million Jews killed by the Nazis, another 5 million were also terminated, raising the total carnage to roughly 11 million victims. The genocide took place for roughly five years, from 1941 to 1945, marking it as one of the most deadly genocides in history.

The process of the Holocaust began in stages, ultimately leading to the "Final Solution." The Nazi Party began to set up concentration camps in 1933, which escalated to ghettos in 1939 shortly following the outbreak of World War II when German forces invaded Poland, sparking Great Britain and France to declare war on Hitler's army. In the year 1941, Germany was able to take control of most of Eastern Europe and Nazi officers murdered approximately 2 million Jews in mass shootings. Once Nazi officers realized that the shootings weren't as efficient and that they were degrading toward the gunmen's mental states, they decided to resort to gas chambers at concentration camps to fulfill their "Final Solution." This final stage of the Holocaust lasted until the end of World War II in Europe, which ended in 1945.

The largest part of the Holocaust that comes to mind when one thinks of this dark period is the subject of concentration camps. Camps existed throughout German territory, existing at Auschwitz, Belzec, Chelmno, Jasenovac, and various other locations. The most deadly of course, was the camp at Auschwitz. Along with direct execution of the prisoners at camps, experiments also took place that resulted in the subjects being frozen, placed in pressure chambers, drug tests, chemical tests, and various surgeries and operations. The obvious horror and lack of respect for the human race as a whole was on display during the Holocaust. The fact that one man's momentum can force an entire country to turn their heads to nearly an entire group of people as they are executed shows how easily something such as this can occur and how horrible the event really was.

An individual who was able to commit acts of righteousness while others were following the tide was Otto Berger, a dentist who was able to save his Jewish colleague from the horrors of the Holocaust. The Jewish man was Fedur Bruck. Bruck lived in Ratibor, Upper Silesia. He served in Germany's army during Der Erste Weltkrieg. After the war, Fedur Bruck studied dentistry and went on to work as a dentist for the school system. But as Nazi activity began to rise in Germany, Bruck was fired and moved to Berlin. Shortly after his migration, he was fired again after the party removed all Jews who held jobs. This motion forced Bruck to treat only Jewish patients. Nearly 9 years later, on 12 October 1942, Fedur Bruck was notified that he was being deported to the east. He refused to present himself and instead went into hiding. He was able to settle with some of his Berlin acquaintances, eventually finding a home with Mr. Berger. Berger himself was also born in Upper Silesia in 1900. Thirty years later he decided to join the Nazi party but he was eventually removed from the party after he began to criticize the movement. Bruck, post war, described how he and Berger met: "I met Otto at the beginning of 1943 through a mutual friend. When he learned that I was living as an illegal because of my being persecuted on racial grounds, he immediately, on our first meeting, supplied me with food and offered to hide me if I had to leave my present hideout." Berger is considered a righteous individual because of his ability to help his colleague while others were busy hunting people like Bruck down. Mr. Berger provided housing for Bruck 21 months straight. He even had to move twice because of the Allies bombing and another time when circumstances at the location became unsafe. Otto was able to give Bruck all his food, complete sheltering, and all the other needs he might've required throughout the entire 21-month stay up until the end of the war.

Upon the war's conclusion, Bruck searched for some of his acquaintances before the war broke out. He was able to locate his former assistant from his times at Upper Silesia who also had to move to Berlin where she worked under a dentist by the name of Dr. Blaschke, who was Adolf Hitler's dentist during the war. Once the war was over in Europe she was called upon by the head of the Russian military force to help locate and identify the Nazi Party leader's remains based upon his dental records. Bruck was able to accompany his former colleague as they searched for Hitler's body, bringing him closer to the force that nearly took his life if it wasn't for the selfless actions of Otto

Berger during the war. Bruck was able to provide some of his expertise as they searched, and was eventually offered to take over Blaschke's clinic by the Soviets. Bruck, however, declined the generous offer and decided to move to the American zone of Berlin and eventually moved to the United States in 1947. After moving, he settled in New York where he stayed until his death in 1982. Throughout his time in New York, he was able to maintain contact with Otto Berger, his rescuer, by exchanging letters.

One can see why Berger is considered and recognized as a Righteous Among the Nations by Yad Vashem. He, as a German citizen during the war, was able to successfully hide, feed and protect Fedur Bruck throughout the entire 21-month period of the war while Nazi officers looking to capture Bruck and any other Jews were breathing down his neck. He was able to successfully move twice while maintaining suitable conditions for Mr. Bruck. He was even able to provide Bruck a false ID. German citizens who were able to stand for what they thought was right while many others were easily pushed to follow the horrors of the Nazi party highlight the fact that there is always righteous among us, and that one idea can never be completely followed by all.

The wounds left by the Holocaust left a large scar on those involved that is still healing today. Those who were fortunate enough to survive the camps found out that it was nearly impossible to return home or reestablish things how they were before the war because in most cases they had lost family members and were still heavily discriminated against even though the Holocaust was no longer in place. This led to a large number of Jewish refugees fleeing across Europe and even around the globe, attempting to escape the past. Although the Allies were not able to help save most of the Jews who were exterminated at camps throughout Germany, they attempted to bring justice to those responsible for so many deaths. The Allies held the Nuremberg Trials in 1945 and 1946, which uncovered the utter horrors of the Nazi Party to the rest of the world. After the trials concluded, nine Nazi officials were executed for their roles and another 12 were imprisoned for their participation. To help out even more, the Allied powers created a homeland for Jewish survivors of the Holocaust, Israel, in 1948. Over the decades that followed the war, German citizens struggled to comprehend the Holocaust's harsh legacy. Survivors and family members of those involved wanted some sort of compensation to replenish the wealth and property which was stolen from the Nazi party before the Holocaust's occurrence. Five years after the creation of Israel, in 1953, Germany's government began to make payments to individual Jews to attempt to recognize and acknowledge the obvious crime that occurred and Germany's responsibility for it.

A question that is often posed is whether or not an event like the Holocaust can re-occur in the future. One would like to think that we have evolved and are much smarter than we were roughly 70 years ago and wouldn't allow such a movement to happen. But if an event takes place that may appear to threaten an entire group that holds similar beliefs, then obviously that group will make an attempt to make a statement, an attempt to fight back. One can see how circumstances currently in the United States rhyme with what took place in Germany post World War I. Many in America believe that the country has fallen to a level far less superior to what was previously held by our country. And because of that assumption, we have people who look for something to blame our downfall on. In comes Donald J. Trump, an entrepreneur and businessman who has begun to make statements that heavily speak to the needs and wants of those who believe America is on the wrong track and needs to be redirected. Trump has the belief that two parties of people, in particular, are responsible for America's downfall. The two parties Trump is referring to are people who follow the Muslim faith in American and illegal-immigrants who have entered the country through America's southern border. Trump often makes radical assumptions about these individuals, painting them all with the same brush, assuming that they all are responsible for such awful crimes we see too often in the news. And because of these assumptions he has created, he believes that America should institute a Muslim ban in America, a ban that sounds awfully similar to one that occurred in the early 1930's. He also wants to build a wall along America's southern border, completely tarnishing our value of being a free nation. These proposals, unfortunately, sound perfect to some people's ears. But like Germany, America has many righteous individuals who would never allow such a thing to take place no matter how many follow Trump's proposals. We can never rule out anything from occurring anywhere on this planet but it is highly unlikely because of the amount of righteous individuals among us today. That is why the chances of seeing another Holocaust take place in our future is so unlikely because of individuals like Otto Berger who helped Fedur Bruck in such a dark period where people were following a movement because everyone else was.

Karl Plagge

Sarah Whipple (Co-Winner)

On the first day of July in 1944, Wehrmacht Officer Major Karl Plagge spoke to the mass of Jewish laborers under his supervision. "In your travel you will be escorted by the SS," he told them, "which as you know so well, is an organization for the protection of refugees, thus you have nothing to worry about." An SS Officer looked on unsuspectingly, but the thousand Jews who Plagge addressed knew better. In the words of Josiph Reches, son of one of the laborers, "When he ended his speech, he looked in the direction of my father and with his eyes he said goodbye."

It may be difficult to justify naming Karl Plagge, a Wehrmacht Officer, as a hero of the Holocaust. Indeed, it took three tries and over a thousand pages of firsthand accounts for the Yad Vashem to recognize him as Righteous Among the Nations. Initially, he joined the Nazi Party willingly, saying in his own words that "I really believed during that time in Hitler's social promises and declarations of peace. I thought to fight for a good thing, because I believed that you are always free to join and leave a party." Plagge, like so many others in his time, was frustrated by the embarrassment Germans felt after the First World War. National Socialism seemed like the only way to restore the dignity and pride in a broken people. Thousands rallied behind promises of a prosperous Germany, allowing Nazi leadership to capitalize on the desperation of the masses.

But Plagge, unlike many other National Socialists, maintained a strong sense of ethical obligation in the rise of Nazi Germany. "I was a man that believed in compromises between political interests and not in the inconsiderate removal of all opponents," he later remarked. He refused to don the Nazi uniforms, a requirement at that time, and in 1939 ended his membership in the Nazi Party. Decades later, as the world continues to wonder how the Holocaust was able to happen, this mentality provides a critical component of our understanding. Those who were originally in favor of the Nazi Party for its promises of peace and unity became committed to a larger ideology and failed to remain critical of the policies adopted by the party. History would look upon this time much differently if the people of the world maintained the same level of ethical responsibility as Major Karl Plagge.

Karl Plagge's education and experience as an engineer gained him great favor in the ranks of the Wehrmacht. Stationed as an officer in Vilnius, Lithuania, he became quickly familiar with the brutal reality of Hitler's Europe. Wielding his position of power in the Wehrmacht to his advantage, he worked tirelessly to protect the Jewish people of Vilnius. When the Vilnius ghetto was scheduled to be liquidated, he travelled to Berlin to convince the SS to allow the creation of an HKP work camp under his supervision. Pearl Good, a Holocaust survivor who credits Plagge with her life, remembers that he "traveled to Berlin to convince the authorities that his highly skilled Jews were indispensable for the Army Vehicle Repair- a bare-faced lie which, if discovered, could have ended in Plagge's execution."

In World War II Vilnius, possessing a work permit was a matter of life or death for the Jewish community. The yellow slip allowed an able bodied man, his wife, and two of his children to avoid execution. These work permits were granted to "useful Jews," and those deemed "unuseful" were sent to the Ponary forest to be shot and killed by the SS. Over 70,000 Jewish people met their end this way. Of this unspeakable atrocity, Plagge later recounted, "I saw unbelieveable things I could not support... it was then that I began to work against the Nazis."

Of his efforts to protect Jewish people, perhaps one of the most significant was the creation and maintenance of his HKP work camp. In a letter to the Kauen Concentration Camp Headquarters, Plagge argued against the proposed liquidation of the Vilnius ghetto and its inhabitants, writing "As the motivation and effectiveness of the Jewish labourers is essentially dependent of the fact that not only the men but also their wives and children can remain in Vilna..." Knowing full well the implications of a work permit, he issued hundreds to unskilled workers, keeping over 1,200 Jews alive in his camp by convincing the SS of their necessity. The women, he argued, were essential to maintain the morale of the men, and were consequential in creating and repairing Nazi uniforms, a lie that could have cost him his life. Lawyer Alfred Stumpff would later testify that "There were a great number of Jews that weren't really useful or necessary for the work that had to be done." Michael Good, the son of two survivors from the HKP camp, told the New York Times that his dad couldn't even change a lightbulb, but was deemed "essential" and allowed to live because of the work permit. By providing these "unuseful Jews" with work permits and protection, Plagge saved hundreds of lives.

Plagge's humanitarian efforts continued not only in his creation of the camp, but in its operation as well. Food rations were scarce for everyone in war torn Europe, and most slave laborers received dangerously little food. Plagge's deep commitment to justice manifested itself in the distribution of food in his camp. "I had the job to observe that the German officers never received better rations than the workers," Heinz Zuene, a subordinate of Plagge, reported. "That's what he always wanted me to check." He required weekly weighings of the laborers to ensure they were getting sufficient food, and searched extensively for extra potatoes, flours, vegetables, and horse meat to sustain the hundreds of families in his camp. Driven by his desire for justice in an unjust world, he never allowed his subordinates or himself to take more rations than were distributed to the laborers. This policy prevented his officers from adopting a superiority complex that could have had dangerous implications for the families in the camp.

Plagge required the utmost conduct from his guards and subordinates, resulting in one of dismally few labor camps with little report of guard abuse. Those who he found to be particularly mean or hateful were disciplined or removed from command. Heinz Zuene observed that Plagge "always required that there would not be any injustice in his park, particularly when it was against Jews." In one striking example, a spiteful sergeant trampled the leg of a Jewish worker in Plagge's camp. When the news reached the major, he openly criticized the sergeant and relocated him to an area of the camp where he could no longer terrorize the laborers. Plagge created a camp where laborers were able to exist in some of the most livable condition for Jews of the time. Although he would later lament that he did not do enough, his bravery and humanity helped to counteract the wave of dehumanization engulfing the European continent.

Major Plagge was often situated in a precarious position. As a German National Socialist, he knew that he could survive the war by remaining silent about the injustices he saw. On the other hand, by speaking up too loudly, he would be removed from his position and likely executed, and the hundreds of lives under his protection would be ended along with him. This internal conflict is embodied in many of his letters and writings. In one letter, he wrote:

As a National Socialist I must say 'yes' to the mass slaughter, to the politics against Poles, which see in these people an inferior class of human being, and to many others more. As a human being, I perceive that it is insanity and that everything must become a heap of ruins, because all of this must lead again and again to the most violent eruption.

In the end, Plagge survived the war and directly contributed to the survival of over 200 Jewish people. Even after his return to his home city of Darmstadt after the war, he remained haunted and horrified by the atrocities he witnessed, and blamed himself for not doing enough.

Those he saved, however, used very different rhetoric. In the denazification trials, those who had survived the Holocaust on account of Major Plagge testified on his behalf, and many later wrote accounts for the Yad Vashem to qualify him as Righteous Among the Nations. One boy remembers a sympathetic police officer referring his family to Major Plagge, telling him "Plagge will be able to keep his Jews alive longer than I can." Survivors Mark and Anna Balber write, "200 survived, we among them. We survived largely through the good deeds of Major Plagge. He was a good man who did his best in a difficult situation. We owe him our lives. He should forever be remembered for his goodness and courage." Survivor Bill Beggel remembers, "Without any financial incentive, he risked being executed to save us." While Plagge suffered with idea that he could have done more, hundreds of families lived on across the world because of his actions.

On that fatal day of July 1st, 1944, tensions escalated in the Plagge camp. As the Red Army approached, the 1,200 Jews in the camp prepared hiding places. They knew the SS was becoming desperate, and would senselessly slaughter the inhabitants of the camp to prevent the possibility of liberation. With the Red Army drawing closer, German authorities ordered Plagge and his ranks away from Vilnius, leaving the camp in the hands of the SS. Before he left, Plagge gathered his laborers in the presence of SS officers, telling them that he must leave and that the SS would take great care of them. The Jewish people understood the warning concealed in his speech. The next day, only half reported to roll call. They were killed immediately.

In the days that followed, sweeps of the camp resulted in the discovery of half of those who hid, adding hundreds more to the list of those who lost their lives in the path of evil. But when the Red Army reached Vilnius, over 200 people emerged from roofs, attics, and storage spaces in the Plagge camp. It was the largest coalition of survivors in Vilnius, with a rate of survival over 15 percent higher than the rest of Lithuania. The world must always remember those who died in the days before liberation, but it is imperative that Major Plagge is also remembered for putting the future of humanity before his own life and safety.

In April of 2005, 48 years after the death of Karl Plagge, the Yad Vashem announced that he would be named as Righteous Among the Nations. Through great personal turmoil and sacrifice, he had saved over two hundred Jewish people. From those two hundred survivors, thousands of children and grandchildren flourished. During his supervision of the camp, he would tell the workers that "Regrettably, this war has destroyed our moral values as well as the material ones." But Plagge himself resisted wholeheartedly the destruction of human values, and in doing so prevented the destruction of generations of Lithuanian Jews to come.

It has been over 60 years since the tide of Nazism ravaged Europe, but the lessons of the Holocaust remain as relevant as they ever were. Millions of refugees continue to suffer as much of the world turns away, fearing the social or economic consequences of involvement. Once committed to a political ideology, people even today feel entrapped to justify the injustices committed by their party, rather than standing up against the wrongdoings of those around them. Of this, Plagge once wrote "I act as I must, as my nature impels me, not because I am a Nationalsocialist, but rather although I am a Nationalsocialist." Remaining critical of all viewpoints and practices, including one's own, is the only way to prevent such crimes against humanity from happening again.

Remembering the Holocaust isn't simply about those who killed and those who perished- it is equally important to remember those who acted and those who fell silent. We must never forget the consequences of allowing dehumanization to happen. We must never forget the millions of innocent people who paid the ultimate price for the silence of those around them. And we must never forget those like Major Plagge, who provided a haven of humanity in a sea of injustice. We can never fall silent, and we can never forget.

Bibliography:

Bill Beggel Testimony to Yad Vashem. Accessed: http://searchformajorplagge.com/searchformajorplagge.com/Plagge_Documents.html.

Cowan, Allison Leigh. 60 Years Later, Honoring the German Army Maj. Karl Plagge, An Unlikely Hero of the Holocaust. New York Times: March 28, 2005.

Good, Michael. The Search for Major Plagge: The Nazi Who Saved Jews. New York: Fordham UP, 2005.

Letter from Major Karl Plagge to SS, 1944. Accessed: http://searchformajorplagge.com/searchformajorplagge.com/Plagge_Documents.html.

Letters Written by Karl Plagge to his wife Anke in June 1944. Accessed: http://searchformajorplagge.com/searchformajorplagge.com/Plagge_Documents.html.

Plagge Denazification File. Accessed: http://searchformajorplagge.com/searchformajorplagge.com/Plagge_Documents.html.

Summary of Plagge Case for Yad Vashem Reviewers. Accessed: http://searchformajorplagge.com/searchformajorplagge.com/Plagge_Documents.html.

Testimony of Mark and Anna Balber. Accessed: http://searchformajorplagge.com/searchformajorplagge.com/Plagge_Documents.html.

Testimony of the Reches Brothers. Accessed: http://searchformajorplagge.com/searchformajorplagge.com/Plagge_Documents.html.

Heroes of the Holocaust

Sigmursson Ngirturong

The tolls of war are sewn deeply in the heart of the human spirt; for war itself has torn apart nations and impacted many lives. The human condition during war is overpowered by crippling fear and anxiety. As a result during these times of war and injustice, one begins to examine their ethical morals to act on an incentive to help others. However, it is said that there are those who are willing to make life altering decisions to take honorable paths of actions, where an ordinary person must brings forth their own courage and integrity to persevere. Ignoring possibilities that death will most likely be their fate, and focusing on a conscious decision to help others in the face of adversity is what sums up the true meaning of heroism.

Centuries of disseminating anti-Judaism, racial anti-Semitism seized Europe and manifested itself into the extermination of the Jewish populace. This was a dark era in human history that is deemed as the Holocaust. When Adolf Hitler became chancellor of Germany on January 30th, 1933 up until the 8th of May in 1945 until the war officially ended, many horrific and unfortunate events took place resulting in altering the lives of many innocent people. Many families were separated, abused, and murdered due to horrific laws and movements enacted under the regime of Adolf Hitler. Furthermore throughout this period of terror, Jews all across Europe were being placed in ghettos. Eventually being sent off to concentration and extermination camps all across Europe. "In 1939 the Jewish population of Ukraine was 1.5 million, or 3 percent of the total population of Ukraine." (Gregorovich) When the German army reached Ukraine the killing squads, also known as Einsatzgruppen, carried out specific orders to exterminate the Jewish people. The end result of this horrendous mission was that an estimated 850,000 - 900,000 Jewish were lives lost. Nonetheless as seen in countless wars across all nations there were those who took a stand against Nazism with an unbreakable faith and courage that propels them into a class of their own. These were the Heroes of the Holocaust, and this is their story.

In Ukraine, the Jewish community made up the largest minority population, and at the time this population had been subjected to persecution and anti-Semitic racism. Yad Veshem has specified that an estimated half of those recognized as "Righteous Among the Nations" are in fact women, and one of those in particular is Ludviga Pukas. Her story is deeper than just a person who rescued Jews. It is a story of how families are not necessarily based only on genetics, but also defined by the choices one makes and the connection it is based upon and that is cultivated throughout time. In addition to developing relationships and helping others, Ludviga Pukas demonstrated acts of selflessness and made immense sacrifices to save a family in need. A person with a human spirit willing to endure the hardships of the Holocaust, serve as a rescuer of Jews and become a mother of two young orphaned Jewish children. An act of bravery that goes above and beyond ones owns life. Ludviga carried out heroic and bold feats independently during dangerous times so that others who were in danger of losing their lives may live. For instance, in 1937, she moved from her hometown to modern day Kheml'nyts'kyy (former Proskuror) and worked as a domestic helper assisting Frima Strenik. Ms. Strenik was a high school teacher who had two young children, Elina and Gennadiy. After three years of being employed with Ms.Strenik, Ludviga gave birth to her daughter, Galya. Ludviga continued working for Ms.Strenik and on July 7, 1941 the East German army conquered Ukraine. During the occupation of Ukraine the East German regime ordered Jewish families to relocate out of their homes. And unfortunately, Frima's property was burned down along with all her family possessions. This event prompted Frima to apply for new identity papers and register her children as Ludviga's, due to the fact that she and her children were in danger because they were Jewish. Afterwards Ludviga, Frima and their children moved into an apartment. However, not long after moving into their new residence, their neighbors began to take notice of their unique family and by the end of 1942 just before the liquidation of the Jews, which is a time when Jews were being killed in large numbers, Ludviga sent Frima to a village where her brother lived. Unfortunately on her travel to Ludviga brothers' village she was captured and eventually killed. The death of Frima left her two young children in the care of Ludviga. Moreover, during the liquidation period the police confronted Ludviga and questioned her about harboring Jews. Aiding Jews was a serious offense at the time, punishable by death. Ludviga and another women told police that they weren't sheltering any Jews. Nevertheless the Germans still turned over her apartment conducting a full search of Jews hiding in her home. Luckily based on their investigation and search they didn't find the children because Ludviga cleverly hidden them. A courageous and skillful act well worth the acknowledgement because concealing Jews during the time was immensely difficult.

In order to prevent Jews from being caught many rescuers, parents, and children would fake the identity those being hidden. Many would do so by mastering languages, dialects, behaviors, and even religious rituals in order to not be caught. If it wasn't possible to fake an identity most would have to hide under floor boards or in attics. Though they were being hidden by rescuers it is said that most were treated poorly and even at times abused. Another common tactic was to counterfeit papers to pass as "Aryan" using forged names and birthdates. The emotions of those go into hiding no more than expressed in a quote by Regine Donner, "I had to keep my Jewishness hidden, secret, never to be revealed on penalty of death. I missed out on my childhood and adolescent years. I was robbed of my name, my religion, my Zionist idealism." Only the mind is left to imagine the heartbreak that Frima's children had to endure. Rescued families would also create a detailed story to ensure the security of those they were saving. Though the situation in Ukraine at the time was especially difficult for rescued families as they were getting caught by collaborators with the Nazi regime, it did not discourage Ludviga to help others in need. During the occupation of Nazi Germany in Ukraine an Auxiliary Police was formed as local police who would conduct raids, executions, and searches. These collaborators range from Nazi battalions to Ukrainian SS volunteers set out to catch Jewish citizens trying to escape or hide. The motivation for those who cooperated with the Nazi regime can be attributed to the buildup of resentment to the Russians for Holodomor (Said to be a manmade famine however holding differing viewpoints between Russia and Ukraine of the genocides origin of it being manmade). This cooperation nonetheless was short lived until the Nazi regime deported hundreds of thousands as slave laborers. By the time the Red army reached Ukraine the viewpoints of many citizens had shifted and a support against Nazism had grown. When the Red Army liberated Proskuror on March 19, 1944 recovery from the Holocaust was allowed to take root. Later that year in September Frima's children Eldina and Gennadiy changed their last name back to Strenik to complete their studies in school. Even when the two children were contacted by their aunts they refused to leave Ludviga's side until they finished their studies. As through the years Ludviga has taken care of them during the Nazi reign successfully concealing the identity of the two children that she took as her own. A bond that couldn't be broken, Eldina and Gennadiy referred to Ludkiga as their mother up until her death in 1984.

Many of these rescuers were just everyday people making a decision that unknowingly influenced thousands to follow the same path. Throughout the Holocaust not only were there those hiding and smuggling Jews, but whole organizations rescuing Jewish refugees all over Europe. Brought together by a force that is unexplainable to make that gesture that perseveres the hope for humanity. That is when even in the worst times known to man. Hope and a single hand to help can save those around the world. A gesture not only seen during the Holocaust but seen throughout history. Heroes of all kinds with the heart that is in words "Righteous Among the Nations". Willing to lay down their own lives for others they didn't know.

Overall until this day there lives on in many forms genuine non-profit organizations and research centers set out to cure diseases, famine, and change the world for good. Heroes like Ludviga Pukas will always be remembered for their kind actions, and valor. The quiet heroes are never forgotten for the true meaning of a rescuer found within the saying "Whosoever saves a life, saves an entire universe." (Mishnah, Sanhedvin 4:5)

Work Cited
Gregorovich, Andrew. Jewish Holocaust in Ukraine. Spring 1995. Print.
www.infoukes.com
www. Jewishvirtuallibary.org
www.ushmm.org/mlc/en/article.php?moduleId=10005519
www.yadvashem.org/yv/en/exhibition/rightous-women/pukas.org

The Holocaust Hero

Wei Jun Chen

The most unforgiveable crime that humans have ever committed was the Holocaust. This tragedy has caused many Jews lives. According to the statistics, it was estimated that the Nazi Regime and it collaborators killed about 6 million Jews. It was Adolf Hitler's plan for the genocide on Jews. Other victims of Nazi crimes included Romanis, ethnic Poles and Slavs, Soviet prisoners of war, communists, homosexuals, Jehovah's Witnesses and the mentally and physically disabled. Almost every arm of the country's bureaucracy was involved in the killing process. In addition, universities in Germany refuses to accept any Jewish students and denied the degrees of those who were already studying in their field.

The Nazis created a plan known as the "Final Solution" to exterminate the Jews, and why remains uncertain. What is certain is that the genocide of the Jews was the peak of a decade of Nazi policy, under the rule of Adolf Hitler. The "Final Solution" plan has many stages. This happened after the Nazi Party rise to power, the state enforced racism resulted in anti-Jewish legislation, boycotts, Aryanization, and the Night of Broken Glass pogrom, all of which aimed to remove the Jews from German society. At the beginning of World War II, anti-Jewish policy evolved into a plan to concentrate and eventually annihilate European Jewry.

After the rise of Nazi regime in Germany in 1933, they built a series of detention facilities to imprison and eliminate the enemies of the state. Most prisoners in early concentration camps were Germany communists, Socialists, Social Democrats, Gypsies, Jehovah's Witnesses, homosexuals, and persons who were accused of social deviant behaviors. These centers were known as "Concentration Camps" because they were concentrated in one location.

After the German invasion of Poland in 1939, the Nazis opened a forced labor camps where many prisoners died from exhaustion, starvation, and exposure. It was known that the SS unit was guarding the camps. During World War II, the camps expanded rapidly. In some of those camps, the Nazis doctors perform medical experiments on prisoners.

The Nazis planned to establish the ghettos in the occupied Poland. The Polish and Western European Jews were being moved into these ghettos. Between the year 1941 and 1944, the Nazis authorities deported millions of Jews from Germany and their occupied territories and from many countries of their allies to the ghettos and killing centers. The Nazis created the killing centers to perform mass murders. This was nothing like concentration camps that served as detention and labor centers or extermination camps. The first killing center was Chelmo, which was located in Warthegau part of Poland. In addition, this happened during the German invasion of Soviet Union in 1941, mobile killing squad began killing many Jewish communities. They mainly shot them or used gas. After the Wannsee Conference in January 1942, the Nazis began to deport the Jews from all over Europe to six extermination camps established in former Polish territory. Almost all of those Jews who got deported and were sent to camp were immediately sent to gas chambers and only small numbers of them were chosen to do special work. According to the statistics, it was estimated that 6,000 Jews were being gassed each day in Auschwitz-Birkenau in Poland. The Auschwitz concentration camp was considered the largest in the Nazi regime. It included three main camps; they all were used for forcing labors on Jews. One of those camps was also considered in the extended period as a killing center. The camps were located 37 miles in the west of Krakow. They were basically near the pre-war German-polish border in the Upper Silesia, an area that Nazi Germany annexed after invading and conquering Poland. It was estimated that 1 million Jews were deported to the camps in Auschwitz-Birkenau and around 900,000 died. Those extermination camps were the killing centers designed to carry out genocide. It was estimated about 3 million Jews were gassed in extermination camps.

The Jews were deemed by the Nazis as a priority danger to Germany, and were the victims of Nazi racism; other victims were 200,000 Roma who also known as the Gypsies. In addition, there were about 200,000 mentally and physically disabled patients, mainly Germans, living in institutional places, who were also being murdered in the Euthanasia Program. The Euthanasia Program was meant good death. It usually referred to painless death. The Nazis, however, used the Euthanasia term as for a clandestine murder program. This program was mainly targeted for mentally and physically disabled patients living in institutional settings in Germany and German-occupied territories. This program was the Nazi Germany's first mass murder program. This predated the genocide in European Jews by two years. This program was intended for restoring the racial integrity of the German nation. In mid-1939, a number of planners organized a secret operation targeting the disabled children. They were led by Philipp Bouhler, who was the director of Hitler's private chancellery, and Karl Brandt, who was Hitler's attending physician. On August of 1939, the Reich Ministry circulated a requirement for all physicians, nurses, and midwives to report newborn infants and children under age of three who show signs of mental or physically disabilities. In October of 1939, the public health authorities encouraged the parents of children who had severe disabilities to admit their young children to one of a number of specially designed clinics throughout Germany and Austria. Consequently, those clinics were designed to kill children. They had specially recruited staff to murder their young charges by using lethal overdoses of medication or by starvation.

During the final years of war, as the Nazis retreated in to the Reich themselves, the concentration camp population suffered tremendous amount of losses including Jewish and non-Jewish prisoners. This was all due to starvation, diseases, and mistreatment. In addition, the SS evacuated concentration camp prisoners to the front approach because the Nazis dids not want them to be liberated. Under the SS guards, the prisoners had to march on foot during the cold and severe winter weather without a good amount of food, sheltering, and clothing. In addition, the SS guards were ordered to shoot those who could not keep up the pace. Other prisoners were evacuated by open freight car during the cold winter.

Between 1944 through 1945, the Allied Forces liberated many of the concentration camps.Consequently, the death in camps continued for several weeks after the liberation. Some prisoners were too weak to even survive. According to the SS reports, it was estimated that more than 700,000 prisoners left the camps in January 1945.

Aside for all these tragic events, there are always heroes who would help others to avoid these tragedies. The hero's name was Elisabeth Abegg. She was born May 3rd, 1882, and she was the cousin of William Abegg, who was known to be the Social Democratic salesman. She grew up in Strasbourg, which was the capital of Alsace and also the hometown of Albert Schweitzer, the great Alsatian theologian, humanist, musician, and medical doctor. He tought Christian universalistic thought that centered on the equality of man and the sanctity of human life, and he had a lifelong influence on Abegg. Elisabeth was a history teacher at the fashionable Berlin girls' school, the Luisen Mädchenschule, Abegg attempt to impress her humanistic beliefs on her students, many of whom came from Jewish homes. After Hitler's ascension to power, she soon came into conflict with the newly Nazi-appointed director of the Luisen Mädchenschule. This had her moved to another, less fashionable school. In 1940, she was forced to retire prematurely and it was for following a denunciation.

Abegg was once marked by the authorities as politically unreliable and summoned by the Gestapo for interrogation. She could not be deterred, however, from maintaining contact with her former Jewish students and friends. With the deportation to the East, Anna Hirschberg was her close friend for 42; she understood the true import of the Nazi persecution of Jews. However, Abegg knew that it was too late to save her friend; Abegg felt she could still be useful in saving other Jews from the murderous clutches of the Gestapo. During that time, she turned the apartment that she shared with her eighty-six-year-old mother and Sister Julie into a temporary shelter and assembly point for the Jews who had gone underground. Abegg was working with her friends in the Quaker movement; she helped many Jews by offering them the temporary shelter in her own home or directing them to hide in places somewhere else. By doing this to help the Jews, she was considered to be a hero at that time and still is today. However, she was still remaining undetected under the Nazis' radar. Thus, this allowed her to buy more time and save more Jews within the vicinity. She skimped on her own food and her sister supplied them with food ration cards; she also invited them for each Friday to full meals in her house. Most of those who knocked on her door asking for help were complete strangers. All of this took place under her neighbors' noses, even though some tenants in the apartment house were active Nazis. Every Friday afternoon, Jews within the vicinity would gather up in Abegg's apartment for a home cooked meal and a bit of companionship. She provided warmth for the Jews.

Abegg did not hesitate to take further risks despite knowing that she could've been taken away from society and potentially killed. Liselotte Perlcs, the director of day-care center in Berlin, could not decide whether to go into hiding with her nine year old niece, Susie. They hid there anyways because the Nazis were on high alert. She visited them in January 1943 in the Jew house to which they been moved. Three apartments had already been sealed off after the residents had been deported to the East. This will allow them to maintain more cover and avoid being discovered by the Nazis. Abegg was persuading them that it was time to go underground and it was successful, and it was the last possible moment, as this was the eve of the last large Gestapo round-up of the Jews of Berlin. Abegg sheltered Jews in and around Berlin, Alsace and East Prussia and provided false identities for them to escape Germany, money and provisions. She even sold her jewelry and other valuables to finance her rescue operations. This allowed her to bribe the corrupted border guards. She organized an underground that smuggled Jewish families to Switzerland. She continued her humanitarian work, never thinking about the risk and danger to herself and her family.

Furthermore, during that time, 1942, many Jewish victims were sent by train to concentration camps. Thus, if they survived the journey, they either got poisoned in the gas chambers or worked as slaves. With Abegg's plan, this was however a turning point, she was able to help hide many Jews, feed them when they faced hunger, and guided them to escape Germany.

Abegg's close friend Anna Hirschberg was taken away by the Nazis. This triggered Abegg's courage to save and hide many Jews within the vicinity despite the failure of saving her close friend Anna. Abegg did not reject anyone from staying in her place because she knew that if she rejected them, they would face the same consequences like her friend Anna. Abegg had an advantage by having extra room in her place because it was a shared room with her relatives and family. This showed the true strength and hope for humanity; and this was made possible by Abegg's plan.

At last, after World War II ended, those survivors who were still in contact with Abegg were dedicated to her 75th birthday, in 1957, a mimeographed collection of memoirs entitled "When One Light Pierced the Darkness." In May 1967, Yad Vashem decided to recognize Elizabeth Abegg as the Righteous Among the Nations. Elisabeth Abegg died at the age 92 in August 8, 1974 in Berlin, Germany. In conclusion, heroes like Elisabeth Abegg are the type of people in this world who bring changes for the good.

Work Cited

United States Holocaust Memorial Museum. United States Holocaust Memorial Council. Web. 25 Feb. 2016. <http://www.ushmm.org/>.

"The Holocaust." Wikipedia. Wikimedia Foundation. Web. 25 Feb. 2016. <https://en.wikipedia.org/wiki/The_Holocaust>.

"Holocaust." Holocaust | Home Page. Web. 25 Feb. 2016 <http://www.projetaladin.org/holocaust/en/homepage.html>.

"Elisabeth Abegg - The Righteous Among The Nations - Yad Vashem." Elisabeth Abegg - The Righteous Among The Nations - Yad Vashem. Web. 25 Feb. 2016. <http://www.yadvashem.org/yv/en/righteous/stories/abegg.asp>.

"The Righteous During the Holocaust." Holocaust Memorial Center. Web. 25 Feb. 2016. <http://www.holocaustcenter.org/page.aspx?pid=514>.

Righteous (Berthold Beitz)

William Gardner

The Holocaust was an event that shook the world. Even though it was hidden from most of the world during the war. After the war was over all the news about these death camps got out and shocked the world. Stories about harsh treatment of the Jews spread, and the death toll was raising every day. By the end of it all the total fatalities of Jews was approximately 6 million. It is the most gruesome event in history and in human in nature. To think that this actually happened and no one stopped it.

Many Germans turned a blind eye to these horrors. But the few, the great, saw what was going on and said they would not sit idly by and let this happen. Just in Germany there are 587 recorded people who risked their lives to save the lives of others. These heroes risked it all to protect what they thought was right. These individuals are known as the righteous. Berthold Beitz was a very righteous man saving as many Jews as he could during World War II. Before learning about Mr. Beitz it is crucial to know about the Holocaust because it illustrates the risks he had to put himself in front of.

The Holocaust was one part of World War II instated by Hitler. The worst man to walk this Earth. He used the Jews as a scapegoat for all of Germany's problems after World War I. He created hate in Germany, using hate of Jews to rise in power. In early 1933 Hitler gained power and began militarizing Germany and creating it into a fascist state. He rebuilt the German economy while blaming Jews for their loss in World War I and used this as a way to justify his militarization and rebuilding of factories to the German people. If he dealt with the Jews and "got rid of them" for Germany, there would be no reason they would lose this war. Germany was disgraced by the Treaty of Versailles. No one likes losing, just like the German people, and they felt crushed and were willing to do anything to restore their power and pride. Hitler wanted to spread his "amazing" regime to the rest of the world, and began by invading Poland. Hitler began his assault on Europe and while this was going on he began requiring Jews to wear patches containing the Star of David, isolating them from the rest of the population. He then ordered the S.S. to round all the Jews up into ghettos and start construction of work camps and concentration camps. Jews from all the Nazi conquered countries began being rounded up and placed into the work camps or concentration camps. The S.S. would line people up and shoot them, like women and children who were not suited to work. Only those who were fit enough were kept alive, barely fed so they could work but not strong enough to fight back. Camps were harsh and demeaning to the Jewish people, disgracing them by tattooing ID numbers and never referring to them by names but just numbers, making them subhuman. As these camps were being used, Hitler began to worry about his empire as the Soviets advanced. Hitler began to instate a much harsher program for dealing with the Jews.

Hitler instated the Final Solution plan in 1942 to completely finish what he started. He was determined to end what he started, the horrible, horrible Holocaust even though it is impossible to think, grew even more bleak. He began shipping the Jews by train car like cattle to six of the new death camps. Rumors surrounded the new camps, harsh work and even less food, but none of them realized what it really had in store. These camps sought to as efficiently as possible kill people. It was murder industrialized. The camps used gas to kill the Jews at alarmingly fast rates. The camps then burned the bodies in ovens of unseen proportions, Thousands of Jews were being killed every day. The Jewish people had no escape from the horrors. It was murder on the largest scale imaginable. To make matters worse, as the war closed in on Hitler and as the Allies drew closer to each camp, the Nazis burnt everything and left the sick, and all who could walk marched to the next camp. When you couldn't walk any longer you were shot or beaten to death to save ammunition. The Nazi Party knew what they were doing and knew they had to burn their records because of the gruesomeness. Hitler, even though he was losing, wanted to complete what he started. He tried to kill as many Jewish people as he could because he wanted to end what he started. Hitler was going to lose all the way, and there was no substitute. In the end the Holocaust is the single worst genocide the world has ever witnessed. This event showed the worst of humanity. It also brought forth some of the most courageous or righteous stories of people trying to save the Jewish people and opposing the Nazi regime. Opposing the Nazi regime was very dangerous as you would face the same punishment and were treated like those that you were trying to hide. Usually they were just shot or sent to a camp like Auschwitz. The people who put their lives at stake live on in the history books as some of the greatest human beings ever to live.

The few, the brave, the mighty, the righteous. There are those who turned their backs to the Holocaust and said that's none of my business. But then there are those who saw what was happening and said "I will not stand idly by while this idiot kills innocent people." It was more than an opposition to the Nazis, it was people taking a stance on morals. They could not bear to see such an injustice happen right in front of their eyes. A fierce man who stood in opposition to this tyranny was Berthold Beitz. Born on September 26, 1913 he was a well known German industrialist. He was responsible for leading one of the largest steel conglomerates after World War I. Before all of this he was a banker from Hither Pomeranian. He soon began working for the Shell Oil Company in Hamburg Germany in 1938. With this experience working for the oil company the Nazi Party saw him as a crucial asset to the Nazi empire. Hitler's war machine was built around oil and needed someone to run the recently seized Boryslaw oil fields in Ukraine in July 1941. Beitz was given responsibility for a large oil field and had to pick essential workers for the plant. He used his power to pick 250 Jewish people from the Boryslaw area, which was a very Jewish region. He named them professionals and essential to the plant. After witnessing the Invaliden-Aktion which was a SS raid of a Jewish orphanage, Beitz was determined to save as many lives as he could from the region. He said that when you see a mother holding her children and being lined up and shot you cannot sit idly by. It is human nature to help them. He was not taking a moral stance against the Nazis he was just outright opposing the inhumanity. He was informed before SS raids by the Nazi heads and with this information he was able to warn Jewish people and people hiding Jews and save them from being caught. By doing this he was risking his life by providing high treason according to the Nazis. He would receive a fate worse than death if the Nazis figured out that he was using his position to compromise them. Whenever the Nazis came to search for the Jews or pick them up, they would have a much harder time finding anyone because they had heeded Beitz's news and left or hid somewhere else until the raid was over. In warning all these people he saved an uncountable number of lives.

In August 1942 he did the most courageous thing in his life. He saw a train full of Jews headed straight for the Belzec extermination camp. A camp which was part of

Hitler's final solution in which all Jews who went there were immediately killed by gas or bullet, then thrown in an oven. It was the most disgusting thing in human history and Beitz had heard about these camps and knew the fate of all the Jews sitting on the train car. He could not sit idly by and watch as these humans were treated like cattle and shipped off on a train car to a slaughter house. And for no reason other than some funny man with a small black moustache said they were evil. He used his position at the oil plant to request that they all stay as they were vital or professional workers at the oil plant. He said that he should have chosen qualified workers for the position but instead he chose tailors, carpenters, and Talmudic scholars. He saved all of them from hell. By hiring these people, he saved all their lives even though they were not suited for the position. By having people who were not well suited to work at this position they did not run the oil plant effectively and in a way this could have helped the allied war effort by not supplying the Nazi army with oil, which was essential to the Nazi war machine. Hitler's army was very mechanical as it used the blitz tactic to lead the army with tanks and cars to break front lines and create chaos. It was one of the reasons that Hitler's army was so effective. The army went through causing as much trouble to the allied lines and it was the reason Hitler was able to take over Europe. With less oil Beitz could have indirectly sabotaged the Nazi Blitz.

He used his power as an oil plant head to issue work permits to Jews in camps. He would send the fake work permits to get them out of the Nazis hands. Many Jews traveled around the continent safely displaying their fake work permits with Beitz's signature. Berthold had to sign many work permits to save all the Jews from camps all over Europe. Even though this system worked very well to save Jews it did in fact come back to almost bite him in the rear. In 1943 two girls were stopped by the Gestapo for having forged Aryan permits on a train. The permits were signed by none other than Mr. Beitz and it led to a Gestapo investigation. Even though the Gestapo investigated him he did not crack. A tough task to do as the Gestapo went by any means necessary to get information that they needed. This was his closest call to be found by the Nazis and most likely executed. Beitz was later drafted to the German army in March 1944. He was credited for saving over 800 Jewish lives over the course of World War II and received the 'Righteous Among the Nations' award from Yad Vashem, which is the highest honor to receive of a non-Jewish person saving Jewish lives. He led a prosperous steel conglomerate after the war and is also credited for being one of the leading rebuilders of Germany's post war economy.

Berthold Beitz risked it all to save the lives of others. He stood up for what he believed was right and that takes courage. He used his power to save countless lives throughout the war-torn continent. He is someone that we should all take a lesson from. You only live life once, and if you want to enjoy it you need to stand up for what's right and not follow the crowd. You can't let a demagogue scare you into doing something their way. It is the only way people like Hitler are able to get so far in the world. If you don't stand up for what you think is right, you are only helping the Hitler's of the world. During the Holocaust only a few were righteous enough to stand up against Hitler and the Nazis but those who did will live on forever as heroes.

Righteous Germans

Zahraa Ahmad

Adolf Hitler, the man responsible for the Holocaust, rose to power 15 years after Germany's defeat in World War I. The Treaty of Versailles made Germany pay reparations for the war and took away some of its land. The Germans also had little confidence in the Weimar Republic because it was a weak government. These conditions led to Hitler's rise to power and the rise of the Nazi Party. Hitler was a very powerful public speaker and he was appealing to the Germans because he promised he would make Germany glorious again. Thanks to Hitler's popularity, the Nazi Party was able to win the 1932 elections and in January 1933, Hitler was appointed chancellor of Germany. Hitler later declared himself dictator of Germany after the Reichstag fire happened.

Hitler gained control over Germany at the end of 1934 and this is when his movement against Jews went into effect. He claimed that the Jews were the reason why Germany lost World War I and they corrupted German culture with their foreign influence. Jews were portrayed to be evil, dishonest, and racially inferior, and the Germans were honest and racially superior. The discrimination against Jews became known as Anti-Semitism and the German were known as the "Aryans." The Nazis justified their poor treatment toward Jews by combining their racial theories with Charles Darwin's theories of evolution. They said that Germans would rule since they were racially superior and the Jew were going to become extinct since they were racially inferior.

Hitler started to exclude Jews with legislation and fear, this included burning books written by Jews, removing Jews from their jobs and public schools, taking away their businesses and property and excluding them from public events. On September 15, 1935, he passed the Nuremberg Laws which excluded Jews from German society. These laws led to Kristallnacht in November 1938, when German synagogues were lit on fire and the windows of Jewish shops were broken. During that night, around 100 Jews were killed and thousands more were sent to jail. Hundreds of thousands of Jews started to leave Germany and those who stayed lived in fear and uncertainty. In September 1939, Germany attacked Poland and started World War II. In 1940, the Nazis started to make ghettos for the Jews of Poland. They were deported from their homes and forced to live in those ghettos. The large population of Jews helped the Nazis deport them to concentration camps. These camps lacked food, water, space, and sanitary facilities that were needed for a large amount of people living in the concentration camps. Many people died due to deprivation and starvation.

In 1941, Hitler decided to put his "Final Solution" into action and formed four mobile killing groups known as Einsatzgruppen A, B, C and D. Their job was to gather Jews from towns and take them to huge pits they had dug earlier, stripped them, lined them up, and shot them with their weapons. They Jews they killed were buried in large graves. The Einsatzgruppen had killed more than 1.3 million Jews by the end of 1942. Although the Nazis killed people from other ethnic groups, only the Jews were doomed for total annihilation. They were the only ones that would receive the "Special Treatment," which meant that all Jewish men, women, and children were going to be killed with poisonous gas. Chelmno (Kulmhof), Belzec, Sobibor, Treblinka, Maidanek, and Auschwitz were the 6 death camps the Nazis had set up in Poland. Ravensbruck, Neuengamme, Bergen-Belsen, Sachsenhausen, Gross-Rosen, Buchenwald, Theresienstadt, Flossenburg, Natzweiler-Struthof, Dachau, Mauthausen, Stutthof, and Nordhausen were the major death camps they had set up in countries that Germany controlled during the war.

Jews who were living in countries that were ruled by Germany had to wear badges that marked them as Jews. The Nazis started to round them up and take them to ghettos or concentration camps and they were later taken to the killing centers. When Jews arrived at a concentration camp, they were stripped of their belongings, killed in the gas chambers by poisonous gas, and then their bodies were burned in crematoriums. Three and a half million Jews were killed in these death camps. Jews who were strong and healthy weren't killed immediately and were reserved for slave labor. They were forced to work for the Nazis in munitions and other factories. They worked from morning to night and were not given an adequate amount of food and shelter, so many of them were literally worked to death. Towards the end of Hitler's rule, the Nazis made the prisoners who were still alive march on the territory they still had and many of them died due to illness and the others were shot.

Concentration camps were liberated as the Allies began to take more territory away from Germany. There were 50,000 to 100,000 Jewish survivors after the war ended and they were living in American, British, and Soviet territory once Germany lost the war. These Jews couldn't go back to the home they had before they were deported because they would be threatened by anti-Semitic neighbors and their homes were filled with bad memories. They later emigrated to Palestine, America, and other countries.

Although Jews were treated inhumanely and discriminated against, there were still people who were willing to help them by hiding them, getting them food, or by helping Jews get forged passports. These individuals did the right thing and helped people who would have been sent to concentration camps and killed. These individuals are also very brave because they would have been sent to a concentration camp if they were caught aiding Jews. Dorothea Neff, Meta Schmitt, and Martha-Maria Driessen are Germans who helped their Jewish friend Lilli Wolff during the World War II.

Antonie Schmid. whose stage name was Dorothea Neff, Meta Schmitt, and Martha-Maria Driessen helped their friend Lilli Wolff, a Jewish dress designer, during World War II and the Holocaust. Lilli's rescue story rotated around three cities:

Cologne, Berlin, and Vienna. All of these women had a common profession and they knew each other before the war started. Lilli met Meta in 1918 and opened a fashion and costume design studio with her in Cologne two years later. Martha-Maria entered the business in 1932 as a volunteer employee and Dorothea was introduced to Lilli by a friend in 1934. During the first years of Nazi rule, Lilli and Meta were allowed to operate and they were allowed to have 40 employees. Lilli was forced to leave their partnership in November 1938.

Antonie was a professional stage actress and was also fired from her local theater in 1933 when she was suspected of political disloyalty. She moved to Cologne, then Königsberg, and she arrived in Vienna in 1939. She joined the Volkstheater, located in Vienna, where they offered her a position and became famous under her stage name Dorothea Neff. She became acquainted with many Jewish people who were connected to the art, this included Lilli Wolff and they became fast friends. Lilli moved to Vienna in September 1940 falsely thinking it would be easier to live as a Jew in Vienna than in Cologne. The lease to Lilli's apartment was canceled by the owner, but thanks to the intervention of the theater director she was able to rent an empty apartment with the cost of furnishing was paid for by Meta and Martha-Maria. Later, Dorothea began to pay a monthly payment so she could keep Lilli off the list of mandatory labor employment. She also began to bribe a local bureaucrat so he wouldn't put Lilli on the list of Jews who were required to work.

Lilli received a deportation notice to the east in the winter of 1941. When she received the notice, they decide that Lilli should go to Berlin to find Lilli a hiding place. Meta went with Lilli so she could help and protect her. Lilli was unable to hide in Berlin, so she returned to Vienna and Dorothea offered her a place to hide inside her home. Lilli found out the authorities were told about her going to Berlin and she had to go to a certain office so they could question her. Meta accompanied her and waited outside for 8 hours. Dorothea helped Lilli pack for her deportation, but at one point Dorothea closed Lilli's suitcase and said "You're not going anywhere! I'll hide you!" Dorothea didn't prepare in advance for this and years later she explained her actions by saying "As I looked into Lilli's pale face, I was so overcome by compassion for this poor abandoned human being that I couldn't let her go off to face the unknown." Dorothea reported that Lilli was missing before the expulsion at the end of 1941. Lilli didn't leave Dorothea's apartment until April 1945 and stayed underground until that day. Both Lilli and Dorothea lived with the constant fear of being discovered. While Dorothea was hiding Lilli in her home, she made sure not develop any close relationships and limited her social life because if she did there would be a higher chance of Lilli being discovered. If a guest would come over, Lilli would go into a hiding place and stay there quietly until the guest left. While Lilli was hiding she became ill in the August of 1944 and had to leave for an emergency operation. She said that she was taken to a hospital because there was a lump in her breast. Dorothea used her old German identification card, took Lilli to the hospital, and said that Lilli is her relative from Cologne named Antonie Schmid, which is Dorothea's original name and she didn't use it in Austria. Thanks to that Lilli received treatment and was able to get better.

Dorothea received help from 2 individual while Lilli was hiding in her home. Those 2 individuals were Meta Schmitt and Martha-Maria Driessen. They would occasionally visit and when they did they brought food rations, clothes, and other small items. Meta also accompanied Lilli to Berlin and when Lilli had to go in for questioning. In 1942, Lilli thought she had an opportunity to get a forged passport for 3,500 marks, so she called Martha-Maria. They decided to borrow money from the owner of the Kölnische Zeitung, also known as the Cologne newspaper, the owner knew whey they were borrowing money. Martha-Maria went to Vienna so she could give the money to Lilli, but the passport didn't come. They found out that the man who was supposed to give it to them was a swindler. Although they were deceived, Martha-Maria and Meta repaid the loan. When the end of the war was nearing, Dorothea told her secret to a young actress who also worked at the Volkstheater. The actress began to collect food stamps for Lilli. Dorothea was endangering herself by hiding a Jew in her home if she was caught she would have been deported to a concentration camp and eventually die there. The chances of them getting caught increased during the aerial bombardment of Vienna because Dorothea took Lilli to the basement of the building and told her neighbors that Lilli was a relative of hers from Cologne. Lilli came out of hiding when the Soviet Union took control of Vienna on April 9, 1945. After the war ended, Dorothea kept working as an actress and eventually went blind. Lilli moved to Dallas, Texas in 1947 and became a well-known fashion designer.

Dorothea's brother and sister-in-law alerted her that she was putting herself in danger and told her not to hide a runaway Jewish woman. Lilli later said "I am unspeakably thankful to her. She has done all she could to make my life easy, to make me feel that I am a human being, that I was worth of her care she bestowed so warmheartedly on me." While Lilli was living with Dorothea she observed Dorothea's nobility of mind and heart with a deep thankfulness. What Dorothea did for Lilli was incredibly courageous because she knew what would happen to them if they were caught. Martha-Maria and Meta were also very generous and willing to help Lilli. These women decided not to listen to Hitler and the Nazis and they made the right choice because they were able to keep their friend Lilli alive. It also shows that there were Germans who were willing to help Jews even though they were told by the Nazis that Jews are inferior to them and they are the reason why Germany lost in World War I. Dorothea once said, "The greater the darkness of a period, the brighter is the light of a single candle." I think she means that even dark times are upon us there will still be people who will work against that darkness and try to make things better again.

Bibliography
"The Holocaust: An Introductory History." Jewish Virtual Library. Web. 23 Feb. 2016. < https://www.jewishvirtuallibrary.org/jsource/Holocaust/history.html >.

"The Holocaust." History.com. A&E Television Networks. Web. 23 Feb. 2016.
< http://www.history.com/topics/world-war-ii/the-holocaust >.

"Introduction to the Holocaust." United States Holocaust Memorial Museum. United States Holocaust Memorial Council. Web. 22 Feb. 2016.
< http://www.ushmm.org/wlc/en/article.php?ModuleId=10005143 >.

"Hitler Comes to Power." United States Holocaust Memorial Museum. United States Holocaust Memorial Council. Web. 22 Feb. 2016.
< http://www.ushmm.org/outreach/en/article.php?ModuleId=10007671 >.

"From the Testimony of Lilli Wolff - The Righteous Among The Nations - Yad Vashem." From the Testimony of Lilli Wolff - The Righteous Among The Nations - Yad Vashem. Yad Vashem. Web. 20 Feb. 2016.
< http://www.yadvashem.org/yv/en/righteous/stories/related/wolff_testimony.asp >.

"Dorothea Neff - The Righteous Among The Nations - Yad Vashem." Dorothea Neff - The Righteous Among The Nations - Yad Vashem. Yad Vashem. Web. 20 Feb. 2016.
< http://www.yadvashem.org/yv/en/righteous/stories/neff.asp >.

"Schmid FAMILY." Yad Vashem. Yad Vashem. Web. 11 Feb. 2016.
< http://db.yadvashem.org/righteous/family.html?language=en >.

Johanna Eck

Zoe Lackemacher

Oppression; the exercise of authority or power in a burdensome, cruel, or unjust manner. A terrible but accurate example of people being oppressed was in World War II, the second time the world has seen such a gruesome, hasty war. This one was known as the war to end all wars, because the First World War did not solve any of the problems, and the thought of giving it a second go somehow made complete sense amongst powerful countries and leaders.

This war was the largest and most violent the world had ever seen, and lasted from 1939 through 1945. After the Versailles Treaty, Hitler and the Nazis gained control over Germany calling for a mass effort to restore the past glory allied to the humiliating situation that the treaty had put Germany and its people in. Hitler, being embarrassed and not wanting to make Germany, his army, or himself look worse than any other, decided to become possibly one of the most infamous dictators the world had ever seen, one of the most cruel in world history.

Massive inflation followed by very high unemployment heightened existing class and political differences that began to undermine the government. On January 30, 1933, Adolf Hitler, leader of the Nazi party was named chancellor of Germany by President Paul Von Hindenburg after the Nazi Party won a significant percentage of the vote in the elections. They had taken advantage of the political unrest in Germany to gain an electoral foothold.

The Nazis incited clashes with the communists and conducted a vicious propaganda campaign against its political opponents - the weak Weimar government and the Jewish people whom the Nazis blamed for all of Germany's problems has a country. A major tool of the Nazis' propaganda assault was the weekly Nazi newspaper Der Sturmer. At the bottom of the front page of each issue, in bold letters, the paper stated, "The Jewish people are our misfortune!" Der Sturmer also regularly featured cartoons of Jews in which they were caricatured as hooked-nosed and apelike. The influence of the newspaper was far-reaching: by 1938 about a half million copies were distributed weekly. Shortly after Hitler became chancellor, he suggested Germany hold new elections so he could gain control of the German Parliament for the Nazis. The Nazis used the government apparatus in order to terrorize everyone else and hold power amongst everyone. They would arrest any other party leaders and ban them from coming back, thereby making it nearly impossible for anyone else to have more power than Adolf Hitler, the leader of the Nazis. The Nazis held the majority of power in the government and won the election. The Nazis then moved quickly to turn their power into a dictatorship.

The Nazis banned all of their critics from being able to post bad things about them and from doing so, for the most part only good word was spread about these Nazis. They were also able to develop a sophisticated military and army force, one of the best in the world. By 1934 Hitler had complete and utter control over Germany. The hatred of Jews by the Nazis was justified in their words that the Jews corrupted the pure German culture with their "foreign" and "mongrel" influence. The Nazis blamed Germany's weakened economy on the Jews since a great number of them held jobs in commerce, finance, the press, literature, theater, and the arts. When in reality Germany was in debt due to wars and spending so much on leaders and military, if anything the Jewish people brought money into Germany.

Between 5 and 6 million Jews - out of a Jewish population of 9 million living in Europe - were killed during the Holocaust. It is impossible to know exactly how many people died as the deaths were comprised of thousands of different events over a period of more than four years. About half of the Jewish victims died in concentration camps or death camps for example, Auschwitz. The other half died when Nazi soldiers marched into many large and small towns in Germany, Poland, the Soviet Union and other areas and murdered people by the dozens or by the hundreds.

In the 1930s, Nazi persecution of Jews and other opponents was common knowledge in Germany. News reels in cinemas around the world at the time showed footage of attacks on Jews, their properties and synagogues in Germany during Kristallnacht. But the Nazis tried to keep the extermination of Jews and their other genocidal acts a secret.

While ordinary Germans knew that the Jews had been deported to the east, large segments of the German population were unaware that they were being murdered. The response of the Allies to the persecution and destruction of European Jewry was inadequate and the strongest moral voice, the Pope's, was silent.

On December 17, 1942, the Allies issued a condemnation of Nazi atrocities against the Jews, but this was the only such declaration made prior to 1944. No attempt was made to call upon the local population in Europe to refrain from assisting the Nazis in their systematic murder of the Jews. It has been suggested that the Allies could have bombed the death camp at Auschwitz to slow down the Nazi murder machine. But it is unlikely that any such measures could have stopped, or even significantly slowed down, the genocide of the Jews.

It is morally unjustifiable to rank human suffering in order to diminish the horror of "lesser" forms of human suffering. Every catastrophe or act of genocide has its similarities and differences with other catastrophes and genocides. But historians emphasize that the Holocaust was unique, because it is the only time in history when one nation tried to systematically murder every man, woman, and child of a certain ethnic or religious minority as a political goal, seeking to find and destroy them everywhere, from the bustling metropolitan centers of Europe to remote Greek islands.

The Nazis created a complete bureaucratic apparatus to accomplish their goal. However, throughout all of this horror and what seems like a hell on Earth, there were still many many good people. One of those being Johanna Eck.

From 1942 until the end of the war, a widowed woman named Johanna Eck sheltered four victims of Nazi persecution. Two of those who found refuge in her home were Jews. In 1942, Jakob, his wife, and their children were deported to the East, never to return. Young Heinz alone had barely managed to escape arrest and was wandering aimlessly in the streets without a plan or place to stay. Everybody he turned to for help refused to have anything to do with a Jewish illegal for fear of being caught. Eck alone, of all his non-Jewish acquaintances, stood by him in this difficult moment, offering him refuge in her home, and sharing her meager food allowance with him. She would spend several days on end away from home in an effort to obtain additional food rations from trustworthy friends.

When, in November 1943, the house was destroyed in an air raid, Eck took it upon herself to locate an alternative hiding-place for Heinz. Even while he was living away from her, Eck kept in close contact with Heinz, providing him from time to time with food-ration cards. It was through Heinz's landlady, Ms. M., that Eck came to be acquainted with Elfriede Guttmann, a Jewish girl who was hiding in her home. In December 1943, the Gestapo, raided Ms. M's house. Elfriede, who had been hiding under one of the beds, barely managed to escape detection.

Shattered by this traumatic experience, the Jewish girl visited Eck and told her what had happened. Eck, who had in the meantime been assigned a single-room apartment, immediately agreed to offer her refuge.

Elfriede's end was very tragic. The Jewish girl, who survived the horrors of the war intact, succumbed to a sudden stomach constriction shortly after the liberation. She passed away in June 1946, on the eve of her projected emigration to the United States. Eck, a nurse by training, sat at her bedside at the hospital until she passed away. She later inquired with the Jewish community as to the names of Elfriede's parents and brother.

Although they had all perished, she had the names inscribed on the gravestone that she set up at her own expense at the Berlin-Weissensee cemetery.

Doing something as dangerous as this would be seen as insane by anybody, but to have it been done by a woman was unheard of. Nobody wanted to revolt against Hitler or at least be public about their hatred towards his views and policies, but there were plenty of people who disagreed with what he preached. Being a woman at this time was already difficult enough as it stands, let alone one who helped illegal people stay safe in an Anti-Jew country. No one would have thought that a woman would have been able to help this much, but they were obviously incorrect.

Bibliography
"The History Place - Holocaust Timeline." The History Place - Holocaust Timeline. Web. 25 Feb. 2016.
"The International School for Holocaust Studies." Women in the Holocaust. Web. 25 Feb. 2016.
"33 Facts You Should Know About the Holocaust." About.com Education. Web. 25 Feb. 2016.

Hermann Friedrich Gräbe, 谢谢您！

YongFen Lei (Sallay)

 你可知道每个时代都留存着一段血腥的历史？你可想象生活在那段历史下的人们是怎么熬过去的？你可体会那些人曾经受过的种种磨难？有人说过去的都已经过去了，但是他们不明白这不仅仅是时间的问题，而是一种对历史的反思，一种对上一辈的尊敬，和一种对已牺牲的英雄的敬佩！

让我们把时间倒流，一起回到那段可怕却又充满勇敢的岁月。

呼！呼！呼！一片又一片的玻璃碎声正在围绕着德国，奥地利和苏台德区。这是1938年的"碎玻璃之夜"，也称"十一月的迫害"。在黑暗的街上，纳粹党的人随处可见，他们面无表情，只是一味地敲碎犹太人们的商店，袭击他们的教堂，和闯入他们的家庭。这无疑是一种可恨可耻的行为！就这样，纳碎党把犹太人们所有的付出和努力都敲碎了。命运有时候就是喜欢捉弄人。谁都没有想到"碎玻璃之夜"只是这场噩梦的开头，更可怕的事情正在等待着那些无辜的犹太人们。

随着纳碎党渐渐地强大了起来，集中营的数目也逐渐地变多了。这些集中营一开始只是用来扣押犹太人，慢慢地就变成了"灭绝营"。有很多无辜的犹太人都被处死在里面，灭绝营的死刑也是极其残酷和惨不忍睹。我相信没有亲身经历过的人是无法真正地体会到犹太人们的痛苦。

　　幸运的是，当上帝把门关掉了，但却给你留了一扇窗。在远离灭绝营的地方大多数都归纳碎党所操控，住在那里的人有很多都想帮助被扣押的犹太人们，但却有心无力因为他们不知道纳碎党会对他们及他们的家庭做出什么恐怖的行为。俗话说得好，世间没有绝对！总会有那么一些人为了和平，为了信念，为了无辜受害的犹太人们站出来与纳碎党抗争。他们是英雄，敢为人之所不敢为，敢当人之所不敢当！

　　英雄无处不在。　在茫茫人海中，我的目光投向了他，Hermann Friedrich Gräbe。

　Hermann出生于1900年，六月十九号。他们一家住在德国的一个叫格拉夫拉特的小镇上。他出身并不富裕，他的爸爸是一名纺织工人，而他的妈妈则是一个佣人。在他24岁那年，他结了婚，并完成了训练成为了一名工程师。那个时候，很多德国的年轻人都选择加入纳碎党，当然，Hermann也不例外。但很快的，他就醒悟了。他不能容忍纳碎党的所作所为，为此他曾公开批评纳碎党的反犹太人活动。随着他的公开评论，Hermann被抓进了监狱及扣押了几个月。但是，好人有好报，他最终没有受到任何审讯，并且被释放了出来。由此可见，他的信念，注定了他从逆境走向了光明，因为他有一颗英雄的心。

　　在1938之1941年，Hermann所在的建筑公司派他到利沃夫，乌克兰去协助一些工事。在1941年的九月，他在乌克兰区域成立了一间分公司，名叫"荣格"。　他的公司雇用了大约5000名犹太男女，这些犹太人都是来自公司附近的灭绝营。　可以说，他是故意雇用这么多犹太人的，因为有了工作的掩护才不会轻易被身边人怀疑，这样他就可以偷偷地帮他的犹太员工们办理伪造的身份证，以便于他们逃离困境。在帮助犹太人逃离的过程，他毫不犹豫第牺牲自己的财产和地位，甚至赌上自己的生命。Hermann把生存的机会留给了他人，自己毅然地挑战着死神，他只是一个凡人，但是他做出了非凡的举动。

其中最惊险的一次就是在1943年。他当时在帮他的25个犹太员工提供伪造的雅利安人身份证。在Hermann用车运送他们到安全部落的过程中，他们的车停在了路上，而更糟糕的是他们当时所在的那个路段有很多的德国路障。也就是说，如果他们被发现了，无论是救人者或是被救者都将会死路一条。幸运的是，他们平安地度过了那个难关。每当我读到这段事迹时，心里都会感到温暖，就如在寒冷的夜里有人给了我一个大大的拥抱。Hermann让我相信了只要有一颗坚定的心，永不放弃，就会到达你所渴望的终点。

终于，1945的到来改变了纳碎党，犹太人和Hermann 的命运。 美军把纳碎党的成员一网打尽。他们把灭绝营里的犹太人们释放了出来，他们无法想象，灭绝营里犹太人们是怎么撑过来的。根据美军的描述，灭绝营里的人个个都骨瘦如柴，面无容光，眼神里充满了绝望。灭绝营里还有很多裸露的尸体，老人的，少妇的，青年的，以及小宝宝的。当时在场的美军都被眼前的一切所惊呆了，虽然他们曾经都经历过残酷的战场，但是他们始终不敢相信眼前的一切是真的，他们的眼泪不由自主地流了下来。

在那之后，Hermann就开始与在纽伦堡的美军战争罪科作了一份证词。这份证词就像Hermann心底的一个秘密，现在也终于是时候说出来了。他在证词上描述了他第一次在乌克兰所见到的暴行，一行又一行的犹太人，裸露着身体，站在一个大坑附近。裸露的人群里有着老人，女人，男人和小孩子。他们有的在哭，有的在和他们的家人说再见，有的在拥抱。。。。。。一切的一切来得太快了。随着阵阵枪声的响起，一个又一个的人倒入了那个大坑里，一滴又一滴的鲜血犹如雨滴般洒满了周围的土地。几分钟过去了，一群无辜的人就这样消失于这个世界上，伴随他们的只有眼泪，鲜血，和枪声。。。。。。

这不仅仅是一份证词，它代表着一段真实的，错误的，以及无可改变的历史。 Hermann是这段历史的见证人，作为唯一一个在纽伦堡作证的德国人，他所承受的压力是很大的。在《罗诺夫的摩西》这本书中，作者赫尼克提到了在战争过后，Hermann被德国给赶了出来，因为他写了这份证词。想必当时Hermann也不好受，但是好人总是会被世界善待的。

在那之后，他带着他的妻子和孩子一起搬到了美国的三藩市。在那里他度过了他的余生，直至到1986年，他去世了。

眨眼间，恰似一缕轻烟。世界变了，但是战争却依然存在，无辜的生命一天天的牺牲，一切的一切其实并没有改变多少。再过几年，那些曾经生存于那段可怕历史的人们就要离开这个世界了，毕竟人类的生命是有限的。但是，我相信他们的故事不会因此而消失，它们将时时刻刻地警惕着不要重踏之前的错路，不要更多无辜的人死去，更重要的是不要迷失了自我。同时，我们要好好的去爱身边的人，珍惜可以在一起的时间，因为我们永远无法承诺明天，永远无法预测生命的终点，也许一刹那后，我们就消失了。

最后，我要向亲爱的Hermann Friedrich Gräbe致敬！虽然，他已离开这个世界，但他的英雄精神却不曾消失过。谢谢您！

Hermann Friedrich Gräbe

YongFen Lei (Sallay)

Do you know the bloody parts in the history? Can you imagine how people living in that period of history survived? Would you like to feel all the hardships people back then faced? Some people say that the past has passed, but they do not understand this is not just a matter of time; instead it is a reflection of history, a sign of respect for the previous generation, and an admiration for the sacrificed hero!

Let us turn the clock back to the terrible part of history.

Boom! The sound of broken glass is everywhere in Germany, Austria and Sudetenland. This is the 1938 "broken glass night", also known as "November's persecution." In the dark streets, the Nazis are everywhere; they look cold and emotionless. The Jewish homes, shops and churches are attacked. This is undoubtedly a hateful and shameful behavior! The night passed by as the Nazis cracked down every effort the Jewish families had earned in years. Fate sometimes likes to tease people. In the meantime, no one thought "broken glass night" would lead to a dreadful nightmare like the death camps; unfortunately, more terrible things are waiting for those innocent Jewish people.

The number of concentration camps has gradually increased as the Nazis have grown stronger and stronger. These camps were initially used only to detain the Jews, and slowly became "extermination camps." Many innocent Jews were executed inside; the killing methods were extremely cruel and appalling. Those who have not personally experienced cannot really say anything about the suffering of the people.

Fortunately, when God closed the door, he always left you a window. Far away from the extermination camps, most of them were under the control of the Nazi Party. Many of the people who lived there wanted to help the Jews, but they were powerless and too afraid of the Nazis would harm their families. However, hope is always there! There will always be some people stands up for the Jews and fight against the Nazis. They are heroes; dare to do anything in order to help.

Heroes are everywhere. In the vast crowd, I saw him, Hermann Friedrich Gräbe.

Hermann was born in 1900, June 19th. The family lives in a small town in Graflatt, Germany. He was not wealthy, his father was a textile worker, and his mother was a servant. At the age of 24, he married, and completed the training became an engineer. At that time, many young people in Germany have to join the Nazi party; Hermann was no exception. But soon, he realized that the Nazis are wrong. He could not tolerate what they had done, for which he had openly criticized the anti-Semitic activities. With his public comment, Hermann was arrested and imprisoned for several months. However, the good man finds his way out; he eventually did not receive any interrogation, and was released. Thus, his belief doomed him from adversity to the light, because he has a heroic heart.

In 1938 to 1941, Hermann's construction company sent him to Lviv, Ukraine to assist in a number of fortifications. In September 1941, he set up a company in the Ukrainian region, named "Jung". His company employed about 5,000 Jewish men and women, all of whom came from extermination camps near the company. It can be said that he was deliberately employed so many Jews, because the cover of the work will help them in the upcoming plans. He secretly helped his Jewish employees to forged identity cards in order to facilitate their escape. In the process of helping the Jews to flee, he did not hesitate to sacrifice his property and status, and even bet on his own lives. Hermann left the chance of survival to others, and had resolutely challenged the death; he was just a mortal, but he did remarkable things.

One of the most thrilling things was in 1943. He was helping his 25 Jewish employees to forge an Aryan identity. Hermann's car was in the process of transporting them to the security tribe, their car parked in the road, but the worse was that they were at that section of the road where there are many German guards. In other words, the Jews or Hermann will die if they are found. Fortunately, they survived. Every time I read about Hermann, my heart feels warm, as in the cold night someone gave me a big hug. Hermann made me believe that as long as there is a firm heart, and never give up; one will eventually reach the desired end.

Finally, the arrival of 1945 changed the fate of the Nazi Party, the Jews and Hermann. The US military defeated the Nazis. They released the Jews in the extermination camps, and they could not believe what had happened inside the camps. According to the description of the US military, the people in the camp are skinny, eyes full of despair. The soldiers saw a lot of exposed bodies, the elderly, young woman, young people, as well as small babies. The US military were all stunned, although they have experienced many brutal battlefields, but they still cannot believe everything is true.

After the defeat of the Nazi party, Hermann began a testimony with the US War Crime Section in Nuremberg. The testimony is like a secret hiding deep inside Hermann' s heart, and now it is finally time to say it. In his testimony, he described the atrocities he had witnessed in Ukraine for the first time, a line of Jews, bare-bodied and standing near a pit; there were elderly, women, men and children. Some of them were crying, some were saying goodbye to their families, and some were hugging each other tightly. . . . . . Everything came so fast. As the bursts of gunfire sounded, one after another fell into the pit; drop by drop of blood like raindrops sprinkled around the land. A few minutes later, a group of innocent people disappeared in this world, along with only tears, bloods, and gunfire sounds. . . . . .

This is not just a testimony; it represents a real, wrong, and irrevocable history. Hermann is the witness of this history, as the only one in Nuremberg to testify to the Germans, he is under great pressure. In the book "The Moorings of Lenov", the author Henik mentioned that Hermann was driven out of Germany after the war because he wrote the testimony. However, the world always treated good people kindly. He moved with his wife and children to San Francisco where he spent the rest of his life until 1986 when he died.

Blink of an eye, like a ray of smoke. The world has changed, but the war is still there, innocent lives sacrifice day by day, all of all actually did not change much. In few more years, those who have survived the bloody parts of the history will leave the world; after all, human life is limited. However, I believe their stories will never disappear. They will always be there to warn people not to walk the wrong path again, no more bloods of the innocents; more importantly, do not lose your faith. At the same time, we need to love the people around us, cherish every minute spent together, because we can never promise tomorrow, can never predict the end of life, perhaps after a moment, we shall be gone forever.

Last but not least, I would like to pay my respect to Mr. Hermann. Even though he already left the world, but his heroic spirit would always remain. Thank you!

Holocaust Essay

Aidan Stivers

During World War Two, there was a horrible tragedy known as the Holocaust. The Third Reich, or Nazi party, was responsible for this great loss of human life, with Adolf Hitler at the helm. The Nazi Party had come to power in 1933 by creating a demagogue, a political leader who seeks support by appealing to popular desires and prejudices rather than rational arguments. Adolf Hitler used Anti-Semitism to gain his power and eventually become dictator of Germany. Hitler and the Nazi's believed that the Jews stood in the way of world domination. One of Hitler's quotes was, "The struggle for world domination will be fought entirely between us, between Germans and Jews. All else is facade and illusion. Behind England stands Israel, and behind France, and behind the United States. Even when we have driven the Jew out of Germany, he remains our world enemy." We can see that Hitler did not want Jews in the way of his domination of the world, and started by getting rid of the Jews at home. This also shows the horrible discrimination against Jews at the time, and the mindset had against them during the Holocaust. Another quote by Hitler, ". . . the discovery of the Jewish virus is one of the greatest revolutions that has taken place in the world. The battle in which we are engaged today is of the same sort as the battle waged, during the last century, by Pasteur and Koch. How many diseases have their origin in the Jewish virus! ... We shall regain our health only be eliminating the Jew." We see here that Hitler doesn't just want to get them out of Germany. He wanted to eliminate them all. This led to the Holocaust that we know today. The death of over 6 million Jews by the Nazi Party.

Many Germans followed Hitler through his dictatorship and agreed with getting rid of the Jews but there were some heroes, some people that went against that belief and helped the Jews. One of the most famous Germans that helped the Jews was Oskar Schindler. He saved more Jews during World War 2 than anyone else. He managed to save over 1,200 Jews from the Nazi Party and gas chambers. Oskar Schindler gave up a lot of his wealth trying to help save the Jews. He spent millions by bribing and paying off the Schutzstaffel and even risked his life trying to help. The Jews that worked for Schindler wrote a letter about him on May 8, 1945, stating, "We, the undersigned Jews from Krakow, inmates of Plaszow concentration camp, have, since 1942, worked in Director Schindler's business. Since Schindler took over management of the business, it was his exclusive goal to protect us from resettlement, which would have meant our ultimate liquidation. During the entire period in which we worked for Director Schindler he did everything possible to save the lives of the greatest possible number of Jews, in spite of the tremendous difficulties; especially during a time when receiving Jewish workers caused great difficulties with the authorities. Director Schindler took care of our sustenance, and as a result, during the whole period of our employment by him there was not a single case of unnatural death. All in all he employed more than 1,000 Jews in Krakow. As the Russian frontline approached and it became necessary to transfer us to a different concentration camp, Director Schindler relocated his business to Bruennlitz near Zwittau." In this letter, you can see the lengths Oskar Schindler went to save the Jews that worked for him. It also shows the amount of success he had in keeping them save. There was not a single case of unnatural death of a Jew under Schindler in Nazi run Germany during the Holocaust. In 1962, Schindler was awarded the title "Righteous Among the nations by Yad Vashem. This gave him recognition for his deeds during the Holocaust. When Oskar Schindler died in 1974, he was almost penniless and unknown, but they Jews that were saved by him lobbied and financed for his body to be taken to Israel, making him the only Nazi to be buried in Jerusalem. To help people remember what he did, the United States Holocaust Memorial Council gave him the Medal of Rememberance in 1993. The Steven Spieldberg movie, Schindler's List, has also helped people remember what he did for the Jews during the Holocaust and how much he put himself on the line to do it.

Another German hero at the time was Albert Goering. Even though his brother, Hermann Goering, was second in command to Hitler and was the one who led the concentration camps, causing the death of 6 million Jews; Albert Goering despised the Nazi Party and risked his life and his career trying to help Jewish during the Holocaust. Albert Goering got Hermann to release Jews from the concentration camps many times. Hermann wanted to show off his power to his younger brother and would do what Albert asked him to do. This lead to the saving of many Jews as Albert would ask for some to be freed. The main way Albert Goering helped Jews leave Germany was by obtaining travel documents, giving them to families so they could escape the horrors of Nazi Germany. Albert Goering was arrested many times by the Gestapo, also known as the Nazi Secret Police, but his brother got him out each time, making him Albert's get out of jail free card. One of the people Albert saved was Tatiana Otzoup Guliaeff, the daughter of a silent movie star, Alexandra Sorina, who later wrote a letter giving thanks to Albert. In the letter, she stated, "Little did I know that you, at the risk of your own life, gave orders in the name of your half brother, a high ranking German official, to release prisoners, to issue exit papers to thousands of Jewish and other ethnic peoples, thus saving their lives. How you forged your half brother's name on the documents, how you changed your voice and bearing to sound like he. Neither did I know that, after saving the life of the composer of the "Merry Widow" Franz Lehar and his family, he composed an important musical piece in your honor. Nor did I know that you were tried in Nuremberg, absolved of all your crimes, and banished to Argentina for a number of years for your own safety, for the name of your half brother was well known and hated by all. Most of this I found out from an article written in the 1950s in the News Call Bulletin of San Francisco, where it stated that all the Jewish families, that you saved, remembered you with kindness, gratitude and respect, that they had sent affidavits to certify of your courageous actions." Albert Goering was remembered fondly by the people he saved, but unfortunately his life was ruined just because he had the same name as his brother Hermann. A few Jewish families took him in after the war because he was not able to get a job, due to his namesake. Albert Goering died in 1966.

Another German hero, a woman this time, named Johanna Eck helped Jews on a smaller scale. She successfully sheltered two Jewish people as well as two others who were victims of the Nazis. The first Jewish person she sheltered was an acquaintance from many years before the war, who went by the name Heinz Guttman. Heinz's father, mother, and his siblings had been deported East, and they never returned, so Heinz wandered the streets in search of help. Everyone he went to turned him down for fear they would be caught except for Johanna Eck. Johanna gave him shelter and some of the little food she had. She even spent days away from home to get additional food from trustworthy sources. In November 1943, Johanna's house was bombed so she took it upon herself to find another hiding place for Heinz, which she did successfully.

313

The second Jew she managed to save was Elfriede Guttman. Although they had the same last name, Heinz and Elfriede were not related. Elfriede was found hiding in Johanna's landlady's house. The German Secret Police raided the landlady's house and Elfriede barely managed to stay hidden. Johanna then took her in after the landlady acquainted them. Elfriede managed to be extremely lucky, as when Johanna and Elfriede were in line at a bakery they met a former classmate of Elfriede, Erika Hartmann, who was eager to help them. Erika gave Elfriede some Aryan documents, including one that said she had work for the labor service. These became very useful on January 30, 1944 when the Allies bombed Berlin. Johanna took advantage of the chaos and registered Elfriede as Erika Hartmann, whose house and documents had been burned during bombing. This allowed Elfriede to live legally with Johanna. She helped them for the rest of the war. Later, when she was questioned about why she did what she did, she answered, "The motives for my help? Nothing special in a particular case. In principle, what I think is this: If a fellow human being is in distress and I can help him, then it becomes my duty and responsibility. Were I to refrain from doing so, than I would betray the task that life – or perhaps God? – demands from me. Human beings – so it seems to me – make up a big unity; they strike themselves and all in the face when they do injustice to each other. These are my motives." She was a courageous and selfless person during the war, which is why Yad Vashem recognized her as Righteous Among the Nations on December 11, 1973.

The last hero I will talk about is another woman. Ludviga Pukas from Ukraine helped a family hide from the Nazi's in the town of Proskurov. She found work as a domestic for Frima Sternik, who had two children, Eldina and Gennadiy. Sternik and Pukas became very good friends during the time she worked there. When the Nazi's took over Proskurov, Sternik's house was destroyed and the family went to live with Pukas. When Sternik went to register for new identity papers, she put Eldina and Gennadiy as Pukas' children, as well as Pukas' own daughter. This allowed them to get an apartment, as Pukas was registered as a mother of three. After a little while, Sternik got noticed, so she wanted to move. Pukas sent Sternik to her brothers house in a nearby village, but on the way, Sternik was caught by the Nazis. Then the police came and searched Pukas' house in search of Jews. They found one that Pukas had allowed to stay, but they never found Eldina or Gennadiy. After the war ended and Ukraine was liberated, Eldina and Gennadiy were able to live normal lives again. The went to school, changed their names back to Sternik, and regarded Pukas as their mother.

There were many heroes during the Holocaust and I know that we don't know all of them, but all the acts of kindness and compassion that we have seen in the deeds of the people we do know shows that people are capable of amazing things, no matter how big or small their contribution was. Many sacrificed their own health and safety for the lives of others. Oskar Schindler lost his fortune, Alfred Goering was hated just for having the same name as his brother Hermann Goering, and Johanna Eck and Ludviga Pukas risked their lives to keep Jews safe from the Holocaust. They all gave up things to help the lives of others and that should never be forgotten. They impact they had on many peoples lives is also seen today. There are many descendants of Schindler Jews and people that have written letters about the good things Albert and Schindler did. Eldina and Genniday are able to live their lives and continue to be grateful to the people who help. We need more people in the world like the heroes of the Holocaust, who will go out of their way to help others, no matter how many.

Works Cited

"Oskar Schindler." Accessed February 26, 2016.
http://www.ushmm.org/wlc/en/article.php? ModuleId = 10005787

"Oskar Schindler: His List of Life." Accessed February 26, 2016.
http://www.ushmm.org/wlc/en/ article.php? ModuleId = 10005787

Auschwitz. "Schindler Letter." Accessed February 26, 2016.
http://www.auschwitz.dk/Schindlerletter.htm

Auschwitz. "Albert Goering: The Good Brother" Accessed February 27, 2016.
http://www.auschwitz.dk/albert.htm

Yad Vashem. "Johanna Eck." Accessed February 27, 2016.
http://www.yadvashem.org/yv/en/exhibitions/righteous-women/eck.asp

Yad Vashem. "Ludviga Pukas." Accessed February 28, 2016.
http://www.yadvashem.org/yv/en/exhibitions/righteous-women/pukas.asp

McCaffrey Middle School, Galt, CA

Ron Rammer

My name is Ron Rammer and I am proud to be principal of McCaffrey Middle School in Galt, California. Our students have learned about the atrocities of the Nazi regime through readings and class discussions. Many 8th graders made the journey to Washington DC and were able to experience the Holocaust Museum. The knowledge they gained from this experience along with the firsthand accounts of Holocaust survivor Bernard Marks at a school assembly has forever impacted their view of what some humans are capable of. Hopefully this piece of their education will motivate them to always stand up for what they know is right.

Mrs. Leann Salamy

Mrs. Leann Salamy is an 8th grade Language Arts Teacher at McCaffrey Middle School in Galt, CA. She majored in Liberal Studies with a minor in English. She attended Holy Names College and California State University of Sacramento. She has studied and taught about the Holocaust since teaching at the middle school level. Ryy Taylor who wrote the story on the Holocaust is a fabulous student with a bright future ahead of her. She is a gifted writer and artist.

Righteous Gentile Ludwig Wörl

Ryv Taylor (Special Award)

The Holocaust dates back in 1933 to 1945 and is notoriously known for the mass killing and persecution of 6six million Jews. Jews were considered as inferior to the racially superior Germans, as Jews were blamed for Germany's problems of war debt and declining economy. This racial discrimination further resulted in the horrendous genocide of Jewish citizens. While this killing and capturing of Jews seemed nearly impossible to avoid, audacious individuals who were not Jewish risked their lives to help rescue captured Jews, despite the severe punishments of doing so. These heroic men and women are referred to as righteous gentiles.

The righteous offered help for the Jews in various ways, such as hiding Jews in their rescuer's homes and providing false identities so that Jews' real identities were not exposed to Nazis. All though that not all of the righteous were recorded, over 24,000 righteous gentiles are honored for their bravery and benevolent behavior, one of which included Ludwig Wörl, an incarcerated German who lived most of his life as a political prisoner in a concentration camp.

Ludwig Wörl was born in 1906 and died at the age of 61 in 1967. Initially, Wörl was arrested by the Secret State Police, otherwise known as the Gestapo, for his attempts in raising awareness about how horrifying the conditions and system of the concentration camps were. In his attempt, he distributed an illegal document for the Jews to warn them about the camps. As punishment for his actions, Wörl was then sent to a detention cell in Dachau for nine months.

After serving nine months at Dachau, Wörl was later assigned to the concentration camp's nursing bay. There he trained to become a medical orderly and learned to care for the ill Jewish prisoners. Because of his success in caring for the ill, Wörl was sent over to Auschwitz with 17 other men to tend to Jewish and German typhus victims. Subsequently, he was appointed as the camp elder of the hospital barracks.

Now appointed as the camp elder in Auschwitz, Wörl insisted that he employ Jewish doctors and nurses, despite it being against the orders of the Schutzstaffel. Wörl also risked unemployment and his own life by wanting to equip the necessary medicines and procedures for treating the sick Jews. He even went as far as forging the selection lists of Jews as well as Jewish children to prevent them from being gassed to death. As a result of disregarding the Schutzstaffel's orders of making living conditions for the Jews as difficult as possible in the camps, Wörl was incarcerated once again in the detention cell.

He was released soon after because of his German nationality, and his seniority; Wörl was then transported to Güntergrube, a labor camp near Auschwitz. In January, 1944, Wörl stood in defense for the suffocating of Jewish victims in a gas chamber. He later went into trial to defend for the children's lives and stop some of the gas killing. Not only that, but Wörl persisted that the Jews had their required shares of food and clothing when necessary. His concern about these Jewish prisoners grew, and he exempted the Jewish nurses he appointed and the Jewish prisoners in the concentration camps so that they wouldn't be inspected and killed by the Schutzstaffel. Wörl made tremendous efforts to help these Jews, such as helping a prisoner and several others with tuberculosis avoid death by the Nazis.

This incident occurred when Wörl made allegations for an ill man by the name of Kopel Boiman, a Polak born in Wolanow, for the sake of keeping Boiman alive. In June of 1944, Kopel Boiman was deported to Auschwitz, just as Wörl did. Boiman was assigned to working in a mine in Güntergrube, which was one of the many individual camps of Auschwitz. After some time working, he became immensely sick with tuberculosis, but was too afraid to say so because he feared of being gassed by the Schutzstaffel. Despite his concerns for others knowing about his illness, Wörl was aware of Boiman's conditions. Wörl willingly admitted Boiman into his hospital headquarters and cared for him over a span of three months. In order to achieve a full recovery in three months, Wörl had to strategically get people in and out of the hospital to make Boiman's presence there reasonable and ordinary to the Schutzstaffel inspectors. Because of this consistent rotation of patients in the hospital, Wörl saved various Jewish and non-Jewish patients' lives from death by noxious gases. In the end, Boiman and 600 other people were saved by Wörl from having their names on the selection list of citizens who would be killed.

These Jews survived and were saved from death because of the courageous actions that were made by Ludwig Wörl. Wörl helped prisoners escape from death marches, stood in their defense in trials, and lied to keep Jewish prisoners from facing suffocating gases. After World War II, the horrendous acts the Nazis in the Holocaust made, thankfully came to an abrupt end. Ultimately, Ludwig Wörl became a righteous gentile, moreover, a hero, to all the Jews that were saved from illness and death.

Works Cited

http://www.yadvashem.org/yv/en/exhibitions/righteous-auschwitz/woerl.asp

http://www.nizkor.org/ftp.cgi/camps/auschwitz/ftp.cgi?camps/auschwitz//worl.aus

https://www.jewishvirtuallibrary.org/jsource/Holocaust/Gestapo.html

http://www.ushmm.org/wlc/en/article.php?ModuleId=10005143

http://www.yadvashem.org/yv/en/exhibitions/righteous-auschwitz/kopel-boiman-testimony.asp

Monterey Trail High School, Elk Grove, CA

Mrs. Tova El-Atrache

Mrs. El-Atrache has been a social science teacher at Monterey Trail High School for the past nine years.

Jay D. Yanos

Jay D. Yanos been teaching social science at the same location for six years.

Captain Gustav Schroeder: One of the Righteous of the Nations

Betty Wang (Co-Winner)

From the time of B.C.E., Jews have been persecuted as being outcasts of the world. They have been accused, dehumanized, and scapegoated for many crises and chaos in their areas in which they lived, one specifically near the end of World War I. In Germany, the Jews were blamed, along with communists and others, of being what was known as "November Criminals," traitors who had led to the downfall of Germany and the armistice of November 11, 1918. (Stewart, 12 – 13). Adolf Hitler was one of Germany's anti-Semitist leaders, who became a chancellor by 1933, after writing his book Mein Kampf, "My Struggle" (Stewart, 16 – 18), impelling the German people to agree with his ideas of the Jews mainly being the problem among the masses. Unjust and excessive Anti-Jewish Laws were made under Hitler, after he was able to persuade the president to pass the Enabling Act, allowing Hitler to pass laws without going through their parliament, the Reichstag (Stewart, 18). Under Hitler's reign, Jews, homosexuals, Roma people (Gypsies), communist, Jehovah's Witnesses, black people, and people with disabilities were persecuted, killed, and deported to ghettos or concentration camps, usually by the SS, or the Schutzstaffel, Hitler's personal police (Stewart, 23). In the Holocaust, there was a plethora of villainous deeds that deems the Holocaust as a dark, malevolent, and melancholy piece of history today. However, there were still heroes, people who were courageous to help the Jews as they could. One in particular was Captain Gustav Schroeder, a German Nazi soldier who manned the S.S. St. Louis, giving passage for 937 Jews that were on board (Boroson, "Wandering Jews."). He deserves the recognition of being one of the righteous because he treated the Jews as human beings, being courteous and caring to their needs.

The voyage of the St. Louis began after the Kristallnacht pogrom of November 9 to 10, 1938, when the Germans accelerated the pace of forced Jewish emigration, along with presenting them to be unfavorable and unimportant towards other countries, being unwilling to give refuge towards them (United States Holocaust Memorial Museum, "Voyage of the St. Louis.") This event caused the Jews to realize and take action upon leaving Germany, as it had become completely unlivable for a Jew. Gustav Schroeder's ship was described as "a German ocean-liner, [with] seven decks that held 400 first-class passengers and 500 tourist class passengers. The cost was high, and first-class passengers had to pay 33 percent more. Of the 937 passengers on the St. Louis, the majority were women. All were Jewish, with just one exception."(Boroson, "Wandering Jews.") Despite the fact that the cost for payment to board the ship was expensive, it did not stop the Jews from trying. Aaron Pozner, for instance, was a passenger who had to buy a ticket through his family obtaining enough money to allow him his chance at freedom, after being released from Dachau, now of the concentration camps, to have been informed of leaving Germany in fourteen days. The Jewish passengers were extremely apprehensive, however, in boarding this ship. They had no idea of the possibilities or consequences that would be in store for them, as they witnessed a "Nazi flag flying above the ship and the picture of Hitler hanging in the social hall did not allay their fears." Nazi Germany terrorized and persecuted Jews, growing further anxiety and suspicion of this German ship. However, their suspicions and worries were all cleared, as Captain Gustav Schroeder had made sure to relay the message to his crew members to treat the passengers as any other, showing compassion and humanity towards them, despite the one crew member who felt disgusted and revolted at such a policy, evoking him to want to cause trouble and problems (Rosenberg, "U.S. Policy During the Holocaust: The Tragedy of S.S. St. Louis.") Captain Schroeder even respected their wishes of putting down the unsettling portraits of Adolf Hitler, despite himself being a Nazi German soldier, set voyage on May 13, 1939, and made their stay on the cruise enjoyable and jovial, feeling liberated in an ironic circumstance. (Krasner, "Voyage Of Freedom Voyage Of Doom.") Ways as to how they were able to enjoy themselves were through good food, movies, swimming pools, and the children creating new friendships and enacting childish pranks, lifting the spirits and moral of the Jewish passengers. (Rosenberg, "U.S. Policy During the Holocaust: The Tragedy of S.S. St. Louis.") During the voyage, a problem rose in terms of the Cuban government. They had enacted on May 5 Decree 937, which had regarded the use of landing permits worthless and requiring new arrivals to obtain written permission from the Cuban secretary of state and of labor, along with a five hundred dollar bond. This caused Captain Schroeder to create a passenger committee on May 23, discussing about their destination, and decided to arrive on Harvana's harbor, hopefully becoming a safe haven for their passengers, albeit stating "I cannot say what will happen when we reach there." As they had arrived to the harbor, feelings of rejoice and celebration risen among the passengers, hope of a bright, beautiful life and an enjoyable, long future awaited them. There was even a trumpet playing "Freut Euch des Lebens," in translation to "Be Joyful About Life," emphasizing the jubilation and exhilaration they were feeling (Krasner, "Voyage Of Freedom Voyage Of Doom."). However, only twenty eight passengers were admitted: twenty two of them were Jewish with valid US visas, and the remaining six were four Spanish citizens and two Cuban nationals with valid entry documents (United States Holocaust Memorial Museum, "Voyage of the St. Louis."). One of the passengers, Max Loewe, felt despair and hopelessness in this situation, realizing how their situation turned horrible on them, attempting suicide about two times, causing Captain Schroeder to form a suicide watch of fifteen men to patrol the decks in two hour shifts, to make sure there would not be another suicide attempt and try his best to remedy the situation to benefit and persuade the Cuban government and the United States to aid them in fleeing to safety. (Krasner, "Voyage Of Freedom Voyage Of Doom.") It was a difficult task, as the Cuban government refused to admit them or to allow them to disembark from the ship. This caused a turn of events to allow the press to unveil the story to millions of reader throughout the world of Cuba's refusal of help, yet only a few

321

journalists and editors suggested that the refugees be admitted into the United States, in response to the US newspapers portraying the plight of the passengers with great sympathy. On May 28, the day after the St. Louis docked in Havanna, Lawrence Berenson, an attorney representing the U.S.-based Jewish Joint Distribution Committee, arrived in Cuba to negotiate on behalf of the St. Louis passengers. His purpose was to persuade Cuban president Bru to admit the passengers into Cuba, but failed in his attempt. Bru had made an offer to admit the passengers for a fee of $435,500 bond, five hundred per passenger, and when Berenson made a counteroffer, Bru rejected the proposal and broke off negotiations, displaying his complete greed of gaining wealth in the Jews' plight of immense need. Passengers tried asking for refuge to another influential figure, Franklin D. Roosevelt, but had refused to take measures into permitting refugees in entering the United States (United States Holocaust Memorial Museum, "Voyage of the St. Louis."). With reluctance, they had to leave the Havana harbor, returning their voyage to Europe. However, Captain Schroeder had planned upon making negotiations with some European countries, who would hopefully take in the Jewish passengers. Miraculously, the JDC were able to find several countries that would take portions of the refugees into safety; 181 could go to Holland, 224 to France, 228 to Great Britain, and 214 to Belgium. (Rosenberg, "U.S. Policy During the Holocaust: The Tragedy of S.S. St. Louis."). However, later on during the World War, Nazi Germany invaded Holland and Belgium, and the refugees who were taken to Great Britain and France were the only ones who were still safe and alive to continue on during the war (Krasner, "Voyage Of Freedom Voyage Of Doom.").

Captain Schroeder was able to make the passengers feel humane and at ease while being on the ship, having the idea and characteristics of a hero, allowing them to have a sort of safe haven in their cruel, oppressed, imprisoning environment of Germany. His specific characteristics of a hero he displays is his compassionate to treat them equally as they deserve to be, because they are human beings like him, and he is able to see that in them, unlike the majority of Nazi Germany who abstain from refuging Jewish people and acknowledging their self-worth. Additionally, his perseverance and inability to allow them to become endangered throughout the whole voyage demonstrates extreme valor and courage as he makes sure his passengers are sent to safety and are not left behind, valuing the lives of his passengers. Captain Gustav Schroeder was rightfully recognized as one of the Righteous Among the Nations because of his ability to have empathy and bravery to support and assist the Jews in their time of need in the Holocaust. It had been exceptionally challenging throughout the voyage, yet he continued on, giving his passengers hope for the future, unwilling to tarnish their small chances that they had. The Cuban government's inability to help felt inconsiderately due to their indifference to the Jews' situation and inability to gain profit from helping them, along with the U.S. being bystanders to their need for the thought of it not seeming to be something that needed to have them become involved in. Despite the unfortunate amount of the passengers that ended up in an unfortunate circumstances, he was still able to save and provided these Jews a sense of humanity, a significant and essential emotion that they were not allowed nor given, being treated as they were inferior beings that could not be considered humans to Nazi Germany, questioning and belittling their self-worth.

Goodness, indifference, evil: they all interconnected to the different sides of the Holocaust. Nazi Germany was a country of all degrees of evil and methods of evil, as Dr. Marks mentioned how they were bullying them, German citizens not doing anything, as bystanders, and that they continued to punish and ridicule them, blaming them and using them as a scapegoat for their country (Dr. Marks, "5 ½ Years Living in Hell). His speech taught me that committing acts of evil, or being the perpetrator, is similar to allowing evil to happen, or being the encourager. The majority of Nazi Germany were unrelenting in terrorizing and annihilating the Jews, creating their lives to be a living hell. Citizens of Nazi Germany usually let them commit these acts, doing nothing about it, abstaining from lending assistance to the Jews, allowing them to continue being treated as they were, being indifferent towards the Jew's situation, and not only the citizens but the United States and Cuban islands also did not partake any action nor shown interest in aiding the Jews, acting as bystanders also. However, there was still goodness during the time of the Holocaust. Captain Gustav Schroeder was one of the Righteous of the Nations, commended and honored as a savior for those Jewish passengers that boarded the S.S. St. Louis, despite being a German soldier, and contributed to their safety and freedom that they longed for. Through Gustav Schroeder, he displayed to us the hope and optimism that can still be shown in the Holocaust, the effort of support and willingness to be of aide to the outcasts, the scapegoats, the inferior beings that had no recognition or self-worth given to them, the people that had been targeted in Germany as the ones that needed to be killed, the disabled, the homosexuals, the Roma people, the blacks, the communists, the Jehovah's Witnesses, and the last but not least of them all, the highly targeted people whose population was extremely diminished, but still growing, the Jews. The Holocaust teaches us the power of scapegoating, the ability to distort the image of a single group to lead an extreme action of genocide, to have no compassion or empathy of the killings of a human being, losing themselves the ability to have humane feelings. However, it also teaches us that heroes such as Gustav Schroeder are real, and to commemorate and celebrate their honorary achievements and actions they took with their integrity to be humane and do the right thing, they aspire us to become aware of all aspects of this tragic event, and how it affects us present and should help shape the future.

Works Cited

Boroson, Warren. "Wandering Jews." The Jewish Standard. The Times of Israel, 4 Dec. 2009. Web. 27 Feb. 2016.

Marks, Dr. Bernard. "5 ½ Years Living in Hell." n.p. Monterey Trail High School, Power Inn Road, CA. 22 February 2016. Guest Lecture

Krasner, Barbara D. "Voyage Of Freedom Voyage Of Doom." American History 49.3 (2014): 54-61. History Reference Center. Web. 23 Feb. 2016.

Rosenberg, Jennifer. "U.S. Policy During the Holocaust: The Tragedy of S.S. St. Louis." Jewish Virtual Library. American-Israeli Cooperative Enterprise, 20 May 2014. Web. 27 Feb. 2016. Stewart, Sheila. Never Again: Survivors of the Holocaust. Pennsylvania: Mason Crest, 2009. Print.

Stewart, Sheila. Never Again: Survivors of the Holocaust. Broomall: Mason Crest, 2009. Print.

United States Holocaust Memorial Museum. "Voyage of the St. Louis." United States Holocaust Memorial Museum. United States Holocaust Memorial Council, 29 Jan. 2016. Web. 27 Feb. 2016.

Hero Amongst Many

Sara Spradley (Co-Winner)

 Hans von Dohnanyi risked his life in order to protect others in less fortunate situations than himself during World War II. Through strategic planning Dohnanyi saved the lives of multiple Jewish people and continued to look after them and his nation as a member of the resistance against Adolf Hitler until his death in 1945. This is why Hans von Dohnanyi is to be considered a hero amongst many.

Hans von Dohnanyi was born on January 1, 1902 in Austria. He continued an average childhood through his parents' divorce and move to Berlin. It was in this move that Dohnanyi met his future brother-in-law and colleague in the resistance against Hitler, Dietrich Bonhoeffer. In the following years Dohnanyi would study law and learn about the imbalance of power in Germany, as well as strengthen his relationship with Bonhoeffer.

Over time Dohnanyi became a well-known in his field as a scholarly lawyer. This lead to Dohnanyi creating connections among men working under Hitler and gained more important roles with politics. By gaining these higher roles, Dohnanyi was given more opportunities to help the resistance. By 1929 Dohnanyi began to work in the Ministry of Justice as a prosecutor. In this ministry Dohnanyi worked under Franz Gurtner, a man well acquainted with Adolf Hitler, but was very against Nazi work. By working under Gunter, Dohnanyi gained knowledge about the Nazis's actions and plans that he would give back to the resistance. Over time, Dohnanyi kept records of Nazi crimes in hope of prosecution after the end of Hitler's dictatorship. Eventually, Dohnanyi's records would help incarcerate multiple officers that had performed harsh acts against Jewish people such as persecution of churches, sterilization, and torture in concentration camps. But, these records would lead to Dohnanyi's downfall.

Through his work in the Ministry, Dohnanyi gained more knowledge of Hitler's plans to conquer new areas, especially Czechoslovakia. Against this idea, Dohnanyi meet with Wehrmacht officers in hopes of stopping Hitler's imperialism and to rid him as dictator. He also became acquainted with more people in the resistance such as, Colonel Hans Oster, who worked in military intelligence, and Admiral Wilhelm Canaris, head of military counterintelligence or Abwehr, in order to help stop more nations from being conquered. Unfortunately, Czechoslovakia was forced to surrender to Hitler's demands in 1938. This loss lead to thousands of Jewish people being deported to concentration camps, the act in which Dohnanyi and the resistance tried to stop.

Although Czechoslovakia as well as Poland had been imperialized by Hitler's army, Dohnanyi continued to work with the resistance to end these crimes. By 1939 he was promoted by Canaris to deputy, subordinate to Oster, of Abwehr. It was in this promotion that the resistance would grow more powerful and their plans would evolve to become more important. This evolution lead to greater consequences for the Nazi army. Dohnanyi's job in this evolution was to recruit more people that were anti-Nazi and ex-Socialist leaders into the resistance. With these new recruits the resistance began to plan the end of Hitler's reign as dictator with the help of his longtime friend Bonhoeffer.

By 1941 the number of Jewish people as well as people from conquered nation's deaths had drastically increased. With this increase, the resistance grew stronger in order to put an end to this extermination of Jewish people. To help more people survive, the resistance began to deport people that were to be killed or sent to concentration camps to places safer than the areas they were currently in or neutral zones.

With these constant death marches, Dohnanyi and Bonhoeffer made a plan to save 13 Jewish people from being sent to a concentration camp. This plan, called U-7, was created to protect fellow lawyer Friedrich Arnold, his family, children, elderly, and those that were considered crippled and send them to safety in Switzerland because it was a neutral zone.

These people were labeled as Abwehr agents so that they could get to Switzerland safely. In September of 1942, the Jewish people arrived in Switzerland, leaving the Gestapo clueless to their exit from Germany. Even after their escape from deportation, Dohnanyi would continue to look after those he rescued. He consistently funded the survivors so they could live in peace, without fear of being sent into a concentration camp and being killed. This act of kindness towards those less fortunate than himself would eventually lead to his downfall.

After the U-7 plan had taken place, the resistance was stronger than in previous years but, came to a realization that people could not live in peace with Hitler and his army still in control of multiple European nations. Therefore, a plan was made to assassinate Adolf Hitler so that there may finally be peace and more Jewish people would remain safe, no longer living in fear that they will eventually be sentenced to death due to their religion.

By March 1943 the plan to assassinate Hitler, called Operation Flash, was put into action. With the help of other members of the resistance Colonel Henning von Tresckow, Canaris, and Fuhrer a bomb was to be planted on Hitler's plane to his headquarters. The bomb was disguised as two bottles of Cointreau and was to go off while Hitler was mid-flight over Minsk. Unfortunately, the bomb did not go off and Hitler arrived at his headquarters without knowledge that he was supposed to die on his flight. On the 21st of March the resistance had another bombing attempt on Hitler's life was to that was take place but was not accomplished due to a change in Hitler's plans.

Within a month the Gestapo became suspicious of Dohnanyi, his wife Christel, and Bonhoeffer. On April 5, Dohnanyi was arrested while he was in his office as was Bonhoeffer and his wife. They were all sent to separate prisons so they would not have the chance to discuss their stories and how they would react in their separate trials. In these prisons both would be forced to endure the treatment that they had spent multiple years trying to stop.

Dohnanyi was left in solitary confinement in a Lehrter Strasse prison meant for German officers. In this prison, Dohnanyi was threatened, and beaten on a daily basis in order for the Nazis to gain information about the resistance, but he never exposed evidence toward his interactions as an officer in Abwehr or those of any of his colleagues. He was consistently asked questions about any interactions with Jewish people in the U-7 plan, and why he sent wired money to Switzerland.

While he was alone in his cell Dohnanyi wrote coded messages to Bonhoeffer stating his regrets, "That I am responsible for you, Christel, the children, and the parents having to bear this pain, that my beloved wife and you are robbed of freedom." Although he saved the lives of many, Dohnanyi still saw himself in fault for actions out of his control. Dohnanyi did not see himself as the hero he has been proved to be over the years, but simply thought he was to help those less fortunate than himself.

After months of verbal and physical abuse, air raids had hit Dohnanyi while he was in his cell, leaving him with brain a embolism that he ended up surviving. Due to this injury Dohnanyi was put under the control of Ferdinand Sauerbruch in November. Sauerbruch had helped him to remain out of the Gestapo's control while he was slowly recovering from his mental trauma. But, on January 21, 1944, army men captured Dohnanyi and transported him to a military hospital in which his care would be much worse. As Dohnanyi healed, he was rearrested and sent back to prison where he would remain until his trial.

While Dohnanyi and Bonhoeffer were in prison, a final attempt on Hitler's life was made. On July 20, Hitler survived the resistance's attempt to assassinate him. Unlike the previous attempts, the Gestapo found out about the attempt and arrested every person that was connected with it. Colleagues of the men such as Oster and Canaris were arrested, leaving them without help from outside their cells. Unfortunately, this would also harm Dohnanyi's case in trials as the arrested men were known as colleagues of him.

After multiple trials in which Dohnanyi was verbally abused, documents were found to accuse him of treason. The documents found were ones that Dohnanyi collected in order help the resistance and persecute Nazi officers that had committed heinous crimes. With these documents, the Gestapo finally had evidence that Dohnanyi contributed to the resistance and could now send him to trial and prove he was guilty.

Although the Gestapo had given this evidence to Hitler, he continued to send officers to abuse Dohnanyi for a confession out of anger. By February of 1945,

Dohnanyi was being constantly tortured by his officers by order, still he refused to give up evidence that would hurt the resistance and others a part of it like Bonhoeffer and Canaris.

Over time Dohnanyi became less dependent on the resistance to help his case. In a letter to his wife, Dohnanyi wrote "They've discovered everything, absolutely everything. I cannot think who has betrayed us...and when all is said and done, I don't care." He grew to understand the situation he was in and that he could not change his past. He did not regret his decisions to help others and did not care what became of himself for doing such.

Over time, Dohnanyi came to the conclusion that things would get worse before they got any better. It had been shown that the revolution would be the only way to end Hitler's reign as dictator over multiple nations. Due to the constant death Hitler had left behind the nation was moving towards a catastrophe of epic proportions. Dohnanyi saw this and knew that the resistance would be the only way put an end to this reign,

But, by March, Dohnanyi was moved once more due to his paralysis from recent air raids to another military hospital. It was in this hospital that he was granted kinder treatment from his doctor, Albrecht Tietze. Tietze was anti-Nazi, leading him to give Dohnanyi proper treatment rather than the abuse he had previously grown to expect from those in past hospitals. Throughout his stay in this hospital Dohnanyi discussed his past and how he hoped the world would change.

After Hitler was shown the documents Dohnanyi had kept of the Nazi officers, he ordered that people associated with the documents to be executed. The day before his trial Dohnanyi was sedated and during his trial he had little consciousness. Due to this lack of consciousness, Dohnanyi lost the little chance he had in winning his case and was sentenced to death. On April 9 1945 Dohnanyi had to be carried to Sachsenhausen concentration camp to be hung for his crimes of treason. Weeks later Hitler's reign as dictator ended and the concentration camp he was hung at was liberated.

Hans von Dohnanyi lost his life in order to protect others who were worse off than himself. He never saw himself as a hero, but as a person that wanted to protect others more than himself. This was proved through every action he made as a part of the Abwehr in the resistance against Hitler and the Nazis. He went through years of verbal and physical abuse to protect those he cared for. He worked to save others in nations far from his own because he knew the actions being done in his country were horrendous acts of terrorism. If others failed and were captured, he blamed himself for their demise. He helped 13 Jewish people to freedom and supported them until his death. He contributed to assassination attempts on Adolf Hitler in hopes of ended the reign of destruction and death he had left. Although he is not as remembered as others, Dohnanyi contributed majorly in the resistance against Hitler and saved multiple Jewish people's lives. This is why Hans von Dohnanyi is a hero amongst many.

Work Cited

"Another Plot to Kill Hitler Foiled." History.com. A&E Television Networks. Web. 01 Mar. 2016.

Nelson, F. Burton. "Family, Friends & Co-Conspirators." Christian History 10.4 (1991): 18. History Reference Center. Web. 4 Mar. 2016.

"A Legacy of Resistance: Recalling the Life and Struggle of Hans Von Dohnanyi - Boston.com." Boston.com. The New York Times. Web. 01 Mar. 2016.

Sifton, Elizabeth, and Fritz Stern. "The Tragedy of Dietrich Bonhoeffer and Hans Von Dohnanyi." The New York Review of Books. Web. 01 Mar. 2016.

"Press Room." Yad Vashem to Recognize Hans Von Dohnanyi as a Righteous Among the Nations. Web. 01 Mar. 2016

Rolling Hills Middle School, El Dorado, CA

Kristin Cheatham has worked in the Buckeye Union School District for the past 8 years. She has taught 8th grade Language Arts for the past 5 years. Her favorite unit to teach is the Holocaust unit. The students really have a strong emotional connection to the unit, and it is the most meaningful.

Otto Busse

Kyle Leonard (Special Award)

Otto Busse was the youngest of seven brothers, born in a family that consisted of farmers. But instead of following family traditions and becoming a farmer, he became a painter and set up an independent business like many other people in the 1930s. He joined an organization called NADSAP and soon leaving it out of disgust of its anti-Jewish policy, only to rejoin it when the Nazi general pressured him to do so. At the age of 39, Busse was assigned to the police station on the German-Polish border.

At the time, the entire Jewish religion, as well as people related to Jewish people was under fire to say the least. There was a lot of radical downright cruel treatment of the Jewish people. This supposedly was because of twisted Nazi ideals that stated that the German race is a superior one and the Hebrews are "inferior". These accusations were based off of science experiments that never happened and Hitler's personal views. The reason anyone believed in Hitler in the first place was a developed anti-Semitism that was happening in many countries years before Nazis ever came to power. In fact, anti-Semitism dates back hundreds of years before the Nazis. The Nazis were just the people who took advantage of this to take it to new extremes. There were few people who helped anyone the Nazis were after because they had so much power. That is what makes the people who did help them so brave. Because they did what many people were too scared to do, which was to rise above the propaganda that the government was shoving down their ears.

After being assigned to a police station, Otto Busse was discharged and set up a paint workshop in Poland in 1943 where he was supposed to be helping in economic reconstruction by renovating buildings. However, that is when he met two Jewish girls hiding. They were in hiding because at the time, it was very dangerous time to be Jewish. Simply by being a Jew, or being related to a Jew you would be sent to a camp where you were either forced to be a slave or be exterminated. Even if you were not sent to an extermination camp, you were very likely to die because there was so little food and often it was not even nutritional. So many Jews lived in hiding, leaving no trace because if they left a trace and got caught they were as good as dead. Back to Otto who had just found two Jews in hiding, he let them go. Not only did he let them go, but he also joined the Jewish resistance and this is where he earned his place in Righteous Among Nations and made history.

The punishment for rescuing and helping Jewish people during that time was the same as being a Jewish person so by helping those two women alone he was risking a lot. But for Otto Busse this was not enough. He also supplied guns, medicine, and clothing at his own expense. He even used his property to store guns and let people who printed anti-Fascist leaflets do their work there. He even attended a partisan meeting in the woods. Unfortunately he could not help them because he had been drafted at the last minute into military service and was captured by Russia as a prisoner of war for five years in a POW camp in Kiev. After his release, he wanted to go back and meet the two women he found years ago. Thankfully, the Jewish organization located Chasia Bilizka and Chaika Grossman so he was able to reconnect with them. He tended to spend prolonged visits in Germany where the girls lived and he did this often until he died in Germany in 1980.

I think anyone who contributed to helping the Jewish people who were being assaulted at the time was a very brave person. If they got caught they suffered the same fate as the people in the Nazi camps. It was the equivalent of being a most wanted criminal on the run except they did their actions out of compassion and trust whereas the average criminal performs their actions out of greed and they did not face a camp where they would most likely die. The average criminal faces a prison with enough food and shelter. And let's not forget that this individual hid guns and Jewish resistance contributors in his apartment. He probably would have continued doing so if he had not been drafted to the military.

One of the truly terrible things about the Holocaust is just how well it worked. Before the Holocaust there were 564,000 Jews in Germany and after, their numbers were reduced to 30,000. They killed 6 million Jews not including people who were not Jewish in about six-and-a-half years.

It is good though that about 300,000 Jews escaped to other countries while they were permitted to through. But numbers do not lie, and if you remember before, there was 6 million more Jews before the Holocaust and that is one of the saddest things ever. Especially when you consider that we did not do much about it until it was way too late.

Work Cites
Busse Family ttps://answers.yahoo.com/question/index?qid=
20091217194734AAA2vQL

Georg Ferdinand Duckwitz, the Nazi Who Saved Jews

Aidan Miesner (Special Award)

I had the pleasure of doing research on Georg Ferdinand Duckwitz as part of an essay competition in honor of Eleanor Marks. To honor his wife, Bernard Marks started this local essay competition as a remembrance to those who lost their lives, lost family or aided in the survival of the Jewish people targeted by Hitler and the Nazi Party. Bernard Marks is a Holocaust survivor himself and I was fortunate enough to have the opportunity to listen to his story at my school. His story and message was a strong one about survival. His story lead to my wanting to take the time to learn about one of the people who helped aid the Jewish people during this time. Georg Ferdinand Duckwitz was an honored recipient of the Righteous Among the Nations award. This award is an official title awarded by Yad Vashem on behalf of the State of Israel and the Jewish people to non-Jews who risked their lives to save Jews during the Holocaust. George was the recipient of this award on March 21, 1971. I will share with you some extraordinary facts about Mr. Duckwitz's life and the risks he took to help the Jewish people.

Georg Ferdinand Duckwitz was born in 1904 in Bremen, Germany. After college, he became a businessman in Scandinavian countries as a coffee trader. He then joined the Nazi Party in 1932. He first worked for Alfred Rosenberg's foreign policy office but eventually left to work for the Hamburg America Line shipping company. In 1939, the Third Reich assigned him to the German embassy in Copenhagen. He was assigned as a maritime attache when the Nazi occupied Denmark. An attache is a person on the staff of an ambassador, typically with a specialized area of responsibility.

While he was working as an attache, Duckwitz worked with Werner Best, who at the time was in charge of the Gestapo. That is when he learned that the Nazis were planning on shipping all of the Danish Jews to concentration camps in Germany. Duckwitz knew this wasn't right and felt a deep need to do something to stop this. He went to Germany, to Hitler's chancellery to protest the deportation of the Jews to death camps. They refused his request because it was against their policies. This did not stop him. He took action by secretly communicating with the Swedish prime minister. He persuaded the prime minister to allow Jewish refugees into Sweden so they could escape the Nazis. He then notified Hans Hedtoft, a Danish politician about the deportation of the Danish Jews. Hedtoft in turn notified senior rabbis of the plan to escort the Jews into Sweden. This allowed the rabbis to notify the community and Jews of the escape plan. Due to Duckwitz's alerting of the Nazi plan, everyone in the Denmark community from the Danish families, students of the university, churches, the police, and even King Christian X helped organize the escape of the Jews into Sweden. The Jews were secretly transported to Sweden in the hulls of hundreds of small fishing boats. These small fishing boats transported the Jews across the Oresund Strait to the Swedish side. The escape was a success in part because of Duckwitz's work behind the scenes with the German Navy. At that time the German Navy was patrolling the strait where the boats were crossing with the Jews. Over a three week span Duckwitz and the Danish resistance rounded up and saved the lives of over 6,000 Jews from certain death. The thing that makes this so amazing is that Duckwitz carried out his mission while still working for the Nazi party. This was a huge risk for him.

After Duckwitz finished the mission he returned to his official work as a Nazi. He never revealed what he had done in fear of losing his job or potentially worse. If you helped Jews you could be punished by death. Some of these deaths were field executions. The field executions were meant to set an example and to prevent people from breaking Nazi laws. After the war he returned to working as West Germany's ambassador to

Denmark. He died in 1973 shortly after receiving the Righteous Among the Nations award in 1971.

Georg Ferdinand Duckwitz was an extraordinary German who turned against his own kind to help the Jews. He helped the Danish Jews from going to concentration camps, or being tortured, or even killed. He risked his own life to help them in the process, because if he were to be caught helping Jews he would have been sent to the concentration camps and potentially killed. Duckwitz said "Everyone is obliged to imagine himself in another person's position in a given situation. I do not think that my life is more important than the lives of 7,000 Jews." Even though it is reported that over 6 million Jewish people were killed during the Holocaust, had there not been people like Georg Duckwitz coming to their aid, the numbers would have been much greater. I had such an amazing time learning about this extraordinary man. It is incredible to think this all occurred a mere 76 years ago. I only wish we could have learned from this devastating time but unfortunately it appears that we just keep repeating history, just in different ways. Georg Ferdinand Duckwitz will always be remembered for his actions which helped save 99 percent of the Jews in Denmark. One last extraordinary fact to leave you with was that he was the highest ranking German officer to organize and execute the escape of Jews to this level. His actions are known as one of the most heroic rescues of the Holocaust. A Nazi saving Jews, who would have thought that possible.

Works Cited

www.yadvashem.org/yv/en/righteous/faq.asp

http://listverse.com/2008/11/06/10-people-who-saved-jews-during-world-war-two/

http://gf-duckwitz.weebly.com/background-and-history.html

http://www.ushmm.org/

http://www.capitalpunishmentuk.org/

https://www.facinghistory.org/

Sacramento Charter High School, Sacramento CA

Patrick Durant
Assistant Principal

Born in Sacramento and raised in Tokyo, Japan,
Patrick Durant earned his degree from UC Davis.In
2007, Patrick became a Social Science teacher at
Sacramento Charter High School where he taught
World Geography, World History, U.S. History
and Government and Economics, also coached
Men's Varsity and Women's Varsity Soccer at
Sacramento Charter High School.In 2014 he earned
his Administrative Credential and his Masters degree
from Sacramento State University.

Heroes of the Holocaust Essay

Alianna Doran

 The Holocaust was a disastrous event in the twentieth century in which Adolf Hitler arranged genocide to destroy European Jewry. There were a number of groups of victims in Nazi Germany. Any group which did not conform to the Nazi rules was persecuted. These included people who disagreed with the Nazi regime, such as Gypsies, and different groups that were considered less than human by the Nazis, like the Jews, they were the main target of Hitler's racial state. This resulted in a devastating arrangement of mass murders of Jews. The exact numbers of victims are difficult to know, however it is known that in the region, 6 million Jewish people were murdered, including 1.5 million children.

While the Holocaust was a disastrous event, there were many cases in which people jeopardized their lives and everything else to help the Jews survive. For instance, Theodor and his wife Hildegard Dipper made a positive impact on Max Krakauer and his wife Ines life during the Holocaust. The Jewish family was endangered, and with the help of Theodor and Hildegard Dipper, they were able to survive through the Holocaust. Unlike Max Krakauer and his wife Ines, others were unlikely to find help. Unfortunately they were destroyed during the Holocaust, and because of their help and aid to this Jewish family, Theodor and Hildegard Dipper were seen to society as heroes. Those who helped rescue Jews during the Holocaust presented a lot of difficulties. Individuals willing to help Jews were also in danger, and they had to serve major consequences if they were caught in supporting people in hiding.

A hero is someone who is brave, who is selfless, and idealized for courage. A hero is anyone who can show courage when faced with a problem. A hero is a person who is able to help another in various ways. A person can become a hero by saving someone who is in danger. A hero is someone who is there to help others and gives them strength to get through life's difficulties. A hero can be someone who gave up his or her life so another could live. A hero does not always have to show courage, he can be afraid but still be a hero through his other actions; I believe that heroes don't have to be afraid to engage in a heroic act. Most of the time heroes are scared because they are human just like the rest of us but they feel a moral obligation or something inside of them that tells them to act, regardless if they are scared or not.

As mentioned before, Theodor and Hildegard Dipper were seen as heroes. In 1944, Theodor and Hildegard Dipper made a heroic act, sacrificing their lives and everything they had by letting the Jewish Krakauer family hide in their home, during springtime for three and a half weeks. Without being affected by the fact that Theodor was a German pastor in Reichenbach, he himself was suspected of opposition to the regime. He was sent to the concentration camp for several weeks in 1938, and the Gestapo forbade him to preach in church. In December 1944 and January 1945 the Krakauer

Family returned a second time, and Pastor Dipper helped them find other hiding places. In 1947 Max Krakauer published a memoir, and described the wartime events portraying pastor Dipper as a central figure in their survivor.

Theodor and his wife Hildegard dipper are portrayed as heroes because they had the courage to help the Jewish Krakauer family. Theodor took it upon himself to find places for the Jewish family to stay, and supplied them with food. Though it became more difficult from one week to the next for Theodor, he still managed to take the risk with helping the Jewish family. Without the help of Theodor the Jewish family would not have survived because unlike Theodor himself, several pastors had agreed before to hide the Jewish family, they changed their mind when they thought about the possible consequences of the Jewish family's capture. Theodor risked his life by protecting the Jews, in every way he could, Theodor and Hildegard Dipper are heroes to the Holocaust for the survival of Max and Ines Krakauer.

Works Cited
http://db.yadvashem.org/righteous/family.html?language=en&itemId=6666802
http://holocausthistory.net/#

Oskar Schindler

Aaron Hunter

 How would you feel if you and/or a group of people you look similar to were to be killed by your physical features? The Holocaust was a genocide that took place in Germany in the 1930s. A genocide is the deliberate killing of a large group of people, especially those of a particular ethnic group or nation. This particular genocide was the German Nazis killing and torturing the Jewish people in Germany. The leader of the Nazis was Adolf Hitler. At the time, the leader was named the Fuhrer. Jewish people were told apart from Germans and other people by their noses. Also, everybody in Germany had to have identity papers. Those of Jews were clearly marked. They were to wear the Yellow Star of David on their arm. Jews couldn't really find a loophole in this because if you didn't have your identity papers, you couldn't eat, work, or travel. Also, Germany was a religion-filled country in the 1930s. Everyone knew what religion you were by where you lived and/or what you did for a living. Jews were easy to identify for the most part.

Through the tragic times of the Holocaust, there was a man named Oskar Schindler, and he was a true hero. A hero is usually a person who displays great courage, outstanding achievements or noble qualities. Oskar was born April 28, 1908, and died October 9, 1974. He was also a German industrialist, spy, and a member of the Nazi party. He showed hero qualities by saving over a thousand Jews, risking his life, and showing great courage.

Oskar Schindler showed hero qualities by saving over a thousand Jewish people. During World War II, Oskar continuously risked his life to protect and "In those years, millions of Jews died in the Nazi death camps like Auschwitz, but Schindler's Jews miraculously survived." Schindler had a factory in which he employed 1,750 people, and 1,000 among them were Jews. He outwitted Adolf Hitler and saved all of his Jewish workers. The factory was in Krakow, Poland and was an enamelware factory. Oskar died penniless and did whatever he can to keep his Jews safe. No one laid a finger on any of Oskar's Jews. He treated them like daughters and sons and made sure they stayed safe. "He surfaced from the chaos of madness, and he spent millions bribing and paying off the Nazis to get food and better treatment for his Jews. Nobody was hit at his factory, nobody murdered, and nobody sent to nearby concentration camps like nearby Auschwitz." This showed the significance of Oskar's character and the fact that he did whatever possible to keep his Jews safe, including spend all of his money.

What grabs my attention out of this is one question: What is Oskar's motive? Some people's motives for saving somebody is that the rescuer loves the person they rescued, they know the people very well, or they just have a great heart and take action when they see something wrong. I don't know Oskar's motive, I think he just had a great heart, but he surely did lots to save these Jewish people.

Schindler showed hero qualities by showing great courage. The saving of the first Schindler Jews began in 1939 when he came to Krakow in the beginning of the German invasion. In Krakow, he took over two companies that used to be under Jewish management that dealt with the manufacture and sales of enamel kitchenware products. In one of the businesses, however, Schindler was merely a trustee. Looking more for his own power, he opened up a small enamel shop right outside of Krakow near the Jewish ghetto. Here, he employed mostly Jewish workers. This, in turn, saved them from being deported to labor camps. Then in 1942, Schindler found out through some of his workers that many of the local Krakow Jews were being sent to the brutal Plazow labor camp. This is where Schindler's connections with the German government were so useful. Using his know-how, he convinced the S. S. and the Armaments Administration, who had set up the Plazow labor camp, to set up a portion of the camp in his factory. They agreed, and Schindler took even those unfit and unqualified for work. In conclusion, he spared 900 Jewish lives from this one action. Schindler could've gotten in great trouble by saving all these Jews, Hitler would've probably killed him. He didn't care, though. His main goal was to take care of and save the Jews. "Schindler, aware of the planned action because of his Wehrmacht contacts, had his workers stay at the factory overnight to prevent them coming to any harm.[47] Schindler witnessed the liquidation of the ghetto and was appalled. From that point forward, says Schindler June Sol Urbach, Schindler "changed his mind about the Nazis. He decided to get out and to save as many Jews as he could."[48]"

The last reason I think Schindler showed hero qualities is that he risked his life. Hitler was a powerful man and killed millions in the Holocaust, Schindler could've easily been another person died if Hitler would've found out about his operation. Eleven million people were killed during the Holocaust (1.1 million children). Six million of those victims were Jewish. Other groups targeted by the Nazis were Jehovah's Witnesses, homosexuals, disabled people, and Roma.

No matter what anyone believes, the story of Schindler touched me. I think to myself, would I have the courage to give up my life for a bunch of strangers? Would I give up all of my comforts and riches with nothing in return? I am a bit bewildered by the story. I wish that I knew exactly why he did the things he did. Yet as the old saying goes, "Some things are better left unsaid." I think that is what Schindler believed. He saw no reason to give a why. I think that is why he is a hero. He did not want all the pomp and circumstance. He did not want the hero status. I think he saw no reason to brag about what he had done. Schindler knew what it meant to himself and those that he saved, and that is all that mattered. Saving those lives was his return for giving up all he had. He died without much fanfare. He was bankrupt and his last few years were rough. He gave up everything he owned, literally. Yet it did not matter. He gave an unselfish love, of sorts, to the Jews. Schindler is indeed a hero for many reasons. Most importantly, he helped to save a race of human beings, just like you and me.

WORKS CITED
http://www.oskarschindler.com/

Holocaust Hero

Alaysha Jackson (Runner-Up)

Anastasia Jaklushina was a great hero because she showed kindness, bravery, and gave protection to someone in need. Anastasia had protected and taken a boy whom she never even met before. She had loved and care for the boy like he was her own, and after she found out the secret he was keeping from her she still provided protection. She had played a major role in the young boy's life. Without Anastasia the boy could have possibly been died before she even had chance to live. She had risked her reputation, freedom, and life for a homeless and orphan boy who needed her help. During this time it was a great risk of your life to try and be a hero to those who became less fortunate. To stand out and be different was prohibited but some brave souls who dared to be brave and save a life or to were the real heroes during this time of horror and terror. The fact that during this time of hate there were still good people is what gave humankind the hope that they can make it through this. For this time and moment hope is everything because it gives people the will to fight on. The Holocaust during this time was a fight for survival especially if you did not agree with what the Germans were fight/ standing for. So the fact that there were still some brave souls secretly trying to make up for all the wrongdoing means the most. In this doing a small good deed can measure out a good hand full of bad deeds.

Anastasia Jaklushina was just a normal woman who had been living with her daughter Tamara in a Ukraine work settlement called Shakhtar Sverdlova, in the district of Stalino (today Donets'k District) during the war. Knowing that Anastasia had responsibilities shows how much she had to lose during this time and the fact that she was willing to risk it all shows a lot of bravery and courage just to have shield and protect a boy who she had never met before. Even when she found out that he had lied about his name she did not turn her back on him but became more careful to his surroundings and shielded him more than ever. She had shown compassion and motherly instincts to a boy who had none. Just imagine the dramatic change the family had to go through all for one boy. How she lied to Germans and forced her family to keep a major secret. When the German citizens became suspect of the boy right around when she had found out that he lied about his name is the time where she get really overprotective of him. She ended up changing her whole life style to keep him safe. Anastasia had put him in the basement, kept the window curtains closed, and bought enough food for him for three years. She had taken him in and treated him like her own. The Jaklushia family made sure Emil was safe with no injuries and was very healthy until liberation day. But even after then she help him find his mom and kept in touch with them until the day she died. That is why I believe Anastasia Jaklushina was a true hero in my eyes. Anastasia never once was selfish and after liberation day she helped Emil to find his mom. When she could have told him to give up on his mom and stay wither because he had become so close to the family it felt like he was he own. Another possible outcome of where she could have been selfish is when they actually found his mom she could have told him how his mom left him behind and that means she did not love him as much as she did. But she did none of this she was always loving and giving him nothing but positive vibes. So many things Anastasia could have done wrong like could've made Emil her work slave or worse could have turned him over but she did not. Anastasia was a good person deep down and on the outside. She was beyond every characteristic of being a hero.

Emil Shilin also known as Yemelyan Savchenko (the boy) one day arrived at Anastasia Jaklushina's house as a complete stranger asking/begging for food. At this time the boy was around eleven and an orphan with adequate clothing on. His name is Yemelyan Savchenko and he had come to her house on November 1, 1941 after the Germans occupied the area and she took him for one or two days which turned out to turn into months; he had fit into the family so while they soon felt that he should stay with them. Soon later the neighbors became really interested in the boy and began to spread rumors that the boy was a Jew. Just imagine being that young, lost, and scared during this time. Yemelyan was doing all that was necessary to survive; AND having to fight for his life at such a young age was smart and created a plan to stay alive. Later on come to find out he had lied about his name was not Yemelyan Savchenko, but in fact his real name is Emil Shilin. Anastasia Jaklushina had already taken in the boy and killed off any and all possible rumors of his true identity that may have occurred while she was protecting him and doing her best to make sure his dangerous secret stays a secret until its safety is a guarantee. Emil most likely knew nothing of the rumors the only major thing that was most likely on his mind was how most of his family had been taking from him including his mother, but also is he going to live to one day find her. Anastasia had shielded him by being aware of what was going on not only around him but herself and her family to make sure they were all safe and secured. Emil was left in a world full of hate until Anastasia and her family came to help guide and make sure he was secured from the bitter hatred. Emil is lucky to have come across someone like her but during the process he took a huge gamble. Both made choices that not many have the courage to make with so much at risk. During the time of the Germans/Nazis every decision you made was LIFE or DEATH situations. Everything was black or white, good or bad, or even bad or worst. There was never a gray or middle or even an Ohkay, but Emil was one of the ones who got close to that common ground all because of the help of the Jaklushina Family helped him to get there. Emil's life could have turned out so differently but in the end it all worked out for him. He was able to stay healthy and find his mother in the end all because of he put his trust into a family he met for the first time but since then they had never let him down and helped him to make it through the toughest time in his life that he would have to go through.

Emil's mom was another example of heroism. She sacrificed a lot almost her life to make sure her son could possibly get away and hide. I couldn't imagine that this woman nor any mom after eleven years would abandon her child and then soon after some years come back in their life after a family already was looking after him and had to very good care of him considering the circumstances. Really could you imagine being a single mom during in the middle of a war where your people/race are being slaughtered like mangy, DISGUSTING, disgraced animals, but also having to look after a child and yourself in survivor mode. The possibilities of how Emil and his mom how they were separated is the terror that might have traumatized her for a long time. Thinking of some of the possibilities it had to be when the Germans were occupying the area and the Germans probably grabbed his mom while she told him to hide. In these moments I believe her motherly instincts kicked and all she could think of is her son's safety. The thoughts the little eleven year old boy probably had going through his head was will this be the last time I ever see my son. If that is what had occurred she probably ended up in a concentration "work" camp. This woman went through hell and back to survive for her son in the hope that one day she would soon find him again. A mom should never have to go through the nightmare of worrying or even wondering if her child is safe and did she do the best possible outcome for her child's safety. The horror her mind, soul, and body went through during this time is something that can never be forgiven. So in this moment Emil's mom stands as another hero of the Holocaust for having to make the toughest decisions that not only affected her but her son too. Over a million people were dying by the hours, soon to be turned into minutes and seconds but yet they were able to survive. Back then you were better off finding ten dead bodies on the streets than it was for someone to survive let alone a full family that involved in treason like facilities and a Jewish family that was being hunted down like wild animals to survive.

I just want to say thank you to Yad Vashem for introducing me to Anastasia's rescue story and showing me the meaning of true bravery. Hope is the factor that keeps everyone alive. Hope causes people to fight for their rights to be free. Hope can open the minds of those who are filled with fear, doubt, and discouragement. HOPE is in you it is that drive that pushes you to make your dreams become a reality. Like hope TRUST played a major role in this story of survival. Emil had to trust he was safe with Anastasia but also trust that his mother was doing the right thing and will come back and get him. Anastasia had to trust that Emil would follow her every instruction. While Emil's mom had to trust herself and trust that her son made the right decisions while she is forced to be absent. She also has to trust that he will still love her and few her no different when she comes back into his life. Trust is a huge factor in a time of crisis because you look for someone to lean on and guide you but trust that they aren't leading you into the ground. The woman in this story line were crazy courageous. They had shown so much compassion, love, and mental strength that it sets a certain bar they have set for a lot of mothers not just during this time but throughout the whole timeline. Parents have a strange way of making sure their children does not get harmed by the big bad world; but soon notice that the children have to find their way and that they cannot shield or protect them from the world but only prepare them for the worst to come. Warning is key because now that the child knows possible outcomes to look out for hopefully they can make the better decision from the parents counseling. There are so many things I have learned from this experience. The Holocaust has change my idea of heroes that you see in the comic books. The people in they are so extraordinary and unrealistic they sale the best fantasies of false hope. Until you time travel through history and look back on the "average" lives and see exactly how they save lives, start revolutions, create all new nations. Everyone has a hero in them you just have to look deep down in yourself and make the decisions to help others see a brighter future in themselves even if they cannot see it at the moment. JUST HAVE TO TRUST, BELIEVE, AND HOPE EVERYTHING TURNS OUT OKAY IN THE END!

Heroes of the Holocaust:-Emil Beer

Destiny Burney (Co-Winner)

Murder...that is what comes to mind for many people when they think about the Holocaust. In January of 1933 Nazis entered Germany believing that Germans were "racially superior" (Wittingham, 2011). Six million Jews were murdered by the Nazi regime, and this terrible act was named the Holocaust, which is of Greek origin meaning "sacrifice by fire" (Wittingham, 2011). The most memorable person of the Holocaust was Adolf Hitler; leader of the Nazi Party during the Third Reich Chancellor of Germany (Bhattacharyya, 2015). He was the dictator and central figure during both the Holocaust and World War II. Although this was a difficult time for most, there were influential people that showed great bravery and displayed heroism. One of those heroes was Emil Beer. Emil is a hero for a few reasons; he helped a Jewish boy Rudi survive a year longer, helped Rudi's Jewish parents survive and supplied them with food, and provided Rudi with a document showing that he had a true Christian education in an effort to give him a better life. Beer also tried to prevent Rudi and his parents from being victims of slave labor and concentration camps. This paper will discuss Emil's background and story; the paper will also go into detail about slave labor and concentration camps to fully understand the heroism that Beer had.

Emil Beer owned a mechanical weaving mill factory that he sold to Joseph Eichler, a Reich German who was part of the Nazi program, for much less than the property was worth because the property was clearly under duress (Dean, 2007). Upon his return from exile after war, he faced a battle with the state over his property, and he finally succeeded in having his rights recognized by the district court which ordered the property back to the original owner (Dean, 2007). The Communist Party of Czechoslovakia reacted immediately and workers in the district went on strike, blocking Beer's return from the outset (Dean, 2007). On March 5th, the day that the factory was to be handed to him, blacksmith Frantisek Havlas grabbed Beer by the throat and threatened him because he and the others felt that Beer had revealed himself as to being a Germanizer and an asocial employer (Dean, 2007). A Germanizer is when a person tries to cause or adopt German customs. None of this was true though. Beer only attended Czech schools, was a member of the Bohemian national society, had financially supported Czech minorities, and during the war had openly declared his affiliation with the Czechoslovak community in London (Dean, 2007). Emil Beer was a Hero.

Emil Beer was from Berg near Koln and a member of the Confessing Church. In 1933, Beer was the only landlord who was willing to offer accommodations to a Jewish family from Koln that had fled from the Nazi persecution rise (2016). The family returned after a year and their son Rudi converted to Christianity along with Beer's daughter Edelgard (2016). They were engaged but Rudi called it off after the Nuremberg Laws made it illegal, but continued to see her. Beer gave Rudi a certificate stating that Rudi had received proper Christian education and was a true Christian (2016). Beer was brave to help him and risked his own life to do it.

Near the end of 1941, the Gestapo was looking for Rudi, who was staying with Beer in Berg. Beer hid Rudi from the police and moved him to a different location within the village (2016). This saved Rudi for a while until he was deported in 1942 where he was then murdered by the Nazis. Beer would also secretly travel to Koln where he would comfort and help Jews who were being held under guard in special assembly camps (2016). He remained in close contact with Rudi's parents and would supply them with food-ration cards that were very hard to get and saved Rudi's parents from starvation. On March 12, 1998 Emil Beer was recognized as Righteous among the Nations.

One of the things that Emil Beer was trying to protect Rudi and his parents from was slave labor. The slave laborers consisted of Jewish workers that were transported from their home states to a variety of concentration camps that were ran by the Nazis

(Lippman & Wilson, 2007). German corporations purposely made use of slave labor because it provided a great return to the investors of the corporations (Lippman & Wilson, 2007). The Nazis made millions of Jews and other groups perform forced labor in conditions that were unbearable at times inside detention facilities and concentration camps (United States Holocaust Memorial Museum). The people who were forced to work often were not rested, had minimal clothing, and had to perform duties that were unnecessary and humiliating (United States Holocaust Memorial Museum). Slave labor also existed outside of concentration camps by the Nazis, and as early as 1937 the Nazis increased the exploitation of the forced labor for economic gain to meet the desperate labor shortages (United States Holocaust Memorial Museum). By the end of that year the majority of the Jewish male population in Germany was required to perform slave labor for various government agencies (United States Holocaust Memorial Museum).

The Jews who were sent to work as slave laborers and were not killed right away because they were strong enough to work, became weak quickly because of the conditions that they worked in. Emil Beer sharing the ration food card with the family saved their life. If they would have been sent to work as a slave laborer they would have lived on starvation ratios. A daily ration of one piece of black bread, a small slab of butter, and a small cup of something that was supposed to be soup is all that the workers would receive each day (Slave labor, 1969). It was not uncommon for something to be floating in the soup. It was also not uncommon for a master to have one of their German Shepherds rip apart a human body to pieces just for fun. To know of such tragedy occurring, Emil Beer could not fathom subjecting people that he cared for to so much pain and suffering.

Concentration camps were a basic feature of the control in Nazi Germany between 1933 and 1945 and occurred right after Hitler and the Nazi Party was given control over the police. (Cagrisi, 2000). They are called concentration camps because the people were physically "concentrated" in one location (United States Holocaust Memorial Museum). The first camp in Germany was established shortly after Hitler was appointed as chancellor in January of 1933. Concentration camps are inhuman forced labor, harsh mistreatment, hunger, disease, and unexpected executions that were a sure way to die or be killed. In the extermination camps more than three million Jews were murdered (Cagrisi, 2000). Typically, concentration camps consist of barbed wire barracks, guards and watchtowers. The Jews had slept in bunk "beds" and worked at an average of twelve hours a day. There were a total of twenty-two concentration camps and they all had killing methods. The most common use of their "killing method" was the gas chambers, they were blocked up in the chambers while the personnel closed the doors then they would release the gas (Cagrisi, 2000). They would also use what they call gas trucks. Jews would be driven by the truck then suffocated with exhaust fumes. They had many methods but I think the ones the guards used the most was shooting. There was a shooting event November 1943, called "harvest feast." In the camps men were separated from women. The first to be gassed were men, the women had their hair cut off before they went to their death. If the older women or children were unable to work they would be executed right then and there but either a shooting or gas suffocation (Cagrisi, 2000). Gas and guns were not the only death strategy as many Jews died from diseases. Many Jews got very ill and they knew the doctors could not help because by the time they got to the doctors it had been too late (Cagrisi, 2000). This type of chaos is what Emil Beer was protecting Rudi and his parents from.

Jews were told coming into the camps that they were going to get jobs and better living conditions, and the Jews brought all their most valuable belongings just for it to get destroyed. The children were taken away from their parents while the parents had to work and do slave labor. They got fed little pieces of bread on the good days if they were lucky, but most days it would be one piece (Cagrisi, 2000). These camps were a big turn for Jews as they had nothing really to begin with, then Hitler made it worse for them. Hitler was looked at as a good person and people looked up to him, for the good. Meanwhile he murdered and enslaved Jews. Between 1933 and 1945, Nazi Germany and its allies established more than 40,000 camps and other incarceration sites; and these sites were used for mass murders, forced labor, and detention facilities for enemies of the state (United States Holocaust Memorial Museum). Most of the prisoners that were help at these locations were: People accused of "asocial" behavior, Gypsies, German communists, and Jehovah's Witnesses (United States Holocaust Memorial Museum). People that survived these camps are lucky but also traumatized. Going through and witnessing all of what they saw would be hard. Being a survivor from that is even more than lucky. Concentration camps were a major turn in Jewish lives and a major part of the Holocaust.

To conclude, the murderous time during the Holocaust responsible for the death of a million Jews killed by the Nazis and led by the most memorable person of the Holocaust, Adolf Hitler was one of the most devastating times in history. Although it was a difficult time for most people alive during that time, there were influential people that showed great bravery and displayed heroism such as Emil Beer. This paper talks about Hero of the Holocaust Emil and how he became a hero by helping a boy Rudi survive a year longer, helping Rudi's parents survive and supplying them with food, while also providing Rudi with a document showing that he had a true Christian education. With the terrible acts of slave labor, and monstrous concentration camps, Beer's efforts tried to prevent Rudi and his parents from being victims of such tragedy. His efforts worked for a while and earned him the rightful title of being a Hero of the Holocaust.

The Heroes of the Holocaust are so significant because they stood up for what they knew was the right thing. Sometimes things happen and just because it is what the majority of the people are doing; it does not mean that it is the right thing to do. The courageous heroes stood up against Hitler and the Nazi Regime, risking their lives for the lives of others during one of the darkest periods in history.

There is a lot that can be learned from Emil Beer and the other Heroes of the Holocaust. The first thing that can be learned is to always do the right thing and to have the confidence and courage to do it. The second thing that can be learned is to be grateful

344

that we live in today's world; that although still displays forms of slavery, but not in the extreme devastating circumstances as during the Holocaust. Lastly, to be learned from such extraordinary people is to help implement change. If we know right from wrong, and we have the power of influence...then there is no reason why we cannot all be heroes in our own right. We do not have to be living during the Holocaust to make a difference or save a life. We all possess the same power as Emil Beer, and all have the opportunity for our stories to be told one day also.

References

Bhattacharyya, K. (2015). Adolf Hitler and his parkinsonism.Annals of Indian Academy of Neurology,18(4) doi:http://dx.doi.org/10.4103/0972-2327.169536

Cagrisi, B. V. (2000). The killing machine. Holocaust a call to conscience, Retrieved fromhttp://www.projetaladin.org

Dean, M. (2007). Robbery and restitution. : Berghahn Books.

Lippman, E. J., & Wilson, P. A. (2007). The culpability of accounting in perpetuating the holocaust. Accounting History, 12(3), 283. Retrieved from http://search.proquest.com/docview/214898712?accountid=458

Slave labor. (1969, December). Holocaust studies, 9(13), Retrieved from http://www.aish.com/ho/o/48961881.html

The righteous among the nations. (2016). Yad vashem, Retrieved from http://db.yadvashem.org/righteous/family.html?language=en&itemId=40 13858

United States Holocaust Memorial Museum. "Introduction to the Holocaust." Holocaust Encyclopedia. www.ushmm.org/wlc/en/article.php?ModuleId=10005143. Accessed on February 24, 2016.

Wittingham, R. (2011). The Holocaust. In A. Andrea, World history encyclopedia. Santa Barbara, CA: ABC-CLIO. Retrieved from http://search.credoreference.com/content/entry/abccliow/the_holocaust/0

Elisabeth Gesslers (Leja)

Dominic Green

The Holocaust was a tragic event in the twentieth century, in which Adolf Hitler organized a genocide to eradicate European Jews. While the Holocaust was a tragic event, there are many cases in which people risked everything to help Jews survive. For instance a hero is someone who is brave, selfless and outgoing. One hero of the Holocaust is Elisabeth Gesslers (Leja), a Polish Catholic woman of ethnic German origin who joined a family as the nanny of the family's three young children, Elek , and Roman. During the Holocaust she saved the children.

When the war started, Elisabeth remain with the Gesslers and help them escape from Beilsko Biala to Lvov, instead of joining her family in safety. Leja assisted Eduard, now a widower with three children. In 1941, Eduard and his son Elek escaped to Hungary, leaving Lili and Roman with Leja. In March of 1942, Leja, Lili and Roman fled Lvov and journeyed to Hungary by going through Carpathian Mountains to join Eduard. Leja sewed her meager valuables into the lining of young Roman's coat, and hired a rickety cart and two guides to take them through the mountains. In the night the group stopped at Gestapo. Leja with her native German successfully convinced the officers that she was hurrying to find a doctor for her sick children. Eventually the group was reunited with Eduard in Budapest.

The approach of the Germans led to mass flight but many had to return to the city when their escape routes were cut off. The German army entered the town on September 3, 1939, and immediately initiated an anti-Jewish reign of terror. On September 4, 1939, the Nazis burned down both synagogues in Bielsko and the H.N. Bialik Jewish cultural home. In the summer of 1940 a ghetto was established in Bielsko. The ghetto was liquidated in June 1942 when the town's remaining Jewish population was deported to the death camp in Auschwitz. Bielsko was amalgamated with Biała in 1950 to form the city of Bielsko-Biała. After the war a few hundred Jews settled in Bielsko-Biała. A children's home for orphans, survivors of the Holocaust, functioned there for a few years. The Jewish Cultural Society ran a club until June 1967 when the Polish government initiated its anti Semitic campaign. After that date almost all the remaining Jews left Poland.

The Auschwitz concentration camp complex was the largest of its kind established by the Nazis. It included three main camps, all three camps used prisoners for forced labor. One of them also functioned for an extended period as a killing center. It is estimated that the SS and police deported at least 1.3 million people to the Auschwitz complex between 1940 and 1945. Like some concentration camps, Auschwitz I had a gas chamber and crematorium. Initially, SS engineers constructed an improvised gas chamber in the basement of the prison block, Block 11.

The Holocaust was the systematic, bureaucratic, state-sponsored persecution and murder of 6 million Jews by the Nazi regime and its collaborators. During the Holocaust there many hero who helped thousands of Jews survive. During the Holocaust they were brave, selfless and outgoing, and these actions saved a lot of people. I think I learn from what they did so that there is not another and if there is another have these same actions.

Citation
Yad Vashem. web. 1/28/2016
United States Holocaust Memorial Museum.web.2/2/2016
Center For Holocaust & Genocide Studies. web. 2/2/2016
The Holocaust : Last We Forget. web. 2/09/2016
Heroes of the Holocaust: The courageous fighters against Hitler's regime.web 2/9/2016

Heroes of the Holocaust

Jazanni Judge

If you were in the Holocaust, do you think you would have survived for long? Why or why not ?The Holocaust was a very sad, unrighteous and evil event that took place in the twentieth century which Adolf Hitler and the Nazi Party set up a killing of many Jewish people and anyone opposing his opinion on things. The Holocaust was such a horrific event, there were still many people who believed in good and risked their lives and the lives of their families to help Jewish families. The Holocaust affected many countries including the Netherlands, Belgium, Luxemburg, France, Denmark, Yugoslavia, Greece and Norway. I would define a hero as risk taking, brave and selfless. Two people who were heroes in my eyes are Anna Jozkiv and Vladimir Jasinski and I am going to gives some details as to why they are heroes. They both have their individual qualities that bring out the "HERO" in the characteristics.

The first person who I believed to be a hero is Anna Jozkiv. Some things I found appealing are "she took a former neighbor's 12-year-old niece back to her home" and put her under a safer environments. Just imagine how scared the 12-year-old girl could have been. That girl didn't let fear affect or stop her from doing good. Anna was brave and selfless for putting her life in the hands of danger. Anna's consequences could have been torture, death, etc. Anna was also "devoted to taking care of that little girl." She took a risk of her life, personal security, and her family's life. This leads to the next person very similar and much of the same qualities.

Another hero is Vladimir Jasinski. He also, like Anna, was selfless, risk taking and brave. One noble act is "painting a huge cross on the front door of their home" to blend in. This is a risk taking quality because if he would Vladmir was caught him as well as his family will face harsh conditions, starvation, and death. Another act he did was "He was caught and cruelly beaten by a Russian guard who suspected him of assisting Jews and given a warning." He showed he was going to stay faithful with his own kind alternately of respecting his rights by what the soldiers instruction him.

They are similar because they both demonstrated by their action by putting someone else's safety and well being above their own. They both show the characteristics of being a hero during this time period of the Holocaust. The difference is Anna didn't experience the tribulations from the Nazi soldiers whereas Vladimir was beaten for being caught and brutally beaten and could have been worse. This could have been the turning point of going against what the soldiers asked of him. Instead he stayed loyal to them by sticking with the same mind set.

In conclusion the Holocaust was a life changing experience to those who survived. If you survived you either obeyed the Nazi soldier's instruction or you didn't get caught doing those opposing actions. One thing that interests me after reading about the Holocaust and some things the survivors that had to do to stay alive is how the majority of the people would keep a very famous musician safe from the enemies like The Pianist. Thanks to heroes like Anna and Vladimir doing those selfless actions, not to many people would have survived. I think if it was for people like these heroes persevering through the tough/ difficult times. Many people may look at the life changing history like it was nothing or it was not that bad. It was worse than anyone could probably picture.

Work Cited Page
http://www.theHolocaustexplained.org/
https://www.google.com/#q=genocide
www.jewishvirtuallibrary.org
www.yadvashem.org

Max Maurer: Hero of the Holocaust This essay needs special review

Jose Mendoza

 Max Maurer was recognized as a hero for saving the lives of 13 Jewish prisoners. Max was brave, wise and optimistic showing a hero characteristics. As a police officer during the Holocaust, Max was entrusted with Jewish prisoners. He disobeyed the SS guard's order to take the prisoners to jail for escaping the death march in Landshut. When Max was ordered to take the prisoners to that jail it meant they would be executed there. The prisoners begged for their lives and Max took the prisoners to a farm owned by one of Max's friends who is also not Jewish and hid the prisoners there for the night. Max was risking his own life to save the lives of 13 Jewish prisoners which was unacceptable for Germans to commit. Max Maurer is a hero because he sacrificed his own life to save 13 others.

As a brave man who was risking his life by not following the SS guard's order by aiding the 13 Jewish escapees. During the Holocaust, saving a Jewish person meant you were asking for your own life to be taken away. It was not allowed to save the life of a Jewish person because getting rid of the Jewish race was the main goal. Max was brave for actually taking the Jews to the farm. Max Maurer was risking his own life for the 13 Jewish prisoners because he knew at that moment that it would be a living hell for the prisoners. Max did not want for the prisoners to be executed because knowing that when he took them to the jail, he did not want to feel guilty of murder. Even though he did not personally kill them, it would be horrific to know that you took them to get killed.

Max Maurer was a wise person for deciding what was right for the prisoners and not for himself. Having to make a decision that does not favor him was a scary situation. While the prisoners were begging for their lives, Max as a police officer tried very hard not to let his emotions get to him. Making a decision that was based on emotions such as what is morally right or wrong is how a police officer should not make a decision.

For example, if a man is shooting at innocent people and the police officers come to protect the people by shooting the man down but in the standoff his brother is there yelling at the police officers to not shoot at his older brother because without him life would be difficult. The police officer's job was to have the man stop shooting at innocent people and have to do anything in their power make it happen. In this example, the police officers shot the man because people were in danger and even though the little brother did not want to lose his brother, the police did their job and protected the citizens. Officer Max Maurer did the opposite of this and let his feelings get to him. That was how the prisoners were able to live. The prisoners did not even bribe Max because everything was taken away from them when first brought to the concentration camps. Max made a wise choice of saving the lives of the 13 Jewish prisoners by providing them with shelter.

Max Maurer was an optimistic person because doing the right thing was what he did. Doing the right thing in a situation like this is what matters the most. The 13 Jewish prisoners lives were saved when Max thought that saving the lives of the escapees were worth dying for. Even though Max knew what would happen to him if the SS guards found out he was illegally transferring prisoners to shelter. Disobeying the SS guard's orders meant that if Max would have been caught he would have been executed right on the spot. What I found interesting was that Max had knew where to hide the prisoners overnight so that he can take them to an area where Jews are not being executed. Also Max's friend who provided the shelter for the prisoners sacrificed his family's and his life to save the lives of the 13 Jewish prisoners. What I wonder is that if anyone in Max's friend family did not want to take in the prisoners because they would lose their lives if someone told the SS Guards. Max did what was right because the odds were in his favor and had a good friend to help him with providing shelter.

Max Maurer as a male police officer helped Josua Lusztig, Moses Kohn, Jancsi-John Weiner and a few other Jewish when they needed it the most because running away from SS Guards in a death march means lives were soon to be taken away. As a police officer, Max was astonished when he was hearing the prisoners beg for their lives. He wondered about his life and what would happen to his family if he spared the lives of the prisoners which was a crime to commit by anyone who is against Adolf Hitler. As the leader of the Nazis Party, he ordered them to exterminate all Jews because he thought the Jews were at fault for losing in World War I. Having to pay to the other countries meant that with a smaller population means that economic stress will not likely happen. All Jews were to be exterminated because everyone, especially Germans, thought that Jews went against Germany and had spies to go back and tell opposing countries during the war what was to be expected . Max had thought that most Jews were already executed and had no personal reason to kill the prisoners. Instead of killing them he spared their lives and provided them with shelter so when the Americans came they would all be liberated just like what they wanted since the beginning of the concentration camps.

After the Jews were driven out of the Ghetto, they were all sent to separate concentration camps and some families were lucky to leave together. What they did not know was that they were soon going to be separated at the concentration camps they were sent to. When only these few words were said by the SS guards, "men to the left, women to the right," families never saw each other again. If Max was there at the concentration camp and saw that Jews were escaping he would have to kill them right on the spot because he was surrounded by other guards. If he would have acted like if nothing was going on he would have been killed because people were escaping the side he was watching. Max Maurer can be seen as a person who not only saved the lives of the prisoners but as a person who does not follow orders when told to for the sake of the lives of others. Max as you can see is a person who not only disobey the orders given to him by the SS Guards but you can also see him as an individual who saw the Holocaust as a sin of life. That was why he chose to spare the lives of the 13 Jewish prisoners.

During the Holocaust, Jews were being exterminated in concentration camps and Max who believed killing was wrong if thre was no purpose for it had thought through the situation and finally came to decision of letting the prisoners live. If the prisoners had not begged for their lives, Max would have not given them a second chance to live. The Jews would have not needed a second chance if it weren't for Hitler but Max considered that if they lived their lives would mean the world to the prisoners because their lives can be taken away from them at any moment. A job of a police officer can be crucial because taking the life of another person means a mom's child will no longer live. It is crucial because it results in a hard decision being made by someone who not know what the effects are going to be on that one person the officer is trying to take down and his family. Max believed that if he let the prisoners live there would be consequences that he and the prisoners would have to face in the near future. What Max was probably thinking was that if all that came in the future would be worth it. That is because he would not have needed to face anything because he was German and the majority of Germans did not have to deal with anything from the SS Guards. As the SS Guards were becoming big in the number of soldiers, it meant that more Jews were more likely to be killed in a matter of time. Max changed this idea the likelihood of a Jew being killed but it was not very big.

Max is a hero of the Holocaust because he is a lifesaver to 13 Jewish prisoners. Saving the lives of these prisoners got Max to be recognized as a hero. The lives of the prisoners was not to throw away but to be given a second chance. A second chance was given to these prisoners because Max believed it was for the best. Instead of being taking the prisoners to jail he gave them shelter so that the Americans can liberate them. After the prisoners were liberated they were the lucky ones to survive the horrible event. The prisoners realized how lucky they were to actually be aided to survive. Max who was a police officer during the time did not want to do what other officers were doing. That was to kill those whom they had to kill in order to survive on their own. Not listening to the SS guard's order means that they were resisting and did not want to view Hitler as a leader. This was a serious problem because more and more people wanted to rescue those who were being executed. Hitler did not want this action to keep on taking place so he had to recruit more soldiers into the army. Those who were helping the Jews were to also be executed without hesitation.

Max was not killed because no one knew about what he did except him and his friend. Max did not want anyone to find out because he knew he was going to die. His action determined that not only can he go against the dictator but also to do the right thing. What was hard to believe was that Max actually helped the prisoners. I can't believe it too. How can one man and his friend be able to save lives of 13 Jews. This was a surprising act and no one thought that during this time, things like this happened.

When the prisoners left the Buchenwald concentration camp to start on the death march the 13 Jewish prisoners escaped. They were trying not to be killed by being shot by an SS guard. They were tired of having to work all day and get fed small portions of food everyday. The rations were not enough and many of the prisoners were dying of starvation. The guards did not care if they died or not because they were going to kill them eventually. Max on the other hand was unlike the SS guards and assisted the prisoners.

The significance of Max's action was to tell about a man who got help from a good friend to save the lives of others. This shows that one can do the right thing when things are not great. One can think different from others and that is okay. During the Holocaust, those who saved lives are now recognized as heroes. Max Maurer is a hero because he saved the lives of 13 Jewish prisoners. By providing them with shelter they were able to live the next day. There would have not been another day for the prisoners but Max was a brave, wise, and optimistic and spared their lives. Today Max is recognized as a hero and has his name imprinted on the Wall Of Honor.

Jewish Leaders

Kierra L. Arafiles (Co-Winner)

Have you ever questioned the position of a hero? Many people think of heroes as people with selfless intentions, play a huge role in the danger, and have a lot of integrity. When in the early 1930's a mass of problems with the Holocaust began to take place for the European Jews. During this time many heroes stood out such as Arnold Alexander, a financial supporter, when trying to free them from the concentration camps, never stopped helping the Jews , and was a person the Jews could trust.

Arnold was a hero in supporting the Jews financially when the Jews were fugitives. Arnold was able to help the Jews because he had a big role in the Jewish community, he was educated in law and public services for the Jews. "When they returned to Nitra, they reestablished themselves thanks to financial assistance from

Arnold" (Yad Vashem.org,Arnold Family) .Arnold helped the Jews even as they were in and out of the concentration camps in those years. Arnold had available supply such as shelter, food, or money for the Jews to use when they needed it and it was given not borrowed. Arnold's input to the help for Jews was the financial support when they were in and out of the camps. Arnold helped Jews in all circumstances because he was a Jew himself. Even as Arnold had his own life at risk he never gave up on the people during his tactics to freeing the Jews. "When Jewish lawyers were forbidden to continue practicing, he continued to employ two Jews in his office and was even fined for doing so," (Yadveshem,1)(2). Arnold was heroic during this time because he was punished for helping the Jews by being placed in the concentration camp himself where he perished. Arnold's had family as well during this time that he had to try to help but didn't feel it was right to leave out anyone.

Alexander Arnold wasn't the only person who helped the Jews in the Holocaust. In the movie The Pianist (2002), we see how the main character, Vladick Szpillman, was helped by the German-chosen Polish police officers, by being taken out of the cattle cars to work at the ghettos. Doing this Vladick was able to live without being in the concentration camps. Even as he was helped to work he still was at risk of being killed, beaten or even taken to the camps. Vladick's decisions while at work in the ghettos was to take down the barriers, clean after the Germans and while doing so he would supply weapons to the Polish on the other side, he would even give out supplies of foods to those without enough. In the pianist the Jews had to endure separation of family, which Vladick did, chosen at any time to die, and lying to survive. Alexander being similar to Vladick endured the same treatments while trying to help Jews but he was actually caught trying to escape to another land.

Alexander was taken to the camps to work where he died but that didn't stop the helping of Jews because they were able to live in Arnold's security homes, and the leftover money he had. Many would say that this act wouldn't necessarily be a heroic thing if he had suffered for the other Jews but just a mistake while doing but Arnold before being separated from the Jews they settled a plan that at any point of danger to go to his home and take any money left for any Jew that needs it.

Also in the movie The boy in the Striped Pajamas (2008) a young boy Bruno discovers a concentration camp were a little boy Shmuel is placed, they become great friends from two different sides. Bruno realizes they aren't supposed to be friends but doesn't stop their relationship. Bruno decides to do a large favor disguising himself as a Jew to look for Shmuel's father in the camp. This was something that questioned the idea of heroism because even as the two boys died while trying to continue the task Bruno wasn't intentional when understanding what actually was going on toward the Jews. The movie The boy in the Striped Pajamas (2008) would be what not to consider as a heroic act for the Jews during the Holocaust. This was similar to Alexander because they both took life risk tasks which did end their lives as an act of helping the Jews. Alexander took a larger extent for the Jews knowing what was happening to them.

Arnold being a person the Jews could trust allowed tasks to be made without as many flaws, at times they were not as successful but never gave up to try. Arnold risked his life to rescue those out of situations. The two then went into hiding in eastern Slovakia (Yadveshem,1). Arnold was able to help a family overcome the atrocious problems happening. "Arnold succeeded in rescuing the Zobels' four-year-old son from the camp and took him to his mother. Arnold got them back together, not allowing things to get any worse. In similarity a princess Sofka Skipwith also experienced a time when she had to do the same." After the first deportation of the Polish Jews, Sofka and Madeleine used their contacts to the resistance movement to arrange getting a number of children out of the camp. They managed to save the life of a Jewish baby "(Yad Vashem,2). Sofka Skipwith was similar to Arnold when being able to rescue children from the concentration camps. They succeeded in the plan but had to risk their lives. This act for the Jewish children was a heroic and life threatening deed that considers them a part in the help for the Jews.

Although we have a general idea of what to consider when titling someone heroic there are many people that do task that are life risking without the title. When saying that Arnold Alexander was a hero he was doing a deed that ended his life, he was able to put a mother and child back together to survive. This was a sacrificing moment that not all would say they would do for another person. Sofka Skipwith would be considered a heroic person because she as well as Arnold rescued a child out of the concentration camps but she was in a different situation where she was a Polish princess which made the situation not as life threatening. Sofka was at an advantage with her resources to getting people away from danger, Arnold was a Jewish man, which would easily get him mistaken as a prisoner in the camps. This is a time where the term hero would be considered on the situation because not all heroes have a story to match.

When telling whether or not a person could be considered a hero you go by the actions that a person takes rather than the words they speak. Arnold Alexander should be considered hero. Arnold Alexander helped Jews financially, never gave up on the Jews while in or out of the concentration camps, and was trustworthy to the Jews. Having these allowed us to understand his heroic acts for the Jews and can consider what he did as a self respecting person.

San Juan High School, Citrus Heights, CA

Shannon Barbarino

I have been teaching at San Juan High School in Citrus Heights for 8 years.

I grew up in Southern California, and attended California State University, Northridge for my BA English degree. Shortly after earning my degree, I moved to Sacramento for the credential program at Sacramento State University, and have been teaching in the area ever since. I enjoy working with high school students, and love it when their curiosity drives their learning. In those moments they truly have the ability to inspire and impress.

Ashley Beach has been teaching English and Drama at San Juan High School for three years. Ashley received her Bachelor's Degree from Cal Poly in San Luis Obispo. Ashley loves her job of working with high school students. She genuinely enjoys seeing them excited about school and learning.

Heroes From Different Walks of Life

Ana Rocio Miranda

Most people think of the Holocaust as a tragic time. In reality, despite the bad things that had happened there were many people who actually helped save the Jews. The rescuers were from different countries, some were even German. Male, female, rich, poor. These heroes came from all kinds of walks of life. According to Hitler's perspective all Jews were worthless and did not deserve to live. He sent Germans to take all Jews and keep them in camps. Some were labor camps and the others were concentration camps. Many people died in those camps; only a handful survived. Some were rescued by other people and some made it out alone. Families got separated and you were lucky if you found a relative. Even though there were many deaths you have to keep in mind those who tried their hardest to help. They had put their own lives at risk for a Jew.

There were many people from Germany and Ukraine who helped Jews survive the Holocaust. Such people were Natalia Zubritskaya and Ivan Moiseyev. She worked as a midwife at a hospital in Zaslav, Kamenets-Podolsk District, today known as Izyaslav, Khmel'nyts'kyy District, with Ivan Moiseyev, the doctor. They were both connected to the Soviet partisans as helping wounded and with the medicine. Natalia Zubritskaya was from Ukraine. Ivan Moiseyev was born and raised in Moldavia, at the time it was part of the Soviet Union.

He was also known as Vanya. Two years in the Soviet army and never did he deny his savior. Ivan Moiseyev was prosecuted for believing in his faith. Tortured and killed as a Christian martyr in 1972 at the age of 20. He had six brothers and one sister all raised by their parent in a Christian home. Finished school in 1968 and got baptized in 1970. He devoted his life to god and read the bible daily. He and his family had to go to an underground Christian church because religion was outlawed. That year he got drafted to serve two years of military training with the Soviet army. He inspired many people there and they became Christians as well. Occasionally she would visit other Jewish families in need and supply basic provisions. Even after the Gestapo suspected the orphanage carried Jews she went on and kept working there. They had taken Pitter for interrogation after their suspicions.

Another hero I would like to honor for putting their lives at risk for another human being despite the race is Olga Fierz. She was from Czech Republic. She was in Praha, Praha Hlavni Mesto, Bohemia, Czechoslovakia during the war. Olga Fierz helped out at an orphanage in the Žižkov quarter of Prague with Přemysl Pitter, the director. In the orphanage there were Jewish children of whom she had helped take care.

During the Holocaust Olga Fierz took care of the Jewish children by supplying shelter, food, and basic goods. She would also go visit the convalescent home in Mýto u Rokycan where they kept other Jewish children and checking on their well-being. She cared and nurtured for these Jewish kids basically like their mother. A heroic act is something you do to help the community or someone else without thinking of yourself or what you get out of it. Being a hero isn't about getting the recognition or being "known" it is about the act that you do for someone other than yourself that makes you a hero. In this case the German and Ukrainians were recognized as heroes due to the fact that they chose to help the Jewish knowing that their lives could end after people find out and yet they rescued them.

Over 6 million people died during the Holocaust and only a handful made it out. There are many more stories from those who got rescued and those who rescued the Jews, from feeding a child to risking your own life to save another.

In 1933 approximately 9 million Jews occupied 21 countries in Europe. During World War II Germany was using those countries from Europe for the military. Two out of every three European Jews was killed by 1945; 1.5 million children were murdered. This number includes more than 1.2 million Jewish children, tens of thousands of Gypsy children and thousands of handicapped children.

Now close your eyes, think about your family having to be in a cart some get separated and some stay together. Imagine having to see guards brutalize your family. Imagine having to go to the restroom in one bucket only, having to go almost two days without food or water. Being a slave for someone you have never meet before. Wondering night and day when you will be free, if that is even a possibility. Knowing that there are hundreds and thousands of Jews gassed, tortured, and beaten to death. Open your eyes now, what do you see? I see my family in this position and I also see many more families. Not only do I think about it every night but it is sad how many elders, handicap, and people with disability were killed just for not being able to be a slave for them. I am so thankful I have my family with me every day. I am so grateful to have many people in my life who care so much about me. I don't know the whole Holocaust story but I do about all the heroes that did good deeds for others.

In honor of all the angels in heaven who look after us now that will save and protect us all. I want to take the time to thank Mr. Marks for coming to San Juan and speaking to us about his survivor story. It was an honor to have him here and all the stories I have heard and read have touched my heart so much. I see the world through different eyes now. Thank you to all the heroes who help them get through that rough time without them the world would have lost so many people.

Thank you to all the heroes from different walks of life.

Works Cited

"11 Facts About the Holocaust." DoSomething.Org. DoSomething.Org. n.d. Web. 25 Feb 2016.

"A Soldier's Higher Allegiance." Living Bulwark. Sword of the Spirit. 2011. Web. 26 Feb 2016.

Gilbert, Martin. The Righteous: The Unsung Heroes of Holocaust. Macmillian. n.d. Web. 26 Feb 2016.

The Holocaust: Crimes, Heroes, and Victims. Louis Bulow. 2015. Web. 26 Feb 2016.

Heroes of the Holocaust

Anthony Isca

 Fritz Heine was born on December 6, 1904 in Hanover, Germany. His father was employed as an organ builder. He was an only child whose mother died of tuberculosis when his father had left to fight in World War I. When his father returned in 1918, his mother's body was turned over to his family. His father remarried. Fritz recalls that his father was a serious worker even though they were very poor. Fritz says his first difficult experience was the loss of his mother. The Heine family had always been supporters of the Social Democrat Party, and followed the Protestant religion. They were very poor, and this left a deep impression on Fritz. He had to attend trade school because the family had no money for high school. He quit going to church because he didn't believe that he was a churchgoer at the age of thirteen. He stated that it was not important in Hanover that people followed other religions and he was sure that he had Jewish friends as well in his childhood.

At the age of 18, Fritz got employed as bank clerk and became active in the Social Democratic Party, (S.P.D.), and by the age of 21 he became the joint secretary of the party. By the age of 25 he had joined the party's executive committee and became an adjunct secretary in Berlin when the SDP needed candidates for office. In 1928 he was recruited for the campaign and information party unit by Hermann Muller and organized the party's propaganda department in 1933.

The S.D.P party was considered a left party, which preceded the Communist Party. After that the S.D.P. became the Liberal Party, then the Catholic's German Missionaries, and after 1923 the party became the Nazis, which was at the other end of the spectrum. Fritz was first secretary of treasury for several years. There were concerns about the rise of the Nazi Party. With 6 million people out of work they became easy prey for brilliant speakers such as Hitler and Goebbels.

Sometime between February and March of 1933, the S.D.P was outlawed and they could no longer work in the open. Before then he helped to publish numerous pamphlets and was chief of propaganda. He relates that in one of the pamphlets an author quoted a passage in the introduction and attributed the quote to the Nazi minister of interior, Goering. However, this was a mistake. The minister went to court to prove himself right. Fritz, who was the chief of propaganda had to go to court to respond to the charges. However, Fritz could not prove that he was not the author of the passage, which misquoted the Nazi minister. Subsequently he received 5 months suspended sentence in 1932.

With the S.D.P. banned altogether, its leaders had to either go underground, abroad or be arrested. Fritz was a very active member in the party and knew he would be a target. Since he was a good skier he brought several dozen of his friends, political and Jewish, over the border on skis to Czechoslovakia. Initially, Fritz was not aware of Hitler's danger. He felt that other Germans were not aware of Hitler's danger either. He pinpointed the period between 1928 and 1930 as the time during which Germans realized Hitler's danger. He spoke of street fights that began occurring. Nazis were provoking and fighting in the street with the public.

He possessed false passports and returned back to Germany between 1933 and 1936 about 10 times to help with the resistance and bring more people out of Germany. Nazis pressed the Czechoslovakian government to also ban the S.D.P. activities and in 1937 were exiled where the party went to Paris to try to continue their work. They were able to smuggle pamphlets back into Germany in toothpaste tubes, which were distributed by resistors and friends. Fritz says that there were 6 secret district secretaries for the S.D.P. around Germany. Four were located in Czechoslovakia. One was located in the Netherlands and one was situated in Denmark. They lived on the frontier of Germany. It was easier for people within Germany to go outside to these people. Most of his friends and himself were expropriated from Germany. They were no longer Germans. They got refugee passports from Czechoslovakia.

In 1941, the Germans stormed Holland, Belgium and then France. After the Germans took over France, many refugees tried to make their way to a "free zone" in southern France. The German airplanes machine-gunned masses of people fleeing, and Fritz was among them. Around the first or second of May, in 1940, he was sent to an internment camp where the French asked them if they would be soldiers without arms. He agreed only to escape the camp, which he was able to do. He escaped 15 miles outside of Paris to build roads for the Petain government. Things worsened which forced him to travel to the south to the free French zone. He did not make it all the way. He reached Marseilles. It was very dangerous there.

It was rumored that he and the others would be extradited to the Nazis. Fritz says he and other S.D.P. members turned to help from friends in New York. The American Federation of Labor was going to assist them. In 1940, 600 American visas were sent. He and other S.D.P. members traveled to Spain, then to Portugal. The "most in danger" got the visas. Fritz says recipients of the visas were not necessarily Jews either. A journalist who spoke out against the Nazis and who was well hated by them was in more danger than a Jewish member of the party. Specifically, they traveled from France over the Pyrenees into Spain, then onto Portugal. In Lisbon, they got a British visa.

In June of 1941 they reached the U.K. They remained there until 1946. In October 1945, he received permission to return to Germany for three days to attend the first conference of the liberated Social Democratic Party. By February 1946, he received a permit to return to Germany for good. In 1943, he went to Algiers at the request of the British government. The British and the Americans defeated the Germans in Algiers. As a result, there were 20,000 to 30,000 German prisoners in Algiers. Fritz's job therefore was to find out the Nazi plan from the prisoners. The camps each held about 4,000 to 5,000 prisoners, who were being supervised by German Nazi officers. Soldiers who said they were not Hitler supporters were mishandled and some were murdered.

Fritz first knew about the situation in the concentration camps in 1933. People died but not directly at the hands of Nazis, but from the conditions imposed upon the people.

A slow death was imposed. He does not remember when the gassing began. His main effort was protecting the party, although he helped some Jews. The main objective of the Rescue Committee was to help those in danger. He and another person helped about 100 to 150 people escape over the course of the war, he estimated that of that number maybe two dozen were Jews. For him his activities centered not so much if one was Jewish or non-Jewish. Fritz stated that the British operated a great intelligence system, although he did not know the particulars of the system.

Yad Vashem awarded Fritz the Righteous Among Nations medal. He was honored for helping Jews out of France and for providing false documents for people to travel as far south as one could go in France. Fritz was glad that the Nazis were dead, or at least some of them were dead. He stated that the Germans did a very "Black Deed." However, he was prepared to return to Germany as soon as the Nazis were out of power. He said as early as 1941-1942 he was ready to return. He had plans for how he would treat the Nazis, rebuild the country, etc. He could not effectuate this until the Nazis were gone. When he did return, he was an executive member of the Social Democratic Party. It consisted of five men and one woman, who was Jewish. He remained in that position until 1958. When he returned he found that Hanover had been completely burned out.

Fritz hoped that the atrocities will be a burden for the generations to come. However, he feared that it will not be. The Holocaust and war activities are only in the books. He felt that the younger generation is not at all interested in history. He warned that we should not be too optimistic about what they, the youth, are learning from the past. His response to, "if Hitler could have happened anywhere," he answered it is hard to say, but one can look at Stalin, who killed many.

He related that he and his wife visited a church in France. There he learned of how some of its followers no longer were believers in God. He talked of 150 people who no longer believed in Catholicism. These people were burned just like the other religions by Nazis. It is the duty of everyone to transport events to the generations about what has happened. It is necessary to prevent any similar drastic, tragic events. Nobody knows the future. We can only hope that experience will teach people not to do such things again. We must do everything in our forces to prevent it. The S.D.P., upon its return, did publish its own papers, which Fritz helped to do. In 1970, Fritz left political life. In 1961, Fritz finally got married. He and his wife knew each other during the war and lived together during and after the war.

Sources:
http://www.westperry.org/cms/lib/PA09000117/Centricity/Domain/422/Germany%20Rescuers%20Packet.pdf - ppg 141 - 145
http://collections.ushmm.org/oh_findingaids/RG-50.012.0037_sum_en.pdf - ppg 1 - 5
http://collections.ushmm.org/search/catalog/irn506520 - 1 - 5
http://db.yadvashem.org/righteous/family.html?language=en&itemId=4015232
http://www.independent.co.uk/news/obituaries/fritz-heine-36172.html

Heroes of the Holocaust: Adolf and Maria Althoff

Carmen Penalva

Adolf Althoff was born in 1913 in Sonsbeck near Dusseldorf. Adolf's father Dominik married Adele Mark and they had eight children: Carola, Sabine, Helene, Franz, Henriette, Minna, Jeannette, and Adolf. His family had their own circus since the 17th century. This means that he was another member of these 300 years circus family. Also his sister Carola, and his brother Franz become a circus directors´. His parents always thought that he was destined to be part of the circus during all his life.

In 1939 Adolf and his sister Helene created their own circus called Circus Geschwister. Their father helped giving them some animals and objects. Afterwards, on his 26th birthday married Maria Von der Gathen. She was part of another famous circus family that were specialized in horse training. She also became a director of the circus.

Their show was a hit between Germans in 1937. His top attraction was a tiger riding on the back of a horse. A couple of years later his sister Helene started her own show, and Adolf and Maria continued as Circus Adolf Althoff. While the Second World War was happening they adopted the sons of Maria's sister. Although they were at war, they continued travelling all over Europe surviving the bombings.

In the summer of 1941, they stopped near Darmstadt in Hesse. Darmstadt is the first city where the Nazis forced Jews to close their stores. While they were there a young girl called Irene Danner visited the circus. Her father and mother were Hans and Alice, and her sister name was Gerda. Her father wasn't Jewish but her mother was. According to the Nazis' laws people who had partial Jewish ancestry since 1750 were called ´mixed´ and considered Jews. This means that Irene, her mother and her sister were Jews. They had a bad time because of discrimination and Irene and Gerda were also expelled from school. Their life changed completely and all their future expectations disappeared.

One day she went to Adolf hoping to have the option to be a part of the circus. By coincidence he had a job for her being a part of the elephants´ show with his wife and with another girl. Later she asked Adolf about the possibility of her mother and her sister working there too, she explained him the reason. He knew that it was dangerous but he wanted to help them. One time he said that circus people don't see difference between races and religions. Shortly after this she fell in love with Peter Storm-Bento who also was a circus artist and they tried to marry but they couldn't because the rules didn't allow them to do it. Later Nazis started to deport Jews to Lublin in Poland. Irene's grandmother didn't have the same fate as Irene did, she was part of those deported people. Adolf was taking care of them during all this time. Irene´s father was sent back home because he was ordered to divorce his Jewish wife but he instead joined his family's existence.

When the Gestapo inspected the circus, they had to hide until it was less dangerous. In some cases a circus worker complained to Adolf that the Jews weren't doing anything there, what Adolf did was dismiss him. The whole circus kept the secret and the war finished with Irene and her family alive.

After the war Adolf and Maria continued travelling and opening their circus in a lot more places of Europe with new and different shows. Unfortunately Carola´s husband died so Adolf decided to join her for a while. He also changed the title of the circus to Circus Friederike Hagenbeck because he thought there were a lot of circuses with the Althoff title. Later he reverted the circus' name again to the initial one, Circus Adolf Althoff, and he closed it in 1965 when it was at its best time.

In 1966 Althoff's son, Franz, was having a great time working in Blackpool but in 1967 all the family went to America because Adolf's show in which his tiger was on the back of the horse had been recognized as The Greatest Show on Earth. When they returned from America the Althoff family created a new circus called Circus Althoff Williams. Franz started with a show that became the first ´containerised´ European circus. This was achieved thanks to the teachings of his father. Although Adolf and Maria had retired, they were also involved with their son´s enterprise. Sometimes they travelled with the show.

Finally, Adolf died the 14 of October in 1998 in his sleep probably because of a heart failure when he was 85 years old. He was in a hospital of Stolberg in Germany.

On January 2, 1995, Yad Vashem recognized Adolf and Maria Althoff as Righteous Among the Nations.

DR. HANS GEORG CALMEYER

Dr. Hans Georg Calmeyer was a German who helped Jews survive the Holocaust. He was born in June 23, 1903 in Osnabruck. Osnabruck is a big city that was bombed extensively during World War II and later reconstructed. He was the son of a judge and he studied Law in different places. His profession was to be a lawyer, a well-known lawyer in his city. He wasn't identified with any political party. He worked privately because he was a self-employed, he only had two employees working with him; one of them was Jewish.

The NSDAP: The National Socialist German workers´ Party known as the Nazi Party was a political party in Germany that fought against the communist uprising. The Nazis´ idea was to unite Germans or those who were physically and intellectually inferior. The leader of this political party was Hitler since 1921. When the power of the party increased in January 1933 they suspected that he was interested in communist intrigues and distrusted him. The reason why they thought this was that he as lawyer had defended communists a lot of times. After that happened, he was seen more and more oriented with the left. Some years later, in May 1940, he arrived in The Netherlands with the invading forces. The German army surrendered after four days. The Netherlands were under German occupation for a long time. In 1945 was finally liberated but they left the city in ruins. Fortunately, when Calmeyer went there he found an acquaintance who offered him the possibility of join a job as administrator.

Aryans were a race considered, for the Nazis, superior to any other and it was only composed of Germans. Now the principal objective for them was to get rid of all those inferior races called alien races who were living there in The Netherlands. They chose a specific office, in which Calmeyer was working, to help in the process. Their essential work was to examine all those cases where it wasn't very clear if they formed part of the Aryans or of the alien races. The people who were examined more were the Jews.

In January 1941 Dutch Jews had the obligation to register with the authorities. At that time the rules were very strict--if you were half or quarter Jews, then you were already included in the list. All those Jews didn't even know why they had to do all of that, they just followed orders. Soon the deportations began and people also began to realize and to understand the significance that had to be written on that list. A lot of people started to go to Calmeyer's office hoping to change their classification, but unfortunately it wasn't so simple. He wanted to help them and he realized that he could do it but he would have to act carefully to avoid suspicions and to get into trouble. He only told his opinion on the deportations and persecutions of Jews and his plans to people who he really trusted. One of the things he did to avoid suspicions was to don't have any kind of relationship with the lawyers who were defending Jews. To start trying to save lives of Jews first he selected his coworkers. Those selected were two lawyers called Dr. G. Wander and J. van Proosdij, a war-invalid, a genealogical researcher, and a man called Henrich Miessen. All of them disagreed with the Nazi regime. The rest of the people who were working in his office were also reliable. Basically, Calmeyer's office was an anti-national-socialist place.

He started thinking about creating a passage for the Jews so they could escape from the German registration trap.

The people who were part of a Jewish community could be considered Jews according to some Germans laws. In this case only the leader was the one who could decide whether that person was Jewish.

In 1941 he said in a memorandum that to belong to a religious community didn't mean having to be religious. He also noted a case in which a man had Jewish grandparents but when he was a kid he had been taken out of the Jewish community. He therefore proposed the change of that, something they approved not realizing that they had created a loophole through which a lot of Jews had the option to survive. Later many Jews began to go to Calmeyer's office and also a lot of petitions started to arrive there.

Some people forged the baptismal certificates because it was something simple for experts familiar with ancient writing. These forgeries were made many times but Calmeyer didn't participate in them.

SS General Raute wanted to appoint a committee in which a Dutch, called Ludo Ten Cate, had to be also a member. During the year, he collected 100,000 cards with information about the Jews. This was dangerous because a lot of the petitions reaching

Calmeyer's office were based especially on the information that Ten Cate had. They suspected him and they demanded him but nothing happened and he continued doing the same things.

Calmeyer also tried to save the mixed marriages. They were safe for a while until the Nazis decided that they also had to be deported.

Finally Calmeyer saved at least 3,000 Jews: He recognized 2026 as half-Jewish and 873 Aryans. This means that 60 percent of the applications were approved.

On March 1992 Hans Calmeyer was recognized as Righteous Among the Nations by Yad Vashem.

OSKAR AND EMILIE SCHINDLER

Oskar was born the 28th of April, 1908 and Emilie was born the 22nd of October, 1909. Both of them were part of a Catholic family. Oskar's father had a factory of agricultural machinery and he was expecting that he would be responsible for it.

The majority of young Germans in his city supported the Nazis. When the war started in 1939, he moved to Cracovia. Cracovia was a city in which a big amount of citizens were Jews. A month later, he took over an old factory where they created cookware for the German army. The factory was working well so in 1942 he enlarged the factory. He needed more workers, he had a total of 800 men and women and 370 of them were Jews.

What differed him from the war profiteers was that he always was a good person with his workers, especially with his Jewish workers. He started to think different when he realized the horrible things Nazis were doing. In that moment the only thing he wanted was to help all Jews he could. When his Jewish workers were threatened by Nazis when they said that they were going to be deported, he told them that he needed all that people to work in the factory or it would be affected. He also forged documents so that Jews could work there and they didn't have to go to the concentration camps. In this way he could keep them alive there. He was arrested several times but he continued trying to save lives. He suggested a commander if he could create a concentration camp next to the factory for his Jewish workers and he accepted. Now he had the possibility of taking care of them and giving them an extra ration.

In the last days of war, Oskar and Emilie hid because they weren't safe there anymore. After the war they lived under continuous threats from former Nazis. They fled to Buenos Aires, Argentina where they worked as farmers and they were supported financially by a Jewish organization. Later, Oskar left Emilie there and he went back to Germany where he lived in poverty. Argentina policemen were guarding her house 24 hours a day to protect her.

In 1962 a tree was planted in their honor in the Avenue of the Righteous Among the Nations at Yad Vashem. Oskar and Emilie were recognized as Righteous Among the Nations in 1993. Finally Oskar died in October 1974, and Emile death was 5 of October, 2001. Both of them died in Germany.

Heroes of the Holocaust

David Shkrobanets

So many people helped Jews survive the Holocaust such as Georg Ferdinand Duckwitz. Georg F. Duckwitz was born in 1904 Germany and had been involved in the international coffee trade before World War II. In 1939 Duckwitz worked in the German embassy in Copenhagen, which helped him get information about the Holocaust. In August 1943 the decision was made to deport the Jews from Denmark to Theresienstadt. When Duckwitz heard of this he flew to Berlin to advocate against the Nazi plan. When the plan failed, he flew to Stockholm to discuss an idea about smuggling the Jews from Danish into Sweden with Prime Minister Hansson.

News about the deportation spread quickly around Denmark. The Danes helped the Jews find places to hide across Sweden. Because of the actions of Duckwitz and the Danish people, almost the whole population of the Danish Jews survived the war. Then after the war, Duckwitz served as the German Ambassador to Denmark.

After all he did to help the Danish Jews survive, Georg Ferdinand Duckwitz passed away when he was 69 in 1973.

Busse Otto another man, Righteous Among the Nations, helped rescue Jews from the Holocaust. Born in Gillandwirszen in East Prussia, Otto was the youngest from seven brothers. He started out a farmer but after a while he went to study to be a master painter. In 1939 he joined the ranks of the NSDAP, but in 1935 he left the party out of revulsion for its anti-Jewish policy, then in June 1939 under pressure of the Kreisleiter he joined again. After the outbreak of war Busse was 38 years old and instead of drafting him into the army he was assigned to a police reserve unit on the German-Polish border.

In March 1943, Busse was discharged from the Gendarmerie, he then went all the way to Bialystok in eastern Poland, where he started a paint workshop. Busse's main task was consisted of renovating hospitals and apartments vacated by Jewish residents. With this task he could employ local Poles and had access to forced Jewish labor. One day Busse was looking for rooms for his labor force, then when he went to check an apartment where two girls were staying. A conversation started that then Busse offered the German-speaking girls secretarial work in his business. He later found out that the two girls, Chasia Bilitzka and Chaika Grossman, were actually Jewish. Because of them Busse first saw the horrors of extermination that the Nazis were doing to the Jews. After thinking about it Busse thought of a way he could help save some of the Jews. Since he was a German employer, he could save some of the imprisoned Jews by claiming them as his workers. It saved the Jews from being included in the transports to the death camps. He eventually became involved in the full ambit of Jewish resistance activity. He obtained pistols for the resistance fighters, gave them warm clothing and medicines, which he paid from his own pocket. He started getting involved with more people who were rescuing the Jews, he let the Jewish underground organization use his apartment as a temporary hiding place for weapons to be delivered to partisans in the woods. Toward the end of 1944, Busse had to leave Bialystok and go back to Germany. He was drafted into military service last-minute, but then captured by the Russians and was held in a POW camp in Kiev for about five years, he was then released from captivity and he returned to the Federal Republic. On June 25, 1968, Yad Vashem recognized Otto Busse as Righteous Among the Nations. Busse became ill in 1978 then died in Germany in 1980.

Another man, Righteous Among the Nations, was Fritz Heine. Born in Hanover in 1904, His mother died when his father was away from home in the war. Early in his career he worked as a clerk, as well as working part-time as an editor of a Hanoverian Sport newspaper.

In 1925, Fritz was 21 years old when he joined the executive committee of the SPD in Berlin as an adjunct secretary. With the Nazi takeover and the SPD getting banned, on June 22 1933, Heine, as well as many others who were the leading members of the SPD, went into exile. He then took charge of the propaganda and publication activities of the SOPADE. The Czech government caved into Nazi pressure and expelled the SOPADE from its territory in 1940, while Heine with the other SPD leaderships who were exile, relocated to Leon Blum's France.

In May 1940, Heine, with most other German immigrants in France, was put in an internment camp and was looking at extradition to Germany. The American Jewish Labor Committee went into the breach, at this juncture, and intervened with President Roosevelt, who gave the commands for the issue of one thousand emergency visitors' visas to the United States. The Jewish Labor Committee compiled lists of persons to be saved and allocated three hundred thousand francs for the purpose. Heine was the youngest member of the SOPADE executive and he spoke both French and English well and because of this he was appointed his liaison and right-hand man.

The Vichy regime was collaborating with Nazi Germany, which made the rescue operation very risky. Many people who did not get French exit visas had to be smuggled over the Pyrenees into Spain, and they even provided some with fake passports. Heine could only remain in France until February 1941, because by then the situation was becoming too uncertain for a German immigrant with his political record. So because of this he traveled a little, first to Lisbon then from there he went to Great Britain. After the war was over he returned to Germany, then he became a member of the new executive committee of the Social Democratic party. Fritz Heine was recognized as Righteous Among the Nations on October 29, 1987.

Peter Friedrich, born in 1889, was also a man righteous among the nations who helped out in the Holocaust. As a socialist and an ardent opponent of the Nazis, he kept Ismar Reich and his mother from August 1943 to the day of the liberation hidden in his cottage on the outskirts of Berlin. Through Friedrich's unmarried daughter Erika the contact was formed. Reich had met her at an apartment where he exchanged/purchased black-market food, and the two young people took to each other instantly. In August 1943, Reich's mother called on Erika, who arranged for her to stay at her parents' cottage on the outskirts of Berlin when Reich was apprehended on the street by the Gestapo. Then the mother's son was soon joined with the mother when he miraculously managed to escape at the last minute before his train arrived in Auschwitz. A double wall was quickly built in the rabbit hutch, which was ideal for both hiding during visits and for keeping warm during winters. In October 1944, Friedrich's daughter Eriks gave birth to a child, which was from a love affair with Reich. After the liberation, Reich was going to leave Germany with his mother for the United States, but Erika would not part from her family and home country at any cost. So from then on they were separated and went their separate ways. Erika died about three years later, which left her child to be raised by his German grandparents. Friedrich died in Berlin in 1967. Peter Friedrich was recognized as Righteous Among the Nations on July 16, 1985.

Apart from all the men who helped the Jews in the Holocaust a woman named Helmrich Donata was also righteous among the nations. Born in 1900, Donata was a mother of four and was married to Major Eberhard Helmrich. Major Helmrich set up an agricultural labor camp near Drohobycz with Jewish inmates as workers in the summer of 1941. In November of 1942, Mrs. Helmrich came for a visit from Berlin. She told her husband there was a shortage of manpower in Germany and had him get forged Ukrainian papers for two Jewish girls who were employed on the farm, which were Susi Bezalel and her younger sister. A few months later a Jewess named Anita Birnbach came to the Helmrich household. This was very risky for a mother of four, because the German police were supposed to have regular control over the Jews. Afraid that one of the children might give up, by accident, that there were Jews with her, Mrs. Helmrich arranged for the Jewish girls to work as housemaids around the neighborhood. She kept looking after the Jewish girls, updating them with what information she had about what was happening in Drohobycz from her husband's letters. When Susi Bezalel got a note that her mother was dead, she looked up to Mrs. Helmrich and started calling her "Mami". On July 7, 1986, Donata Helmrich was recognized as Righteous Among the Nations.

Born 1881, Max Kohl, a German who helped rescue Jews from the Holocaust, was descended from an old tanner family from Thuringia. Continuing the family tradition, Max devoted himself from a young age to the leatherwear industry, then in 1921, founded his own tannery in Burscheid. Because of his excellent qualifications, Kohl in 1941 was posted as the acting manager of a leatherwear factory in Lwow. The factory produced goods for the German army and the SS. The work force mainly consisted of Polish forced-laborer and about 40 Jews. The workers were recruited from the Lwow ghetto to work in the factory for a few months until they were sent to their death in the Belzec camp. In 1942 Cecilia Abraham, the only known Jew who survived the tannery, met Kohl. Kohl wasn't like all the other people that treated the Jews inhumanely, he was treating them humanely, and doing his best to make them have the most favorable working conditions. The kindness he showed to the Jews under his command was so great that the jealous Polish workers gave him a nickname of "Jewish uncle." Every time the SS wanted to get a Jew out of this group, to put them on the death sentence, Kohl would bribe them with tanned hides or leather products and obtain a reprieve. In the spring of 1943, Kohl was commanded to lay off all his Jewish workers he was commanding and to direct them to the Gestapo. Instead of following what they told him, Kohl told the Jews to hide while he himself went to the Gestapo headquarters to arrange a deferment. He got a written permit that allowed him to continue to retain his Jewish worker, he was overjoyed when he returned. This didn't last long, on June 1, 1943, the Lwow ghetto was liquidated. The SS thugs rounded up all the Jews in the factory then a few days later they were all murdered. Abraham herself did not go to work in the factory on that day, she was busy trying to save her mother's life because she was trying to commit suicide. In her desperate time she turned to Kohl for help, who ordered a horse and a cart to drive her and her mother to the ghetto hospital. Because of this Abraham was not present in the factory premises at the time that the Jewish workers were being handed over to the SS and were murdered. With the help of a German acquaintance, Abraham was able to escape. After the war Abraham visited her rescuer in Germany. Max Kohl, on December 16, 1969, was recognized Righteous Among the Nations. Kohl's home town, Burscheid, decided to name a street after him in 1982.

Many people helped Jews during the Holocaust, many people brought hundreds to freedom while others maybe one or two. People who risk their life like this should be recognized more often even if they do only rescue one person's life. The Holocaust can be a great reminder that things happen under people's noses without them even realizing until it's too late. What would you do if you could save a life or two, but risk your own life in the process? Would you do it, even when you might not even be recognized as Righteous Among the Nations?

Works Cited

"Rescue Story; Busse, Otto." YadVashem. Yad Vashem The Holocaust Martyrs' and Heroes' Remembrance Authority, Web. 8 February 2016

"Rescue Story; Heine, Fritz." YadVashem. Yad Vashem The Holocaust Martyrs' and Heroes' Remembrance Authority, Web. 9 February 2016

"Fritz Heine." wikipedia. Wikimedia Foundation, Inc, 4 January 2016. Web. 9 February   2016

"Rescue Story; Friedrich,Peter ." YadVashem. Yad Vashem The Holocaust Martyrs' and Heroes' Remembrance Authority, Web. 15 February 2016

"Rescue Story; Helmrich, Donata." YadVashem. Yad Vashem The Holocaust Martyrs' and Heroes' Remembrance Authority, Web. 15 February 2016

"Rescue Story; Wieth, Irmgard." YadVashem. Yad Vashem The Holocaust Martyrs' and   Heroes' Remembrance Authority, Web. 16 February 2016

Some of the Ukrainians who helped Jews in the Holocaust were:

Emma Lugovskiy

Alabusheva-Brandt, Mariya

Mariya lived in Mariupol, next to a Jewish family, by herself. When the Germans came, Mariya took the Jewish family's daughter, Ira and took care of her. The next day Mariya took Ira back to her parents because her name was on the list of local Jews. While the Germans were taking the Jews, Ira's grandma managed to convince a German guard that Ira wasn't a Jew and the Germans let her stay nearby so they would go double check and see if she was really a Jew or not. But later that night, Ira was able to run back to Mariya's home. While Ira was staying at Mariya's house, a German officer was put into Mariya's home as well for six months. The German believed that Ira was Mariya's daughter. When the officer left, Ira moved to an orphanage under a fake name, and Mariya would visit her once a week to give her food and teach her to behave as a Christian. After the war, Ira's mom came back and found Ira and lived next to Mariya until she passed away. Later on they moved to Israel.

Aleksyuk, Nadezhda

Nadezhda lived alone with her young son in Dibrovka. While the war was going on, a man, Boris Polishchuk, claimed to be an escaped prisoner of the war. He asked if anyone would let him live in their homes and in exchange he would help the villagers out with their work. Nadezhda let him stay at her house, but she didn't know that he was really a Jew who was hiding from the Germans. Whenever the Germans would come to Dibrovka, he would go to the forest to hide. Nadezhda asked him why he would do that and he told her who he really was and that his actual name wasn't Boris but was Gogerman. Nadezhda still provided food and shelter to him even after she found out the truth, and in return, he helped her out with her daily works. After the war, he was reunited with his family but remained in close contact with Nadezhda even though he left to Israel with his family.

Babich, Mariya

During the Holocaust, Mariya took a Jewish baby under her care for four years and after the war, the baby's mother had died but her father was still alive and was very grateful that Mariya spent four years taking care of his daughter. She was the only member of her extended family to survive.

Ambruzhuk and Chemeriskaya Families

The Ambruzhuks' neighbors, Leontiy Gelin and his family, were Jews and were taken away from their homes, and moved into ghettos. Later on, the majority of the Jews in that ghetto were murdered, except some of the stronger ones who were fit to do laborious work. Among those were Leontiy and his son, Boris. Leontiy was able to escape and make it back to Morozovka, where he lived and where the Ambruzhuks lived. He stayed with them for a night, and then moved to the Chemeriskayas' home.

After a few days he moved again to Luchinets with Nina, one of the members of the Chemeriskaya family, and before he left he gave Anna, part of the Ambruzhuk family, a note to pass onto his son, Boris. Anna was able to pass the note to Boris, which she wrapped in clothes as she gave it to him. Later, Boris too was able to escape from the ghetto and moved to the Ambruzhuks' home where he stayed for a week, and later on moved to Chemeriskayas' home. Later on Boris received another note from his father saying it was safe to move to Luchinets, and two days they found each other and moved to a ghetto in Kopaygorod. A little while later, the Chemeriskayas took in Boris's cousin and he too eventually moved to Kopaygorod.

Danilyuk, Leonida

The Leonidas' friend from school, Lusya Gorinshtein, was a Jew and when the Germans occupied Berdichev, the city they lived in, Lusya hid at Danilyuk's home while her mother, Faina Gorinshtein and two sisters moved into a ghetto. In September, many of the Jews living in the ghettos were killed, but Faina was able to hide herself and her children in an attic. Danilyuk and Lusya found them and took them into their home where they hid for three months. Faina was able to get a fake ID that said she was Polish and moved. Faina was a seamstress and told Lusya to go to Berdichev to get one from a friend. When she got there, she went to Danilyuks' home to visit, and they went out for a walk. However they accidently bumped into an old classmate who called the police and told them that there was a Jew in town. Two officers came to the Danilyuks' home to see if there was a Jew but Lusya was not spending the night at the Danilyuks' home and since the officers didn't have enough evidence that there really was a Jew in town, they left the Danilyuks alone and Lusya was able to make it back to her mother.

Datsko, Olga

Olga Datsko lived in Myslowa. Two years after the Germans invaded the area, Olga found a man hiding in her barn. The man asked her if he could stay there. He told her that he was a Jew and that he fled from his camp. His wife was pregnant and was able to avoid getting taken into a ghetto or camp. Michail (the man Olga found in her barn) was planning on escaping and seeing his wife and baby, and Olga let him stay and hide in the barn. When the area was liberated, Michail dressed as a peasant woman just to be safe and so no one would notice he was really a Jew, and made his way to Tarnopol with Olga. When they arrived, they found Michail's wife and daughter, all safe and sound.

Kurdus, Gorpina

Gorpina lived in Chizhovka during the war and Holocaust. One day during the winter, she found Bunya Gokhbarg, a Jew, with her daughter in her barn. Gorpina let them stay at her home, and during the day, they would stay in the barn but when it was nighttime, they went inside her home to stay warm and sleep. Bunya and Ida, Bunyas daughter, would often visit the camps to visit their relatives. One day, when Bunya was making her way back to Chizhovka from visiting someone in the camps, she was followed and murdered. Afterwards, when Ida was coming back to Gorpina's home after a visitation, she too was followed and Gorpina and Ida got arrested, but Gorpina was released because Ida said that Gorpina didn't know that she was staying in her barn. Ida got sent back to a concentration camp, but managed to escape again and hide until liberation happened.

Minkova-Shtepan, Svetlana

Svetlana was a student at Odessa University, and when the war broke out, the university was closed so she had to tutor herself. One day, a girl came up to her and asked her if she could be her roommate. Svetlana agreed, and once they became close, the girl who claimed her name was Olga told her that she was really a Jew and her real name was Yevgeniya Sherman. Before she was hiding in her husband's hospital, but then it became dangerous for her to stay there, so she got a false ID and that was why she really moved in with Svetlana. Yevgeniya would sometimes visit her husband, and also her kids who too were hiding. One time, Yevgeniya was recognized by someone and they said that they wouldn't turn her into the police if Yevgeniya and Svetlana would pay them. For many months, Svetlana and Yevgeniya kept paying the person to keep silent, and they did. Yevgeniya stayed with Svetlana until the war was over, and after it was they stayed close friends.

Nesterenko, Ivan and Kucherenko, Nadezhda

Ivan and Nadezhda lived in apartments next to a Jewish family with three children. When all the Jews were being taken out of their homes, two of the older sons ran away from the city, but the parents and little girl stayed and were taken to the ghettos. One day, when the Jews were being taken to the shooting pits, there was a large crowd of people watching and Raisa, the little girl, was pushed into the crowd by her mother. She didn't know where to go, so she went back to her apartments where she lived before. When she entered, a man saw her and took her into his home to protect her. However, he had a large family himself, and wasn't able to take care of her for too long, so he gave her over to Ivan and Nadezhda so they could take care of her since they didn't have any children in their homes at that time. When the war was over, the little girl met up with her brothers again, but choose to stay with Ivan and Nadezhda. Eventually, they adopted her officially and she lived with them.

Ryabaya, Akulina and Bessmertnaya, Akulina

When the war between the Germans and the USSR broke out, and Jews were put in concentration camps, Ryabaya would come to the fences at the camps and throw over cooked potatoes for the prisoners to eat. She met a family, the Klauz family, in the camp but they were moved to another camp after a while and Ryabaya lost contact with them. In December 1943, Josef was killed by the Germans, and so the rest of the Klauz family fled to Ryabaya's home for protection. They stayed in her attic, but since there were four of them, there wasn't enough food for Ryabaya and her mother and Ryabaya's mother threatened to inform the police on the Jews if they wouldn't leave. The Klauzes moved to Bessmertnaya's home where they stayed until liberation.

Zhurba, Sofya-

Sofiya lived next to a Jewish family, and one day the all disappeared and she didn't know what happened to them for the next few months. Then in November of 1941 she saw Chayim and Fira Knizhnik, two of the children from the Jewish family.

They fled from a camp after their parents were killed, and Sofya took them into her home to hide them. The next morning Chayim was missing and later they found out that he left the house at night and was spotted and killed. Sofya then told Fira to keep quiet and hide in the basement during the day, and only at night come into the house. Later police got information that Sofya was hiding a Jew in her home, but she knew they knew before they came to her home, so she sent Fira to a friend's house until it was safe for Fira to return back to Sofya's home. Fira stayed with Sofya until liberation and since Fira was little when she moved in with Sofya, she thought Sofya was her mother. In 1948 Sofya got married and Fira moved into to live in her aunt's home. Even after that Sofya and Fira stayed in close contact, and Fira still called Sofya her mother.

Ludviga Pukas

Pukas worked as a housekeeper in Frima Sternik, her high school teacher's home. The two were very close, and stayed at Sternik's home even after Pukas had a child. When the war broke out, Sternik's house was burned down and everything in it, including documents and ID's. Pukas got a new ID and registered Sternik's two children as her own. Pukas moved into a new apartment with Sternik, but the neighbors noticed her and she had to move to a ghetto. One day, Sternik tried to escape to her brother's house but got caught and was killed. Another time, someone reported Pukas for hiding Jews, and the police came to see and they found a Jewish woman Pukas was helping, but the woman said Pukas didn't know she was Jewish. They searched her house for any more Jews but didn't realize the children were Jews. After the war was over, the children changed their names back to Sternik but still stayed with her until they finished school. They too, like Fira, referred to Pukas as their mother.

Works Cited

"Ludviga Pukas." Yad Vashem. Yad Vashem The Holocaust Martyrs' and Heros' Remembrance Authority, 2016. Web. 23February, 2016.

"Glushniova FAMILY." Yad Vashem. Yad Vashem The Holocaust Martyrs' and Heros' Remembrance Authority, 2016. Web. 22 February, 2016.

"Ryabaya FAMILY." Yad Vashem. Yad Vashem The Holocaust Martyrs' and Heros' Remembrance Authority, 2016. Web. 22 February, 2016.

"Nesterenko FAMILY." Yad Vashem. Yad Vashem The Holocaust Martyrs' and Heros' Remembrance Authority, 2016. Web. 22 February, 2016.

"Minkova FAMILY." Yad Vashem. Yad Vashem The Holocaust Martyrs' and Heros' Remembrance Authority, 2016. Web. 22 February, 2016.

"Kurdus FAMILY." Yad Vashem. Yad Vashem The Holocaust Martyrs' and Heros' Remembrance Authority, 2016. Web. 22 February, 2016.

"Datsko FAMILY." Yad Vashem. Yad Vashem The Holocaust Martyrs' and Heros' Remembrance Authority, 2016. Web. 22 February, 2016.

"Daniliuk FAMILY." Yad Vashem. Yad Vashem The Holocaust Martyrs' and Heros' Remembrance Authority, 2016. Web. 22 February, 2016.

"Ambruzhuk FAMILY." Yad Vashem. Yad Vashem The Holocaust Martyrs' and Heros' Remembrance Authority, 2016. Web. 22 February, 2016.

"Babich FAMILY." Yad Vashem. Yad Vashem The Holocaust Martyrs' and Heros' Remembrance Authority, 2016. Web. 22 February, 2016.
"Aleksiuk FAMILY." Yad Vashem. Yad Vashem The Holocaust Martyrs' and Heros' Remembrance Authority, 2016. Web. 22 February, 2016.
"Brandt FAMILY." Yad Vashem. Yad Vashem The Holocaust Martyrs' and Heros' Remembrance Authority, 2016. Web. 22 February, 2016.

German Heroes of the Holocaust

Isis Solorzano

 This essay will discuss some people who in wartime had great courage and brotherhood to help other people who perhaps were different, but regardless of religion, culture and language, they helped those people who were being discriminated by government, they risked of being discovered with Jews and that the arrest but more importantly they lost their family.

There were many Germans who helped Jews survive the Holocaust. One such person is Berthold Beitz born in 1913 in Zemmin, Hither Pomerania. He began his career as a banker at the Pommersche Bank in Stralsund and started to work for Shell Oil Company in Hamburg in 1938.

Beitz started to helped to the Jews when he was credited with helping to lead because the re-industrialization of the Ruhr Valley and rebuilding Germany into an industrial power.

Beitz had a big task that was able to designate workers as essential to the war effort, also assigned to supervise the Carpathian Oil Company operating the Boryslaw oil fields. Boryslaw area was a large Jewish population, with many Jews holding position as chemical engineers, laboratory assistants, laborers, and mechanics in the area's oil industry. When the "Invaliden-Aktion" was more calmed, an SS-led evacuation of a Jewish orphanage in Boryslaw, is when Beitz become determined to act to save local Jews. In that moment he was saving some 250 Jewish workers.

Beitz had an important position. He had a notification of the plans and actions of the Nazis against the Jewish community he could prevent to the Jewish community, also had the opportunity to select suitable workers from Jews who were being held at transfer different points for deportation to concentration camps. Beitz saved 250 more people like men, women from the transport train to the Beitz extermination camp by claiming them as professional workers. After taking Jews to the camp with the support of his wife he decided hide more Jews in their home, regardless of discovery, besides risking his family, he was also issued and signed fake job permits for save more Jews from the death camps. It was several days after the extermination of the Jews when Beitz efforts were nearly exposed by a problem when two Jewish girls were arrested on the train to Hungary with forged "Aryan" for permits that had signed false. Beitz survived

372

despite a Gestapo investigation into the incident, but after few months he was drafted into the German army.

In total, Beitz had been credited with saving the lives of 800 Jews. Beitz explained his motivation: "I saw how people shot, how they were lined up in the night, also her motives were not political, they were purely humane, moral motives." I think Beitz had great support for Jews in those times of war, however for people was one of the most prominent people to help.

There were many Germans who helped Jews survive the Holocaust. One such person is Luise Meier, born 13 January 1885 in Porch as Luise Bemm. She was a German housewife. During World War II she helped Jews escape to Switzerland. She married Karl Meier, a merchant; lived with him from 1909 in Soest and had four children. In 1930 the family moved to Cologne to Berlin in 1936. Her husband died in 1942 of stomach cancer, and two of her sons fell in the war.

She began helping Jews after the tragic death of her husband and children. When Luise moved to Berlin was a vibrant city but before Luise Meier, the devout Catholic was allowed them first to make calls from their apartment after Jews owning telephones had been prohibited.

Among the inhabitants belonged to the couple Felix and Herta Perls, with whom the couple Meier was known, and then Luise Meier had aided during her husband's illness. She and others escaped with false papers to Switzerland to but not long for that a Swiss delegate of the International Red Cross was looking Luise Meier in early 1943 with the request on to help other Jews and brought her fake ID documents of Fedora Curth and Ilse francs. In Gottmadingen they met Josef Höfler and his Swiss wife Elise, who henceforth formed a network to help escape. Lotte Kahl reached Switzerland.

Luise Meier and her husband helped 27 total other Jews to flee. Emmi Brandt, who should be brought together with a young girl, with the support of the network in Switzerland, fell in their flight on account of their extensive baggage; both were arrested. Emmi Brandt told the names of the smugglers, they survived the war in the Ravensbrück concentration camp.

Hofler escaped yet to Switzerland before the intended arrest, Josef Hofler and Luise Meier were arrested on 24 May 1944th Luise Meier sat first in singing a, from February 1945 in Stockach. For a conviction, it did not come. In Stockach she was freed on 21 April 1945 by Allied troops, also Josef Hofler survived. She saved 25 Jews.

She can no longer do anything for the Jews that before the war ended Luise Meier spent the rest of their lives and died in Soest 1979.

There were many Germans who helped Jews survive the Holocaust. One such person is Gustav Schröder born Hadersleben, September 27, 1885 who was a sea captain. He was very interested in Embaçada so Schröder began his seagoing career in 1902 at the age of 16, on board the training ship Großherzogin Elisabeth, also Schröder began studying languages as a hobby and eventually became fluent in seven but after a long time Schröder finally reached the position of Captain. He was posted at Calcutta, India, but was interned there as an enemy alien throughout World War I.

When Schröder returned to Germany in 1919, he found himself without a job, due to the forced demilitarization and the limit placed on the number of warships in the German Navy by the Treaty of Versailles. Schröder was hired by the shipping company HAPAG (Hamburg-Amerikanische Packetfahrt-Aktiengesellschaft).In 1935, was promoted to 1st officer on the Hansa. But one year later he became master of the MS Ozeana.

Schroder first thing he did to help the Jews was that with the help of Louis had to do a boat in 1939 from Germany to Cuba carrying 937 German Jewish refugees seeking asylum. The first insisted Schroder was that Jews were treated with respect and allowed them to conduct religious services on board, no matter how this would be viewed unfavorably by the Nazi Party then in power. Unfortunately it was a problem to get to Cuba, the Jews were rejected and so, forcing Schroder to return to Europe with them. But Schröder not remember Dominican Republic had offered him asylum by some officials in Evian Conference in July 1938 were offered to accept 100,000 German Jews. But finally passengers were disembarked in Belgium and all were accepted with gratitude and fraternity by Belgium, France, Holland, and the United Kingdom.

Still in command of the St. Louis, Schröder prepared for another transatlantic voyage, but his passengers were not allowed to board. En route, war was declared on Nazi Germany by both Britain and France. Returning from Bermuda, Schröder evaded a Royal Navy blockade and docked at then neutral Murmansk. After a few years Gustav Schröder died in 1959 at the age of 73.

Works Cited
Beitz, Berthold, Wikipedia, Last edited 24 days ago by Bertuio.
Meier, Luise, Wikipedia,Updated 2 days ago by morning frost.
Schroeder, Gustav,Wikipedia, Last edited 1 month ago by Mpaulson (WMF).

German Heroes of the Holocaust

Jacqueline Roman

The Holocaust was a state-promoted persecution and massacre of 6 million Jews. These tragic executions were caused by the Nazi regime and their helpers. In January 1933, when the Nazis came to power in Germany, they believed they were "racially superior" and that the Jews were less important. They believed that the Jews were a threat to the so called German racial community. The German government also directed other groups of people because of their "racial inferiority". Around 1945, nearly two out of every three European Jews were murdered by the Germans and their collaborators, which was part of the "Final Solution. The Final Solution was the Nazi procedure to kill the Jews of Europe. Even though the Germans wanted to get rid of the Jews there were still Germans risking their lives and money like in the case of Oskar Schindler and other German Heroes of the Holocaust.

There were many brave Germans who helped Jews survive the Holocaust. One such person was Dr. Albert Battel. Albert Battel was born in Klein-Pramsen, Prussian Silesia on January 21st 1891. He studied economics in Munich and Breslaw. Battel then was a German Wehrmacht Army lieutenant and lawyer. The 51-year-old was put in Przemysl in South Poland as the adjutant to the local military commander, Major Max Liedtke. This happened when the SS was preparing to take action against the Jews of Przemysl on July 26, 1942

Dr. Albert Battels actions saved many lives of the Jews from the Nazis. When the SS started to begin their first liquidation against the Jews, Albert demanded that the bridge over the River San to be blocked or he would open fire at them. This bridge was the only way into the Jewish ghetto. Battel evacuated up to a hundred Jews and their families to the local military command. In there they were protected by the Wehrmacht after Dr. Albert Battel saved them from the Nazis.

A hundred Jews were saved by a very brave man, Dr. Albert Battel. He used army trucks to move the Jews from the ghetto to their local military command when he scared away the SS before they got ahold of the Jewish people. The authorities of the SS decided to investigate the army officer. After, Battel made them leave without the Jewish people. Even though Battel was a member of the Nazi Party since May 1933 he was still being investigated. Albert Battel has brought attention to himself before when he was being kind to the Jews. He was also known that he extended a loan to a Jewish colleague before the war. Albert was then unemployed from military service when he was found of heart disease. In his homeland Breslaw he was taken into Volkstrumand and got captured by the Russians. When Battel went back to Germany he was not allowed to practice law according to the denazification court. Dr. Albert Battel's actions of bravery to save the up to a hundred Jews were recognized long after he died. He was recognized as a hero thanks to the Israeli researchers and the lawyer Dr. Zeev Goshen. Yad Vashem recognized Dr. Albert Battel as Righteous Among The Nations 30 years after his death on January 22, 1981.

Oskar Schindler was another Holocaust hero with the help of his wife, Emilie Schindler. Oskar was born on April 28, 1908 in Zwittau. His wife, Emilie Schindler, was born on October 22, 1907. He was born into a middle class family and Oskar Schindler was expected to follow onto the footsteps of his father, which was to be in charge of the family farm machinery plant. In 1938, Schindler became a member of the Nazi Party. The 31- year-old went Krakow, a city populated by about 60,000 Jews. Oskar Schindler took over a factory that had belonged to a Jew, which made him a lot of money and he had some Jews working there for him. Oskar Schindler didn't like the idea of the Nazi persecution of the Jews. He was willing to risk his life and money for his Jews.

Schindler kept the Jews, who were working in his factory, safe from getting deported to Auschwitz. When the SS threatened to deport his Jews to Auschwitz he would not allow them and argued that if they were removed it would affect his efforts to keep up production essentials for the war. Oskar smuggled food and medicine into the barracks with less chance of getting caught because he had his own sub-camp and took care of his Jews. Oskar Schindler was making money in his camp and no one was being beaten, everyone was being fed, and no one was killed.

Oskar and Emilie Schindler saved up to 1,000 Jews. Both Emilie and Oskar were recognized because of an act of bravery when 120 male prisoners were being transferred westward in cattle wagons without any food or water by the SS. When these Jewish male prisoners were traveling on a seven-day journey in the middle of winter, Emilie Schindler stopped them at Brunnlitz just in time and begged the SS commandment that she needed the Jewish prisoners for work. As they were about to rescue these Jews, they took 107 of the Jewish survivors who were with frostbite and helped them back to life. The dead bodies were then buried with full Jewish religious rites, thanks to Oskar and Emilie. For some of acts of bravery, Oskar was arrested several times for being in favor with the Jews, but he never confessed. After Oskar Schindler died in Hildesheim, Germany, in October 1974, he was buried in Israel by the Jewish survivors he helped. On his grave, he had an inscription that says: 'The unforgettable rescuer of 1,200 persecuted Jews.'

Another courageous German hero of the Holocaust was Georg Ferdinand Duckwitz. This man was born on September 29, 1904 in Bremen, Germany. Duckwitz was born into a patrician family in Hanseatic City. After going to college, he started working in the worldwide coffee trade. Georg Duckwitz was a businessman who traded with Scandinavian countries in the 1930's. In the year 1932 he joined the Nazi Party and worked for a foreign policy office of Alfred Rosenburg. He eventually left to work a shipping company called Hamburg America Line. When Duckwitz was aware of Hitler's real intentions against the Jewish community, he became really disappointed.

This German hero, Georg Ferdinand Duckwitz, warned the Danish Jews about the Nazis' intentions against them. Duckwitz helped the Jews to escape from the Nazis before they were deported to concentration camps where they could have suffered and died. Georg Duckwitz saved thousands of Jews. Georg became very close to the new Nazi Reich Representative for Denmark, his name was Werner Best. Best was a former deputy chief of the Gestapo and was a Nazi ideologue. Werner never followed the policies of the predecessors, but Hitler ordered a policy toward the "Final Solution" and he followed. Werner Best became confident about the plan for the deportation and taking actions against more than 6,000 Jewish people on September 28, 1943. Georg risked himself and began to warn his Danish friends who then informed the leader of the Danish Jewish community. This helped out the Danes to begin their rescue mission and transported 7,000 Jews overnight in ships and boats across the sea to a safer place in Sweden.

Georg Ferdinand Duckwitz saved many more than 6,000 Jews. In about two months it was estimated that 99 percent of Denmark's Jews were saved. Then the Gestapo decided to finish with the plan to take out the Jews, but most Jews were in the safe land of Sweden. There were still about 500 Jews who were mostly elderly and sick. They were caught and deported to the camp of Theresienstadt around October 2nd. Georg Ferdinand Duckwitz died on February 16, 1973. Two years before his death he was known as Righteous Among the Nations by Yad Vashem on March 29, 1971.

Works Cited

"Albert Battel." Wikipedia. 6 August 2015. Web. 17 Feb. 2016

"Holocaust." The Shalom Show Tv. Rcp Productions, n.d. Web. 18 Feb 2016.

Bulow, Louis. "Oskar Schindler Rake - & Savior." The Holocaust, Crimes, Heroes, & Villians n.d. Web. 18 Feb 2016.

Bulow, Louis "Emily Schindler." Oskar Schindler, His List Of Life. n.d. Web. 19 Feb. 2016   "Introduction to the Holocaust." Holocaust. n.d. 19 Feb. 2016

Heroes of the Holocaust

Kayla Jespersen (Special Award)

We should never forget those who risk their own lives to save others. During the Holocaust the Jewish people were being persecuted by the Nazi government. Many men and women played a very important role in the rebellion to save them. Women played a very important role in the fight against the Nazis. The Nazis saw women as weak and felt they should be home bound with children and be submissive to their husbands. This stereotype helped women from immediately suspected of being Jews. Here you can meet three women who were chosen as the Righteous Among the Nations. In a world of total moral collapse there was a small minority who mastered extraordinary courage to up hold human values.

Gertrud Luckner was born on September 26, 1900 in Liverpool, England and died August 31, 1995 in Freiburg in Breisgay Germany. As a small child she was orphaned at seven years old her foster parents changed her name from Jane Hartman to Gertrud Luckner. In 1933 when the Nazis came into power Gertrud joined the German Catholics peace association and she did free-lance work with the Catholic aid where she arranged exit opportunities for the Jews.

With international contacts she was able to secure safe passage for the refugees. Gertrud was able to organize aid circles for Jews, assisted many escape, provide food and clothing, and found addresses where Jews could hide from Nazi's. It is unknown the total number of Jews she saved. When World War II broke out she was given the task to trace missing people and give aid to prisoners of war. Gertrud's heart was taken captive by the Jews whose civil rights were being stripped away. She used money from the archbishop to smuggle Jews over the Swiss border.

With Gertrud's help the Catholic Church is credited with saving 700,000 to 860,000 Jews. Until 1943 she was arrested by the Gestapo. She was taken to Ravensbruck concentration camp and Gertrud spent 19 tormenting months in there.

The camp was liberated on May 3, 1945. Gertrud spent the rest of her life devoted to building bridges between Jews and Christians. In 1951 Gertrud was one of the first Germans to visit Israel with an invitation to recognize her as righteous among the nations.

Jean Kowalyk Berger was born in Ukraine in 1909. Early in life she earned her living as a seamstress. Jean was a religious person who always felt what the Nazis were doing to the Jewish community was wrong. When her mother became ill they both begin helping the Jews.

At the times her mom became ill the Germans had labor camp built across the street from her house. Jean convinced a German officer to allow a doctor from the labor camp treat her mother. The doctor was Doctor Berg. While he was treating Jean's mother he asked if he was able to escape from the camp would they hide him. One night he showed up at their door with people to hide in a tiny house. In order to hide them Jean had a wall built in the attic to hide them behind it.

Jean was able to save all 15 people who showed up that night. The house was raided several times by the Gestapo but they never found anyone. After the war was over Jean married Doctor Berg. Jean received a threatening letters after the war because she saved Jews, so Jean and her husband moved to the United States. Even after moving, helping Jews was very important to her. In 1985 her deeds where recognized by Yad Vashem. Jean died in September of 1998.

Countess Maria von Maltzan was born March 25, 1909 to German to nobility at Militsh place in Silesa Germany. She was raised on 18,000 acre estate and the youngest of eight children. Before the war she was starting school to become a veterinarian. In 1933 that schooling was put on hold until 1943. In 1933 she joined the resistance against the Nazis. For years she worked as an underground fighter. When Hitler's plans for total extermination of Jews dawned on Maria she knew what she had to act immediately.

Since 1935 she always responded to calls for help and took Jews into her own home feed them and protected them right under the Gestapo noses. Maria probably got away with this because of who her family was and she had family fighting with the Nazis. Throughout the war the countess con Maltzan with the help of Swedish church provided a safe haven to more than 60 Jews deserters and forced labors, arranging for them to escape. From 1942 to the end of the war she sheltered Hans Herschel. She hid him in a special hiding place in a couch in her living room. One time when the Gestapo came they wanted her to open it. She told them it was stuck. She even gave them permission to shoot it. They decided to leave.

She is credited with saving more than 60 people. Her story Maria let the world know in 1986 when she wrote her memoirs. Due to the horrors of the war Maria had many difficulties, but was forever grateful the Jews who never forgot her heroism. During the war she lost a baby who was in an incubator at a hospital that was bombed during an air raid. She became addicted to drugs. After her husband died in 1975 she built a new existence as a veterinarian in Berlin. There she became famous for cost free treatment of dogs owned by local punks. In 1987 she was recognized by Yad Vashem. She died in November 12, 1997.

Works Cited

Wikipedia, Gertrud Luckner December 20,2015
https://en.wikipedia.org/wiki/Gertrud_Luckner February 25, 2016

The Righteous Among The Nations, Gertrud Luckner 2016 Yad Vashem The Holocaust and Heroes Remembrance Authority
http://www.yadvashem.org/yv/en/righteous/stories/luckner.asp February 25, 2016

Jean Kowalyk Berger, The Jewish Foundation for the righteous 2016
https://jfr.org/rescuer-stories/berger-jean-kowalyk/ February 27, 2016

Wikipedia, Countess Maria von Maltzan, December 30, 2015
https://en.wikipedia.org/wiki/Maria_von_Maltzan February 27, 2016

The Righteous Among The Nations, Countess Maria von Maltzan 2016 The Holocaust and Heroes Remembrance Authority
http://db.yadvashem.org/righteous/family.html?language=en&itemId=4043010 February 27, 2016

Justice

Lasha'e Harden

In the 8th grade most people hear the minimum amount about the Holocaust. All they learn is that in the late 1930"s into the 1940's a man named Adolf Hitler ordered for all Jewish people living in Germany to be forcibly incarcerated, but what you don't find out is that there were a lot of people who risked their lives to help Jews escape, or who gave them a chance at survival.

There were many people who helped Jews survive the Holocaust. One person was a German man named Hans Hartmann. Hartmann was born December 12, 1913 in Villnachern, Switzerland. He first started working in an advertising office of a shoe business for 7 years in 1931, when the war started he became a senior officer of Heeres Kraftfahrzeug in 1942 in Lwow.

Hartmann was approached by a woman named Gitel Goldberg who was trying to have her son and husband released from the death camp. After he was approached by Mrs. Goldberg he went to the camp and found the son and husband and drove them right through the gate. He took them home and the family tried to thank him by giving him their last prized possession, which was a gold plated pelican writing set. He declined and went back to his station.

That day he saved not just two people but a whole family. Hans' story was admitted onto Yad Vashem on July 16, 1963. Hans was caught for letting Wolfe and Abraham Goldberg free and he was ordered to leave to Lwow and join a repair unit and which made him unable to help anyone else. After the war was over he became a postmaster. Wolf and Abraham Goldberg decided to located their rescuer and they found him in small Bavarian town called Wolfratshausen. Abraham moved to Israel and to this day their families still keep in touch.

Another hero who changed the lives of many families was a German man, Woerl Ludwig. Ludwig was born February 28, 1906 in Germany. He was trained by the Germans to be a medical orderly. Ludwig was held as a political prisoner for 11 years in a Nazi concentration camp, then he was arrested again in 1934 for handing out flyers informing Jews on what concentration camps where and what the Nazis were doing to Jewish people.

After he was released for handing out the pamphlets he was transferred to a camp joinery and trained to be a medical orderly and then was transferred to the camp's infirmary. At the infirmary he helped hundreds of Jews by making sure they had enough rations of food and if they were sick he would make sure that their workload was lessened so they could heal. Ludwig also employed multiple Jewish doctors, saving them from death.

Over roughly six years Ludwig saved over 600 hundred Jews by taking them under his protection, employing them and saving them from the severe working environment. He made sure people under his supervision were fed properly, and if they were injured he made their workload was cut down. He also helped multiple people escape the death marches, he made sure they had proper medicines to treat their sickness, and he forged selection papers to save Jews from being gassed. At the time of the liberations he helped multiple Jews escape the death marches. But these actions did not go unseen by the Nazis.

Ludwig was caught twice helping and saving Jews and the first time he got caught he was locked away in an isolated detention cell in the dark for nine months. After forging the selection papers the Nazi had, he was incarcerated in a dark cell by himself again. After every living Jew was liberated there was a key witness in the trial against Auschwitz. When the trail was over he became the chairman of organization of former Auschwitz prisoners and he dedicated his life to bringing Nazis to justice.

Woerl Ludwig was recognized by Yad Vashem on March 19, 1963. There were many men who were heroes during the Holocaust, but there were also very heroic women such as Marie Burde.

Marie Burde was born in 1892 in Germany. Burde was a poor woman who lived in a dark cellar/basement and she sold newspaper, empty bottles and old cloth to make a living. Marie took in three Jewish men during World War II. Alfred and Rolf Joseph went on into hiding after their parents had been arrested and they later on ran into their friend Arthur and were told that a woman by the name of Marie Burde was known for showing sympathy and secretly helping persecuted Jews. They found Burde's house and she quickly took them in and insisted that they stay inside during the day. The house that Burde lived in was destroyed by an air raid so she took the men to a lot that she owned. She then relocated them back to Berlin and Alfred was arrested and sent to a camp where he survived and later reunited with his brother. After the war was over the brothers Alfred and Rolf took care of Marie until she died in the 1950's.

The affect Marie had on the Joseph brothers ended up in her favor when she needed help later on in her life and the brothers knew what she did for them and they took care of her.

There is no way to justify what happened during the Holocaust. It was wrong and should not have happened, but it happened and there were a lot of people who silently and publicly rebelled against it, such as the people listed above and many more, who show that what was happening wasn't right and never would be.

I learned a lot from my research but my biggest lesson was that one person or group of people are not superior to another and that you shouldn't look down on people.

Heroes of the Holocaust

Liana Shilo

Adolf Hitler was a wicked man. He killed 6 million Jews! He made himself look like an animal, even worse. From concentration camps to burning flames to suicide to gas chambers, he was responsible for the suffering and the deaths of the Jews. Not many from the millions tortured survived, but the ones who did have a story to tell from personal experiences. You get to feel terror, surveillance, fear, restrictions and yet risking everything to help their Jewish friends.

Andreas Friedrich Ruth, born on September 23, 1901 in Berlin was part of an informal Berlin resistance group. In 1922, she completed her training as a welfare worker and then a bookseller. She wrote reviews and feature articles for the newspapers. In 1924, she married a West German president. In 1925, she bore to him a daughter, Karin. After six years of marriage, they both divorced. In the 1930's she lived with a conductor. After the Nazis took power, the group was founded. But their uncle Emil helped keep them hidden away; he provided them food and got them false papers. Their daughter Karin helped the group. In 1948, Ruth moved to Munich and married Walter. Then 1945, Borchard died, Walter Seitz director of the Munich University Hospital. On September 17, 1977 she committed suicide, leaving a note before her self-chosen death, she writes: "Many die late - some die too early ... It seems to me now come a good time to die." We remember her today because she is Righteous Among the Nations.

Leonard Bartlakowski, born on August 31,1916 was the Berlin-born son of a Polish family that had been a foreigner in Germany. He was on a mission, on a plane to attack Warsaw, when he jumped off the plane by parachute. Somehow he reached Lwow and the Soviets there imprisoned him. In June 1941, Germans overpowered Lwow and they let the political prisoners go, including Bartlakowski himself. Without any papers they knew him as Robert Krysinski, which was his alias, and was placed at a nearby Rawa

Ruska as a German-Polish interpreter and a soldier for the local Gestapo. It was there that Abraham Weidenfeld first met him. Bartlakowski/Krysinski was standing guard with a German soldier over the Jews waiting in line for a piece of bread. The next day as the German interpreter entered Weidenfeld's pharmacy to ask for razor blades, there Weidenfeld pleased himself and offered him a pack of blades without charging him. Then against all odds began a worthy friendship.

Bartlakowski, whose office was located at the railway station, was well placed to obtain a well amount of information about the transports and raids. He would notify Weidenfeld, who passes along the information in codes to sorts of Jewish Councils in the area near or surrounding a particular place. One day Bartlakowski heard that the local Gestapo received instructions from the Lwow Gestapo to have empty cattle trucks ready for the transportation of the Rara Ruska to Belzec. He immediately notified Weidenfeld but he himself went during the night into the ghettos and warned the people. Bartlakowski offered to shelter his friend and his family, but Weidenfeld, who still had a hiding of his own in his pharmacy, refused and asked him to hide his sister-in-law, Romana Kessler, and Dr. Stephanie Reicher instead. It was only a few months later, mid-June 1943, when the Weidenfleds joined them. Until the liberation of Rawa Ruska on July 27, 1944, they stayed hidden in the small apartment. It wasn't a place of comfort, you had to squeeze into a hole about 3 cubic feet deep dug underground under the bed. Having food was a challenge, they couldn't buy the amount of food for five people without triggering suspicion. Bartlakowski was pressured to steal food from his work place at the railway station. The rumors about hiding the Jews were so widespread that the Gestapo came to inspect the place with a dog. He managed to trick them off with liquor. After the war, he returned to Germany to join his family in Berlin. Bartlakowski died of a disease in 1953, at the age of 36, of tuberculosis contracted while he was in the Soviet prison in Lwow. The Weidenfelds, who had emigrated to Australia, had sent him letters for some time until they learned that he had died. On September 4, 1979, Bartlakowski was recognized as Righteous Among the Nations.

Dr. Albert Battel, born on January 21, 1891. As a 51-year-old reserve officer and lawyer from Breslau, he was stationed in Przemysl in South Poland as a military officer who acts as an administrative assistant to the local military commander, Major Max Liedtke. One July 26, 1942, when the SS prepared to launch their first large extensive area resettlement action against the Jews of Przemysl, in spouse with his superior, ordered the bridge over the River San, the only access into the Jewish ghetto, to be blocked. As the SS Commando attempted to cross to the other side, the sergeant in charge threatened to open fire unless they backed off. All this happened in broad daylight, to the amazement of the locals. Later that same day, an army objected under the command of Oberleutenant Battel broke into the cordoned-off area of the ghetto and used army trucks to whisk off up to 100 Jews and their families to the house of the local military command. These Jews were placed under the protection of the Wehrmacht and were sheltered from deportation to the Belzec extermination camp. The remaining ghetto partners, including the head of the Judenrat, Dr.Duldig, underwent resettlement in the days to come.

After this incident, the SS authorities began a secret investigation into the crazy conduct of the army officer who had dared defy them under such embarrassing circumstances. It turned out that Battel, even though he was a member of the Nazi Party since May 1933, had already been suspicious in the past by his friendly behavior toward the Jews. Later, in his services in Przemysl, he was officially given a warning for shaking hands of the chairman of the Jewish Council, Dr.Duldig. The uprising reached the attention of the highest level of Nazi power. No less a figure than Heinrich Himmler, took a lively interest in the results of the investigation and sent a photocopy of the incriminating documentation to Martin Borman. In the letter, Himmler swore to have the lawyer arrested immediately after the war. All this was kept a secret against Battel. In 1944, he was discharged from military service because of a heart disease. He returned to his hometown in Breslau, only to be drafted into the Volk Storm and fall into Russian captivity.

After his release, he settled in West Germany but was prevented from returning to practice law by a court of de-Nazification. In 1952, he died in Hattersheim near Frankfurt. On January 22, 1981, he was recognized as Righteous Among the Nations.

Sam Igiel, one of the Jews rescued by Battel's intervention, describes Battel's courage. After the war he reported about Monday, July 27, 1942:

"Dr. Battel did not limit himself to the intervention, by which he rescued 2,500 Jews from being evacuated. As the action was in progress, staying in the quarter at the time, in the face of the Gestapo's lawlessness and violence, could result in evacuation at any moment anyway. Therefore, to avoid complications Oberleutenant Battel stopped about ninety of his workers with their families in the command's backyard as early as Sunday. Also he sent two police-protected lorries to fetch the workers from more distant quarters. The lorries set off five times and every time they came back with a new group of Jews until the number reached 240. When one of these transports got stopped by the SS, Dr. Battel intervened personally. Under the threat of manning the town he made the lorry go free. Then he had all Jews installed in the Kommandantur basement where they were kept the whole week under his protection during the action. On his order they were protected with bags of biscuits, meat and even milk for the children. He ordered that we get lunches."

Otto Berger, born on 25 of April, 1900. Fedur Bruck's family lived in Ratibor, Upper Silesia, where he studied dental medicine and worked as a dentist in the schools of Liegnitz. With Nazi activity rising even before 1933, Bruck was fired and moved to Berlin. He continued to work as a dentist for the school system, but not for long. In 1933, when all the Jews were removed from government positions, he too lost his job. He was permitted to treat only Jews. On October 12, 1942, Bruck heard that he was going to be deported to the east. He decided not to present himself, and go hide himself. He managed to find shelter with some Berlin allies, and finally reached the home of another dentist, Otto Berger. After the war, Bruck described how the contact was made:

"I met Otto at the beginning of 1943 through a mutual friend. When he learned that I was living as an illegal because of my being persecuted on racial grounds, he immediately, on our first meeting, supplied me with food and offered to hide me if I had to leave my present hideout." Berger continued to hide Bruck for 21 months, even after he had to move twice. Once was after his home had been bombed by Allied airplanes, and another time was when the apartment became unsafe. As Bruck had no official identification card and no ration cards, Berger not only sheltered him but also provided food and all his needs. He eventually managed to get Bruck a fake card, but continued to shelter him until the war ended.

After the war, Bruck began to search for his pre-war friends. He found his former assistant from Upper Silesea who too moved to Berlin, where she worked for a Dr. Blaschke. Blaschke was Adolf Hitler's dentist. When the war was over, she was called by the Russian commander to help identify Hitler's remains with the help of his dental records. Bruck accompanied her and provided some of his expertise. Nevertheless, and even though the Soviets offered him to take over the Blaschke clinic, Bruck moved to the American zone of Berlin and in 1947 emigrated to the United States. He settled in New York, where he lived until his death in 1982. He kept in touch with his rescuer, and kept sending letters to each other. Otto Berger was from the Upper Silesea. In 1990, He had been born in Oppeln. In 1930 he joined the Nazi party and the SA. But soon after he became discouraged, he began to criticize Nazism. For that reason, he was forced out from the SA and the party ranks.

After 36 years in jail, on the 20 of November 2003, Berger committed suicide by hanging himself in Straubing prison. The suitableness of Berger's 36 years in jail was questioned in his obituary by the Sueddeutsche Zeitung, as he never killed anybody and even murderers in Germany tend to be released after much shorter sentences. Burger was buried at the Alten Friedhof in Neuburg an der Donau. On 11 of August 2009, Otto Berger was recognized as RIghteous Among the Nations.

Works Cited

Yee, Danny. "Berlin Diaries:Berlin Underground, 1938-1945, Battleground Berlin, Andreas-Freidrich, Ruth." Danny Reviews. Danny Yee's Book Reviews. 2003. Web. 20 February 2016.

Gretter Susanne. "Ruth Andreas-Friedrich." Fem Bio. Frauen.biographieforschung.6 June 2008. Web. 22 February 2016.

Yad Vashem. "The Righteous Among The Nations." Yad Vashem. Yad Vashem The Holocaust Martyrs' and Heroes' Remembrance Authority. 2016. Web. 20 February 2016.

Yad Vashem. "The Righteous Among The Nations." Yad Vashem. The Holocaust Martyr's and Heroes' Remembrance Authority. 2016. Web. 21 February 2016.

Yad Vashem. "The Righteous Among The Nations." Yad Vashem. The Holocaust Martyrs' and Heroes' Remembrance Authority. 2016. Web. 20 February 2016.

Louis. "The Few Good Men, Where Wargaming and History Collide." The Few Good Men. XenForo. 2010-2016. Web. 17 February 2016.

Yad Vashem. "The Righteous Among The Nations." Yad Vashem. The Holocaust Martyrs' and Heroes' Remembrance Authority. 2016. Web. 23 February 2016.

Heroes of the Holocaust

Liliya Litvinchuk

There were many Ukrainians who helped Jews survive the Holocaust. One such person was Sofka Skipwith. She was born in 1907, in St. Petersburg, Russia. As a Russian refugee, she lived both in England and France with her husband, Leo Zinovieff, who was from another exiled family. She and Madeline White, another detained British citizen, tried to help the best that they could. After the first deportation of the Polish Jews, Sofka and Madeline used their contacts to the resistance movement to arrange to get numbers of children out of camps and save them. They even managed to save a life of a Jewish baby.

Sofka Skipwith is recognized for saving several Jewish people. She will always be remembered and never forgotten. In the beginning of 1943, 280 Polish Jews holding Latin American passports or visas arrived in Vittel from Warsaw. Some of these passports were forged or had been received through consulates in other countries without the authorization of the Latin American governments. Sofka was deeply moved by the tragic stories she heard from the Jewish prisoners and she decided to help them out.

Another person who is recognized for helping Jews survive the Holocaust was Anna Igumnova. She was born in Russia into an aristocratic family.

In 1917, she and her husband left for a vacation in Europe and could not return home when the October Revolution started. The October Revolution was followed by the Russian Civil War and the creation of the Soviet Union in 1922. Anna received her Ph.D.in Chemistry in Berlin, and then moved with her family to Slovakia. The Igumnovas had two children, an older daughter and a younger son. Later on in in the late 1920's Anna's husband committed suicide. From the mid-1930's Anna lived in Piestany, a famous spa town, working in the research institute there. In 1942, a new colleague joined the institute, Alice Winter nee Tandlich from Bratislava. Although Jewish, Alice was given "exception papers" because she shared in a secret prescription for the treatment of rheumatic disease.

Germany occupied Slovakia following the Slovak national uprising. With Soviet troops approaching the country's borders, the deportations of the Slovakian Jews resumed on September 30, 1944. It was then that Anna became more actively involved in helping her Jewish Acquaintance.

There were lots of people who helped the Jews survive the Holocaust. Another person who helped a lot was Ludviga Pukas. In 1937, Ludviga (NIna) Pukas left her hometown and moved to the town of Proskurov (today Khmel'nyts'kyy), where she found a job as a domestic with Frima Sternik, a high school teacher who lived with her children, four-year old Eldina and one-year old Gennadiy.

During the war, Pukas was still a maid to a Jewish woman named Firma Sternik. She herself was not Jewish but wanted to stay loyal to her employer, so Pukas hid her and her two children (4 year old Eldina and 1 year old Gennadiy). Their house was burned to the ground, thus making Pukas take matters into her own hands. She registered her daughter and Sterkin's children as her own, then she was given a new apartment. A day before destructions of Jews of Proskurov, she sent Sterkin to her brother's home but was caught halfway there and killed. Ludviga allowed Jews into her house despite the danger of being exterminated.

On March 25, 1944, the Red Army liberated Proskurov and, in September of that year, Gennadiy and Eldina changed their names back to Sternik and returned to school. They made contacts with their aunts but they refused to leave Pukas until they completed their studies, in the 1950s. Until her death in 1984, Gennadiy and Eldina regarded Pukas as their mother.

Another person who played a major role in our history was Antonina Gordey. She was born on 1 January 1907 and died on 1 January 1978. She lived in Minsk, Belarus (USSR).

Antonina Gordey worked as a nanny for the Ledvich family, a Jewish family that lived in Minsk. She took care of six-year-old Rafail and three-year old Raya. Mordukh Ledvich, the head of the family, had a profession as an engineer, his wife Fanya was a kindergarten manager. On the day when the war became really bad, Mordukh was enlisted into the Red Army, while Fanya was told to move the kindergarten to the east.

The apartment building where the Ledvich family used to live put down to the ground. Fanya went to stay at her friend's house while leaving her two kids at the orphanage, assuming that they would be fed better. Soon the Ledvich kids and many other Jewish children were transferred to the ghetto orphanage. Antonina continued visiting them in the orphanage, brought them food and promised to take them as soon as she would find a job and a place that they could live in. Several months had passed by. One day Antonina came to see her children in the ghetto orphanage and did not find Rafail. Children from the orphanage told her that Germans had been drawing blood samples from him, which caused his death. Very scared about losing Raya, Antonina took her out of the ghetto orphanage the same day she found out that Rafail was gone.

Another hero of the Holocaust was Julian Bilecki. Julian Bilecki was a small bony teenager when he and his family hid and saved 23 Jews under the ground, to save them from the Nazis' death. In 1943, nearly 3,000 Jewish families were slaughtered by Nazis. Some of the Jewish children ran away from the Nazi extermination and survived. They ran away to the Bilecki farm. In June, 1943, 23 Jewish people came to the Bilecki door and they were seeking for refugee from Nazis. The Bilecki family accepted all the Jews and decided to build a bunker in the woods; they would be camouflaged and not noticed at all. The hardest thing was providing the food. Food in villages was very hard to find, and the Bilecki family somehow maintained to feed an extra 23 people without any suspension.

The Bilecki family showed the Jews were to hide, helped them move from place to place when they were found, brought them food once in a while to help them survive. After living under the ground for more than a year, the group of the Jews heard gun shots around the bunkers. They already knew that this was the last bit of the war and that freedom would be just right around the corner. The Russian army liberated the area on March 27, 1944, and the Jews all separated from each other. Some immigrated to the U.S and to other countries.

As time passed by, many of those who survived sent lots of packages in the mail of clothing and food. The Bilecki family remained poor in the Ukraine still living on a farm. More than half a century later Julian Bilecki (70 year-old) and another five survivors are residents of New York. These heroes were honored and recognized and will never be forgotten.

From 1941 to 1945, Jews were efficiently murdered in one of the deadliest genocides in history. The use of extermination camps equipped with gas chambers for the efficiency mass extermination of people was an unprecedented feature of the Holocaust. Many people died. Either they got put into the gas chambers or they became very weak and could not survive. Many became very sick and their sicknesses could not be treated because of the lack of medicine that was available to them. Men were being separated from women, wives from husbands, and children from parents. Most kids who were very young and women got put into the gas chambers and they were gassed.

Another Holocaust hero was Anton Sukhinski. Anton Sukhinski was a loner and an outcast. Many people called him an idiot. He never ended up getting married, always seemed to be living on the verge of poverty in a small little house in Zborow. His neighbors always made fun of him because of the love that he had toward gentle nature and love of all living creatures. But at that time when everything started collapsing, when many of the people started participating in the murder of Jews or turned their backs on their neighbors, it was Anton Sukhinski (the village idiot) who stood up for what he had believed in and preserved human values. Without getting any help from anyone he was responsible for the survival of six people.

Anton Sukhinski offered his help to the Zeiger family, which consisted of a father, mother, and their two small sons. The Zeiger family brought along a woman who was their family friend and Eva Halperin a young girl whose family was all killed and dead. She was alone in the world. Sukhinski was already hiding a 16-year old girl in a room below the ground level (basement). Eventually the neighbors found out that Anton was hiding people and then they started harassing him and the people who he had been hiding in his basement. Anton Sukhinski was always a loving warm-hearted person and he always welcomed everyone into his home.

For nine whole months they all remained in that little hole, cramped up, no room to move, and a small kerosene lamp. The fear of being found and shot was huge among all people, so nobody came out of the hiding place. Anton would bring them whatever food he could find and a chamber pot. Providing food for six people was very hard for a poor man like Anton. In addition he lived under a constant fear of being discovered by his neighbors and by the Germans.

When the day of liberation came the door to the room where they were trapped opened. Being in that small whole changed the lives of those six people. They were not used to walking on land and they were being blinded by the sun since they were in darkness for a whole nine months. After liberation the six people stayed together very close for a while. Then they set out to build their own lives. The Zeiger family immigrated to the USA, Eva Halperin went to Uruguay, and Zipora left to Israel.

Irena Sendler was a 29-year-old who was a social worker, employed by the welfare department. After the German occupation she took advantage of her job in helping the Jews. She tried her best to help out the Jews, but that did not end up lasting for a very long time. She somehow got into the ghetto where the Jews were transferred to, and maintained to help out the dying and suffering Jews. Irena helped to take out Jews secretly out of the ghetto and found hiding spots for them. On October 20, 1943 Irena Sendler was arrested. She was sentenced to death and was sent to a prison, but the bribe officials managed to get her out and then she was released from the prison. She had very little yet has done so much in our history. She will always be honored because she is a very important person, and helped out the Jews a lot. She did a lot to save the Jews that's why she will never be forgotten. She will always be honored in the history of the Jewish nation.

Works Cited

Anna, Igumnova. ¨Women of Valor¨. Stories of Women who rescued Jews during the Holocaust. Yad Vashem, 19 October 2010. Web. 28 January 2016.

Saruwatari, Kayleigh. "The Life of Ludviga Pukas". Prezi, 18 February 2015. Web. 22 February2016.

Antonina, Gordey. "Women of Valor". Stories of women who rescued Jews during theHolocaust. Yad Vashem, 9 May 2007. Web. 22 February 2016.

"Both Victim and Predator". Ukraine's Problematic relationship to the Holocaust. Baltic Worlds, 1August 2011. Web. 23 February 2016.

Julian Bilecki. "A Holocaust Survivor". Julian Bilecki and his Jews. Web. 23 February 2016.

"The Holocaust". Wikimedia inc, 17 February 2016. Web. 23 February 2016.

Irena, Sendler. "Women of Valor". Stories of women who rescued Jews during the Holocaust.

Yad Vashem, 19 October 1965. Web. 24 February 2016.

Righteous

Michael Kinda

The Holocaust was a bureaucratic state-sponsored persecution of over 6 million Jews. The Nazi regime believed that Germans were "racially superior" and the Jews interfered with their supremacy. During the Holocaust the Nazi regime planned to eliminate anyone who stood in their way. The Jewish people were targeted for ethnic, racial, and national reasons. Adolf Hitler started a world war to acquire world domination. His driving force and perhaps the only thing that moved him forward was his hatred for Jews. The "Righteous Among the Nations" refers to the non-Jewish people who risked their own lives to go against the racist Nazi regime to provide aid to Jews during the Holocaust. These people ranged from factory workers to German military commanders. They changed the lives of many Jews who were facing a morally unjustified nightmare that became a reality.

Adolf Weigel

There were many Germans who helped Jews survive in the Holocaust. One such person was Adolf Wiegel. Adolf was born on June 6, 1882 in Berlin, Germany. He was a lifelong banker and a committed member of the Social Democratic Party of Germany. His process of helping Jews began when he encountered disagreements in politics. He later retired from the Democratic Party of Germany to pursue a different career.

In 1915 he founded a bindery and printing plant that was recently established in the city of Kopenickerstrasse. His wife, Frida Wiegel, was placed as the managing director of the office supplies factory that her husband owned. Here they employed Jews to keep them from persecution. He also helped Jews that were persecuted by printing fake IDs to those who were in hiding and needed to acquire a different identity to escape suffering. Werner Scharff and Gertrude Scharff were both Jews who were employed at Adolf's bindery and printing plant. They were both in hiding after they had been deported to Theresienstadt and later escaped. In autumn of 1943, Adolf with the support of Werner Scharff set up a resistance group called the "Community for Peace and Reconstruction," which was a group operated in Luckenwalde, Brandenburg.

Adolf Weigel along with his acquaintances hired and helped over 30 Jews escape from persecution. On October 12, 1944, the couple was arrested because of "suspicion of treason and Jew favoring." Adolf Weigel was assigned to a "work camp" in Wuhlheide. On March 24, 1945 he was then transported toward Dachau, because of the lack of transport they were continued on foot. In April, when the "death march" was near Sonneberg in Thuringia, the SS shot Adolf Weigel and got rid of his body in a mass grave near the roadside along with others suspected of favoring Jews. Adolf Weigel was 62 years old.

Paula Wendt

Factory owners were not the only ones to help the Jewish people, but workers in the factories did as well. One such person was Paula Wendt. Paula was born on August 25, 1897 in Germany. She married Heinrich Wendt, but they soon divorced. After the separation she moved back with her parents in Bublitz. Paula was a German national hired by Adolf Weigel to work in his bindery and printing plant. Weigel was a factory owner who hired Jewish laborers to work in his factory to avoid persecution. In view of the fact of Germany's racist doctrine and laws, Paula Wendt remained friendly with Weigel's Jewish laborers.

Working alongside Jewish laborers, she helped them escape persecution. Paula even offered to hide Jewish laborers in her house. Werner Scharff set up a resistance group called the "Community for Peace and Reconstruction." From time to time Werner Scharff and Gertrude Scharff hid in Paula Wendt's house. She also helped them print anti-Nazi propaganda in the printing press to spread the word to form an uprising in support for the "Community for Peace and Reconstruction."

Paula Wendt, alongside Adolf Weigel and Frida Wiegel, helped saved over 30 Jews from persecution. Paula alone rescued three Jews from persecution. Paula Wendt was together with her sister, Ida Roscher, Adolf Weigel, and Frida Weigel when the Secret State Police arrested them on October 12, 1944. First they were taken to prison at Alexanderplatz. There they were subjected to interrogation and mistreatment by the State Police. Then the three women came into the town of Arbeitserziehungslager Fehrbellin, where they were forced to work in a factory. On April 24, 1945 they were liberated by the Red Army. The three women were devastated by the Camp. Once liberated, Paula Wendt moved back to her apartment in Lausitzer Platz. She has been recognized as a victim of the Nazi regime.

Willi Ahrem

Not everyone in the Nazi regime was influenced by Hitler's hatred for Jews. Some placed themselves in position of authority to offer help to Jews that were suffering. One such person is Willi Ahrem. Ahrem was born on January 1, 1902 in Germany. He was a German member in the armed forces. In 1941 he became a Commander in a forced labor camp in Ukraine. Ahrem distinguished himself by his humane behavior towards the laborers.

Willi Ahrem illegally transferred and placed Jews into hiding. He even provided basic goods and arranged safe shelters. Ahrem helped every Jew he could save without gaining too much suspicion. He placed himself in great personal risk by smuggling Jews to safe houses, he even provided shelter at his own residence. Ahrem would personally warn Jehoshua Menzer; a German-speaking Jew who would spread the word to other Jewish people when attacks directed against them were approaching. This allowed many Jews to flee into the forest and to nearby villages. Ahrem sheltered the Menzer family along with two other Jews in a cellar in his house. Willi Ahrem provided them with blankets and food, along with other necessaries.

The total number of Jews Willi Ahrem rescued is unknown. We do know he saved a family and two more Jews from persecution in one event. Ahrem was a commander in a forced labor camp, and his humane behavior towards the laborers meant he treated them with care and must have saved more Jews than we are informed of. In the meantime, Ahrem's position as a commander became very vulnerable. He had trouble proving he was not helping Jews. He barely cleared himself from these allegations. Following that experience, in 1943, he moved back to Germany from Ukraine until the end of the war. Willi Ahrem was in a position of power, and he chose to save those he was hired to torment. His humane behavior meant it all to a lot of people who faced their demise.

Vladimir Chernovol

Germans were not the only people rescuing Jews. Many Ukrainians placed themselves in danger by providing their helping hand to save the lives of innocent Jews. One such person was Vladimir Chernovol. In the year of 1921, Chernovol was born in the Kirovograd District in the village of Vodyana. His family's property was confiscated by the Soviet regime during the 1930s. He pursued and later graduated from a teachers training course and began to work as a teacher in a village. Soon after the Germans occupied their village, he decided to return to his birthplace to continue this teaching career.

Vladimir Chernovol hid and provided shelter for the Jews evading persecution. Vladimir bribed the local police, and gave them protection under the Red Army. While Chernovol was returning to his birthplace after the Germans occupied his village, he met Grigoriy Lantsman. Lantsman identified himself as a Soviet pilot who had fallen into German hands and escaped. After a while Lantsman revealed to Chernovol that he was a Jew. Vladimir Chernovol then immediately suggested that Lantsman should join him. Once the men arrived in Vodyana, Chernovol invited him into his former home and secretly obtained the required verification of Lantsmann's identity from a military commander in Dobrovelichivka. This document allowed him to live in the village until the fall of 1943, when the Germans invaded and took the Ukrainians into forced labour camps. A few months later, Lantsman was able to escape and find Chernovol's house. Once again Vladimir took him in and hid him in his house. Lantsman was eventually discovered, but Chernovol bribed the local policeman to keep his secret. After the area was liberated in March of 1944. Lantsman joined the Red Army and fought until the end of the war. Chernovol and Lantsman kept in touch for many years later.

Vladimir Chernovol saved the life a Jew in critical and desperate times. We only know of one confirmed life that was saved, but there could be many more. Vladimir Chernovol was a teacher and a hero who came into the life of a person in need. Chernovol operated in secret and did anything necessary to keep a life safe. After the war Chernovol continued his teaching career for many years. From the Holocaust to this moment now, Vladimir Chernovol will be dearly admired as a teacher who came to the rescue of a Jew in a time of immense despair.

Maria Babich

Ordinary everyday Ukrainians also reached out to imprisoned Jews. One such person was Maria Babich. Babich was born in the 1900s in Ukraine. She worked minor jobs to sustain herself. During the German occupation, Maria Babich helped Jews who were imprisoned in a ghetto at Rowne Wolyn.

Maria Babich provided supplies and resources to Jews incarcerated in the ghettos. She helped in any way she could. Babich took to the extremes and sheltered a Jewish baby whose parents were in desperate need. Maria sheltered and took care of the baby's needs for four years. On November 6, 1941 the baby's mother, Mina Osipow, perished during Operation Reinhard. Operation Reinhard was a codename to eliminate millions of Jews in the general government. It began with the deportation of Jews to extermination camps. The baby's father, Itzhak Osipow, served in the Red Army and later returned to Rowne after the war to find his daughter, Irit, still alive thanks to Maria Babich. Irit was the only surviving member of the entire Osipow family.

Maria Babich saved a Jewish baby's life. Without Maria, Irit's life would be a question with a devastating answer, and that answer is not the result of Maria Babich. Babich went out of her way to raise a baby in a time of great hate. While the Nazi regime was trying to eliminate Jews, Maria was raising one. Babich survived the war and later on became part of the Osipow family. She then immigrated with them to Israel. Babich gave an opportunity to a desperate life. Maria Babich was one of the first ones to become part of the institutions Avenue of the Righteous Among the Nations.

Works Cited

"Wiegel Family." Yad Yashem. Yad Vashem The Holocaust Martyrs' and Heroes' Remembrance Authority, 2016. Web. 15 Feb. 2016.

"Adolf Wiegel." :: Kreuzberger Gedenktafel Für Opfer Des Naziregimes 1933-1945. Web. 15 Feb.2016.

"Willi Ahrem." Wikipedia. Wikimedia Foundation, 20 Aug. 2015. Web. 16 Feb. 2016.

"Ahrem Family." Yad Yashem. Yad Vashem The Holocaust Martyrs' and Heroes' Remembrance Authority, 2016. Web. 16 Feb. 2016

"Ahrem Willi (1902 - 1967)." Yad Yashem. Yad Vashem The Holocaust Martyrs' and Heroes' Remembrance Authority, 2016. Web. 16 Feb. 2016.

"Teachers Who Rescued Jews During the Holocaust." Vladimir Chernovol. Yad Vashem The Holocaust Martyrs' and Heroes' Remembrance Authority, 2016. Web. 16 Feb. 2016.

"Chernovol Family." Yad Yashem. Yad Vashem The Holocaust Martyrs' and Heroes' Remembrance Authority, 2016. Web. 16 Feb. 2016.

"I Am My Brother's Keeper." The Dedication of the Avenue of the Righteous Among the Nations."Drops of Love in an Ocean of Poison" Yad Vashem The Holocaust Martyrs' and Heroes' Remembrance Authority, 2016. Web. 16 Feb. 2016.

"Babich Family." Yad Yashem. Yad Vashem The Holocaust Martyrs' and Heroes' Remembrance Authority, 2016. Web. 16 Feb. 2016.

"Holocaust | Basic Questions about the Holocaust." Projetaladin. Projetaladin, 2009. Web. 17 Feb. 2016.

Willy Kranz

Oleksandr Bilskyy (Co-Winner)

William Kranz was a married man who was born in Berlin in 1889. This man was the lessee of the canteen at the Berlin Tegel prison. He was living his normal life during the times of the Holocaust and one day a little girl came to him who was named Rita. She came to him with her mother and they had just escaped from Nazi soldiers who were rounding up the Jews for the concentration camps. The mother asked him to take care of her daughter, Rita Cohn. Kranz talked to his wife and they decided to take care of Rita. And for Rita's mom, Kranz got a job for her so she could earn money and run away. Kranz took care of Rita for over half a year. He was investigated for harboring a fugitive but he introduced Rita to everyone as his adoptive daughter.

After he was investigated, he almost lost his job and his home. After Rita's mother earned enough money to take care of Rita, but Kranz kept on helping them with money and food after they left his house. Until he knew that they were fully safe in another country. After he helped Rita and her mom, he liked helping people who were on the run from the Nazi soldiers that he helped over five more families. After two years of helping families, his neighbors got suspicious of him adopting so many children during a small period of time. That they talked to the general of the Nazis and they came to his house and killed him and his family

This man shows courage and bravery that a lot of us have never seen. He knew that harboring Jews could get him killed and his family and any one of his friends and family. After helping Rita and her mother and getting the feeling that he changed someone's life for the good and possibly saved her life, he continued to help more and more families and he ignored the risk because he knew it outweighs saving people's life. His wife also was brave to go along with this, even though a mother always wants to protect her child and at the moments that Kranz was helping Rita and her mom he had a five year old child who was getting sick all of the time.

When Kranz was under investigation, they tossed his house every time. Every time they messed with his family and relatives. They made life hard for them and made want to give up Rita and her mother to the German army. But Kranz managed to convince all his relatives that Rita was an actual child that he adopted. So they believed him and never spoke another word to the German officers. In my eyes this man is a hero. He made it his duty and job to protect this girl from any harm coming to her. He acted like she was his own daughter.

Next, I'm going to talk about the Bielski family overall. All of these people are my relatives. Fruma is my great-grandmother. Dedek is my great-grandfather. It's a great honor knowing that I have relatives from the past who have made a change in this world and helped people out who were in need. Fruma rescued three people out of these concentration camps. They were Benjamin Blitzer, Sonia Blitzer and another Blitzer family member but the first name is unknown to this day. Fruma rescued them by hiding out in the wood and then helping them escape the camp and took them to a safe place to take cover from the German officers searching the woods and villages for them. Fruma herself lived in Nadworna, Stanislawow, Poland during the war.

After the officers passed by and didn't find the Blitzer family, Benjamin proposed to Sonia. They had a wedding at Frumas house and got married. Because of Fruma's courage she made it possible for a family to have a real love life and have children. Fruma was an honored guest at their wedding and the Blitzer family felt forever in their debt.

Next I want to talk about the Bielski partisans and the work they have done. All of these people are related to me from my father's side. All of these people have made a big difference during the time of the concentration camps and the war. These people first started off with four of the Bielski brothers who escaped themselves from the German officers when they were gathering the Jews for the camps. The rest of her family got killed in the ghetto in August of 1941 and they wanted to retaliate so they did and they started rescuing who they could on their way. The names of the four Bielski brothers were Tuvia, Alexander (also known as Zus), Asael and Aron Bielski. They started small with whatever they could and they started a camp in the forest. They started with 13 neighbors and themselves. The group originally started at the size of 40 people but it grew very quickly after they started rescuing people. That is how this group formed.

A little background of the Bielski family is that they were millers and grocers in Stankiewicze near Nowogrodek, an area at the beginning of the Second World War that belonged to the second Polish Republic and was occupied by the Soviet Union in September 1939 in accordance with the Molotov-Ribbentrov non-aggression pact between Nazi Germany and the Stalinist Soviet Union. The Bielski family served as low-level administrators in the new government set up by the Soviets, who strained their relations with the local Poles, to whom the Soviet Union was an occupier. Following the Germans' Operation Bararossa, the invasion of Soviet Union that began on June 22, 1941, Nowogródek became a Jewish ghetto, as Nazis took over those lands and implemented their genocidal policies.

The partisans lived in underground dugouts or bunkers. In addition, several utility structures were built: a kitchen, a mill, a bakery, a bathhouse, a medical clinic for the sick and wounded, and a quarantine hut for those who suffered from infectious diseases such as typhus. Herds of cows supplied milk. Artisans made goods and carried out repairs, providing the combatants with logistical support that later served the Soviet partisan units in the vicinity as well. More than 125 workers toiled in the workshops, which became famous among partisans far beyond the Bielski base. Tailors patched up old clothing and stitched together new garments, shoemakers fixed old and made new footwear, leather-workers labored on belts, bridles and saddles. A metalworking shop established by Shmuel Oppenheim repaired damaged weapons and constructed new ones from spare parts. A tannery, constructed to produce the hide for cobblers and leather workers, became a de facto synagogue because several tanners were devout Hasidic Jews. Carpenters, hat-makers, barbers, watchmakers served their own community and guests. The camp's many children attended class in the dugout set up as a school. The camp even had its own jail and court of law.

The Bielski group's partisan activities were aimed at the Germans and their collaborators, such as Belarusian volunteer policemen or local inhabitants who had betrayed or killed Jews. They also conducted sabotage missions. The Nazi regime offered a reward of 100,000 Reichsmarks for assistance in the capture of Tuvia Bielski, and in 1943, led major clearing operations against all partisan groups in the area. Some of these groups suffered major casualties, but the Bielski partisans fled safely to a more remote part of the forest, and continued to offer protection to the noncombatants among their band. Like other partisan groups in the area, the Bielski group would raid nearby villages and forcibly seize food on occasion, and peasants who refused to share their food with the partisans were the subject of violence and even murder. This caused hostility towards the partisans from peasants in the villages, though some would willingly help the Jewish partisans.

The Bielski partisans eventually became affiliated with Soviet organizations in the vicinity of the Naliboki Forest under German platoon (Vasily Yefimovich Chernyshev). Several attempts by Soviet commanders to absorb Bielski fighters into their units were resisted, and the Jewish partisan group retained its integrity and remained under Tuvia Bielski's command. This allowed him to continue in his mission to protect Jewish lives along with engaging in combat activity, but would also prove a problem later on. The Bielski partisan leaders split the group into two units, one named Ordzhonikidze, led by Zus, and the other Kalinin, commanded by Tuvia. Fighting on the Soviet side, they took part in clashes between Polish and Soviet forces. Notably, they took part in a disarmament of a group of Polish partisans by the Soviets on 1 December 1943. According to partisan documentation, the Bielski fighters from both units claimed to have killed a total of 381 enemy fighters, sometimes during joint actions with Soviet groups.

In the summer of 1944, when the Soviet counteroffensive began in Belarus and the area was taken over by the Soviets, the Kalinin unit, numbering 1,230 men, women and children, emerged from the forest and marched into Novogrodek. Despite their previous collaboration with the Soviets, relations quickly worsened. The NKVD started interrogating the Bielski brothers about the rumors of loot they had reportedly collected during the war, and about their failure to "implement socialist ideals in the camp." Asael Bielski was conscripted into the Soviet Red Army and fell in the Battle of Konigsberg in 1945. The remaining brothers escaped Soviet-controlled lands, emigrating to the West. Tuvia's cousin, Yehuda Bielski, was sought by the NKVD for having been an officer in the pre-war Polish Army, but managed to escape with Tuvia's help and made his way to Hungary and then to Israel.

After the war, Tuvia Bielski returned to Poland, and then immigrated to present-day Israel in 1945. Tuvia and Zus eventually settled in New York where they operated a successful trucking business. When Tuvia died in 1987, he was buried in Long Island, New York, but a year later, at the urging of surviving partisans in Israel, he was exhumed and given a hero's funeral at Har Hamenuchot, the hillside graveyard in Jerusalem. His wife, Lilka, was buried beside him in 2001. The last living Bielski brother, Aron Bielski, immigrated to the US in 1951. He changed his name to "Aron Bell." The remainder of the Bell family now lives in upstate New York and California. Aron lives in Florida. None of the Bielskis ever sought any recognition or reward for their actions. Yehuda Bielski, their first cousin and fellow partisan, moved to Israel to fight in the Irgun.

Some of the members of the Bielski partisans (but not the Bielski brothers themselves) have been accused of war crimes on the neighboring population, particularly for alleged involvement in the 1943 Naliboki massacre of 129 people, committed by Soviet partisans. Though some witnesses and some historians do place members of the Bielskis' unit at the massacre, former members of the brigade and other historians, dispute this asserting that the partisans did not arrive in the area until several months later. The Polish Institute of National Remembrance has been investigating the massacre since the early 2000's. As of April 2009, it has not issued official findings. Some historians working at the Institute have asserted in other publications, however, that the Bielski brothers had not been involved in the massacre.

After knowing all of this I have pride in my last name and I can now tell people the story of my ancestors. And I just want to compare Willi Kranz and the Bielski brothers and family. They both did something great, both helped out people in need, but both had different ways and methods. Kranz was a peaceful man who did not want trouble but wanted to make a difference The Bielski brothers just wanted to help people and did this in a more violent way because they wanted revenge for their parents that were killed in the ghettos by the German officers. Both of these sides are heroes for what they did for the people in need.

Works Cited

"Kranx Willi." Yad Vashem. The Holocaust Martyrs' and Heroes' Remembrance Authority. 2016. Web. 15 February 2016.

"Bielski Partisans." Wikipedia, The Free Encyclopedia. Wikimedia, Inc. 2016. Web. 15 February   2016.

German/Ukrainian Heroes

Shelby Jones (Co-Winner)

 "The motives for my help? Nothing special in a particular case. In principle, what I think is this: If a fellow human being is in distress and I can help him, then it becomes my duty and responsibility. Were I to refrain from doing so, than I would betray the task that life – or perhaps God? – demands from me. Human beings – so it seems to me – make up a big unity; they strike themselves and all in the face when they do injustice to each other. These are my motives. "

The Holocaust was one of history's deadliest genocides, which killed 11 million people under the communist rule of Adolf Hitler and the Nazi Regime. Over one million children and five million non-Jewish victims were also killed during his time including homosexuals and the physically disabled. While all of Germany was occupied with darkness and fear, it was the acts of valor displayed by fearless everyday heroes that gave people a glimpse of humanity in a devastating time. By offering food or supplies to Jewish victims, to even lying to authorities and hiding Jews in their homes, these ordinary people became known as remarkable by their selfless displays of courage.

Countless brave people risked their lives to rescue those imprisoned by the Nazi soldiers during the Holocaust. One such heroin was a German widow Johanna Eck, born in 1888. This courageous woman succeeded in yielding refuge to four Jewish victims of the abuse of the Nazi regime. Eck was acquainted with Heinz Guttmann before the war, as Heinz father, Jakob, was comrades-in-arms with Eck's deceased husband.

In 1942, Jakob along with his wife and children had been deported to the east and never returned, leaving the very young Heinz abandoned. After wandering around aimlessly and barely escaping arrest, Heinz began to seek refuge but was denied on the argumentation of obtaining an illegal Jew. Johanna Eck was the only person to provide support to Heinz in this dangerous time by giving him shelter and even sharing her meager food allowances with him. In November 1943, Eck's home was demolished in an air raid and Johanna continued to protect Heinz by relocating him to a safer hiding place and continued to keep in contact with him. She provided food ration cards and important contact information to him even after he was relocated.

Johanna Eck became familiar with a Jewish girl named Elfriede Guttmann through Heinz's landlady at the time. In 1943 Eck agreed to provide shelter to the Jewish girl after she was told about her traumatizing experience with the Gestapo. While standing in a line at a bakery one day, Guttmann was approached by a girl around the same age as her, a former classmate. After hearing about the Jewish girl's circumstances, she was eager to help by giving her some personal Aryan documents confirming that she had done work for the labor force. This proved to be invaluable on the night of January 30, 1944 when their house was burned down in an air strike in Berlin. Elfriede's life ended tragically in 1946 when she developed a sudden stomach constriction shortly after her liberation, even after surviving the horrors of the war. Eck, a trained nurse, sat at her bedside before she passed away.

In 1937, a Ukrainian woman named Ludviga Pukas found a job in the town of Proskurov as a domestic for a high school teacher named Frima Sternik who lived with her two children ages one and four. Pukas and Sternik grew to be good friends, and Pukas continued to stay with Sternik even after giving birth to a child of her own. Sterniks home along with all of her possessions were burned down when the German conquered Proskurov on July 7, 1941. Sternik registered her two children, Gennadiy and Eldina, as well as Ludvigas child Gayla as Pukas' children. Now posing as a mother of three, Pukas was assigned a new apartment in which she lived with Sternik. While living in this new apartment Sternik began to feel noticed by the neighbors which compelled her to move to a ghetto. At the end of 1942, the eve of the liquidation of the Jews of Proskurov, Sternik was caught and killed while attempting to move to a home in the village that Pukas' brother owned.

After the ghetto was liquidated, German police went to search the home that Pukas was residing in with the three children. During the search they found another Jewish woman living with the family that Pukas had offered refuge to. They proceeded to do an intense search of the entire house, unaware that two of the children registered as Pukas' were Jewish themselves.

The Red army liberated Proskurov on March 25, 1944, and Gennadiy and Eldina returned to school after changing their names back to Sternik. The two children always regarded Pukas as their mother and remained with her even after they came into contact with two of their biological aunts.

Born in 1914, Yelena Gayevskaya was a young Russian artist living with her parents. Yelena was from a once noble family who had lost their wealth in 1917 during the Bolshevik revolution, and was living in a communal apartment. Gayevskaya met Anna Tarakanova and her husband, an opera singer and conductor of the theater choir in the late 1930s, as well as Anna's sister Yuliya Galpernia and her four-year-old daughter Tamara.

On September 29, 1941, the day on which the Jews of Kiev had been ordered to make their way to the ravines of Babi Yar, Gayevskaya went to Tarakanova very early in the morning and met her and her family on their way to the gathering point. Gayevskaya offered to hide the family in her apartment after managing to persuade them that it was a trap. Anna and Yuliya and Yuliya's daughter took Gayevskaya up on this offer, and Tarakanova's husband, who was not Jewish, returned home. After time had passed, rumors were spreading that Gayeskaya was hiding Jews in her home. After discovering that she was in risk of getting caught, she changed the data in Yuliya's identity documents and sent her to a home in the city that belonged to one of her friends.

The friends she was staying with began to suspect her of being Jewish, which caused her to leave the home under an assumed identity she used to work as a laborer until the liberation. In the meantime, Anna Tarakanova's husband obtained false identity papers for his wife and she and her niece Tamara returned home. Tarakanova was obliged to report once a week to the police station. Shortly before liberation, Tarakanova was killed after returning from signing these papers. Yuliya returned to Kiev and was reunited with her daughter in 1944. In 1965, she immigrated to Israel. Tamara continued to be in touch with Gayevskaya after her mother's immigration.

Luise Wilhelminee Elisabeth Abegg (Elisabeth Abegg) was a German educator and resistance fighter against Nazism born in 1882. Abegg was born to Friedrich Abegg, a jurist, and Marie Caroline Abegg in Strasbourg, which was then a part of Germany. Elisabeth Abegg studied history, classical philology and romance studies at Leizpig University in 1912 and graduated with a doctorates degree in 1916. She moved to Berlin in 1918 when the Alsace region was reclaimed by France. In Berlin, she became involved in postwar relief work organized by the Quaker community. She was an active member of the Garman Democratic Party and became a teacher at the Luisengymnasium Berlin-Mitte in 1924.

Abegg openly criticized the Nazi regime after Adolf Hitler assumed power in 1933. She was questioned by the Gestapo and was punished for this open criticism by being transferred to another less fashionable school. In 1941, she was forced to retire from teaching and officially converted to Quakerism in 1941. In 1942, Elisabeth began to help persecuted Jews by offering shelter. She relied on her Quaker friends and former students to help find safe option of shelter for the Jews she would rescue. Abegg would temporarily house dozens of Jews in vacant homes but found safer and more permanent options for housing in Berlin, East Prussia and Alsace. She sold her jewelry to pay for some Jews' escape to Switzerland and tutored hiding Jewish children at her apartment.

Between 1942 and 1945, Elisabeth Abegg rescued close to 80 Jews. After the Second World War, Abegg resumed teaching in Berlin. She became a member of the Social Democratic Party of Germany and was active in Quaker groups. In 1957, a group of Jews whom Abegg had rescued during the Holocaust published a book, titled And a Light Shined in the Darkness, in dedication to her. She died in 1974.

"I swore never to be silent whenever and wherever human beings endure suffering and humiliation. We must always take sides."
— Elie Wiesel

The Holocaust was one of the world's most devastating tragedies, leaving many feeling like all hope for humanity was absent. It was the brave heroes: Every day men and women, moms, dads, Jews, non-Jews, and many other sacrificial human beings that brought the sense of humanity back into a hopeless nation. The effects Adolf Hitler and the Nazi Regime left on the world will forever be a scar on the world's past. But like the painful memories of this genocide will forever linger in the minds of many, so will the shining legacy of those who chose to risk their lives for another human being despite of their race, religion, or beliefs.

Work Cited

Eck, Johanna. "Johanna Eck; Germany." Women of Valor. Yad Vashem The Martyrs' and Heroes' Rememberance Authority, 2016. Web. 22 February 2016.

Pukas, Ludviga. "Ludviga Pukas: Ukraine." Women of Valor. Yad Vashem The Holocaust Martyrs' and Heroes' Rememberance Authority, 2016. Web. 22 February 2016.

Abegg, Elisabeth. "Elisabeth Abegg." Wikipedia The Free Encyclopedia.Wikimedia Foundation, Inc. 30 December 2015. Web. 24 February 2016

"The Holocaust." Wikipedia The Free Encyclopedia. Wikimedia Foundation, Inc.17 February 2016. Web. 24 February 2016.

Yad Vashem. Yad Vashem The Holocaust Martyrs' and Heroes' Remembrance Authority. 2016.   Web. 24 February 2016.

T. R. Smedberg Middle School, Elk Grove, CA

Kalli Carvalho is a native of Sacramento, California. She graduated from University of California, at Davis in 1983. Her passion for teaching began in 1989, when she started her career as an educator. Since day one, Carvalho has always felt as though teaching the mandated curriculum (although critically important) is secondary to teaching life lessons that will help our young adults become compassionate, empowered citizens who will step up to change the inequities and injustices in our society and world.

This is why the teaching of the Holocaust has become one of the most important units for her 8th grade students. By using the Diary of Anne Frank, as well as the first-hand experience of honored Guest Speaker, Mr. Bernard Marks, students learn about tolerance, resilience, and resistance to ideologies which are destructive and hate-filled. The research paper (many submitted to the Eleanor Marks Essay Contest) is the culminating event, asking students to research and reflect upon the lessons taught.

When the Temple B'Nai Isreal was the target of a hate crime in 1999, Carvalho and her students took a field trip to the temple, to offer support and help to the Jewish community which was targeted.

Ms. Carvalho is a proud Greek-American who finds her joy in family, traveling to the Greek Islands, and reading. She looks forward to the future, as she is confident that the students of her past will be ready to build communities that show understanding and acceptance for all.

Hate Crimes in America

Angelyn Nguyen

 If you saw someone getting beat up on the streets, would you stop it? Of course you most likely said yes, but you probably won't actually stop it. Hate crimes were created by ancient civilizations, the Roman Empire was one of the first. Hate crimes are crimes that are motivated by racial, sexual, or other prejudice, and they usually involve violence. This type of crime is all over the world and it's hard to stop. Hate crimes are as old, if not older than the Roman Empire and are still here today. People around the world could learn valuable lessons from the heroes who stood up to Hitler's hate because Nazism is still in existence today, our world is facing religious based hate, and if it is not stopped unspeakable outcomes could occur. Therefore, Hitler's hate for the Jews still exists today.

First off, Nazism is still in existence today. Neo-Nazi is what people call the Nazis of the modern time. For example, Neo Nazis are often publishing material and host Internet servers and the Neo-Nazis in America are protected by the first amendment (https://www.splcenter.org). This shows that Nazism is still active and is use the internet to their advantage. Another piece of evidence is, Neo-Nazis are responsible for up to 45 deaths in the last 20 years (http://archive.adl.org). This evidence demonstrates that Neo-Nazis are around and have been killing at least 2 people a year. The Jewish Library states, "Neo-Nazi activity has surged and declined in unpredictable waves in Germany, France, England, Russia, the Scandinavian countries, the United States, Canada, South Africa, and elsewhere" (www.jewishvirtuallibrary.org). This evidence shows that Nazism exists and that it is very hard to predict how strong it would be. Keep in mind, that the Jewish religion is one of the many religions that are hated on.

Remember, our world is facing religious-based hate. To begin with, 18.6 percent of hate crimes are due to religious bias in 2015 (www.fbi.gov). This shows that there are people who commit crimes because of someone's religion. Furthermore, hate crimes motivated by religious bias accounted for 1,014 incidents and 1,092 offenses, involving 1,140 victims in 2014 (www.jewish-virtuallibrary.org). This shows that over a thousand people were hurt because of their religion in one year alone. Another piece of evidence is that Muslims are target more often since 9/11 (www.washingtonpost.com). The evidence not only shows that the Muslims are hated more often because of 9/11. It also shows that we fear them and the one way to react is to attack them. We attacked them so we feel better and we don't care what happens to the other group of people. This can go for anything like, sexuality, religion, ethnicity, etc. For this reason, we need to stop our attacks against certain groups of people.

Gradually, if hate crimes aren't stopped, the unspeakable will happen. For instance, Jews are still a big target for hate: 59 percent of religious bias hate crimes are anti-Jewish (http://forward.com). This means that the Jewish people are more likely to get attacked than any other religion. The Jew is at the risk of getting killed due to the high religious bias rate. This means that there is a risk for genocide of the Jewish people to happen once again. To prove the reason, the pyramid of hate needs to be explained (http://www.culturefreedomradio.com/). The pyramid has five levels of hate. The first level is prejudiced attitudes. This is where we are okay with stereotypes of any kind, make jokes that make people feel unimportant and most of us won't challenge it, and even blaming a whole group of people where most of them didn't do anything. The second level is acts of prejudice. Where our society will do these things to a group of people: call them names, mock them, make mean jokes, ban them for doing certain things and avoid them in general. The third level is discrimination. We discriminate them with education, employment, and housing. Plus, harass them and most of us won't help the groups of people that have it happen to them. The forth level is violence, the stage we are at. With violence against the group of people themselves we have thrown threats, attack, terrorized and murdered them because they weren't like us. We even destroy their property to prove we are stronger than them. The fifth and final level is genocide. Which is where we kill an entire group of people .We are one stage away from genocide happening because of the hate crimes we committed. There are certain groups of people that are more likely to have genocide against them. Plus, hate crimes may look like it has a steady rate but its slowly rising. The reason is hate groups are decreasing but the hate crimes are at the same rate (www.washingtonpost.com). This shows that hate crimes are increasing but most people are ignoring it. People ignore it because it's not affecting them but that is how Hitler gained power. People ignored the problem and it weakened the protest's power against Hitler and it could happen to us sooner or later. The risks of genocide happening is getting closer and closer, yet not many people are trying.

People around the world could learn valuable lessons from the heroes who stood up to Hitler's hate because if it is not stopped unspeakable outcomes could occur, our world is facing religious based hate and, and Nazism is still in existence today, Hitler's hate is growing stronger and it's getting more difficult to stop. You can help to stop this hate. It may not seem like much but if you can stop someone getting hurt, it might prevent a hate crime. If possible, you can conduct peaceful protest, this may be silly to you but it does help your cause. Now with the knowledge you have now, help stop hate crimes before it is too late.

Works Cited

Anti-Defamation League. "Neo-Nazi Skinheads." Stop Hate. Anti-Defamation League, 1999. Web. 17 Feb. 2016. < http://archive.adl.org/hate-patrol/njs/neonazi.html >.

Eric, Brotha. "The Pyramid of Hate." Culture Freedom Radio Network. Culture Freedom Radio Network, 11 Nov. 2015. Web. 17 Feb. 2016. < http://www.culturefreedomradio.com/apps/blog/entries/show/43628903-the-pyramid-of-hate >.

F.B.I. "Latest Hate Crime Statistics Available Report Contains Info on Offenses, Victims, and Offenders." FBI. U.S. Department of Justice, 16 Nov. 2015. Web. 17 Feb. 2016. <https://www.fbi.gov/news/stories/2015/november/latest-hate-crime-statistics-available/latest-hate-crime-statistics-available>.

Ingraham, Christopher. "Anti-Muslim Hate Crimes Are Still Five times More Common Today than before 9/11."Washington Post. Fred Ryan, 11 Feb. 2015. Web. 17 Feb. 2016. <https://www.washingtonpost.com/news/wonk/wp/2015/02/11/anti-muslim-hate-crimes-are-still-five-times-more-common-today-than-before-911/>.

Ingraham, Christopher. "The Ugly Truth about Hate Crimes - in 5 Charts and Maps." Washington Post. Fred Ryan, 2016. Web. 17 Feb. 2016. <https://www.washingtonpost.com/news/wonk/wp/2015/06/18/5-charts-show-the-stubborn-persistence-of-american-hate-crime/>.

Jewish Library. "Anti-Semitism in the United States: Statistics on Religious Hate Crimes." Jewish Library. Jason Levine, 2016. Wcb. 17 Feb. 2016. <https://www.jewishvirtuallibrary.org/jsource/anti-semitism/hatecrimes.html>.

Jewish Library. "Anti-Semitism: Neo-Nazism." Jewish Library. Fred Ryan, 2016. Web. 17 Feb. 2016. <https://www.jewishvirtuallibrary.org/jsource/anti-semitism/neonazism.html>.

Markind, Johanna. "Jews Are Still the Biggest Target of Religious Hate Crimes Read More: Http://forward.com/news/325988/jews-are-still-the-biggest-target-of-hate-crimes/#ixzz40TvYtQrn." Forward. The Forward Association, Inc., 2016. Web. 17 Feb. 2016. <http://forward.com/news/325988/Jews-are-still-the-biggest-target-of-hate-crimes/>.

Southern Poverty Law Center. "Neo-Nazi." S.P.L. Center. Alan B. Howard, 2016. Web. 17 Feb. 2016. <https://www.splcenter.org/fighting-hate/extremist-files/ideology/neo-Nazi>.

Ukrainian Heroes

Frank Kutsar (Special Award)

Have you ever heard about the Holocaust and what happened in that event?

The Holocaust was an action led by a ruthless leader named Adolf Hitler. This horrible action lasted from 1933-1945. Adolf Hitler was a genocidal killer who went after those of Jewish ethnicity. Hitler thought that there was a master race and he would have to create it. He didn't only go for the Jewish, but also after the cripple and gays. Hitler tried many ways to exterminate these people, but he figured it was too expensive. So he came up with the idea of "The Final Solution." This was where Adolf Hitler cremated the dead and living. Hitler's reign ended when the Soviet Union came in and freed all of the people. At this point, Hitler knew that the Soviets were

404

coming for him, so he committed suicide. Even though Hitler did so many horrible things, many Jewish people were saved because of the courage, bravery and humanity of the Ukrainian heroes who fought against Hitler. One of the main things that Ukrainians did to help the Jewish was their courage.

Many of the Ukrainians during the Holocaust were very courageous. For example, Ludviga Pukas was a Ukrainian maid who remained faithful to her employer, hiding her and her children (www.yadvashem.org). This evidence supports my thesis because if the Germans found out that Ludviga was hiding her Jewish employer, they would kill her and her family for helping a Jew. "However, before long, the neighbors noticed Sternik and she felt compelled to move to the local ghetto." (www.yadvashem.org) Secondly, "Julian Bilecki was just a skinny teenager when he and his family hid 23 Jews in an underground bunker, saving them from Nazi death squads" (www.auschwitz.dk). Julian Bilecki showed courage because not any ordinary teenager would try to risk his or her life hiding Jews. Lastly, Julian Bilecki's and the 23 other Jews' shelter was discovered, so Julian created a whole other bunker that they stayed in and survived (www.auschwitz.dk). This is courageous because if he didn't build one in time, they would all have to perish. Another important fact about courageous Ukrainians is that there were also very brave ones too.

Another act shown by Ukrainian heroes from the Holocaust was bravery. First off, Irena Sendler took advantage of her job in order to help the Jews. It became impossible once the ghetto was sealed off. She went into the ghetto to help the dying Jews. (www.yadvashem.org) Sendler gave up her own life to help something that she wasn't even a part of. Secondly, Anna Igumnova got her Ph.D. in chemistry and secretly gave out prescriptions to sick Jews (www.yadvashem.org). Luckily, Anna didn't get caught but if she did, it would be the end for her. Thirdly, Lois Gunden rescued Jewish children by taking care of them (www.yadvashem.ory). Lois gave a part of herself to be with children who she didn't know and had a different ethnicity than her. Although many Ukrainians showed bravery, much of them also showed humanity towards the Jews.

Thirdly Ukrainian heroes showed humanity. Starting with Karolina Juszczykowska, she hid Jews in her home to protect them from the Nazis (www.yadvashem.org). "The two fugitives were shot on the spot, and Karolina was arrested and interrogated" (www.yadvashem.org). Although she saved some of them, the police raided her house and found them, no one was left alive to testify the rest of what happened, Karolina really loved the Jewish ethnicity. Second, Sofia Kritikou was a single mother who took an 18, 16, and eight year old into hiding. They had fake identity cards bearing Greek orthodox names (www.yadvashem.org). This shows how a Ukrainian woman saved Jewish lives and how much she cared for them. Third of all, Antonia Gordey worked as a nanny for a Jewish family. She took care of a six year old and a three year old once the civil war broke out. (www.yadvshem.org) Antonia helped two kids survive so that the Jewish nation would prosper. These are the three main points of how Ukrainians showed courage, bravery, and humanity during the Holocaust.

Many Jewish people were saved because of the humanity, bravery and courage of the Ukrainian heroes of who fought against Hitler. There was once many of these heroes. Where are they now?

The Final Solution

Jonathan Vargas (Special Award)

Imagine you are in a place people call concentration camps. You're just barely surviving off one piece of bread a week. You're all alone because of one man named Adolf Hitler. He took your family from you in a blink of an eye, but you know you can't give up. You spend a majority of your teen life hoping one day all this would end. The Holocaust was a horrifying period of time beginning in 1938 in which a man named Adolf Hitler became Chancellor of Germany. He came up with the idea that Germans were the superior race. He wanted to wipe out all non-German human beings. By 1945, Hitler killed millions of people. The Jews were treated like they didn't mean anything because the Nazis treated them like they weren't human, they were sentenced to death through places called concentration camps, but there were still people willing to help the Jews. They never did anything wrong yet they were still being killed by the Nazis.

The Jews were killed through places called concentration camps. The Nazis had the Jews sent to these camps to be killed in gas chambers, cremation ovens, and they were killed by diseases that were spreading throughout these camps. One of the diseases at these camps was typhus, which is the disease that Anne Frank died from. These were only a few of the different ways the Nazis murdered millions of people (www.ushmm.org).

Many of these people never made it to the gas chambers or ovens. They died by starvation or dehydration. These death camps were located all over Germany, France, Berlin, Italy, and many others (www.jewishvirtuallibrary.org). These camps cut the hair of the people they held captive to demoralize them. To some people, their hair is a part of who they are and the Nazis took that away from them (www.projetaladin.org). However, concentration camps were only one way the Jews were treated cruelly by the Nazis.

The Jews weren't even treated as if they were human. The Nazis cut their Jewish hair and stripped them of their clothes. Nobody should've ever treated another person this way
(www.ushmm.org). The Nazis threw the Jews into cremation ovens where they were burnt alive. No person would ever do something so cruel to another, but Hitler did (www.yadvashem.org).

After death, their bodies were thrown into pits piling on top of each other stripped of their clothes. We usually bury our dead, not stack them like a pile of dirt. When we bury our dead, it helps us acknowledge the importance of the people that pass away, but Hitler did not give them that (www.clecem.org). Nevertheless, there were people willing to stand up to the Nazis.

There were people who stood up to the Nazis like a man named Adolf Althoff. He helped a girl named Danner hide from the Nazis and their twisted ideas. If he were to not help them, they would've been sent to a concentration camp (www.yadvashem.org). He provided Danner, her mother, and her sister with food, shelter, and supplies. Without these things, Danner and her family would have died (www.yadvashem.org).

Adolf was taking a big risk in hiding them because he could've gotten caught at any time. If he were caught, he would be killed or even sent to a concentration camp where he would be killed (www.yadvashem.org). "I couldn't leave them in the hands of these murderers" (Althoff).

Nonetheless, the Jews were wrongly accused of crimes they didn't commit.

The Jews were treated like they meant nothing because of how inhumanely the Nazis viewed them, they were murdered in places called concentration camps, but there were some people who saw the evil in Hitler's ideas and did something about it. The Jews never did anything to deserve such a horrible life. They were sent to these camps because of what they believed in. The people that stood up to the Nazis were a very brave group of people because if they were caught, they could've been tortured or even killed. This was a horrible period of time for our world and we need to make sure it does not happen again. We need to not discriminate people just because of the color of their skin or what their beliefs are. Hitler believed that the extinction of the Jewish people and many others was the Final Solution, but I believe that equality for all people of different color and religion is the Final Solution.

WORKS CITED

"Introduction to the Holocaust." United States Holocaust Memorial Museum. United States Holocaust Memorial Council, 29 Jan. 2016. Web. 16 Feb. 2016.
< http://www.ushmm.org/ >.

"Le Comité Aladin Femmes a Participé à La Projection Du Film « Fatima» Réalisé Par Philippe Faucon." Projet ALADIN. N.p., 2009. Web. 16 Feb. 2016.
< http://www.projetaladin.org/ >.

Vashem, Yad. "The Righteous Ones." YadVashem. The Holocaust Martyrs' and Heroes' Remembrance Authority, 2016. Web. 16 Feb. 2016.
< http://www.yadvashem.org/ >.

"Welcome to the Catholic Cemeteries Association." Catholic Cemeteries Association. Catholic Cemeteries Association, 2014. Web. 16 Feb. 2016. < http://www.clecem.org/ >.

Living In a Biased World

Maya Ledezma

Have you ever witnessed a cruel and hateful situation? If you did not know, the Holocaust was a very crucial, hateful and cruel time for the Jewish people and others. The Holocaust was led by a man named Adolf Hitler. The Holocaust was a very cruel and hateful time that took place between 1938 and 1945 in Germany and in Eastern Europe. This whole tragedy was caused by a man named Hitler because he wanted to rule the world and make it better. Many people rejected the ideas of Hitler's final solution, which is one of the things that led to the Holocaust. They rejected it because they recognized the hate involved and witnessed the cruelty of the Nazis and how some of the people who weren't harmed, didn't help. When it comes to acts of hate, ignoring it should never be the answer.

Many people rejected the ideas of the final solution because they recognized the hate involved. "On September 22, 1939 Jewish people were excluded from many things such as The Chamber of Cultures" and other important events (Gilbert). Even though this wasn't a very big deal, this was the beginning of the Holocaust. "They thought that the Jewish community were biologically and racially distinct, and also a struggle for dominance out of everyone else" (ww2history.com). This supports the thesis because it shows how they thought about them and why they hated them. "Hitler ... also ... thought that the Jewish people were directly responsible for Germany's many problems" (www.hitlerschildren.com). This supports the thesis because, it shows that Hitler dislikes them very much that he blames them for any and all problems that arise in Germany and in the world. Most of the people who weren't harmed witnessed the cruelty executed by the Nazis and never helped.

Many people rejected Hitler's ideas because they realized how cruel and wrong he was. "During the final solution, Hitler sent disabled, elderly, mentally ill people" ... and children ... "who weren't like him to concentration camps where they would suffer" (www.KatKinson9.tripod.com). On the other hand, this applies to the thesis, because they were cruel to people who they didn't like. To make them feel dehumanized, the Nazis "tattooed numbers on them that would become their names" during their time in the camps (www.KatKinson9.tripod.com).To sum up, this sentence supports my thesis because it shows that they wanted to make them feel worthless and that is an act of cruelty. During the long time they spent at the concentration camps, "many Jews were punished, by receiving jobs working the crematories watching their own people die" in front of their eyes (www.KatKinson9.tripod.com). As you can see, this is an act of cruelty because they wanted to scar and make them feel frightened. Since mostly all the people were worried and scared, they didn't want to help.

Many people rejected helping the Jewish people and many others who were in danger for many reasons. One reason why some of them didn't help was because "they didn't want to get" ... caught or ... "in trouble by the Nazis", and suffer a painful consequence (www. /why-didn't-everyone-help-the-Jews/). Therefore, this evidence proves that people denied helping, so they wouldn't get in trouble. In addition, "most of the people didn't ... actually ... "know what was happening at that time" (www./why didn't-everyone-help-the-Jews./). They weren't aware of the gruesome occasions that were happening, so they didn't have a chance to be able to help the people who were in danger. Last of all, the reason why most people didn't want to help is that because the "Germans saw nothing wrong in this situation" (www.enotes.com). Moreover, my piece of evidence supports the thesis because, it shows that certain people didn't think what Hitler was doing, was wrong, which makes them not want to help. Foremost, most people refused or were not aware to help Jews and others who were targeted.

To sum up my research, the events that took place during the Holocaust and the final solution were very cruel and hateful. The Holocaust took place during the years 1938-1945, led by a man name Adolf Hitler. The people of Germany and Eastern Europe recognized the hate involved, witnessed the cruelty of the Nazis and also how some of the people who weren't targeted or in danger didn't help. I have learned that when some people in power, commit crimes against humanity, and others look away because it's convenient or they are afraid it can lead to cruel acts like the Holocaust and the final solution. We should all try to make the world a less biased and racial place. Thus, have you, ever witnessed a cruel and hateful situation?

Works Cited

Martin Gilbert, Never Again a history of the Holocaust, Universe, June 17, 2000, print

No author, www.enotes.com, 2016. Web

No publisher, No author, www.Katkinson9.com, 12 Feb. 2016

"Why Didn't Anyone Do Anything to Stop the Holocaust? Why Didn't Anyone Do Anything to Stop the Holocaust? - Homework Help - ENotes.com." Enotes.com. Enotes.com, n.d. Web. 17 Feb. 2016.

"Hitler's Children." Hitler's Children. N.p., n.d. Web. 16 Feb. 2016.

A World I Would Choose

Shelley Du

Did you know that 6 million people were killed in the Holocaust because they weren't thought of as perfect? Could this happen again in today's age? The Holocaust lasted from 1933 to 1945 and was led by a man named Adolf Hitler. The Holocaust started in Germany when Hitler and the Nazis began to rise in power due to political and social circumstances that characterized the interwar period. The Holocaust began with hatred of Jewish people and the thought that they were an inferior race. This time of the Holocaust has the ability to teach people what hatred can lead to: would it be enough to stop it from happening again in today's society? The lessons of the Holocaust are still important today because many in our nation still face persecution, this hate sometimes can result in violence, and there are many to struggle to promote love and understanding. America will never persecute people like Nazi Germany did, right?

Many in our nation still face persecution. Many Christians are persecuted by abuse, kidnappings, and deportation because it's an assumption that persecution is part of the Church's past (www.opendoors.org.za). This shows that people are persecuted because of their religion. Religious hate isn't the only way people hate others: homosexual people are also persecuted by people (www.carm.org). People are being persecuted because of their sexuality and not thought of as just another person. Ten Baptist families were expelled from their community for not giving up their faith, which was Christianity. The families were not willing to give up their religion for someone else therefore they were expelled from their community; this is one of the many ways hate can spread. With this in mind, this hate may intensify into more.

This hate can sometimes result in violence. The Nazis' propaganda was that Jewish people were their misfortune (www.jewishvirtuallibrary.org). This is how the Nazis were able to convince people that it was okay to push out the Jewish from their society and eventually, it turned into brutal violence. "Darkness cannot drive out darkness; only light can do that. Hate cannot drive out hate; only love can do that." (Martin Luther King, Jr). During the Holocaust, 6 million Jewish people were murdered by the Nazis (www.yadvashem.org). This example is a perfect way of showing people how hate can turn into violence because the hate against Jewish people gradually got worse to the point of people gathering them up and killing them. Hate violence crimes are those directed against persons, families, groups, or organizations because of their racial or religious background (www.socialworkers.org). These crimes originate from hate that people hold for other just because they have different racial and/or religious background. In the end, can people really learn how to stop hating others?

There are many people who still struggle to promote love and understanding. Racism and discrimination are used to encourage fear and hatred of others (www.humanrights.gov.au). These acts show that people can't promote love and understanding but they can promote hatred and fear of people. The Darfur genocide is one of the many ways hatred is still around, even today. It refers to the mass rape and killing of Darfur men, women and children that began in 2003 that continues today. "The killings began in 2003 and continue still today, as the first genocide in the 21st century" (www.worldwithoutgenocide.org). This new genocide makes us ask each other: "Has anything really changed? Have we really become something different?" African Americans are one of the most frequent victims in the United States of hate crimes. Is this really something that should be going on, knowing that it will do nothing but just bring more hate onto the world and make people feel as if they're worthless; simply for being people of what group they're in? On the whole, have we really grown and realized that all of this results in and will continue to result nothing more than just violence?

The lessons of the Holocaust are still important today because many in our nation still face persecution, this hate sometimes can result in violence, and there are many to struggle to promote love and understanding. There are still many who struggle to promote love and understanding, this hate can result into violence, and there are many in our nation that still face persecution. Is this the kind of world you'd want to live in? If not, make sure you stop the person when you see or hear them hating on someone else just because they are different from them in one way or another.

Works Cited

"Australian Human Rights Commission." Admin. Www.humanrights.gov, 2012. Web. 18 Feb. 2016.

Ephross, Paul H. "The Impact of Hate Violence on Victims." The Impact of Hate Violence on Victims. Arnold Barnes, May 1994. Web. 18 Feb. 2016. <http://www.socialworkers.org/pressroom/events/911/barnes.asp>.

"How Vast Was the Crime." Yadvashem. N.p., n.d. Web. 18 Feb. 2016. <http://www.yadvashem.org/yv/en/holocaust/about/index.asp>.

Kuntz, D. "Nazi Propagnda Tactics." Jewishvirtuallibrary. Www.yadvashem.org, n.d. Web. 18 Feb. 2016. <https://www.jewishvirtuallibrary.org/jsource/Holocaust/propaganda.html>.

"Peace & Inspiration: Great Quotes." The Peace Alliance. N.p., n.d. Web. 18 Feb. 2016. <http://peacealliance.org/tools-education/peace-inspirational-quotes/>.

Slick, Matt. "Examples of Persecution of People Who Do Not Agree with Homosexuality." CARM. Matt Slick, n.d. Web. 16 Feb. 2016. <https://carm.org/homosexual-persecution-of-christians>.

"Ten Baptist Families Expelled for Refusing to Recant Their Faith." « Persecution News. J. Schnabel, 28 Jan. 2016. Web. 16 Feb. 2016. <http://www.persecution.org/2016/01/28/breaking-news-ten-baptist-families-expelled-for-refusing-to-recant-their-faith/>.

Discrimination in Modern America

Trentt Parker

On a quiet night in a peaceful neighborhood, a racist slur is shouted by a band of white supremacists. Breaking the window of a peaceful and small house is a brick with a threthning message that warns the happy family to leave town. This kind of discrimination doesn't just happen in countries far away; it happens in America. Though death camps aren't involved, this hate is often reminiscent of the discrimination that happened during the Holocaust. The Holocaust was a 7-year period in which the Nazi Party, led by Adolf Hitler, killed 6 million Jewish people and 5 million non-Jewish people. This mostly took place in Germany, but the death camps, such as Auschwitz, were built and run outside of Germany. The Holocaust, or "The Answer to the Jewish Question," started in 1938 and ended in 1945. The lessons of the Holocaust are still important today because many on our nation are still facing persecution, this hate can sometimes result in violence and yet, there are many who struggle to promote love and understanding.

Even in America many groups of people are discriminated against, persecuted, and made to feel like they are less than other people. The Washington Post`s research shows that 65 percent of LGBT affiliates feel that they are discriminated against while 54 percent of African-Americans feel as though they are discriminated against as well (www.washingtonpost.com). These are important numbers because even though we've grown more accepting, we still are discriminatory. InterNations states "Due to zero-tolerance policies in schools, disadvantaged black youths quickly end up being pushed out of school and into the juvenile and criminal justice systems" (www.internations.org). Black youth are not given a fair chance to get out of the stereotypical box they are put in. InterNations also states "After the September 11 terrorist attacks, Islamophobia has increased in the US, fueled by ignorance and the faulty belief that all Muslims are fundamentalists" (www.internations.org). Muslims are one of the most discriminated groups in the U.S. because of faulty stereotypes. This discrimination hurts emotionally and is unjustified, but sometimes this discrimination can lead to violent hate crimes.

Discrimination can sadly lead to violent hate crimes, even in America. The Human Rights Campaign states "In more than half the country – 29 states – employees lack explicit workplace protections on the basis of sexual orientation" (www.hrc.org). In these states it is viewed as "fine" to discriminate a co-worker because of their sexual orientation, America may be making major progress but there is still a long way to go. The Leadership Conference "On Election Night 2008, Ralph Nicoletti and Michael Contreras, both 18, and Brian Carranza, 21, of Staten Island, New York decided shortly after learning of Barack Obama's election victory "to find African Americans to assault," according to a federal indictment and other court filings. The men then drove to a predominantly African-American neighborhood in Staten Island, where they came upon a 17-year-old African American who was walking home after watching the election at a friend's house. One of the defendants yelled "Obama!" Then, the men got out of the car and beat the youth with a metal pipe and a collapsible police baton, injuring his head and legs. The men went on to commit additional assaults that night" (www.civilrights.org). This is a major reason that children of African American descent grow up afraid of what people could do to them. Forward`s research shows that 59 percent of religious-based hate crimes were directed toward Jewish people (www.forward.com). Even though the Holocaust is over discrimination against Jewish people certainly is not. Through this discrimination there are people who struggle to advocate and promote peace.

People who try to spread love and understanding are blocked out because many people are unwilling to listen or cooperate. The Human Rights Campaign states "The

412

Human Rights Campaign represents a force of more than 1.5 million members and supporters nationwide" (www.hrc.org). Though this is a large number it is upsetting how miniscule it seems when you find out that over 300 million people live in the United States. Yad Vashem states: "The mainstream watched as their former neighbors were rounded up and killed; some collaborated with the perpetrators" (www.yadvashem.org). If this discrimination doesn't sound familiar to what is going on right now in many countries, including the U.S., you should open your eyes to the real problems in society. Biography Online says about Martin Luther King Jr. "On April 4th 1968, King was assassinated" (www.biographyonline.net). Martin Luther King Jr. just wanted to spread messages of love and togetherness, and instead he was shot dead.

The lessons of the Holocaust are still important today because many on our nation are still facing persecution, this hate can sometimes result in violence and yet, there are many who struggle to promote love and understanding. In conclusion if this discrimination continues, America could be in danger of a senseless tragedy like the Holocaust.

Works Cited

"An Important Step Toward Workplace Equality: An Executive Order on Federal Contractors."   <i>Human Rights Campaign</i>. N.p., 2016. Web. 3 Feb. 2016. <www.hrc.org>.

Berman, Mark. "Americans See a Lot of Discrimination against People Who Are Muslim, Black   or Gay." <i>Washington Post</i>. The Washington Post, 17 Nov. 2015. Web. 2 Feb.   2016. <http://www.washingtonpost.com/>.

Hate Crimes Against African Americans." The Leadership Conference. N.p., n.d. Web. 4 Feb.   2016. <www.civilrights.org>.

"HRC Story." Human Rights Campaign. N.p., 2016. Web. 18 Feb. 2016. <http://www.hrc.org/>.

"Martin Luther King Biography." Biography Online. N.p., 2016. Web. 18 Feb. 2016.   <www.biographyonline.net>.

Norris, Brian, and Caroline Stiles. "Racism and Discrimination in the US." InterNations. N.p., n.d. Web. 2 Feb. 2016. <www.internations.org>.

"The Righteous Among The Nations." Yad Vashem. N.p., 2016. Web. 18 Feb. 2016.   <http://www.yadvashem.org/>.

America: Future Heroes or Bystanders?

Vincent Tang (Special Award)

"The world is a dangerous place to live; not because of the people who are evil, but because of those who don't do anything about it" (Einstein). Adolf Hitler became Fuhrer of Germany in 1934. Later he started what became known as the Holocaust, which, when translated, means "burn it all." All, referring to the Jewish people, as well as other people who Hitler saw as inferior. The reason for Hitler's anti-Semitism is unknown, other than using the Jewish population as a scapegoat for Germany's failures. Hitler's efforts to exterminate the "undesirables" were not completely successful because many saw the wrong doing, refused to stand by and watch, and even took life-threatening risks to make a change. Perhaps, witnessing these acts of hate inspired people to do something about it.

Many people saw Hitler's wrong doing. The Nazis sentenced groups of women to death by starvation and women awaiting for their sentence were only given food rations to eat, only every other day, which was just fake bread and vegetable soup. They were also crammed into small rooms with about 60 women in each room. This shows just a small fraction of the cruelty that the Nazi government is capable of inflicting upon others. Most Jewish armed resistance formed after 1942 as an attempt to resist the Nazis, despite their lack of training, after it has become clear that the Nazis had murdered their families. The Jewish armed resistance showed that the Jewish people were aware of what the Nazis were doing to them. The war of self- defense was carried out on three levels: armed uprisings in ghettos and camps; escape and smuggling of Jews from towns and ghettos to the forests for partisan warfare; and by hiding individuals in various hiding places. The Jews who had been captured realized that the Nazis were an evil government, and had chosen to fight for their right to live, rather than let themselves slowly die out. So they chose to help fight against the Nazis secretly.

People who had seen Hitler's wrong doings refused to stand by. Many Jewish workers sabotaged the German factory goods often by sewing clothes and making them nearly impossible to wear, and by using too many nails on the soles of shoes, making them nearly impossible to wear. This shows that Jews were able to secretly sabotage the Nazi factory, without being caught. Ludmilla Page and other Jewish workers would purposely make flaws on ammunition shells made of enamelware for months while in Bruennlitz. This is a more effective sabotage on German goods, because the Nazi army would not be able to fight back, if their ammunition was flawed. Nazi-sponsored persecution and mass murder fueled the resistance to the Germans in the Third Reich itself and throughout occupied Europe, although Jews were the Nazis' primary victims, they also resisted Nazi oppression, so they escaped.

Many individuals took life threatening risks for a change. Jewish prisoners were able to successfully launch uprisings, even the worst conditions, in many camps, including Auschwitz. This shows the power of the Jewish people, when they work together. Ivan Shevchenko, Ukrainian Holocaust Jew smuggler, met Yakov Sukhenko on a trip to Zdulbunow and when the two became friends, they hatched a plan to help their Jewish family and comrades escape to Eastern Ukraine. This shows the bravery of the people who knew what was right, who would take the risk of losing their lives for doing what was right. Despite the indifference of most Europeans and the grouping of others in the massacre of the Jews during the Holocaust, people of all neighboring countries, of all ethnicities and religious backgrounds still chose to help the Jews. Those who helped the Jews knew the risks of death for helping, but they also knew that what Adolf Hitler and the Nazis were doing was wrong, so they chose to do what was right.

Hitler's effort to exterminate the "undesirables" was unsuccessful. People took life threatening risks for change, refused to stand by, and many saw the wrong doings. When wrongs occurs here, in America, will we just stand by or will we take action?

Works Cited

"Armed Jewish Resistance: Partisans." United States Holocaust Memorial Museum. N.p., 29 Jan. 2016. Web. 18 Feb. 2016. <
http://www.ushmm.org/wlc/en/article.php?ModuleId=10005441

"Armed Jewish Resistance: Partisans." United States Holocaust Memorial Museum. N.p., 29 Jan. 2016. Web. 18 Feb. 2016.
<http://www.ushmm.org/wlc/en/article.php?ModuleId=10005441>.
http://www.ushmm.org/wlc/en/article.php?ModuleId=10005441

"Oral History." United States Holocaust Memorial Museum. United States Holocaust Memorial Council, n.d. Web. 18 Feb. 2016.
http://www.ushmm.org/wlc/en/media_oi.php?MediaId=3185

"Jewish Uprisings in Ghettos and Camps, 1941–1944." United States Holocaust Memorial Museum. United States Holocaust Memorial Council, 29 Jan. 2016. Web. 18 Feb. 2016.
http://www.ushmm.org/wlc/en/article.php?ModuleId=10005407

"The Righteous Among The Nations." The Righteous Among The Nations. United States Holocaust Memorial Museum, n.d. Web. 18 Feb. 2016.
http://db.yadvashem.org/righteous/righteousName.html?language=en&itemId=4017457

"Rescue." United States Holocaust Memorial Museum. United States Holocaust Memorial Council, 29 Jan. 2016. Web. 18 Feb. 2016.
http://www.ushmm.org/wlc/en/article.php?ModuleId=10005185

Overseas Schools

Private Gymnasium Dr. Richter, Kelkheim, Germany

Marion Polydore

Principal

Manfred Rennenberg

Teacher sports and mathematics

Ilse Sonja Totzke

Katharina Scherer (Co-Winner)

"Das Vorgehen gegen die Juden halte ich nicht für richtig. Mit diesen Maßnahmen kann ich mich nicht einverstanden erklären. Hierzu möchte ich betonen, dass ich keine Kommunistin bin. Mir ist ein jeder anständige Mann recht, ganz gleich welcher Nationalität er angehört."1

Aussagen wie diese waren zu Zeiten des NS Regimes gewiss nicht alltäglich. Diese stammt von einer Frau, die zu Zeiten des Nationalssozialismus bereit war, ihr Leben zu riskieren, um die damals verfolgten Juden vor einem ungerechtfertigten grausamen Schicksal zu schützen. Sie ist bekannt unter dem Namen Ilse Sonja Totzke, geboren ein Jahr vor Ausbruch des Ersten Weltkriegs am 4. August 1913 in Straßburg und geehrt seit 1995 als „Gerechte unter den Völkern" in der Holocaust Gedenkstätte Yad Vashem.

Aufgewachsen ist sie bei ihren Eltern Sofie Wilhelmine Totzke, einer Elsässerin mit Abstammung aus einer angesehenen Künstlerfamilie und von Beruf Schauspielerin, sowie Ernst Otto Totzke, einem Lehrersohn aus Westpreußen und von Beruf Kapellmeister. Die protestantisch getaufte Ilse verließ das Elsass in Begleitung ihres Vaters und sie zogen nach Mannheim, vorerst ohne Sofie, die kurz darauf nachfolgte. Dieser Beschluss war Folge des 1919 zurückgefallenen Elsass-Lothringen an die Franzosen. Otto Totzke, der fest entschlossen war seine deutsche Nationalität zu behalten, war nun gezwungen Straßburg zu verlassen. Ilse verzieh ihrem Vater nie, dass er ihre Mutter einfach so zurückließ. 1920 starb Sofie sehr jung im Alter von nur 30 Jahren. Es kam zur erneuten Heirat des Vaters und die nun 19 Jahre alte Ilse bekam 2 Stiefschwestern, entschied sich jedoch 1924 ihr Zuhause, für ein Leben im Internat in Bamberg, zu verlassen.

Das Verhältnis zu ihrem Vater lässt sich keinesfalls als harmonisch bezeichnen, denn in noch minderjährigem Alter klagte Ilse vor Gericht gegen ihn. Die Beschuldigung, er verschwende ihr mütterliches Erbe, erntete Zuspruch und ein Vormund sollte von nun an die Erbschaft verwalten, bis zu ihrer Volljährigkeit, da das Erbe ja nun Ilse zustand.

Nach erfolgreicher Absolvierung der Schulausbildung in Ludwigshafen und Mannheim, zog Ilse in die Heimat ihrer Stiefmutter, die in Bamberg gelegen war und schrieb sich im März 1932 am Bayerischen Staatskonservatorium für Musik in Würzburg ein, um Klavier, Violine und Dirigieren zu studieren. Nicht selten wechselte sie ihre Adresse und lebte als Untermieterin bei jüdischen Familien. Die Machtübernahme der Nationalsozialisten 1933 brachte Ilse nicht dazu, von ihrer ablehnenden Einstellung gegenüber der Judenverfolgenden Bewegung abzuweichen und

---

1 http://www.fembio.org/biographie.php/frau/biographie/ilse-totzke/

auch den Hitlergruß verweigerte sie. Dies führte zu Misstrauen und der Überwachung der mittlerweile 20 Jahre alten, überzeugten Gegnerin Hitlers.

1934 erwarb sie mit dem Erreichen ihrer Volljährigkeit den ihr zustehenden Teil des mütterlichen Erbes , welcher einen Flügel, 42.000 Reichsmark2 und wertvolle Einrichtungsgegenstände beinhaltete. In den nächsten 2 Jahren wohnte Ilse dank ihrer Beziehungen auf Gut Keesburg im Grünen und kam in den Besitz einer Kamera, mit der sie ihre Vorliebe für Landschaftsfotografie entdeckte. Doch feindlich gesinnte Beobachter ,wie damals ein Sport-Professor, sahen in ihr das Motiv einer Spionin. Die Sommerferien verbrachte sie in Österreich und Italien, bekam jedoch auch Besuch von Bekannten, zu denen auch „Jüdinnen im neuen BMW-Wagen" zählten, wie der Gutsverwalter berichtete. Im November 1935 beschloss sie, ihre Stiefschwestern in Bamberg zu besuchen, doch das Schicksal ließ ihr Ziel unerreicht und es kam vermutlich aufgrund des schlechten Wetters zu einem Unfall, der für Ilse Totzke später der offizielle Grund der Beendigung ihres Musikstudiums wurde. Da sie einen Schädelbruch erlitt, musste sie sechs Wochen lang im Juliusspital bleiben, kehrte dann jedoch wieder nach Gut Keesburg zurück. Sie geriet ins Visier der Gestapo , aufgrund ihrer sich von den anderen unterscheidenden , protestantischen Verhaltensweise, bei der sie sich von ihrem Umfeld abkapselte und immer mehr zurückzog, den Hitlergruß verweigerte und Kontakte zu Juden pflegte. Diese, damals als respektlos empfundene Lebensweise konnte vom Konservatorium nicht toleriert werden und ist der wahre Grund der Zwangsrelegierung Ilses. Handfeste Beweise gab es nie, doch ihre Nachbarschaft denuzierte sie, mit teilweise lächerlichen Beschuldigungen. Ihre Angewohnheit bis zur Mittagsstunde zu schlafen, sowie ihre hervorragenden französischen Sprachkenntnisse, machten sie scheinbar verdächtig. So manch einer stufte Ilse sogar als männerfeindlich ein. Das war zu dieser Zeit jedoch keineswegs ungewöhnlich. Bestätigt wird diese Annahme durch vielerlei Zitate. Ein Beispiel hierfür stammt von einem Mann namens Gellately : „ Manchmal war die Bevölkerung radikaler als die Nazis. Es gab so viele Denunziationen, dass die Gestapo am Ende nicht mehr hinterherkam."3

Es wurde sogar eine Akte für sie angelegt, die ihren Lebenswandel dokumentierte und von der kontaktfreudigen jungen Frau bis hin zur scheinbar isolierten Rebellin berichtet. Auch ein erneuter Umzug 1938 änderte nichts an Ilses ausweglosser Lebenssituation, denn nun lebte sie zurückgezogen in einem Häuschen mit zwei Zimmern und Küche auf dem Grundstück eines Textilkaufmanns. Einer bedeutsamen Tätigkeit ging sie zu dieser Zeit nicht nach und beschäftigte sich überwiegend mit dem geerbten Flügel ihrer Mutter und Büchern, doch der finanzielle Notstand zwang sie zu einer Beschäftigung im Wandergewerbe , für die Ilse sich schämte. Doch im Jahr 1939, aufgrund des Einmarschs in Polen, wird ihre Tätigkeit aufgelöst und es herrscht wieder Krieg. Mit ihm wuchs auch das Misstrauen gegen alle Verdächtigen und somit auch gegen

---

2 https://books.google.de/books/IlseTotzke

3 http://daserste.ndr.de

Ilse, da sie für ihre Ablehnung der herrschenden politischen Richtung bekannt war. Ihre isolierte Wohn- und Lebenssituation sowie ihre Arbeitslosigkeit und ihr gegen Normen verstoßendes Verhalten , zum Beispiel ihre Liebe zu Frauen und Vorliebe für männliche Kleidung, sowie ihr jüdischer Freundeskreis brachten sie erneut ins Visier der Gestapo. Es folgte ein Verhör, in dem ihr die Einweisung in ein Konzentrationslager angedroht wurde, falls sie den Umgang mit Juden nicht zukünftig unterlassen würde.

Die Nürnberger Gesetze des Jahres 1935 führten zur Freiheits- und Rechtseinschränkungen der Juden. Ein erster Schritt zum Ziel, die Juden aus der Volksgemeinschaft auszugrenzen, war mit dem Verbot einer Ehe zwischen Juden und Ariern getan. Dieses Gesetz verschärfte sich 1941 stark, als das Verbot einer freundschaftlichen Beziehung zwischen Juden und Deutschen durchgesetzt wurde. In diesem Jahr wird auch Ilse Totzke näher unter die Lupe genommen, als man erneut ihre Post überwachen ließ und es folgte ein Zusammentreffen zwischen Ilse und der Gestapo am 5. September. Nachdem man ihre Wohnung durchsucht hatte und keinerlei Indizien fand, außer ein paar Büchern die von jüdischen Schriftstellern geschrieben wurden, verhörte man sie und Ilse gestand den Kontakt den sie zu Juden pflegte. Die Politik betreffend äußerte sie sich sehr bescheiden, mit der Begründung, sie habe nicht viel für diese übrig.

„Wenn aufgrund meiner jüdischen Bekanntschaften unterstellt wird, dass ich den Nationalsozialismus ablehne, so antworte ich,dass ich mich nicht um Politik kümmere."

Das waren ein paar der mutigen Worte die an diesem Tag von Ilse gesprochen wurden.

Mit dem weiteren Verlauf des Gesprächs, leugnete Sie ihre Judenbekanntschaften keineswegs, sondern betonte ihre Meinung, indem sie verkündete, dass das Vorgehen gegen die Juden nicht richtig sei. Dort sprach Ilse auch die einleitenden, aufrichtigen Worte, die eingangs erwähnt wurden.

Da jeder kriegsfähige Mann seinen Platz in der Armee eingenommen hatte, wurde jede Arbeitskraft benötigt. Die dann folgende Weigerung Ilses, Ihre Dienstverpflichtungen zu erfüllen , wobei sie sich auf die Spätfolgen ihres Schädelbruchs im Jahr 1935 berief, rückte Ilse in kein besseres Licht und ließ sie als arbeitsscheu gelten. Diese Taktik schützte sie jedoch vor den drohenden Strafen, die damals bei Kriegsdienstverweigerung üblich waren. Doch Ilses wahre Begründung war der Gewissenskonflikt ,mit dem sie zu kämpfen hatte. Einen Einsatz für die Kriegsmaschinerie, konnte sie mit sich selbst unter keinen Umständen vereinbaren.

Inzwischen war Ilse so uneins mit ihrer deutschen Staatsangehörigkeit, dass sie ihren Ausbruch in die Schweiz plante, aber vorerst mit dem Ziel den Juden bei der Flucht zu helfen und das Schicksal dieser vor ihr eigenes zu stellen.Später gab sie bekannt, es sei schon lange ihr Wunsch gewesen aus Deutschland zu flüchten. Die damals herrschenden Umstände machten ihr diese Entscheidung leicht. Der erste erfolgreiche Grenzübertritt rettete 2 jüdischen Frauen das leben.Beiden verhalf sie über die Grenze in die Schweiz, kurz vor deren drohender Deportation. Ilse scheiterte jedoch beim zweiten Versuch 1943. Der nachfolgende Text beschreibt die beiden Fluchtversuche:

Es ist die Nacht vom 26. zum 27. Februar 1943: In der Dunkelheit waten zwei junge Frauen durch das eiskalte Wasser der Lützel. Das ist ein idyllisches Flüsschen, das am anderen Ufer "Lucelle" heißt. Die Lützel / Lucelle bildet die Grenze zwischen dem Süd-Elsass und dem Schweizer Jura. Die beiden Flüchtlinge klettern über den Drahtverhau, der Nazi-Deutschland von der Schweiz trennt, und suchen sich im Dunkeln ihren Weg in die Freiheit.

Ruth Basinski ist Jüdin. Ihre Deportation in ein Konzentrationslager stand unmittelbar bevor, als Ilse Totzke sie überredete, die Flucht zu wagen. Ein paar Monate zuvor schon hat Ilse Totzke zwei andere jüdische Frauen über die Grenze gebracht und ihnen damit das Leben gerettet. Diesmal jedoch misslingt der Fluchtversuch. Die beiden Frauen werden gefasst und nach Deutschland ausgeliefert.

Warum Ilse nach dem ersten erfolgreichen Fluchtversuch nach Deutschland zurückgekehrt ist, bleibt unklar. Vielleicht hatte sie sich schon verpflichtet weitere Fluchthilfe zu leisten. Die Möglichkeit Asyl in der Schweiz zu beantragen nutzte sie nicht und kehrte auf eigenen Wunsch über die Grüne Grenze ins deutsche Reich zurück.

Ihr Schicksal ließ jedoch keinen erfolgreichen Fluchtversuch mehr zu und die Folgen waren für beide Beteiligten Frauen gravierend.

Was sie dann beim Verhör zu Protokoll gibt ist den Nationalsozialisten Grund genug sie in ein Konzentrationslager zu schicken :

„Der Fluchtplan war mein eigener Entschluss, ich wurde von keiner Seite unterstützt (...) Ich möchte nochmals erwähnen, dass ich aus Deutschland flüchten wollte, weil ich den Nationalsozialismus ablehne. Vor allem kann ich die Nürnbergergesetze nicht gutheissen. Ich hatte die Absicht, mich in der Schweiz internieren zu lassen. In Deutschland wollte ich unter keinen Umständen weiterleben."

Mit diesen Worten konnte sie ihre Komplizin Ruth Basinski jedoch leider nicht beschützen, denn diese wurde nach tagelangem Verhör nach Ausschwitz deportiert. Sie waren ebenso die Ursache für Ilses Deportation im Juni 1943, ins Konzentrationslager Ravensbrück, wo sie den Namen Sonia Totzki ,aus bis heute unbekannten Gründen, annahm. Sie gab sich als polnische Staatsangehörige aus , vermutlich aufgrund ihre ablehnenden Haltung gegenüber ihrer deutschen Wurzeln.

Die nun zur Schwerstarbeit gezwungene Frau musste unter miserablen Bedingungen leben, was Auswirkungen auf ihre seelische und gesundheitliche Verfassung hatte . Das NS Regime wusste sich nur mit der Vergasung mehrerer Tausenden Gefangenen zu helfen, um die Zahl der Häftlinge zu reduzieren, was für unmenschliche Zustände sprach. Ilse, nun Sonia, konnte jedoch durch eine Rettungsaktion des Schwedischen Roten Kreuzes aus der Lagerhaft befreit werden und überlebte.Nach der Gefangenschaft trat sie einen Erholungsaufenthalt in Schweden an und zog anschließend nach Paris.

Nach ihrer nun zerstörten beruflichen Zukunft bleibt Sonia nichts anderes übrig als ihren Unterhalt 9 Jahre lang mit Gelegenheitsarbeiten zu verdienen. Dieses Schicksal wurde von ihr jedoch nicht akzeptiert und sie beschloss 1954 nach Würzburg zurückzukehren um von den Behörden eine Entschädigung zu verlangen. Schon früher hatte sie ihre Anwältin beauftragt einen Wiedergutmachungsantrag zu stellen, doch Ergebnisse ließen lange auf sich warten. Letzten Endes erhielt sie 8750 Mark für einen traumatischen Schicksalsschlag, der sie für alle Zeiten geprägt hat.

Bei all diesen Ereignissen verlor Ilse den Kontakt zu ihrer Familie und nahm diesen auch nicht wieder auf. Im März 1957 erreichte eine Mitteilung das bayerische Entschädigungsamt per Luftpost, in der Ilse schrieb, sie sei auf einer Studienreise in Pakistan. Über die letzten 30 Jahre ihres Lebens ist bislang nichts konkretes bekannt, jedoch zur besseren Vorstellung des äußeren Erscheinungsbildes dieser Widerstandskämpferin, dürfen ihre Größe von 159 Zentimeter, sowie ihr schlanker Körperbau und die langen dunkelblonden Haare und grau-blaue Augen, nicht unerwähnt bleiben. Diese Informationen entnahm man ihren Akten während ihrer Inhaftierung in Würzburg, kurz bevor sie ins Konzentrationslager geschickt wurde.

Ihre Sterbeurkunde verrät ihren Tod am 23. März 1987 im elsässischen Haguenau. Wie genau sie starb und woran ist unklar, jedoch besagen Quellen, sie sei ermordet worden, wie beispielsweise ein Zitat von Schott während eines Interviews preisgibt: „Frau Totzke war keine Jüdin." Aber am Ende wurde auch sie umgebracht, weil sie Juden geholfen hat".[4]

Doch eine zu ihrem 100. Geburtstag nach ihr benannte Straße in Würzburg lässt ihren Namen nicht in Vergessenheit geraten,sowie ein für sie gepflanzter Baum in der „Allee der Gerechten" in Jerusalem.

Quellenangaben

http://www.mainpost.de/ueberregional/politik/zeitgeschehen/Zerstoerter-Traum-von-Freiheit;art16698,7608227

http://wuerzburgwiki.de/wiki/Ilse_Totzke

http://www.br.de/radio/bayern2/bayern/land-und-leute/ilse-totzke-wuerzburg-yad-vashem-koerner-keuler100.html

http://tatteredremnants.blogspot.de/2009/10/014-ilse-sonja-totzke-1913-1941.html

https://books.google.de/books

http://www.fembio.org/biographie.php/frau/biographie/ilse-totzke/

http://daserste.ndr.de/panorama/archiv/2001/erste7664.html

---

[4] http://daserste.ndr.de/panorama/archiv/2001/erste7664.html

Wilhelm Adalbert Hosenfeld

Nele Schwarzenberger (Co-Winner)

Wilhelm Adalbert Hosenfeld wurde am 2. Mai 1895 in dem kleinen Dorf Mackenzell in der Nähe von Fulda geboren. Er war das vierte von sechs Kindern. Sein Vater war Lehrer. Die Familie war streng katholisch, was ihn von Kind an sehr prägte. Als Jugendlicher trat Wilhelm, genannt Wilm, in eine Schüler- und Studentenbewegung namens „Wandervogel" ein. Mitglieder dieser Bewegung bevorzugten ein Leben in der freien Natur und setzten wichtige Impulse für die Reformpädagogik und die Freikörperkultur in Deutschland. Außerdem wollten sie ein starkes National- und Gemeinschaftsgefühl bei den deutschen Bürgern wecken. Gegenüber der Politik verhielt sich die Wandervogelbewegung neutral. In dieser Bewegung fühlte sich der junge Wilm sehr wohl. Ihre Prinzipien und Ideale hatten für ihn auch in seinem weiteren Leben eine hohe Bedeutung.

Eine Woche nach Beginn des ersten Weltkrieges beendete Wilm Hosenfeld sein Lehramtsstudium. Die Lehrerausbildung legte in der damaligen Zeit einen besonderen Schwerpunkt auf eine patriotische Erziehung der Schüler. Wilm Hosenfeld meldete sich danach freiwillig als Soldat zum Einsatz. Während des Krieges wurde er schwer verwundet und kehrte 1917 schließlich in sein altes Heimatdorf zurück. Sein Referendariat absolvierte er dann ab 1918 als Lehrer in verschiedenen Gemeinden rund um Fulda.

Im Jahr 1920 heiratete Wilm Hosenfeld die 22-jährige Pazifistin und Protestantin Annemarie Krummacher. Annemarie stammte aus einer Kunstmalerfamilie in der Nähe von Bremen. Ein Jahr nach ihrer Hochzeit bekamen die beiden das erste von insgesamt fünf Kindern.

1927 wurde Wilm Hosenfeld nach längerer Arbeitszeit als festangestellter Lehrer einer Volksschule in Hessen zum Direktor dieser Schule ernannt. Damit bekam er auch die Chance und den Raum, seine ehrgeizigen reformpädagogischen Ziele umzusetzen.

Die Machtübernahme 1933 von Adolf Hitler begrüßte Wilm Hosenfeld. Seine Begeisterung galt vor allem Hitlers Vorhaben, Deutschland vom Versailler Friedensvertrag zu befreien. Der Vertrag war 1919 verabschiedet worden und sah sowohl die wirtschaftliche als auch militärische Schwächung Deutschlands vor. Außerdem fand Hosenfeld, dass Adolf Hitler mit seiner starken Persönlichkeit und Zielstrebigkeit ein guter Politiker sei, der Deutschland sowohl innerlich als auch nach außen hin wieder stärken würde. Zusätzlich erhoffte er sich, dass durch die vielfältigen Großveranstaltungen und Aktionen und durch die Rhetorik der NSDAP eine einheitliche Volksgemeinschaft entstünde, so wie es auch schon immer sein persönliches, als auch ein Ziel der Wandervogelbewegung gewesen war. Den Antisemitismus, der fester Bestandteil des Parteiprogrammes der NSDAP war, schien Wilm Hosenfeld dabei vollkommen ignoriert zu haben. Mehr Sorgen bereitete dem bekennenden Christen, die während der dreißiger Jahre zunehmende Bekämpfung der katholischen Kirche durch Adolf Hitler. Trotzdem trat Hosenfeld 1933 zuerst der SA und nach der Zwangs-Auflösung des Katholischen Lehrerbundes auch dem Nationalsozialistischem Lehrerbund bei. Mitglied der NSDAP wurde er 1935. Hitlers Massenveranstaltungen, wie zum Beispiel die Nürnberger Reichsparteitage, faszinierten Hosenfeld sehr, doch einen erneuten Krieg wollte er nicht. Da er die Sorge vor einem neuen Krieg auch offen vor seinen Schülern vertrat, wurde ihm die Lehrerlaubnis für den weltanschaulichen Unterricht entzogen. Die Nationalsozialisten hatten befürchtet, Wilm Hosenfeld könnte seine Schüler zu Pazifisten erziehen.

Zu Beginn des Zweiten Weltkrieges 1939 meldete sich Wilm Hosenfeld freiwillig zum Militärdienst in Polen. Seine Frau Annemarie war strikt gegen den Einmarsch in Polen und auch dagegen, dass sich ihr Mann daran beteiligte, konnte ihn jedoch nicht davon abhalten. Wilm empfand den Einsatz in Polen zwar nicht als angenehm, aber als gerechtfertigt und notwendig. Er fühlte sich verpflichtet, dort zu kämpfen, um Deutschland wieder zu einer starken Nation zu machen, die von der Welt respektiert und anerkannt würde. Außerdem hoffte er, nach dem Krieg auf einen große und glückliche Zukunft Deutschlands unter Hitlers Führung. Nach dem Sieg über Polen wurde er, ohne an einem Gefecht teilgenommen zu haben, zum Offizier befördert. 1940 wurde Hosenfeld nach Warschau versetzt. Dort lernte er polnisch und nahm direkten Kontakt zu den Polen in Warschau auf. Wilm Hosenfeld zeigte sich respektvoll den Polen gegenüber. Für ihn spielte es keine Rolle, ob sie Gefangene, Juden, Kommunisten oder einfache Bürger waren. Für Wilm Hosenfeld galt die christliche Maxime, dass alle Menschen gleich seien und gleich zu behandeln seien. Außerdem ging er bei jedem Menschen unvoreingenommen erst einmal von dem Besten aus.

1941 wurde Wilm Hosenfeld Leiter der Wehrmachtssportschule in Warschau. Zu dieser Zeit erfuhr er auch das erste Mal vom Warschauer Ghetto. Was sich genau hinter den meterhohen Mauern und Stacheldrahtzäunen abspielte, fand er nach kurzer Zeit heraus. Unter welchen miserablen, schrecklichen und menschenverachtenden Bedingungen die Juden dort lebten, schockierte und entsetzte ihn zutiefst. Wilm Hosenfeld begann sich für die Deutschen zu schämen, aber vor allem schämte er sich vor sich selbst. Dafür, dass auch er tatenlos zuschaute. In einem Brief an seine Ehefrau Annemarie schrieb er damals: „Ich sehe viel Rohheit und Dummheit und Lügen und Verblendung. Dieser Krieg ist mit Unrecht über Unrecht beladen, keine hohe sittliche Idee ist da."

Nach einigen weiteren schlimmen Einblicken und dem Miterleben vieler Gräueltaten, die die Nationalsozialisten an Juden und der polnischen Zivilgesellschaft begingen, veränderte sich Wilm Hosenfeld. Er suchte mehr Halt in seinem katholischen Glauben und begann mutiger zu werden. Er fing an jüdischen Kindern im Ghetto heimlich Essen zu zustecken, obwohl er damit riskierte, selbst hart bestraft zu werden. Auch ließ er sich zusammen mit Juden und Polen fotografieren, um offen zu zeigen, dass sie für ihn, entgegen der nationalsozialistischen Ideologie, keine Untermenschen waren.

Wilm Hosenfeld befand sich in einem ständigen Konflikt mit sich selbst. Auf der einen Seite hielt er den Krieg immer noch für gerechtfertigt. Er wünschte sich auch weiter aktiv als Frontsoldat kämpfen zu dürfen und war stolz auf die Verantwortung, die er mit der Sportschule trug. Auf der anderen Seite sah er jedoch die unzähligen Gräueltaten und Kriegsverbrechen der Nationalsozialisten, die er überhaupt nicht mit seinem Gewissen und seinen religiös geprägten Idealen vereinbaren konnte. In einem Tagebucheintrag aus dieser Zeit notierte Wilm Hosenfeld: „Wenn das wahr ist, was in der Stadt erzählt wird, und zwar von gläubigen Menschen, dann ist es keine Ehre, deutscher Offizier zu sein, dann kann man nicht mehr mitmachen [...] Aber das ist ja alles Wahnsinn, das kann doch nicht möglich sein."

Wilm Hosenfelds innerer Konflikt wurde immer größer, bis er es nicht mehr aushielt, seine Augen vor Misshandlung, Deportation und Vernichtung der Juden zu verschließen. Er begann, sich vom Nationalsozialismus abzuwenden, und mit dem polnischen Widerstand zu sympathisieren.

Im April 1943 war Wilm Hosenfeld auf Heimaturlaub in Deutschland. Dort berichtete er seiner Familie von den kaum in Worte zu fassenden Verbrechen der Nazis an den Juden, wie zum Beispiel den unzähligen Massenhinrichtungen in Konzentrationslagern. Während Wilm Hosenfelds Heimaturlaub fand ein großer Aufstand, der wenigen noch nicht deportierten Juden, im Warschauer Ghetto statt. Er wurde von den Nationalsozialisten blutig niedergeschlagen. Weitere hunderte Juden verloren ihr Leben.

Für Wilm Hosenfeld war der Aufstand im Warschauer Ghetto offenbar ein letzter entscheidender Wendepunkt. Er schrieb am 16. Juni 1943 in sein Tagebuch: „Diese Bestien. Mit diesem entsetzlichen Judenmassenmord haben wir den Krieg verloren. Eine untilgbare Schande, einen unauslöschlichen Fluch haben wir auf uns gebracht. Wir verdienen keine Gnade, wir sind alle mitschuldig. Ich schäme mich, in die Stadt zu gehen, jeder Pole hat das Recht, vor unsereinem auszuspucken."

Als Wilm Hosenfeld von seinem Heimaturlaub zurück nach Warschau kam, begann er seinen persönlichen, einsamen und verzweifelten Kampf. Er versuchte, so viele Menschen wie möglich zu retten, die sonst potentielle Opfer der Nazis hätten werden könnten. Damit ihm das gelang, nutzte er seine Position als Leiter der Wehrmachtssportschule in Warschau. Er fälschte die Dokumente und Pässe etlicher vom Tode bedrohter Polen und Juden, um sie dann unter falschem Namen in der Sportschule anstellen zu können. Insgesamt hatte die Sportschule 27 Angestellte.

Das letzte Treffen zwischen Wilm Hosenfeld, seiner Frau und seinen Kindern war im Mai 1944. Wilm Hosenfeld notierte damals in seinem Tagebuch, dass er der festen Überzeugung sei, dass die Taten der Nazis einer Welt ohne Gott entsprächen. Und dass das deutsche Volk eines Tages dafür büßen müsse.

Die Lage in Warschau änderte sich abermals, als sich am 1. August 1944 die Widerstandsgruppe „Polnische Heimatarmee", gegen die deutsche Besatzung Polens erhob. Die deutsche Armee ging sehr aggressiv gegen die Widerstandsgruppe vor, große Teile Warschaus wurden völlig zerbombt. Wilm Hosenfeld hatte die Aufgabe, die gefangenen, oft sehr jungen, Widerstandskämpfer zu verhören. Während dieser Verhöre versuchte Wilm Hosenfeld alles Mögliche, um die Widerstandskämpfer so gut wie möglich zu entlasten. Denn er persönlich bewunderte zutiefst ihren Mut, sich gegen die deutsche Diktatur zu erheben. Außerdem veranlasste Wilm Hosenfeld gegen den Willen der SS-Führung, dass die Verletzungen der Gefangenen versorgt wurden und dass die Gefangenen nach den Genfer Konventionen behandelt wurden. Unter hohem Risiko, selbst bestraft oder sogar getötet zu werden, gelang es Wilm Hosenfeld einige Widerstandskämpfer mit gefälschten Pässen als seine Mitarbeiter in seiner Dienststelle anzustellen. Nur durch Wilm Hosenfelds mutiges Handeln gelang es, ihr Leben vor dem Terror des Nationalsozialismus zu retten. Unter diesen Personen befanden sich auch einige Juden.

Bekannt wurde Wilm Hosenfeld vor allem durch die Rettung des jüdischen Pianisten Wladyslaw Szpilman. Ende 1944 entdeckte Wilm Hosenfeld den vollkommen ausgehungerten Mann, der sich seit einigen Monaten in den Ruinen von Warschau versteckt hatte. Wilm Hosenfeld versorgte ihn mit Essen und versteckte ihn bis Kriegsende auf dem Dachboden einer Villa. Die Geschichte von Szpilman wurde 2002 in Roman Polanskis Oscar gekröntem Film „Der Pianist - Mein wunderbares Überleben" weltbekannt.

Trotz der unbeschreiblichen Verbrechen der Deutschen in Polen genoss Wilm Hosenfeld bei seinen Angestellten bis zu seinem Verlassen von Warschau 1944 ein hohes Ansehen. Doch er selbst war psychisch am Ende. Denn obwohl er Menschenleben retten konnten, konnte er sich sein Mitwirken und Mithelfen an den Verbrechen der Nationalsozialisten nicht verzeihen. Er fühlte sich schuldig, weil er jahrelang an Hitlers Drittes Reich geglaubt hatte, es unterstützt und dafür gekämpft hatte. Und dafür, dass er nicht schon früher angefangen hatte, die Ideologie Hitlers anzuzweifeln. Schon am 28. März 1943 schrieb Wilm Hosenfeld in sein Tagebuch: „Und wir Toren glaubten, sie könnten uns eine bessere Zukunft bringen. Als Schande muss jeder Mensch es heute empfinden, daß er auch nur im geringsten dieses System bejahte."

Im Januar 1945 wurde Wilm Hosenfeld von Soldaten der Roten Armee in der Nähe von Warschau gefangen genommen. Nach jahrelanger Inhaftierung wurde Wilm Hosenfeld 1950, ohne den Nachweis eines Verbrechens, aber wegen seiner Zugehörigkeit zur „Abteilung Ic", zu 25 Jahren Lagerhaft verurteilt. Die Sportschule gehörte organisatorisch zu der „Abteilung Ic" von Wilm Hosenfeld und war unter anderem auch für nachrichtendienstliche Tätigkeiten zuständig, was der Hauptgrund für seine Inhaftierung war. Die von Wilm Hosenfeld geretteten Menschen durften nicht vor Gericht aussagen und konnten ihn deshalb auch nicht entlasten. Auch die verzweifelten Versuche seiner Frau und eines von ihm geretteten Polen, Wilms Freilassung zu erwirken, scheiterten.

Schon während der Inhaftierung und vor seiner Verurteilung erlitt Wilm Hosenfeld mehrere Schlaganfälle, die dazu führten, dass er halbseitig gelähmt wurde. Außerdem litt Wilm Hosenfeld unter den enorm strengen Haftbedingungen, die in seinem Fall Isolationshaft bedeuteten. Er versuchte immer wieder vergebens, sich in eine polnische

Haftanstalt verlegen zu lassen. Auch die von ihm während des zweiten Weltkrieges geretteten Polen und Juden versuchten während seiner gesamten Inhaftierung und bis zu Wilm Hosenfelds Tod immer wieder seine Freilassung zu erwirken. Doch all das blieb vor den russischen Richtern wirkungslos. Keiner von Ihnen schien sich auch nur im Ansatz dafür zu interessieren, was Wilm Hosenfeld während des zweiten Weltkrieges für die von Nazis verfolgten Menschen getan hatte und dies zu seinen Gunsten auszulegen.

Am 13. August 1952 starb Wilm Hosenfeld nach weiteren Schlaganfällen im Kriegsgefangenenlager Stalingrad. Er wurde 57 Jahre alt.

Im Februar 2009 wurde Wilhelm Hosenfeld von der israelischen Gedenkstätte Yad Vashem zu einem „Gerechten unter den Völkern" ernannt. Wladyslaw Szpilman beantragte diese Ernennung schon 1998. Es dauerte aber noch elf Jahre bis die Unschuld von Wilm Hosenfeld bewiesen wurde und bis belegt war, dass er nie an Kriegsverbrechen der Deutschen, während der NS-Zeit, beteiligt gewesen war.

Zu Wilm Hosenfeld Entlastung konnten auch die vielen Tagebücher und Briefe beitragen, die er während seiner Stationierung in Polen an seine Frau Annemarie geschickt hatte. In diesen von großer Verzweiflung und innerer Zerrissenheit geprägten Dokumenten hielt Wilm Hosenfeld detailliert fest, was er in Warschau Tag für Tag erlebt hatte. Auch scheute er sich darin nicht, deutliche Kritik am Umgang der Nazis mit den Polen zu üben. Er verurteilte Hitlers Gräueltaten. Vor allem aber schäme er sich zutiefst für sein eigenes Zutun zum Gelingen der Naziherrschaft und für das Handeln und Wegschauen aller Deutschen.

Wilm Hosenfelds Briefe und Tagebücher wurden im Jahr 2004 in dem Buch: „Wilm Hosenfeld, Ich versuche jeden zu retten" veröffentlicht.

Quellen:

Tom Ockers - Dokumentationsfilm: „Vater, Mutter, Hitler- Vier Tagebücher und eine Spurensuche"

Stefanie Maeck –„Der Nazi, der Juden und Polen rettete" - 23.11.2015 - www.spiegel.de

Marian Bretz - Biografie Hosenfeld- www.lemo.de

Arne - Wilhelm Hosenfeld -„Ich versuche jeden zu retten, der zu retten ist" - www.bündische-vielfalt.de

Wilm Hosenfeld- www.wikipedia.de

Manfred Füge – „Der Offizier, der nicht nur den Pianisten rettete"- www.welt.de - 03.07.2004

Arrigo Beccari (Giorgio Perlasca)

Livia Antonella Parisella
Fondi, Italy

Arrigo Beccari nacque a Castelnuovo Rangone il 14 agosto del 1909 e all'età di 14 anni entrò in seminario divenendo successivamente sacerdote nel 1933, anno in cui svolse anche la carica di insegnante ed economo nel Seminario Minore di Nonantola.

Oltretutto dal 1939 al 1980 ricoprì anche l'ufficio di parroco nella chiesa di San Pietro a Rubbiara, una frazione di Nonantola e dal 1980 al 1986 fu parroco di Nonantola, dove rimase fino alla morte, nel 2005[2].

Don Arrigo ebbe un ruolo principale nella vicenda storica di Villa Emma infatti nel 1942 l'organizzazione ebraica di assistenza ai rifugiati DELASEM riuscì a ottenere il permesso affinché un gruppo di una cinquantina di ragazze e ragazzi ebrei rifugiatisi in Slovenia, potesse essere accolto in Italia e il delegato bolognese Mario Finzi prese in affitto la spaziosa Villa Emma, a Nonantola, per dare sistemazione al gruppo. Ad essi in seguito se ne aggiunsero altri, raggiungendo una novantina di ragazzi di varie età e varie provenienze e la villa divenne oltre ad un luogo abitativo, una scuola in cui venivano svolte attività pratiche in condizioni di sostanziale tranquillità, come ad esempio la coltivazione delle patate.

L'8 settembre, con l'occupazione nazista, in meno di 36 ore, don Arrigo Beccari e il suo amico, il dottor Giuseppe Moreali provvidero a nasconderli, affidandone una parte a una trentina di famiglie locali, già da un anno coscienti dell'esistenza di Villa Emma, collocandone molti altri nel Seminario Abbaziale vestiti da seminaristi, mentre alcune ragazze vennero affidate alle suore come finte novizie. Tutti i ragazzi, provvisti di documenti falsi, poterono espatriare in Svizzera a piccoli gruppi tra il 6 e il 17 ottobre 1943. Uno soltanto tra i piccoli ospiti di Villa Emma, malato e ricoverato in ospedale, fu deportato e perì ad Auschwitz e la stessa sorte toccò anche a Goffredo Pacifici, il bidello di Villa Emma, che fu arrestato e deportato una settimana dopo mentre guidava in Svizzera altri ebrei, molti dei quali nel dopoguerra raggiunsero Israele. Nel frattempo la parrocchia di Rubbiara divenne una centrale importante della Resistenza emiliana ove si stampavano nel solaio documenti falsi e materiale di propaganda antifascista, e si dava rifugio a partigiani e ebrei, non solo modenesi e ferraresi ma anche quelli mandati da don Leo Casini e dalla curia fiorentina, i quali venivano sistemati nelle campagne circostanti.

Il sacerdote purtroppo venne arrestato il 16 settembre 1944 per una delazione, assieme a don Ennio Tardini, e passò sette mesi, senza mai confessare la sua attività, nel carcere bolognese di San Giovanni in Monte fino alla Liberazione.

Il suo impegno verso i rifugiati venne premiato con il titolo di Cavaliere dell'Ordine al merito della Repubblica Italiana il 2 giugno 1961, di Giusto tra le Nazioni il 18 febbraio 1964 e di Prelato d'onore di Sua Santità il 23 ottobre del 1989.

Don Ivo Silingardi, al centenario dalla sua nascita, lo ricordò come un semplice parroco di campagna , incrollabile di fronte a tutte le difficoltà anche quando venne arrestato e non smise di agire contro il fascismo rubando le lenzuola per chi ne aveva bisogno e trovando informazioni su altri detenuti per farle avere ai loro parenti liberi. Un uomo che rincuorava i suoi parrocchiani, incitandoli a resistere e a non abbattersi, spesso usando questa frase: "Nei momenti di malinconia pregate, lavorate e pensate che dopo la tempesta viene sempre il sereno". Un uomo che non si lamentava mai, che al contrario ha sempre accettato tutto quello che la vita gli poneva innanzi prendendolo come una prova, un'occasione per rafforzarsi.

Un uomo che giustificava il suo dovere di aiutante nei confronti del popolo ebraico dicendo ai giovani sopravvissuti:"Se siamo riusciti ad aiutarvi, anche un poco soltanto, Dio ne terrà conto. Ma non l'abbiamo fatto per questo, l'abbiamo fatto perché lo dovevamo fare".

Il 17 gennaio, festa di S. Antonio Abate patrono degli animali, era tradizione che il parroco andasse a benedire le stalle e consegnasse al contadino un immagine 'nuova' di S. Antonio circondato dagli animali domestici. Rubbiara di Nonantola fino a quaranta anni fa era una terra agricola con stalle e case coloniche. Don Beccari amava particolarmente questa festività e lui considerava questo giorno un'occasione preziosa per incontrare i suoi parrocchiani chiamando tutti i contadini per mangiare insieme il cotechino e i ciccioli del maiale appena macellato, accompagnato da un bicchiere di Lambrusco, il tipico vino emiliano e perciò quest'anno è stata scelta la stessa data per inaugurare una statua realizzata in suo onore dallo scultore Romano Buffagni, suo ex allievo divenuto poi maestro nella scuola di artigianato fondata dal sacerdote, quest'ultimo dimessamente vestito, sorridente, con una mano sotto il mento, in un atteggiamento che era solito avere nei momenti di tranquillità conviviale tra la sua gente. History written by Livia Antonella Parisella from Fondi, Italy

Itailian Historical Page

Giorgio Perlasca (Arrigo Beccari)

Livia Persila

A hero is someone who helps people and someone who risks his/her life for other people. Heroes in the Holocaust would risk their lives for other people.

A man who had saved thousands of Hungarian Jews, he made protective passes for them which are fake passports so they could go to a different country for them to be safe and this hero's name was Giorgio Perlasca.

Giorgio Perlasca was born on January 31, 1910 in Como, a city located in Lombardy, Italy. He was raised in Masera, Province of Padua. He fought in the Second-Italo Abyssinian War and in the Spanish Civil War in the area of East Africa.

In World War II, Perlasca helped get supplies for the Italian army. After a while, he was put into an official delegate of the Italian Government. The Italians would send him to Eastern Europe to get supplies for the Italian army. On 8 September 1943,

Dwight Eisenhower, an american general had said about the surrender of Italy to the allied forces. The Italians had to decide to joing Mussolini's Italian Social Republic or stay on the side of the King and fight on the Allies' side. Perlasca had chosen to stay on the king's side and that had cost his freedom which meant they had to take him as a prisoner. He was put in a castle for diplomats. He was given a christian name 'Jorge.' A few months passed by and he had a medical pass which let him travel in Hungary; he took advantage of it.

Giorgio worked with a man named Angel Sanz Briz and of course other diplomats. Giorgio's job was to make protective passes. Angel Sanz Briz was taken to Switzerland on November 1944, and he had asked Perlasca to go with him to safety on a note Briz had left. But he decided to stay. Immedeatley Perlasca had lied to the Hungarian government that Angel Sanz Bris would only be leaving for a short period of time and that he would be back and in the meantime he would substitute. All throughout the winter, Perlasca would hide, shield and feed thousands of Jews in Budapest, and he would make them protective passes since a law had passed for onlyJews of Sephardi orgin could get but he made it too save as many Jews he could. He would bribe and beg officials and police men into helping him with protecting as many Jews as he could save. Also, in that time with the Russians approaching Budapest, the last remaining Spanish diplomat fled the capital, leaving the embassy officially closed down. Everything he had been doing had worked, even though he had to patrol the houses night and day to make sure that roving bands of Hungarian Nazis did not break in and murder or kidnap the protected people. But that only happened once when 300 people under Spanish protection were carted off to the Budapest for deportation to Auschwitz.

On December 1944, he had rescued 2 boys from going on a train convincing the German army with the protective passes. From December 1, 1944 to January 16, 1945, he had saved over 5,000Jews by himself, more than the famous Oskar Schindler had saved. After the war, Perlasca went back to Italy, but didn't tell what he had done to anyone, not even his own family. But then in 1987, a group of Hungarian Jews had found him.

He was a man who was proud of himself to have saved all those innocent lives. He may have not saved them all but he did do the best he could. There are many Holocaust heroes but Giorgio Perlasca was the most inspiring and interesting to know that any of the Holocaust heroes would risk their own lives to help other those are true heroes. It's sad to know how this world had been through before knowing that people could be so heartless to kill own man kind. Giorgio Perlasca is yet to be one of the best in history. He was blessed with a gift, a gift to save people but unfortunately he has passed away on August 15, 1992 in Padua. But yet again he has left a great history for himself. Added to all those heroes, he will not be forgotten. That is why people keep this alive. People need to know about these great heroes. Sad and unbelieveable things always happen, you never know what you will face and all you can do is hope for the best and help the best and be the best you can. Like Giorgio knowing he could loose his life for helping out Jews that weren't from the certain origin they needed to be from the law. He knew that he was putting himself in danger and he knew he would not have the chance to see his family again but he worked for them. He had to stay, and he did not like to see innocent lives being taken. Children, women, men, elderly, every one of those people who didn't make it could have been something great in life. They could have saved lives also, big things. Especially the children, they weren't able to live the rest of their lives because of selfish maniacs. They never got the chance to even think about what they wanted to be, all they might have thought is that everyone in the world was like the Nazis. They couldn't do anything but get killed, but Perlasca was at least able to save many and important lives. The reason I picked to write about Giorgio Perlasca is I knew every other unsung hero did the same by saving Jews but Giorgio Perlasca's story was interesting, it was something that helped Jews get out of it completely with a protective pass. A man who would help all throughout his life, Hitler was his enemy. He had chosen the right path for himself and his future. He couldn't have chosen better, after everything Giorgio Perlasca in my opinion is one of the best unsung heroes of the Holocaust.

Technical University

Праведники Народов мира

Zlata Arestova

День Катастрофы (ивр. יום השואה, **Йом ха-Шоа**) — национальный день памяти и траура в Израиле и за его пределами, установленный Кнессетом в 1951 году. День, в который по всему миру вспоминаются евреи, ставшие жертвами нацизма во время Второй мировой войны.

Холокост или как его называют в еврейских кругах - Шоа, величайшая из трагедий прошлого! Слово *"холокост"* — греческого происхождения, оно означает *"жертва всесожжения"*.

В 1933 году еврейское население Европы превышало девять миллионов человек. Большинство европейских евреев жили в странах, которые во время Второй мировой войны были оккупированы Германией или находились под ее влиянием. К 1945 году немцы и их сподвижники убили почти две трети из числа евреев, живших в Европе, в рамках программы "Окончательное решение еврейского вопроса" – плана уничтожения европейского еврейства.

Хотя евреи, которых нацисты считали главной угрозой Германии, были основными жертвами нацистов, среди обреченных на смерть были и около 200 000 цыган.

Число уничтоженных людей с умственными и физическими недостатками (главным образом немцев, живших в лечебницах) - жертв программы "эвтаназия" также приближается к 200 000. Коммунисты, социалисты, Свидетели Иеговы и гомосексуалисты, все они подверглись гонениям по политическим или поведенческим мотивам.

Украинские евреи всегда имели большое значение как для самой страны так и для ее жителей. Во все времена евреи Украины занимали важную роль в культуре, образовании, бизнесе и становлении Украинского государства. Большие еврейские общины и маленькие семьи были расположины во всех Украинских городах также в маленьких местечках и селах. Одним из таких городов был город Проскуров (нынешний Хмельницкий).

Первые сведения о евреях Плоскирова (именно так называлось местечко до своего переименования в 1795 году в Проскуров и в 1954 году — в

Хмельницкий) можно найти в документах Ваада четырех земель за 1627 год [*центральный орган автономного еврейского общинного самоуправления в Речи Посполитой, действовавший с середины XVI до половины XVIII веков*]. В разные периоды он был частью территорий и Речи Посполитой (затем Польского царства), Оттоманской, и Российской Империи. В период восстаний, 1648–54 гг., этот тогда польский городок был стерт с лица земли казацкими отрядами под предводительством Максима Кривоноса и Данилы Нечая. Так как казаки не слишком любили евреев, то шансов остаться в живых у последних было очень мало. Несмотря на жестокость повстанцев к евреям, ходили слухи, что гетман Хмельницкий по каким-то причинам был более миролюбив к еврейской общине Плоскирова, что давало следующим возможность жить и вести свой бизнес в более удоволетворяющих условиях.

В 1740-е гг. расположенное в 30 км от Плоскирова местечко Меджибож стало важнейшим центром хасидизма и сегодня является одним из главных мест паломничества иудеев. Вскоре приверженцами хасидского движения стали все евреи города.

По переписи 1765 г., в городе проживало 750 евреев. После первого раздела Польши (1772), по данным Подольских епархиальных ведомостей, в Плоскируве из 300 дворов 184 были еврейскими.

В 1775 г. город получил право на проведение дважды в год двухнедельной ярмарки, это оживило его экономику и способствовало притоку евреев.

Одним из красочных примеров Проскуровских евреев 18 века был раввин и основатель хасидизма Бааль Шем Тов (Исраэль бен Элиэзер), он поселился в Междибоже в 1740 г., и тут же протекала его основная деятельность. До переезда в этот поселок он уже стал известным, хотя жизнь его нельзя было назвать простой.

Он был еврейским учителем, много времени уделял духовному развитию, но продолжал зарабатывать на жизнь тяжелым трудом — добывал известь. Когда ребе переехал в Междибош он уже был известен как целитель и святой.В своей ешиве он собрал десятки учеников, которые продолжили его традицию и стали лидерами хасидизма.

В Проскурове и соседних к нему городах было по истине много талантливых евреев, многие из которых к сожолению стали частью ужасных событий. Но важно знать, что все они внесли огромный взнос в культуру и повседневную жизнь всего еврейского населения Украины и других стран. Яркими примерами стали Гершеле Острополе(1757-1811) комик и шут – советчик родившейся в Острополе, он был известен на всю Восточную Европу. Еще одним примером стал живописец и график

Абрахам Вейнбаум (1890–1943) родившейся в Каменец –Подольском и многие многие другие.

Городу пришлось пережить не только военные перипетии, но и страшный пожар в мирное время: в 1822 году Проскуров сгорел, и, несмотря на одобрение царя Александра I 1824 в году восстановить город, финансирования так и не поступило. Проскуров зажил новой жизнью только тогда, когда в 1870 году было завершено строительство железной дороги.

В те годы представители еврейской общины были обеспечены финансово, но не социально — в частности, право на светское образование было ограничено.

Из-за того, что количество еврейских студентов в училищах не должно было превышать 10%, у евреев возникла необходимость в создании своего учебного заведения подобного уровня — и в 1908 году по инициативе и на средства еврейской общественности города в Проскурове открылось первое коммерческое училище. В новом учебном заведении количество детей-евреев было больше 50%! Город не перестовал развиваться и причиной этому была большая еврейская община.

В конце 19 в. в Проскурове было 29 фабрик и заводов, хозяевами или арендаторами многих были евреи, например, владелец сахарного завода, потомственный почетный гражданин города Лев Мозель, владелец чугунолитейного завода Бейриш Ашкенази, владелец бакалейной лавки Блувштейн, купец Шейнберг и другие. Все врачи и дантисты города были евреями; многие евреи работали учителями, страховыми агентами и провизорами.

В городе действовали синагога и семь молитвенных домов, еврейская больница, еврейский клуб и общество помощи бедным «Гмилут хасадим».

В 1907 г. Еврейское население города составляло 17 тыс. Человек и несмотря на то ,что 80 % налогоплательщиков составляли евреи, в 1912 году в училища не было принято ни одного еврея.

Февральская революция, ослабление центральной власти и большевистский переворот в октябре 1917 г. резко обострили национальные отношения на Украине. Уже осенью 1917 г. крестьянские сходки в Проскуровском уезде приняли решение о выселении евреев из деревень.

Положение стабилизировалось с приходом в город немецких войск весной 1918 г., однако в ноябре 1918 г., после отступления немцев, Проскуров переходил из рук в руки в нем управляли то большевики, то крестьянские банды. С февраля 1919 г. по ноябрь 1920 г. Проскуров оказался под властью Директории, одним из руководителей которой был С. Петлюра. К тому времени население города составляло около 50 тыс. жителей, 25 тыс. из которых были – евреи. В 1920-е гг. случилась «проскуровская резня», погибло окло 1650 евреев и ранено 600 , события этой ужасной ночи впоследствии отразились в картинах М. Сима. Жертвам этого кровавого погрома был установлен памятник.

После установления советской власти (1920) в Проскурове проживало 13500 евреев, что составляло меньше половины населения города, не все евреи поддержали политику новой власти, в 20-е – 30-е годы у общины были отобраны Большая хоральная синагога, еверейский театр (в последствии переделанный в украинский) и единственная государственная школа на идише была закрыта в 1939г..

 Во время немецкой оккупации (нацисты вошли в город 8 июля 1941 г.) евреи были согнаны в два гетто: общее и для «специалистов». Общее гетто немцы ликвидировали в октябре 1941 г.: 8000 человек под конвоем были выведены на свалку за скотобойней и группами расстреляны у заранее вырытых ям. Гетто для «специалистов» было уничтожено 30 ноября 1942 г. Нацисты и их местные пособники убили в этот день 7000 евреев из Проскурова, многие погибли ранее от болезней и голода.

Одной из чудом спасшихся стала 14 -летняя *Этя Бренштейн*, выжившая в Акции, ее спасителями стала *семья Островских*. Алексей и Сабина Островские проживали в Проскурове, во время немецкой оккупации в 1942 Алексей работал на железной дороге, а его молодая жена заботилась о их новорожденном ребенке. В ноябре 1942 в их дом пришла Этя, Алексей был другом отца Эти – Герша, за долго до этой Акции отец Эти показал ей дом Островских и сказал, что в случае опасности она может спрятаться там.

Этя была единственной кто выжел из ее семьи. Она пряталась у Островских влоть до середины 1943года, когда потом она услышала,что в трудовых лагерях Транснистирии еще остались выжившие евреи. У Эти была тетя в Копайгороде, и девочка попросила переправить ее туда.

Островские орендовали телегу спрятали в ней Этю и перевезли ее в город под названием Бар, на южном берегу реки Буг, там проходила территориальная граница между Румынией и Германией. Втроем они перенчевали в доме у сестры Сабины и на следующий день переправились через реку.

Вскоре Этя нашла свою тетю, они оставались вместе в гетто вплоть до освобождения, наступившего 20 марта 1944г. После войны Этя пересилилась в Киев и продолжала поддерживать связь с семьей Островских.

В 1990-х Этя Беренштейн (в то время Стежеринская) иммигрировала в США.

Эта история является одним из величайших примеров как мало стоит человеческая жизнь, когда людьми управляет ненависть и как много она стоит для тех кто знает ей настоящую цену, а настоящей цены нет! Жизнь – безценна! И семья Островских это понимала. Эта семья поставила интересы жизни другого человека, привыше своих собственных. Алексей и Сабина не отвернулись он маленькой Эти, которая так нуждалась в их помощи. Алексей и Сабина Островские может не так известны, как некоторые другие Спасители, они не смогли укрыть от смерти десятки или сотни людей, но то, что они сделали поистине безценно! В 1940-е годы, во времена Сталинизма и Нацизма, когда люди так трепетно держались за собственные жизни отчаянно пытаясь не видеть, что происходит вокруг, а в некоторых случаях были пособниками убийц, Островские пошли на величайший риск! Именно поэтому можно с городостью сказать, семья Островсих – герои, герои прошлого и великий пример героев настоящего и будущего!

В Украине примеров таких благородных людей - 2544 человек, все эти люди заслужили почетное звание **«Правидники народов мира».**

История показывает как во время Второй мировой войны германские нацисты и их союзники убили около <u>шести миллионов евреев</u>. Эту методичную, бюрократическую, организованную на государственном уровне операцию по преследованию называют **Холокостом.**

«Очень важно никогда не забывать о событиях прошлого и о людях, которые в них участвовали, о спасителях и тех, кто был хлоднокровно убит!»

Примечание: После Холокоста многие оставшиеся в живых нашли прибежище в лагерях для перемещенных лиц, находившихся в ведении Союзников. Между 1948 и 1951 годами почти 700 000 евреев иммигрировали в Израиль, включая 136 000 перемещенных лиц еврейской национальности из Европы. Другие из них иммигрировали в Соединенные Штаты или другие страны. Последний лагерь для перемещенных лиц был закрыт в 1957 году. **Преступления, совершенные во время Холокоста разрушили большинство европейских еврейских общин и полностью уничтожили еврейские общины в восточной части оккупированной Европы.**

Ссылки:

http://jewishnews.com.ua/ru/publication/evreyskaya_ukraina_10_faktov_o_evre
yah_hmelynitskogo

http://db.yadvashem.org/righteous/family.html?language=ru&itemId=4035714#

http://spigel.km.ua/article/read/uezdnyi-goro-prosurov.html

http://yvng.yadvashem.org/nameDetails.html?itemId=1872742&language=de

http://jewishkrasilov.org.ua/kolichestvo-pogibshix-v-period-shoa-xolokosta-v-
xmelnickoj-oblasti.html

http://www.jewish.ru/history/press/2008/04/news994262043.php

https://www.ushmm.org/wlc/ru/article.php?ModuleId=10005143

A Survivor's Voice

Bernard Marks was born in Lodz, Poland. Following the occupation by the Nazis in 1939, all Jews of Lodz were forced to move into the slum area of Lodz, a small area that formed the ghetto. Bernard spent four years working in a factory as a cloth cutter, while his father, Joseph, was the chief designer and pattern maker. In August, 1944, Bernard and his family were transported out of the Ghetto to Auschwitz. He never saw his mother or brother, or any of his 200 relatives, again.

When he and his father arrived at the selection ramp in Auschwitz, Joseph presented his young son's work permit and Gestapo registration to an S.S. officer to prove that Bernard had been working for the German government in the Ghetto. The officer then permitted Bernard to join his father at the selection ramp; both were assigned to work commandos in the Auschwitz/Birkenau camp. Later, it was learned that his father had been speaking to Dr. Mengele, the infamous doctor who performed hideous medical experiments on twins in Auschwitz.

Soon, Bernard and Joseph were transferred to the Dachau concentration camp and then to one of sub-camps to work as slave laborers building the Weingut II Bunker, an underground factory which was designed to produce Germany's ME262 jet planes. Beginning April, 1945 Bernard contracted Typhoid fever in camp Hurlach. (Kauferig IV)

On April 27, 1945, Bernard and his father were liberated by the U.S. Army 12th Armored Division. Bernard spent the next two years in Bavaria attending high school, trade schools, and university to catch up on studies he had missed during the five years living under the brutal Nazi regime.

Bernard Marks immigrated to Kansas City, Mo., in 1947 where he graduated for the second time from high school. He served in the US Army in Europe and Korea and was awarded the Army's Presidential Unit Citation, the Korean Presidential Citation and two Bronze Stars for bravery. He recently received a special medal from the President of Korea for the work he did with the local population, especially with children in need of medical attention.

Following his military service, Bernard graduated from Finley Engineering College in Kansas City, Mo., with a degree in Electrical/Nuclear Engineering.

In 1954, Bernard moved to Sacramento to work for the Aerojet General Corporation as a senior engineer on the Delta Rocket for the moon landing, Titan I and II ballistic missiles and various other research projects for both military and civilian applications.

Currently, Bernard is semi-retired as an environmental engineer, widowed, with two daughters and four grand children. In 2008, after 66 years of waiting for the right time and the right place, he finally achieved his goal of having a Bar Mitzvah at Congregation B'nai Israel., Sacramento.

Every year, Mr. Marks travels around the world to give presentations about the Holocaust from his first-hand perspective.

Bernie served for many years as President of B'nai Brith David Lubin Lodge, he is also a PP of Central California B'nai Brith District Grand Lodge #4, a recipient of the coveted AKIBA AWRD for community service.

Served in the U.S. Army with SHAEF Hdq. European theater as a translater and witness to the Dachau Trials. Also, served in Korea/Japan in the medical field. Recipient of the special Korean Presidential Medal for the work with children during the conflict. Recipient of many military medals including 2 bronze stars and the U. S. Presidential Unit Citation

Eleanor (Ellie), Bernie's wife of 56 years, passed away on April 15th, 2008. She served as President of B'nai B'rith Women, Sacramento Chapter #15.

Their daughters are active in Temple Beth El Sisterhood in Fresno, California.

Acknowledgments

I hereby wish to truly thank the teachers who encouraged their students to write these essays, the judging committee and proof-readers, editors and anyone else who helped with this project.

Judging Committees

Chief Judge: Nadine Muench
Finance Operation, Leadership for Verizon Corporate

Senior Rabbi Mona Alfi, Congregation B'nai Israel, Sacramento, California

Danise Crevin
Education Administrator Congregation B¹nai Israel
Sacramento, California

Margo LaBayne . Has lived in Elk Grove , California for the past 6 years with her husband and two children is working for the Elk Grove Unified School District for the past 3 1/2 years .

Laine Josephson Native Sacramentan,. Lifetime member Congragetion B'nai Israel, Community Volunteer and wife to Gregg and momie to Ellie

Bruce Deutsch is a Sacramento native who is daily grateful for his responsibility to the California teachers in his role as Associate Portfolio Manager with CalSTRS. Along with his wife, Morgan, and their family, Bruce enjoys being an active part of the Jewish community

Erica Cassman. CBI TEACHER -

Erica is a California State credentialed teacher. She taught at the elementary school level for ten years in Los Angeles before starting her family and moving to Sacramento. She is currently staying at home with her 3 year old daughter Lilah and 1 year old son Gavin. Since moving to Northern California Erica has become an active member in the Jewish community. Erica's educational background includes a Bachelor of Arts in Liberal Studies with a Concentration in Art and a Master's degree in Educational Administration, both from California State University, Northridge.

Joel Gruen works and lives in Sacramento, CA. He is a a full-time accounting student at American River College and works part time teaching Hebrew and Judaica at B'nai Israel Congregation.

Bina Lefkovic -- Bina Lefkovitz, has worked in various capacities in the youth and community development fields for the past 35 years. Her expertise is in policy, program and partnership development, community planning and youth development. Currently she is part time faculty at CSUS, and consults with organizations on youth engagement strategies.

Brie Bajar has been teaching at B'nai Israel Congregation since 2010, and is a Middle School administrator during the week. She lives in Elk Grove, California with her husband Billy and son Ethan. She enjoys reading, practicing Yoga, and spending time with family and friends

Chuck Rosenberg Retired for five years. Former school psychologist for 26 years

Shoshana Steel, Project manager global financial investments firm and mother of three boys.

 Leslie Oberst is a long-time member of Congregation B'nai Israel. She is currently the Early Education Specialist and teaches Hebrew classes.

 Sunny Rommer, Graduate with Masters degree, Hebrew Union College, Los Angeles in Jewish Education. Worked 36 year as a Jewish Educator. 2000 - 2009 Jewish Educator Director at Congregation B'nai Israel. Presently employed by the State of California

 Hope Rabinovitz – Long-time member of Congregation B'nai Israel and past president of CBI.

 Rachel Stern is a member of the California Juvenile Parole Board. Prior to this she was staff counsel at the California Department of Corrections and Rehabilitation, working on improving the treatment and conditions of confinement for juvenile criminal offenders in state custody. She, her husband Eric, and their two sons live in Sacramento.

 Eric Stern is a budget manager at the California Department of Finance. He previously worked for the Little Hoover Commission, and before that was a newspaper reporter and editor in three states, primarily covering state politics and government. He, his wife Rachel, and their two sons live in Sacramento.

 Stephen Prunier of Carmichael, California is a member of Congregation B'nais Israel along with his wife Jody and 3 sons: Hudson, Harris and Holden. He is Group Counsel for Guardian Life Insurance Company.

Jody Schwab Prunier, MSW, JD is a retired Assistant District Attorney from Worcester, MA and trained mediator. She is currently a stay-at-home mother and volunteer at-large in the local community.

Nicholle Collins works for human resources at the DMV. In her spare time she enjoys spending time with her daughter and playing drums.

Nick Collins works for the registration department at DMV. He enjoys playing guitar and spending Ike with his family

Matthew Archer, Professor of Anthropology at Sierra College, Rocklin, CA. Graduate of UCLA and UT-Austin.

Mahala Archer has been an educator for 20 years having worked as a teacher, administrator, consultant and researcher primarily focusing on issues of literacy, curriculum reform, and equity. Mahala graduated with an environmental science degree from UCLA and has a Master's in education from UC Berkeley.

Jamie Cavanaugh

Laurel Rosenhall. Current CAL matters graduate UC Berkley School of Journalism, correspondent Sacramento Bee, correspondent Los Angeles Times.

Susan Orton Attorney, retired

Carolyn Brokshire-- State Water Resources Control Board, Associate Governmental Program Analyst

Patricia Phenizy, Sac Room volunteer

Zlata Arestova Mechanical Engineer, Graphic Designer

Jody Cooperman- I have been teaching 8th grade English and U.S. history at Sutter Middle School for teen years. My commitment to teaching about the Holocaust came as a result of poorly it was done in our anthology book. I have been on a quest to learn more ever since. Currently a fellow for the Central Valley Holocaust Educators Network and U.C. Davis. Have studied at the United States Holocaust Memorial Museum, Museum of Tolarance and USC's Shoah Foundation. The underlying theme throughout my teaching is "What You Do Matters." I challenge my students to go deeper in their thinking during study.

J. Gordon Dean teaches Animation and Graphic Design in a public high school in Elk Grove, California. He lives in Sacramento with his wife and their two sons.

Mandy Greene, Administrator, Congregation B'nai Israel, Sacramento, CA

Steven Millner, Vice President, US Bank, Rancho Cordova, CA

Bernie Goldberg, Educator/Author/Activist

Rachel Zerbo, Public Health Educator

Laura Mahoney, Staff Correspondent for Bloomberg
News
Both here and collage

Joel Schwartz, Senior Research Analyst, California State
University, Sacramento

James Scott, Librarian, Sacramento Public Library.

Joe Spink, Library Assistant, Sacramento Public Library

Geoff Rohde, Librarian, Sacramento Public Library

Roxana Puerner, Administrative Analyst, Sacramento
Public Library

Rachael Horsley -- State Water Resources Control Board, Associate Governmental Program Analyst

Elaine Hussey has taught about The Holocaust for over ten years. She studied with the Museum of Tolerance in Los Angeles, and received a Fellowship to study at Yad Vashem. She primarily taught middle school children, and more recently has been giving lectures to adult study groups.

B. Carl Miller – Teacher/Author/Researcher

John Jackson – Retired teacher, California General Contractor, Music Lover and Member of Congregation B'nai Israel choir and two other choirs.

Elise Huggins – Teacher -French Translator

David Ayotte – Librarian/French Translator

Celine Sankar CPA retired - French translators.

Nina Bochilo – Library Assistant, Sacramento Public Library, Russian Translator

Ken Chau – Library Assistant, Sacramento Public Library/ Chinese Translator

Bernard Marks - Author/Russian, German, French Translator

I am most appreciative to all the teachers and the judging committee for their dedication and work with the students from the many schools who contributed essays to this volume.

I am also greatly appreciative to the proof-readers listed below. And thanks to the Sacramento Public Library's I Street Press and Gerald Ward who helped assemble and publish all Volumes of these essays.

Laura Mahoncy, Staff Correspondent for Bloomberg News

Gerald F. Ward, Librarian, Sacramento Public Library, I Street Press

446

Past Judges

Jessica Braverman-Birch , Don Burns, Ilene Carroll , Melissa Chapman ,
Wendy Fischer, Teena-Marie Gordon , Rabbi Shoshanah D. King-Tornberg,
Tuula Laine, Shirley Lange, Rabbi Michal Loving, Wendy Miller, Ann
Owens, Bonnie Penix, Elissa Provance , Susan Ross, Sara Sault, Frank
Severson, Katherine Severson, Tom Tolley, Gary Townsend, Heather Wilde,
Leslie Wilde